American Media and Mass Culture: Left Perspectives

American Media and Mass Culture

Left Perspectives

EDITED BY Donald Lazere

UNIVERSITY OF CALIFORNIA PRESS

BERKELEY   LOS ANGELES   LONDON

University of California Press
Berkeley and Los Angeles, California

University of California Press, Ltd.
London, England

Printed in the United States of America

1   2   3   4   5   6   7   8   9

Library of Congress Cataloging-in-Publication Data

American media and mass culture: left perspectives / edited by Donald Lazere.
    p.   cm.
  Includes bibliographies.
  ISBN 0-520-04495-9 (alk. paper).   ISBN 0-520-04496-7 (pbk.)
    1. Mass media—United States.   2. United States—Popular culture.
I. Lazere, Donald.
P92.U5A48   1988
302.2′34′0973—dc 19   87-22182

CONTENTS

Preface   ix

Introduction: Entertainment as Social Control
    DONALD LAZERE   1

Further Readings   24

Part I. MEDIA AND MANIPULATION

Introduction   29

Further Readings   32

Reshaping the Truth: Pragmatists and Propagandists in America
    ALEX CAREY   34

Selling to Ms. Consumer   CAROL ASCHER   43

The Blockbuster Decades: The Media as Big Business
    WALTER POWELL   53

The Corporate Complaint Against the Media
    PETER DREIER   64

Conservative Media Criticism: Heads I Win, Tails
    You Lose   DONALD LAZERE   81

Part II. CAPITALISM AND AMERICAN MYTHOLOGY

Introduction   97

Further Readings   104

Doublespeak and Ideology in Ads: A Kit for Teachers
    RICHARD OHMANN   106

Stars, Status, Mobility   JEREMY TUNSTALL   116

From Menace to Messiah: The History and Historicity of Superman
    THOMAS ANDRAE   124

Domesticating Nature   TODD GITLIN   139

The Infantilizing of Culture   ARIEL DORFMAN   145

Part III. MOMENTS OF HISTORICAL CONSCIOUSNESS

Introduction   157

Further Readings   161

Shirley Temple and the House of Rockefeller   CHARLES ECKERT   164

Frank Capra and the Popular Front   LEONARD QUART   178

The Politics of Power in *On the Waterfront*
PETER BISKIND   184

Machismo and Hollywood's Working Class   PETER BISKIND AND
BARBARA EHRENREICH   201

Gimme Shelter: Feminism, Fantasy, and Women's Popular Fiction
KATE ELLIS   216

Part IV. THE MASS-MEDIATION OF POPULAR AND OPPOSITIONAL CULTURE

Introduction   233

Further Readings   237

Television's Screens: Hegemony in Transition
TODD GITLIN   240

The Search for Tomorrow in Today's Soap Operas
TANIA MODLESKI   266

The Blues Tradition: Poetic Revolt or Cultural Impasse?   CARL BOGGS AND
RAY PRATT   279

Working People's Music   GEORGE LIPSITZ   293

Rock and Popular Culture   SIMON FRITH   309

Part V. IDEOLOGY IN PERCEPTION, STRUCTURE, AND GENRE

Introduction   323

Further Readings   329

Representation and the News Narrative: The Web of Facticity
GAYE TUCHMAN   331

Daffy Duck and Bertolt Brecht: Toward a Politics of Self-Reflexive
Cinema?   DANA B. POLAN   345

Women and Representation: Can We Enjoy Alternative Pleasure?
JANE GAINES   357

Masterpiece Theatre and the Uses of Tradition   TIMOTHY BRENNAN   373

The Liberating Potential of the Fantastic in Contemporary Fairy Tales
for Children   JACK ZIPES   384

Part VI. MEDIA, LITERACY, AND POLITICAL SOCIALIZATION

Introduction   407
Further Readings   417
The Teachings of the Media Curriculum   NEIL POSTMAN   421
Class as the Determinant of Political Communication
    CLAUS MUELLER   431
Charting the Mainstream: Television's Contributions to Political
    Orientations   GEORGE GERBNER, LARRY GROSS, MICHAEL MORGAN, AND
    NANCY SIGNORIELLI   441
Mass Culture and the Eclipse of Reason: The Implications for
    Pedagogy   STANLEY ARONOWITZ   465

Part VII. FROM THE HALLS OF MONTEZUMA TO THE SHORES OF TRIPOLI: CULTURAL IMPERIALISM

Introduction   475
Further Readings   478
Ambush at Kamikaze Pass   TOM ENGELHARDT   480
Sports and the American Empire   MARK NAISON   499
Introduction to *How to Read Donald Duck*
    DAVID KUNZLE   516
The Great Parachutist   ARIEL DORFMAN AND
    ARMAND MATTELART   530
Media Imperialism?   JEREMY TUNSTALL   540

Part VIII. ALTERNATIVES AND CULTURAL ACTIVISM

Introduction   555
Further Readings   558
Should News Be Sold for Profit?   CHRISTOPHER JENCKS   564
An Alternative American Communications System   ROBERT CIRINO   568
Pacifica Radio and the Politics of Culture   CLARE SPARK   577
A Course on Spectator Sports   LOUIS KAMPF   591
Rethinking Guerrilla Theater, 1971, 1985   R. G. DAVIS   599
Public Access Television: Alternative Views   DOUGLAS KELLNER   610

PREFACE

This anthology brings together the multiple strands of recent leftist criticism concerned with the role of mass culture in both shaping and reflecting twentieth-century American political consciousness. The emphasis is less on direct relations between mass media and politics (as in news reporting on political events) than on the broader suffusion of political ideology throughout everyday life in news and entertainment media, advertising, sports, music, and other branches of the culture industry.

Most of the selections appeared originally in limited-circulation left journals and presses within the past decade or so. Some, such as those by Neil Postman and George Gerbner's research group, are not written from a left or any other partisan viewpoint but are included because their findings substantiate the lines of argument presented here. The length of the book was dictated by two needs: to convey the impressive scope of this critical school, and to marshal a comprehensive counterstatement to the conservative thinking that has been in ascendancy since the seventies in both American cultural criticism and electoral politics. Even in this large a collection, many worthy possible selections have had to be relegated to recommended further readings. Articles were selected on the basis of literary quality, humanistic approach to cultural issues, and contribution toward a cogent overview. In keeping with the dialectical and unifying principles of the critical movement represented here, readings are grouped within and among sections to create thematic continuity from beginning to end, so that the individual works increasingly reflect off one another. My general and section introductions stress these continuities and suggest other possible groupings of included and recommended further readings for comparison and contrast.

This collection originated with a special issue of *College English*, a journal of the National Council of Teachers of English, entitled "Mass Culture, Political Consciousness, and English Studies" (April 1977). Favorable response and the subsequent proliferation of criticism in this mode prompted expansion and updating, with the goal of a book addressed to a wide readership of college students and teachers in all mass media or popular culture subject areas. Although emphasis has shifted from the teaching to the criticism of mass culture, this volume is intended to be a textbook as well as a scholarly collection, and an eye to issues concerning education has been retained. While the interdisciplinary range needed to do the subject justice is stressed—the contributors represent a dozen fields of scholarship and media activism—the style of most of the readings continues to be that of the critical essay rather than of social-scientific research; their focus on literary, rhetorical, and semantic aspects of mass culture highlights the distinctive contribution English and modern language studies can make to media scholarship.

The general political position shared by the editor and most contributors is what, in America, is labeled "radical." We accept that label mainly in its literal sense of going to the roots of problems, in opposition to the liberal tendency toward superficial, ad hoc expedients. Although this book does not provide "equal time" for conservative or liberal views, it does attempt to present those views accurately and judiciously in the course of disagreeing with them. In terms of pedagogy, most American textbooks (like most American news media) purport to express a neutral or balanced viewpoint, which often simply conceals the authors' biases and fails to clearly delineate differing ideologies. We believe it is more conducive to learning to expose students and teachers to a comprehensive, first-hand expression of one particular viewpoint and let them evaluate it against sources representing other ones—conservative, liberal, libertarian, and so forth.

The "left perspectives" here, then, refer to a position generally to the left of mainstream, Democratic-party liberal capitalism as it has developed in the twentieth century. That is, most contributors favor some degree or variety of socialism—but socialism as defined in its democratic forms, not the perverted version associated with Soviet Russia and other Communist dictatorships. Similarly, Marxist cultural theory (whose main lines are summarized in my general introduction) predominates here, but this fact needs to be qualified by recognizing the multiple meanings of the term *Marxism* and its abuses by both left and right. All Marxists are socialists, but neither all socialists nor all the leftist contributors to this book are Marxists, although most draw to a greater or lesser extent from Marxist theory. In other words, one can take Marxist theory seriously and find value in its critique of bourgeois society[1] without necessarily espousing it whole (though some writers herein do so) or becoming enmeshed in the endless disputes over fine points of doctrine that often blight Marxist theorizing. Furthermore, although all Communist parties claim to be Marxist, not all Marxists are Communists; indeed, most worthwhile Marxist criticism in recent decades has been written in the cause of political and cultural freedom and in vehement opposition to the propagandistic "Marxist culture" and "socialist realism" imposed in Russia under Stalin. Finally, although Marxist cultural criticism cannot authentically be merely an academic endeavor detached from active political commitment, neither does it necessarily have any affiliation with all the governments, parties, and individuals around the world today that make claims to Marxism, often in the most vulgar if not thuggish manner.[2] So although there is a great deal of criticism of the United States and capitalism in this book—along with a great deal of affection for the country's better self—the criticism is motivated by the desire to see America live up to its democratic potential and is not meant to imply that any present-day communist society presents a preferable alternative to American democracy.

At the same time, however, opposition to communism does not justify the blind rejection of every form of Marxism. It does not justify a monolithic good-versus-evil view of the cold war or of Third World revolution. It does not justify the stifling of radical voices—whether communist or anticommunist—in American public discourse. Above all, it does not justify the collapse of critical standards in regard to capitalism, the United States, and right-wing forces both here and abroad that has increasingly characterized neoconservative thought. (This trend is typified by *Commentary* magazine's recent panegyrics to John Wayne and Clint Eastwood as true-blue Americans, its making of common cause with the Moral Majority, and its defenses of right-wing dictatorships that sound like parodies of the wide-eyed enthusiasm of American leftist visitors returning from tours of cosmeticized Potemkin villages in Soviet Russia.)

This clarification of the book's politics is necessary because, in the present American political climate, it is depressingly predictable that those who dare to assert the slightest validity in Marxist thought will not encounter substantive evaluations of their arguments but shrill invective drawn from an arsenal of stock responses, including accusations of doctrinaire, jargon-ridden writing, hatred for American democracy, and guilt by association with every communist or terrorist atrocity. (Here again, conservative rhetoric has tended to become an echo of the very vices conservatives attribute to leftists.) We can only hope that stating our position on these matters clearly at the outset will help avert prejudiced responses to this book.

The fact is that recent left cultural criticism encompasses not only a diversity of precise political positions but a wide variety of topics, analytic methods, styles, and tones. The attempt has been made here to convey this diversity, and particularly to avoid sectarianism and dogma. The editor does have a bias, however, against jargon and in favor of clearly written, concrete analysis. Although the Frankfurt School has been the dominant influence on the writers here, its leading figures viewed American culture through foreign eyes and generally wrote of it in German or a Germanicized English that put off many readers. The contributors to this collection have assimilated Frankfurt School and other recent European, Latin American, and British criticism, but most of them are Americans speaking in their native voice about their native culture. This bias in favor of clarity and familiarity also explains the minimal inclusion of the more arcane varieties of recent Marxist, structuralist, and post-structuralist cultural theory (much of it written in the most tortured academic French or in imitation thereof), which in any case have received more than adequate attention in the past few decades in comparison to the lines of left criticism emphasized here. The distinctive mission of leftist intellectuals is to translate theory into practice and into discourse that, at some stage of mediation, is relevant to the daily life of ordinary people and intelligible to them. If this anthology succeeds in its intentions, readers will find in it a fulfillment of that responsibility.

Thanks are due to Richard Ohmann, who commissioned the original *College English* issue on which this book is based, and to Ernest Callenbach, my sponsoring editor at the University of California Press, whose patient support and wisdom about film and other cultural theory were invaluable, and whose Ecotopian optimism for the future somewhat tempered my own pessimistic bent. Two great mentors, Dwight Macdonald and Herbert Marcuse, died while this book was in progress. Macdonald first stimulated my interest in mass-culture criticism in an undergraduate writing class at Northwestern, and he continued in later years to encourage me and many younger critics, prodding with his inimitably acerbic editorial comments. Marcuse has been unjustly denigrated since the sixties, largely on the basis of a couple of foolish sentences in *Repressive Tolerance*, which his attackers invariably dredge up in order to dismiss the whole body of works by one of the most important thinkers of our time. We hope that this book will mark one step toward restoring due stature to Marcuse and his Frankfurt School colleagues. Among the contributors, Charles Eckert is no longer living and Robert Cirino is too ill to write; the fine work of both will be missed. The editors at Pantheon Books, and especially Tom Engelhardt, are to be commended for singlehandedly accounting for a large percentage of the books by leftist political and cultural critics published by major American trade presses since the end of the sixties; several of our selections have also appeared, usually in different versions, in Pantheon Books.

Brandon Jones, Michael Pemberton, Greg Parras, Hope Myers, Connie Davis, Linda Porter, and Nancy Hart contributed valued research and clerical assistance. My indefatigable editorial assistant, Sauny Dills, merits special commendation, as does Charles Dills for helping cope with word-processing complications. Finally, thanks to Barbara Ras and Anne Canright at the University of California Press for scrupulous manuscript editing.

A source note for each article identifies the journal or book in which it was originally published. These articles are reprinted with the permission of the original copyright holders.

Notes

1. Much confusion results from the fact that in common American usage "bourgeois" refers to the middle class, whereas in Marxist terminology it is synonymous with "capitalist"; thus "the bourgeoisie" refers to the ruling class of capitalists, and the middle class is designated "the petite bourgeoisie." The Marxist usage is generally followed throughout this book, with "bourgeois" used descriptively, not pejoratively.

2. In Western European politics and Third World revolutionary movements, a diversity of left parties—democratic socialists, national and international Communists, and other varieties of communists—sometimes allied and sometimes vying with one another, all claim to be Marxists. Such conflicts make these situations far more problematic than they are conventionally made to appear by American politicians and media, and they cause much division of opinion among American leftists. These issues are not directly pertinent to this book, however, except in relation to the political influence of American culture abroad and to the image in American media of other countries and of our foreign interventions, dealt with mainly in Part 7.

INTRODUCTION: ENTERTAINMENT AS SOCIAL CONTROL

DONALD LAZERE

I

One of the more durable offshoots of the American New Left in the sixties was a revival of mass culture criticism, which by the eighties has grown into a full-blown theoretical movement. The distinctive emphasis of this movement is on the central role of the culture of everyday life in shaping political consciousness, not only through the subject matter of cultural works but also through their structures, genres, linguistic and perceptual patterns, and the class relations embodied in cultural institutions, creators, and audiences.

Other approaches to mass culture have, to be sure, proliferated in the academic world, under a bewildering array of labels: mass media, communications, popular culture, the popular arts, and so on. Unfortunately, *Media* and *Communications* seem to have carried the day as rubrics for university courses and markets for scholarly books, thus inhibiting a broader emphasis on cultural issues. The departmentalization of academic studies has further obstructed a coherent, humanistic perspective. Departments of journalism, communications, and speech—at least until recently—have typically focused mainly on media institutions and technology, and their curricula have emphasized empirical research or pre-professional training more than criticism.[1] Media sociology and political science have produced a large, useful body of scholarship, but here again, much of it has consisted of "value-free" and quantitative studies detached from critical evaluation.[2] Mass culture has become a productive but still small subfield in history, philosophy, and American Studies. In English, popular song lyrics have been studied as poetry, while film, science fiction, comic books, and other popular genres have been studied for dramatic, semiotic, or social-psychological significance. Freshman English anthologies have incorporated various popular writing genres as models for expository techniques, style, and rhetoric, and essays *about* mass media as models for critical analysis. Mass culture as a whole, however, remains extremely marginal in English undergraduate and graduate curricula and in the professional organizations and prestige critical journals—especially considering how many leading twentieth-century literary figures have written criticism on the subject.

In these various academic approaches to mass culture, the prevalent attitude has been the accepting, often affirmative, and even celebratory one best exemplified by the Popular Culture Association and the *Journal of Popular Culture*, which were founded in 1969. This approach tends to reject or ignore the distinctions earlier critics made among highbrow, middlebrow, and lowbrow culture and between folk or popular culture—the spontaneous expression of common individuals, directed to their peers—and mass culture, manufactured and marketed commercially by impersonal business interests. (I will henceforth use the term *popular culture* in reference to critics to designate the affirmative position, in contrast to *mass culture*, connoting the more negative attitude.) The sources for the popular culture attitude include Marshall McLuhan, Susan Sontag's "One Culture and the New Sensibility" (both of which have been somewhat over-simplified and vulgarized), the countercultural mutations of the 1960s, and "new journalists" like Tom Wolfe and Hunter Thompson, who satirize but ultimately validate mass culture by appropriating its own language.

The popular culture approach has provided a legitimate corrective to criticism by such cultural elitists as Ortega y Gasset, Q. D. and F. R. Leavis, Dwight Macdonald, T. S. Eliot, Ernest van den Haag, and the Marxists of the Frankfurt School, a body of criticism that considered the effects of mass culture to be wholly negative. Certainly national publications, film, radio, television, and the phonograph, along with the spread of higher education, have made millions of Americans, especially in provincial locations, more worldly and critical-minded. The last few decades in particular have seen the most widespread diffusion of cosmopolitan tastes in American history—one positive feature of the "yuppie" (young urban professional) phenomenon. The old highbrow/middlebrow/lowbrow and popular culture/mass culture distinctions have had to be revised at least somewhat as a result of the improved artistic quality in some products of commercial culture, such as Hollywood films and the more inventive popular music of the sixties, with a concomitant increase in appreciation of these forms on the part of highbrow critics. High art has increasingly incorporated popular culture and vice versa, often with vitalizing effects for both. Middle America has discovered Baryshnikov and Brie, while intellectuals praise "Hill Street Blues" and Larry Bird. In Los Angeles, long synonymous with everything lowbrow, the 1984 Olympics were accompanied with predictably vulgar hucksterism but also with a first-rate international festival of classical music, ballet, theater, folklore, and painting.

Even with all that is valid in the affirmation of popular culture, however, its recent advocates have tended to play down persistently troublesome aspects of the politics of culture. (In this respect the rise of the popular culture movement forms part of the general depoliticizing of American academic discourse, as well as of both high and mass culture themselves, that has characterized the cold war period.) In their intensified study of popular culture, left analysts have maintained a more critical political and aesthetic perspective than has the Popular Culture Association school—a distinction that tends to be ignored by the editors of journals like the *New Criterion* and *Partisan Review*, who seem to equate increased attention to popular culture with the abandonment of critical standards toward it. The scholars in the present collection bear little resemblance to the leftist intellectual straw man created by neoconservatives, who is alienated from and misunderstands everything American. On the contrary, they share with the popular-culturists an aficionado's immersion in the national lore that inescapably shapes us all, for better and worse; they are simply more cognizant of the worse, particularly on the political plane.

The changing critical focus has served to stimulate leftists to reformulate the political issues in ways that were overlooked by the older Marxist critics. The highbrow/lowbrow issue, for example, is no longer confined simply to distinguishing quality culture for the elite from kitsch for the masses. Recent left critics have attempted to systematically delineate in cultural works, producers, and audiences the relation of "taste cultures" (Herbert Gans's term for highbrow, lowbrow, and intermediate levels of aesthetic appreciation) to social class and political attitudes.[3] Some have focused on how corporate capitalism has appropriated high- and middlebrow culture, as in Timothy Brennan's "Masterpiece Theatre and the Uses of Tradition" (Part 5), which discusses the takeover of the Public Broadcasting System by corporate Medicis like Mobil Oil and the ideological consequences in programming. Others have similarly analyzed the recent co-option by capitalism of the modernist and avant-garde culture that was championed by Macdonald and the Frankfurt School. (Conversely, neoconservative critics have seen high culture as being corrupted neither by capitalism nor by the pretentiousness of "midcult," as Macdonald saw it, but by the left-leaning counterculture that peaked in the sixties; this controversy could provide a sequel to the present volume.)

Some flavor of the popular culture approach can be conveyed by looking at one textbook, the widely adopted *Popular Writing in America* (1974), edited by Donald McQuade and Robert Atwan, and one professional journal, an *Arizona English Bulletin* issue entitled "Popular Culture and the Teaching of English." Both volumes intentionally skirt the issue of the commercial production of mass culture, with the resulting possible oppositions of interests between producers and audience. McQuade and Atwan explain that their selections "were intended to illustrate how various kinds of writing shaped by quite different commercial purposes and intended audiences interact with and modify each other to produce what we can reasonably call a common culture." They go so far as to avow, "We wanted to avoid introducing such essentially futile, if not paralyzing, questions as 'Is the news truly objective?' and 'Is advertising an abuse of language?' "[4] In his introduction to "Popular Culture and the Teaching of English," Michael T. Marsden of Bowling Green University, home of the Popular Culture Association, writes, "If Popular Culture is a reflection of our society, as indeed it is, then the products it produces can be said to be mirrors of that society. The mirrored images may be somewhat distorted, but the image will be generally accurate. We can know a people by what they consume, and we are what we enjoy!"[5] Again, the unquestioned assumption is that the mirror reflects the values of the people, not the values the producers impose on them.

In presenting a section on advertisements as models of popular writing, McQuade and Atwan proclaim, "Advertisements constitute a lively repository of American vocabulary, idiom, metaphor and style, in short, a fairly reliable index of the state of public discourse."[6] At the risk of raising "futile, if not paralyzing, questions," one must observe that if "Reach Out and Touch Someone" and "Times Like These Were Made for Taster's Choice" are McQuade and Atwan's idea of a reliable index of the state of our public discourse, either they have a tin ear or, if they are correct, the fact is cause for distress, not celebration. To the extent that some people now do talk like commercials, they have learned their language from those commercials, not lent it to them. Marsden is even more rhapsodic about advertising as literature:

The television commercial, for example, which I have christened the sonnet form of the twentieth century, operates much like a sonnet within very definite and strict limitations. . . . Like the sonnet, the television commercial is a highly rigorous structure within which there is immense freedom for the creative mind. . . . It is not difficult to find commercials that beautifully illustrate the writing techniques of comparison and contrast, argumentation and persuasion, and even more esoteric devices such as definition and classification. What better examples of good description are there than television commercials?[7]

Authors like McQuade, Atwan, and Marsden undoubtedly believe that by regarding advertising and mass culture in general simply in literary terms, they are legitimately keeping their discussion within the boundaries of English and out of political science or economics. However, by taking for granted and tacitly endorsing the role of mass culture in the American political and economic status quo, these authors are in effect taking a partisan position that validates that status quo. Furthermore, the prevalence of this and other approaches restricted to one or another isolated dimension of mass culture has contributed to a lack of attention, inside and outside the academic world, commensurate with the preeminent role of mass culture as a whole in contemporary society. (The radical right wing has, to date, been the most vocal group in calling public attention to the all-pervasive influence of news and entertainment media. The validity of the rightist critique will be examined in Part 1.)

II

The critical tradition that has dealt most fully with the politics of mass culture is Marxist theory. Foremost among its continuing appeals is that it is one of the few critical schools still viable that maintain the organic worldview of nineteenth-century humanists like Matthew Arnold in insisting on seeing life steadily and whole. Even the breadth of concerns of such neoconservative cultural critics as Daniel Bell, Norman Podhoretz, and Daniel Boorstin owes much to the influence of Marxism in their backgrounds. To be sure, there is always the danger in a comprehensive philosophy like Marxism of degeneration from totalism to intellectual totalitarianism, a procrustean bed of reductionism and dogma. In its more refined exponents, however, Marxist theory has produced distinctive perceptions about problems such as the various kinds of fragmentation in both modern culture and academic study referred to above; it has further provided a plausible explanation both of the major cause of this fragmentation—capitalist division of labor and social organization—and of its consequence—helping to reproduce the social order by impeding the articulation of a coherent oppositional consciousness.

Applied to any aspect of culture, Marxist method seeks to explicate the manifest and latent or coded reflections of modes of economic production and social organization, political ideology, relations of class and power (racial or sexual as well as political and socioeconomic), and the political consciousness of people in a precise historical or socioeconomic situation viewed as a moment in the dialectical flux of history. (Although Marxist critics sometimes apply the judgments "regressive" or "progressive" in interpreting such historical moments, the more refined contemporary critics use these terms not to lay down a correct party line but rather to delineate objectively the often complex and conflicted mix in cultural works of nostalgic appeal to obsolete values and acknowledgment of dialectical change. For example, Kate Ellis, in her analysis of contemporary popular women's fiction (Part 3), traces the strains between evocations of precapitalist familial and sexual roles and accommodations to feminist advances.) Marxist criticism frequently includes a corollary critique of other schools of thought that neglect the above subjects of study, bringing to light the significant gaps and mystifications this neglect leads to, as in my above discussion of the shortcomings of the popular culture school and other mainstream academic thought in addressing the political dimensions of cultural topics.

Marxist analysis has provided an incisive tool for studying the political signification in every facet of contemporary culture, including popular entertainment in television, film and photography, music, mass market books, advertising, newspaper and magazine features, comics, fashion, tourism, sports and games, architecture and city planning, as well as such acculturating institutions as education, religion, and the family. For example, Fredric Jameson, the most distinguished contemporary American Marxist literary critic, has also written highly nuanced interpretations of films, including *The Godfather*, *Jaws*, *Dog Day Afternoon*, *The Shining*, and *Diva*, in terms of their reflections—largely unintentional—of recent changes in class relations and world political economy and of corresponding shifts in the consciousness of their creators and characters. Indeed, the significance of Jameson's insights has frequently transcended the ephemerality of the films themselves.[8] Stanley Aronowitz can ingeniously explicate children's games,[9] methods in different countries of painting a door, or the sexual-political folkways of a San Francisco billiards bar. In England, Richard Hoggart, Raymond Williams, Stuart Hall, and the critics associated with the Centre for Contemporary Cultural Studies at the University of Birmingham have emphasized the problematics of the relation between working-class culture and mass culture.[10] Roland Barthes devoted one book, *The Fashion System*, to the semiotics of fashion, and another, *Mythologies*, to such diverse topics as wrestling, striptease, cars, toys, margarine, and plastic. T. W. Adorno, Walter Benjamin, John Berger, Raymond Williams, Ariel Dorfman, Armand Mattelart, and their followers in this volume have studied the embodiment in mass media of our ideologically determined perceptions of time and space, the natural and the artificial, work and leisure. Sociolinguistic studies such as those by Lev Vygotsky and A. R. Luria on cognitive differences between oral and literate cultures or by Basil Bernstein on language and class have been applied to media discourse and audience reception, as Claus Mueller does here (Part 6). Marxist feminists, represented here by Kate Ellis (Part 3), Carol Ascher (Part 1), Jane Gaines (Part 5), and Tania Modleski (Part 4), have focused on cultural reflections of historical moments in the political economy of sex roles; they have also scrutinized the distinctive mediation between patriarchy and capitalism and its shaping of our thought, language, and cultural forms.

A large body of cultural criticism has come out of structuralism, semiology, deconstructionism, and the Marxism of Louis Althusser and his followers.[11] Much of this work derives in part but also departs from the lines of Marxism emphasized here. Barthes and Umberto Eco in particular have written many useful, concrete analyses in the semiotics of mass culture. Many structuralist and Althusserian works, however, are at a level of abstract theory irrelevant to the concerns of this collection. At its worst, this kind of metacriticism seems to consist mainly of endless dreary permutations of the jargon of Saussurean linguistics, phenomenological philosophy, and Lacanian psychoanalysis. Whatever concrete insights such works contain rarely derive directly from linguistic-phenomenological theory, and stripped of their verbal excess baggage, they rarely make points significantly different from more accessible Marxist criticism, such as Gaye Tuchman's jargon-free structural analysis of television news (Part 5) or Norman O. Brown's psychoanalytic-Marxian interpretation, in *Life Against Death*, of the relation between the development of childhood language, gender identity, and adult neurosis, which in 1959 anticipated much of Lacan and Derrida but which seems to have been read by few of the fashionable French theorists or their American acolytes. Moreover, the structuralists' separation of the phenomenological from the sociological and historical study of language and consciousness runs contrary to the essential integrativeness of Marxism. And although their emphasis on the generation of ideology by impersonal social structures is valid in itself, it has led to underestimation of the deliberate efforts the culture industry makes toward social control (surveyed in Part 1). The dubiousness of the claims of structuralism and deconstructionism to be politically radical modes of thought was confirmed by their eager assimilation, in the most politically sanitized versions, into the American academic mainstream during the seventies and eighties. For this collection, then, pieces have been selected—most notably those by Tania Modleski (Part 4), Dana Polan, and Jane Gaines (Part 5), and my introduction to Part 5—that present some of the more concrete themes common to structuralist analysis, such as the revelation of ideological effects hidden in conventional structures of cultural perception and of significant absences in those structures. These pieces also convey a clear political thrust, and their analytic points are not smothered by excessively abstract theory or vocabulary.

III

The most prominent theme in Marxist and other recent left cultural criticism is the way the prevalent mode of production and the ideology of the ruling class in any society dominate every phase of culture, and more specifically, at present, the way capitalist production and ideology dominate American culture as well as the cultures of countries throughout the world that have been colonized by American business and culture (see Part 7). In the left view, this domination is perpetuated both through overt propaganda in political rhetoric, news reporting, advertising, and public relations and through the often unconscious absorption of capitalist ideology by creators and consumers in all aspects of the culture of everyday life.

The preeminence of ideology as a means of political control was emphasized early in the century by Georg Lukács in *History and Class Consciousness*, in which he analyzed the false consciousness that capitalist ideology imposed on the working class, causing them to accept beliefs against their own self-interest, and by Antonio Gramsci in his formulation of "ideological hegemony," whereby the interests of the capitalist class are made to appear to all other segments of society as the natural, immutable order of the world. By the 1930s the role of modern mass culture as a key agent of ideological hegemony became a central concern of the Frankfurt School, which included Max Horkheimer, T. W. Adorno, Erich Fromm, Leo Lowenthal, Herbert Marcuse, and Walter Benjamin, all of whom (except Benjamin, who died fleeing the Nazis) emigrated to the United States after the rise of Hitler and subsequently focused their attention on American mass culture.[12] The Frankfurt School critics perceived that, in the twentieth century, mass culture has surpassed the church and challenged the family and the state (with which it has increasingly merged) as the most influential socializing forces. They also saw certain similarities between all modern mass societies, whether in totalitarian dictatorships or capitalist democracies. Whereas in fascist and communist states police repression and blatant propaganda are used to control the masses, in ostensibly free countries like the United States mass production and communication have created the less heavy-handed and brutal but equally efficient weapon of cultural conditioning, whereby capitalists are able to regiment mass consciousness toward a society of compliant citizens, workers, and consumers through what Marcuse terms "the systematic moronization of children and adults alike by publicity and propaganda."[13]

Similar critiques of mass society were, of course, made through the forties and fifties—by Orwell in *1984* and Huxley in *Brave New World Revisited*, by C. Wright Mills and Fromm (preeminently in the underestimated *Sane Society* in 1955) and by the "New York intellectuals" associated with journals such as *Partisan Review*, *Politics*, the early *Commentary*, and *Dissent*, including Dwight Macdonald, Clement Greenberg, Edmund Wilson, Paul Goodman, Leslie Fiedler, Irving Howe, Mary McCarthy, Norman Mailer, and James Baldwin. Thus the views on mass culture of the New York intellectuals and the Frankfurt School dominated the monumental 1957 collection *Mass Culture*, edited by Bernard Rosenberg and David Manning White. Most of the New York intellectuals, however—with the exception of Goodman, Baldwin, and, to some extent, Mailer—by the fifties had backed away from their earlier Marxism and muted their criticisms of capitalism and the United States under the exigencies of cold war anticommunism; they now, like the elitist cultural conservatives, tended to hold the masses themselves, rather than their capitalist manipulators, responsible for their benightedness.

The decreasing emphasis on political manipulation as a factor in mass culture that characterized "end of ideology" criticism during the cold war can be seen in three versions of the same passage written between 1944 and 1960 by Dwight Macdonald—even though Macdonald remained more critical of capitalism than most cold war liberals. "A Theory of 'Popular Culture,' " published in 1944 in Macdonald's journal *Politics*, compared traditional folk art with "Popular Culture," a term he later replaced with "mass culture" and still later with "masscult":

Popular Culture is imposed from above. It is manufactured by technicians hired by the ruling class. . . . It manipulates the cultural needs of the masses in order to make a profit for their rulers. . . . Politically, Folk Art was the common people's own institution, largely independent of their masters' culture; while Popular Culture is an instrument of social domination. . . . If one had no other data to go on, a study of Popular Culture would reveal capitalism to be an exploitative class society and not the harmonious commonwealth its apologists say it is.[14]

In the second version, "A Theory of Mass Culture" (1953), *businessmen* is substituted for *the ruling class* in the second sentence, and a revision of the next sentence reads, "The Lords of *kitsch*, in short, exploit the cultural needs of the masses in order to make a profit and/or to maintain their class rule—in communist countries, only the second purpose obtains."[15] In the third version, "Masscult and Midcult" (1960), the corresponding passage begins: "Masscult comes from above. It is fabricated by technicians hired by businessmen." (The change from *is imposed from above* to *comes from above* is typical of cold war semantics, in which American political issues were depersonalized and fault displaced from specific agents.) Neither of the earlier versions of the next sentence, about the manipulation or exploitation of the cultural needs of the masses, appears in this text, although phrases from it appear in the next paragraph, in the context of a relatively benign judgment of American masscult in comparison with the Russian version, which exploits the masses "for political rather than commercial reasons."[16] The favorable contrast with Russia, where "it is as if Hearst or Colonel McCormick ran every periodical," is well taken, but Macdonald's disjuncture here between political and cultural or commercial manipulation in America is evasive and unsupported. This evasion runs throughout the essay, visible in several other changes from the earlier essays where, without justification, terms like *class rule* and *exploitative* get cut or transferred to a cultural rather than political context.

A similar rejection of the manipulation thesis is apparent in David Riesman's *The Lonely Crowd* (1950) (see the introduction to Part 1 below) and Daniel Boorstin's *The Image* (1962). Boorstin, after a brilliant 260-page exposition of mind manipulation by business and politicians, concludes lamely, "While we have given others great power to deceive us, to create pseudo-events, celebrities, and images, they could not have done so without our collaboration. If there is a crime of deception being committed in America today, each of us is the principal, and all others are only accessories. . . . Each of us must disenchant himself, must moderate his expectations, must prepare himself to receive messages coming in from the outside."[17] This conclusion is a classic example of the "What You Mean 'We,' Paleface?" evasion that Richard Ohmann analyzes in "Doublespeak and Ideology in Ads" (Part 2). In rejecting the manipulation thesis, cold war liberal critics prepared the way for the popular culture school, which, with McLuhan as mediator, simply focused on the positive rather than the negative aspects of what McQuade and Atwan accept as the "common culture" of commercial producers and consumers.

After the virtual moratorium on criticism of the United States and capitalism during the cold war, the New Left movements of the sixties—in civil rights, campus protest, opposition to the Vietnam War, and feminism—charged that this moratorium had blinded intellectuals and the public to the manipulativeness, dishonesty, and increasingly monopolistic power of the American state and corporate capitalism. Beginning with Marcuse's *One-Dimensional Man* in 1964, the titles of several subsequent books indicate this renewed concern among cultural critics: Hans Magnus Enzensberger's *The Consciousness Industry*, Guy Debord's *Society of the Spectacle*, Stanley Aronowitz's *False Promises: The Shaping of American Working Class Consciousness*, Herbert Schiller's *The Mind Managers* and *Communication and Cultural Domination*, Stuart Ewen's *Captains of Consciousness* and (with Elizabeth Ewen) *Channels of Desire: Mass Images and the Shaping of American Consciousness*, Bertram Gross's *Friendly Fascism*, and Patrick Brantlinger's *Bread and Circuses: Theories of Mass Culture as Social Decay*.

In the eighties, the cycle has been repeated with the reheating of the cold war and attendant conservative attempts to stifle or denigrate left criticisms of America and capitalism. Neoconservative sociologist Nathan Glazer wrote a book about the sixties entitled *Remembering the Answers*, based on a quip by a former Old Leftist from the thirties that it had been so long since he had heard the left arguments that were being revived in the sixties, he had forgotten the answers. It seems that each side must periodically make the effort to remember and reformulate its answers. The present volume marks such an attempt: a left response to the current conservative offensive.

IV

The French situationist Debord's notion of *la société du spectacle* has become central in recent left cultural criticism. As Norman Fruchter puts it,

The spectacle is the continuously produced and therefore continuously evolving pseudo-reality, predominantly visual, which each individual encounters, inhabits and accepts as public and official reality, thereby denying as much as is possible, the daily private reality of exploitation, pain, suffering and inauthenticity he or she experiences.[18]

The colonization of leisure time in the twentieth century, the manufacture of mindless distraction to fill people's every spare moment, is a more pervasive means of keeping the masses diverted from critical political consciousness than any bread and circuses devised by earlier ruling classes—even though the culture industry's immediate motivation may not be political control so much as the maximizing of profits through what Henri Lefebvre, in *Everyday Life in the Modern World*, terms "the bureaucratic society of controlled consumption." In the fifties, American households averaged four hours of television viewing a day; by the eighties, it was seven hours. The majority of Americans (certainly the majority of college students I have taught) are more knowledgeable about and emotionally involved in the latest television melodrama, sports championship, electronic game, or pop music superstar than they are about their society's most urgent problems.

This value system is both pandered to and perpetuated by the whole system of commercial mass communication. Critics of mass culture are frequently accused of wanting to replace the lowbrow dictatorship of the market with that of their own highbrow, puritanical, or commissarial tastes. This accusation misrepresents most current left critics, who seek not to restrict media content but to expand it and who would not wish to eliminate trivia but simply to prevent it from eclipsing quality culture, as almost inevitably happens in commercial media needing to maximize audiences and profits. The unfulfilled potential of television drama, for example, to address issues of social substance is illuminated by the rare exceptions like "Roots" and "The Day After." The artistic or ideological merits of these programs may be debatable, but they are significant in that, for at least a few days after their showing, all around the country people could be heard discussing race relations or nuclear war instead of pro football. This response provided a hint of what a civically conscious American common culture might be like.

Not even the staunchest defenders of the commercial mass media can deny the inadequacy of these media as our primary source of public information. Especially on television, trivia expands endlessly, to the exclusion of broadcasts of legislative deliberations, investigative reporting and documentaries, in-depth commentary, forums and debates, and unrestricted questioning of public officials by opponents or press beyond the charade of presidential press conferences and "Meet the Captive Press." [19] An hour-long discussion or lengthy print analysis of a current political issue, commonplace in the academic world and serious journalism, is rare today in the mass press, television, or radio (network radio at least used to feature daily, fifteen-minute commentaries before the television era)— although the Cable News Network, C-Span, and the "MacNeil-Lehrer Report" on PBS did make some progress in this direction in the eighties. Our public information system is what the public schools would be if education were made a commercial enterprise, with teachers and course content selected for their entertainment value as measured by Nielsen Ratings among students.

Another aspect of the spectacle is that today politics is show business and show business is politics. Statesmen responsible for world survival run for election on the basis of physical glamor, ritual appearances at sports events, and association with entertainment celebrities. Election campaigns are packaged by advertising agencies; campaign oratory has largely been reduced to glitzy, thirty-second spot commercials accessible only to candidates who can afford to pay for the production and air time; and televised "debates," consisting of hurried exchanges of platitudes and unsupported claims, are judged by press pundits and voters mainly on the basis of the candidates' acting performance. It was in the normal course of events that in 1982 Gen. Alexander Haig stepped from the office of secretary of state to the boardroom of MGM-United Artists Entertainment Company. And no one remarked on the incongruity when an earlier secretary of state, Henry Kissinger, was interviewed by Howard Cosell on the telecast of the baseball playoffs and declared in his German accent, "I've been a Yankee fan all my life." All political sectors, from the president to the Symbionese Liberation Army, have learned every trick for getting maximum media exposure. One of the Croatian nationalists who skyjacked a jetliner to publicize their cause summed it up when, on surrendering, he broke in half the fake stick of dynamite he had used to terrorize the passengers, and cracked, "That's show business." For the television generation, the lines have become blurred between reality and make-believe, between news, drama, and advertising. The events of Watergate did not have the full stamp of authenticity in the public's mind until they were aesthetically shaped on film as *All the President's Men*; the real reporters Robert Woodward and Carl Bernstein were fated ever after to look like second-rate imitations of Robert Redford and Dustin Hoffman. The ascent of Ronald Reagan from sportscaster and movie actor to president epitomized show business politics. Regardless of his merits as a politician, it is unlikely that he would have gotten anywhere in politics without his celebrity identity; indeed, his skills in substituting image manipulation for substantive policies and in viewing world politics in the good guys versus bad guys terms of a western were virtues in the eyes of a public conditioned to accept a B-movie vision of reality.

As news mingles with entertainment and advertising, political issues succumb to planned obsolescence along with other material and cultural commodities. Both politicians and news media set the public agenda with an eye to issues that can be presented in a catchy, tabloid manner. The professional consultants who developed the rapid-fire "top-forty-stories" format for local newscasts justified it by claiming, "People who watch television the most are unread, uneducated, untraveled and unable to concentrate on single subjects more than a minute or two." [20] William Safire reports that when he was a speechwriter for President Nixon, Nixon told him, "We sophisticates can listen to a speech for a half hour, but after ten minutes the average guy wants a beer." [21] One issue at a time gets singled out for headlines and possible legislative action and then gets shuttled out of sight, often falsely implying that the problem has been resolved. Since the sixties this sequence has included the issues of civil rights and black power, poverty, campus protest, Vietnam, feminism, environmentalism, abuse of power by security agencies, nuclear power, and opposition to nuclear weapons. As I write, the decline of public education is getting the headline treatment, after decades of political neglect; by the time this book is published, however, the issue will probably have receded once again into oblivion.

As Stanley Aronowitz argues in "Mass Culture and the Eclipse of Reason: The Implications for Pedagogy" (Part 6), the ultimate "literacy crisis" today is not the decline of mechanical skills stressed by the back-to-basics movement, but the socially induced destruction of the capacities to learn, remember, think critically, and distinguish meaningful language from doublespeak and hype. Indifference to the quality of language and reasoning is further engendered by the one-way communication of mass media; the absence of personal interaction between audiences and distant celebrities, politicians, corporate officials, news reporters, and advertisers stifles dialogue, debate, and any sense of control over public policy. Other readings in Part 6, "Media, Literacy, and Political Socialization," document the authoritarian effects of the restricted linguistic patterns of television and other mass media. As Neil Postman and George Gerbner's research group report, even the capacity to have genuine emotions may be diminished by the culture of the spectacle. Gerbner suggests that the most detrimental effect of violence in media is not in provoking violent behavior in audiences but in deadening sensitivity to real-life violence. After the graphic depiction of nuclear war on "The Day After," teachers reported disappointed reactions from junior high students to the effect that "it wasn't as gory as *Friday the Thirteenth*," and viewing videotapes of the fatal 1986 explosion of the Challenger space shuttle has reportedly become a form of entertainment among teenagers.

All these aspects of the society of the spectacle—the arbitrary obsolescence of every issue, confusion of the important and the trivial, fragmented discourse, audience passivity, deadening of sensitivity by the glut of senseless violence in television and film entertainment, the sheer overload of media messages—are bound ultimately to leave people in a state of confusion and apathy, unable to make critical distinctions or to engage in meaningful political action. These states of mind in high school and college students are all too familiar to teachers struggling to enable them to develop, or even care about developing, critical thinking abilities.

V

Current left analysts do not unanimously accept the Orwellian-Marcusean vision of an irremediably stupefied, controlled society, which some consider undialectical in its bleakness. These critics, including several in Part 4 and elsewhere here, argue that the bureaucratic agencies of state and corporate control are too cumbersome and internally conflicted to be completely effective. The hegemony of these agencies is "leaky," as Gitlin puts it, and faces constant challenges from unpredictable historical currents and audience responses. These critics acknowledge a substantial presence in mass media of progressive political views and liberatory aesthetical appeal; they also cite cases in which the media inadvertently generate oppositional forces and, emphasizing areas where the hegemony of the dominant powers is contestable, point to instances of indigenous expressions of working-class culture and "counter-hegemonial practices." Some look to the progressive potentialities in new communications technology as well.

These openings certainly must be acknowledged; leftists can ill afford to ignore any progressive possibilities in mass culture. But neither should the chronic leftist predisposition toward wishful thinking about prospects for the Revolution allow such possibilities to be overestimated. No one today except the most paranoid leftists and rightists believes that the media are monolithic in intent or effect. If television was largely responsible for the selling of President Nixon and the Vietnam War, it later was also largely responsible for their unselling. And the most inane feature of mass media can backfire on their producers. The insertion of commercials in "Roots" and "The Day After" brought home to audiences the grotesqueness of commercial sponsorship. For example, a commercial on "Roots" showing a suburban woman taking Rolaids to ease her upset stomach during an

exciting furniture auction, which followed the harrowing depiction of an eighteenth-century slave auction, inadvertently dramatized the contrast between the
affluence of middle-class society and the degradation that blacks past and present
have suffered. It can equally well be argued, however, that the triviality of the
commercials nullified the programs' dramatic and political power.

As for the "revolution" in communications technology, although the proliferation of cable and satellite TV systems and home video recorders has, at this writing, somewhat weakened the monopoly the networks and major producers have
enjoyed in television, programming remains safely within corporate hands, dictated by commercial ends. The democratizing potential of the new communications systems has also been limited so far because of high cost and restricted
geographical access. Further, the expansion of these media has been offset by a
general tendency toward oligopolistic concentration of ownership, as Walter
Powell documents in "The Blockbuster Decades: The Media as Big Business"
(Part 1).[22]

There is no denying that, in general, freedom of cultural expression has expanded in America since the dismal period of the fifties. Hollywood films, television dramas, and documentaries dealing with serious political issues now appear with some frequency, and conservatives are correct in claiming that most of
them express liberal viewpoints. These films include *Network*, *The Godfather*
(especially Part II), *Chinatown*, *One Flew Over The Cuckoo's Nest*, *The China
Syndrome* (and most of Jane Fonda's other films), *Serpico*, *Prince of the City*,
Reds, *Missing*, *Ragtime*, *Daniel*, *Silkwood*, and *Under Fire*, and the television
programs "The Selling of the Pentagon," "Return to Manzanar," "Fear on Trial,"
"Love Canal," "Roots," "The Day After," "A Case of Rape," "A Matter of Sex"
(about job discrimination against women), "60 Minutes," "Lou Grant," and several documentaries, mainly on PBS, critical of United States policy in Vietnam,
El Salvador, and Nicaragua. The eventual popularity of "Hill Street Blues" and
"Cagney and Lacey," after initially low ratings, was also a progressive sign, not
because these programs had a strong leftist viewpoint but because their breaking
down of the stereotyped content and technique of most previous dramatic serials
and the relatively high caliber of their writing, direction, and acting challenged
commercial TV's stupefying norms.

The expansion of free expression in America is somewhat cyclical, though,
and must be constantly fought for. Every assertion by the cultural left is countered by a strong reaction from the right—in the late sixties by the Johnson and
Nixon administrations and in the eighties by Reaganites, the Moral Majority, and
a host of organizations attacking alleged left-wing biases in education, news, and
entertainment media. The inevitable cultural backlash is now visible in films like
Red Dawn and *Rambo* or television programs like "Amerika," their version of
anticommunism as infantile and hypocritically exploitative as the "red menace"
films of the fifties. (The right turned Sylvester Stallone, like John Wayne before
him, into a patriotic hero for the Vietnam vigilantism of his Rambo character,
even though Stallone, like Wayne, never saw military service, having managed to
avoid the draft during the Vietnam War.)

Moreover, pointing to any number of disorganized oppositional tendencies does not amount to concluding that the system as a whole is shakable. From the Marcusean viewpoint, social control has been so highly developed that the ruling powers can allow opposition a fairly loose rein; they thus perpetuate the semblance of a free, pluralistic society while ensuring that the opposition lacks sufficient force to break through the constraints of the society of the spectacle. The history of the sixties shows that the system is willing to tolerate opposition precisely to the extent that it poses no real danger. When the Johnson and Nixon administrations began to feel seriously threatened by the New Left, repression was quickly instituted; after the Vietnam War ended and militant protest subsided in the seventies, tolerance reemerged.

It must be stressed that Marcuse never denied that repressive tolerance is vastly preferable to straight repression; and American leftists today have universally repudiated the attempts by some in the sixties to provoke repression as a means of priming the dialectical pump. Leftists can be grateful for and take advantage of the present degree of cultural freedom while maintaining a realistic sense of the limits of leftist expression in America and the multiple ways in which oppositional messages get disarmed in mass media. Some of the more optimistic leftist critics lack this sense, as do the conservative cultural critics who view with alarm the same tendencies leftists are hopeful about. (Their arguments are addressed in Peter Dreier's "The Corporate Complaint Against the Media" and my "Conservative Media Criticism: Heads I Win, Tails You Lose," in Part 1.)[23]

VI

Whatever degree of freedom and effectiveness opposition culture has in the United States, its ultimate constriction is the stifling of any mass-circulated, fundamental questioning of the capitalist economic system or advocacy of socialist alternatives. The model of socialism advocated by most recent American leftists and assumed throughout this book is a libertarian mixed economy in which the largest, monopolistic industries and corporations would be socialized and operated on a nonprofit basis, owned or democratically controlled by workers, voters, and communities, at the local level wherever possible. The profit motive in business and professions, though not entirely supplanted, would be restrained in favor of eliminating extremes of wealth, poverty, and power differentials by means of electoral politics, tax policy, guaranteed employment and minimum income, free or low-cost health care (including preventive medicine) and education at all levels, child-rearing and old-age benefits, and other such necessities as economic progress allowed. Under this system, small businesses and farms would be encouraged with government subsidies, as against the present American system, in which big business has the advantage; food production would be undertaken for nationwide and worldwide need, with no farmer being discouraged from raising crops to prop up profits while much of the world goes hungry. The defense and arms industries would be socialized to eliminate conflicts of interest and profiteering from war or weapons trade. Financial incentives would be used to reduce geographical inequities by developing depressed areas and relieving congested ones. Environmental protection, not high on past socialist agendas, is now moving to the fore as it becomes manifest that the artificial stimulation of demand and unrestrained growth of modern capitalism is destroying the earth's resources and ecological balance and working against population control. (Socialism, like capitalism, must face conflicts in which conservation has to be balanced against increasing production in areas of actual need, but a socialist economy can at least aim at striking that balance without having to artificially stimulate demand or restrict supply.) Other democratic countries have long since taken for granted many of these policies that have been made to seem out of the question in the United States (for example, public ownership of communications media, utilities, and transportation) and, in at least some cases, most notably in Scandinavia, have implemented basic welfare services and income equalization that have proved more effective than American efforts in this direction. The standard response—that American free enterprise is better at delivering the goods—has been weakened in recent decades by the relative decline of the American economy and quality of life; indeed, the Scandinavian and other quasi-socialist countries have equaled or surpassed America's standard of living.

The actual history of socialism to date has undeniably fallen short of democratic socialists' hopes, though it has never been fully implemented, either in the European countries with social democratic parties implementing controls on an essentially capitalist economy or—least of all—in states headed by Communist dictatorships. Indeed, socialists have often been socialism's own worst enemy. Socialism has not, however, been the total disaster painted by capitalist propagandists, especially in unbiased comparison to the more sordid chapters in the past and present of capitalism; in fact, a strong case can be made that capitalism has owed its survival to the incorporation of socialist measures. By the same token, many socialists acknowledge that a mixed economy may at present be the most workable policy and best guarantee of political and cultural freedom. In any event, socialism is far from being a dead issue throughout the contemporary world; socialist ideas and ideologists certainly merit something better than the facile chorus of ridicule, even toward modest social democrats like Irving Howe and Michael Harrington, that has become the American conventional wisdom of the neoconservative age.

The pros and cons of socialism itself, however, are not at issue in this book; the central point here is that socialist criticisms of capitalism, though often substantial, are excluded from the agenda of mass public discourse in contemporary America, to the detriment of the health of democracy. Organizations like the Democratic Socialists of America and journals like *Socialist Review*, *Dissent*, *In These Times*, *The Nation*, *New Politics*, and others, including those in which many of the articles in this volume first appeared, serve as forums for much valuable information and for exchanges of opinions that are frequently representative of a broader ideological range than is allowed in the bland mainstream media— as proved by the fact that the major media frequently pick up stories or report on disputes at second-hand from the left press (see Peter Dreier's "The Corporate Complaint Against the Media" in Part 1). Yet socialist views are currently limited in their circulation to a small audience, mainly of intellectuals.

In most other democracies today, socialists form a majority or near majority of the population; they have access to mass media and a respected place in political, cultural, and academic life; disagreements among diverse socialist parties— social democrats, Communists, and many other varieties of Marxists—form part of the national dialogue. Only in America are communists and anticommunist socialists undifferentiated in the public mind; only in America are social democrats labeled "radical" or "extremist" and lumped together in the crackpot fringe with Birchers and the Moral Majority; indeed, extreme right-wing groups have become *more* respectable than social democrats in the Reagan years, closer to the mainstream.

To be sure, Marxist and other socialist scholars have gained increased presence in some sectors of the American academic world in recent years—giving rise to the hysteria of Accuracy in Academia and other conservative groups who claim that Marxist fanatics have overrun the universities. (Readers of this volume can judge for themselves how fanatic its contributors are.) But prejudice against leftists is still so strong in many schools and departments that in them socialism remains the ideology that dare not speak its name. Inside and outside of academic circles, socialists are intimidated into using code-words such as *critical theory* (the euphemism for Marxism adopted by the Frankfurt School members when they came to America), *progressive*, or *economic democracy* (in Tom Hayden's California organization, Campaign for Economic Democracy, *socialism* is reportedly shunned as "the 'S' word").[24]

One means by which socialist views are excluded from American public discourse is a semantic ploy whereby capitalism as an economic system is confused or falsely equated by definition with political democracy, freedom, and patriotism. (In a 1986 court case in Tennessee, fundamentalist parents won the right to keep their children from being exposed to public school textbooks that presented views differing from their own, among which is the belief that "capitalism was ordained by God.") Advocates of all varieties of socialism, then (many of whom believe that a socialist or mixed economy can be more conducive to these political values than capitalism is), become defined as "antidemocratic" and "unAmerican." As a result, American political debate is parochially confined to the terms of liberalism versus conservatism or the Democratic versus the Republican party rather than capitalism versus socialism; capitalism is exempt from criticism, simply taken for granted on all sides, to the point where it is virtually invisible as a political entity or issue. Favoritism toward capitalism, as toward the status quo in any social order, is not perceived as a form of partisanship. Thus the Advertising Council, in effect a propaganda agency for corporate capitalism, can ingenuously assert that its public service announcements are "non-commercial, non-denominational, non-partisan politically, and not designed to influence legislation."[25] In a similar vein, the obituary for Walt Disney in the *Los Angeles Times* claimed that "his characters knew no politics, and received affection from the young at heart of whatever political persuasion or ideology."[26] Compare this judgment with Michael Real's analysis, in *Mass-Mediated Culture*, of Disneyland as a microcosm of capitalist ideology, or with Dorfman and Mattelart's book *How to Read Donald Duck* (excerpted here in Part 7), in which the Disney comics distributed in Latin America are seen as filled with propaganda for American corporate imperialism. Real's communist version of Disneyland or Robert Cirino's scenario for an American socialist television newscast (Part 8) might cause readers to snicker at what they perceive to be blatant propaganda. And yet, is it not an indication of how indoctrinated we have been that we do not recognize the real Disneyland or commercialized newscasts as equally blatant propaganda for capitalism? These examples illustrate perfectly Marx's definition of ideological hegemony, the capacity of any ruling class "to represent its interests as the common interest of all the members of society, put in an ideal form; it will give its ideas the form of universality, and represent them as the only rational, universally valid ones" [27]—indeed, as the only conceivable ones.

Only when capitalism falls into a period of manifest economic crisis, as it has since the mid-seventies, do organs of the status quo go on the defensive explicitly—as in *Time* cover articles entitled "Can Capitalism Survive?" [28] and "Socialism: Trials and Errors" (subhead: "An ideology that promises more than it delivers") [29]—thereby making the momentous concession that capitalism is a contestable entity, not invisible and inalterable as the air we breathe. When President Nixon had to drop his facade of blithe obliviousness toward his attackers and insist, "I am not a crook," it was clear he was in big trouble.

The basic problem of culture under capitalism is that capital is needed to finance it. High culture as a commodity is typically targeted for modest profits and a limited, cosmopolitan audience with a relatively high tolerance for political dissent. But the content bias of commercial mass media is almost of necessity conservative: audience must be maximized, and advertised products must appeal to the lowest common denominator of cognitive development, that of people most susceptible to oversimplified and repetitious appeals to authority, ethnocentrism, religion, and stereotyped good guys versus bad guys morality, as Gerbner and Mueller document in Part 6. It is generally easier to rally people at this level to patriotism, aggression, and retribution against alleged atrocities by the Enemy than to international cooperation and pacifism. (Demagogic emotional appeals can certainly be used for left-wing causes, as Stalin and Mao did, or to rally the masses against the status quo as well as in support of it, as Hitler did in his rise. But for such appeals to succeed, either there must be massive, active discontent, or else the opposition forces must be able to control communications media, education, and so on—as, for example, if socialists were able to expose American children to 350,000 propaganda messages by the age of eighteen, as they are now exposed to comparable propaganda for capitalism in the form of that many television commercials.)

Virtually any right-wing cause, no matter how loony, can find either a profitable market or backing by capitalist ideologues. American leftists attempting to start news or cultural enterprises, however, can rarely muster enough investors or advertisers to break even. Most operate with largely volunteer staffs and depend on small individual contributors, university or government subsidies, or a few wealthy patrons willing to go against their class interests for principle or tax write-offs—all inclined to be fickle. (Shortly before this writing, Max Palevsky, prototypical capitalist angel of leftist causes, arbitrarily pulled the plug on the journal *democracy*, which he had financed, and *Inquiry* was scuttled by its Libertarian party backers for being too leftist.) Lack of capital and advertising precludes mass distribution; thus at most newstands you can find right-wing tracts like *Plain Truth*, the magazine of the Worldwide Church of God, with its rosy-cheeked, socialist-realist cover portraits of Marcos and Pinochet, and *Soldier of Fortune* (the Magazine for Mercenaries), as well as a staggering array of journals catering to every market from hang-gliding to bondage-and-discipline, but not *The Nation*, *In These Times*, *Dissent*, the *Progressive*, *Socialist Review*, or even—outside of large cities and college neighborhoods—slicker efforts such as *Mother Jones* and the *Village Voice*. Granted, conservative highbrow magazines like *Commentary* and *National Review* are not much easier to find, but then their politics are not that different from *Reader's Digest*, *TV Guide*, and *Time*. It is a major anomaly of contemporary American politics and culture that socialist thought has become restricted mainly to highbrow circles—circles in turn restricted mainly to the upper social classes, whose self-interest is ultimately inimical to socialism.

Defenders of capitalism argue that if an opposition movement, even one for socialism, becomes so widespread that catering to it becomes profitable, the culture industry will do so, thereby proving that the profit motive guarantees free expression. This theory was borne out to some extent in twentieth-century America prior to the cold war. But all forms of socialism were subsequently discredited, by association with Stalinism and by other factors, some legitimate and some not, to such an extent that a widespread socialist revival may now be permanently precluded, even if conditions someday warrant it. Socialist writers accumulate large files of rejection letters praising their work but regretting that it does not have sufficient profit potential. Catch-22. It is unlikely that a market for socialist views can ever develop, given the absence of public access in the first place. Moreover, long-range self-interest is likely to motivate capitalists to use their control of the media to block socialist opinion from regaining wide circulation—a much easier task than in the past or in other democracies that still have strong leftist constituencies.

How far would American corporate capitalism go in publicizing a movement for its own abolition? The experience of recent decades provides some light on this question. When business is thriving and capital amply available, as in the sixties, some corporations take a chance on finding a market for leftist books, films, and records. But when investment money gets tight, as it has since the seventies, the survival of such projects comes to depend on a few maverick producers or publishers secure enough to risk losses with leftist works. Furthermore, corporate support for oppositional works diminishes quickly in any period when public opinion swings to the right or the political establishment is cracking down on dissent. All these cases indicate that the prospects for socialist, or any other, opposition are not promising if its survival has to depend on the good health of the system it seeks to replace.

Possible democratic socialist alternatives to the present system of American mass culture are explored in Part 8 of this collection. Full implementation of such alternatives is as remote at this time as the coming to power of a socialist

party. Not quite so remote is the goal of overcoming the present capitalist monopoly by the inauguration or expansion of at least some of these alternatives, as
well as by the increased inclusion of socialist viewpoints in teaching—in ways
suggested in the introduction to Part 8—as part of a generally expanded range of
expression. At issue now is the survival of any significant socialist presence in
American public life and of any possibility that alternatives to capitalist solutions
might be considered, or even imagined, on particular public policies, including
cultural ones. In the eighties, American labor has, for the most part, either accommodated to management hegemony or been overpowered; the minorities are
quiescent; feminists have been stymied; and intellectuals are more subdued than
at any time in recent history. Neoconservatives deride left intellectuals who criticize America and capitalism while enjoying all the comforts thereof. But on the
other side of the coin, intellectuals' personal comforts can easily blind them to
persistent injustices in their country's domestic and foreign policies that do not
directly impinge on them. Many conservatives and some liberals would not in the
least regret the disappearance of a radical left from America. One can only urge
them to consider that the antiutopian accommodation to American realities on
which they pride themselves may be contributing to the extinction of all capacity
for social renewal. America's electoral process, government, and industry currently appear to be suffering from paralytic inability to make the most modest
reforms—even in the direction of more workable models of capitalism like the
Japanese one—while the main political momentum seems to be in the direction
of the antidemocratic right. Even if for no other reason, the radical left would
merit preservation as a critical standpoint outside the mainstream of American
ideology.

This collection, then, is part of the current movement to reintroduce the discussion of socialism into American political, cultural, and academic discourse,
by presenting critical perspectives on mass culture under capitalism that can be
assimilated by students and scholars, even if their own political beliefs differ. It is
not our intention to try to indoctrinate students, or to argue that this is the only
defensible viewpoint, that there is nothing good to be said for capitalism, or that
any variety of socialism provides the answer to every political or cultural problem. Rather, the weighting of this book is intended to demonstrate that the bulk
of American mass cultural media, and of scholarship in the field, is equally one-
sided in favor of capitalism, thereby constricting our capacity for objective criticism or for conceiving of possible alternatives to established modes of thinking.

VII

One of the most extraordinary moments in the recent history of mass media
comes in the climactic scene of the Paddy Chayefsky–Sidney Lumet film *Network*. Howard Beale (played by Peter Finch), the ex-newscaster who is turned
into the populist Mad Prophet of the Airways as a media hype, has told his viewers about the sale of the network to Arab capitalists and incited them to send
millions of protest telegrams to the White House to block the sale. He is brought
before the chairman of the board of the master conglomerate that owned the net-

work, the archcapitalist Arthur Jensen (played by Ned Beatty). In a monologue that echoes Dostoevsky's "The Grand Inquisitor," Jensen paternally chastises Beale for his naiveté and then reveals the Mystery: all of the ideals propagated by governments and the media—democracy, liberty, patriotism—are a fraud. The ostensible oppositions between the United States and the Arab countries or the Soviet Union, between the "free world" and totalitarianism, are illusions. The ultimate reality underlying world politics is money—dollars, petrodollars, rubles, francs. There are no nations, there is only the worldwide network of finance and corporations, whose workings have the impersonal inevitability of the primal forces of nature.

Arthur Jensen's corporate cosmology is a satiric oversimplification of world politics; it overlooks the very real conflicts between and within capitalist, Communist, and Third World blocs, the domination of the world's economy by American-centered corporations, and the immeasurable differences between living in Western democracies and in dictatorships of either the left or the right (even though most of the latter depend on Western support). Nevertheless, what is stunning about the scene is that it transcends the platitudinous account of world politics that is normally promulgated without challenge in American politics and mass media; it at least comes close to what most Americans must sense vaguely to be the truth, as is indicated by the gasps and applause of audiences watching the scene.

The subsequent denouement of *Network* merits further analysis, for it sums up the central issues in the relationship between mass culture and political consciousness. The chastened Howard Beale returns to his program as the apostle of Arthur Jensen's corporate cosmology. But the message he has gotten and conveys to his viewers is that the individual is insignificant and powerless to resist the impersonal forces of corporate politics. As a result of his taking this counter-revolutionary line, he is shot, on the air, by the leftist Ecumenical Liberation Army. Ironically, though, it is not his counterrevolutionary message per se that incites the assassination, but the fact that his defeatism has caused the network's ratings and profits to drop. The revolutionaries, granted airtime by the network, have been co-opted into the ratings-profits rat race; they are recruited for the murder by the network executives beneath Jensen, for whom short-term profits—even garnered through anticapitalistic programs—are more important than the unprofitable preaching of the corporate ideology of Arthur Jensen.

It can be argued that Chayefsky's black humor and cynically ironic twists about the media's capacity to jumble the political left and right have at this point gotten out of hand, reducing the serious political left theme of the film to absurdity, discrediting the entire left as an oppositional force, and leaving an unduly defeatist impression. Still, the satire on the symbiotic relation between the media and radical crackpot groups like the Symbionese Liberation Army is not all that far from reality.

The ultimate ironic twist in *Network* comes in the film's final scene. Howard Beale's bullet-riddled body is shown on the TV studio monitor next to another monitor showing a familiar children's cereal commercial. The studio audience (and presumably the home viewers), who have sat impassively through the shooting, continue impassively to watch the commercial, numbed by steady television exposure to the differences between violence on crime shows and in real life, between commercials and news, between images and reality. They—we—are finally like the protagonist in Antonioni's *Blow-Up*, for whom a murder is only a scene to be impersonally photographed, or like Jean-Baptiste Clamence in Camus's *The Fall*, for whom "fundamentally, nothing mattered. War, suicide, love, poverty got my attention, of course, when circumstances forced me, but a courteous, superficial attention. . . . How shall I express it? Everything slid off—yes, just rolled off me." [30] And over the scene of the monitors the film's final credits are superimposed, drawing the film audience into complicity with the television audience—an effect compounded when *Network* itself is shown on TV.

Is the audience of *Network* expected to leave the theater thinking, as Howard Beale has earlier exhorted his viewers to shout, "I'm mad as hell, and I'm not going to take it any more"—and then to do something about it in the way of political action? Or are they expected distractedly to let the film's political truths roll off them, washed away in the daily torrent of media trivia? Would the film have a stronger effect if its conclusion were unequivocally, affirmatively revolutionary? Would the corporate executives who finance films and television allow a show to go all the way in advocating the overthrow of capitalism—if the show was profitable? They might indeed, given the likelihood that the paralyzing overload of media messages is sufficient to defuse even the most subversive message.

The contradictions between content and institutional context in a production like *Network* illustrate the necessity (and, of course, the difficulty) of determining whether everything valuable in American mass culture justifies everything meretricious, as in the popular culture view, or whether the meretricious ultimately nullifies the valuable. The survival of oppositional tendencies in both mass culture itself and scholarship about it does show that the United States is still far from being a closed society. Whether these tendencies will prevail or eventually be swallowed up in the effective totalization of the society of the spectacle will depend on many unpredictable variables, political and economic more than cultural—foremost among them the rapidly shifting balance of worldwide power and the fluctuating American and international economies. In the meantime, if humanistic education is to be faithful to its professed responsibilities, it must foster, in the ways suggested here and in every other possible way, critical consciousness in opposition to all political and cultural forces that threaten to close our universe of discourse.

Notes

1. *The Journal of Communication*, the journal of the International Communication Association, has provided a forum for critical as well as empirical approaches; see especially the symposium on these two approaches in a special issue, "Ferment in the Field" (*Journal of Communication* 33, no. 3 [1983]). The Speech Communication Association began publication in 1984 of the journal *Critical Studies in Mass Communication*. The Union for Democratic Communications is a recently formed left-critical caucus in communications scholarship.

2. See Todd Gitlin, "Media Sociology: The Dominant Paradigm," *Theory and So-*

ciety, no. 6 (1978): 205–253, a detailed historical critique that focuses on the influence in media research of Paul Lazarsfeld and his associates.

3. Herbert Gans, *Popular Culture and High Culture* (New York: Basic Books, 1974). Gans's provocative but sketchy connections between taste cultures, social class, and political attitudes require further development by other scholars. Recent studies in this direction include the selections by Claus Mueller and George Gerbner's group in Part 6 below; Harold L. Wilensky, "Mass Society and Mass Culture: Interdependence or Independence," *American Sociological Review*, no. 29 (April 1964): 173–196 (also excerpted in *The TV Establishment*, ed. Gaye Tuchman [Englewood Cliffs, N.J.: Prentice-Hall, 1974], pp. 139–160); and most recently, by the French sociologist Pierre Bourdieu, *Distinction: A Social Critique of the Judgment of Taste* (Cambridge, Mass.: Harvard University Press, 1984), a more comprehensive study of these questions than any American work to date.

4. *Popular Writing in America*, 2d ed., ed. Donald McQuade and Robert Atwan (New York: Oxford University Press, 1980), p. xxxi.

5. Michael T. Marsden, Introduction to "Popular Culture and the Teaching of English" (special issue), *Arizona English Bulletin* 17, no. 3 (1975): 3.

6. McQuade and Atwan, *Popular Writing*, p. 7.

7. Marsden, "Introduction," p. 7.

8. See Fredric Jameson's "Reification and Utopia in Mass Culture," *Social Text*, no. 1 (Winter 1979): 130–148; "Class and Allegory in Contemporary Culture: *Dog Day Afternoon* as a Political Film," *College English* 38, no. 8 (1977): 843–859; "The Shining," *Social Text*, no. 4 (Fall 1981): 114–125; "On *Diva*," *Social Text*, no. 6 (Fall 1982): 114–119. None of Jameson's articles were available for inclusion here because he was in the process of revising them into book form.

9. Stanley Aronowitz, *False Promises* (New York: McGraw-Hill 1973), pp. 61–69.

10. For a survey of the work of the Birmingham critics, see Michael Green, "The Centre for Contemporary Cultural Studies," in *Re-Reading English*, ed. Peter Widdowson (London: Methuen, 1982), pp. 77–90.

11. The key work in Althusser's cultural theory is "Ideology and Ideological State Apparatuses," in *Lenin and Philosophy and Other Essays* (London: New Left Books, 1971), pp. 121–73. Althusser's work is placed in the history of Marxist cultural criticism by Stuart Hall in "Culture, the Media and the 'Ideological Effect,'" in *Mass Communication and Society*, ed. James Curran, Michael Gurevitch, and Janet Woollacott (London: Arnold, 1977), pp. 315–348. An informative survey of Althusserian and related French Marxist cultural criticism is found in *Praxis*, no. 5 (1981). Among attacks on Althusser's school by other Marxists are E. P. Thompson's *The Poverty of Theory* (London: Merlin Press, 1978) and Simon Clarke et al., *One-Dimensional Marxism: Althusser and the Politics of Culture* (London: Allison & Busby, 1980); the latter work criticizes the group of British semiologists around the journal *Screen*, which has, as it happens, subsequently merged with its more down-to-earth companion journal *Screen Education* and become less doctrinaire. For an exceptionally lucid summary and critique of Althusserian-Lacanian cultural theory, see Terry Eagleton, *Literary Theory: An Introduction* (Minneapolis: University of Minnesota Press, 1983).

12. A thorough account of the Frankfurt School's personalities and theories of mass culture is found in Martin Jay, *The Dialectical Imagination: A History of the Frankfurt School and the Institute of Social Research, 1923–1950* (Boston: Little, Brown, 1973), esp. pp. 173–218.

13. Herbert Marcuse, "Repressive Tolerance," in Robert Paul Wolff, Barrington Moore, Jr., and Herbert Marcuse, *A Critique of Pure Tolerance* (Boston: Beacon Press, 1969), p. 83.

14. Dwight Macdonald, "A Theory of 'Popular Culture,'" *Politics* 1, no. 1 (1944): 20.

15. Dwight Macdonald, "A Theory of Mass Culture," in *Mass Culture*, ed. Bernard Rosenberg and David Manning White (New York: Free Press, 1957), p. 60.

16. Dwight Macdonald, "Masscult and Midcult," in *Against the American Grain* (New York: Random House, 1962), pp. 14–15.

17. Daniel Boorstin, *The Image; or, What Happened to the American Dream* (New York: Harper Colophon, 1962), p. 260. In my opinion, *The Image* remains the best book on American mass culture, in both content and style, anticipating many lines of recent left criticism. It is regrettable that Boorstin, in his cold war conservative mood, pulled his punches on direct criticism of capitalism and failed to acknowledge the Marxist sources of his analysis from his Old Left past. It is equally regrettable that as a consequence recent leftists have not adequately acknowledged Boorstin.

18. Norman Fruchter, "Movement Propaganda and the Culture of the Spectacle," *Liberation*, May 1971, pp. 4–17.

19. The political timidity of reporters on television interview programs is documented by Mindy Nix in "The Meet the Press Game," in Tuchman, *The TV Establishment*, pp. 66–71.

20. *San Francisco Sunday Examiner and Chronicle*, 16 March 1975, p. 14.

21. William Safire, *Before the Fall* (New York: Quadrangle Books, 1974), p. 314.

22. Among many leftist critiques of cable and other new communications technology, see Vincent Mosco, *Pushbutton Fantasies: Critical Perspectives on Videotex and Information Technology* (Norwood, N.J.: Ablex, 1982), and Vincent Mosco and Janet Wasko, eds., *Labor, the Working Class and the Media* (Norwood, N.J.: Ablex, 1983).

23. Douglas Kellner, in "Network Television and American Society," *Theory and Society*, no. 10 (1981): 31–62, judiciously analyzes the intersections between the left and right positions, with a more optimistic conclusion for left prospects than mine. A reiteration by Kellner of his position and a critique of it by Moishe Gonzales along the same lines as mine appeared in *Telos*, no. 62 (Winter 1984–1985): 196–209. Patrick Brantlinger concludes his *Bread and Circuses: Theories of Mass Culture as Social Decay* (Ithaca, N.Y.: Cornell University Press, 1983) on a similar optimistic note for progressive tendencies in mass culture, but the weight of his prior analysis, through nearly three hundred pages spanning the history of Western cultural theory, leans more toward Frankfurt School pessimism.

24. Bertell Ollman and Edward Vernoff, eds., *The Left Academy: Marxist Scholarship on American Campuses* (New York: McGraw-Hill, 1982) and *The Left Academy, Volume Two* (New York: Praeger, 1984), survey the present status and scope of the academic left.

25. See William D. Lutz, " 'The American Economic System': The Gospel According to the Advertising Council," *College English* 38, no. 8 (1977): 860–865.

26. Quoted in Herbert Schiller, *The Mind Managers* (Boston: Beacon Press, 1973), p. 99.

27. Karl Marx and Frederick Engels, "The German Ideology," in *Reader in Marxist Philosophy*, ed. Howard Selsam and Harry Martel (New York: International Publishers, 1963), p. 200.

28. *Time*, 14 July 1975.

29. *Time*, 13 March 1978, p. 24.

30. Albert Camus, *The Fall* (New York: Knopf, 1957), p. 49.

Further Readings *

General Theory of Mass Culture

Adorno, Theodor W. "Culture Industry Reconsidered." *New German Critique*, no. 6 (Fall 1975): 12–19.

Arato, Andrew W., and Eike Gebhardt, eds. *The Essential Frankfurt School Reader*. New York: Continuum, 1982.

Aronowitz, Stanley. *The Crisis in Historical Materialism: Class, Politics, and Culture in Marxist Theory*. New York: Praeger, 1981.

Barber, David. *The Pulse of Politics: Electing Presidents in the Media Age*. New York: Norton, 1980.

Barthes, Roland. *Mythologies*. New York: Hill & Wang, 1972.

Baudrillard, Jean. *In the Shadow of the Silent Majorities*. New York: Foreign Agents Series, Semiotext, 1983.

———. *Simulations*. New York: Semiotext, 1983.

Bell, Daniel. *The Cultural Contradictions of Capitalism*. New York: Basic Books, 1976.

Benjamin, Walter. "The Author as Producer." *New Left Review*, July–August 1970.

Berman, Marshall. *All That Is Solid Melts into Air: The Experience of Modernity*. New York: Simon & Schuster, 1982.

Blume, Keith. *The Presidential Election Show: Campaign '84 and Beyond on the Nightly News*. South Hadley, Mass.: Bergin & Garvey, 1986.

Brantlinger, Patrick. *Bread and Circuses: Theories of Mass Culture as Social Decay*. Ithaca, N.Y.: Cornell University Press, 1983.

Brenkman, John. "Mass Media: From Collective Experience to the Culture of Privatization." *Social Text*, no. 1 (1979): 94–109.

Debord, Guy. *Society of the Spectacle*. Detroit: Black & Red, 1973.

Enzensberger, Hans Magnus. *The Consciousness Industry: On Literature, Politics and the Media*. Translated by Michael Roloff. New York: Seabury Press, 1974.

Ewen, Stuart. *Captains of Consciousness: Advertising and the Social Roots of the Consumer Culture*. New York: McGraw-Hill, 1976.

Ewen, Stuart, and Elizabeth Ewen. *Channels of Desire: Mass Images and the Shaping of American Consciousness*. New York: McGraw-Hill, 1982.

Fromm, Eric. *Escape from Freedom*. New York: Rinehart, 1941.

———. *The Sane Society*. New York: Holt, Rinehart & Winston, 1955.

Giroux, Henry A. "The Politics of Technology, Culture, and Alienation: An Overview of Neo-Marxist Thought in the Twentieth Century." *Left Curve*, no. 6 (Summer–Fall 1976): 32–41.

Gouldner, Alvin W. *The Dialectic of Ideology and Technology: The Origin, Grammar, and Future of Ideology*. New York: Seabury Press, 1976.

Gramsci, Antonio. *Prison Notebooks*. New York: International Publishers, 1971.

Gross, Bertram. *Friendly Fascism*. New York: Evans, 1980.

Habermas, Jürgen. *The Legitimation Crisis*. Boston: Beacon Press, 1975.

---

*The Further Readings sections provide bibliographical information for citations not footnoted in the introductory essays and articles; by the same token, footnoted citations have generally not been repeated in Further Readings. The vast number of pertinent works has necessitated some arbitrary placements of citations in order to minimize duplication among different Further Readings sections, even though many works could fit into more than one, especially since the book's readings are grouped by theme rather than by genre.

————. *Toward A Rational Society*. Boston: Beacon Press, 1970.

Hauser, Arnold. *The Sociology of Art*. Chicago: University of Chicago Press, 1982.

Horkheimer, Max. *Eclipse of Reason*. New York: Seabury Press, 1974.

Horkheimer, Max, and T. W. Adorno. "Art and Mass Culture." In *Critical Theory*. New York: Herder & Herder, 1972.

————. "The Culture Industry: Enlightenment as Mass Deception." In *Dialectic of Enlightenment*. New York: Seabury Press, 1974.

Lefebvre, Henri. *Everyday Life in the Modern World*. New York: Harper & Row, 1971.

Marcuse, Herbert. *An Essay on Liberation*. Boston: Beacon Press, 1968.

————. *One-Dimensional Man*. Boston: Beacon Press, 1964.

————. "Repressive Tolerance." In Robert Paul Wolff, Barrington Moore, and Herbert Marcuse, *A Critique of Pure Tolerance*. Boston: Beacon Press, 1969.

Mills, C. Wright. *The Power Elite*. New York: Oxford University Press, 1959.

————. *White Collar*. New York: Oxford University Press, 1951.

Postman, Neil. *Amusing Ourselves to Death*. New York: Viking, 1985.

Real, Michael R. *Mass-Mediated Culture*. Englewood Cliffs, N.J.: Prentice-Hall, 1977.

Robinson, Lillian S. *Sex, Class and Culture*. Bloomington: Indiana University Press, 1978.

Rosenberg, Bernard, and David Manning White, eds. *Mass Culture: The Popular Arts in America*. New York: Free Press, 1957.

Schiller, Herbert. *Communication and Cultural Domination*. White Plains, N.Y.: International Arts and Sciences Press, 1976.

————. *The Mind Managers*. Boston: Beacon Press, 1970.

Sobel, Robert. *The Manipulators: America in the Media Age*. New York: Doubleday-Anchor, 1976.

Williams, Raymond. *Communications*. New York: Barnes & Noble, 1967.

————. "Conclusion." *Culture and Society, 1780–1950*. New York: Columbia University Press, 1958.

————. *Problems in Materialism and Culture*. London: Verso, 1980.

————. *The Sociology of Culture*. New York: Schocken Books, 1982.

Williamson, Judith. *Consuming Passions: The Dynamics of Popular Culture*. London: Boyars, 1986.

The Culture of Everyday Life

Adorno, Theodor W. "The Stars Down to Earth: The *Los Angeles Times* Astrology Column." *Telos*, no. 19 (Spring 1974): 13–90.

————. "Theses Against Occultism." *Telos*, no. 19 (Spring 1974): 7–12.

Ascher, Carol. "Narcissism and Women's Clothing." *Socialist Review*, no. 57 (May–June 1981): 75–86.

Barthes, Roland. *The Fashion System*. New York: Hill & Wang, 1983.

Brown, Bruce. *Marx, Freud, and the Critique of Everyday Life*. New York: Monthly Review Press, 1973.

Certeau, Michel de. *The Practice of Everyday Life*. Berkeley and Los Angeles: University of California Press, 1985.

Eco, Umberto. *Travels in Hyperreality*. New York: Harcourt Brace Jovanovich, 1986.

Goldman, Robert. "We Make Weekends: Leisure and the Commodity Form." *Social Text*, no. 8 (Winter 1983–1984): 84–103.

Haug, W. F. *Critique of Commodity Aesthetics: Appearance, Sexuality and Advertising in Capitalist Society*. Minneapolis: University of Minnesota Press, 1986.

Ollman, Bertell. *Class Struggle Is the Name of the Game: True Confessions of a Marxist Businessman*. New York: Morrow, 1983.

Silverman, Deborah. *Selling Culture: Bloomingdale's, Diana Vreeland, and the New Aristocracy of Taste in Reagan's America*. New York: Pantheon, 1986.

Tufte, Virginia, and Barbara Myerhoff, eds. *Changing Images of the Family*. New Haven: Yale University Press, 1979.

Turim, Maureen. "Fashion Shapes: Film, the Fashion Industry and the Image of Women." *Socialist Review*, no. 71 (September–October 1983): 79–96.

Bibliographies

Bullock, Chris, and David Peck, eds. *Guide to Marxist Literary Criticism*, pp. 148–168. Bloomington: Indiana University Press, 1980.

Marxism and the Mass Media: Towards a Basic Bibliography. 7 vols. New York: International General, 1976–1980.

Real, Michael R. "Media Theory: Contributions to an Understanding of American Mass Communications." *American Quarterly* 32, no. 3 (1980): 238–258.

Anthologies

Curran, James, Michael Gurevitch, and Janet Woollacott, eds. *Mass Communication and Society*. London: Open University Press, 1979.

Fischer, Heinz-Dietrich, and Stefan R. Melnik, eds. *Entertainment: A Cross Cultural Examination*. New York: Hastings House, 1979.

Gardner, Carl, ed. *Media, Politics and Culture: A Socialist View*. London: Macmillan, 1979.

Gurevitch, Michael, Tony Bennett, James Curran, and Janet Woollacott. *Culture, Society, and the Media*. New York: Methuen, 1982.

Hall, Stuart, Dorothy Hobson, Andrew Lowe, and Paul Willis, eds. *Culture, Media, Language*. London: Hutchinson, 1980.

Hall, Stuart, and Paddy Whannel. *The Popular Arts*. New York: Pantheon Books, 1965.

Modleski, Tania, ed., *Studies in Entertainment*. Bloomington: Indiana University Press, 1986.

Mosco, Vincent, and Janet Wasko, eds. *The Critical Communications Review*. Annual. Norwood, N.J., 1983–.

Special Issues of Journals

College English 38, no. 8 (April 1977). "Mass Culture, Political Consciousness, and English Studies."

democracy 1, no. 4 (October 1981). "Culture vs. Democracy."

Humanities in Society 2, no. 4 (Fall 1979). Symposium on Theodor W. Adorno.

Humanities in Society 4, no. 4 (Fall 1981). "The Politics of Literacy."

Praxis, no. 5 (1981). "Art and Ideology, Part I."

Praxis, no. 6 (1982). "Art and Ideology, Part II."

Radical Teacher, no. 8 (May 1978). "The Politics of Literacy."

Radical Teacher, no. 13 (March 1979). "Mass Culture."

Tabloid, no. 6 (Summer–Fall 1982). "Special Issue on Music."

Telos, no. 31 (Spring 1977). "On Gramsci."

Telos, no. 39 (Spring 1979). "On Habermas."

Telos, no. 40 (Fall 1980). "More Habermas."

Telos, no. 45 (Fall 1980). "On Lowenthal."

Telos, no. 62 (Winter 1984–1985). "Debates in Contemporary Culture."

Part I
Media and Manipulation

INTRODUCTION

Marxist and other leftist accounts of mass culture as manipulation have been challenged since the 1950s from three quarters: liberal and Popular Culture Association pluralists who discount the effects of manipulativeness; conservatives who believe that mass culture *is* manipulative, but in leftist interests; and leftists who themselves have modified the manipulation theory in diverse ways. The first two positions are addressed by the readings in this section; the last is covered in Part 4.

Beginning in the early sixties, much New Left scholarship has been devoted to refuting the liberal pluralist position. In line with the general reaffirmation by intellectuals of American society—as opposed to Stalinist Russia—during the high cold war years of the late forties and early fifties, liberal social scientists and cultural critics tended to view contemporary America as a refutation of Marx's model of bourgeois society dominated by a capitalist ruling class; in this pluralist view, the growth of a diversity of contending interests has guaranteed a balance of power. (Since the sixties, some liberals have shifted closer to the New Left position, whereas others have been designated neoconservative—"Old Liberal" might be a more accurate term—partly by virtue of holding fast to the pluralist view and rejecting New Left critiques of it.)

A classic expression of the liberal pluralist position is found in *The Lonely Crowd*, one of the most influential books of the fifties, published in 1950 by David Riesman with Reuel Denney and Nathan Glazer. (Glazer later became a leading neoconservative; Riesman swung to the left during the Vietnam War.) In this book Riesman presents a long list of interests who he claimed had come to divide power in America, beginning as follows: "The future seems to be in the hands of the small business and professional men who control Congress, such as realtors, lawyers, car salesmen, undertakers, and so on; of the military men who control defense and, in part, foreign policy; of the big business managers and their lawyers, finance-committee men and other counselors . . . ; [and] of the labor leaders." [1]

Trends in the second quarter of the century had seemed to bear out Riesman's ranking; subsequently, however, it has become evident that the pluralistic trend has been offset by a regression toward consolidation of power by multinational corporations and the military-industrial complex whose growth President Eisenhower warned against in his farewell address in 1961. Concerning manipulativeness by corporate powers in mass media and other sectors, Riesman's answer was that the corporate elite were no longer robber barons with a public-be-damned attitude, but had, just like middle-class Americans, become "other-directed"— they were now so many Willy Lomans wanting only to be well-liked by the masses. While it is undeniable that wealthy individuals and corporations have become more concerned with their public image under the glare of modern media coverage, it is not so certain today as it appeared to Riesman that their substantive behavior has drastically changed rather than simply being cosmeticized by elaborately engineered public relations campaigns.

Indeed, one of the main contributions of New Left scholarship has been the uncovering, through historical case studies, of large-scale corporate manipulation of the workforce, political processes, the economy, consumers, and media audiences—dating back to the late nineteenth century and growing steadily to the present, and at levels far greater than acknowledged by the pluralists. These historical studies include Harry Braverman's *Labor and Monopoly Capital*, Stanley Aronowitz's *False Promises: The Shaping of American Working Class Consciousness*, Stuart Ewen's *Captains of Consciousness: Advertising and the Social Roots of the Consumer Culture*, and David Noble's *America by Design: Science, Technology, and the Rise of Corporate Capitalism*. Their argument is that if manipulation has decreased in terms of brutal exploitation of labor, political machines, and media management in the Hearst style, it has increased in terms of corporate concentration and "engineering of consent" (a term coined by its proponent E. L. Bernays).

Following similar lines, the first three articles in this section trace the progression since the early part of this century (a span also covered, through analyses of individual cultural works in the various decades, in Part 3). Alex Carey, in "Reshaping the Truth: Pragmatists and Propagandists in America," studies the origins in America of the industries of public relations and propaganda—a word that, as Carey shows, its early American advocates used more freely than do more recent politicians, journalists, and scholars, who have often discussed its operation in fascist or communist societies, but rarely in our own. Addressing the same period and industries that Carey does, Carol Ascher focuses in "Selling to Ms. Consumer" on the corporate effort to engineer a shift in consciousness in middle-class women from homemaking to consuming. (S. J. Kleinberg's article "Success and the Working Class" supplements Ascher in documenting how the turn-of-the-century literature of success denigrated working-class men and—even more so—women, and how the journalism produced by workers opposed proletarian militancy to the doctrine of upward mobility into middle-class consumership.)[2] Walter Powell's essay "The Blockbuster Decades: The Media as Big Business" delineates the immense acceleration into the 1980s of corporate conglomeration and oligopoly in every phase of the culture industry. This trend has brought us ever closer to the society of total administration depicted in Marcuse's *One-Dimensional Man* and that of passive consumption outlined in Christopher Lasch's *The Culture of Narcissism*.

A vivid narrative tour of the cultural landscape produced by the society of controlled consumption is found in Jeffrey Schrank's 1977 book *Snap, Crackle, and Popular Taste: The Illusion of Free Choice in America*. Schrank extends such studies as Vance Packard's *The Hidden Persuaders* and Wilson B. Keys's *Subliminal Seduction*, on the advertising industry's exploitation of depth psychology, in a survey of the packaging, programming, and standardizing of consciousness in franchised chain stores, supermarkets, and shopping malls, all designed to the same nationwide pattern to induce a sequence of purchasing impulses; in Muzak's similar sequencing of music keyed to rhythms of shopping or work; in television programming, packaged tours, sports spectacles, and the culture of the automobile; in prefabricated housing and other architecture and decor; and in cheaply manufactured imitation foods such as Country Time ("Tastes Just Like Good Old-Fashioned Lemonade").

It would seem difficult to maintain, as liberal pluralists and conservatives both do, that the culture industry is only giving the people what they want, when the people are deceived about what they are getting—by business with regard to commodities they buy, and by government (Vietnam and Watergate, for example). As Dwight Macdonald observed, "To the extent the public 'wants' it, the public has been conditioned. . . . It is easier to say the public wants this than to say the truth which is that the public gets this and so wants it." [3] It might be even closer to the truth to say the public takes what it gets, like it or not. The constant lengthening of sports seasons leading to a glut of simultaneous televised baseball, football, and basketball is a prime example of initiative coming not from audience demand, but from the media pushing to see how much the audience will put up with. Even though the public is free, at least in theory, to take it or leave it, this is at best a negative freedom. The corporations still set the agenda of what is offered. Moreover, the mood of passive consumption fostered by the one-way communication of mass culture combines with ever-growing economic obstacles to stack the deck against active audience initiatives or attempts by any but the rich to launch alternative businesses or cultural enterprises.

Another standard conservative and liberal-pluralist line of defense is to point to numerous instances in which attempts at commercial or political manipulation have failed, or to case studies in which the subjects have denied being influenced by media. The flop of Ford Motor's Edsel car in spite of heavy promotion is always cited, but the Edsel Defense evades the issues. To begin with, campaigns of public relations, advertising, and programmed shopping or labor obviously have a high enough success rate to warrant constantly increasing corporate and political investments in them. As for the social scientists who, following Lazarsfeld and Katz's *Personal Influence*, minimize the direct influence of mass media, they do not seem to have spent much time listening to conversations in playgrounds, bars, or beauty shops. The influence of this or that particular campaign is less significant than the all-pervasive influence of the system as a whole. The ultimate point of the left position is not whether near-total control of consciousness has been or ever can be achieved by American capitalism, but whether it is socially beneficial for wealthy corporations and individuals to have inordinate, undemocratic power, combined with their compulsion by the profit motive, to *attempt* to gain systemic control. Can we not envision a more desirable social order than one in which the dominant institutions and a huge share of national resources are dedicated to manipulating the populace, and to constantly seeking more sophisticated ways of doing so?

The factitiousness of many of these standard defenses of the culture industry has become manifest since neoconservative business interests and cultural critics devised the ultimate PR campaign—to persuade the public that American news and entertainment media have a leftist bias. Using the "heads I win, tails you lose" rhetoric analyzed here by Peter Dreier ("The Corporate Complaint Against the Media") and Donald Lazere ("Conservative Media Criticism"), the neoconservatives are now pushing all of the same arguments about media manipulation that they staunchly rejected when leftists were making them.

Notes

1. David Riesman, with Reuel Denney and Nathan Glazer, *The Lonely Crowd* (Garden City, N.J.: Doubleday/Anchor Books, 1956), p. 257.

2. S. J. Kleinberg, "Success and the Working Class," *Journal of American Culture* 2, no. 1 (1979): 123–138. Kleinberg's article and the cluster of articles on working-class culture with which it appeared in this issue of *JAC* were noteworthy exceptions to the political blandness of most Popular Culture Association publications—including *JAC*.

3. Dwight Macdonald, "Masscult and Midcult," in *Against the American Grain* (New York: Random House, 1962), pp. 9–10.

Further Readings

Aronowitz, Stanley. *False Promises: The Shaping of American Working Class Consciousness*. New York: McGraw-Hill, 1973.

Aronson, James. *Packaging the News: A Critical Survey of Press, Radio, TV*. New York: International Publishers, 1971.

Bagdikian, Ben. *The Effete Conspiracy*. New York: Harper & Row, 1972.

———. *The Media Monopoly*. Boston: Beacon Press, 1983.

Baran, Paul and Paul Sweezy. *Monopoly Capital*. New York: Monthly Review Press, 1966.

Barnouw, Erik. *The Sponsor: Notes on a Modern Potentate*. New York: Oxford University Press, 1978.

———. *Tube of Plenty: The Evolution of American Television*. London: Oxford University Press, 1975.

Brantlinger, Patrick. "Giving the Public What It Wants." *NCTE, Public Doublespeak Newsletter* 3, no. 2 (1976): 1.

Braverman, Harry. *Labor and Monopoly Capital*. New York: Monthly Review Press, 1974.

Brown, Les. *Television: The Business Behind the Box*. New York: Harcourt Brace Jovanovich, 1971.

Bunce, Richard. *Television in the Corporate Interest*. New York: Praeger, 1976.

Cirino, Robert. *Don't Blame the People*. New York: Random House, 1971.

———. *Power to Persuade: Mass Media and the News*. New York: Bantam Books, 1974.

Cohen, Stanley, and Jock Young, eds. *The Manufacture of News: Social Problems, Deviance, and Mass Media*. Beverly Hills, Calif.: Sage, 1981.

Compaine, Benjamin M. *Who Owns the Media? Concentration of Ownership in the Mass Communication Industry*. New York: Harmony Books, 1979.

Coser, Lewis A., Charles Kadushin, and Walter W. Powell. *Books: The Culture and Commerce of Publishing*. New York: Basic Books, 1982.

Ellul, Jacques. *Propaganda*. New York: Knopf, 1965.

Gans, Herbert J. *Deciding What's News: A Study of CBS Evening News, NBC Nightly News, Newsweek, and Time*. New York: Vintage Books, 1980.

Gitlin, Todd. *Inside Prime Time*. New York: Pantheon Books, 1983.

———. *The Whole World is Watching: Mass Media in the Making and Unmaking of the New Left*. Berkeley and Los Angeles: University of California Press, 1980.

Jhally, Sut. *The Codes of Advertising: Fetishism and the Political Economy of Meaning in the Consumer Society*. New York: St. Martin's Press, 1987.

Kostelanetz, Richard. *The End of Intelligent Writing: Literary Politics in America*. New York: Sheed & Ward, 1974.

Leiss, William. *The Limits to Satisfaction: An Essay on the Problem of Needs and Commodities*. Toronto: University of Toronto Press, 1976.

Leiss, William, Stephen Kline, Sut Jhally. *Social Communication in Advertising*. New York: Methuen, 1986.

Noble, David. *America by Design: Science, Technology, and the Rise of Corporate Capitalism*. New York: Knopf, 1977.

Paletz, David L., and Robert M. Entman. *Media Power Politics*. Glencoe, Ill.: Free Press, 1981.

Parenti, Michael. *Inventing Reality: The Politics of the Mass Media*. New York: St. Martin's Press, 1986.

Randall, Richard S. *Censorship of the Movies: The Social and Political Control of a Mass Medium*. Madison: University of Wisconsin Press, 1968.

Riesman, David. *Abundance for What? and Other Essays*. Garden City, N.Y.: Doubleday, 1964.

Schiller, Dan. *Objectivity and the News: The Public and the Rise of Commercial Journalism*. Philadelphia: University of Pennsylvania Press, 1981.

Schrank, Jeffrey. *Snap, Crackle, and Popular Taste*. New York: Dell, 1977.

Schudson, Michael. *Advertising, the Uneasy Persuasion*. New York: Basic Books, 1984.

————. *Discovering the News: A Social History of American Newspapers*. New York: Basic Books, 1978.

Stein, Ben. *The View from Sunset Boulevard*. New York: Basic Books, 1979.

Stein, Robert. *Media Power: Who Is Shaping Your Picture of the World?* Boston: Houghton Mifflin, 1972.

Talbot, David, and Barbara Zheutlin. *Creative Differences: Profiles of Hollywood Dissidents*. Boston: South End Press, 1984.

Theberge, Leonard J., ed. *Crooks, Conmen and Clowns: Businessmen in TV Entertainment*. Washington, D.C.: The Media Institute, 1981.

Wasko, Janet. *Movies and Money: Financing the American Film Industry*. Norwood, N.J.: Ablex, n.d.

Whiteside, Thomas. *The Blockbuster Complex: Conglomerates, Show Business and Book Publishing*. Middletown, Conn.: Wesleyan University Press, 1981.

Wolfe, Alan. "Magazine Merchants of Death." *The Nation*, 4 July 1981, pp. 26–29.

RESHAPING THE TRUTH: PRAGMATISTS AND PROPAGANDISTS IN AMERICA

ALEX CAREY

At the end of World War II the United States of America enjoyed a preeminence in power, prestige, and worldwide moral regard that is perhaps unprecedented in the history of human societies. Since then, however, American prestige and moral authority have suffered an almost ceaseless sequence of damaging revelations. Cumulatively these revelations have produced an immense gulf between the claims expressed in popular images and official rhetoric and the increasingly visible and increasingly ugly reality behind the images and rhetoric. Hence the new euphemism for telling lies and being found out—the credibility gap.

Consider for a moment the symbols by which Americans defined their dream and picture reality: the Statue of Liberty with its Christ-like promise of succor and compassion to all the poor and wretched of the earth; the Declaration of Independence with its noble proclamation of respect for the equal and inalienable rights of all men and women; the unending public litany of adulation for American freedom, American individualism, and American democracy; a near religious commitment to the American form of the free enterprise economic system, with its supposed almost immaculate joining of private interest to public well-being.

Consider now the harsh lines of the reality that has broken through the dream-time image so long cherished. Some few of these lines are listed almost at random:

• the elitist contempt of high American officials for the ordinary people they are supposed to serve that is implicit in the decades of sophisticated deceit and urbane barbarity revealed by the Pentagon Papers, deceit and urbanity that enabled those officials to wrest from the American people "democratic" authority to desolate peasant societies;

• then the very nadir of systematic abuse of minds and bodies by American institutions and policies that is revealed in Lieutenant Calley's trial plea after the My Lai massacre: "nobody ever told us they were human";

• the discovery that General Motors, Standard Oil, and Firestone Tires, publicly among the most patriotic and self-righteous of American corporations, had privately conspired together to destroy much of America's public transport system in order to boost the sale of their products;[1] and that ITT had not only continued during the war to operate factories in Germany that built bombers for the German air force, but subsequently collected $27 million indemnity from

From *Liberation*, July–August 1977.

the American people because the American air force bombed ITT's German factories;[2]

• finally, the most crushing blow of all: the corruption that enveloped an American president (and in no small measure the American presidency also, when it was cynically traded for a lawless pardon)—most crushing of all, because the American president and presidency had been promoted, over several decades, to the status of a more-than-royal embodiment of two hundred years of democratic, humane, and generally edifying rhetoric and imagery.

Moreover Nixon was, in 1972, no mistrusted or unwanted president. Since his fall it is common to hear people recall Nixon's history of deceit, ruthlessness, and corruption running back twenty years. But in 1972 he was still the new, warm almost lovable Nixon who (as responsible commentators observed in their role of official image-makers to his presidency) had grown, had gained a new stature, almost a new personality, under the sanctifying influence of the responsibilities of presidential office.

While the image-makers thus re-created and projected Nixon so that he won more popular votes than any previous presidential candidate in American history, in this very period, the presidential tapes reveal, the president and his highest aides and ministers were plotting, in the diction and the moral temper of a clique of mafia thugs, how they might use the powers of the presidency even further to corrupt and deceive. Nor is there any longer, unfortunately, substantial reason to believe that, if Kennedy or Johnson had been reckless enough to put the reality behind their public images on as many spools of tape as Nixon, their credibility gaps would have been notably less.

The corruption of American ideals and American power that the past decades have revealed is an American tragedy. But, given the scale of American power, they constitute also a world problem of a quite different order of magnitude: an unpredictable source of exacerbation to the risk of nuclear annihilation. For this reason it is of the first importance to try to understand how the tragic deterioration in the American democratic system has come about—and whether and how it might be remediable.

Insofar as cultural history is continuous, any starting date for an explanation of the contemporary American malaise must be arbitrary. That point acknowledged, I shall, for reasons I hope to make clear, start at the beginning of this century. The most influential social thinkers in the recent history of American society have been William James and John Dewey. Both were men of exemplary character and generous humane intent. But just as Marx did not intend Stalin, so the intentions of James and Dewey have not determined the consequences of their theories. Both were pragmatists; that is to say, they made the truth of a belief depend not on the evidence that leads to its adoption, but on the consequences that follow that adoption.

Because they were also popular evangelists for pragmatism, it is convenient to refer to James and Dewey for a summary characterization of the pragmatic outlook. American culture has, of course, a much longer history of pragmatic preoccupation with appearances and consequences. As Boorstin succinctly observes, "The whole American tradition of pragmatism, from Benjamin Franklin, who insisted that it was less important whether any religious belief was true than whether the consequences of the belief were wholesome, down to William James . . . has expressed a consuming interest in the appearance of things." [3] James held that an idea is "true" so long as to believe it is profitable to our lives and that " 'the true' . . . is only the expedient in the way of our thinking, just as 'the right' is only the expedient in the way of our behaving." He maintained, for example, that if the belief that God exists "works satisfactorily in the widest sense of the word, it is true," and added "experience shows that it certainly does work." [4]

Dewey similarly holds that beliefs should be distinguished as "good" and "bad," not as "true" and "false." Beliefs are good if believing them has beneficial consequences. [5] "Facts" do not exist for Dewey, Bertrand Russell observes, "in the sense that 'facts' are stubborn and cannot be manipulated." [6] For Dewey proposed to replace the notion of truth with the notion of "warranted assertibility": [7] any belief that can be claimed to bring useful consequences may acquire "warranted assertibility" on that ground alone.

The notion of "warranted assertibility" already has an air of Watergate about it. For the moment we shall not follow that particular lead, except to cite Russell's warning about any philosophy that, by making the consequences of a belief the test of its truth, delivers to those powerful individuals or nations who are able to determine consequences the right to say what beliefs shall be called "good" or "true." Russell observes:

In all this I feel a grave danger. . . . The concept of "truth" as something dependent on facts largely outside human control has been one of the ways in which philosophy hitherto has inculcated the necessary element of humility. When this check upon pride is removed, a further step is taken on the road toward a certain kind of madness—the intoxication of power. . . . I am persuaded that . . . any philosophy which, however unintentionally, contributes to [this intoxication] is increasing the danger of vast social disaster. [8]

For twenty years from about 1900 there was, in the American press, a "flood of . . . articles on pragmatism." This flood was started by James and Dewey. James employed much vivid rhetoric, such as "truth is what works," "the true is the expedient," and "faith in a fact helps create the fact." [9]

James and Dewey's evangelism *coincided* with the growth of a "problem" for business corporations to which their pragmatic viewpoint authorized a congenial "solution": it was closely *followed* by the development of a mass communications technology (especially radio and television) that greatly assisted the implementation of that solution.

The pragmatic viewpoint—denying the existence of a world independent of human belief—advocated that, within wide limits, human beings should resolve their problems and frustrations by adopting and promulgating any belief that "works" to that effect. The following observations by V. O. Key, professor of government at Harvard University, indicate the congeniality of this viewpoint to American corporations in the political context that developed after 1900:

Businessmen are a small minority highly vulnerable to political attack. . . . They . . . have to depend on something other than their votes. They have to use their wits—and their money—to generate a public opinion that acquiesces in the enjoyment by business of its status in the economic order. . . . To gain public favor business associations employ in large numbers public relations experts, those masters of the verbal magic that transmutes private advantage into the public good . . . [and] continuing propaganda calculated to shape public attitudes favorably toward the business system.[10]

Thus "as industrial power grew . . . the conscious policy of managing public attitudes to retain that power came to be adopted";[11] and, from about 1920, increasing numbers of business corporations appointed public relations executives whose "function . . . was . . . to deal with words . . . designed to influence the public without necessarily involving any basic change of attitude or action on the part of the company."[12]

By the mid-1930s there developed an "organized, nationwide business-propaganda for the sale of ideas to the American people dealing with . . . the values and merits of the [free] enterprise system." Rapidly "such generally accepted, if not almost hallowed, ideas [of contemporary advertising] as . . . 'all the traffic will bear,' 'repetition is reputation,' and 'truth is believability' . . . [were] focused on the sale of ideas."[13]

By 1939 a Senate committee (the La Follette Committee) reported:

The National Association of Manufacturers has blanketed the country with a propaganda which in technique has relied upon indirection of meaning, and in presentation on secrecy and deception. Radio speeches, public meetings, news, cartoons, editorials, advertising, motion pictures, and many other artifices of propaganda have not, in most instances, disclosed to the public their origin within the Association.[14]

After World War II "business interests more and more utilized their public relations resources for the dissemination of political ideology . . . [until they produced] an almost overwhelming propaganda of doctrine . . . [and] saturation of the media with advertising calculated to sell ideas rather than merchandise."[15]

By 1948 American business's anti–New Deal/socialist/communist propaganda campaign was costing $100 million a year for such advertising alone.[16] The year 1950 brought an interim dividend in Senator Joe McCarthy; and that dividend, duly cultivated, brought in 1952 the final dividend to which the campaign was ultimately directed[17]—an end to twenty years of Democratic administrations (an unbroken period equal to the sum of *all* Democratic administrations in the ninety years prior to 1933).

One general point should not escape notice. There is a remarkable correspondence in attitude to truth between pragmatists and propagandists. Both justify the promotion of false beliefs wherever it is supposed that false beliefs have socially useful consequences. Indeed, the principal difference between them consists perhaps in this: the ordinary propagandist may know that he is telling lies, but the pragmatist-propagandist, having redefined truth to make it indistinguishable from propaganda, is likely to become inescapably trapped in the supposedly "useful" deceptions and illusions he approves as "warranted assertibilities."

I wish now to trace the growing accommodation of intellectuals associated with American industry to the partisan and pragmatic values of business; and the convenient rationales by which (as true pragmatists in their own right) they preserved their pretensions to integrity without handicap to their career chances.

Until 1900 American business corporations took a contemptuous attitude to public opinion. But from 1900 to 1910 Upton Sinclair and others so effectively exposed the exploitation and brutality of American industry that, as *Fortune* magazine wrote later, "business did not discover . . . until its reputation had been all but destroyed . . . that in a democracy nothing is more important than [public opinion]." [18]

This discovery led rapidly to the development of a profession of specialists in "public relations" whose task it was to ensure that public beliefs about industry were such as to keep both industry and the public happy. (It should perhaps be recalled that, according to James and Dewey, *any* public belief that has such consequences is true.) Ivy Lee was the first great PR man. He taught business to use the press. But his "best known feat," as *Fortune* observes, "was to convert John D. Rockefeller, in the public mind, from an ogre to a benefactor." [19]

Following Ivy Lee, Edward L. Bernays was the next major figure in the new propaganda–public relations field, a field he would develop and dominate for the next thirty years. By 1937 *Business Week*, after noting that Bernays was "a nephew of Sigmund Freud, the great Viennese psychoanalyst," observed that "Mr. Bernays has attained corresponding stature in his own sphere of psychology," which *Business Week* described as the motivation and control of "the 'mass mind.'" [20]

The next major application of the pragmatic conception of truth came in 1917. With American entry into World War I, a Committee on Public Information (better known as the Creel Committee) was formed. Bernays, who worked with the committee, reports that "every known device of persuasion and suggestion (was employed) to sell our war aims to the American people," who were initially unenthusiastic. Bernays observes of the Creel Committee's activities that "reports that the Germans were beasts and Huns were generally accepted. The most fantastic atrocity stories were believed." The Creel Committee was credited with producing by such methods "a revolutionary change in the sentiments of the nation." [21]

At the end of the war, Bernays continues, businessmen realized "that the great public could now perhaps be harnessed to their cause as it had been harnessed during the war to the national cause, and that the same methods would do the job." Thus, when Bernays and others associated with the Creel Committee "returned to civilian life [they] applied [on behalf of business] the publicity methods they had learned during the war." [22]

The use of propaganda by corporations and industries to control public opinion grew, and Bernays prospered. *Fortune* magazine later observed that "the 1920s . . . were notable for the rise of E. L. Bernays [who] . . . became known for what he called 'the engineering of consent' and for 'creating news.'" [23] By 1923 Bernays was giving courses in public relations and propaganda at New York University. [24] In 1928 the *American Journal of Sociology* published a how-to-do-it article by Bernays entitled "Manipulating Public Opinion," in which Bernays paid tribute to sociologists for the help he obtained from their work. [25]

From 1930 to 1960 Professor Harold Lasswell held a position of academic leadership in the field of propaganda and communication comparable with Bernays's leading role as a practitioner in the business world. [26] In 1933, in an article for the *Encyclopedia of the Social Sciences*, Lasswell observes that since the "masses" are still captive to "ignorance and superstition," the arrival of democracy, in America and elsewhere, has "compelled the development of a whole new technique of control, largely through propaganda." For, Lasswell continues, propaganda is "the one means of mass mobilization which is cheaper than violence, bribery or other possible control techniques." Moreover, propaganda is essential in a democracy because "men are often poor judges of their own interests" and must therefore be swayed by propaganda to make choices they would otherwise not make.[27]

Until the mid-1930s conscientious objection to the engineering of consent had been quite widely in evidence; by 1947 objection on ethical grounds had almost completely disappeared. Large numbers of social scientists and university departments were actively engaged with the practice of consent-engineering—largely on behalf of corporations—and with related research.

In 1947 an article by Edward Bernays entitled "The Engineering of Consent" was published in the prestigious *Annals of the American Academy of Political and Social Sciences*. In this article Bernays offers a rationale for the use of propaganda in a democracy, which *Fortune* magazine and others later adopted. The rationale consists in equating "propaganda" with "persuasion," and hence with "democracy." "The engineering of consent," Bernays firmly asserts, "is the very essence of the democratic process, the freedom to persuade and suggest."[28]

By this date Bernays displays the same elitist contempt for the ordinary citizen we observed in Lasswell in 1933. "The average American adult," he observes, "has only six years of schooling. . . . [Therefore] democratic leaders must play their part in . . . engineering consent. . . . Today it is impossible to overestimate the importance of engineering consent; it affects almost every aspect of our daily lives."[29] In 1949 Bernays was honored by the American Psychological Association for his contributions to science and society.[30]

In the same year, *Fortune* magazine, following Bernays's lead, observed that "it is as impossible to imagine a genuine democracy without the science of persuasion [i.e., propaganda] as it is to think of a totalitarian state without coercion." That point established, *Fortune* continued: "The daily tonnage output of propaganda and publicity . . . has become an important force in American life. Nearly half of the contents of the best newspapers is derived from publicity releases; nearly all the contents of the lesser papers . . . are directly or indirectly the work of PR departments."[31]

In 1950 a particularly mordant description by Lasswell of the role of propaganda in (American) democracy was republished in readings "representative of the best work in the field": "Conventions have arisen which favor the ventilation of opinion and the taking of votes. Most of that which formerly could be done by violence and intimidation must now be done by argument and persuasion. Democracy has proclaimed the dictatorship of [debate], and the technique of dictating to the dictator is named propaganda."[32]

In 1956 Professor William Albig of Illinois University reviewed the work of the previous twenty years on public opinion and related subjects. He observed that in that time "there has been more organized study of public opinion in the

U.S. . . . and more special pleading and propaganda . . . than in all previous cultural history." [33]

Albig found that, whereas before 1936 there had been continuous concern "with questions of ethics in relation to the formation and effects of public opinion," this concern had largely disappeared from later writing and research. By contrast he found in the later work "evidence of the intense excitement of professionals at the vision of the possibility of increased psychological control of their fellow men," and evidence, also, of "further degeneration of respect for their target, the common man." Albig concluded his review with the warning that "many of the younger social scientists" had not "adequately pondered" the likely political results of the values and assumptions expressed in their work. [34]

In 1960 an American historian, Daniel Boorstin, published a book entitled *The Image; or, What Happened to the American Dream.* Boorstin, who is now librarian of the Library of Congress, was much concerned about the effects of the huge growth in advertising and associated propaganda. One major effect, in Boorstin's view, had been a popular shift from concern with "ideals" to concern with "images." [35] It is instructive to compare his description of American society in 1960 with the ideas about truth promoted by James and Dewey fifty years earlier.

Boorstin observes that "the 'corporate image' . . . is, of course, the most elaborately and expensively contrived of the images of our age," and that "the momentous sign of the rise of image-thinking and its displacement of ideals is, of course, the rise of advertising." Boorstin considers that Americans "have underestimated the effect of the rise of advertising. We think it has meant an increase of untruthfulness. In fact it has meant a reshaping of our very concept of truth." [36] In consequence of this reshaping, "not truth but credibility is the modern [American] test. We share this standard with the advertising men themselves," and "all of us . . . —all American citizen-consumers—are daily less interested in whether something is a fact than in whether it is convenient that it should be believed." As a nation, Boorstin observes, Americans have come to think

that our main problem is abroad. How to "project" our images to the world?
Yet the problem abroad is only a symptom of our deeper problem at home. We have come to believe in our own images, till we have projected ourselves out of this world [so that] now, in the height of our power . . . we are threatened by a new and peculiarly American menace. . . . It is the menace of unreality. . . . We risk being the first people in history to have been able to make their illusions so vivid, so persuasive, so "realistic" that they can live in them. We are the most illusioned people on earth. Yet we dare not become disillusioned, because our illusions are the very house in which we live; they are our news, our heroes . . . our very experience. [37]

Thus, by 1960, some thirty years after the *American Journal of Sociology* published Bernays's article "Manipulating Public Opinion," American public opinion has been manipulated, in Boorstin's phrase, "out of this world." In less than another decade, the pragmatic displacement of "truth" by beliefs it was judged desirable people should hold, and of stubborn facts by "warranted assertibilities," had played a manifest part in producing the outcome Russell warned about in 1945: "a certain kind of madness—the intoxication of power . . . increasing the danger of vast social disaster."

And so to Vietnam and Watergate and the slow, slow difficult road back to truth and sanity, a road that cannot be traversed until the subject of propaganda and its control in American society—almost entirely neglected for fifty years by political scientists—is afforded a high and urgent priority in the nation's affairs. For the key political problem confronting the United States has neither changed nor ameliorated since Professor Robert Dahl defined it in 1959 in the following terms: "How much of the generally favorable attitude of Americans toward business"—and the consequent "absence of any well-defined alternative, in the United States to the present order"—

can be attributed to deliberate efforts to manipulate attitudes. . . . Much in the way of political theory . . . depends on the assumptions one makes about the sources of political attitudes. . . . If one assumes that political preferences are simply plugged into the system by leaders (business or other) in order to extract what they wish from the system, then the model of plebiscitary democracy is substantially equivalent to the model of totalitarian rule.[38]

If government of the people by the people for the people, in any meaningful sense, is not to perish from the American earth; if the American Dream is not to end in a better appointed, more adroitly managed, version of 1984; then it is of cardinal importance that the problem described by Dahl not be buried out of sight and out of mind by celebrations and symbols that glorify images and ignore realities.

Notes

1. B. C. Snell, *American Ground Transport* . . . (Snell Report), U.S. Senate Committee of the Judiciary, Subcommittee on Antitrust and Monopoly, Washington, D.C.: GPO, 1974.

2. A. Sampson, *The Sovereign State: The Secret History of ITT* (London: Coronet, 1974), p. 45.

3. D. Boorstin, *The Image; or, What Happened to the American Dream* (London: Weidenfeld & Nicolson, 1961), p. 212.

4. W. James, *Pragmatism* (New York: Longman Green, 1907), pp. 75, 222, 299.

5. J. Dewey, *Reconstruction in Philosophy* (New York: Holt, 1920), pp. 128–130.

6. B. Russell, *History of Western Philosophy* (New York: Simon & Schuster, 1945), pp. 825–826.

7. J. Dewey, *Logic: The Theory of Inquiry* (New York: Holt, 1938), pp. 7–11, 118, 546.

8. Russell, *History of Western Philosophy*, p. 828.

9. C. S. Peirce, *Values in a Universe of Chance*, ed. P. Weisner (New York: Doubleday, 1958), p. 180.

10. V. O. Key, *Politics, Parties and Pressure Groups* (New York: Crowell, 1958), p. 103.

11. Ibid., p. 108.

12. E. L. Bernays, *Public Relations* (Norman: University of Oklahoma Press, 1952), p. 87.

13. R. Brady, *Business as a System of Power* (New York: Columbia University Press, 1943), pp. 292–293. See also E. C. Bursk, "Selling the Idea of Free Enterprise," *Harvard Business Review*, May 1948, pp. 372–384.

14. U.S. Congress, Senate Committee on Education and Labor, *Report of the Committee on Education and Labor*, no. 6, pt. 6, pursuant to Special Resolution 266, 76th Cong., 1st sess., 1939, p. 218.

15. Key, *Politics, Parties and Pressure Groups*, pp. 106–107.

16. C. D. MacDougall, *Understanding Public Opinion* (New York: Macmillan, 1952), p. 568; and "Is Anybody Listening?" (editorial), *Fortune*, September 1950, p. 78.

17. "Is Anybody Listening?" p. 79; and H. G. Moulton and C. W. McKee, "How Good Is Economic Education?" *Fortune*, July 1951, p. 126.

18. "Business Is Still in Trouble" (editorial), *Fortune* 39, no. 5 (1949): 198.

19. Ibid., p. 70.

20. "Public Relations—First in the Order of Business" (editorial), *Business Week*, 23 January 1937, p. 34.

21. Bernays, *Public Relations*, pp. 71, 75, 74.

22. Ibid., p. 78.

23. "Business Is Still in Trouble," p. 200.

24. Bernays, *Public Relations*, p. 84.

25. E. L. Bernays, "Manipulating Public Opinion: The Why and the How," *American Journal of Sociology* 33, no. 6 (1928): 961.

26. "Lasswell is the most well-known of contemporary American political scientists . . . he has probably influenced more work in other people than any political scientist alive today" (B. Crick, *The American Science of Politics* [London: Kegan Paul, 1959], p. 176).

27. H. D. Lasswell, "Propaganda," in *Encyclopedia of the Social Sciences* (New York: Macmillan, 1930–1935; reprint, 1954), pp. 523, 524, 527.

28. E. L. Bernays, "The Engineering of Consent," *Annals of the American Academy of Political and Social Sciences* 250 (March 1947): 114.

29. Ibid., pp. 114–115.

30. See "Edward L. Bernays Intergroup Relations Award Meeting," *American Psychologist* 4 (1949): 265.

31. "Business Is Still in Trouble," p. 69.

32. H. D. Lasswell, "The Theory of Political Propaganda," in *Reader in Public Opinion and Communication*, ed. B. Berelson and M. Janowitz (New York: Free Press, 1950), p. 180.

33. W. Albig, "Two Decades of Opinion Study: 1936–1956," *Public Opinion Quarterly* 21, no. 3 (1957): 14.

34. Ibid., pp. 21–22.

35. Boorstin, *The Image*, pp. 197–200, 239ff.

36. Ibid., pp. 184, 205.

37. Ibid., pp. 227, 212, 241, 240.

38. R. Dahl, "Business and Politics: A Critical Appraisal of Political Science," in R. Dahl et al., *Social Science Research on Business: Product and Potential* (New York: Columbia University Press, 1959), pp. 37–38, 42.

SELLING TO MS. CONSUMER

CAROL ASCHER

Consumerism and its handmaiden, advertising, developed in the late 1900s and the first decades of the twentieth century. Like many historical trends, these two grew largely outside of any direct decisions by those who were most affected by them—in this case, women. The period around the turn of the century was a time when, in fact, fewer women held professional roles than they had only two or three decades earlier. Moreover, active women of the period threw their energies into either the suffrage movement or various social welfare fights. Even Florence Kelly, executive secretary to the Consumer Union in the early 1900s, saw it as her role to generate pressure to improve the working conditions in which products were made rather than to create a movement to fight the growth of advertising or buying.

Without women's participation at higher levels in business and industry or an active women's movement concerned with these issues, the home was increasingly shaped by forces whose interests were not its own. As one woman argued in 1908, "Perhaps the real danger to the home lies in the fact that women . . . are not free to control the industrial changes which affect it, and that these changes are being determined too largely by commercial interests." [1]

Nonetheless, there was much about the condition of women that made them receptive to the changes taking place. It is this receptivity that I want to explore. For history is never completely beyond people's control, even when they are not at the helm where decisions are made.

Between 1890 and 1920, when America became transformed into a consumer society, women's lives continued on the almost runaway course of change begun much earlier in the nineteenth century. For those women who moved outside the home, new supports and new possibilities for selfhood became potentially available, though none were easily won or even easy to live with once attained. But for women in the home, the period had a shattering quality, much as the late sixties and early seventies have had for housewives today. And the loss of old norms and ties made these women vulnerable to solutions posed by the world of commodities.

In the early 1900s central heating, gas appliances, and running hot and cold water lightened housework for a growing number of women, particularly in the middle class. Water no longer had to be boiled for washing, nor irons heated on a stove, and coal didn't have to be brought in from a cellar and stoked throughout the day. The introduction of the fireless cooker (gas stove) was a milestone for women of this period; it meant that temperature could be controlled, and cooking done more efficiently and with greater certainty than ever before.

In the next decade, many women were able to purchase washing machines, ice boxes, and vacuum cleaners. These household appliances lightened work inside

From *College English* 38, no. 8 (1977).

the home, but they also necessitated a reordering of women's sense of housekeeping. An example can be given with the vacuum cleaner. Here much of the early advertising consisted of retraining women to see cleaning as the rather undramatic suction process, rather than as the visually reassuring display of stirred-up dust they were used to.[2] Christine Frederick, one of the few women working with industry, expressed the disequilibrium the housewife was experiencing in the late 1920s when she said that manufacturers had to help women transform their work from the "hand-craft age" into the era of the "machine operative."[3]

The spread of the kindergarten and compulsory schooling in the first decades of the twentieth century also took some of the old childrearing responsibilities away from women. More important, these new institutions, as well as their intellectual underpinnings, began to shift the notion of who knew best how to care for children. Emerging fields of child development and education offered new methods of mothering and critiqued the old. Early standardized tests, such as the Binet, measured "objectively" how smart the child was, rendering inadequate a mother's sense of her daughter or son. Although mothers still spent years caring for their children, they increasingly did so with the specter of professional judgment hanging over them.

Women in the home were also affected by the changing order of the work world. The early home economists—domestic scientists, as they were then called—had hoped to strengthen the family and improve the woman's place in it by also insisting on the authority of the husband-father. But the new organization of industry made it difficult for men to hold on to their old controls, either at work or at home. The geographic separation of the home and work worlds made it impossible for the father to maintain the authority he had once held when he worked inside the home alongside his family. At the same time, work for most men lost its craft, and an increasing proportion of men worked for wages in large, anonymous situations where they retained little control over their work. This breakdown in the material base for male authority gave a spurt to feminism. But it also made daily life more uncertain for those women who tried to adjust old patterns to new realities.

As men's work on the outside lost its dignity, their role inside the family turned from that of patriarch to that of provider. Not only did the home have to offer solace from the workday world, but women had to bolster the wounded egos it was causing in their menfolk. It was as if by making the home a castle, women could transform their husbands back into kings.

Given the hierarchical patterns women were used to, the decreased dominion of the husband-father opened the way for women to accept a new locus of authority. This authority was being developed by science and industry. Both would have new rationales for right and wrong, and both would turn all the family, including the father, into children, to be taught, teased, and coerced. One of the most self-conscious statements of this shift in authority came toward its end, in 1931, when Edward Filene, head of the great Boston department store, wrote,

since the head of the family is no longer in control of the economic process through which the family must get its living, he must be relieved of many ancient responsibilities and therefore of many of his prerogatives. . . . Women . . . and children are likely to discover that their economic well-being comes not from the organization of the family but from the organization of industry, and they may look more and more for individual guidance, not to their fathers, but to the *truth* which science is discovering.[4]

Birth control also undermined old authority patterns as well as transformed women's work in and outside the home. The shrinking of family size had started in the early nineteenth century, but it became a public "problem" in the later decades of the century when a number of social movements advocated some form of birth control and when it became a common fear that the middle class would simply cease to reproduce itself. Margaret Sanger's first clinic, which opened in 1916, was the culmination of decades of struggle for public access to birth control.[5] By the 1920s 70 to 80 percent of all middle- and upper-class women were assumed to be using some form of contraception.[6] For the first time, sex became separated from reproduction. The 1920s was a time of tremendous sexual experimentation—a time in many ways as free as today. But along with increases in sexual freedom, divorce grew rapidly. Whereas in 1890 there had been only three divorces per thousand, by 1920 the number had risen to nearly eight per thousand.[7]

Even the older feminists were caught off base by the new sexuality. Jane Addams, for example, who had grown up in the period when womanhood meant motherhood—or its more liberated variant, social housekeeping—spoke publicly of her discontent with the emphasis on sexual gratification. And Charlotte Perkins Gilman condemned the risqué clothing of the flappers. Although she felt bound to endorse sexual liberation, she believed women were displaying a "backlash of primitive femininity" that stood in the way of real sexual equality.[8]

Birth control generated the potential for women's economic independence, but it also caused a great deal of uncertainty and retrenchment. By 1920 every third worker was a woman, and 20 percent of all married women worked.[9] The proportion of single women (including those widowed and divorced) had also increased significantly in the preceding thirty years.[10] Moreover, single women were holding jobs and living outside families, rather than doing chores in return for room and board with relatives, as had been the case several decades earlier. However, Charlotte Perkins Gilman was not wrong to fear the backlash of "primitive femininity." In the first decades of the twentieth century the proportion of professional women declined. Between 1910 and 1930, for example, women doctors declined by 7 percent and women musicians and composers by 6 percent.[11] By the time the Nineteenth Amendment was passed, women posed no threat as a voting block, and few women in the 1920s ran for political office. Although many women worked, they did not aspire to the heights they once had.

Changes in work and the family had made women at home insecure; but this insecurity was exacerbated by women's increasing isolation. An important source of this isolation stemmed, in turn, from changes in the organization of the home and its relationship to the outside world.

By the turn of the century, although apartments were being built in every city, the single-family home was becoming a reality as well as an ideal for more people. Public transportation had enabled housing to spread out from city centers. Suburbanization made it possible for workers' families to live with their own separate roofs over their heads. And industrialists, home economists, and social reformers alike argued the importance of providing such dwellings for workers and their families. The *Ladies' Home Journal*, the most influential of the women's magazines, featured a model house plan for a single-family home in each of its issues.[12] Many of the industrial towns built in the late 1800s contained single-family homes in order to develop in their workers a sense of the right way to live. Some went so far as to offer courses in home economics for the wives; these courses reinforced the importance of the single-family home and the role of women in it.[13]

After World War I, the automobile furthered the sprawl of residential areas outside the cities. Thousands of men were already traveling to work over an hour each way, and neighborhoods were becoming devoid of men during working hours. While most urban women emigrées to the suburbs complained of loneliness, the idea that suburban living was important to family life, and particularly to raising children, kept the flow of families outward from the cities.

With a revolution going on in Russia and the potential for social upheaval obvious in this country, single-family dwellings became fused with a vision of preventing revolution and communism. The women's magazines supported this vision. A 1920 issue of the *Ladies' Home Journal*, for instance, "intimated that the Bolsheviks wanted most of all to destroy the single-family house and replace it with 'nationalized woman' in mass housing." The magazine also connected feminism and communism as foes of the home and motherhood, asserting that women who selfishly chose not to have children or not to raise them by themselves at home were "aiding the red cause."[14]

Along with the ideal of the single-family home came new housing styles, which lessened the housework but opened the way for commodities to enter the home. The parlor, the repository of tradition, had been the first to go, aided by a virulent campaign against it in the 1890s by the editor of the *Ladies' Home Journal*, Ed Bok. The parlor symbolized holding on to old family heirlooms and relating to guests in old, formal ways. The living room, by contrast, was to be "lived in." It could embrace new styles in commodities and human relationships.

Along with the number of rooms, room size also shrank steadily. This trend was most obvious in the kitchen, a room that had once been the center of household production. Following the industrial ideal of specialization, architects now stripped all but food preparation from the room. The ideal size for a kitchen in the early 1900s had already shrunk from its nineteenth-century expansiveness to ten by twelve feet.[15] By the end of World War I, kitchenettes began to appear.[16] The elimination of laundry space in the kitchen went along with the growth of the commercial laundry, one of the few ultimately unsuccessful campaigns to commercialize what had been women's work.[17] Small kitchens and kitchenettes also eliminated the possibility of eating inside them, and by the early 1930s one author was noting that small kitchens had forced "a good deal of eating outside the house."[18]

Small kitchens were a sign of prestige, as they both followed the ideal of efficiency and specialization and were a visual display of the fact that the husband's salary enabled the family to buy, rather than produce, most of what it used. The inverse relationship between kitchen size and workers' incomes was drawn out with exquisite detail by a Harvard social scientist. In his view, among families whose income was ten dollars a week or less, the wife spent her time "cooking, washing, caring for the children, and doing outside washing or going herself to work." The kitchen in these homes was "perforce the family living room and should be made proportionately ample." In families whose weekly income approached eighteen dollars, while the family still ate in the kitchen, it would probably want "a 'best room' in which to receive callers, actual or hoped for." Among "families of a higher income class," however, a small kitchen was most appropriate. Here, in this analyst's view, "the housewife is quite willing to carry food and dishes into the dining-room in order to escape eating the food in the place where it was cooked; also a separate dining-room is deemed more comfortable by the rest of the family." [19] Thus the middle-class housewife paid for the greater gentility of her family by preparing food alone, in a small kitchen, and carrying it to and from the dining area.

By 1920, the isolation caused by single-family homes and the specialization of rooms within them had apparently caused enough widespread distress among women at home that a book could be written entitled *The Nervous Housewife*. The book combined popular psychoanalytic notions of human needs, an ideological commitment to the single-family home with its specialized quarters, and—despite the contradiction—a detailed study of the damage it was wreaking on women. In a poignant chapter called "The Housework and the Home as Factors in the Neuroses," the author, Abraham Myerson, listed as sources of women's contemporary neuroses not only their raised expectations but also, and more important, the isolation and monotony of their work:

All work at home has the difficulty of the segregation, the isolation of the home. Man, the social animal who needs at least some one to quarrel with, has deliberately isolated his household—on a property basis. There has grown up a definite, aesthetic need of privacy; all of modesty and the essential feeling demand it.

This is good for the man, and perhaps for the children, but not for the woman. Her work is done all alone, and at the time her husband comes home and wants to stay there, she would like to get out. Work that is in the main lonely, and work that on the whole leaves the mind free, leads almost inevitably to daydreaming and introspection. These are essentials in the housework—monotony, daydreaming, and introspection. [20]

Because Myerson assumed that the need for privacy and segregation were worth nurturing in their current form, his solution to "the nervous housewife" was tentative and piecemeal. Like Charlotte Perkins Gilman, Myerson suggested that some of housework would probably have to be made cooperative; but he was cautious to insist that this be done within the confines of the nuclear family and the single-family home.

Isolation inside the home began to impel women into shops and stores. Yet shopping itself provided less and less succor for isolation. For it too was becoming bereft of personal contact.

In the 1880s and 1890s department stores sprang up in all major cities. Since several hundred clerks could not be trusted to bargain in the manner of a shopkeeper, department stores began to institute the "fixed price." With the fixed price, the clerk was relegated to showing items and making change. In the same period, F. W. Woolworth began his five-and-dime stores. These further limited the contact between salesperson and customer by instituting open counters and displays. Woolworth's salespeople now only made change for purchases already chosen.

In food retailing, packaged foods around the turn of the century left the grocery store clerk without measuring functions, and shifted the focus from the actual product and the relationship between clerk and shopper to the product's appearance in its package. Brand names became the source by which the customer chose—and increasingly received her "human" contact. With packaging of food items, "self-service" came into existence. Now, instead of the storekeeper serving a woman as she filled her order, the woman was left to roam through the store while clerks stocked shelves and took inventory. Contact with the customer became limited to the checkout.

In the small shops, women had been allowed to charge and pay as their money came in. As the chain stores became the major self-service operators, the self-service stores demanded cash. The motto was "pay as you go," and nobody's personal relationship with the proprietor was good enough to warrant informal debts and charges. Instead, the larger stores began to offer installment plans, which—after some investigation of her or his personal finances—allowed the consumer to pay on time, at interest. Like self-service, installment buying aimed at stimulating purchases. But it did so without either the personal trust of the old charge account or the economic risks to the storekeepers.

Advertising developed its modern appeals during this period of upheaval and estrangement. The very technological improvements that furthered women's uncertainty and isolation also created the possibility for more effective selling. As old roles and relationships weakened, consumerism and advertising took upon themselves the burden of offering contact and promising love, trust, and security. Some of the changes in selling and advertising techniques—such as certain forms of packaging or the use of color photography—necessitated technological advances. But the dramatic alterations in the style and meaning of the messages had less to do with technology than with an increased understanding of human psychology, as it developed through psychoanalysis and its derivative movements, and with a conscious decision by businessmen to play an active role in helping to form what women and men wanted.

Before 1880, advertising messages had consisted largely of detailed instructions, diagrams and descriptions of the product by the manufacturer, or lengthy testimonials by its users. Images only indirectly connected to the product generally did not come into play. Around the 1890s, advertisers began to loosen up and experiment with new forms. Jingles and human interest trademarks appeared. Jingles told a story, often absurd, but focused on a phrase or an image that embedded the product in the customer's mind. While the emotional appeal of jingles was often their silliness, it was clear to sellers that catchy, emotionally appealing ideas, rather than long descriptions, were good selling devices. Human interest trademarks also followed the device of the simple message but began the trend of more "subjective" advertising. Human interest trademarks, such as the Wool

Soap Kids or the H-O cereal baby, were characters who became known and loved for themselves.

Advertisers used images of children self-consciously in the 1890s, directing them specifically at women. *Printer's Ink*, the advertising trade journal, announced in 1896 that "the picture of a healthy, pretty child rivets the attention of most people, especially women. This fact is now generally recognized by advertisers, and the use of a multitude of child-faces as eye attractors is the result." [21] The effectiveness of children as an advertising device was heightened because motherhood had become a choice for many women. At the same time, the images served to draw women back in toward their mothering role.

From the outset, advertising theory, like much of psychoanalysis, was developed largely through experience with women. The psychology of advertising as a discipline has been dated as early as 1903, and certainly numerous insights about what motivated women were being developed around the turn of the century. However, it was with the end of World War I that an accelerated need to increase consumption and the spread of psychoanalysis in this country joined to create a new, scientific study of women as consumers. Notions about the nature of women quickly became embedded in analyses of how the consumer functioned.

Many advertising theorists took Freud's notion of the sexual drive or instinct and used it for their own purposes. Whereas Freud postulated only sexuality as an instinct that transcended history (and even this had a quite broad meaning, almost at the level of a life force), advertising theorists began to produce long lists of "instincts" that were clearly products of a specific culture and whose aim was to further embed people in that culture. For example, Christine Frederick, in her book *Selling to Mrs. Consumer*, listed eighteen "female instincts," among which were sex-love, mother-love, love of homemaking, vanity, love of mutation or change (that is, fashion), love of prestige, and love of reputation. [22] She even elevated the love of trading to an instinct in her attempt to rationalize and justify women's new consumer role. Designating all these traits as instincts removed them to a place where the society no longer had to take responsibility for their existence. Instead, those traits that would be developed, accentuated, and reinforced by advertising could be blamed on the instinctual structure.

Whatever the specific "instinct," emotionality and irrationality became the mainstay of advertising's notion of human or female nature. This was the vulgarized version of the psychoanalytic notion that the individual was driven by unconscious drives. And as emotionality and irrationality became embedded in the common sense of advertising practice, advertising language and imagery drew more and more on prestige, sexuality, isolation, and the alternative, love and contact. Carl Naether, in his classic *Advertising to Women*, argued that advertising should always "strike a personal note," because women were always involved in "the personal"; he suggested using "fanciful expressions" and "chatty tones" with women. [23] His suggestions implied an understanding that the messages of advertising would have to convey the personal contact lost to most people's lives. Like Naether, Christine Frederick also emphasized woman's emotionality. In Frederick's view, woman had a "natural" intelligence, which was "instinctive" and "practical"; but living emotionally, she often revived her spirits with "foolish purchases." Both Frederick and Naether were aware, however, of the changes women were experiencing. Whereas Naether warned industry that they must appeal to the "growing class of business women," Frederick told advertisers that "the present generation of women are not bound much by religious controls, nor by the feeling of being below men in political rights, mental ability or sex inhibition." [24]

Even in their most freedom-loving images, however, the advertisements of the 1920s never incorporated the full implications of the working woman or the possibilities of women living outside of families. Freedom was connected to leisure and romance; stability, to the family and the home. Women might hold jobs, but their main fantasies were still directed toward the family configuration. Whereas women had earlier produced the objects of their daily lives, now they were to buy them—from the objects that made them lovable (marriageable), to those that created a healthy family or a secure home life.

An analysis of the most common themes in advertising in the late 1920s is worth quoting in full, because of the clarity with which it outlines the new images of advertising. Based on a study of the *Woman's Home Companion*, the author, Otis Pease, reported two themes as paramount: "the American family at home" and "the importance of romantic love":

1. *The American family at home.* Home is never an apartment but a house, usually owned. It sanctifies leisure and recreation. It is invariably a "white collar" home. No one works or sweats; families only play at home. A housewife plays with her kitchen and her laundry; the husband plays with his boys or his radio. Homes usually have two cars and a dog. Mothers-in-law, uncles, and grandfathers live elsewhere. Single men and women do not exist. A successful man is a husband who is unfailingly cheerful, "sincere," and upwardly mobile. He may often acquire these virtues by correspondence courses and by other expenditures of money, but his failure to possess them would be a sign not of poverty, but of defective character. The worries, insecurities, and fears of modern men and women stem from failure to be liked, to adjust to one another, to find adequate sexual satisfactions, but especially from failure to live amid the accoutrements of leisure. These criteria of security are surpassingly important to all families. To possess them is to be free from tension and misery. Harmony and happiness in fact depend on the rate of consumption of gadgets. Friends are always dropping in to view the Frigidaire or dance to the Philco. No more than a good meal and a quiet deodorant are needed to keep the affection of one's husband and children. The preparation and serving of food, to be sure, is a complex function; but the housewife may trust the food industry for advice and guidance. Other large institutions perpetually bolster the family: banks, insurance companies, and utilities stand ready to protect its security and preserve its happiness. Money spent in these institutions is never an expense but an investment.

2. *The importance of romantic love.* The satisfactions of sex and the criteria of romantic love are inextricably intertwined; but whereas romantic love is indispensable to sexual satisfaction, the reverse is not the case: romantic love is desirable in and of itself and is bound up with other ends, such as prestige, social success, power and wealth. The criteria of romantic love can be acquired cheaply by purchase: youth, smoothness of skin, a prominent bust, a deodorized body, a daily ritual of body care, handsome or alluring clothes, outward manners, and a ready affirmative response to these criteria in the other person. (Some women age so young and fade out—constipated. The wife of the Pretender to the throne of France is irresistible; she possesses the power to love; she commands attention; she uses Pond's. Look like a schoolgirl all your life; use Palmolive for your skin—it is made from natural African beauty oils.) Romantic love is available only to those who retain the appearance of youth. Men and women over forty are Mothers, Fathers, Grandmothers, Grandfathers, Business Executives, Professional People; they are no

longer capable of romantic love or, therefore, of sexual interests. They seek, instead, prestige and social success; they are content merely to conform to their assigned roles as
Mother, Father, etc. Romantic love is also a function of wealth and the ability to consume
it. Romantic love depends on leisure time, shopping, parties, sports, vacations, cruises,
night clubs, and usually on the premise that the pair are not yet married. Real satisfaction
is attainable from sex only upon acquiring the criteria of romantic love.[25]

As women shopped, these images drew them in. They promised solutions to
unfulfilled needs and escapes from anxieties. For isolation, there was the promise
of contact and communication; for uncertainty, a world where values and ideals
were clear. Adventure and freedom could be gained through romantic love; security, protection, and nourishment, through family life. The concrete solution to
these desires, however, was to be mere things—commodities that had taken on
the emotional overtones conveyed by the ads.

And if the anxieties and insecurities aroused naturally by contemporary life
were not enough to sell products, then these feelings were provoked and drawn
out by the advertisements themselves. Commodities from mouthwash to life insurance used the possibilities of marital disaster to sell their products. Women's
beauty products, which became a major industry during the twenties, helped to
inject into physical beauty much of the uncertainty about being a woman and
maintaining a marriage. Advertisements were increasingly aimed at heightening
women's insecurity so that their product might then be sold as a solution. As
Stuart Ewen, who studied advertising in the 1920s, put it,

Keen and critical glances constantly threatened her. As her home-making skills had become reconstituted into a process of accumulating possessions, her sexuo-economic capacities were reinforced on a commercial plane. An ad for Woodbury soap (1922) offered
women "the possession of a beautiful skin" which might arm them to meet a hostile world
"proudly—confidently—without fear." Another Woodbury ad warned women that "a
man expects to find daintiness, charm, refinement in the woman he knows," and that in
order to maintain his pleasure, a woman must constantly spend on her appearance.[26]

Without an alternative vision, women were easily caught in the solutions that
advertising offered. If femininity was valued in a period of great instability between women and men, then the loveliness that cosmetics offered was hard to
resist. If marriage seemed the only alternative in a time when so many forces
made it less secure, then anything from life insurance to mouthwash might be
grasped at. Commodities appeared to fill the cracks of a shattered world, and
promised to make that world secure in an exciting new way.

The individual that psychoanalysis and psychology were discovering was rapidly channeled into a narrow range of possible wishes and desires. The liberating
potential inherent in the loosening of family ties was transformed into a romance
of sexuality and family life. Life choices would increasingly be seen in terms of
choices about commodities, whose images would symbolize to the isolated, insecure consumer the satisfaction of her well-chiseled desires.

Notes

1. Caroline Hunt, *Home Problems from a New Standpoint* (Boston: Whitcomb & Bar-
rows, 1908), pp. 143–144.
2. Frank G. Hoover, *Fabulous Dustpan* (Cleveland: The World, 1955).

3. Christine Frederick, *Selling to Mrs. Consumer* (New York: The Business Course, 1929), p. 181.

4. Edward Filene, *Successful Living in the Machine Age* (1931), p. 96; quoted in Stuart Ewen, "Advertising as a Way of Life," *Liberation*, January 1975, p. 17.

5. Linda Gordon, *Woman's Body, Woman's Right: A Social History of Birth Control in America* (New York: Viking Press, 1976).

6. Norman Himes, *Medical History of Contraception* (1963), p. 340; quoted in Mary P. Ryan, *Womanhood in America from Colonial Times to the Present* (New York: Franklin Watts, 1975), p. 268.

7. Paul H. Jacobson, *American Marriage and Divorce* (New York: Holt, Rinehart, 1959), pp. 1–19.

8. Ryan, *Womanhood in America*, p. 262.

9. Margaret Mead and Frances Bagley Kaplan, eds., *American Woman: The Report of the President's Commission on the Status of Women, and other Publications of the Commission* (New York: Scribner, 1965), pp. 46–47.

10. Mary Ross, "The New Status of Women in America," in *Women's Coming of Age: A Symposium*, ed. Samuel D. Schmalhausen and V. F. Calhoun (New York: Horace Liverwright, 1931), p. 537.

11. Sophonisba Breckinridge, "The Activities of Women Outside the Home" (1933), p. 723; quoted in William O'Neil, *Everyone Was Brave: A History of Feminism in America* (Chicago: Quadrangle, 1961), p. 305.

12. An analysis of these homes, as well as other reforms proposed by the *Ladies' Home Journal* editor, Ed Bok, can be found in Helen Woodward, *The Lady Persuaders* (New York: Ivan Obolensky, 1960).

13. G. W. W. Hanger, *Housing of the Working People in the United States*, Bulletin of the Bureau of Labor no. 54 (Washington, D.C.: GPO, 1904); quoted in Gwendolyn Wright, "A Woman's Place Is in the Home; Changes in Domestic Architecture and in American Family Life, 1880–1915" (UCLA, 1976, typescript).

14. Quoted in Wright, "A Woman's Place."

15. Isabel Bevier, *The House, Its Plan, Decoration and Care* (Chicago: American School of Home Economics, 1907), pp. 86–87.

16. Stuart Ewen, *Captains of Consciousness: Advertising and the Social Roots of the Consumer Culture* (New York: McGraw-Hill, 1976), p. 28.

17. Heidi Hartman, *Capitalism and Women's Work in the Home, 1900–1930* (Ph.D. diss., Yale University, 1974).

18. Albert Farwell Bemes, *The Evolving House*, vol. 2: *The Economics of Shelter* (Cambridge, Mass.: MIT Press, 1934), p. 69.

19. Winthrop Hamlin, "Low Cost Construction in America" (Cambridge, Mass.: Department of Social Ethics, Harvard University, 1917); quoted in Wright, "A Woman's Place."

20. Abraham Myerson, *The Nervous Housewife* (Boston: Little, Brown, 1920), pp. 77–78.

21. Frank Presbrey, *The History and Development of Advertising* (1928; New York: Greenwood, 1968), p. 387.

22. Frederick, *Selling to Mrs. Consumer*, p. 45.

23. Carl Naether, *Advertising to Women* (New York: Prentice-Hall, 1928).

24. Frederick, *Selling to Mrs. Consumer*, p. 23.

25. Otis Pease, *Responsibilities of American Advertising* (New Haven: Yale University Press, 1958), pp. 38–40.

26. Stuart Ewen, *Captains of Consciousness*, p. 178.

THE BLOCKBUSTER DECADES: THE MEDIA AS BIG BUSINESS

WALTER POWELL

Over the past two decades, the information and entertainment business has come to be dominated by a characteristic American institution: the giant corporation. Publishing, recording, and broadcasting firms are now owned, in large measure, by publicly traded companies that rival huge manufacturing and financial conglomerates in size. Control over their operations rests, to a growing extent, in the hands of corporate managers rather than individual entrepreneurs. In most sectors of the business, a small number of these mammoth corporations effectively control the market. Three networks, for example, control television programming, and seven companies dominate the film industry. Newspaper chains own more than half of America's daily papers, and these papers account for over 70 percent of daily circulation. Six companies control more than 85 percent of the U.S. record market. And multimedia complexes that combine film, newspaper, or magazine operations with hardcover and paperback publishing are transforming the face of that former "cottage industry," book publishing.

Objections to this concentration of power have come from both ends of the political spectrum. Ralph Nader and other liberal reformers, on the one hand, argue that bigness is inherently bad—both because it hampers innovation and potential competition, and because it fosters cozy back-scratching agreements among subsidiaries of the same conglomerate. Bigness, these critics contend, also contributes to an awareness of common interests among large corporations, and hence tends to squelch political and economic diversity. And big corporations, more than small ones, can ignore the needs of particular groups of workers or consumers without feeling the pinch.

Conservative critics, on the other hand, argue that economic concentration in the media has created an elite stratum of political liberals—the "mediacracy," in Kevin Phillips's term, the "new class" in Irving Kristol's—that is insensitive to the concerns of ordinary Americans. The media that this new elite controls, worse yet, provoke public instability and alienation by focusing on corruption,

From *Working Papers*, July–August 1979. Since the time this article appeared in 1979, the trend toward increased concentration of ownership of the mass media has continued, noticeably picking up speed in the mid-1980s. In part, this development was triggered by a relaxation of the ownership restrictions enforced by the Federal Communications Commission. In the past, a company could own no more than seven radio or television stations; the number now permitted is twelve. In general, the Justice Department during the Reagan administration has looked favorably on media mergers and cross-media ownership. The department's view has been that bigness promotes efficiency. Although the empirical validity of this view is subject to much debate, there is little question that ownership of the media is now concentrated in fewer hands and that the number of independently owned newspapers and broadcasting stations has continued to decline. One new twist in media competition is the rise of new media conglomerates, such as Capitol Cities and Fox, who are challenging the once-dominant independent companies.

poverty, and everything else that's "wrong." Phillips contends, in fact, that we have entered an age where communications corporations and the knowledge industry have replaced manufacturing as the major element of the U.S. economy. In an article in *Society* magazine a couple of years ago, for example, he noted that "celebrity is shifting. The old type of celebrity was a general, a local landholder, a big businessman. Now the celebrities come from the world of knowledge, artistic performance, and media. The difference is quite real." *

In the industry itself, there is widespread disagreement over whether concentration is good or bad. According to traditional thinking, the job of producing books, films, and the evening news is both qualitatively and practically different from that of producing automobiles, bars of soap, or food processors. The suspicion lurks that the new companies in the field, like big companies everywhere, will be primarily responsible to their stockholders and security analysts, not to their readers, viewers, or listeners. Yet critics are just beginning to examine what specific effects the new corporate structures might have on the business of providing entertainment and information. Are independently owned companies preferable to chains and conglomerates? Is family control of a newspaper better than management by professional administrators? Who gains and who loses?

Answering these questions is not easy, partly because the changes are often more apparent than real. In any given area, for example, competition heats up during the process of concentration. Yet the peculiar nature of that competition—a handful of companies spending huge sums to promote a small number of products—means that the public won't necessarily benefit. Then, too, mergers and acquisitions are not all alike. In some cases, two companies in the same line of business simply merge: a morning and an afternoon newspaper in the same city, for instance. In other cases, a company seeking to diversify its holdings acquires a firm in a wholly different line of business. This was a characteristic trend in the 1960s, when large corporations like Litton, ITT, RCA, CBS, IBM, Raytheon, and Xerox began acquiring media properties, particularly publishing companies. (These mergers were fueled by expectations that new computer technology could profitably be combined with the older business of printing information—an expectation that has only partially been borne out.) Finally, acquisitions and mergers may occur between companies in related fields—such as book publishing and movie making, or newspapers and broadcast media. This trend has been most common in recent years.

The effects of economic concentration in the media will doubtless vary, depending on what the new structure of ownership is and on which segment of the industry is under consideration. A look at some specifics may reveal what the real effects in each case may be.

The newspaper industry, once made up of many competitive, local businesses, is now dominated by chain ownership. Most American communities to-

---

*The conservatives, not surprisingly, focus almost exclusively on the power of the mass media, ignoring concentration in other industries. And they concentrate on the celebrities, glossing over the fact that the capital for media mergers comes from the banks, insurance companies, and investment firms that make up the country's financial elite. (A widely publicized example is the role played by a consortium of banks in the unsuccessful attempt by American Express to take over McGraw-Hill.)

day have only one daily paper, but even where there is more than one, the same company often puts out the morning and evening editions. Moreover, this development must be placed in the context of a general marked decline in the number of daily papers published in this country.

In 1940, 60 newspaper chains owned 319 daily papers, or 17 percent of all dailies. By 1977, 167 chains controlled 1,082 papers, or 61 percent of the total. (The number of daily newspapers in the United States had dropped about 6 percent in the interim.) Chain papers, on the average, reach a much larger circulation than independently owned papers and are more likely to be located in larger markets: chains, in fact, account for about three-quarters of total daily-newspaper circulation in the United States.

No single chain has the power that the Hearst empire once possessed—in 1946 Hearst papers alone accounted for about 10 percent of daily-newspaper circulation—but the facts of concentration are nonetheless startling. The twenty-five biggest chains own 31 percent of all dailies and account for 52 percent of circulation. The six largest—in order of circulation they are Knight-Ridder, Newhouse, Chicago Tribune, Gannett, Scripps-Howard, and Times-Mirror— alone control more than a quarter of total circulation. And chain-owned papers are frequently the only game in town. Not one of the seventy or eighty papers owned by Gannett, for example, faces any local competition.

The figures for television station ownership are quite similar. Despite Federal Communications Commission regulations prohibiting any one group from owning more than seven stations (and only five of them VHF), 57 percent of all television stations in the country are owned by groups. Like chain-owned newspapers, these stations are in the larger markets. On the average, a total of 132.1 million households tune in to a group station every day, compared with 37.3 million for independent stations; group-owned stations thus attract 77 percent of the daily television audience.

The nine largest groups alone attract close to a third of that audience. The biggest of these are the network groups themselves—ABC, CBS, and NBC— each of which owns five stations, including one each in the country's three largest markets (New York, Chicago, and Los Angeles). The other large groups include Metromedia (six stations), RKO General (a subsidiary of General Tire and Rubber, four stations), Westinghouse (five stations), Storer (seven stations), Field Communications (five stations), and Capital Cities (six staions).

Some of the same economic forces encourage concentration of ownership in both the newspaper and the television business. The primary incentive, according to Stanford economists James Rosse and James Dertouzos, writing in a Federal Trade Commission report, is the U.S. tax laws. Under current IRS regulations, they note, a firm's undistributed earnings are not taxed as personal property; hence, it pays to find somewhere to invest them. And family-owned businesses may be prime candidates for acquisition by other companies because of the need to expedite settlement of a family's estate. Chain ownership of newspapers eases each paper's adaptation to changes in typesetting and printing technology; new equipment can be adopted by chain members one at a time, thereby smoothing investment patterns and minimizing risk for the parent company. In television, group ownership gives stations some tax benefits and other financial advantages, and may provide some economies of scale through centralized management.

By and large, though, Rosse and Dertouzos believe that joint ownership provides few, if any, true economic efficiencies. Most advertising revenue, for example, is derived locally, so chain ownership doesn't provide any advantage there. Labor negotiations, too, are generally conducted at the local level. They conclude that there is "little evidence of significant social benefit accruing as a result of chain ownership" of newspapers or television stations.

Book publishing, in general, is not heavily concentrated. In 1972, the fifty largest publishers accounted for 75 percent of the industry's sales. Publishing, however, is an industry with a number of submarkets—book clubs, college textbooks, and mass market paperbacks—which are highly concentrated. Ten companies, for example, operate seventy-eight book clubs. These accounted for 89 percent of total book club sales in 1976.

Prentice-Hall, McGraw-Hill, CBS Publishing, and Scott, Foresman & Company are the big four of the college textbook market. The ten largest college publishers (in addition to the four above, they include Harcourt Brace Jovanovich, John Wiley & Sons, Macmillan, Richard D. Irwin, Harper & Row, and Addison-Wesley) accounted for over 70 percent of total sales, while the top twenty publishers controlled over 93 percent of the college market in 1975. In *The College Publishing Market, 1977–1982*, Dantia Quirk writes, "There are decided economies of scale in the college market; publishers with annual sales of over $20 million have higher gross margins, lower selling, editorial, and promotion expenses and higher net income than text publishers with smaller annual sales." Wall Street publishing analyst J. K. Noble found that, as a general rule, the larger the publisher, the higher the profit margin, and that this was "clearest in college textbook publishing."

In mass market paperback publishing the emphasis is on quantity. The books are sold in supermarkets, drugstores, airports, and anywhere else a bookrack can be squeezed in. A minimum print run is fifty thousand; the maximum is several million. Mass market paperback houses compete furiously with each other for the rights to hardcover best sellers, with bids often topping a million dollars. The sums involved mean that even relatively large publishers can't compete with the giants. William Jovanovich, in his 1978 fourth-quarter report to stockholders, commented on the sale of his mass market line to MCA: "We sold Jove Publications, Inc., at a net operating loss of $2,000,000 and a net loss on disposal of $7,720,000. HBJ does not intend to publish a monthly series of popular paperback books under the present conditions of mass market distribution."

In 1978, the Justice Department brought suit against CBS, which already owned the Popular Library paperback line, asking that it be required to divest itself of Fawcett Publications. In 1976, the department contended, the eight largest firms accounted for approximately 81 percent—and the four largest firms, 53 percent—of total sales. CBS subsequently sold off its Fawcett line. But even with Fawcett, CBS was not the biggest mass market publisher; both Bantam and Dell were and are larger. New American Library, Ballantine, and Pocket

Books follow CBS, each with closely equivalent shares of the market, and Avon is next. None of these paperback firms is independently owned. Their combined sales in 1977 were estimated at $392 million, or 76 percent of the industry's total.

Another characteristic of the book industry is the growth of large, vertically integrated publishing complexes. Doubleday, for instance, a major hardcover trade publisher, also owns the paperback company Dell and its hardcover affiliate Delacorte, as well as Anchor Press, Dial Press, and at least twelve book clubs, including the Literary Guild. Harper & Row, a large publisher with trade, juvenile, and college and high school text divisions, owns Basic Books, Barnes & Noble Books, and the college division of Dodd, Mead & Company. And it recently purchased both T. Y. Crowell, a trade publisher that controlled six small textbook companies, and J. B. Lippincott, another trade publisher that also owned Ballinger Publishing, a scientific monograph house.

In the recording business, the major companies have built up such powerful distribution networks that smaller firms, which depend on wholesalers, find it difficult to compete. Not long ago, a record that sold a hundred thousand copies was considered profitable. This figure has climbed to two or even three hundred thousand today. Moreover, the emphasis is now on blockbusters—recordings that, in industry parlance, "go platinum," or sell a million copies.

Six major companies—CBS, Capitol, MCA, Polygram, RCA, and Warner Communications—controlled more than 85 percent of the U.S. record market last year. The most profitable company—Polygram, with its subsidiary, RSO Records—released only ten albums. A recent *Fortune* magazine article shed some light on Polygram's strategy. RSO was dissatisfied with the modest success of soul singer Linda Clifford, so executives decided to "repackage" her. The company will spend more than $100,000 on photo sessions, new clothes, makeup artists, and hair designers to provide a new image for Clifford. RSO's president noted, "We try to design the music in the album to the widest demographics possible."

Four of the six largest record companies—CBS, MCA, RCA, and Warner—are affiliated with corporate parents who are also involved in films and book publishing. Here we find the major development in the knowledge and entertainment business during the seventies: in the growth and expansion of multimedia enterprises. One of the biggest of recent combinations illustrates the trend. Gannett, the huge newspaper chain, is merging with Combined Communications Corporation in a $370 million deal. CCC owns two successful papers, the *Cincinnati Enquirer* and the *Oakland Tribune*, which will join the Gannett galaxy. But it also has seven television stations and thirteen radio stations, thus giving Gannett a strong foothold in broadcasting.

Perhaps the most troubling sort of multimedia venture is joint ownership of a newspaper and a television station in the same city. The FCC has forbidden such combinations in the future, but in June 1978 the Supreme Court overturned an appeals court ruling that required the divestiture of existing cross-ownerships. Currently, more than 25 percent of the 718 television stations in this country are owned by newspaper chains; only 28 percent have no affiliation with any other media establishment, and these independent stations are likely to be located in smaller markets, their audience amounting to only 15 percent of the industry total.

Cable television has been heralded as a medium that will bring great programming diversity to the public, yet over half of existing cable systems are already controlled by other media. Broadcasting companies own 30 percent of all cable systems, newspaper interests 12 percent, and publishers of books or magazines 13 percent.

Executives within the media business use terms such as "cross-fertilization" and "synergy" to explain cross-media mergers. Film companies, for example, look to book publishers as sources of materials and as outlets for novelizations of successful films. Book publishers "see more material in a week than a film producer does in a year," according to one multimedia executive. And novels have advantages over screenplays. As Peter Guber, producer of the film *The Deep*, explains,

Someone comes in and tells a 15-minute yarn, and you have to make the assessment of whether or not to gamble from $10,000 to $200,000 to develop the property for filming. But you read a novel and you can make that assessment based on a fully fleshed-out series of characterizations, a fully articulated plot and a clear indication of those incidents which make for exciting and successful films.

Another reason for multimedia tie-ins is the desire companies have to own a work from the outset, thus eliminating the middleman. The association of movie companies and paperback publishers is particularly profitable in this respect. Release of a successful paperback novel shortly in advance of a movie based on the novel helps build anticipation for the movie, and joint promotion of the film and the book has major advertising advantages for each. Additionally, paperback publishers are finding a profit in novelizations—quickly written, fleshed-out versions of successful screenplays such as *Star Wars* or *Close Encounters of the Third Kind*.

If executives of large media conglomerates are interested only in the bottom line, will quality and diversity suffer? Does the emphasis on multimedia blockbusters work to the detriment of serious or experimental writing, filmmaking, or records? Research on chain ownership and "conglomeratization" provides at least some partial answers.

One conclusion is that there are few, if any, blatant abuses to match those of earlier times. For many years, William Randolph Hearst used his newspapers, magazines, and wire services to urge the United States to declare war on Mexico because he feared expropriation of his mining properties there. Overt propagandizing is very rare today. In fact, William Gormley, in his research on newspaper-television cross-ownership for the Institute for Research in Social Science at Chapel Hill, North Carolina, uncovered an opposite tendency. Newspaper-owned television stations, he found, are much less likely to editorialize than stations not owned by newspapers.

But Gormley also found that joint ownership of a newspaper and a television station in the same city restricts the variety of news available to the public. A common arrangement is for the newspaper to share the carbons of its stories with the television station before the papers hit the streets. That practice lessens diversity and exacerbates the problem of pack journalism. Moreover, the homogenizing effects of cross-ownership are most noticeable (and damaging) in cities with populations under 125,000 since there are seldom any competing local news sources.

Cross-ownership does work to the advantage of employees. They can move more easily from one medium to another while still retaining pension and medical benefits, vacation time, and seniority privileges. Gormley notes that newspaper and television stations under the same ownership are apt to be located in the same complex of buildings. While sharing a parking lot or cafeteria entails nothing sinister, it does encourage employees to think of themselves as belonging to the same corporate parent. That, in turn, encourages cooperation and, ultimately, greater story overlap. The resulting look-alike coverage may not be glaring, but as Judge Learned Hand wrote in *United States* v. *Associated Press*, "Right conclusions are more likely to be gathered out of a multitude of tongues."

John Norton, newspaper analyst for the investment firm of John Muir and Company, believes that chain-owned papers, like cross-owned media, are also more homogenized. Quoting from an article by N. R. Kleinfield in the *New York Times Magazine*, he says, "They look alike and read alike. . . . There'll be fewer papers that print and raise hell. You'll see fewer gadflies. Newspapers, I think, are going to have less distinctive personalities. All papers are becoming more service oriented, and the chain-owned papers, with their sophisticated market-research techniques, are most aggressive in this area."

Confirming this trend, Gannett president Al Neuharth says, "Basically we respond to our reader studies. Whatever diet the readers want, we custom tailor the paper for that diet. If the readers in Ithaca want to know the school menus for all the schools in the area, we'll give them that. That's no great practice of journalism, but it's what the readers want."

Supporters of media concentration argue that chain-affiliated papers are better because they have more resources at their disposal. Kristine Keller, however, in a 1978 master's thesis at the University of California, compared twenty-eight chain-owned papers with independently owned papers having the same circulation and time-of-day publication. The independently owned papers contained 16 percent more national news, 35 percent more international news, and 25 percent more local and state news than the chain papers. They also featured more of the most expensive kind of news, staff-written stories (as opposed to syndicated news). Other studies report that chains often raise both the newsstand price and advertising rates of papers they acquire, but that they do little to improve content.

In book publishing, blatant abuses of conglomerate power are not a problem either. Even a group critical of the industry, the Authors Guild, concedes that "it is not that fewer books are being published than formerly, or even, at least not provably, that books of exceptional merit are going unpublished." The Association of American Publishers goes further: many mergers led to the survival of imprints that would otherwise have disappeared, the association argues, and publishing could not have expanded as rapidly as it did over the past twenty years without the infusion of the substantial capital that the mergers provided. To back these claims, the association offers statistics showing that the number of book publishing firms has increased by 25 percent over the past twenty years. During this period as well, the number of books released annually increased by more than 200 percent—from eighteen thousand to forty thousand.

The nature of the work process in publishing has changed as mergers have taken hold of the industry. The Authors Guild doesn't like the changes, calling them a "degradation of the publishing process itself." Says the guild:

The author used to find in his publishing firm an editor anxious to edit, to suggest, to be a midwife to excellence. Now, if his firm is a merged or a conglomerated one, he's apt to find instead someone called an acquisition editor. This person is hardly an editor at all. He or she is too concerned with acquiring the next book, with achieving a better balance sheet for his or her satrapy against others in the firm, to have much time or taste for editing. An acquisition editor is really a book broker.

In the course of our research for *Books: The Culture and Commerce of Publishing*, Lewis Coser, Charles Kadushin, and I learned that many writers now turn to outside agents rather than to publishing-company editors for "hand holding" and support. Agents today not only market manuscripts for an author, but they also serve as financial advisers, marriage counselors, real estate agents, and tax consultants. One agent puts it neatly: "I hold hands all day, pat hands, make nice. Agents are date bureaus, travel bureaus, mothers, psychologists. We are a writer's closest friend, sometimes his only contact with the outside world. . . . You have to get him started again if he stops . . . , you have to go through his divorce with him, find him dates."

Agents repeatedly told us that it is much more rewarding today to be a literary agent than an editor. As an editor, says one agent, "you are structured by the publishing house. As an agent, however, I can take on anything I want. I can represent anyone I want." "I would go crazy dealing with in-house politics," says another agent. "The things that confine me as an editor would bug me too much," says a third.

Other changes have also taken place in the internal structure of publishing firms. Hardcover trade houses today depend for their very survival on subsidiary rights sales (to book clubs, paperback houses, film companies, or television). Increasingly, the key people in publishing firms are not editors but whoever is in charge of subsidiary rights deals. Although best-selling hardcover books are auctioned off to the highest-bidding book clubs and paperback publishers—and are not sold "on the cheap," as it were, to corporate siblings—more subtle forms of corporate favoritism do exist.

"Of course, best sellers go to the highest bidder. We have no problems there," says one publisher. "But take a look at the smaller books, the respectable works that don't have mass market potential written all over them. I have a hell of a time selling the rights to them, but my competitors who have affiliated paperback lines and book clubs seem to be doing just fine." This, obviously, is a difficult charge to substantiate. However, a perusal of the subsidiary rights roundup columns in several industry newsletters over a six-month period did support the charge. In an inordinate number of cases, where paperback rights sales were in the low range (from $30,000 to $100,000), the acquiring paperback house was a corporate relative of the hardcover publisher.

Recently, Random House, a subsidiary of RCA, appointed a new chief financial officer and treasurer whose previous experience was not in books but with a major Detroit automobile company and with another division of RCA. At Bantam Books, president Oscar Dystel, who has decried the failures of publishers to "live up to their cultural and social responsibilities," is nearing retirement. Alberto Vitale will become the new chief operating officer. Vitale is from IFI International, the Agnelli family Fiat holding company that owns 49 percent of Bantam. The question that troubles critics of conglomerates is this: Will an editor be able to persuade someone like Vitale that a book by an unknown writer, a book with a limited market, should be published on a hunch that the author's third or fourth book just might be a best seller? Would such a book—which would have few subsidiary rights possibilities—be worth the time and effort of a slick publicity department?

For many years, publishing was a quiet and neglected business. Now it is a "glamor" industry, very much a part of the entertainment business. Conglomerate ownership has provided higher salaries as well as better health and retirement benefits in a field where people traditionally labored for "psychic" income. Moreover, employees have far greater job opportunities and possibilities for corporate mobility.

But concentration does not always work to the advantage of employees. When Harper & Row completed its acquisition of Lippincott, two hundred employees of the latter firm lost their jobs. Authors have also been affected. Concentration has meant big money for some authors, but not for most. And the excessive attention paid to books with tie-in possibilities may work to the detriment of other smaller projects, particularly when the search for blockbusters is conscious and planned rather than accidental.

The film *Superman* is a good example of how the system works. Warner Communications, the entertainment conglomerate, launched what it called a "megamillion-dollar campaign to sell Superman through every medium in every market in the United States." A Warner executive vice-president, quoted in *American Film* magazine, said that "the difference between this and other films is that all these things are taking place up front." Warner Books was very much a part of the multimedia binge: the company released not one but eight Superman-related "non-books" as part of the tie-in.

The Superman case illustrates another trend: the development of highly sophisticated and expensive publicity departments and market research divisions in a variety of media. The film industry, for example, manipulates movie endings before test audiences in search of the one that gets the right audience response. Record companies and newspapers also are resorting to more scientific kinds of market analysis so they can come up with products that appeal to the widest possible audience. Following their media partners, book publishers now pay more heed to artwork for a book's cover and to the accompanying publicity campaign. Many lament that the media are becoming a hit-or-miss business: the goal is to find the big book, film, or record, and everything else gets lost in the process.

The money that is spent on promotion and market analysis might be put to better use funding a diversity of new materials instead of the costly one-shot projects. The media used to be characterized by their shotgun approach: marketing a wide variety of products in hopes that a few would land on target. Today's approach more closely resembles a cannon, wherein much time, energy, and money go into one big product that is expected to appeal to a huge audience and offer spin-off possibilities for other media. These trends are most pronounced in companies that own several traditionally competing media.

The changes taking place in the mass media are subtle and not immediately cause for great worry. But the available evidence suggests that concentration and cross-ownership lessen diversity, add to the number of homogenous products, and impede the chances for serious work to come to the attention of a national audience. In 1945, Supreme Court justice Hugo Black stated that the First Amendment "rests on the assumption that the widest possible dissemination of information from *diverse* and *antagonistic* sources is essential to the well-being of the public." The threat to the marketplace of ideas today is not overt or diabolical, but it is real. What can or should be done to arrest and reverse this trend, however, is a question not easily answered.

One solution is simply to forbid concentration by legislative means. The media, of course, may not be at the top of the priority list here. There are many industries, in particular the oil industry, where antitrust arguments are far more compelling and of much greater immediate concern to the public. Promotion of competition by removing trade barriers in a number of protected industries— from steel to television sets—would have a more significant impact and would benefit consumers more directly than any activity we might propose for changing media ownership. Nonetheless, it is worth considering what the options are.

The Federal Communications Commission, as noted earlier, has prohibited any future joint ownerships of a newspaper and a television station in the same town. It has also limited the number of radio and television broadcast stations that one company can own. Yet, with bureaucratic fuzzy-headedness, it has allowed existing cross-ownerships to continue. The FCC declared that it is "unrealistic to expect true diversity from a commonly owned station-newspaper combination." But, it added, "a mere hoped-for gain in diversity is not enough" to warrant the "possibility of disruption for the industry and the hardship for individual owners" that divestiture would entail. Furthermore, it contended that divestiture would be unfair, since the FCC itself encouraged cross-ownership in the 1960s.

The Federal Trade Commission and the Justice Department will continue to scrutinize media concentration, but they probably will limit their actions to individual cases—and these actions will doubtless spend years in the courts. Public sentiment for direct government subsidies for independent or alternative media organizations is strong in Canada, but not in the United States. Nor are there any proposals to create public organizations such as the National Film Board of

Great Britain to encourage experimental and innovative work. Government sources argue that a number of granting agencies already provide substantial public and private support for individual artists—so action in this direction is also unlikely.

A revision of the tax laws, particularly those that apply to inheritance and the reinvestment of profits, might have helped preserve some independent newspapers five or ten years ago. Today, there are so few independent newspapers of any size left that such legislation would have minimal impact.

One possible starting point, based on the legislated breakup in the 1940s of the Hollywood film studios' control of film distribution, is to examine the current methods of distribution of both books and records. The clout of the major record companies, with their powerful in-house distribution networks, seriously impairs entry by smaller or independent firms. Mass market paperback publishing operates under a system of exclusive distribution contracts requiring that no "competing" line of books be distributed. This arrangement sets up an almost impenetrable barrier to new firms trying to enter mass market paperback publishing. Elimination of current exclusive distribution arrangements would give a number of smaller firms access to the national market.

Every media executive contends that he or she is "only giving the public what the public wants." However cynically we may view that sentiment, in the end change may come only when the public makes greater—and more vocal—demands.

THE CORPORATE COMPLAINT AGAINST THE MEDIA

PETER DREIER

In a series of advertisements currently featured in newspaper op-ed pages and major magazines, Mobil Corporation takes on the bias of the news media. In one of them, entitled "The Myth of the Crusading Reporter," Mobil cites a study purporting to show that "leading reporters and editors of major newspapers and television networks have distinct hostilities toward businessmen." These journalists, utilizing "publicity-hungry critics of business" and anonymous sources, may then "use the press to 'crusade' on behalf of these [personal] beliefs." Worse yet, Mobil informs us, the next generation of journalists is even more hostile to business, if another survey, of Columbia University Graduate School of Journalism students, is any guide. Only one-quarter of them believe that the private-enterprise system is fair.

America's business community did not need Mobil's public-relations department to warn it that the media are hostile to business. Since the later 1960s, when public opinion polls began to report a dramatic decline in public confidence in big business, corporate leaders have discovered a convenient scapegoat—the news media. In speech after speech, business spokespersons have accused reporters of being "economically illiterate," of sensationalizing stories to attract (and frighten) readers and viewers, and of wanting to put business out of business.

At every turn, they see the wrongdoings of big business—windfall oil profits, nuclear power plant accidents, chemical waste disposal hazards, bribery of public officials, death and injuries from unsafe automobiles—splashed across the front pages and the evening news. Business leaders worried that in a hostile climate, elected officials would translate what they saw in the polls into anti-business legislation. They viewed the gains of progressive groups—embodied in the activities of such bureaucracies as the Environmental Protection Agency, the Equal Employment Opportunity Commission, the Occupational Safety and Health Administration, and the Federal Trade Commission (all but the latter products of 1960s activism)—as obstacles to corporate profits and a healthy economy.

Corporate captains genuinely felt maligned and misunderstood. And they were firmly convinced that the public's disapproval of their performance was based almost entirely on misunderstanding rather than on corporate behavior. If those responsible for shaping public opinion (particularly journalists) were accurately informed about the benefits of our economic system, they believed, business's standing in the polls and among elected officials would improve.

The study cited by Mobil—conducted by political science professors Stanley

From *The Quill*, November 1983.

Rothman of Smith College and S. Robert Lichter of George Washington University—simply confirms what corporate leaders have long suspected.[1] Their findings, though not significantly different from those of a decade's worth of academic research on journalists' backgrounds and attitudes, are being widely circulated. Their research has appeared in magazines, been quoted in mainstream newspapers, and summarized in an op-ed column syndicated by the *Washington Post*. This study should be seen not simply as a fact-filled academic report, but as ammunition in a full-scale propaganda war being waged by the business community to make the news media more sympathetic to corporate America.

Since the mid-1970s, big business has been on the ideological offensive to change the public's perceptions of the profit system, the role of government, and the dangers of alternative ideas and arrangements. *Business Week* sounded the battle cry in 1974: "It will be a hard pill for many Americans to swallow—the idea of doing with less so that big business can have more. . . . Nothing that this nation, or any other nation, has done in modern economic history compares in difficulty with the selling job that must now be done to make people accept this new reality."

The business community began a five-part "selling job" that is still in progress, but has already had a significant impact. The campaign has been only loosely coordinated. It is not headquartered in any one boardroom or led by any one business clique. There have been, however, a common message and common targets.

The most obvious approach has been the emergence of "advocacy advertising" by large corporations, particularly the oil and energy companies that have been under the closest scrutiny by public interest groups and government. Their expensive ads in major newspapers and magazines (Mobil's are the most visible) extol the virtues of free enterprise capitalism and decry the dangers of regulation. To deflect their Robber Baron image, they promote themselves as socially responsible corporate citizens—selling the system rather than specific products. Or, they ask people to view them not as impersonal corporate giants but—as reflected in Bob Hope's TV ads for Texaco—as enterprises owned by folks like you and me. Growing corporate sponsorship of public television is designed both to reveal business's civic-mindedness and to divert public television from controversial (and potentially anticorporate) programming. Ads for the corporate-sponsored National Right-to-Work Committee, in major magazines, depict powerful trade unions trampling on the rights of beleaguered individual workers. Corporate public relations departments place ads in major magazines that reach opinion makers and journalists, urging them to call to get the facts on industry-related public issues.

Second, corporations and corporate-sponsored foundations organized a variety of forums at which corporate executives and media executives could discuss the media's "antibusiness" bias. An early effort was a series of exclusive seminars, sponsored by the Ford Foundation in 1977, that brought together high-level corporate executives and lawyers (most of them from Fortune 500 firms), executives of the major national media, and a few reporters to engage in frank, off-the-record discussion for two days. The results are summarized in *The Media and Business*, edited by corporate lawyer Joseph Califano and the *Washington Post*'s Howard Simons. Similar seminars soon followed. Also, corporate executives and media executives increasingly were invited to speak to each other's organizations on the general topic of "détente" between business and the media. Gannett's Allen H. Neuharth addressed the Cincinnati Chamber of Commerce in 1979 on "Business and the Press: Why We Ought to Understand Each Other." A few months later, Thomas J. Donohue, vice-president of the U.S. Chamber of Commerce, told media executives and journalists at the First Amendment Congress that "business and media must respect each other's First Amendment rights." The American Society of Newspaper Editors chose as its 1976 convention theme, "Is the press giving business the business?"

The corporate executives' message—that the media needed to become more sensitive to business and to improve their business coverage—obviously had an impact. Since 1978, almost every major newspaper in the country has expanded its business pages and added reporting staff to cover business. A few, such as the *New York Times*, the *Boston Globe*, the *Washington Post*, and the *Chicago Tribune*, have added special business sections. (In contrast, there are only about twenty-five full-time labor reporters on American newspapers.) Although news executives justify this trend as a response to the public's demand for more in-depth news about the economy, the timing of the expanded business coverage appears to be more than coincidental. Much of it is simply boosterism—glowing stories of new investment plans, fawning profiles of corporate executives, summaries of quarterly and annual corporate reports. Stories about personal finance—how to start a new business, where to invest your savings, problems of finding a second home—take up much of the remaining space. There is almost no investigative reporting on these pages and little good to say about unions or consumer groups. Their focus is on "upscale" readers, not inflation-pinched working folks.

Third, big business began cultivating current and future journalists directly. Programs in business or economics journalism are among the fastest growing additions to journalism school curricula. Corporations and their foundations have targeted journalism schools with endowments for undergraduate, graduate, and midcareer programs to improve journalists' understanding of business and economics. The National Association of Manufacturers joined with the American Newspaper Publishers Association and the Association for Education in Journalism to develop a program to "improve business reporting" through workshops at journalism schools. Because most economics departments and business schools communicate a narrow range of ideas, most journalists and students are exposed primarily to mainstream thoughts. They may improve their technical competence in economics, but the hidden curriculum is never identified in the course outlines.

As Gar Alperovitz, director of the National Center for Economic Alternatives, says,

In the United States the economics profession is dominated by a debate between moderate conservatives and conservative conservatives. In the business schools and economics departments, they tend not to talk about the social consequences of economic decisions and economic arrangements, so they miss new intellectual ideas. The range of economic debate in the press in Western Europe and Japan is much broader and more sophisticated than in the U.S. There they talk about planning—not whether, but how—and about worker control, industrial strategy, and credit allocation.

Fourth, business realized that as a profession, journalism—highly individualistic and competitive, but with few agreed-upon standards to evaluate performance—equates prizes with excellence. As a result, the number of awards for excellence in some aspect of business reporting has spiraled upward in recent years. Not surprisingly, most of these contests are sponsored by corporations, industry groups, or business schools with a particular view of what constitutes high-level business reporting. The prestigious Loeb Awards, the "Pulitzer Prizes of financial journalism," are administered by the Graduate School of Management of UCLA. The Media Awards for Economic Understanding program, which annually receives more than one thousand entries from eager journalists, is supported by Champion International Corporation and administered by the business school at Dartmouth College. Westinghouse offers an award for science reporting, Carnation for nutrition reporting, and the National Association of Home Builders for housing reporting. The list of similar prizes fills pages each year in *Editor & Publisher*. Almost all the prizes include cash awards.

The sponsors may claim that they do not meddle in the contest, that winners are chosen by impartial judges, but the invisible hand surely operates. The corporate-backed awards help, subtly, to shape the kinds of stories journalists pursue and the kinds of standards editors recognize. This influence is less blatant than the more traditional means of seduction by which businesses finance luxury trips to various conferences revealing the wonders of corporate technology, new food products, new auto models, and so on, but it has the same intention and—to some degree, at least—the same effect.

Finally, big business, convinced that ideas have consequences, launched a massive effort to provide journalists with "research" and to make friendly "experts" more accessible. Best known are the recent activities of the American Enterprise Institute, a well-endowed right-wing think tank, which has a small army of neoconservative social scientists and economists grinding out studies that "prove" the harmful effects of government regulation, corporate taxes, and labor unions; the misguided or subversive motivations of consumer and labor advocates; and the weakness of the United States's current defense posture. Similar think tanks—the Hoover Institution at Stanford, the American Institute for Public Policy Research, the Institute for Contemporary Studies, the Heritage Foundation, among others—provide the same message and ammunition. Their reports, books, magazines, and pamphlets are sent to journalists on newspapers and magazines around the country. Their authors are promoted and made available for interviews and background briefings with reporters. For journalists— always hungry for "informed sources" with the stamp of scholarly legitimacy— these corporate-sponsored, conservative think tanks and intellectuals are a gold mine. Their ideas became the ideological underpinning and policy guidelines of the Reagan administration.

Enter Rothman and Lichter. The two political scientists had earlier conducted research on the New Left (leading to their book, *Roots of Radicalism*), concluding that student activism was rooted in personality problems, not idealism. Previous studies had found that most sixties activists were bright, emotionally healthy, and dedicated to pragmatic change. Rothman in particular was well known in conservative academic circles for his efforts to discredit this view and thus lend comfort to those who viewed such challenges to the establishment as the work of misguided and selfish malcontents.

Rothman viewed journalists in a similar way. Two years before he began his interviews with reporters and editors, he wrote an essay for a book published by the right-wing Hoover Institution, blaming liberal journalists of the national media for "the decay of traditional political and social institutions." The essay then repeated the familiar litany of criticism against the so-called liberal media.

When the two professors proposed conducting a large-scale study of various leadership groups (including journalists, business executives, television and film producers, corporate lawyers, clergy, federal judges, government officials, and Pentagon officials), they had little trouble finding support from right-wing foundations. They received grants totaling more than $300,000 from several conservative sources, among them the Scaife Foundation, a major funder of New Right organizations. The research project was headquartered at Columbia University's Research Institute on International Change, a cold war outpost.

Their initial findings, focusing on business-media comparisons, have already found a home in several conservative publications, including *Public Opinion* (sponsored by the American Enterprise Institute), *The Public Interest* (a leading organ of neoconservatism, edited by Irving Kristol), *Across the Board* (the magazine of the business-sponsored Conference Board), and *Business Forum* (a journal of the School of Business at California State University, Los Angeles). Obviously, their agenda went beyond earning academic credits by publishing in limited-circulation scholarly journals.

Rothman and Lichter's study is fairly straightforward. They interviewed 240 reporters and editors of major national media—the *New York Times*, the *Washington Post*, the *Wall Street Journal*, *Time*, *Newsweek*, *U.S. News & World Report*, the three commercial television networks, and public television. They also interviewed 216 top- and middle-level executives at seven Fortune 500 companies. The gist of the study is a comparison of the social backgrounds, personality characteristics, and opinions of these media and business elites.

Their story is grounded in a theory formulated in the 1970s by conservative intellectuals to explain, and discredit, the growing influence and visibility of the environmental, consumer, women's, and peace movements. Irving Kristol, Daniel Bell, and others began to argue that postwar America has produced a stratum of well-educated, upper-middle-class, cosmopolitan professionals, which they label the "new class." These professionals are products of urban, affluent families; they are based in the universities, government regulatory agencies, legal services offices, public interest movements, and the media. It is this "new class," the analysts argue, that is responsible for the challenges to business power that emerged in the 1970s—the followers of Barry Commoner, Ralph Nader, Gloria Steinem, Tom Hayden, Helen Caldicott, Daniel Ellsberg, and their counterparts. Despite their claims of altruism, however, this group is actually out for itself; cleaner air, new sexual morality, and expansion of government social programs (but not the Pentagon) mean greater happiness and more jobs for the elite, according to the "new class" thesis.[2]

Spiro Agnew foreshadowed this theory when he attacked the liberal media as "nattering nabobs of negativism." Joseph Kraft lent it credibility in an article, "The Imperial Media," for the neoconservative opinion journal *Commentary*. Now Rothman and Lichter have translated Agnew's rhetoric, Kraft's self-confession, and the neoconservatives' "new class" theory into social science.

Journalism's elite, they found, consists primarily of highly educated, well-paid white males. They come from educated, high-status families: 40 percent of their fathers were professionals and an equal number were businessmen; only 12 percent were blue-collar workers. The business executives, too, are primarily educated, affluent white males, but only 53 percent came from business or professional families while 28 percent had blue-collar fathers.[3] More journalists than businessmen attended prestigious colleges and graduate schools, and more come from big cities. Business leaders were only slightly better off economically than the journalists. Fifty-seven percent of the businessmen, compared to 48 percent of the journalists, reported annual family incomes of $50,000 or more. (Of course, since more male journalists than businessmen are married to professional women, *family* income may be misleading. Business execs generally make more than even top reporters. And the inclusion of leading network TV news anchors may skew the journalists' income toward the high end.)

Not surprisingly, the journalists' social and political views are to the left of the businessmen's. For example, 88 percent of journalists, compared to 65 percent of businessmen, believe that the U.S. legal system favors the wealthy; 48 percent of journalists, but only 29 percent of businessmen, believe that government should guarantee jobs; 68 percent of journalists, compared to 29 percent of business execs, think the government should substantially reduce the income gap between rich and poor. Journalists were more likely to favor government regulation of business, to believe that corporations put profits before the public interest, and to believe that the United States is responsible for Third World poverty and gobbles up too much of the world's resources. As Rothman and Lichter acknowledge, journalists are hardly socialists; only 13 percent think large corporations should be publicly owned. (As did 7 percent of businessmen—these guys should be fired!) Instead, these elite journalists are "welfare state liberals."

In terms of their social orientations, journalists are clearly more influenced by the post-1960s "new morality." Few attend church or synagogue. Ninety percent believe that a woman has a right to an abortion, as compared to 80 percent of the business execs, only a slight difference. However, 47 percent of the journalists, but 76 percent of the businessmen, think adultery is wrong; and 25 percent of the journalists, but 60 percent of business execs, believe homosexuality is wrong.

Their social orientations are consistent with the two groups' personality characteristics. Rothman and Lichter administered Thematic Apperception Tests to their respondents. The psychological profiles are fascinating; briefly, the businessmen were straight-laced, achievement-oriented, and more self-controlled.

Journalists were more "narcissistic," personally insecure, and thus likely to build themselves up by devaluing other people. They also scored higher on a "fear of power" scale, which the researchers suggest reveals that they want power but are afraid to pursue it directly, so they attack those who already have it.

Rothman and Lichter interpret their findings in terms of a widening conflict between the media and business in American society, and more broadly as part of the growing rift between the "new class" and the traditional establishment. The hostility, Rothman and Lichter report, is real: "We asked all of them to rate the influence of various groups in our society and to express their preferences for the power that each group should have. Each group rates the other as the most influential group in America; moreover, each wants to reduce substantially the power of the other and to take its place as the most influential."

But what really worries Rothman and Lichter, and their corporate sponsors, is that the ascendancy of the "new class" has not only tainted the public's faith in business, it has also eroded businessmen's confidence in themselves and the system of which they are a part. In the ideology of capitalism, business pursuit of profits was compatible with *and* helpful to the public interest. Entrepreneurs had a sense of "calling," and the self-made businessman was a cultural hero. The rise of big business at the end of the nineteenth century—and with it the so-called Robber Barons like Rockefeller, Ford, and Carnegie—turned public opinion against corporate leaders, their brutal labor relations, and their giant holdings. The businessmen responded with a concerted public relations effort to transform their public image. They set up philanthropic foundations, donated money for libraries and colleges, and established other "good works." The campaign was mostly successful, especially after the Depression. With the post–World War II economic expansion, most Americans agreed with Charles Wilson that "what's good for General Motors is good for America." Prosperity restored public faith in business and gave businessmen themselves a much-needed shot of self-esteem.

How, then, to explain the sharp drop in public confidence in big business since the late 1960s, which accelerated during the past decade? One answer would be to relate it to the sagging performance of the American economy. Simultaneous high inflation and rising unemployment—"stagflation" in economists' jargon—can certainly shake a family's belief in free enterprise. Business, of course, has a different answer. The "new class" assault on business as well as on business-oriented values has undermined public confidence in corporations as institutions and in free enterprise as an economic system. The media, they claim, share much of the blame.

Conservatives worry that there is no longer the widespread sharing of key values that helps hold society together. Many divergent "interest groups" are pursuing their own political and economic agendas; the growing pluralism of life-styles has replaced the mythic church-going nuclear family. As the economic pie stops growing, people begin to compete for slices of what economist Lester Thurow has called a "zero-sum society." These competing values, life-styles, and interest groups can have a contagious effect, even on top and middle corporate management. If leaders begin to doubt their own role in society, and society's commitment to their business values, the entire social fabric begins to unravel.

As Richard Nixon told C. L. Sulzberger of the *New York Times* in 1974, the trouble with the country is the weakness and division among "the leaders of industry, the bankers, the newspapers. . . . The people as a whole can be led back to some kind of consensus if only the leaders can take hold of themselves."

This lack of confidence explains, in part, why business has devoted so many resources to its ideological mobilization and schizophrenic efforts to both seduce and discredit journalists. The Mobil ad that cited the Rothman/Lichter study, as well as much of business's advocacy advertising and self-promotion, is designed not only to influence journalists, and, through them, the public, but also to reassure business people themselves that they are not to blame for the nation's economic tailspin—it's the fault of ill-informed or hostile journalists, a confused public, and opportunistic or misguided politicians. Without faith in themselves, corporate leaders and conservative intellectuals worry, business people will be ill prepared for the challenges of the coming decades.

Still, Rothman and Lichter's survey begs an important question. We have known for a long time that journalists, in general, are more liberal than the general population. The ranks of journalism have always been filled with reformers and crusaders. Recent sociological studies, such as Gans's *Deciding What's News*, Epstein's *News from Nowhere*, and Johnstone, Slawki, and Bowman's *The Newspeople*, only confirm what Leo Rosten observed in his 1937 book, *The Washington Correspondents*. If journalists have *always* been reform-minded, then what explains the increase of investigative and muckraking reporting during the past fifteen years? Perhaps reporters and editors used to keep their political views to themselves but recently have allowed more of their personal beliefs to spill onto the news pages. Some say that the emergence of "interpretive" journalism, replacing the "just the facts" school of reporting, gives journalists greater leeway to introduce their own biases in the selection, editing, and writing of news. The growing acceptance of "advocacy" journalism since the 1960s perhaps gave credence to a generation of reporters who wanted to be agents of social change, not simply chroniclers of the passing scene.

These explanations share a common thread: The national media's growing criticism of traditional centers of power, particularly big business, stems from changes within the profession of journalism and among journalists themselves. This is clearly the message of the Rothman/Lichter study, even though the authors themselves never explicitly make the leap of saying that the journalists' values influence their reporting and editing. (They are, however, now completing a study of news coverage that, Rothman indicated in an interview, is likely to discover a liberal bias in news coverage on such controversial issues as busing, abortion, human rights in Latin America, nuclear power, and the energy crisis.)

A somewhat different explanation, however, emerges out of the past decade's sociological research on how "news" is created. This includes Herbert Gans's *Deciding What's News*, Michael Schudson's *Discovering the News*, Steven Hess's *The Washington Reporters*, Gaye Tuchman's *Making News*, Mark Fishman's *The Manufacture of News*, David Altheide's *Creating Reality*, Leon Sigal's *Reporters and Officials*, Todd Gitlin's *The Whole World Is Watching*, and David Paletz and Robert Entman's *Media Power Politics*. Earlier studies, including Warren Breed's

1955 "Social Control in the Newsroom" and Bernard Cohen's *Press and Foreign Policy*, reached similar conclusions. According to these studies, "news" is a product of the daily organizational habits of journalists and their contact with sources. Most daily news stories originate from *routine* channels—press releases, official proceedings (Congressional hearings, courtrooms, regulatory agencies), reports, staged media events such as press conferences, and background briefings. With limited staff, the media station reporters at "beats" where they expect "news" to happen.

Newsgathering then, of course, becomes a self-fulfilling prophecy. Under deadline and competitive pressures, reporters file stories from these beats rather than venture off the narrow track. When reporters spent most of their time hanging around at precinct stations, crime stories dominated the news. Today, news tends to flow from reporters positioned at city hall, the state house, the White House, Capitol Hill, the Pentagon, and other centers of power. In addition, as a result of their day-to-day routines, reporters develop cooperative relations with regular news sources. The reporter wants a story and the source wants his or her version of reality reported. Thus the tendency to promote an establishment-oriented flow of news is reinforced. Finally, because high-level government, corporate, and foundation officials have greater resources to use in reaching reporters, they are able to initiate and dominate the flow of what becomes "newsworthy." These powerful organizations have the resources not only to stage events and hire public relations staffs, but also to fund and publish reports and books by "experts" who can become "reliable sources." In contrast, the poor, the powerless, and the unorganized lack the resources to command such routine access to reporters and the media. To make news, they must disrupt "business as usual." Labor relations becomes news only when strikes become violent or inconvenience the public. Ghetto conditions become news only when the poor tenants riot or boycott. Nuclear power becomes an issue only when demonstrators occupy a nuclear construction site. Otherwise, reporters rarely go to union halls, ghettos, or offices of activist organizations.

The accumulated findings of these studies indicate that, as Tom Wicker wrote in *On Press*, objective journalism is essentially "establishment" journalism. News tends to flow from powerful sources and reflects their version of reality. Whatever their personal values, journalists tend to adjust to these professional standards and daily routines.

There appears to be a conflict between the angry complaints of conservatives and business leaders that the press is hostile to the establishment and the overwhelming consensus among sociologists that the press serves as a transmission belt for establishment views. The paradox, however, is not difficult to resolve. The press, the sociologists agree, goes to where the power is. During the past fifteen years or so, the political and business establishment has been deeply divided over how best to cope with foreign policy, economic crisis, and social upheaval. Thus, journalists' high-level sources are telling different sets of stories.

Similarly, the past fifteen years have witnessed a growing upsurge of grassroots political activism. Although the student New Left has disappeared, many of its adherents—as well as a new and more heterogeneous group of activists—

have built a more sophisticated range of social movements than existed in the 1960s. These include the women's and senior citizens' movements, the consumer and public interest groups like Common Cause, the environmental, nuclear freeze, and peace movements, and such community and neighborhood groups as Massachusetts Fair Share and ACORN; there is even growing militance in some segments of organized labor, especially among working women (like Nine-to-Five) and on issues of workplace health and safety. Although some of these groups certainly fit the conservative stereotype of the "new class" adherents, much more of the upsurge has truly been a grassroots phenomenon of what we once called "middle America." This activism has not gotten the headlines of its counterpart on the other end of the spectrum, the "New Right," but it has been a major influence in politicizing average citizens and shaping the political agenda.

In the light of these two trends—a widening split within the establishment and the upsurge of grassroots protest—the press has shown a greater tolerance for controversy and conflict. What some view as the national media's "antiestablishment" bias is, in fact, a reflection of the canons of objective journalism.

In the 1950s and early 1960s, when there was a national bipartisan consensus on cold war foreign policy and domestic welfare-state goals, the press mirrored this concord in a celebration of Pax Americana and Luce's "American Century." The Vietnam War, however, produced a lasting split within the establishment over the conduct of foreign affairs, a split between a conservative wing pushing for greater military strength and tough talk with the Soviets, and a moderate wing, concerned about bloated defense budgets and the potential for global conflict. The conservative wing is best represented by such groups as the Committee on the Present Danger and the Hoover Institution at Stanford, groups favored by the Reagan administration in filling State and Defense Department slots. The moderate wing is best represented by the Council on Foreign Relations and the Trilateral Commission, corporate-sponsored policy groups whose leaders have filled high-level slots in every administration since Truman's. In domestic economic and social policy, likewise, a conflict developed between laissez-faire advocates like Milton Friedman and his ideological friends at the American Enterprise Institute and the U.S. Chamber of Commerce, and the moderate Keynesians at the Brookings Institution and the Business Roundtable.

These organizations are simply surrogates for ideas and perspectives. In the real world, the lines between competing establishment points of view are blurred and overlapping. But the national media still report conflict within very narrow limits. In the entire spectrum of American political and economic thought, the distance between the Committee on the Present Danger and the Council on Foreign Relations on foreign policy, or between the American Enterprise Institute and the Brookings Institution on domestic policy, is relatively short. But the conservatives treat the views of the experts at CFR or Brookings—and the politicians who take their advice—as the left end of the spectrum and then, because the major national media are more in tune with these groups, harass the press for its "liberal" bias. But, in the broad range of political views, these moderate groups are hardly "antibusiness," or even "antiestablishment." Rather, they reflect a struggle *within* the American power structure.

According to Whom? . . . The Spectrum of American Politics: A Sampling of Sources

Topic	Left	Liberal	Moderate	Conservative
Foreign policy	Institute for Policy Studies Institute for Food and Development Policy Coalition for a New Military and Foreign Policy	Center for Defense Information Jobs with Peace Amnesty International Committee for SANE Nuclear Policy	Council on Foreign Relations Trilateral Commission Club of Rome	Committee on Present Danger Hoover Institution Georgetown Center for Strategic and International Studies
Domestic economic and social policy	National Center Economic Alternatives Council on Economic Priorities Conference on Alternative State and Local Policy	Brookings Institution Urban Institute Center for Social Policy	National Bureau of Economic Research Committee for Economic Development Business Roundtable	U.S. Chamber of Commerce American Enterprise Institute Heritage Foundation
Legal institutions	National Lawyers Guild	American Civil Liberties Union	American Bar Association	Mountain States Legal Foundation
Foundations	Stern Fund Field Foundation of New York Haymarket People's Fund	Stewart R. Mott Foundation Ford Foundation Rockefeller Family Fund	Rockefeller Brothers Fund Charles Stewart Mott Foundation Twentieth Century Fund	Scaife Foundation Smith Richardson Foundation Lilly Endowment

It is worth recalling that when currently fashionable conservative ideas were put forward by Barry Goldwater in 1964, they were considered extremist. The right-wing think tanks have benefited from a decade of heavy financial support from friendly business groups and respectful media coverage that have brought them off the fringe and into the mainstream.

The accompanying table indicates what a real spectrum might look like. Obviously, the left side of the table is conspicuously absent from the daily flow of national journalism (except, perhaps, among guest contributors to the op-ed pages). Mary McGrory, perhaps the most progressive national columnist, is at most a McGovern-style liberal. Evans and Novak are Henry Jackson Democrats. There are plenty of right-wing opinion shapers, such as George Will, William Buckley, and James Kilpatrick. But not *one* nationally syndicated columnist is a socialist, or, in European parlance, a "social democrat," such as Michael Harrington or Barry Commoner. When journalists look for experts on foreign policy,

Topic	Left	Liberal	Moderate	Conservative
Opinion journals	The Nation The Progressive In These Times	The New Republic Washington Monthly N.Y. Review of Books	Foreign Affairs Harper's The Atlantic	The Public Interest Commentary National Review
Major new books	Rebuilding America (Alperovitz and Faux) Beyond the Wasteland (Bowles, Gordon, and Weiskopf) Deindustrialization of America (Bluestone and Harrison) Economic Democracy (Carnoy and Shearer)	The Zero-Sum Society (Thurow) The Next American Frontier (Reich) Winning Back America (Green)	Energy Future (Yergin and Storbaugh) Theory Z (Ouchi) Industrial Renaissance (Abernathy, Clark, and Kantrow)	Wealth and Poverty (Gilder) Post-Conservative America (Phillips) The Way the World Works (Wanniski) American Politics: Promise of Disharmony (Huntington)
Political organizations	Democratic Socialists of America Citizens Party Citizen/Labor Energy Coalition	Democratic Party (liberal wing) Common Cause Americans for Democratic Action	Democratic Party (moderate wing) Republican Party (moderate wing) Ripon Society	Republican Party (conservative wing) National-Conservative PAC Moral Majority

they rarely go to the Institute for Policy Studies, a well-respected left-oriented think tank. When it's economic expertise they're looking for, few turn to the new generation of left-oriented academics (such as Samuel Bowles at the University of Massachusetts, David Gordon at the New School for Social Research, Bennett Harrison at MIT, Barry Bluestone at Boston College, or Gar Alperovitz at the National Center for Economic Alternatives). The farthest left they travel is Harvard (to talk to Robert Reich) or MIT (to interview Lester Thurow).

Reporters doing stories about the nation's housing crisis or issues like rent control typically go to groups like the National Association of Realtors, the National Association of Home Builders, or the Mortgage Bankers Association of America for statistics and analysis. The two most frequently quoted "experts" on the subject are George Sternlieb, a Rutgers University professor, and Anthony Downs of the Brookings Institution, both of whom have close ties to the real estate industry. Grassroots groups like ACORN, Citizen Action, and National

Peoples Action and left-oriented housing experts like Chester Hartman of the Institute for Policy Studies and the Planners Network, Peter Marcuse of Columbia University, Cushing Dolbeare of the National Low Income Housing Coalition, and John Atlas of Shelterforce are virtually invisible to the national news organs. And the same could be said for any number of issues—food policy, environment, labor relations, health care, welfare, and many others.

The "left" is not totally left out, of course. There are occasional feature stories on "new trends" among intellectuals that note the growing influence of radicals and democratic socialists. And when a social movement begins to pick up steam and can mount large demonstrations and rallies—the nuclear freeze campaign, for example—the press quotes its leaders and reports its ascendancy. But in the daily routine of journalism, these "left"-oriented views do not come into journalists' line of vision, and journalists rarely go out looking for them.

In the past decade, journalists have covered the major issues and events that cast doubt on the wisdom or managerial skill of American business. The Santa Barbara oil spill, Hooker Chemical's Love Canal problems, and the Three Mile Island power plant incident were all technological accidents that became grist for journalists' mills. Questionable business practices may be hard to uncover, but corporations that violate labor law (J. P. Stevens), that knowingly manufacture and sell unsafe products (the Dalkon Shield or Ford Pinto), or that violate trade embargoes or bribe foreign officials (ITT) do find themselves subject to journalistic scrutiny.

It is interesting, however, that most of the so-called antibusiness stories were initially uncovered not by the major media but by either social movement organizations or politically oriented publications. Conditions in J. P. Stevens's textile plants were brought to public attention by the union and its national boycott, not a crusading reporter investigating workplace atrocities. The Love Canal episode—which triggered a national concern over toxic chemicals—came to public attention because of a grassroots effort by working-class neighbors (led by Lois Gibbs) concerned about their children's health. Both the Ford Pinto story and the exposé of the dumping of unsafe birth control devices (the Dalkon Shield) on Third World nations were uncovered by the leftist *Mother Jones* magazine.

Most journalistic exposés focus on the public sector—primarily conflicts of interest on the part of public officials, and primarily with local entrepreneurs, real estate, insurance, and construction firms. This is relatively small-time, low-level corruption. The information is usually dug out of public documents. But unless government regulatory agencies—frequently the source for investigative reports—have done the work already, documents about wrongdoing by major corporations and industries are hard to come by.

By fighting for legislation that makes information on both government and corporate practices accessible, reform movements have aided journalists. Common Cause, for example, helped win passage of laws requiring disclosure of campaign financing, enabling journalists to link wealthy individuals and corporations to elected officials and their voting patterns. The neighborhood movement won passage of the Home Mortgage Disclosure Act requiring banks to disclose lending patterns, thus permitting urban reporters to investigate "redlining" practices. The Freedom of Information Act has been extremely useful in allowing access to information about FBI infiltration of protest groups, government reports about exposure to nuclear radiation, and many other issues. Reporters interested in piercing the corporate veil, however, still face many legal obstacles. Our legal system protects private businesses from having to disclose very much about their inner workings, even though their decisions have significant public consequences.

For many reasons, journalists tend to avoid the hard work required to investigate corporate behavior. Their employing organizations provide few resources, or incentives, to do so. As Mark Dowie, who investigated and wrote the Pinto story for *Mother Jones*, explained, the story was available all along to anyone who knew how and where to look for it. "Stories like this are very much like photography," Dowie said. "It's not enough to know how to use the camera. You have to know what you're looking for."

What conservatives view as the press's "antibusiness" hostility is, in reality, a quite tame form of objective journalism. Journalists report different views *within* the establishment, and they report the views of protest groups when those groups are able to make a stink, but they rarely go beyond exposing what Herbert Gans has called violations of "responsible capitalism." The national press may criticize or expose *particular* corporate or government practices or *particular* corporations or elected officials who violate the public trust. Thus, a scandal like Watergate (with its many counterparts at local and state levels) or a Pentagon weapons boondoggle lends credence to the view that these violations are *exceptions* to an otherwise smoothly running system. The bad apples are purged, and the good ones remain. Even the so-called liberal media view such occurrences as "situations needing to be managed," not as basic flaws in an unjust or inefficient economic and political system.

Business leaders, obviously, have little patience for the "bad apple" theory. Any public exposure of corporate wrongdoing can taint the entire profits system. And when these stories appear in a context of economic hard times, the bad publicity can become contagious. As a result, what some may view as the media's occasional slap on the wrist, business feels as a punch in the jaw.

If the national media have contributed to the public distrust of big business, it is not because reformist reporters and editors have waged a war on corporate America. Whatever their personal beliefs (and, to my mind, Rothman and Lichter failed to capture the somewhat muddled, wishy-washy, nonideological character of journalists' reformism), journalists are constrained from a consistent assault on corporate America by the routines of daily journalism and the conventions of objective reporting.

The United States has many conservative and right-wing newspapers and a host of moderate liberal papers that take their cue from the *New York Times* and the *Washington Post*. But no major daily today is as far to the left as the New York *PM*, the York, Pennsylvania, *Gazette*, the Madison, Wisconsin, *Capital-Times*, or the Chicago *Sun* were in the 1940s. At that time these papers were hardly out on a political limb. The 1948 Progressive party campaign by former vice-president Henry Wallace (more progressive, in context, than McGovern's 1972 platform), the stands of the leftist CIO, and even President Truman's call for national health insurance, although opposed by most daily papers, were popular with millions of

American citizens. The cold war consensus and McCarthyism soon set in, however, and the "left" voices in American life quieted down. Today, with both conservatives and moderate liberals unable to find any solutions to gnawing political and economic problems, there is a resurgence of protest and intellectual ferment on both the left and the right. But while the national news media find it easy to cover the right flank (if with little sympathy), they have all but ignored the left side of the debate.

Moreover, while the media may occasionally expose both government and corporate wrongdoing, they are even less interested in examining possible solutions to chronic social, economic, and political problems. For example, the United States is one of only two industrialized nations (the other is South Africa) without a system of national health insurance; but while Americans can read a great deal about the problems of Britain's national health program, they know very little about its effectiveness in reducing major health problems, and much less about the overwhelming success of Canada's, Sweden's, or Germany's health measures. Experiments with consumer cooperatives, worker-owned or publicly owned enterprises, and other "social democratic" reforms—in the United States and elsewhere—might help Americans see the possibility of light at the end of our narrowing economic tunnel, but even though, as Rothman and Lichter report, 13 percent of elite journalists believe that "large corporations should be publicly owned," they certainly aren't getting their ideas into the news. With few exceptions, the national media are blind to reforms that challenge basic economic arrangements.

The series of Mobil ads attacking the media is designed to intimidate journalists into greater caution in reporting the wrongdoings of big business and the flaws of private enterprise capitalism. By portraying liberal journalists as motivated by irrational subconscious impulses, Rothman and Lichter's study contributes to three objectives on the corporate agenda: It discredits journalists as being politically and socially out of touch with the readers and viewers and the advertisers; it shores up the confidence of the business community by identifying an "outside" source of its problems; and it helps make journalists doubt themselves by replacing credo ("Afflict the comfortable and comfort the afflicted") with ego and Rorschach blots.

If there is room for improvement—and I think there is—the direction must be not toward making journalists more cautious in scrutinizing the workings of our economy and its central institutions, but toward giving journalists the resources to do so better. Perhaps this is too much to expect when the major national media are themselves big business, as Ben Bagdikian notes in his recent *The Media Monopoly*. But it would certainly be worth the effort.

I READ THE NEWS TODAY. OH BOY!

Imagine turning on the Six O'Clock News and hearing something like this:

Good evening. The quarterly economic indicators released today suggest a continuing downturn in quality of life. Prices of the four basic necessities—

housing, health care, energy, and food—were up a substantial 7.6 percent on an annual basis as a result of economic concentration and corporate and government mismanagement in those sectors, according to the National Center for Economic Alternatives. The poor suffered the most, while corporate profits soared. Unionized workers fell behind.

In the OSHA Report, another 3,241 workers were killed and 637,000 suffered disabling injuries in workplace accidents during the third quarter. During the quarter, an estimated 25,000 workers died of long-term occupational diseases, according to the Center for Responsive Law, which said the toll was the equivalent of a DC-10 airliner crash every day. As usual, meatpacking, construction, lumber, and mining led the list of the most unsafe industries.

The Consumer Product Safety Commission survey of hospital emergency rooms disclosed 7,482 fatal accidents involving household consumer products during the three-month period, and another nine million nonfatal accidents with public and private costs totaling $2.4 billion for the quarter.

The Plant Shutdown Monitor of the Data Center in Oakland reported that 98,025 workers lost their jobs as a result of plant shutdowns, of which 47,400 were described as temporary layoffs. Of the thirty-seven plants involved, most were profitable, but the parent firms, most of them multinational corporations, were concerned about the price-to-earnings ratio of their stocks and decided to eliminate marginal profit centers or transfer operations overseas or to nonunion areas, according to AFL-CIO economists. As we have reported previously, significant increases in suicide, alcoholism, family violence, and other stress-related problems are likely to follow in the wake of the plant shutdowns. The mayor of Mentor, Ohio, where Caterpillar laid off a thousand workers, said in a joint statement with the Lake Country Federation of Labor that several schools, fire stations, dental clinics, and libraries will have to close as a result.

And that's the way it is, Tuesday, November first, 1983.

Sound ridiculous? Of course. Such a recitation would be considered biased (although the figures given here are actual numbers or reasonable estimates from recent periods). By focusing on corporate decisions and their impact on workers and communities, these statistics paint what some might call an "antibusiness" portrait. And the sources of information—citizen and labor organizations— might be suspect as well.

Consider, however, our regular diet of economic indicators: nightly Dow Jones averages—higher means good, lower means bad; monthly Consumer Price Index reports—explained as if inflation were a product of nature with no structural causes except, perhaps, wage increases or "government spending"; periodic corporate announcements (and explanations) of layoffs—citing foreign competition, union demands, or environmental regulations, but never monopoly or mismanagement. These are no less one-sided, and the sources no less questionable, than the others. But our acceptance of Dow Jones and CPI, and our suspicion of information provided by labor and citizen groups, suggest how much the media have come to accept a corporate version of reality.

Notes

1. The Mobil ad includes Linda Lichter as a third researcher, but the published articles are co-authored by the two males. Lichter headed the study of the Columbia students. (The authors of the book based on these studies, *The Media Elite: America's New Power-brokers* [New York: Adler & Adler, 1986], are listed as S. Robert Lichter, Stanley Rothman, and Linda Lichter. For another critique of the Lichter-Rothman studies, see Herbert J. Gans, "Are U.S. Journalists Dangerously Liberal?" in *Columbia Journalism Review*, November–December 1985, pp. 29–33.—Ed.)

2. Although the "new class" theory has some merit as an explanation for expansion of a sector of professional employees in certain institutions, to view this group as a rival "elite" is misleading. The American economy is dominated by a small upper class based in the largest banks and corporations; stock ownership is highly concentrated, and income distribution is heavily skewed as well. The capitalist class may be under attack, but it is in no danger of being replaced by this "new class." See *Who Rules America Now?* by G. William Domhoff (New York: Simon & Schuster, 1983) for a full discussion.

3. All sociological evidence indicates that corporate directors and top management come overwhelmingly from upper- and upper-middle-class backgrounds (see Domhoff's *Who Rules America Now?*). Rothman and Lichter's business sample must be heavily skewed toward middle management. Their claim that big business is open to upwardly mobile blue-collarites is thus misleading.

CONSERVATIVE MEDIA CRITICISM: HEADS I WIN, TAILS YOU LOSE

DONALD LAZERE

Up until the 1960s, most criticism of mass media in America and Europe took the form of attacks on the "culture industry" as part of an Orwellian mass society; these attacks came both from the leftists of the Frankfurt School and New York intellectual circles and from cultural and political elitists. In the last two decades the media have come under attack from American conservatives as well. This criticism has not been of the highbrow elitist variety, however, disdaining the media for fostering kitsch and stupefied chauvinism. Whether representing the vulgar neoconservatism of Spiro Agnew in his speeches about the "effete corps of impudent snobs" in the eastern liberal media and universities or the more intellectual neoconservatism of Agnew's mentors Irving Kristol and Norman Podhoretz, these critics are avowed populists and patriots who accuse the media of being at once elitist and radically subversive.

This movement has been highly successful in swaying public opinion toward the conservative view. Its most recent forays have involved libel suits such as the abortive one mounted by Gen. William Westmoreland against CBS over an allegedly left-biased documentary on Vietnam, a film produced by Reed Irvine's Accuracy in Media rebutting another such documentary on PBS, various attempts to buy out CBS and other news organizations perceived to be excessively liberal, and the reemergence into public prominence of Patrick Buchanan, the most abusive of all conservative media critics, as President Reagan's communications director. Previous expressions have included periodic diatribes against leftist-intellectual media bias in Mobil Oil's institutional ads and *TV Guide* (published by Nixon and Reagan ally Walter Annenberg, who also helped instigate Westmoreland's suit against CBS), Kevin Phillips's *Mediacracy*, Benjamin Stein's *The View from Sunset Boulevard*, and the Media Institute's *Crooks, Conmen, and Clowns: Businessmen in TV Entertainment* (whose unidentified authors, Linda S. Lichter, S. Robert Lichter, and Stanley Rothman, have also conducted less polemical studies along similar lines for the American Enterprise Institute, discussed above by Peter Dreier). Stein's book was commissioned by Irving Kristol as editor of Basic Books; Stein, Phillips, and Buchanan are all former speechwriters for Nixon and Agnew as well as frequent contributors to *TV Guide*.

On one level, the conservative attack has been a calculated campaign of winning through intimidation, coordinated within the circles of corporate-sponsored New Right foundations, research institutes, and journalists and propagated with the same kind of doctrinaire incantations and slanted oversimplifications that the conservatives attribute to their leftist adversaries.[1] Grist for this propaganda mill, however, has been provided by an undeniable leftward tendency and intellectual upgrading in the political content of American mass culture since the fifties, the landmarks of which have included the news media's critical coverage of the Vietnam War, journalistic exposés of Watergate and intelligence agency abuses, the rise of a counterculture in popular music and films, and a modest increase in the sensitivity of the media to minority, feminist, and gay viewpoints. I will argue here, however, that the chagrin conservatives express over the leftward shift in the media exaggerates its significance and underestimates the multiple ways in which leftist elements get neutralized by mass culture.

The conservative critique contains many valid elements that serve to temper the tendency toward hyperbole and selective vision in the fixation of some leftists on reactionary aspects of mass culture, but it falls into the same faults on the opposite side. For example, conservatives, like leftists, attack manipulativeness by media elites, who are considered to favor the political left rather than the right. In this view, media personnel form a key part of a powerful "new class" or "adversary culture" of intellectuals, artists, and professionals allegedly hostile to America and capitalism. This analysis focuses on the points of conflict between media and the state, not on the points of collaboration, which leftists consider to be far stronger, and it locates media power in liberally inclined reporters, performers, writers, and other employees rather than in conservatively inclined corporate management and advertisers or in the profit-seeking imperatives of media as capitalist enterprises.[2] (Conservative theory has similarly ignored those aspects of the two other key new-class institutions, government and the university, that serve corporate interests.) An analysis is needed that evenhandedly examines the clashes between these opposed factions in the daily workings of media (or the university or government) to determine which ideology prevails on balance, and how. No conservative study as yet approaches this ideal so nearly as Todd Gitlin's *The Whole World Is Watching* and *Inside Prime Time* or Herbert Gans's *Deciding What's News*, both of which find the balance in the major American media ultimately leaning rightward.

The conservative critics' tendentiousness leads to multiple equivocations. First, they disingenuously fail to acknowledge that many of their populist arguments against the liberal media, new-class elite have been appropriated from the critique of corporate liberalism launched by the New Left and its mentors like C. Wright Mills and the Frankfurt School. Second, when conservatives perceive leftist attitudes in mass media, they attribute them to manipulativeness and bias by the media elite. But when it comes to those negative aspects of media that enforce conservative values or serve business interests—TV commercials (especially on children's programs), for example, or violence, sensationalism, and generally trashy programming keyed to maximizing profits—conservative critics shift gears and *defend* the media on the grounds that in the free market of ideas they are simply giving the people what they want, and besides, people really aren't influenced all that much by the media.[3] This little game of "heads I win, tails you lose" precludes the possibility that the people might ever want leftist ideas. After all, one obvious factor in the leftward tendency in the media is a shift in audience demographics from small towns to cities, from whites to minorities, and toward more open-minded attitudes; thus the media, in good capitalist fashion, are merely following the market.

Conservatives similarly refuse to grant the possibility that when media reportage accords with left attitudes, it may, at least on occasion, be a reflection not of bias but merely of the facts—albeit unpleasant ones, for which the media messenger becomes a scapegoat: Vietnam *was* a disaster, Nixon *was* guilty, poverty *does* persist in America. Moreover, the "liberal bias" of media personnel in many cases merely reflects their higher level of professionalism compared to earlier generations of journalists and producers of popular entertainment; they are liberal in the sense of being liberally educated and broadly informed on the issues they are dealing with—one can only wish they were more so. What conservatives sometimes seem to be calling for in media, as in teaching, is equal time for the ignorant and prejudiced. (To be sure, the domination of information media by those better educated and better informed on world affairs than most of their audience—which is perhaps inevitable, to some extent—poses an equal dilemma for left populists who see the bias of corporate liberalism and professionalism discriminating against the working class and poor; neither the left nor the right has addressed this problem very realistically.)

Patrick Buchanan is the ultimate practitioner of "heads I win, tails you lose." After years of attacking liberal journalists for lack of impartiality, he managed to remain unscathed by revelations that he, along with George Will, not only knew—and kept silent—about the purloined Carter debate papers in the 1980 election, but used them to help coach Reagan and later lauded his performance in the guise of impartial journalist. He was similarly unscathed by his role in the Watergate conspiracy, in which, according to William Safire's memoir, he was a leading architect of Nixon's stonewalling strategy and of his effort to attribute all the incriminating charges to liberal media bias, while at the same time feeding whole news stories and columns pushing this line to friendly conservative journalists. Shortly after Nixon resigned, Buchanan wrote a *TV Guide* "News Watch" column blasting academics and the media for their "liberal intellectual pandering to the biases of the black and poor—at the expense of the American middle class." [4] Of course, conservatives like Buchanan never pander to the biases of the white and middle class, let alone of rich folk like Walter Annenberg or Nixon's and Reagan's financial backers. This kind of rhetorical ploy typifies the mean-spiritedness of American neoconservatives, who champion traditional moral and religious values yet constantly ridicule affluent liberals for displaying compassion for those less fortunate. Buchanan's invective could equally well be applied to Jesus Christ, notorious panderer to the biases of the poor and meek.

The position of neoconservative intellectuals of the current *Commentary* persuasion, such as Podhoretz, Kristol, Van den Haag, Michael Novak, Hilton Kramer, and Joseph Epstein, is especially equivocal. They pose as defenders of high, impartial critical standards against leftist fuzzy-thinking and sentimentality in politics or culture, yet they get all misty-eyed when it comes to Nixon, Reagan, and the know-nothing right in America and among our foreign allies. They are associated with the New York intellectual circles that in past decades were most critical of mass culture, but because of their ever-increasing reluctance to criticize any aspect of capitalism, they either have stifled their criticism of the culture industry altogether (except for joining in the attacks on the influence of new-class leftists in it, in as single and simple-minded a manner as Agnew or *TV Guide*) or have recycled their previous lines of criticism against the New Left–aligned counterculture of the sixties and its permeation of mainstream culture, both high and mass. Neoconservatives berate left intellectuals on the one hand for being elitists alienated from mainstream America (i.e., capitalist mass culture) and on the other hand for betraying high-cultural standards when they praise mass-cultural figures like the Beatles. Very crafty, these leftists!

The identification of the counterculture with the New Left dates back to a flirtation between the two that lasted only a few years in the late sixties. Since then, leftists have for the most part dissociated themselves from the counterculture, recognizing—as most neoconservatives have not—that it was in many ways a product of consumer capitalism, which, since well before the sixties, has increasingly dragged the whole national culture down to the level of subadolescence, and that its ostensibly rebellious aspects were quickly absorbed into the dominant system, watered down into hedonistic commodities. By now the rednecks who killed the hippies in *Easy Rider* have adopted the latter's long hair, dope, rock, and bikes, yet remain just as politically conservative as ever, much as the college students of the eighties get stoned, listen to Bruce Springsteen—and vote for Ronald Reagan. (Some left critics, such as Simon Frith, Ellen Willis and George Lipsitz, continue to find oppositional elements in pop music, but with a sobered sense of their limitations.)[5]

Although leftists are divided over the enduring liberatory power of the sexual revolution, they are unanimous in condemning the commodification of sexual liberation in pornography, *Playboy*, advertising, and what television executives cynically label "tits and ass" programming. Yet the left continues to be stigmatized by the public association of the libertinism of "Dallas" and the smutty humor of TV talk shows with liberalism, even though what these programs depict (with a degree of realism that is, if anything, understated) is the mores of conservative upper classes now and throughout history. The present politics of licentiousness is misperceived as a left-versus-right issue; it more closely resembles the conflicts of seventeenth-century England, with Moral Majority Puritans and middle American Viguerie Whiggery in opposition to the Cavalier sybarites of the jet set. In short, the left response to accusations that it is responsible for the culture or counterculture of narcissism is to lob this ball back into the court of the defenders of capitalism.

Conservative critics see television, rock music, and video games as negatively affecting literacy and learning and undermining worker efficiency, social cohesion, and respect for authority; leftist intellectuals are more inclined to focus on how the stupefying influence of mass culture contributes to conformity and authoritarianism. The left and right interpretations are not mutually exclusive. It is quite possible that a decline in reasoning capacities and the resultant worker ineptitude is simply an unforeseen by-product of a whole national culture dedicated to the engineering of docile consumers and employees. Conservatives believe that the disrespect for authority reflected by mass media in recent years has caused young people to withdraw from civic duties into hedonistic narcissism, apathy, and cynicism toward public institutions, including government, business, and law enforcement. I submit that the growing credibility gap undermining the American establishment's claim to legitimate authority (whether that claim is warranted or not, and whatever the role of the media in producing or reflecting cynicism toward authority) has in only a passive sense created the legitimation crisis perceived by many critics on both left and right.

Erich Fromm wrote about the authoritarian effects of mass society in his 1941 classic *Escape from Freedom*:

The result of this kind of influence is a twofold one: one is a skepticism and cynicism towards everything which is said or printed, while the other is a childish belief in anything that a person is told with authority. This combination of cynicism and naiveté is very typical of the modern individual. Its essential result is to discourage him from doing his own thinking and deciding.[6]

In other words, people (especially those whose memory span has been stunted by mass media) may voice skepticism toward authority in general yet still be gullible in each new manipulation by authorities, like Charlie Brown and his perennial hope that Lucy won't pull the football away *this* time. Likewise, Americans today may be cynical toward the status quo, but they are equally cynical toward any alternative, particularly of a leftist variety. The resulting apathy, then, simply leaves the field of social control open to those powerful enough to exercise it, and the masses, like those in Dostoevsky's "The Grand Inquisitor," gratefully cede the burden of authority to those more clever, be they scrupulous or not. Cynicism toward authority has indeed frequently been the tone of entertainment media in the last few decades, but rather than being turned toward organized leftist political alternatives, it has most often been channeled into the right-wing vigilantism of James Bond, Charles Bronson's *Death Wish*, Clint Eastwood's Dirty Harry, Sylvester Stallone's Rambo, and *The A Team*, or the know-nothing anarchism of punk rock, "MASH," "Saturday Night Live," *Animal House*, and *Porky's*.

The whole neoconservative critique ignores the capacity of mass culture to disarm opposition through co-option, planned obsolescence, framing, time lag, and dilution. A recent, prototypical example of the co-optive process was the series of IBM commercials that turned Charlie Chaplin's beleaguered proletarian in *Modern Times* into the efficient manager of a computerized factory; the commercials were so well produced and good humored as to disarm indignation over the perversion of Chaplin's politics. Similarly, the San Luis Obispo County Board of Realtors recently sponsored a Private Property Week, taking as their theme Woody Guthrie's socialist anthem "This Land Is Your Land." Ronald Reagan, too, preempted Guthrie by making "This Train Is Bound for Glory" a theme of his 1984 campaign, and later he seized on Bruce Springsteen's "Born in the U.S.A." for its "patriotic" title, much to Springsteen's dismay. Springsteen's cynical song also spawned an orgy of commercials patriotically pushing cars and beers "Born and Brewed the American Way." "Mack the Knife," the theme song from Brecht and Weill's anticapitalist *Threepenny Opera*, has become a hamburger commercial for "Mac Tonight." In the late sixties, shortly after the Oakland Black Panthers coined the rebellious expression "Right On," the Oakland *Tribune*, owned by the Panthers' archenemy, ultraconservative William Knowland, ran ads reading, "The *Tribune* Is Right On!" And in a similar vein, the Reagan administration's Voice of America appropriated the name of a hero of the Cuban left for its "Radio Marti" anti-Castro broadcasts.

Political opposition has been commodified by the media and subjected to planned obsolescence like every other commodity. Conservatives deplore the media's attraction to novelty and sensation that results in undue publicizing of socially disruptive movements, such as occurred with the counterculture and New Left in the sixties. Regardless of the merits or demerits of the sixties movements, alarm over the threat they posed to social stability now appears to have been greatly exaggerated, considering how easily the counterculture was co-opted into consumer culture and how quickly the New Left disintegrated under external and internal pressures. Concerning the media's fixation on novelty, Todd Gitlin aptly identifies it as part of the paradox of corporate capitalism's growth imperative: "The stability of the system is predicated on the institutionalization of change and speed."[7] Some of the more forthright conservative critics, such as Daniel Bell and Michael Novak, have conceded the same point, viewing the attachment to sensation as a flaw in capitalism but one that might be remedied through moral exhortation. Leftists like Gitlin, however, consider it an incorrigible feature of the system, pernicious not only because it hypes meretricious innovations but even more so because it aborts potentially worthy ones, promoting both indiscriminately for a brief time and then discarding the latter like the former when their novelty wears off.

The publicizing of oppositional movements is contained, moreover, as is the introduction of novelty in general, within the structural and ideological frames of the media, in ways analyzed in Gitlin's *The Whole World Is Watching: Mass Media in the Making and Unmaking of the New Left* and *Inside Prime Time* and Gaye Tuchman's *Making News: A Study in the Construction of Reality*. One example that Gitlin presents is the way the news media framed campus and antiwar demonstrations in the mode of crime coverage, to the neglect of background events and issues involved. Gitlin's own frustrating experiences watching media distortions of the more responsible factions in Students for a Democratic Society, of which he was a leader in the early sixties, are poignantly reflected in this observation:

Just as people *as workers* have no voice in what they make, how they make it, or how the product is distributed and used, so do people *as producers of meaning* have no voice in what the media make of what they say or do, or in the context within which the media frame their activity. The resulting meanings, now mediated, acquire an eery substance in the real world, standing outside their ostensible makers and confronting them as an alien force. The social meanings of intentional action have been deformed beyond recognition.[8]

The ultimate implication of *The Whole World Is Watching* is that no oppositional movement today, of the left *or* right, regardless of its merits, could get its message across intact through the distorting lenses of the media.

Another brake on the effectiveness of opposition culture is time lag: rarely is much media attention given to radically controversial issues until well after the moment when their coverage might pose a serious threat to the status quo. Not until years following the American withdrawal from Vietnam did films and television dramas appear that were critical of the war—while it was going on, we got John Wayne's *Green Berets*. Provocative as ABC-TV's "Roots" was in 1976, it is unlikely that a comparable program could have been produced twenty-five years earlier, when its impact might have changed the course of both American race relations and television quality. The avowal of white viewers that they "never knew" the true meaning of slavery before "Roots" was certainly an affirmation of the political power of art, but it also raised a troubling question—why *didn't* they know? Slavery is not exactly an obscure episode in American history, and television must bear a large burden of blame for previously—and subsequently —obscuring not only black history but the whole sense of historical continuity and cause and effect for a generation of Americans.

A similar case of too little too late has been the popularity since the seventies of films, books, and television programs critical of fifties blacklisting, including the Woody Guthrie revival that featured a Hollywood film of his autobiography, *Bound for Glory*. In 1960 I submitted an article to the then-liberal *New York Post* in an attempt to gain some recognition for Guthrie, who was slowly dying in poverty and obscurity in a state hospital. Although the article mentioned nothing about his politics, it was killed after initial acceptance when the editors learned that Guthrie was an unregenerate communist. The article was later published by the *World Telegram and Sun*, whose editors weren't politically astute enough to dispatch a reporter to administer a loyalty oath at Guthrie's bedside, as the *Post* had done. A liberal might be defined as one who takes courageously leftist stands just as soon as they have ceased being dangerous.

The liberal slant of most American films, television newscasts, and dramas dealing explicitly with political issues in recent years is further offset by the fact that such productions still form a minute percentage of the total outpouring of films or television programs and commercials; the dominant climate of apolitical distraction dissipates any political message. Moreover, regardless of how liberal, or even radical, the message of a particular production might be, its point will be lost if audience members lack coherent understanding of differing political ideologies that will allow them to interpret it. Such understanding is discouraged by the absence of a consistent ideology in either the Republican or the Democratic party, as well as by the nonideological official stance taken by American mass media, which extends to the exclusion of clearcut ideological viewpoints from nearly all areas of programming; in the same way, such viewpoints get blurred in American education by the convention that teachers and textbooks are expected to be blandly neutral. Aside from Christian channels, there is no mass-circulated, nationally accessible equivalent in print, film, or broadcasting of a *Commentary*, *American Opinion*, *Inquiry*, *In These Times*, or Pacifica Radio that might frame "Roots" or "The Day After" within a cogent political perspective rather than simply presenting them as random statements. The status quo is likely to prevail by default in the absence of any clearly articulated ideological alternative or organized political opposition.

Above all, the random criticisms of business people in the media that conservative critics complain about do not add up to any fundamental criticism of capitalism or of the political monopoly of our two capitalist parties, which remain givens of American culture, inconspicuous and unquestionable as the air we breathe. The outer limit of recent media leftism is what Michael Novak, in his pre-neoconservative days, aptly termed "a vague and misty liberalism."[9] Throughout the cold war it has been virtually forbidden for any successful politician, any mass-circulation journalist (including muckrakers like Woodward and Bernstein and "60 Minutes"), any Hollywood film or television show, to attribute any problems in America to intrinsic faults in the capitalist economic system, to voice the need for a labor party here, or to openly advocate socialist policies in general or on particular issues. There were some exceptions in the late sixties and early seventies, as part of the millennialism that was in fashion that season, but since then the politicians and media have beaten an embarrassed retreat and tried to suppress all traces of that lapse from national memory. McGovern's disastrous 1972 presidential campaign was the last gasp of any movement for a guaranteed minimum income or national health insurance, social rights long taken for granted in other industrial democracies.

Indeed, *all* issues related to political economy have been played down in every realm of American consciousness and culture since the cold war began, as though even to consider issues addressed by Marxism is a sign of softness on communism. The continued existence of gross extremes of wealth and poverty; the role in domestic and foreign policy of high finance and corporate competition for markets, resources, and labor; influence-peddling and special-interest legislation; the growing post–World War II dependency of the American economy on waste, environmental destruction, and military spending; monetary and tax policy, inflation and unemployment—no issues influence our lives so directly yet are so little understood and so inadequately reported, analyzed, or dramatized in popular media. The inner workings are mystified: "It's all too complicated for us; only the president and the chairman of the Federal Reserve Board can understand it."

The conservative critics may be right when they say that big business is often portrayed negatively in television and other media—when it *is* portrayed. But more significant is the fact that it rarely appears at all, that it is so sheltered from view and from criticism in the media's blandly middle-class worldview, relative to its actual role in modern America. Probably the most prominent feature of postwar American society, the centralization of the economy and culture under a few hundred national and multinational corporations that also exert enormous political influence, has been virtually invisible as a subject in mass news and entertainment media (and in serious literature, too; even the most biting fictional critique of postwar American capitalism, Joseph Heller's *Catch-22*, was transposed to World War II Europe). Much more public fuss is made over television-network oligopoly than over the larger pattern of corporate oligopoly, of which it forms only one part. Corporate capitalism, both the most powerful agent of elite control and the most radically disruptive force in twentieth-century America, has managed to identify itself with populism and conservatism, even joining in on populist-conservative attacks against the media that are its own subsidiaries. Modern capitalism is conservative in no concrete sense of the word except conserving established hierarchies of wealth and power. Its ethos of profit-stimulating destruction and waste has combined with the deep-seated violence in American history to breed a sense of disposability, not only of the natural environment but also of human life—in Vietnam, the euphemism for killing was to "waste" someone. It has debased seasons and holidays into an endless cycle of merchandising campaigns. It has ruined the country's nutritional health by promotion of a junk-food diet from childhood on. It has radically transformed the American workplace, turning an ever-increasing percentage of workers into employees of organizations whose bureaucratic impersonality often equals that of big government. It has radically altered American demographics, engineering industrial, housing, and transportation policies that have been major contributors to urban overcrowding and rural atrophy. It has leveled the topography of the American heartland, turning local communities and cultures into endlessly repeated clusters of the same franchises in the same freeway interchanges and shopping malls, whose products are endlessly advertised on the same TV commercials from coast to coast. The passionate loyalty to local sports teams is a poignant expression of the fact that they are virtually the only thing that still differentiates one locale from another. My family in Iowa speaks proudly of being "up-to-date" now that their towns and TV-guided lifestyles are indistinguishable from those everywhere else—Des Moines even has a Playboy Club. This standardization has its benefits, to be sure, and is preferable in many ways to the parochiality it has replaced; still, one can wish there were alternatives besides parochiality on the one hand and the great continental wall of Colonel Sanders Holiday Inn Texaco McDonald's Burger King Bob's Big Boy Wendy's Carl's Jr. on the other. Is this what the American Founding Fathers, always invoked by conservatives, had in mind?

My point here is not to indict American capitalism totally—it can be defended on many legitimate grounds, especially relative to communist societies—but only to point out how exempt it is from many equally legitimate grounds for criticism, from a conservative as well as a leftist viewpoint, in the mass media and in the minds of most Americans who consider themselves conservatives. True to Fromm's characterization, Americans, when polled, may voice cynicism toward big business in the abstract yet remain wholly gullible on particular issues concerning the public role of corporations. Many of the college students I have polled believe the television networks are owned by "the government." Moreover, nearly all these students, who attend college in San Luis Obispo, site of the controversial Diablo Canyon nuclear power plant, believe that the plant operator, Pacific Gas and Electric Co., is owned by the State of California; in dozens of student papers summarizing the pros and cons on the plant, whose opening was delayed for years after it was discovered that it was built on an earthquake fault, no one has considered as a possible motivation in the push to open it the multi-billion dollar investment made by the stockholders of PG & E. Such is the success of decades of propaganda by corporations, their political fronts, and public relations agencies, including the totality of American mass media, sanitizing their own social role and sullying that of government and public employees in every activity except corporate-subsidizing ones like national defense.

The condition of American labor has improved vastly over the course of the twentieth century, to be sure (although with some large setbacks in the last few decades), but media images of labor give scant indication that American workers are still ever exploited or alienated. Workers and management on television shows like "Mary Tyler Moore" and "Taxi" are one big happy family, while commercials (the American equivalent of socialist realism, as Michael Schudson has noted) regale us with Juan Valdez loyally scrutinizing the coffee beans he's picking in Colombia for Hills Brothers or the gang of happy workers at the factory or construction site knocking off at closing time for a Miller's.[10]

Occasionally topics related to political economy turn up as the premise of a movie or television show—*Norma Rae* (union organizing in a Southern mill), for instance, or *Trading Places* (the arbitrariness of wealth and poverty), *The Formula* (international energy cartel), *Deal of the Century* (American arms trading abroad), *The China Syndrome* (nuclear power hazards and media trivialization), *Nine to Five* (exploitation of women office workers), or *Rollover* (international finance)—the latter three appearing thanks to Jane Fonda's tenacious efforts against the Hollywood bureaucracy. But these stories usually soon degenerate into pretexts for slapstick comedy, melodramatic or romantic plot twists showcasing glamorous stars. Even media leftists must play the glamor game: Fonda's heroines cannot look like Plain Jane, and Southern mill union organizer Norma Rae has to look like Sally Field instead of the real-life, plump Crystal Lee Jordan. What is missing is not grim socialist realism but simply a degree of truth to life and analytic depth in addressing socioeconomic themes, whether in drama or in comedy. (Capitalism can provide prime material for satire, as shown by *Catch-22*, the San Francisco Mime Troupe, Italian radical *farceur* Dario Fo, *Network*, or Mel Brooks's gag about the corporate conglomerate named Engulf and Devour.)

The notion that television entertainment presents a negative image of big business and the wealthy—advanced by Ben Stein, Accuracy in Media, the Media Institute, Mobil Oil, and the American Enterprise Institute—is based largely on such dramas as "Dallas." Although the popularity of these programs probably does lie largely in their promise of demystifying glimpses into the higher circles of political and financial power, this promise is constantly deferred. Beneath the veneer of criticism of J. R. Ewing's personal villainy, the glorification of business and wealth in "Dallas" is as transparent as it is in "Lifestyles of the Rich and Famous." J. R. is presented as the one rotten apple in the barrel; most of the other oil barons are pillars of virtue, driven on occasion to deviousness only in their noble attempts to foil J. R. Benevolent paternalists all, few ever demonstrate greed—indeed, their lack of compulsion to gain ever more money and power resembles few wealthy people or corporations I have encountered. They are almost never shown trying unduly to influence the political process or public opinion for selfish interests, and they are good buddies to the few workers in their oilfields or ranches ever shown. Labor conflicts are nonexistent. Year after year these prime-time soap operas tug at viewers' hearts with the trials and tribulations of the rich and powerful, with never a hint of questioning why their tragedies should be considered more compelling than those of less privileged people.

The association of beauty and sex with wealth on "Dallas" and its imitators is highly sentimentalized and vastly underrepresents the incidence of lechery and prostitution in the upper classes. Nowhere in the real world outside of Hollywood studios is there the concentration of beautiful people, elegant clothes, and grooming portrayed in the fictitious world of these dramas; yet only the villains, male or female, are ever motivated by lust, vanity, or mercenary sex. Most of the central characters seem oblivious to their movie-star appearance, untouched by the narcissism and gold digging common to professional beauties. *Playboy* reifies beauty, presenting beautiful women as sexual commodities for the affluent male, but the "Dallas" genre gives the characters acted by Playmate-of-the-Month types the demure personality of soap opera heroines seeking only true love and domesticity—although domestic love on these programs is expressed through gifts of diamonds and sports cars. Even the Machiavellian J. R., as portrayed by Larry Hagman, is roguishly charming, and his manipulation of people and financial power is exciting to many women viewers. But imagine how audience response to "Dallas" would differ if J. R. Ewing looked like his real-life model, Nelson Bunker Hunt.

Above all, the "Dallas" genre raises political and economic issues (J. R. subverts a Southeast Asia government or sells oil illegally to Cuba) only to evade them by shifting them from the public into the personal sphere. The corporations on these programs are invariably family businesses, which allows their producers to dramatize their workings not as impersonal bureaucracies driven by internal power struggles and the external imperatives of profit and growth, but as arenas for intrafamilial relations, settings for private psychodrama rather than for the conflict of public interests. Here again, the plain folks appeal: multinational corporations have the same problems our family does. As Gitlin's *Inside Prime Time* documents in fuller detail, television drama, like sitcom, keeps political conflict all in the family. Thus, although individual businessmen may be depicted as villains (melodrama and slapstick, after all, need villains, and Mr. Big is a more plausible candidate than Mr. Little), rarely does TV drama focus on the shadier political or economic activities of corporations as such.

The scrupulous research of Gitlin and George Gerbner, which shows a preponderance of favorable depictions of business in television drama, puts to shame the skewed pseudoscholarship and procorporate special pleading of Stein, the Media Institute, and Mobil Oil. One Mobil ad, "The Myth of the Villainous Businessman," began by citing Gerbner's studies indicating that television violence contributes to an abnormally fearful mentality in heavy viewers. "Other independent studies," Mobil continued, "show that if TV watchers are wary, they are *most* wary of businessmen." [11] The ad then cited Stein and the Media Institute, implying that Gerbner's studies were in accord with them; but in fact Gerbner finds that the effect of TV-bred fear is to make viewers more willing to accept the authority of government, the military and police, and big business, and that the general image of businessmen on television is relatively favorable. Furthermore, when the ad refers to "a 1980 study by the non-profit, research-oriented Media Institute," it neglects—of course—to mention that the Media Institute is funded and directed by New Right businessmen including trustee Herbert Schmertz, Mobil vice-president and mentor of its antimedia ads.

In spite of every evidence that liberal influences in mass culture are generally offset by conservative ones, conservatives have managed to convince the majority of the American public that the media, as well as government and education, have a leftist bias. The ultimate explanation for the success of this sleight-of-hand is that American consciousness is skewed so far to the right that conservative bias is not even generally recognized as such but is accepted as the norm of neutrality. The American situation is an extreme illustration of a general truth of political rhetoric in any social order: partisanship toward the status quo is customarily perceived as nonpartisan. In America, the very notion of criticism is so alien to the national creed of positive thinking that "bias" is widely believed to *mean* criticism of the status quo. Virtually every facet of American socialization, especially prior to the last few decades, has been grossly biased in favor of Americanism, boosterism, organized religion, and the norms of middle-class, white patriarchy. Nor has public concern over bias ever been stirred up about the corporate propaganda produced by massively financed lobbies, managed news and entertainment media, and advertising and public relations agencies. Only when news and entertainment media or educators have deviated from the conservative consensus—Vietnam and Watergate being the most prominent instances —have conservatives and the general public cried bias. The slightest attempts to provide some counterweight to conventional indoctrination are thus singled out by conservative critics and blown up into "hatred of America" and "vicious anti-business distortion." [12]

Any number of further examples could be cited in support of the thesis that conservative biases are considered the norm of neutrality in America. The nationalistic ritual of the pledge of allegiance to the flag is taken for granted, but headlines and public outrage erupt when the Berkeley City Council replaces it with a pledge for world peace. We similarly take for granted a plethora of Sunday religious broadcasts and newspaper sections, most with an explicitly or implicitly conservative slant, but imagine the uproar that would greet "The Atheist Hour" or "The Liberation Theology Page." (Conservatives are correct when they say that beyond explicitly religious programming, American media project an essentially secular view—i.e., that of corporate capitalism; still, few figures in media or politics dare not conform to the charade of professing deep religious faith.) Elementary school teachers in the San Luis Obispo area were required to give their students handouts on the safety of nuclear power—along with an emergency evacuation plan in case of accident at Diablo Canyon—devised by Pacific Gas and Electric. It never occurred to the administrators to question the objectivity or veracity of the PG & E material, but when some teachers proposed to balance it with material from citizen organizations critical of the plant and evacuation plan, the administrators refused on the grounds that *that* viewpoint was partisan.

Neoconservative intellectuals boast about being attuned to that moderately liberal "real America" so misunderstood by the adversary culture, but their own vision of America is a distorted projection of the liberally tinged circles that they—no less than the leftists they criticize—are confined to in eastern metropolises and the Ivy League. Having lived most of my life in various middle American communities, I can testify that the Chamber of Commerce view of reality, in which what's good for business is good for America and the world, is the only one most people in such communities are ever exposed to. Any questioning of this viewpoint, locally or in the mass media, is simply dismissed as maladjustment or communist propaganda.

Even those conservatives who are sincere rather than guileful in their professed alarm over the disintegrating social fabric fail to understand what an unshakably conservative country the United States has become. In a society where most people are insulated from manifest political oppression and at least passively accept the established order, whether for sound or for unsound reasons, the sheer weight of inertia is a stronger force than any movement for change or principled ideology of either the left or the right. It is a struggle for most people just to get by from one day to the next; social stability and the force of habit and routine ease the anxieties of everyday life. For people who are afraid to bite the corporate hand that feeds them, who do not want to be bothered with complicated analyses of intangible social ills or with the threatening assertions of previously disfranchised groups, a simplistically conservative ideology provides a welcome rationalization—and there will always be plenty of opportunistic politicians and profit-seeking media to purvey that ideology. An index of the apparently inexorable rightward drift of American politics in recent decades is that conservative reaction against left movements such as the campus rebellion and counterculture of the sixties has generally far exceeded the original action, while debacles of conservative policy have usually provoked a reaction not to the left but further to the right—thus the widespread current opinion that quiche-eating liberal politicians, journalists, and academics lost the Vietnam War and hounded Nixon unjustly from office. Right-wing statists like Reagan now get elected by posing as libertarian, populist opponents of big government that their constituents believe is socialistic, although in fact it is plutocratic and becoming more so with the election of every antigovernment conservative.

The left in America has long been reduced to a defensive position; its main activities are not, realistically, attempts to gain power or implement its programs, but are perforce holding actions against right-wing offensives: Vietnam, restrictions on civil liberties, denial of equal rights for minorities and women, rollbacks of labor gains from earlier decades, and attacks on media and educational liberalism. At this moment the American left is in the weakest state it has experienced this century except for the fifties, yet conservatives continue to pose as a persecuted minority bravely standing up to the "left establishment," not only in media but also in government, business-labor relations, and education. It seems a plausible inference in these circumstances that the covert aim of this pose is not to even an imbalance but to increase it, to the point of effectively obliterating any left influence in this country.

All in all, then, conservatives are in little danger of losing control, over mass media or any other major realm of power in America. The media, in their perpetual drive to find novelty and to renew exhausted formulas, have indisputably discovered a market for nontraditional viewpoints. But the inroads of adversarial forces signify little more than that the culture industry has learned to assimilate and contain such forces in the pursuit of its essential, unchanging mission: that of delivering consumers to corporate producers, which in turn entails fostering a mentality of compliancy and diversion that stifles oppositional political consciousness.

Notes

1. For an investigative report that updates Dreier on the organizational sources of conservative media criticism, see Walter Schneir and Miriam Schneir, "Beyond Westmoreland: The Right's Attack on the Press," *The Nation*, 30 March 1985, pp. 361–367.

2. Effective refutations of neoconservative new-class theory in general have been presented in Peter Steinfels, *The Neoconservatives* (New York: Simon & Schuster, 1979), pp. 285–290; Christopher Lasch, *The Culture of Narcissism* (New York: Norton, 1978), pp. 232–236; Alvin Gouldner, *The Future of Intellectuals and the Rise of the New Class* (New York: Seabury Press, 1979); Noam Chomsky, *Towards A New Cold War* (New York: Pantheon Books, 1982), pp. 60–114; and David Bazelon, "How Now 'The New Class'?" *Dissent* 26, no. 4 (1979): 443–449.

3. A classic example of this kind of flipflop was a *TV Guide* article, "Does TV Violence Affect Our Society? No" (14 June 1975, pp. 22–28), by Edith Efron, whose constant theme in other *TV Guide* articles and books of that period was the diabolic manipulation of the public by the liberal news media.

4. Patrick Buchanan, "News Watch," *TV Guide*, 2 August 1975, p. A-4.

5. Simon Frith, *Sound Effects: Youth, Leisure, and the Politics of Rock 'n' Roll* (New York: Pantheon Books, 1981); Ellen Willis, *Beginning to See the Light* (New York: Knopf, 1981); George Lipsitz, "Ain't Nobody Here But Us Chickens: The Class Origins of Rock and Roll," in *Class and Culture in Cold War America* (South Hadley, Mass.: Bergin, 1982), pp. 195–225.

6. Erich Fromm, *Escape from Freedom* (New York: Rinehart, 1941), p. 250.

7. Todd Gitlin, *The Whole World Is Watching: Mass Media in the Making and Unmaking of the New Left* (Berkeley and Los Angeles: University of California Press, 1980), p. 237.

8. Ibid., p. 3.

9. Michael Novak, "Television Shapes the Soul," in *Mass Media Issues*, ed. Leonard L. Sellers and William L. Rivers (Englewood Cliffs, N.J.: Prentice-Hall, 1977), p. 47.

10. For a union viewpoint on the image of labor in television news and entertainment see *Television: Corporate America's Game* (Washington, D.C.: Union Media Monitoring Project, 1981).

11. *Los Angeles Times*, 23 August 1983.

12. Kevin Phillips, "News Watch," *TV Guide*, 13 July 1975, p. A-4.

Part II
Capitalism and American Mythology

INTRODUCTION

Much has been written by critics of every political persuasion about the abiding myths of American society; the distinct approach of left critics, as represented in this section, is to examine these myths in relation to capitalist ideology. This is not to reduce the whole American mythology to a capitalist conspiracy, although historical evidence for the calculated promotion of an idealized image of America by and for business interests is greater than is generally acknowledged. In the most common pattern, the myths are reproduced either as uncalculated reflections of the ideological assumptions of capitalism or as appropriations of pre-existing ideals molded into accord with those assumptions. Contemporary conservatives pride themselves on their tough-minded realism, ridiculing socialist ideals as utopian and sentimental. As we shall see, though, the image of capitalism propagated in American mass culture is at least equally utopian. The summary that follows of some key myths synthesizes ideas from the readings in this section and from other sources, including a similar taxonomy in the chapter "Manipulation and the Packaged Consciousness" in Herbert Schiller's *The Mind Managers*. These analyses are based mainly on the classic period of American mythology prior to the sixties; the widespread revisions since then are discussed in the general introduction and in Part 3.

1. *There Are No Class Divisions or Conflicts in America.* As Jeremy Tunstall indicates here, the ideal that American mass culture projects is that of a homogeneous, middle-class society—an ideal at odds with statistical realities, as confirmed in the studies by George Gerbner's research group (Part 6) of political messages on television and their reception by audiences. Simon Frith finds even in the quasi-rebellious popular culture of rock music, as in earlier bohemian and avant-garde movements, an essentially petit-bourgeois consciousness (see his article in Part 4). In this ideal, poor people and militant workers have low visibility, as do upper-class elites—including the barons of mass culture who propagate the myth of the universal middle class. The quest for wealth or power is reconciled with middle-class norms by images of "good" rich people or political leaders who thwart the stock-villainous ones and reinforce Hemingway's retort to F. Scott Fitzgerald that the rich are different from you and me only in having more money: the billionaires of "Dallas" drive their own cars and go first thing every morning to the office, where their secretaries call them by their first names; and the matriarch Miss Ellie, wearing K-Mart dresses, putters around the kitchen of an unguarded ranch house attended by only two servants.

The middle-class ideal is also preeminently a white, Anglo-Saxon one. As Robert Chrisman points out in "Blacks, Racism, and Bourgeois Culture," minorities and working-class ethnics are typically—even in the recent liberal trend in media—constituted through the eyes of and affirm the norms of middle-class whites.[1] In the conventional media view, minorities and ethnics are suitable for portrayal mainly as the butts of humor or as subordinates to WASPs, rarely as dramatic or romantic heroes. Todd Gitlin found in interviews with producers of television network entertainment, many of them Jewish, that fear of perceived audience anti-Semitism led, at least until the seventies, to taboos on New York settings and on characters with mustaches; one producer described the evolution of a classic series out of a project proposed by Carl Reiner, with himself as the star: "They de-Jewished it, Midwestized it, and put Dick Van Dyke and Mary Tyler Moore in the leads." [2]

The very substantial realities of class lines in America are rarely presented in our high or mass culture with anything near the verisimilitude of such British dramas as "Upstairs, Downstairs"; the few abortive attempts to do so—the television series "Beacon Street," for example, or "The Best of Families"—would seem to indicate that American dramatists congenitally lack this aptitude. The convergence toward the middle class conveniently erases any sense of opposing interests between workers and management, who are typically portrayed, especially in commercials, in metaphors of a family or sports team. All hints are expunged of Marx's theory that labor is the primary source of economic value and that capital is unjustly accumulated from a surplus in the selling price of commodities over their cost of production. Left critics including John Berger, Roland Barthes, Judith Williamson, Ariel Dorfman, and Armand Mattelart have analyzed the mystification of production processes, which are reduced to brief incantations of technical know-how by management spokespersons. The role of labor is elided by jumping the gap from resources in their natural state straight to their delivery to the consumer as commodities; Williamson points out that metaphorical images of this jump are among the most common techniques used in advertisements. [3] This mode of commodity fetishism ties in with certain attitudes toward time, history, and nature: all the contingent, contestable processes of production and historical direction are collapsed into a view of the capitalist order as an immutable, natural essence (see the quote from Barthes in the introduction to Part 5).

Corollary to the erasure of class rule and conflict is an image of corporations and their major stockholders and executives as nonpartisan public benefactors rather than as part of a ruling class or power elite, and of government, the military, the judiciary, and the police as neutral institutions free from class interests, as opposed to Marx's characterization of them as the administrative branch of the bourgeoisie. (By an adroit bit of doublethink, neoconservative rhetoric, which otherwise plays down the influence of class interests in America, has singled out the more liberal members of the professional-managerial ranks as an all-powerful, self-interested "new class" and has stigmatized as "special interest lobbies" unions, educator organizations, feminist, civil rights, environmentalist, and consumer groups that democratically represent millions of ordinary constituents.) Richard Ohmann's "Doublespeak and Ideology in Ads" presents a definitive repertory of the semantic ploys that corporations use in advertising (and that are equally common in news and entertainment) to equate their interests with those of the public.

Among the myths asserting the neutrality of elites is that, as Rose K. Goldsen puts it, "the state is the good guy." [4] Only villains and terrorists use unwarranted violence; only evil scientists, our foreign enemies, and invaders from outer space use technology for malevolent ends. Our side and its heroes always come up with the superior technological know-how in the end and can always be counted on to use it benevolently.[5] This time-honored myth was dealt a serious blow in the sixties and seventies with the disillusioning revelations of American use of napalm and Agent Orange in Vietnam, of sophisticated techniques of illegal government surveillance and subversion of opposition groups domestically and abroad, and of experiments by our intelligence agencies in high-technology assassination, torture, and mind control. Nevertheless, the myth has persisted in recent heroes like the Six Million Dollar Man and Bionic Woman, and it has been transported to outer space in the technological-mystical Force used by the defenders of the Republic against the evil Empire in the *Star Wars* films.

   2. *Social Ills in America Are Neither Endemic to the Capitalist System nor Historically Determined.* Literary critic Frederick Crews, in the course of discussing the ideological illusions of academic liberals, observes:

Liberalism takes the most recent phase of capitalism to be reality itself in all its mysterious complexity, and then improvises ad hominem explanations for whatever social dysfunctions it perceives. (Conservatism, not minding the dysfunctions so long as the profits are coming in, goes through fewer mental gymnastics and has a simpler, sterner vision.) The morally overwrought quality of much liberal thinking derives, I believe, not merely from indignation but from the strain of trying not to perceive that capitalism's logical tendency is to preserve inequality, deplete resources, pollute the elements, keep an underclass out of work, and tyrannize over the economies of other nations. The attempt to address such problems without calling attention to property relations yields a confused, symbolic, and hortatory thinking which seizes on immediate occasions for outrage or sympathy while neglecting structural factors.[6]

Thus, as Ohmann notes here, American pragmatic philosophy frequently becomes an item of ideological stock-in-trade, perpetuating the belief that none of our social problems are systemic and that all are amenable to solution through ingenious Yankee enterprise. Ad hoc liberal analyses and programs concerning poverty, racism, sexism, or opposition to American interests in areas such as Indochina and Central America chronically evade tracing such problems to their institutional bases or to the imperatives of capitalist political economy.

   Similarly, in the ideology of any class or country that has attained power, the belief in a dialectical view of history becomes suppressed; we choose to believe that history stopped at the moment our side acceded to power. (In countries where the Communist party has gained power, the Party must resort to particularly convoluted doublethink in reconciling its self-designation as the agent of historical change with the fact of its having become the domestic status quo.) If vulgar Marxism is inclined toward simplistic appeal to historical inevitability, American idealism is equally simplistic in its denial of any force of necessity. When our politicians and media analyze the cold war and Third World or black American uprisings, they tend to disregard as a factor the natural cycle of historical change that may be leading to the end of world dominance by the United States, Western Europe, and the white race. As James Baldwin eloquently expressed it in *The Fire Next Time*, "Behind what we think of as the Russian menace lies what we do not wish to face, and what white Americans do not face when they regard a Negro: reality—the fact that life is tragic. Life is tragic simply because the earth turns and the sun inexorably rises and sets, and one day, for each us, the sun will go down for the last, last time."[7] Thomas Andrae's interpretation here of various versions of Superman's exploits ("From Menace to Messiah") finds in their ahistoricity a reinforcement of American resistance to a dialectical view of history, a point reiterated in countless aspects of American mass culture. Similarly, Dorfman and Mattelart, in *How to Read Donald Duck* (see Part 7), find in Disney's unsexed characters a fantasy of timelessness in prolonged infantile narcissism; the denial of aging and sexual regeneration, especially in the context of the Disney comics distributed in Latin America, models a denial of the possible decline of bourgeois hegemony and colonialism and their replacement by a generation of autonomous native peoples. Dorfman and Mattelart suggest a connection between labor as work and labor as childbirth: capitalist mythology tries to expunge the dialectical processes and painful struggle involved in both economic production and biological reproduction, thereby also avoiding any hint of class struggle.

3. *Heroism and Villainy Are Purely Individual Personality Traits.*   If, in American mythology, social ills are neither endemic to the capitalist system nor historically determined, it follows that evil must result from purely individual malice and conversely that virtue consists of heroic individuals defeating evildoers and subduing their threat to the social order. This view of good and evil forms part of the larger pattern of mystification that reduces every social or political conflict to the level of personal drama. American media heroes tend to be more vaguely situated sociologically than the heroes of other cultures. Indeed, Robert Jewett and John Shelton Lawrence, in *The American Monomyth*, and Will Wright, in *Sixguns and Society*, develop the case that the legendary American superhero (the Lone Ranger, Superman, Shane) comes from *outside* society, stays only long enough to defeat an immediate threat, then disappears again; this formulation thus reconciles the myth of the autonomous individual with the need for social order and at the same time evades the problems inherent in the potential of the hero to become either a leader of organized opposition to systemic evils or a tyrant perpetrating them. Andrae finds exactly this pattern of evasion in the history of the Superman comics, in which Superman is first portrayed as becoming a tyrant, then during the thirties as a class-conscious social reformer, and finally, since the fifties, as vague defender of "truth, justice, and the American way of life" against stock villains like the mad scientist Lex Luther.

Nonconformity in twentieth-century mass culture has frequently been depicted in working-class, lowbrow figures such as cowboys, tough-guy private eyes, Marlon Brando's Stanley Kowalski and Wild One, Elvis, Fonzie, Rambo, punk rockers, and so on. But such characters are viewed through the eyes of middle-class creators and audiences at a romantic distance from working-class life; in this view, the proletarian is a noble savage, the last rugged individualist in a bureaucratic society, but rarely an individual who has a class identity in common with other workers. The idealized image of the working-class rebel has long functioned in middle-class American culture as a momentary dream, never to be realized in real life, of breaking out of routine existence. This myth is most transparent in the current charade of rock musicians and followers of punk fashion enacting ever more bizarrely antibourgeois behavior for the titillation of otherwise conformist middle-class youth (the musicians enriching themselves in the process, like countless previous media mimics of working-class rebels, including such liberals as Mark Twain and Charlie Chaplin). And, as through the whole history of American serious and popular literature, the mythical rebel typically either goes down to gallant defeat, like McMurphy in *One Flew Over the Cuckoo's Nest*, or flees society, like Huck Finn heading for the Indian Territory or Yossarian for Sweden—both patterns serving as cathartic escape fantasies that leave the social status quo intact.

The myth of the lower classes as instinctual noble savages functions further in opposition to intellectuality, invariably associated with upper-middle-class stodginess and often with Jewishness. A recent variant on classic American anti-intellectualism, reflecting neoconservative attacks on "new class" intellectuals, has shown up in several films depicting stock comic-villain characters who are nerdish scientists or government bureaucrats, often portrayed by unmistakably Jewish actors. In the film of neoconservative journalist Tom Wolfe's *The Right Stuff*, the NASA bureaucrats—of whom the most inept is played by Jeff Goldblum—and bland middle Americans chosen to be the first astronauts are contrasted to the heroic cowboy–test pilot Chuck Yeager (played by Sam Shepard, a Greenwich Village playwright whose actor alter-ego has been typecast as the rough-hewn westerner). In *Splash*, the scientists led by Eugene Levi almost murder the WASP-featured mermaid–nature girl by dissection, but in the classic escape-fantasy ending she is rescued by the hero and they escape both scientific rationality and his dull petit-bourgeois career by returning together to her watery Arcadia. Levi's role in *Splash* was a variant on that of the scientist Keys in *E.T.*, played by Peter Coyote, an actor who, as a member of the San Francisco counterculture of the sixties changed his name from Kahane—yet another wish-fulfillment transformation: from middle-class Jew to noble Indian savage. In a sense, these trends may not reflect older forms of American anti-intellectualism or anti-Semitism so much as constitute a grudging acknowledgment that the bookworm, prototypically Jewish, has become a model for middle-class aspirations in the technocratic age and, simultaneously, a target for the often ambivalent feelings of those—including bookworms themselves—who have bought into those aspirations.

Daniel Boorstin noted in *The Image* that, in America, heroes have largely been replaced by celebrities, whose public personalities and adulation are fabricated as commodities. As Jeremy Tunstall suggests here in "Stars, Status, Mobility," mass culture's excessive emphasis on celebrities and stars compensates for the de-emphasis of class. Celebrity worship reconciles democracy with authoritarianism. On the one hand, anyone can become a star—although, as with winning the jackpot at Las Vegas or striking it rich in business, American mythology downplays the prohibitiveness of the odds and the social imbalance that results from one person being enriched at the expense of a thousand others. On the other hand, stars are set up as bigger-than-life figures, and fans, by worshiping these stars, diminish their own sense of self-worth.[8] Furthermore, shows such as "Lifestyles of the Rich and Famous" that emphasize show business and sports celebrities—who often do come from the lower classes—also distract attention from superrich capitalists, who are more powerful and more often have inherited wealth but who tend to keep a low media profile.

Regarding the virtue of individualism in general, Louis Kampf wrote in 1967 about twentieth-century highbrow literature and literary criticism, "A totally self-centered individualism is not necessarily a sign of heroism or nobility; it may, in fact, serve as a mask for the competitive depredations of capitalism. The narcissistic obsession of modern literature for the self, the critical cant concerning the tragic isolation of the individual—these are notions which tie our hands and keep us from the communion necessary for meaningful action."[9] Kampf's arguments were dismissed by many critics at that time as merely strident Marxism, but in the eighties, similar points made by social analysts such as Christopher Lasch, in *The Culture of Narcissism* and *The Minimal Self*, and Robert Bellah, in *Habits of the Heart: Individualism and Commitment in American Life*, have been met with wider agreement.

Villains in American mass culture are even more vaguely situated sociologically than heroes. The gratuitous evil of the stock villain, whether psychopathic killer, horror-movie monster, or Darth Vader–like heavy, deflects public consciousness from evils rooted in the social system. Individual violence is viewed out of context from, and magnified out of proportion to, the violence that, in the words of Marcuse, "is built into the very structure of this society: as the accumulated aggressiveness which drives the business of life in all branches of corporate capitalism, as the legal aggression on the highways, and as the national aggression abroad which seems to become more brutal the more it takes as its victims the wretched of the earth—those who have not yet been civilized by the capital of the Free World."[10] Moreover, the centering of deviancy in vampires, psychos, and invaders from outer space, whom the hero, as surrogate for the state, can blow away without regard for legal niceties, fosters a general disregard for the civil liberties of social deviants. In *The Empire's Old Clothes*, Ariel Dorfman argues that the innate maliciousness and amorphous social identity of American media villains serve further to preclude consideration of antisocial behavior as a response to socioeconomic deprivation. (The intention of Dorfman, and most current left critics, is not to exonerate proletarian criminals, but rather to point out the tendency of right-wing culture to wholly exonerate capitalist society.) Above all, according to Dorfman, the equation of opposition to the social order with criminality serves to discredit any revolutionary movement, a point confirmed by Gitlin's account in *The Whole World Is Watching* of the way the media defined the protest movements of the sixties in the vocabulary of crime coverage.

4. *Capitalism Is Natural; Nature is Capitalistic.* "Everywhere," writes Gitlin in "Domesticating Nature," "nature is consumed by capital, and everywhere the middle class reaches for its private share of the vulnerable and disappearing wildness." A prime contradiction of contemporary capitalism, which its mythology must try to reconcile, is that on the one hand it must endlessly deplete natural resources and wilderness and invent synthetic novelties in order to avoid a declining rate of profit, while on the other hand it wants to present the capitalist

order as being in harmony with the order of nature—hence the labeling of so many artificial products as "natural." (Likewise, while endlessly promoting social flux, capitalism professes to represent a conservative, stable society.) As Barthes put it, "The bourgeois class has precisely built its power on technical, scientific progress, on an unlimited transformation of nature: bourgeois ideology yields in return an unchangeable nature." [11]

Gitlin's "Domesticating Nature," in this section, considers the recent tendency in corporate architecture to introduce nature into high-rise buildings, providing both a gesture to environmental preservation and a shelter for those inside from the deteriorating urban environment in which the corporations have pitched their mansions. In the same way, Disneyland's Main Street, U.S.A., filled like the rest of the park with commercials for the multinational industries that have obliterated small-town local identity, is emblematic of corporations' ingenious capacity to sell back to the consumer a nostalgic replica of everything they have contributed to destroying in nature and society—and to reap praise for their civic-mindedness in the bargain. [12]

Moreover, that nostalgic replica is itself doctored to accord with bourgeois ideology, giving rise to a vision that might be called Capitalist Pastoral. All of nature becomes commodified and tamed—the site for a packaged tour, a worldwide version of Marie Antoinette's peasant hamlet at Versailles. In *The Empire's Old Clothes*, Dorfman discusses several adventures of the Lone Ranger that exemplify the mythic role in the American West of white men and capitalists. Like their Puritan ancestors, these men serve as stewards of both wealth and nature, trustworthy in protecting the environment while policing a reasonable degree of profit-making development, and as natural masters over native peoples, who are portrayed less as noble savages than as helpless children craving to become servants of Anglo know-how. Indeed, both Tonto and Silver were initially saved by the Lone Ranger and consequently volunteered to serve him for life—a conceit reminiscent of Renaissance pastoral poetry in which fish joyously jump out of the streams and into the fisherman's net.

In his conclusion to *The Empire's Old Clothes*, reproduced as "The Infantilizing of Culture," the concluding essay in this section, Dorfman discusses the ways in which twentieth-century politicians and capitalists appropriated the mythology of America as Eden. Whatever degree of authenticity there was in the original myth, he says, was traded on in perpetuum by an infantilizing culture that not only assumes pastoral innocence in all our international interventions but that panders to the wistful desire voters and audiences have to maintain the child's ingenuous view of all reality. Dorfman's analysis is reminiscent of Leslie Fiedler's *An End to Innocence* and *Love and Death in the American Novel*, written in the fifties—except that Fiedler turned his critique of American ingenuousness to the purposes of the cold war, focusing on liberal sentimentalizing of the working class, Communists like the Rosenbergs, and the Soviet Union. Dorfman presents the other side of the coin: the right-wing sentimentality throughout American history that has rationalized racism and imperialism—a theme further developed in Part 7.

Notes

1. Robert Chrisman, "Blacks, Racism, and Bourgeois Culture," *The Black Scholar*, January–February 1976. Reprinted in *College English* 38, no. 8 (1977): 813–822.
2. Todd Gitlin, *Inside Prime Time* (New York: Pantheon Books, 1983), p. 185. Irving Howe, in *World of Our Fathers* (New York: Harcourt Brace Jovanovich, 1976), pp. 567–568, traces the "de-Semitization" of American show business back to the years of World War II.
3. Judith Williamson, *Decoding Advertisements* (London: Boyars, 1978), pp. 133–134.
4. Rose K. Goldsen, *The Show and Tell Machine* (New York: Delta, 1978), pp. 223–235.
5. See Robert G. Dunn, "Science, Technology and Bureaucratic Domination: Television and the Ideology of Scientism," *Media, Culture and Society* 1, no. 4 (1979): 343–354.
6. Frederick Crews, *Out Of My System* (New York: Oxford University Press, 1975), p. 111.
7. James Baldwin, *The Fire Next Time* (New York: Dell, 1964), p. 123.
8. The relation between celebrity worship and authoritarian character structure in democracies was a frequent theme of the Frankfurt School, addressed most directly by Leo Lowenthal in "The Triumph of Mass Idols," in *Literature, Popular Culture, and Society* (Englewood Cliffs, N.J.: Prentice-Hall, 1961), pp. 109–140.
9. Louis Kampf, "The Scandal of Literary Scholarship," in *The Dissenting Academy*, ed. Theodore Roszak (New York: Random House, 1967), pp. 56–57.
10. Herbert Marcuse, *An Essay On Liberation* (Boston: Beacon Press, 1969), pp. 75–76.
11. Roland Barthes, *Mythologies* (New York: Hill & Wang, 1972), pp. 141–142.
12. On Disneyland as a microcosm of capitalist mythology, see Michael Real, *Mass-Mediated Culture* (Englewood Cliffs, N.J.: Prentice-Hall, 1977), pp. 44–89; and Louis Marin, "Disneyland: A Degenerate Utopia," in *Glyph 1* (Baltimore: Johns Hopkins University Press, 1977), pp. 50–67. Also see Alexander Wilson, "The Betrayal of the Future: Walt Disney's EPCOT Center," *Socialist Review*, no. 84 (November–December 1985): 41–53.

Further Readings

Bellah, Robert N., Richard Madsen, William M. Sullivan, Ann Swidler, and Steven M. Tipton. *Habits of the Heart: Individualism and Commitment in American Life*. Berkeley and Los Angeles: University of California Press, 1985.

Friedman, Lester. *Hollywood's Image of the Jew*. New York: Ungar, 1982.

Jewett, Robert, and John Shelton Lawrence. *The American Monomyth*. Garden City, N.Y.: Anchor Press/Doubleday, 1977.

Lasch, Christopher. *The Culture of Narcissism*. New York: Norton, 1978.

———. *The Minimal Self: Psychic Survival in Troubled Times*. New York: Norton, 1984.

Leiss, William. *The Domination of Nature*. Boston: Beacon Press, 1974.

Long, Elizabeth. *The American Dream and the Popular Novel*. Boston: Routledge & Kegan Paul, 1985.

Marwick, Arthur. *Class—Image and Reality in Britain, France, and the U.S.A. Since 1930*. New York: Oxford University Press, 1980.

Merelman, Richard M. *Making Something of Ourselves: On Culture and Politics in the United States*. Berkeley and Los Angeles: University of California Press, 1984.

Powers, Richard Gid. *G-Men: Hoover's FBI in American Popular Culture*. Carbondale: Southern Illinois University Press, 1983.

Rapping, Elayne. *Looking Glass World of Nonfiction Television*. Boston: South End Press, 1986.

————. "The View from Hollywood: The American Family and the American Dream." *Socialist Review*, no. 67 (January–February 1983): 71–91.

Robertson, James Oliver. *American Myth, American Reality*. New York: Hill & Wang, 1980.

Schiller, Herbert. *The Mind Managers*. Boston: Beacon Press, 1970.

Slotkin, Richard. *Regeneration Through Violence: The Mythology of the American Frontier, 1600–1860*. Middletown, Conn.: Wesleyan University Press, 1973.

Smith, Henry Nash. *Virgin Land: The American West as Symbol and Myth*. Cambridge, Mass.: Harvard University Press, 1950.

Weston, Jack. *The Real American Cowboy*. New York: Schocken Books, 1985.

DOUBLESPEAK AND IDEOLOGY IN ADS: A KIT FOR TEACHERS

RICHARD OHMANN

How can business defend itself? The answer is not distant. . . .
Pick up the weapon lying idle at your side, your advertising
budgets.

PATRICK BUCHANAN

Mr. Buchanan, a speechwriter for former President Nixon, was talking about difficulties the oil companies had in 1974 in telling the public their views on energy and the environment. He went on to say, "Oil companies spend billions each year in advertising. Mobil's creation of 'idea advertising,' in lieu of the happy-motoring nonsense, is a first step." Whenever Mobil follows Buchanan's advice—as it has often done and will doubtless continue to do—it uses money spent by consumers for gas in order to educate those same customers in Mobil's *ideas*. Having neither the billions nor the organization of oil companies, there's little that consumers can do to control such education except be alert to and critical of such ideas.

The following material, an abbreviated version of a teaching kit prepared at a workshop in Amherst in the summer of 1974, is about the kind of advertising that Patrick Buchanan had in mind, and about any ads that sell ideas, with or without products. It offers ways to help alert students to business's ideas, and to ways of expressing them that are misleading, confusing, deceptive, manipulative. In other words, to what members of this National Council of Teachers of English committee have come to call "doublespeak."

You could think of the kit as an aid to self-defense, since without critical instruments a student has a handicap in sorting out the hundreds of messages she or he gets daily from advertisers. But we hope that the kit will be more than that. We'd like it to help you help students understand how ideology works, *whoever* the seller or giver. We'd like it to help you and your students define and understand the widespread phenomenon we call doublespeak. And we think it will be useful in teaching some general points of rhetoric and semantics.

One obvious deficiency of the kit needs mentioning. We haven't been able to reproduce the photographs or layout of print ads, or the music or voice of radio ads, or the visual sequences of TV ads. These modes of presentation may contain nonverbal doublespeak, if you will, and we hope you will supplement the kit with whatever criticism you can bring to bear on the sounds and sights of advertising.

The explanations, checklists, and analyses here are addressed to you. They

From *Teaching About Doublespeak*, ed. Daniel Dieterich (Urbana, Ill.: National Council of Teachers of English, 1976). This article was compiled by Richard Ohmann and the Amherst Conference on Public Doublespeak, Summer 1974; the latter part of the article, not reproduced here, suggests writing exercises for students analyzing doublespeak.

are no more than a sketch of the one- to three-week unit we imagine you might teach on doublespeak. And most of this material will need expansion or simplification, depending on the level of your college or high school students. Further—and perhaps this goes without saying—an effective unit on this subject cannot be "canned" for students. Everything depends on their becoming actively critical, finding their own instances, doing their own analyses.

BASIC PRINCIPLES

Ideology is the whole of ideas of a group of people with common interests—a nation, a party, a government, a social or economic class, an occupational group, an industry, etc. The most common tactic of ideology is to show how the interests of the group are "really" the same as the interests of the whole society or of humanity in general. The famous remark of Charles Wilson some years back, "What's good for General Motors is good for the country," encapsulates the root principle of ideology. General Motors, the American Medical Association, the AFL-CIO, the National Rifle Association, garment workers, English teachers, college professors, businessmen—any group that is organized and conscious of a common interest turns out ideology.

Ideological talk does not always amount to doublespeak, but it easily can. And for a simple reason: the interests of various groups in a society are *not* all compatible—not all the time in all respects. Poll taxes were good for white politicians but not for black tenant farmers. Higher faculty salaries at a private university with finite resources may mean *lower* salaries for secretaries or less scholarship money for students. And so on. Usually the conflict of interest is not so dramatic. Then ideology has its best opportunity—and runs its greatest risk of doublespeak—for then it can be rather abstract, hitching on to generally accepted ideas like (in this society) freedom, technological problem-solving, individualism, the family, "ecology." And if conflicts are obscure or buried, the grand concepts smooth a surface over them. Oil companies and consumers are both for a clean environment, and also for free choices in the marketplace; so (say the oil companies) let us work together to solve our problem. To paraphrase an anecdote of Lincoln's, the wolf and the sheep are both for liberty. So long as the discussion remains on this level, bystanders might be content to let the wolf and the sheep resolve their own differences, not noticing that the wolf's desired liberty is to eat the sheep, the sheep's not to be eaten. One person's solution may be the other person's problem—not *always*, but often—and in such a situation ideology is often doublespeak.

It's an important kind of doublespeak for people to study, for three reasons: (1) If they can't decode it, they are likely to make major social choices for bad reasons, and against their interest. (2) Powerful groups in a society have an ideological advantage over the poor, weak, or unorganized. Welfare mothers doubtless have an ideology, too, but lacking the resources to buy prime TV time they are less able to confuse us with doublespeak than are groups that *can* buy prime time. (Remember Buchanan's advice to business.) Ideological doublespeak always tends to keep power where it is in a society. So in the Soviet Union it would be well if young people could detect Communist party doublespeak. Here, the doublespeak of the U.S. Communist party is less a force to contend with than is that of the Pentagon. Ideology detection is a weapon mainly of those without much wealth or power—for example, most of us and most of our students. (3) For all that, much ideology does not *intend* to deceive. People often deeply believe their own doublespeak—and sincerity and goodwill make ideological doublespeak especially hard to detect.

. . . .

THIRTEEN ITEMS OF IDEOLOGICAL STOCK-IN-TRADE

Here's a highly selective list of ideological themes to look for in what American industry says:

1. Anything wrong in our society is a problem, amenable to a solution in the interest of all.
2. Corollary: all conflicts of interest are only apparent.
3. We'll all be best off if business manages the development of resources in the future.
4. It can do this only if (a) profits are high and (b) there is a minimum of government interference.
5. Solutions to problems are generally technical; we need new technology, but not any change in the system.
6. Hence, what the experts decide is best for all. The people are often deficient in understanding.
7. However, neither business nor technocrats have much power: in the present system, *the people* are the ones who decide.
8. They decide best through individual purchases in a free market; voting is secondary, and other kinds of politics a potential threat to free choice.
9. The United States can solve its problems apart from those of the rest of the world, and do so without creating problems elsewhere.
10. Freedom is good for both individuals and corporations, and pretty much the same thing for both.
11. Growth and productivity are good for all.
12. Our needs—for pleasure, love, approval, security, etc.—can best be met by consuming products.
13. Consumption should generally be done by units no larger than the nuclear family. And the nuclear family is the social ideal.

(Remember: Taken as ideas, these themes are of varying merit. They can be openly debated. Certainly they are not in themselves doublespeak. What earns them a place on this list is their very wide acceptance, coupled with their loose formulation: they can easily be appropriated for almost any purpose, honest or dishonest. It is their abuse we should attend to.)

SHORT GUIDE TO IDEOLOGICAL
DOUBLESPEAK

Look for doublespeak in these areas of semantics and rhetoric:

1. *What you mean "we," paleface?*   The homogenizing "we," and "us," and "our." Watch particularly for shifts in the reference of "we," and for instances where "we" purports to refer to everyone in society but where what is said is in fact true only of some. (Recall the Lone Ranger's saying, "There are Indians closing in from all sides, Tonto: we're in trouble," and Tonto's reply: "What you mean 'we,' paleface?")

2. *"America."*   And "the people," "our society," and so forth.   When you read "America needs . . . ," stop and ask if all Americans need it, or only some, or some more than others. The use of *America* is often coercive, not referential.

3. *Abstraction away from people.*   When someone proposes to fight "poverty," does that mean getting more money to poor people, and perhaps less to the wealthy? If not, what? Again, can we be for "ecology" without being against those who upset the ecological balance?

4. *Liberty; or, the sheep and the wolf.*   Both the sheep and the wolf are for liberty, but one's liberty is the other's death. Watch for plus-words like *liberty*, used as if they had the same meaning for all. In many situations they conceal conflict of interest.

5. *It's a problem.*   An American habit of mind conceives any difficulty, crisis, disaster, social conflict—ANYthing BAD—as a problem. This move always implies that we're in it together, faced with the same problem, and all with the same interest in a solution. Remember that your solution *may* be my problem, or that your problem may even be *me*. Be watchful, especially, for disinterested formulation of "problems" by those who have helped create them, and whose livelihoods are at stake. Another thing: labeling something a problem obviously implies that there *is* a solution—but in some situations there may be no approved solution, or even no solution at all.

6. *The technological fix.*   Fusion will solve our problem—or a new emission control device will, or a new ingredient, or a new kind of glass, or just "research." The technological fix is usually aimed at symptoms, not causes. Now, technical solutions sometimes are what we (all of us) need. But often they're *more* needed by those who supply the technology. And very often the technological fix is offered as remedy for social or political problems. When some technological term is the subject of an active verb, try to put people back in the picture: Technology does nothing by itself. *Who* will set the machine going? With what interest?

7. *Experts know best.*   A corollary of the above, this idea always merits some skepticism. But it leads to doublespeak, especially when the ideologue says (a) the people must decide, but (b) the people don't-can't understand what the experts understand, so (c) let the experts decide.

8. *Hard facts or iron laws.*   "The hard fact is that America progresses only if business prospers." But what makes a fact hard? And what issues are excluded from debate by this hard fact? Well, the equation of progress with economic

growth, for one; and the question of alternatives to free enterprise for another. The hard-fact move leads to doublespeak when it treats a present social arrangement as iron law, and so rules out choices that might not be good for the advertiser. Watch for lawlike statements in present tense (like the invented one above), which foreclose discussion of the system itself and its assumptions. And watch for coercive uses of words and phrases like *necessary, only possible, required, essential to economic health*, and *inevitable unless*.

9. *There's nobody here but us chickens.*   Watch for formulations like "the people will decide," or "we will all be ruled by free choices in a free market." They imply that no one has more power than anyone else in determining the future—or even that big corporations have *less* power than ordinary people. Check these formulas against the facts of how decisions will be made on a particular issue. And remember to ask who paid for the ad, and whether ordinary people have any matching power.

10. *What can one man do?*   To stop pollution, buy brand X gasoline. To handle the trash menace, dispose of your bottle properly. To deal with the energy shortage, turn off your lights when not using them. Some of this may be good advice (but not *all* of it), but none of the individual actions proposed will make a dent in the "problem." Watch for ads that urge independent acts of consumers and stay silent about broader "solutions," like new laws or regulations of industry.

11. *Corporations equal people.*   A blend of points 9 and 10. "We're all in this together—*you* conserve heat in your house, and *we'll* build more nuclear plants." Beware of hearty invitations to collaborate in making America better; ask whether the proposed "partnership" is one of equals, or one of chickens and foxes.

12. *Blurred ownership.*   "The people's coal." "Your power company." "America's resources." "Our industrial system." And so on. Ask who, in cold financial and legal fact, owns the thing in question, who has power to determine its future, and why the possessive noun or pronoun is so generalized.

KINDS OF ADS, AND HOW THEY SELL
IDEAS (NOT JUST PRODUCTS)

Probably all advertisements contain or imply some ideology. They are trying to get the audience to do something or believe something that is in the advertiser's interest. One natural meeting ground of audience and advertiser is broad ideas or images of the good life, the good society. As lots of people have said, advertising taken as a whole conveys some important ideological messages:[1] commodities can solve just about all human problems; business is meeting "our" deepest needs; the American way of life is OK basically as it is; there are always problems, but they will be solved by business and consumers in league with each other—and solving problems is progress.

But these and other points of ideology appear very differently in different kinds of ads, and only some involve doublespeak. It helps, then, to have a classification of ads. The following is a handy one, moving from specific to general rhetorical aims.

1. Ads that make a factual claim about a product to persuade you to buy it. (Our razor blade lasts longer; our car gets the best mileage.) Subject to empirical test; no ideology in the foreground; doublespeak at a minimum.

2. Ads that sell a product by making vague and untestable claims about it ("gets teeth whiter") or by associating it with some reliable image—the happy family, youth, sexual success, etc. There's a good deal of deception in such ads through implied associations (cigarettes don't make you young, fresh, and healthy, in spite of what the picture suggests). Doublespeak here resides mainly in vagueness, evasion, and empty language, rather than in ideology.

3. Ads that invoke current social concerns and the anxieties they stir in order to increase the motivation for buying the product. (Your house will be cold this winter: buy sweaters.) Ideology in the background, except for the usual implication that social problems can be solved by individuals, for themselves.

4. Ads that refer to the same current problems but say that the consumer can help solve them—not just for the individual, but for all of us—by making the right purchase. (You can help the energy crisis by buying our gas.) Much ideology here, and often much doublespeak.

5. Ads that sell a company or an industry, not a product, by showing how its activities benefit all. These ads are a gold mine of ideological doublespeak.

6. "Responsible" ads that state the manufacturer's concern about the social consequences of the use of a product. The product, say the ads, is beneficial to all—*if* used properly. Where does responsibility lie for abuse, bad side effects, and the like? In the area of this question there is much room for doublespeak.

7. Explicitly ideological ads that defend high profits, argue against government regulation, etc.

8. And the most general, what we might call "philosophy of life ads." They seem not to be about a product, a company, an industry, *or* the American way of life, but to offer disinterested wisdom. Great ideas (of Plato, Shakespeare, etc.) presented as a public service by the X Company. Ideology is deeply buried here.

A unit on ideological doublespeak in ads should concentrate on types 4–6, but we'll at least glance at the doublespeak potential in each category.

1. Watch for the general motto that sometimes accompanies Class 1 ads. An insurance company ad describes the economic difficulties a small business can encounter when its owner is disabled; then it offers a policy to prevent such difficulties—all factual. The motto at the end is "We add assurance to life in an unsure world." Here is ideological doublespeak of the "hard fact" type. *Is* the world simply "unsure"? Well, yes, continued life and good health are always unsure. But no, the world is not inherently unsure in the other sense required here—economic consequences of accidents could be absorbed by the entire society, not left to individuals. The ad makes a social choice seem an inevitability. Why? Insurance companies, of course, have an interest in keeping the world economically unsure, and in convincing us that it *is* intrinsically unsure. Therefore, the role of insurance companies is in the interest of all of us.

2. A Colgate ad explains that Billie Jean King wins friends as easily as tennis tournaments. "Liking people comes naturally to Billie Jean. Which is one reason she's a long-time user of Colgate." The ideology is in the casual connective,

which not only sells Colgate as a friend-maker (garden-variety doublespeak) but also reinforces the idea that social anxieties, personal failures, and loneliness can all be resolved by buying something. Ideology in Class 2 ads is mainly on this level of abstraction. Get students to ask what assumptions these ads make about the kind of society we have, and how to face problems within it.

3. We are getting closer to ideology here. Libbey-Owens-Ford titles an ad "Insulation You Can See Through, From LOF," and goes on to cite rising energy costs as a reason for buying two special kinds of glass, to keep your view and still "save . . . energy dollars." Here the garden-variety doublespeak is in the implication that glass insulates better than other materials. "Save energy dollars" compared to what? Not to insulated walls, but only to ordinary, cheaper glass— which is not "insulation." The ideological doublespeak lies in the casual connection: energy crisis—buy glass. No real sacrifice is necessary, no change in our pattern of life or the economic system, not even the loss of your picture window. The crisis is presented as an individual, not a social, problem. LOF asks us to rely on patchwork technological remedies, and on the market. This approach rules out, of course, the possibility of legal limitations on the amount of glass in new buildings, and so forecloses the possibility of a conflict between LOF's interests and ours. In Class 3 ads, get students to look at the casual implications about how the individual should act in order to ameliorate the social crisis: what possibilities for action are omitted, and why?

4. What Class 3 ads imply, Class 4 ads more directly state.

> What can one man do, my friend,
> What can one man do,
> To fight pollution in the air,
> That's closin' in from everywhere?
>
> There's a lead-free gasoline, my friend,
> And its name is Amoco,®
> Two lead-free brands, one for every car,
> The one sure way to go.

Lots of doublespeak here.

a. Abstracting: not "fight polluters," but "fight pollution"; not "that's coming from combustion of gas," but "that's closin' in from everywhere."

b. The "one person" ploy is common in free enterprise ideology. The point is to defer collective action in favor of individual action. Needless to say, one person can't do anything to fight pollution so long as he or she is restricted to choosing among brands, disposing of containers "properly," and the like. But encouraging this approach leads a consumer to (1) feel personally responsible, (2) overlook the advertiser's responsibility, and (3) accept the present means of making social decisions. "One person" is led to believe he or she has power that in fact could be possessed only in league with many men and women.

5. Here's an example of a sort common today:

What's My Electric Company Doing about the Energy Problem?
America's fuel shortage problem is so big that it seems difficult for one individual or even one industry to influence it very much. And there are no quick and easy solutions to the fuel shortage facing the nation.

But almost every individual and every company uses energy, so we all should try to help by using fuels wisely.

The electric light and power industry is helping because we have some degree of flexibility in the way we can design our plants to use various fuels now and in the future.

Using Fuels Wisely

At the present time, about half of America's electric power is generated with coal. Natural gas and oil account for a little more than a third.

As we all know, supplies of oil are limited.

So, where changes are feasible, electric companies are burning coal in some of their power plants that once depended on oil. And the expanded utilization of coal, America's most plentiful fuel, is an important goal in our immediate and long-term generating plans. Along with the increased use of nuclear energy.

Searching for New Ways

The electric companies, in partnership with the federal government and others, are involved in research and development in a wide variety of new methods of power generation: developing nuclear "breeder" reactors that would create more usable nuclear fuel than they consume; experimenting with fusion, which would create energy by combining the atoms available in ordinary water; producing electricity directly from the sun's energy; using the earth's heat, deep underground, as a generating source.

Research has been going on in these areas for a number of years, and it will continue long into the future, for there are no instant answers.

But the important thing is, we in the electric companies are doing everything we can today to find ways to ease the energy problem. We are also doing everything we can for tomorrow.

Outlook for the Future

The time is past when any of us can use energy carelessly. But if everyone uses energy wisely in his home, or at his place of business, or when he travels, he will be helping with the nation's fuel shortage problem.

And if we in the electric industry can use those fuels to generate power that best conserve the nation's reserves, America will have gone a long way toward assuring an ample supply of energy for generations to come.

The people at your Investor-Owned Electric Light and Power Companies.

Places to look for doublespeak:

a. The generalization of a problem: "America's fuel shortage problem." The power companies' problem is, in part, to stay in command of this economic area, to keep Nader-like consumers from interfering with free choice and profits. The consumer's problem is, in part, to get the power companies to be more far-sighted and public spirited in the future than in the past. (The wolf and the sheep again.)

b. Equating corporations and individuals through the familiar doublespeak "we": "we all should try to help by using fuels wisely." But "we" consumers can only choose among fuels and technologies made available to us by the power companies and others. The we're-all-in-this-together approach is particularly misleading here.

c. Excluding the layman: See the paragraph about new ways to generate power. Only big industry in "partnership" (suppression of conflict again) with government could do research on this scale. No effort is made here to explain to consumers what the experts are doing, or what consequences can be expected from one or another of these technologies. In what sense is it, then, "my" electric company?

d. The technological fix. This is so universal in American society that it passes almost unnoticed. We read that the power companies are "doing everything we can today to find ways to ease the energy problem." What is that "everything"? Trying out technological solutions. But other possibilities occur: helping to reduce our dependence on power (who encourages us to buy all those appliances in the first place?); submitting energy decisions to voters; changing the companies from "investor-owned" to public. Ads like this treat technology as the only way out and do not explain why the technological fixes of the future will be better than those of the past, which created the "problem" in the first place. They assume that technology is, simply, good. Look in such ads for the presentation of social and political problems as purely technological. This tactic makes it seem that our interest is in leaving the problem to the companies, since they are the ones with the technical expertise.

e. America as abstraction. "America's electric power," "America's most plentiful fuel," "America will have gone a long way toward assuring an ample supply of energy for years to come." Who, specifically, uses the power? produces it? owns the fuel? will make the crucial decisions about energy in the future? Confront these aggregates with questions that make the concrete situation visible, and like as not you'll uncover doublespeak.

6. An ad of the Distilled Spirits Council of the United States:

What's the best way to enjoy a drink? Slowly.
A social drink with good food and good friends. That's a traditional custom observed by most people in this country.
Like any other custom, of course, it can be abused.
Hastily downing glass after glass, for example. Or drinking with no food and no company. That's hardly the way to enjoy the products we make so carefully.
Most Americans, fortunately, make responsible decisions in this respect—drinking and dining leisurely in a relaxed setting.
And with ordinary common sense, that's what liquor is—a pleasure, not a problem.
If you choose to drink, drink responsibly.

This ad trades mainly on "There's nobody here but us chickens" and "What can one man do?" Liquor is traditional, a "custom," etc. But "it can be abused." So you individual drinkers should moderate your drinking, and that will make liquor "a pleasure, not a problem." In other words, no social control is needed; the problem is some people who abuse alcohol, and it can be solved by continuing the free economic relationship between drinkers and distillers—if the drinkers will just be reasonable. (As usual in this type of ideology, the people are held responsible for all problems.)

"If you choose to drink, drink responsibly." Is the word "choose" appropriate, for many drinkers? Is this really an area where the concept of free individual choice applies? The *New York Times* on July 11, 1974, carried a front-page story headlined "Alcoholism Cost to Nation Put at $250 Billion a Year." Among other things, the study suggested that "alcohol control laws and regulations are grossly ineffective in dealing with alcohol problems." But it's in the interest of the distillers to conceive of these as basically individual problems; hence, matters of free choice; hence, not amenable to social control.

7. In these ads, the argument is openly ideological. A United States Steel ad

(written by the chairman of the General Electric Co.) explains that "we" need to have higher profits between now and 1985 so that "we" can meet the "capital needs of this country," so that "we" won't have to live with worsening shortages. Note shifts in reference. The homogenized "we" are also asked "to improve our personal productivity on the job. . . . This will not only help industry earn more and invest more in America's future, it will also help each of us earn more as we produce more." The "personal productivity" of assembly line workers may be in the interest of the board, but is the Board's productivity so certainly in the interest of workers? It's a debatable question, side-stepped by "we" and "our." The same ad also relies heavily on the hard facts approach: In the next twelve years our capital *needs* will come to $3 trillion, most of which "will *have to* be raised and invested by the business community." And the iron-law approach: "The capital available to business comes *only* from profits. . . . The *higher the profits, the higher the levels of investment* that are *possible*" (italics added). Ask students to imagine alternatives to these hard facts and iron laws, and to consider why the language might be excluding these alternatives. And in such ads, watch also for leave-it-to-the-experts, for the portrayal of conflicts as "problems," and for blurred ownership. (On this last: an ad of the American Electric Power system asks the government to "release" the resources of coal it "owns" in the West. "This coal is the people's coal and the people need it." Query: Is the government the people? Are the power companies the people? Just who is to release whose coal and to whom?)

8. The Atlantic Richfield Company has a series of philosophy-of-life ads under way at this writing. One begins with "the real": "People become obsolete before their time in our assembly line culture"; talks about how "we" have made the aged into a problem; offers examples of achievements by old people (Churchill, Sandburg, Grandma Moses, Frank Lloyd Wright, Schweitzer); and ends with "the ideal": "The maturity and social flexibility to recognize that for some, life reserves its greatest rewards until later." In such ads doublespeak is muted or absent. But they bear examination for the usual marks of ideology. How did "our assembly line culture" get that way? Whose interest is served by automatic retirement? by making it hard for older people to find work? What do "maturity and social flexibility" boil down to? What attitude do such ads encourage toward social "problems"? Toward the status quo? And, of course, why is Atlantic Richfield spending money in this way?

Note

1. See, for instance, Herbert Marcuse's *One-Dimensional Man*; or Ronald Gross's short essay "The Language of Advertising," in *Language in America*, ed. Neil Postman, Charles Weingartner, and Terence P. Moran (New York: Pegasus, 1969).

STARS, STATUS, MOBILITY

JEREMY TUNSTALL

The American media appeal to the great middle market of the United States by emphasizing personalities, personal celebrity, the individual achievement of success. This is especially true of the video media and of entertainment, and the view of social inequality thus presented is a status view. This lack of emphasis on class and caste divisions is found not only in Hollywood output but also in much American literature and social science. The idea is typically American and un-European. Less often noticed is the point that, although un-European and somewhat unreal even of the United States, this status view of inequality is still immensely appealing in Europe. Europeans have a long tradition of thinking of America in terms of geographical and social mobility, of the United States as the land where the unreal might become real. Both English and German writers wrote about the American West long before the first cowboy films. And since the beginnings of Hollywood, even the most serious of European writers have been influenced by media portrayals of American social reality. Bertolt Brecht was continually returning to Chicago gang warfare as a metaphor for capitalism, and although Brecht did spend some time in the United States, his knowledge of Chicago gangs seems to have been derived from press and film coverage. Franz Kafka's gothic novel *Amerika* is a parable of social success in the New World and full of visual melodrama straight out of Hollywood.

Even in Hollywood portrayals, traditional forms of social inequality such as class and caste are not entirely absent—clearly upper-class and lower-class people sometimes come on stage, but they usually play minor parts. One's personal qualities matter more than whether one is rich or poor, it is implied. Success has to be earned. Status and personal qualities are vital, too, in being successful as a man or woman, as a child or parent; immigrants and members of minorities can also succeed, but if you are black you may have to try even harder than the rest. This status message is portrayed in news and political coverage, in entertainment, and in advertising. Such a status view of inequality accords well with the middle-of-the-market thrust of American media.

This status view of American society is essentially urban—it is a top-fifty-markets view. The countryside, whether in westerns or in Disney cartoons, is the countryside as seen by urban dwellers. This is also an extremely mobile view of society. People are socially mobile, with sympathetic characters usually moving up the success escalator. Geographical movement is rapid—there are always new guys in town. And media people are also physically mobile—they are forever arriving and departing via spacecraft, aircraft, cars, trains, ships, or horses. Physical mobility provides "events" in news-value terms, and something to film in video terms.

In this status view of society there are still some dilemmas to be solved—but in solving them the individual shows his personal qualities, achieves his status.

From Jeremy Tunstall, *The Media Are American* (New York: Columbia University Press, 1977).

American media output is heavily peopled with professionals and executives—there are three times as many lawyers, policy officers, private detectives, doctors, and business executives in the television labor force than the U.S. Census indicates there are in actuality.[1]

National advertising has long been aimed more at women than men; the woman as consumer has long been a staple editorial topic. Radio invented the daytime radio drama serial, or soap opera. Any television series that is watched by a relatively high proportion of young affluent married women receives the ultimate commercial accolade—"good demographics." A continuing theme in American entertainment has been the American woman's "dilemma" or "two roles." The result was Hollywood's "good-bad" girl;[2] in 1940s American soap operas the protagonists were middle-class women who depended on their personal qualities for solving their dilemmas.[3]

The characteristic dilemmas and ambivalence of American media output aimed at men are highlighted in *Playboy* and its many American and European imitators. The ambivalence of *Playboy* (like that of the traditional women's magazines) encourages the reader to dream that somehow it's always possible to solve dilemmas and play two or more apparently contradictory roles. Once again the material stresses *personal* qualities—it is the task of the individual to try to "have it both ways," to be both housewife and heroine, or to be both Casanova and suburban husband.

American media's stress on reaching young people dates from attempts of the English-language press to wean young immigrants away from foreign-language papers. Certainly Hollywood always recognized that it had a young audience.[4] The preference of advertisers is for reaching the young, who are regarded as better "prospects" for new products and for switching their "brand loyalty." The part played by jukebox and record purchases in radio hit selection produced an enormous bias toward youthful preferences and the intricacies of teenage love in America. Much American material aimed at children was, like comic strips, also aimed at the children's parents.

All of these themes—status, individual qualities, social and geographical mobility, contradictory roles for women and men, youth against age—are literally embodied in the star. This is true of both the fictional characters the star portrays and also the "factual" portrayal of the star in other media and publicity material.

Stardom was forced first on the early filmmakers by the public. Not until 1910 did the promotion of actors' names and the publication of fan magazines begin. But this public demand for stars to worship had been known in the theater and in literature. American society, however, had some special characteristics that predisposed both it and its media system to focus on personal celebrity. The American political system encouraged voters to see politics in terms of a few individuals—such as the president, the state governor, and the two U.S. senators from one's own state. The American popular press from its early days stressed personality and celebrity. The Associated Press, when it appeared, was the perfect mechanism for imprinting a few prominent names on the minds of all Americans. Press agentry grew up around the promotion of theatrical celebrities.

American magazines long concentrated heavily on biography;[5] the best-selling magazines of the 1890s averaged more than one biographical article per number. By 1940–41, three-quarters of all biographical subjects in the *Saturday Evening Post* and *Collier's* came from "consumption" areas—almost entirely from the movies, entertainment, sports, newspapers, and radio. American media have continued to present the media industry itself as one of the main spheres in which "success" can be earned.

Radio helped the same celebrities to appear across the entire range of news, entertainment, and advertising. Stars "endorsed" products and politicians; politicians adopted the styles of entertainment-advertisers. Franklin Roosevelt, a master of the newsreel statement and the radio "chat," found himself in 1940 confronted, in Wendell Wilkie, by a Republican opponent whose main claim to fame was the pleasant sound he made on radio. Television has led to yet further overlapping of politics and Hollywood. C. Wright Mills pointed out that the stars always intermingled: "All the stars of any other sphere of endeavor or position are drawn toward the new star and he toward them. The success, the champion, accordingly is one who intermingles freely with other champions to populate the world of celebrity."[6] One celebrity meeting another is in news-value terms an event; "guest star" A appearing on star B's television show is a theme for the week; putting six stars into one film is an expensive form of accident insurance; getting a film star to attend a political rally may avoid the embarrassment of empty seats.

Celebrities can bid up their star value by appearing in some suitable setting with other countries' stars. The fact that America has more and bigger stars—as well as more and bigger ways of beaming them around the world—is an irresistible attraction for stars from other lands. European and other stars are constantly crossing the Atlantic to confer with, star with, make a show with, or cut a disc with suitable American stars. Hollywood from its earliest days imported both ready-made and not-yet stars. Especially prominent among these were stars of British origin. In this panoply of Anglo-American celebrities, the British royal family appear as the most celebrated of guest star family acts.

Personal qualities can also be negative. And whereas financial success in Hollywood output often correlates with pleasant personal qualities, so also the wicked rich man, the evil personality, recurs again and again in the American media. He appears especially in the western and the crime film; in the western he is the big bad farmer who controls the land, the women, and the hired guns, while in the crime film he is the sinister Mr. Big hovering in the background. In American fictional coverage of politics—as in the news presentation of politics—we are often confronted with a sinister and corrupt Mr. Big. This presentation of sinister wealth and power in terms of a single deviant personality relieves the American media of having to make general statements about social inequality, or class, or wealth, or power. Such a formula for personifying evil maximizes audience appeal while minimizing offense.

It is not difficult to see that many of these themes, although popular within the United States itself, may be even more appealing in Europe and the urban populations of Latin America and Asia. The enormous inflow of population into American cities, the great increases in education and in white-collar employment—these trends have also been experienced in Europe, Latin America, and in the great cities of Asia. Stress on personal qualities, social mobility, status, youth, role conflict for urban women, the tyranny of the boss at work—all of these can be expected to have a strong appeal.

But the appeal of American media in other countries may relate more to the pace or "grammar" of films or television, comics or advertising. American output emphasizes pace, brevity, and terseness. The American media, compared with those of other lands, have bigger production budgets, are more involved with advertising, and operate in a more media-saturated society. Pace is a device to seize audience attention. Hollywood horses always seem to set off at a gallop on even the longest journey and under the hottest sun—not because horse or rider ever favored such lunatic speed, but because the audiences did. Outdoor "action" sequences are obviously more expensive to produce than are studio "talking heads" (or the talking bodies of sex films). The "action adventure" style on television derived from the ABC network's pursuit of a more competitive style of television in the late 1950s.

Many devices that stress brevity and speed are simply intended to catch the attention of the jaded American public. Comic strips are an obvious example of material suitable for readers with little time and perhaps not much reading ability. The pyramid style of news agency writing spills the guts of the story into the first sentence, and each descending sentence contains less and less essential material. The advertisements, which also assume a short attention span and limited interest, to some extent compete with the other material, even though they are intended primarily to complement it.

These themes tend to reinforce each other. Their appeal has been so great in other lands that all film industries have tended to adopt or copy the Hollywood themes. The various mini-Hollywoods, outside the communist world, then start making their own stars, their own status, mobility, and action themes. Popular as some of these themes are locally—especially if linked with some local myth or tradition—they cannot easily compete on the world export stage with Hollywood, because Hollywood has chosen ground on which it seems unbeatable. It has more stars, more mobility, more action.

There have been many imitations of the western, but these have reinforced as much as they have rivaled the authentic American western. The same point is even clearer with science fiction—whether books, films, television series, or comics. When the American astronauts put their footprints on the moon, they also—here media fact and fiction, as often, merged—put American footprints on science fiction. The Japanese and others can, and do, make science fiction films, but they lack the "authenticity" of American ones. Thus, Hollywood cornered the media market in space, that ultimate sphere of stars and mobility.

THE ETHNIC MIX: BLACKS, JEWS, LATINS, WASPS

The ethnic composition of the American media industry must reflect the overall character of the American melting pot and presumably must partly account for the popularity of American media around the world. Isaac Goldberg, in his book *Tin Pan Alley* (1930), emphasized the importance of Negroes and Jews in American jazz, which he related to their common experience of oppression:

The spiritual is religious; the blues are secular, and, as their words readily prove, sexual. Jazz, then, has a decidedly sexual significance. We touch now the root of the antagonism to it. That antagonism, that dour, symptomatic aversion, was largely non-musical, non-esthetic at bottom. It was the evidence of a caste, and, as we now see, a purity complex. For jazz is the sexual symbol of an inferior race.

Is it merely fanciful if I find, in these selfsame observations, the reasons why the Jewish composers of America have been so important in the development of jazz? Read such a novel as Carl Van Vechten's *Nigger Heaven*, and you may be struck, time and again, by certain traits of character that are quite as Jewish as they are Negro; more, the prejudices which the Harlem intellectual has to contend with have their counterpart in Jewish-American life. The Jew, racially, is also an Oriental and was originally much darker than he is today. He has the sad, the hysterical psychology of the oppressed race. From the cantor grandfather to the grandson who learns "mammy" songs is no vaster a stride than from the Negro spiritual to the white "blues." The minor-major, what we might call amphibious, mode of the typical blues, with its blue notes, is by no means a stranger to the Jewish ear. The ecstatic songs of the Khassidim—the pietist sect of the Polish Jews—bear striking psychological analogies to the sacred and secular tunes of the Negro. I have heard Jimmy Johnson imitate a singing colored preacher, and the cantillation could have passed—almost—for the roulades of a Jewish precentor. The simple fact is that the Jew responds naturally to the deeper implications of jazz, and that as a Jewish-American he partakes of the impulse at both its Oriental and its Occidental end. The Khassid, too, walks all over God's heaven.[7]

American popular music has played an enormous part not only on radio and records around the world, but also in films and television. American black music has not been entirely Afro-American in origin; English folk music contributed much to most southern U.S. music upon which both whites and blacks drew. Nevertheless, the black origins of American popular music have been greatly muted in its media presentation—Irving Berlin, George Gershwin, Bing Crosby, Frank Sinatra, Elvis Presley, and most other leading names in such white music acknowledged having drawn heavily on black material.

And throughout most of the nineteenth century the Minstrel Show—featuring the black man as spectacle and all-purpose object of humor—was the predominant form in popular entertainment. Even here the black part was usually played by a white man.

Minstrelsy's unprecedented success demonstrated the great, almost unlimited, demand for popular entertainment that spoke for and to the great mass of middling Americans. . . .

Lambasting aristocrats and making extensive use of frontier language and lore, minstrels asserted the worth and dignity of the white American common man. They created ludicrous Northern Negro characters that assured audience members that however confused, bewildered or helpless they felt, someone was much worse off than they were. . . .

If Negroes were to share in America's bounty of happiness, minstrels asserted, they needed whites to take care of them. To confirm this, minstrels created and repeatedly portrayed the contrasting caricatures of inept ludicrous Northern blacks and contented, fulfilled Southern Negroes . . .

Beginning with early blackface entertainers who adapted aspects of Afro-American music, dance and humor to suit white audiences, minstrelsy also brought blacks and at least part of their culture into American popular culture for the first time. The enthralling vitality of this material, even as adapted by white performers, accounted in large part for minstrelsy's great initial impact. Although minstrel use of black culture declined in the late 1850s, as white minstrels concentrated on caricatures of blacks, when Negroes themselves became minstrels after the Civil War, they brought a transfusion of their culture with them. Again, Afro-American culture intrigued white Americans. But black minstrels had to work within narrow limits because they performed for audiences that expected them to act out well-established minstrel stereotypes of Negroes.[8]

The minstrel tradition was a major formative influence on American vaudeville and subsequently all American media entertainment. D. W. Griffith's *Birth of a Nation* (1915) represented southern white stereotypes of blacks. But the most commercially influential of the early sound films, *The Jazz Singer* (1927), explicitly followed the minstrel tradition—Al Jolson, a white American Jew, played the part of a blacked-up minstrel, as he had often done with enormous success in vaudeville and on Broadway. The following year another minstrel-derived show, *Amos 'n' Andy*, began on radio and became the first great popular success of network radio; it featured two simple but lovable southern blacks—played by whites.[9] *Amos 'n' Andy* subsequently appeared on television and was the focus of many early efforts to remove racial caricatures from American television.

In more recent years black faces have appeared on American television in larger numbers—and in less caricatured form. The more recent approach to them has been the familiar one of personal qualities, of the individual achieving success—and status. Many blacks, we are told now, are nice people, 100 percent American, with college degrees, holding down fine jobs, doctors, lawyers, policemen, and private eyes. Some of them are rotten apples too, but there are always a few such in any barrel.

American Jews and American blacks clearly share the historical legacy of oppression. But the Jews have played various go-between, creative, organizing, and performing roles that have been denied to blacks. Most obviously, Jews have often been the interpreters and transposers of black music for white America and for the world. Jews have also spanned the gap between the rich and the poor—with the first-generation Hollywood tycoons being perhaps the most startling example. Jewish immigrants also settled disproportionately in the go-between city of New York.[10] American Jews have also often spanned the gap between educated and illiterate, between high and low culture, and between popular and serious music; George Gershwin, a Jewish boy born in Brooklyn, was a Tin Pan Alleyman, but he also wrote the black musical *Porgy and Bess*, the first American music ever performed at La Scala, Milan.

Most important of all—from a world media perspective—American Jews were well suited to a go-between role linking Europe and America. Not only did many first-generation Jewish immigrants have psychological scores to pay off in Europe, they also had friends and relatives in Europe and a deep feeling for European culture, aspirations, and prejudices. And although Hitler destroyed the majority of central European Jewry, his regime also drove a further wave of migrants to New York—some of whom returned to Europe after 1945.

How important have Jews been in the overall direction of the American media? Clearly, in nearly all aspects of films, radio, and television they have played a large part. In the press Jewish influence has been smaller, although the *New*

York Times and some other important newspapers are controlled by Jewish families.

In order to decide how powerful the Jews have been in shaping American media one would need to look also at the WASPs, the White Anglo-Saxon Protestants. Undoubtedly people of British and other north European Protestant origin have been the single most powerful ethnic force; for example, when the movies switched to sound in the late 1920s, they also came much more closely under the direction of Wall Street WASPs. The bulk of American daily newspapers and magazines appear to be WASP controlled, and this also applies to a large extent to the news agencies and top 150 television stations.

The WASP-Jewish alliance involves also a division of labor within the media. For example, Edward Jay Epstein, in his study of the New York network television news operations, found that 58 percent of (thirty-six) network producers and news editors he interviewed were Jewish;[11] however, of correspondents who appeared on the television screen, the "predominant" pattern was of Protestant parentage, and there were also some Catholics. A similar division of labor seems to have worked in Hollywood's golden age. While there were many Jewish performers, there was prejudice in favor of Hollywood's having a mainly WASP face. One of the simplest but most important values of the Anglo-American media is the status given to north European physical appearance. The first human faces to become literally known around the world were those of Hollywood stars such as Mary Pickford and Douglas Fairbanks. Their faces, and those of a thousand other northern stars, have ever since looked out from the screens and billboards of the world's cities, establishing a nearly universal notion of physical beauty.

But there is also a fourth important ethnic strain in American media. This Latin strain comes partly from Mexico and Latin America and partly from Italy. Mexico, at least as subject matter, has been incorporated into the Hollywood system. Italy was the original home of the supercolossal film (around 1914) and the Italian industry has been the only one in the world to match Hollywood's carefully flamboyant ways. American film tycoons move to Rome and Italian tycoons to New York with equal ease. Not accidentally, the Hollywood offshore industry has had its biggest foreign base in Rome. Puerto Rican and Mexican Spanish are now the second languages of New York and Los Angeles. The Latin bravura of American films and television accounts in part for their success, not just in Latin America and southern Europe but everywhere in the world; these larger-than-life qualities are, quite simply, suited to the visual media, or to the dominant forms into which these media have been developed.

Latin and Jewish looks tend to merge. This gives the American visual media their three characteristic skin colors: white WASPs, slightly darker Jews and Latins, and black blacks. And along with this ethnic visual typology often goes an ethnic division of labor as simple as heroine, seducer, and slave, or policeman, criminal, and servant. This ethnic division of labor is capable of endless manipulation—the black man as hero is drama itself—and it also seems to have been copied by the film industries of other nations, such as Mexico, Egypt, and India. The white/light brown/black hierarchy was already deeply embedded in each of these societies, but another appeal of this division must have been that it allowed the stars of these infant film industries to look like Hollywood stars—pale spotlit figures surrounded by supporting players with darker skins. This WASP/Jewish/Latin/Black ethnic mix could scarcely have been better arranged had its sole purpose been to appeal to Europe, the white British Commonwealth, and Latin America. But it is a less obviously appealing ethnic mix for Asia. Most countries, when they import American material, *select* quite heavily. It is therefore possible to select those parts of the ethnic mix that seem most appealing locally.

Notes

1. Melvin L. De Fleur, "Occupational Roles as Portrayed on Television," *Public Opinion Quarterly* 28 (1964): 57–74.

2. Martha Wolfenstein and Nathan Leites, *Movies: A Psychological Study* (Glencoe, Ill.: Free Press, 1950).

3. Rudolf Arnheim, "The World of the Daytime Serial," in *Radio Research 1942– 1943*, ed. Paul Lazarsfeld and Frank Stanton (New York: Duell, Sloan & Pearce, 1944).

4. L. Handel, *Hollywood Looks at Its Audience: A Report on Film Audience Research* (Urbana: University of Illinois Press, 1950).

5. Leo Lowenthal, "Biographies in Popular Magazines," in Lazarsfeld and Stanton, *Radio Research 1942–1943*; and Theodore P. Greene, *America's Heroes: The Changing Models of Success in American Magazines* (New York: Oxford University Press, 1970).

6. C. Wright Mills, *White Collar* (New York: Oxford University Press, 1956), p. 74.

7. Isaac Goldberg, *Tin Pan Alley* (New York: Day, 1930), pp. 293–294.

8. Robert C. Toll, *Blacking Up: The Minstrel Show in Nineteenth Century America* (New York: Oxford University Press, 1974), pp. 270–273.

9. Erik Barnouw, *A Tour in Babel* (New York: Oxford University Press, 1966), pp. 225–231.

10. The Jewish population of the United States reached one million in 1898. A generation later the most heavily Jewish area was no longer Manhattan but the Bronx. See Irving Howe, *World of Our Fathers* (New York: Harcourt Brace Jovanovich, 1976).

11. Edward J. Epstein, *News from Nowhere: Television and the News* (New York: Vintage Books, 1974), pp. 222–223.

FROM MENACE TO MESSIAH: THE HISTORY AND HISTORICITY OF SUPERMAN

THOMAS ANDRAE

> *We were against revolution. Therefore we waged war against*
> *those conditions which make revolutions—against those resent-*
> *ments and inequalities which breed them. In America in 1933 the*
> *people did not attempt to remedy wrongs by overthrowing their*
> *institutions. Americans were made to realize that wrongs could*
> *and would be set right within their institutions.*
>   FRANKLIN D. ROOSEVELT, 1936[1]

One cannot help being struck by the current of fear, anger, and disillusionment that gripped the vast majority of Americans during the period between the stock market crash of 1929 and the inauguration of Franklin D. Roosevelt in 1933. The Great Depression raised questions not only about the ethics of capitalists but about the viability and legitimacy of capitalism itself. Although studies of the period show the country more mired in despair and ennui than clamoring for a radical restructuring of the economy, the nation was closer to revolution than at any other time in recent history.[2] Much has been written about this period politically, economically, and historically; however, little is yet known about the matrix of cultural forces that helped contain potentially oppositional and disruptive elements within the mass psyche and prepared the way for the peaceful transition from a collapsed Horatio Alger ethos of individual success to the collectivist ethic of the "totally administered society" of the corporate welfare state. This essay will describe the origin and evolution of the concept of the superman in American mass culture. The transformation of the superman will be shown to be central to the mass media's maintenance of ideological hegemony during the crucial institutional shift from entrepreneurial capitalism to the state-regulated monopoly capitalism of the New Deal.

Superman is one of the most popular fictional creations of all time. In a period spanning little more than forty years he has become apotheosized into a folk hero, been the motive force behind the rapid burgeoning of the comic book industry, and has recently been the subject of a series of multimillion dollar movies. An essential element of this popularity has been his canonization as an archetypical representative of the nation's highest ideals, the defender of "truth, justice, and the American way."[3] Yet few commentators have noticed that the superman figure was not always depicted as the bastion of establishment law and order and the avatar of Americanism he was later to become but, until recently, was usually portrayed as a social menace who threatened fundamental American values and institutions.

. . . .

Excerpted from *Discourse*, no. 2 (Summer 1980).

The superman theme first appeared in American science fiction around the beginning of the twentieth century, but it did not really catch on until the early thirties, when a flood of stories about mental and physical supermen hit the newsstands as either booklength novels or short stories in the gaudy science fiction pulps that had begun to seize the popular imagination during the years immediately preceding the Depression. . . . The idea of the superman was in the air during the early thirties, oppressively evident in the Nazis' distorted use of the Nietzschean concept of the *Übermensch* to glorify Aryan racial superiority and to justify their program of totalitarian domination. . . . Most often, the superman is a sinister figure who is so obsessed with his power and so contemptuous of mankind that he threatens to dominate and enslave the world; he becomes the evil genius of science fiction cliché. In Stanley Weinbaum's story "The Adaptive Ultimate," for instance, a superwoman attempts to gain world domination by exerting a sexually hypnotic control over the secretary of the Treasury of the United States. In order to avert world catastrophe, her powers are stolen by the same scientists who had made her superhuman by injecting her with an experimental serum thereby saving her life. Tragically, she returns to the tubercular, mousey, and unattractive figure she once had been. The message of the superman stories is always the same: whether savior or destroyer, the superman cannot be permitted to exist. Most of the stories of mentally and physically superior human beings end tragically and futilely. Whether he becomes an outcast, a pathetically lonely creature who is ostracized, or a tyrannical monster so dangerous that he threatens to enslave the world, convention dictates that he either die or be robbed of his power.

Appearing for the first time in *Action Comics*, no. 1 (June 1938), Superman represents an innovative break with science fiction tradition. Superman was created by two seventeen-year-old high school students, Jerry Siegel, who invented the character and wrote the strip, and Joe Shuster, who drew it. Siegel and Shuster's Superman differs from his predecessors in science fiction by being neither alienated from society nor a misanthropic, power-obsessed menace but a truly messianic figure—"a champion of the oppressed . . . sworn to devote his existence to those in need." [4] Unlike his predecessors, Superman not only chooses a place for himself in society, he also identifies with and aids his fellows and in turn is accepted, even glorified, by them. He is the embodiment of society's noblest ideals, a "man of tomorrow" [5] who foreshadows mankind's highest potentialities and profoundest aspirations but whose tremendous powers, remarkably, pose no danger to its freedom and safety.

What kind of changes did the popular mind undergo in order to accept a figure who seemed monstrous and threatening in the early thirties but could be accepted as a heroic ideal in the late thirties? One way of understanding this transformation is by interpreting it as a response to the collapse of the Horatio Alger ethos of laissez-faire individualism and its replacement by the experimental collectivism of the New Deal. Americans have had a basic, almost spiritual commitment to the principles of free enterprise and the self-reliant individualism of the Protestant ethic. For millions of Americans—laborers, clerks, small businessowners, and professionals—the Horatio Alger ethic of hard work, frugality, and temperance, if applied long and hard enough, with the right touch of "Yankee ingenuity," would inevitably culminate in their wealth, happiness, and independence. Shored up by constitutional safeguards of free speech and association, of justice and equality, failure to climb the ladder of wealth and status implied a failure of nerve and was an outward sign of sloth, indulgence, or outright incompetence.

As early as the turn of the century this picture was rapidly becoming obsolete, corresponding to an America of the 1840s and 1850s when the majority of the population who worked owned productive properties and were independent farmers, merchants, and professionals or, if they struck it rich, wealthy members of a leisure class. This was a time when individuals could more easily make the major decisions about their work and life, when a poor wage earner or immigrant could still head for the frontier and acquire his own holdings. Since then an increasingly urban, organized, and bureaucratized society has grown up at the expense of what once was a decentralized system of small enterprises and independent owners. This transformation spelled the erosion of Americans' dreams of upward mobility, classlessness, and personal autonomy and signaled the individual's submergence in the mass.

. . . .

During the Depression years, popular writers expressed even greater disillusionment with laissez-faire individualism, launching an implicit attack on the dangers of excessive individualism. This attack is nowhere better expressed than in Jerry Siegel and Joe Shuster's first superman story, which was based on the lurid model of the science fiction pulps. Siegel's story, "The Reign of the Superman," illustrated by Shuster, and written under the pseudonym Herbert S. Fine, appeared in one of the earliest science fiction fan magazines, *Science Fiction: The Advance Guard of Future Civilization*, which Siegel edited while still in high school. The story appeared in January 1933, about six months before Siegel and Shuster's first version of Superman was created. Superman was to undergo a number of small changes before finally emerging in 1938 as the blue-suited, red-caped character we are familiar with today. During this period, Siegel and Shuster hawked their creation to every major newspaper syndicate and comic book publisher, only to be rejected. Dismissed because their character was too fantastic, Shuster's artwork too amateurish, and their concept of a lawless, superpowerful individual a threat to values of law and order, the hottest commercial property in comic books lay on the shelf for nearly six years.

The connection between the stark economic facts of the Depression and the development of a superman mythos in the thirties is evident in the opening pages of Siegel's first superman story. A leering, bald-headed scientist looms over the city like a vulture as hundreds of men stand waiting in the breadline below. The scientist, Professor Smalley, takes a poor, raggedly dressed man off the breadline and coaxes him up to his apartment with an offer of food and a new suit of clothes. At the apartment the young man drinks a cup of coffee laced with Smalley's secret drug and falls asleep. But before Smalley discovers the results of his experiment, the young man disappears; only later does the scientist learn that he has created a mental giant, able to tell the future, assimilate all the world's knowledge, read and control people's minds, and transport himself at will to anywhere in the galaxy. As a consequence, Smalley decides to eliminate the super-man and to assume superhuman powers himself. "Only one Superman can exist and that will be me," he declares.[6] However, the superman reads his mind, and when Smalley attacks him he kills Smalley instead.

The bitterness and frustration caused by the Depression and the desire to gain power and mastery over a chaotic economic situation provide the focus for the superman's character. When people disdain his dirty, disheveled appearance, he humbles them through demonstrations of his devastating mental superiority. De-claring himself "a veritable god," the superman at first mentally forces people to give him money, amasses a fortune through mysterious gambling enterprises, and finally plans to conquer the world by forcing the armies of the major powers into an internecine war that would result in their annihilation. The world is saved only when he loses his powers and is forced to take his place again in the breadline. The ex-superman muses to an astonished reporter, "I see, now, how wrong I was. If I had worked for the good of humanity, my name would have gone down in history with a blessing—instead of a curse."[7]

Superman stories like Siegel's revealed both the attraction and disillusionment Americans felt toward the success myth during the Depression. On the one hand, these stories exposed the Horatio Alger ethic as a sham, belied by the failing economic and inept political situation of the early thirties. The superman is often situated within this context, being initially rejected, hopeless, and down-and-out, like Siegel's evil genius or Weinbaum's voluptuous superwoman. On the other hand, the superman stories, like the gangster film, helped keep alive America's fantasies of upward mobility by showing that success was still possible, but only by going outside the law and established institutional channels. "That Americans were attracted to outlaws during the Depression's most wrenching years is an un-deniable and useful fact," writes Andrew Bergman about the gangster film. "But the manner in which outlaws operated only reinforced some of the country's most cherished myths about individual success. The outlaw cycle represented not so much a mass desertion of the law as a clinging to past forms of achievement. That only gangsters could make upward mobility believable tells much about how legitimate institutions had failed."[8] But, as Bergman concludes, "mobility was still at the core of what Americans held to be the American dream."[9] The desire to be a success, to "be somebody," was even more central to the superman story than to the gangster film. The superman was not simply a success; he was so successful that his existence posed a threat to the entire planet—he was poten-tially the most powerful and wealthy person on earth.

Although the superman's meteoric success makes him an attractive figure, he is invariably condemned as evil and power-mad because, like the outlaw hero, he becomes successful only through criminal means. The superman thus becomes the quintessential evil agent of the Depression: his rampant economic individ-ualism is perceived as the source of the nation's political and economic chaos. He is the epitome of the individual who is totally self-seeking, with no sense of moral or social responsibility. This depiction of excessive individualism as lead-ing to social and economic chaos and possible tyranny mirrors Franklin D. Roosevelt's account of the Depression as a result of "a decade of debauch." "Today we shall have come through a period of loose thinking," announced Roosevelt in 1932, "declining morals, an era of selfishness among individual men and women, and among nations. Blame not governments alone for this. Blame ourselves in equal share." [10]

The social irresponsibility of the entrepreneur, the archetypical hero of laissez-faire individualism, had become oppressively transparent during the Depression. William Leuchtenberg writes: "At a time when millions lived close to starvation, and some even had to scavenge for food, bankers like Wiggin and corporation executives like George Washington Hill of American Tobacco drew astronomical salaries and bonuses. . . . And in Chicago, where teachers, unpaid for months, fainted in classrooms for want of food, wealthy citizens of national reputation brazenly refused to pay taxes—or submitted falsified statements." [11] It was the social irresponsibility, not the financial manipulation, of the entrepreneur that was the target of the New Deal's political and economic reforms.

The New Deal signaled an end to nineteenth-century individualism and placed a new emphasis on social security, governmental regulation, and collective action. This new collectivist ethic pervaded American society. "In the Twenties, America hailed Lindbergh as the Lone Eagle," writes Leuchtenberg. "In the Thirties, when word arrived that Amelia Earhart was lost at sea, *The New Republic* asked the government to prohibit citizens from engaging in such 'useless' exploits. The NRA sought to drive newsboys off the streets and took a Blue Eagle away from a company in Huck Finn's old town of Hannibal, Missouri, because a fifteen-year-old was found driving a truck for his father's business, Josef Hofmann urged that fewer musicians become soloists, Hollywood stars like Joan Crawford joined the Screen Actors Guild, and Leopold Stokowski cancelled a performance in Pittsburgh because theater proprietors were violating a union contract." [12] During the New Deal the ideal of individual success was transformed into an organizational ideal of success through self-sacrifice and collective effort under the direction of a strong leader. This new ethic was espoused by Roosevelt in his inaugural address of 1933: "We now realize as we have never realized before our interdependence [*sic*] on each other; that we cannot merely take but must give as well; that if we are to go forward, we must move as a trained and loyal army willing to sacrifice for the good of a common discipline, because without such discipline no progress is made, no leadership becomes effective." [13] This new collectivist ethic was utilized to justify the increasing subordination, conformity, and regimentation entailed by the bureaucratization of society and increasing state intervention into all areas of private life during and after the New Deal.

Yet the superman stories were not concerned with the irresponsibility of entrepreneurs; rather, they dealt with the excessive individualism and self-seeking behavior of the masses. It is the resentful and downtrodden individuals on the dole who become maniacal, power-mad tyrants: the lowly electrician who hates his boss with the college education and high-paying job in Taine's "Seeds of Life," the starving, tubercular girl in Weinbaum's "Adaptive Ultimate," or the dour young man on the breadline in Siegel's "Reign of the Superman." The destructive

individualism of the entrepreneur is thus projected onto the masses whose potentially revolutionary impulses are stigmatized as deriving from the same causes as
the nation's economic ills.[14] Coming during the Depression, these stories must
have exerted a profoundly conservative influence. Power is depicted as debilitating and consequently is better left alone. The warning at the end of a story like
Siegel's is clear—people should not dream, in their bitterness and disappoint-
ment, of tampering with the failing institutional apparatus for fear of courting a
greater catastrophe.

The superman stories typified what was, in fact, a groundswell of paranoia
that pervaded early thirties popular culture. As Joyce Nelson notes, between
1931, when economic collapse had begun seriously to affect ordinary people's
lives, and mid-1933, when the confident and activist stance of the newly elected
Franklin Delano Roosevelt began to bolster the national mood, three major film
genres were created—the gangster, horror, and fallen woman genres.[15] In each
case, the genre depicted the tragic consequences of departing from the status quo
and the exigency of its restoration: criminals who threatened law and order were
mercilessly gunned down, monsters who ravaged virginal girls or murdered the
innocent and helpless were ceremoniously destroyed, and promiscuous and jaded
fallen women were proven wrong and shown their rightful places as wives and
mothers. Far more serious, however, was the threat of revolutionary insurrection
which was invariably perceived as a chaotic, wantonly destructive frenzy that
would result in complete social dissolution. Perhaps the classic example of revolutionary paranoia was Merian C. Cooper and Ernest B. Schoedsack's *King
Kong*. *King Kong*, contemporaneous with Jerry Siegel's first superman story, was
released in March 1933, at the nadir of the Depression. The famous climactic
scene of Kong bursting his captor's chains and going on a destructive rampage
through New York City is an apt symbolic equivalent for what thirties audiences
most feared (and perhaps secretly enjoyed), the liberation of the lawless, primitive, and bestial forces that were presumed to lie dormant within the collective
unconscious during the Depression.

The superman stories thus fulfilled the role that Andrew Berman sees as the
basis of early thirties films; they defused widespread feelings of discontent with
the system and deflected the potential for revolution by suggesting that the problems of the Depression could be set right within existing institutions.[16] Here they
echoed Roosevelt's assumption that a just society could be secured by grafting a
welfare state onto what remained a capitalist foundation; existing institutions
need not be abandoned if excessive individualism and mass selfishness could be
curtailed. The superman stories thus helped ease the transition from a collapsed
laissez-faire ethic of individual success to a belief in the benevolence of a strong
central authority under the New Deal. From 1935 on there would be a careful and
deliberate attempt by the purveyors of mass culture to reestablish a faith in law
and order and to legitimize the mushrooming powers of the federal government.[17]
Gangster heroes of the early thirties like James Cagney and Edward G. Robinson
were ceremoniously transformed into the G-men heroes of the later thirties in
order to instill a belief in the automatic benevolence and expertise of federal au-

thorities and to establish their preeminence over state and local agencies. No longer portrayed as merely a neutral arbiter, the federal government came to be viewed as an infallible protector of society's welfare.

Siegel and Shuster's adaptation of the superman for comic books reveals a transitional phase in this development. In the earliest episodes, Superman is still not incorporated into the establishment and retains his predecessor's demonic qualities. At first he is a lawless individual who is wanted by the police, who freely resorts to violence or threats of violence to extort information or confessions from suspects, and who kills his adversaries whenever the situation demands it. Unlike his predecessors, however, Superman is selflessly dedicated to the public good. His most deeply held conviction, that he should never use his superpowers for profit or personal ambition, reflects the collectivist ethos of the nascent welfare state. This conviction is manifested in Superman's struggle for social justice and his "dedication to assisting the helpless and oppressed" (*Action*, no. 6 [November 1938]) in the early episodes. In his first two appearances (*Action*, nos. 1 and 2), Superman saves an innocent woman from being electrocuted, stops a wife-beating, and halts corrupt politicians and an avaricious munitions manufacturer from fomenting an international war for their personal gain. Other early issues deal with the rights of accused persons to fair and impartial justice, with crooked unions and corrupt municipal officials, and with prison brutality, slum conditions, and other pressing social issues.[18]

In these early issues Superman is clearly the champion of the underdog, displaying a sense of class consciousness virtually absent from later comic book stories. In one episode (*Action*, no. 3 [August 1938]), Superman exposes the unsafe working conditions in a coal mine caused by the owner's greed and neglect. Disguised as a miner, Superman rescues workers trapped by a cave-in. Confronted with his irresponsibility by Kent, the owner callously declares, "I'm a businessman, not a humanitarian." To teach the owner and a group of his spoiled, affluent friends, who go on a slumming party to the mines, to appreciate the worker's plight, Superman causes a cave-in that traps them in the mine. He clears a path to freedom only when they collapse from exhaustion after vainly attempting to dig themselves out, having learned that the safety devices have become inoperative due to the owner's neglect. "Henceforth my mine will be the safest in the country," boasts the owner to Kent, "and my workers will be the best treated." Although Kent congratulates him on his decision, he muses to himself, "If you don't, you can expect another visit from Superman."

The early Superman's fight for social justice often puts him at odds with the law. In one story (*Action*, no. 8 [January 1939]), Superman, convinced that juvenile delinquency is caused by stifling slum conditions, overtakes a paddy wagon and releases an arrested delinquent from the hands of enraged police in order to save the boy from a life of imprisonment. Then he proceeds to destroy the dilapidated houses of an entire slum area to force the government to erect modern, low-cost housing and to undertake a campaign of massive public aid. Scores of National Guardsmen and a squadron of aerial bombers are ordered to annihilate him to put an end to the destruction, but the bullets of the National Guardsmen bounce off his chest harmlessly, and the bombs unleashed by the planes serve only to complete his task of destruction. In another story (*Action*, no. 12 [May 1939]), Superman, after hearing of the high auto fatality rate, swoops down on a large automobile company and barges into the owner's office, accusing him of using inferior metals and parts in order to make profits at the cost of human lives. Then he gleefully destroys the factory's manufacturing equipment and reduces the factory itself to rubble. Afterward, he abducts the mayor, takes him to the city morgue, and forces him to look at the mangled corpses of the auto victims, accusing him of killing them by not strictly enforcing the speed laws. Repentant, the mayor promises to see to it that the city's traffic laws are stringently obeyed.

Superman's struggle for social justice and his radical tactics suggest an antiestablishment posture that transcends the revolutionary paranoia of the early thirties yet remains unassimilated to the statist ethic of the New Deal. Indeed, Siegel originally conceived of Superman as a thorn in the side of the establishment, and Superman's concern for social change and the plight of the oppressed is unequaled even in recent comic book stories. However, as the expansion of federal power is legitimized and government becomes perceived as a benevolent protector of society's welfare, the radical individualism of the early Superman is displaced by a wholesale identification with the state. By mid-1942, when the war effort demanded unquestioning loyalty to the state and increased collaboration between government and industry, Superman no longer operates outside the law but is made an honorary policeman. Ironically, Superman's chief nemesis becomes the evil genius Luthor, a mad scientist bent on world domination, whose personality is the replica of Siegel's first superman. In the corporate era, Superman must repress those elements of radical individualism for which he once stood. This incorporation of Superman into the establishment culminates in what becomes a major convention of the comic books: social evil is transmuted into personal evil. As Umberto Eco notes, Superman has a civic conscience, not a political one.[19] His struggle against evil becomes confined to the defense of private property and the extermination of criminals; it is no longer a struggle against social injustice, an attempt to aid the helpless and oppressed.

This incorporation of Superman into the establishment has its basis in the early stories, which naively operate within a framework of accepted social and political concentration and thus fail to go beyond reformist politics. Siegel was greatly influenced by the Warner Brothers social consciousness films of the thirties, heavily oriented toward Roosevelt in their politics.[20] The social changes prescribed by the early Superman stories are easily assimilated into the New Deal philosophy of expanded governmental power to regulate the abuses of the economic system and discipline industry, provide social security and public relief, and protect the rights of workers and minorities. Indeed, Siegel acknowledged that listening to Roosevelt's "fireside chats" helped inspire his creation of Superman.[21] Yet the radical individualism and lawlessness of the early Superman was too dangerous not to be contained. Initially, the publishers were unaware that Siegel had cast Superman as an outlaw. When they discovered this fact inadvertently, Siegel was told to make Superman operate within the law and to confine his activities to fighting criminals. All controversial social issues were to be avoided. Siegel left for the army in mid-1943, losing control over Superman to freelancers during his absence. After his return, Siegel attempted to regain full creative control over Superman and launched the first of a long series of unsuccessful lawsuits against his publisher, National Publications, to obtain the legal rights to his creation. Siegel left Superman in 1948. With his departure his name was stricken from the title page as the creator of Superman; it was put back only recently, when he concluded a legal settlement with National. With the exception of a few years after the war, Siegel never wrote Superman again until the period 1959–1966, when he was hired as one of a number of anonymous ghost writers on the strip. In the interim Siegel was blacklisted in the comics industry and forced to write under various pseudonyms. After his control over Superman ebbed and he ultimately departed the strip, Siegel's original vision of Superman was radically subverted, with a vapid establishmentarian hero substituted in his place, which the public, ironically, came to accept as the "real" Superman. The memory of Superman's existence as an outlaw and champion of the oppressed would be virtually extinguished.

The erosion of individual autonomy under monopoly capitalism is, however, apparent from the beginning. The introduction of an alter ego into the Superman stories shows this change. Superman differs from his predecessors in science fiction by being able to exist within society by disguising himself as the self-deprecating and mild-mannered Clark Kent. It is the Kent alter ego that is supposedly a fiction, while the Superman personality is taken as real. This schizoid situation both reflects and distorts the corporate context within which the stories take place. On the one hand, the stories expose a degenerate power structure that turns Kent into an archetypical organization man. In his job as a reporter, Kent is unmercifully bullied and humiliated by his boss, editor Perry White, and must endure cut-throat competition with co-worker Lois Lane for news stories. Kent must continually disguise his powers, conceal his true thoughts and personality, and lie to protect his identity. His longing for acceptance is callously rebuffed by Lois Lane, who can see only his weakness, and not the slumbering giant within. Kent's powerlessness, alienation, and inauthenticity are symptomatic of the status frustration of the new middle class of salaried employees who can neither find fulfillment and dignity in their professional life nor expect to achieve the security and independence that once came with proprietorship. As C. Wright Mills notes, during the last half century there has been a marked shift in the pattern and content of success: "In the older pattern, the white-collar job was merely one step on the grand road to independent entrepreneurship; in the new pattern, the white-collar way involves promotions within a bureaucratic hierarchy." [22] With the decline of entrepreneurial capitalism, success and achievement are redefined in organizational terms: loyalty and conformity to superiors are more important than hard work and self-discipline, who you know is more important than what you know, and identification with the organization is more important than personal virtuosity and independence.

On the other hand, the Superman stories also radically distort the corporate context within which they take place. By portraying the Kent identity as a mere sham, the narrative negates the effects of the organizational context on Kent and affirms instead the illusory reality of a phantasmagoric existence beyond daily life as Superman. The stories thus affirm a form of pseudoindividualism, which disguises the actual facts of corporate power. This is accomplished through a paradoxical function performed by the narrative: it exposes the powerlessness of the individual in modern society and simultaneously effaces it by affirming an escape into a realm of fantastic adventure beyond the repressions of daily life. By identifying with both the impotent Kent and the invincible Superman, the reader can acknowledge the facts of power in daily life but need not confront the painful necessity of changing his or her situation to achieve that power. Indeed, the pivotal point of many adventures is the aversion of such a confrontation, which is anticipated with overwhelming terror and anxiety; a mandatory ingredient of each story is a prohibition on Kent's using his superpowers in his civilian identity, that is, on the job.

The Superman stories thus promote an acceptance of powerlessness in one's daily life for the sake of an ersatz existence beyond it. They reproduce the consumerist ideology of late capitalism—that labor is inherently unsatisfying and only an instrumental means to the freedom obtainable in leisure time. They reflect the purely symbolic character of individualism under monopoly capitalism, where formal public freedom, political equality, and leisure-time consumption mask the hierarchy, repression, and inequality endured daily in the workplace. They function as what French situationist Guy Debord calls the spectacle, a "continuously produced and therefore continuously evolving pseudo-reality, predominantly visual, which each individual encounters, inhabits, and accepts as public and official reality, thereby denying as much as possible the daily private reality of exploitation, pain, and suffering, and inauthenticity he or she experiences." [23] The spectacle is endemic to advanced capitalist commodity production, Debord claims; it functions to divert the masses from a critical political awareness of the day-to-day facts of power that oppress them.

The ersatz quality of Kent's existence as Superman is exposed in the text itself. The attempt to portray Kent as merely a fabrication and Superman as a real personality results in the creation of paradoxes in the narrative. A prime example is the strange ménage à trois between Kent, Lois, and Superman. Kent loves and pursues Lois but is bullied and rejected by her. As Superman he rebuffs her advances yet shows an inordinate concern for rescuing and protecting her. Since Superman and Kent are the same person, this behavior demands an explanation. In numerous stories, Kent experiences the wish that Lois would love him for himself, that is, as Kent. Since this would mean loving a purely fake, fabricated personality, it does not make sense. The only logical conclusion is that Kent is not merely a put-on, and Superman the true identity, but that both identities are aspects of a single personality, each autonomous in its own realm.

The schizoid relationship between Kent and Superman is similar to the behavior of clinical cases of schizophrenia, although Kent is not psychotic or psychopathic. According to R. D. Laing, the schizoid perceives his true identity as a false self, which he attempts to transcend by creating a more authentic personality. He withdraws from relationships with others, attempting to obtain a sense of omnipotence by substituting a fantastic, privatized existence for the world of interpersonal relationships in which he feels impotent.

Such a schizoid individual . . . is trying to be omnipotent by enclosing within his own being, without recourse to a creative relationship with others, modes of relationship that require the effective presence to him of other people and of the outer world. He would appear to be, in an unreal, impossible way, all persons and things to himself. The imagined advantages are safety for the true self, isolation and hence freedom from others, self-sufficiency and control.[24]

Like the schizoid, the superhero attempts to escape the pain and anguish of everyday life by creating a fantastic world beyond interpersonal relationships where he is totally free and in control. This feeling of mastery, however, is only a fantasy bought at the cost of a tragic alienation from himself and others. His feeling of power is based on the renunciation of all pleasure, sexuality, and emotional involvement. Thus, although he freely expresses his love for Lois in his Kent identity, as Superman he must rigidly reject all domestic and emotional attachments. Because he isolates himself from others and renounces the pleasures of friendship, love, and sexuality, his inner world, like that of the schizoid, becomes increasingly impoverished. Side by side with a sense of omnipotence is a feeling of impotence and emptiness. The withdrawal from daily life and emotional involvement only culminates in failure. "The more this phantastic omnipotence and freedom are indulged," writes Laing, "the more weak, helpless, and fettered it becomes in actuality. The illusion of omnipotence and freedom can be sustained only within the magic circle of its own shutupness in phantasy."[25]

During the past two decades, the emotional impoverishment of Superman's existence has become increasingly overt. No longer does he look on the role of isolated hero as overwhelmingly attractive, or on the Kent identity as drab. More than ever before, Superman has the sense of being a lonely outsider, an alien from another world who can be human only in his Kent identity. As a result, the schizophrenia latent in the earlier stories is more strongly expressed. Often Kent decides to give up his Superman identity and totally become his Kent personality.[26] In other stories, Kent reverses roles with his alter ego, becoming a public hero, with Superman reduced to the despised weakling.[27] More than ever before, Superman expresses a yearning for love and domesticity, emotions he has traditionally repressed. In one story (*Lois Lane*, no. 34 [July 1962]), he plaintively watches Lois, now married to his archenemy Luthor, as they play with their children. He muses sadly, "Maybe I'd better marry Lana Lang before she marries someone else." In the fortieth-anniversary issue, the Kent identity totally takes over, and he forgets his Superman identity and marries Lois (*Action*, no. 484 [June 1978]).

The apogee of this tendency is reached in the recent film *Superman—The Movie*, where the latent schizophrenia of the comic book stories is muted and the chaste ménage à trois between Kent, Lois, and Superman uncoupled. Superman is presented as a thoroughly human, vulnerable, and even sexual character. His love and sexual desire for Lois is poignantly expressed in a sensuously erotic sequence in which he takes Lois for a flight over the city. No longer confined to expressing his vulnerability and emotions only in his Kent identity, Superman becomes a man of superpassions who finds his identity as Superman frustrating and limiting. When Lois is killed at the film's climax, for example, Superman cries out in anguish when he arrives too late to save her (having been detained by saving another life elsewhere). He resurrects Lois by breaking one of his father Jor-El's most sacred commands—not to intervene in the course of human history; he flies so fast around the globe that he changes the direction of its rotation, thereby reversing time. The ultimate dénouement of this tendency is revealed in the sequel to the film, when Superman makes love to Lois Lane and relinquishes his superpowers for the rewards of human vulnerability and romantic bliss.

With the malaise of Vietnam and Watergate, Superman has also become increasingly more self-conscious and questioning of the use of individual power. For example, when he tries to stop a civil war in the fictional republic of Borotavia (a pseudonym for Vietnam), Superman comes to realize that "there are natural forces at work in the world that can't be stopped" (*Action*, no. 467). He concludes that "the world needs a balance and though some things can be repressed for awhile, they can't be gotten rid of regardless of how much we try." Like the United States in Vietnam, he becomes a pitiful giant who can no longer impose his will on the world. In another story, "Must There Be a Superman?" (*Superman*, no. 247 [January 1972]), the heroic role itself is questioned. After Superman stops a farmer from beating a migrant worker for striking, the other migrants become lazy and dependent, asking Superman to solve all their problems for them. Superman comes to realize that charity, however much it aids the oppressed, can impede social progress. "If you rebuilt every ghetto and arrested every slum landlord, what then Superman?" he muses. He concludes that to become self-sufficient and independent, people must free themselves, not rely on paternalistic power.

Yet despite the radical questioning and self-doubt, the old formulas remain essentially unchanged. Superman is still basically omnipotent, establishment-oriented, and sexually unfulfilled. The problem, as Umberto Eco notes, is that the Superman concept itself is inherently problematic. This is manifested in the paradoxical treatment of time in the stories. Like the heroes of ancient mythology, Superman is invulnerable and seemingly invincible. Like the characters of a timeless myth, he is a perfect being who does not err, change, age, or develop. Unlike mortals, writes Eco, he does not exist in time and thereby does not "consume" himself in his actions. Superman is a mortal human being, though, not a god, and he is thus tied to the temporal flux of human life in which time is irreversible and each action is a further stage leading to degeneration and ultimately, death.

According to Eco, this paradox leads to a breakdown in the structure of temporality in the stories.

In Superman stories, the time that breaks down is the time of the story, that is, the notion of time which ties one episode to another. In the sphere of the story, Superman accomplishes a given job (he routs a band of gangsters); at this point the story ends. In the same comic book, or in the edition of the following week, a new story begins. If it took Superman up again at the point where he left off, he would have taken a step toward death. On the other hand, to begin a story without showing that another had preceded it would manage, momentarily, to remove Superman from the law that leads from life to death through time.[28]

This destruction of time is evident in the case of many comic strip characters, such as Little Orphan Annie, who has been an ageless child for over fifty years.

Eco argues that Superman stories take place in an oneiric climate in which there is little connection between present, past, and future. The narrative picks up the strands of events without connecting them to previous or future actions. Consequently, the stories take place in a perpetual present that excludes all notions of change and development. The solution the authors have devised to depict change in an essentially static universe is to invent "imaginary tales," stories describing possible developments that do not actually take place but occur in an imaginary time frame, such as Superman's marriage to Lois Lane or his retirement in old age.[29] If Superman actually married Lois Lane or became elderly, this would indicate an irreversible progression in character development that would necessarily implicate him in the temporal flux of events. By utilizing the device of purely imaginary stories, the authors are able continually to invent new plot developments to compensate for the static limitations of Superman as a character. The imaginary stories thus allow Superman to remain a fixed character relegating all development to a spectral realm. Eco claims that only through the maintenance of a confused notion of time can Superman stories be made credible. Superman comes off as a myth only if the reader loses awareness of the temporal relationships in the story and renounces the need to reason on their basis, succumbing to the apparent flux of events while in actuality holding to the illusion that events can take place in a continuous and immobile present.

The paradoxical treatment of time in Superman stories reflects the commodity structure of mass culture in late capitalism. The commodity itself has a seemingly paradoxical structure; it is fixed, repetitive, and standardized yet also apparently constantly changing, evanescent, and unpredictable. It reveals a fixed core that is impervious to substantial change, thereby becoming a vehicle for the stable reproduction of social relations, while its surface structure follows ephemeral changes in style and fashion, making it an enticing article for continuous consumption. Standardization and planned obsolescence are thus twin aspects of the commodity in our high-consumption society. This duality is reproduced in the narrative structure of Superman stories—while Superman remains an essentially fixed, atemporal character, the authors invent "imaginary stories" in order to give him the apparent aura of temporal development and to captivate an audience that demands continuous novelty and unpredictability.

This destruction of temporality cannot, however, take place with impunity. Eco argues that in maintaining a notion of events that are no longer tied together by any strand of logic or necessity, the reader, without realizing it, loses all notion of temporal progression. When events no longer have a structure such that one event follows another in a linear sequence, concepts like causality, which presupposes a sense of temporality, also collapse. "In growing accustomed to the idea of events happening in an ever-continuing present," Eco writes, "the reader loses touch of the fact that they should develop according to the dictates of time. Losing consciousness of the notion of development, he forgets the problems which are at its base—the existence of freedom, the possibility of planning and changing situations and the gains and losses such actions entail."[30] Most of all, notes Eco, the reader loses not only the notion of an existence that is different from that of the present but also the concept of historical change and develop-ment upon which a progressive society is based. The Superman mythos thus im-plicates the reader in an immobilistic metaphysics.

The disintegration of time in Superman stories has ominous psychosocial im-plications. It exemplifies what Theodore Adorno described as the key attribute of mass culture, its substitution of mythic repetition for historical development, the replacement of "the immobility of an ever-identical moment" for time.[31] The destruction of time was connected to the decline of the autonomous individual, claimed Adorno, because temporal development was a crucial attribute of indi-viduality. To paraphrase later Marxists, one could argue that the destruction of time undermines the individual's capacity to become a self-constituted subject— the ability to emancipate oneself from the inhibitions and distortions of the past and to create a future that authentically expresses the individual's needs and de-sires.[32] It promotes a psychologically regressive state in which the reader is re-duced to a condition of impotence and passivity, becoming a perfect pawn for the bureaucratic chessboard.

Notes

1. *The Public Papers and Addresses of Franklin D. Roosevelt*, vol. 5 (New York, 1936), pp. 386, 389–390.

2. Cf. William Leuchtenberg, *Franklin D. Roosevelt and the New Deal: 1932–1940* (New York: Harper & Row, 1963), p. 26; and Studs Terkel, *Hard Times* (New York: Pan-theon Books, 1970).

3. Introduction to the Superman television show, which aired from 1951 to 1957.

4. E. Nelson Birdwell, ed., *Superman: From the 30's to the 70's* (New York: Crown, 1971), p. 21.

5. Ibid., p. 51.

6. Herbert S. Fine [Jerry Siegel], "The Reign of the Superman," *Science Fiction: The Advance Guard of Future Civilization* 1, no. 3 (1933): 12.

7. Ibid., p. 14.

8. Andrew Bergman, *We're in the Money: Depression America and Its Films* (New York: Harper & Row, 1971), p. 6.

9. Ibid., p. 17.

10. Quoted in Ben Zevin, *Nothing to Fear* (New York: Popular Library, 1961), p. 23.

11. Leuchtenberg, *Roosevelt and the New Deal*, p. 21.

12. Ibid., p. 17.

13. Quoted in Mark Roth, "Some Warners' Musicals and the Spirit of the New Deal," *The Velvet Light Trap*, no. 77 (Winter 1977): 4.

14. This type of projection was commonplace during the Depression. For example, John Edgerton, in his presidential address to the National Association of Manufacturers in 1930, blamed the poverty of the jobless on their lack of "habits of thrift and conservation" (Leuchtenberg, *Roosevelt and the New Deal*, p. 21). In an individualistic society that be-lieved that every person rose on his own merits, unemployment was viewed as a personal failure and the unemployed worker almost always experienced feelings of guilt and self-depreciation (ibid., p. 21).

15. Joyce Nelson, "Warner Brothers' Deviants: 1931–1933," *The Velvet Light Trap*, no. 15 (Fall 1975): 7–10.

16. Bergman, *We're In the Money*, p. 167.

17. Ibid., p. 84. See also Richard Gid Powers, *G-Men: Hoover's FBI in American Popular Culture* (Carbondale: Southern Illinois University Press, 1983).

18. For a summary of the early Superman's concern for social justice and his relationship to the law-enforcement establishment, see Michael Fleisher, *The Great Superman Book* (New York: Warner Books, 1978), pp. 422–428.

19. Umberto Eco, "The Myth of the Superman," *Diacritics* 2, no. 1 (1972): 22.

20. For a discussion of the politics of Warner Brothers' social consciousness films, see Bergman, *We're In the Money*, pp. 92–109.

21. Jerry Siegel, press release 13 October 1975.

22. C. Wright Mills, *White Collar* (New York: Oxford University Press, 1956), pp. 262–263.

23. Norman Fruchter, "Games in the Arena: Movement Propaganda and the Society of the Spectacle," *Liberation*, May 1971, p. 5; Guy Debord, *Society of the Spectacle* (Detroit: Black & Red, 1977).

24. R. D. Laing, *The Divided Self* (Baltimore: Penguin Books, 1965), p. 75.

25. Ibid., p. 84.

26. *Superman Comics*, no. 297 (March 1976); *Superman Comics*, no. 209 (August 1968).

27. *Action Comics*, no. 461 (July 1976).

28. Eco, "Myth of the Superman," p. 17.

29. For a summary, see ibid., p. 18.

30. Ibid., p. 19.

31. Quoted in Martin Jay, *The Dialectical Imagination: A History of the Frankfurt School and the Institute for Social Research 1923–1950* (Boston: Little, Brown, 1973), p. 187.

32. Jürgen Habermas, *Knowledge and Human Interests* (Boston: Beacon Press, 1971).

DOMESTICATING NATURE

TODD GITLIN

Everywhere nature is consumed by capital, and everywhere the middle class reaches for its private share of the vulnerable and disappearing wildness. The spirit of the seventies whispers: If the wilderness is going to be stripped away, plowed under, and paved, let's grow our own. Markets develop to make private appropriations of that which is growing scarce. We know or—however dimly—sense that nature is at risk, so we hasten to possess what we can of it. Restaurants and coffeehouses install the loveliest potted plants in their windows as invitations and assurances. From a tenth-story window on the Upper West Side of Manhattan, I've seen houseplants growing in every single visible window of the building across the street. Southwestern entrepreneurs drive truckloads of rare cactus out of the Arizona desert by night to serve the great market for exotica; so thoroughly do they know their market, so insatiable is the demand, that some species are reportedly endangered. The *New York Times* of April 2, 1978, reports a study by several conservation groups: "A hundred million wild birds are being trapped each year to satisfy the growing world-wide craze for exotic household pets, pushing several of the most costly species toward extinction." Poachers thrive, especially on Caribbean islands where a single parrot might bring a year's wages to an impoverished farmer. Several commodity transactions away, at the other end of the world economic chain, inflation-riddled collectors have fused the love of rare, exotic things—which is one of the grand traditions of bourgeois culture—with the love of vanishing nature, contributing to the depletion of that very nature which is so acquisitively loved. In bourgeois society, the living room seeks to take in what the public space will no longer afford. The private acquisition masks the precariousness of the public world.

Of course, the history of capitalism is the history of a humanly constructed world extending its dominion over nature. The equation of the desirable and the scarce, and the shifting of taste to adapt to this equation, have long been the basis of the market system in luxuries, and the Romantic taste for nature has long been organized into an enthusiasm for parks. (The very term *park* has been taken over into its opposite: "industrial park" and now "nuclear park." Corporations seek simultaneously to control and to sentimentalize their unruly creations.) In Weimar Germany, Leo Lowenthal tells me, it was also the fashion to incorporate nature into social spaces: hanging gardens were popular, restaurants installed aquariums, and apartment house lobbies sprouted trees. Now, I suggest, a new note has been sounded within this process. The *scale* on which civilization acquires nature is new; so is the widespread and scientifically grounded consciousness that the environment is in jeopardy; and so is the deliberateness with which a business civilization seeks not only to contain but also to reproduce nature. Recent American architecture stretches the trend still further. New architectural

From *Theory and Society*, no. 8 (1979), with minor changes.

spaces enshrine the principle that the corporate space can and should appropriate nature by enclosing it.

One method uses the indirect means of art. Several years ago there was a show of paintings in the lobby of San Francisco's Transamerica pyramid entitled "A Sense of Place: California Landscape Painting, 1870–1930." In the lobby of this concrete-and-glass monument, where a landmark plaque commemorates the location of a historic building that no longer exists, "A Sense of Place" was celebrated with banal naturalist pictures of much-toured picturesquerie. The building could have been plunked down anywhere; there were no smells, no colors, no topographical features to signify any particular place on earth. In this lobby there was *no* place. Appropriately, when I went back a couple of weeks later, the paintings were gone; "A Sense of Place" had been uprooted, had moved on.

The other method for possessing and exhibiting some version of nature is more direct. If a living room can aspire to become a room in a hypothetical forest, why shouldn't a hotel try to incorporate the forest itself? Some such strategy lies behind the design of the Hyatt Regency Hotel at the foot of Market Street in San Francisco, across the Embarcadero from the bay, a few blocks from the Transamerica pyramid. Opened in 1973 and already a major tourist attraction and the seed of many imitations, this slab of reinforced concrete looks from the waterfront like the stands of a stadium seen from the inside, sloping up twenty stories at forty-five degrees. You climb a steep flight of shallow steps to get into the hotel. The steepness of the climb, as inside a ball park, is perhaps a deliberate architectural signal that one should prepare to enter into a different space; perhaps it is meant to divert you to the Market Street side, where the entrance is easier; perhaps this entrance has been made a trifle forbidding to deflect passersby and tourists who are not guests of the hotel. Whatever the reason, the steep steps amount to a signal: Expect something. Even: Expect spectacle.

Then you are inside, where the public world has been transplanted, behind closed doors. You walk into a cool green pyramid of space twenty stories high. Instead of the conventional hotel lobby, meant to provide an airlock for guests on the way in or out, the Hyatt Regency grants an atrium, a place to *be*, a huge space entirely enclosed but for a faint skylight.

The space is dazzling. Already at first glance this is a hotel lobby unlike any other, an open space meant for walking, sitting, eating, gawking: an urban space that feels spacious, enormous. The space soars, the world opens up before you. Where the typical contemporary lobby imitates an office building—or rather, each lobby imitates the others, all of them marginally distinguishable, homeless places away from home—the Regency imitates the fusion of nature and the city. The city manifests itself as twenty stories of continuous guest-room balconies bounding the pyramid of space. Their effect is to stripe the space and to swell it as it climbs gloriously toward the pinnacle, which is faintly luminous with natural light. You sense space, then enclosure, the feeling of glass walls rushing toward you as they rush toward the top. There is something of the mixed pleasure and vertigo you feel in Manhattan when you look up from the street at skyscrapers, surrendering your eyes to the rush up those walls toward the summits.

You return to ground level to discover not traffic but amenities of city life:

cafés of varying price and ambience, bars, shops, clusters of couches, a floor of geometrically regular ceramic tile. Once inside, people stroll, eat, converse: this is public space. In the center, four stories of sculpture, a hollow sphere-shaped piece made of aluminum tubes. The lobby is three hundred feet long and oddly quiet; everyone wants to hush, respecting the interiority of this space, lending it the semblance of a cathedral. Into this vacancy, from time to time, trickles piano-bar music of a blanched sort known commercially as Easy Listening. The lighting in the lobby is a uniform dark green everywhere but at the summit, as if sunglasses had been clamped over your eyes when you stepped inside.

Quickly you are aware that this city has absorbed nature. A stream flows through over a bed of pebbles, its concrete container bounding the corridor past the shops. The sphere-sculpture stands in the middle of a continuous-flow fountain. Whole trees grow in rows, spotlit from below. There are exotic birds, caged, and twelve hundred (not eleven hundred, not thirteen hundred, according to the official fact sheet) potted chrysanthemum plants. Hanging gardens of vines adorn the balcony walls. The stream flows within ruler-straight banks, the trees are in perfect rows: this is distinctly nature domesticated, relocated onto a reservation. The critic Leo Marx has noted that American writers have always been haunted by the theme of America as a garden being invaded by a machine; by the 1970s, the machine has become an exoskeleton, and in the Hyatt Regency the garden has been contained within it.

We are meant to imagine that this is California incarnate, its famous nature enfolded within the advanced design and sophistication appropriate to the vanguard state. California is the state of aerospace and electronics, Disneyland, the vast irrigated fields of agribusiness, as well as Yosemite, and the Regency atrium incorporates features of all of them. The stream is even marked "Recycled Water," to reassure California's large population of ecology buffs. San Francisco proves it can be what the Chamber of Commerce once called "Executive Headquarters West" without losing its natural soul. But in another way, within the artificial world of the Regency, you forget where you actually are; you might as well be anywhere; actually you are nowhere. Since capital knows no boundaries and respects no local entropies, style is no longer regional, no longer even national, but international. (Some day it may even be interplanetary, as Stanley Kubrick had the wit to suggest with his stylized version of a space-station Hilton in *2001: A Space Odyssey*.) The "uniqueness" of the Regency is capital's idea of a San Francisco landmark; in fact, the Regency is owned by a New York banker (David Rockefeller owns the controlling interest) and was designed by an Atlanta architect (John Portman). Similar structures have been erected in Atlanta, Los Angeles, on Memorial Drive in Cambridge, Massachusetts, even in Rockville, Maryland. We must take seriously the pride with which, at the opening of his Istanbul branch in 1955, Conrad Hilton bragged: "Each of our hotels is a 'little America.'" (The quotation appears in Daniel Boorstin's *The Image*, whose capsule history of the hotel and routinized tourism remains potent despite Boorstin's nostalgia for "the lost art of travel.") Regencys, like Hiltons, acquire nationality as a last-minute "flavor" or "atmosphere," as if it were a disinfectant spray. The One World of the global corporation constructs its version of unity out of simulations of locality. Nature brought indoors, the Regency is indeed utopia; but this utopia is located in the original Greek meaning of the world—noplace.

Over the last century and a half, the hotel has become an important public space. Earlier, throughout the centuries of horse-drawn traffic, the inn was modest and without comforts, essentially a watering and feeding station for travelers and horses. The earliest hotels, in the fifteenth century, were palaces away from home for the mobile nobility. Then the railroad called forth the modern hotel in the nineteenth century, and a combination of Depression mobility and the super-highway engineered the motel in the mid-twentieth. Now it becomes possible for tourists to circumvent the city entirely, to stay in the indistinguishable business strip just out of town. Against this competition, the hotel recoups its losses with monumentalism. The Hyatt Regency is one of the first hotel structures to suit the age of the jet plane. Like the airport, it promises adventure and at the same time packages it to remove any sign of the unpredictable. Its structure reaches upward, promising grandeur and delivering coldness.

The Regency presents travelers with a simulacrum of nature and a simulacrum of the city, both at the same time, yet it permits a circumventing of the variety, and troubles, of either. Architect John Portman has said that one motive for his design is to seal the hotel off from inner-city decay. It turns out that most of the clientele is white, in a city mostly not white. That is one point of this pseudo-plaza: to keep out the poor, which means disproportionately the people of color. In this false city enfolding a simulated nature, strollers watch each other with arranged faces, suggesting that they grasp the artificiality of the scene, they know it was built for this purpose and none other, and that they are here provisionally. The great strolling boulevards of Paris and streets like Las Ramblas in Barcelona and upper Broadway in New York turn into theaters every day because the streets are thoroughfares; all manner of people pass through on their various errands, working, shopping, going to school, hanging out. Thus they bring to the scene some trace of their private intentions as well as their public displays. They are all kinds, all classes and races. As Walter Benjamin noted in his peerless book on Charles Baudelaire, the Baudelairean *flaneur*—the stroller who inspected society with the fine instrument of his feeling—thrived in such a space. In those streets he could run across *tout le monde*, the banker and the whore, the workman and the shopper; he could uncover all the dirty secrets in all the dark corners of the society if he walked far enough and kept his eyes trained and open. But the Regency is a sealed-off world pretending at totality. At $159 a night minimum for a single room, $203 for a bay view (1986 prices), the visitors form a predictable assortment; no wonder they do not scrutinize each other with vast curiosity. Even at the Friday dinnertime "tea dances" in the lobby, where middle-aged couples dance to big bands and single men on the make try to furnish their weekends with companionship, the voyeurs and hustlers look more awkward and distracted than adventuresome. Helen Baehr, a visiting English sociologist, remarked to me that the dance looked like "a big party to which no one has been invited."

Pyramidal grandeur dwarfs even the individuals to whose greater glory the hotel caters. To make the hotel look more habitable, to correct for the monumental, is the point of the five glass elevators visible at the far side of the atrium, sliding soundlessly up and down like cardboard toys. Adorned in Art Nouveau style with rows of small electric bulbs rimming the glass cases, their decorative fancy tempers the Regency's one-world modernity. Without the nostalgia this style evokes, visitors might feel utterly disoriented in the brave new world of geometric slopes. (A similar nostalgia for nobility is served by outfitting the bell-boys in cutaway suits and derby hats, which makes it hard at first to tell who is a bellboy and who might be a member of a visiting rock group.) One of the elevators carries you up over the atrium and then *through* the skylit roof to the rotating glass-walled rooftop restaurant; the elevator shaft actually, amazingly, *supports* the restaurant. Eating there, looking out over the city—now the bay, a few minutes later the financial district—you might experience the truth of the economic system that the Regency serves by flattery: there's room at the top, but not for long; always there's another customer waiting.

The four other glass elevators, meanwhile, are accessible only to hotel guests holding documents the hotel calls "passports." And only these four stop at the hotel-rooms floors. The balconies are thus reserved as hotel space proper, presumably because one commodity the guests are buying is a certain privacy and freedom from robbery. Indeed, during a break in the tea dance, the band leader cautions as casually as he can manage: "Watch out for your purses, ladies and gentlemen, keep an eye on your wrists." The urban reality outside cannot be entirely suppressed.

So much for faint reminders that, outside the Regency, other worlds still exist. But even the world of nature cannot be contained within the temple built to house it for the greater glory of the current civilization. Among the hotel guests, I like to imagine there are some whose children must be heaving on their aluminum-framed nylon backpacks and heading off into the wilderness the Regency parodies: heading off in such numbers, indeed, that they are required to make reservations with the National Park Service for the heaviest-trafficked trails, prone to erosion. As the Regency packages nature, backpackers use high-technology products to ease their access to whatever nature remains, however tamed this nature is by bureaucratic management of the national parks. (The manufacturers and merchandisers of backpacks might well hold their conventions at the Regency.) Even the sterility of the Regency atrium—after $300,000 spent on landscaping!—pays backhanded tribute to the public hunger for a sense of place in the natural world. It is possible in our society to spend one night sitting in a rotating restaurant above San Francisco and the next day clambering up waterfalls. These are two faces of life in a single society, one that refuses to set limits to human power. And the possibility of optimism about the prospects for human society rests partly on our ability to discover a difference between the consequences of these two experiences.

In *The Domination of Nature*, William Leiss refers to Western civilization's drive toward "the subjection of all of nature to the status of being purely an object for human satisfaction." In the Regency, nature has been recreated into a technological order, a pseudopark and pseudoplaza, and the result is to impoverish not only nature and public space but their human inhabitants as well. In aspiring to the limitless, imitating a version of Egyptian eternity and Babylonian splendor, it succeeds finally in evoking nothing but boredom. The novelty of the Regency is quickly consumed, leaving the blank-faced visitors dissatisfied with a nature that has been subjected and simulated precisely to satisfy them. The utopia that subsumes nature kills the life of it.

Acknowledgment

For conversations that bore some fruit here, thanks to Helen Baehr, Marshall Berman, Alvin Gouldner, Leo Lowenthal, and José Luis Pérez Arnaiz.

THE INFANTILIZING
OF CULTURE

ARIEL DORFMAN

Ponce de León couldn't find the fountain of youth in Florida, so Walt Disney created it ten years ago. My congratulations on Walt Disney World's Tencentennial.
—BOB HOPE

If I could be someone else, I'd like to be Mickey Mouse because he never does anything wrong and he's loved by everyone.
—MIKE DOUGLAS

Childhood—or a certain perception of it—has dominated this book.

This should not strike us as strange. Many of the works we have looked at were originally meant for youngsters, even though afterward their elders were included in that cheerful category of children-of-all-ages. Of course, along with this we have noted a tendency to infantilize the adult reader, to diminish the most complex dilemmas to simplified and simpleminded formulas. In fact, most of what we have been examining appears generally childish, in the specific sense that it uses its self-proclaimed innocence as a way of whitewashing—or is it rose-washing?—the world.

It's no accident that this infantile core emerges time and again in these essays dealing with some of the major successes of mass media culture. It has been constantly observed that the cultural industry, tailored to answer the simultaneous needs of immense groups of people, levels off its messages at the so-called lowest common denominator, creating only that which everybody can understand effortlessly. This common denominator (as has also been pointed out frequently) is based on a construct of—what else?—the median, quintessential North American common man, who has undergone secular canonization as the universal measure for humanity. What has not been so clearly stated is this: When that man is reduced to his average, shaved of his adult faculties and conflicting experiences, handed solutions that suckle and comfort him, robbed of his future, what is left is a babe, a dwindled, decreased human being.

Perhaps it is inevitable that the consumer should be treated as an infant, helpless and demanding, in societies such as ours. As a member of a democratic system, he has the right to vote and the even more important right and obligation to consume; but at the same time he is not really participating in the determination of his future or that of the world. People can be treated as children because they do not, in effect, control their own destiny. Even if they feel themselves to be utterly free, they are objectively vulnerable and dependent, passive in a world commandeered by others, a world where the messages they swallow have originated in other people's minds.

This is the concluding chapter of Dorfman's *The Empire's Old Clothes: What the Lone Ranger, Babar, and Other Innocent Heroes Do to Our Minds* (New York: Pantheon Books, 1983).

Logically, the childishness of the media might be seen as having its source in this particular structure. Such an explanation, though interesting, is insufficient, for the procedure by which the spectator is dwarfed to an infantile status has another component. It is accompanied by a strategy intent on enhancing and rewarding this reduction. It cannot be a coincidence that Disney, the superheroes, and *Reader's Digest* all propose to their readers, in one way or another, a rejuvenation of the tired adult world, the possibility of conserving some form of innocence as one grows up. Not only the characters, but also those who absorb them, are offered a fountain of eternal youth, Ponce de León in a pill. This is not the idea that prevails, let us note, in the world of Babar. There the children are miniature adults who must be kept in their places and helped to tread, without nostalgia, the road to maturity with the least possible pain. This may be due in part to the fact that Babar was not intended to be a standardized weekly or monthly production on the assembly line. But the real reason seems to lie elsewhere. The adult-as-spoiled-child of Donald Duck, or the innocent-in-the-body-of-the infinite-adult in Superman, or the reader-as-Adam-with-all-the-knowledge-of-Faust in the *Digest*—all complement and answer the needs of a subservient and passive consumer. They are also, significantly, all products of the United States of America, whose global preeminence—or perhaps I should say "coming of age"—has coincided with this century's technological leap in mass communication and left the United States in a very special position to use its media art to engender its most lasting and popular symbols. It is not simply a question of American economic power and know-how or the control of production and distribution by American multinationals. There is something else as well. The history of America, of the very particular sort of empire it became, seems to have allowed the process of the infantilization of the adult to be accompanied by images or intimations of innocence that were uniquely powerful and all its own. It may well be that such American images were reinforced by the magical, fairy-tale, ubiquitous quality of the media themselves, which could instantaneously transmit dreams and beliefs. The mass media added a new frontier, an unlimited, nonviolent one, to the prior unrelenting expansion of physical boundaries over a vast territory that could not be defended forever by its native inhabitants. Communication is a "peaceful" way of extending, of reaching out to those planetary outposts where military interventions previously had been the preferred way of ensuring free trade.

America has been interpreted, time and again, as the domain of innocence. In a sense, a more extraordinary feat than changing thirteen colonies into a global empire in less than two centuries is that the United States managed to do it without its people losing their basic intuition that they were good, clean, and wholesome. Its citizens never recognized themselves as an empire, never felt bound by the responsibility (or the moral corruption) that comes with the exercise of so much power. Unlike the Spanish, the French, and the English, they did not create permanent institutions with a set of rules, regulations, and doctrines to deal with their possessions, and, because it was more a question of the marketplace than an occupation of territory, did not feel the need to do so. It was enough if trade was regulated and armed might respected. The Americans wanted (and if William

Appleman Williams is right, were almost doomed to want) the spoils of empire, but they were not ready to assume the excruciating dilemmas that went with the knowledge of what they were imposing on others. They desired the power that can only come from being large, aggressive, and overwhelming; but simultaneously, they only felt comfortable if other people assented to the image they had of themselves as naive, frolicsome, unable to harm a mouse. Unlimited frontiers, abundance and plenty, the feeling of being reborn at every crossroads, led to the belief that growth and power need not relinquish, let alone destroy, innocence. Whatever obstructed or contradicted this vision was painted over by a curious sort of memory that reshaped the recent and receding past into myth as it moved. Conflicts could be cleaned up—by the brain if not by the body—before they become part of the future.

Americans felt themselves to be new and young, a country as recent as dawn, created by a break with the tyrannical past and the errors of yesteryear, by a revolutionary war that became a struggle for democracy, liberty, and a Bill of Rights. Along with this, of course, they, like all imperial peoples, upheld the concept of themselves as superior to, and certainly different from, the rest of humanity. Americans nurtured the belief that they were the last best hope for man, the saviors, the City on the Hill. But their dream of converting the heathen to the "true" way of life had a peculiar color to it, because they were inspired by the paradoxical certainty that they presented an example anyone could imitate as long as the whole world was turned into a marketplace. Deep inside, they believed alien cultures and lands were, or could be, identical to them. All those foreigners had to do was consume their products and they would become their exact mirror and equivalent.

If later on North Americans conceived of themselves as a "melting pot," they were animated from the beginning by the notion that the world could, in fact, be melted. Everybody and anybody could be renewed just as the United States had been. America imposed its experience of its own growth from anonymity in the wilderness onto the rest of humanity. If the world is a global village and we are all a family joined by tubes, wires, and voices, and moreover, if everybody is substantially an innocent, an unfinished, incomplete being waiting to unfold, then we can all evolve toward the same adulthood. We can become North Americans, unseparated by culture, interests, religions, creeds, races, ages. To become one, all we have to do is consume and dream the good dream.

It is this combination of infantilism and expansiveness, permitting Americans to view themselves as untainted children and the world as redeemable in their image, that may be the hidden fountain of much of America's mass media popularity. I am not denying the importance of production, ownership, artistic technique, talent, marketing practices, the use of simpleminded success formulas. I only think it's also true that, due to its own self-image, its historic development and what it learned about humankind during that development, America was able to project a universal category—childhood—onto alien cultures that were subjected politically and economically, and to seek in them infantile echoes, the yearning for redemption, innocence, and eternal life that, to one degree or another, are part of the constitution of all human beings. American mass culture appealed to the child the audience would like to be, the child they remembered, the child they still felt themselves at times to be.

There may, in fact, be more than an economic, psychological, and social basis for this sort of success. In spite of resistance from national cultures and diverse subcultures that have rejected homogenization, in spite of overwhelming elite and intellectual criticism of these works of fiction, the infantilization that seems to be such an essential centerpiece of mass media culture may be grounded in a certain form of human nature that goes beyond historical circumstances. The way in which American mass culture reaches out to people may touch on mechanisms embedded in our innermost being.

We are the only species, according to Stephen Jay Gould, that possesses neoteny.[1] *Homo sapiens* carries the features of the child into adult life. By doing so, it retains the evolutionary trend of primates, which led to our development. Other species change their faces radically, while humans conserve an amount of juvenility in them during their whole life span. Gould notes that Mickey Mouse followed this law of nature in his own evolution on the drawing table. He began his career in the late 1920s as a mischievous rascal with snoutlike, disreputable, elongated adult features; but as he "became increasingly well behaved over the years, his appearance became more youthful. Measurements of three stages in his development revealed a larger relative head size, larger eyes, and an enlarged cranium—all traits of juvenility." Mickey was accepted in society, became an adult, an ambassador, a symbol to one and all, a logos in the sky, and did so in the measure that he visually progressed—or, to be accurate, retrogressed—into childhood characteristics. Obviously, this was not something decided by anybody in particular. As Gould points out, it was a process that took fifty years. The draftsmen themselves were probably unaware of it.

Mickey does nothing more than go the way of all North American mass culture. He joins power and infantilization, expands his influence and at the same time retains (or regains) ingenuousness, lords it over everybody, and lets an innocent smile disarm all criticism. The famous mouse, like the mass culture into which he was born, automatically reconciles the adult and the child by appealing to a biological attribute in us, the fact that humans are instinctually conditioned to protect their young and are prepared by nature to react well to anything that resembles juvenility. The mass media, as we have defined them, may use and abuse this sense of inner or moral neoteny of the species, if I can venture such bizarre terms, to ensure their development and domination. It may be that just as our faces carry the traits of a certain youthfulness forever, so our minds and hearts also, in whatever culture, may open up to that which addresses our most tender feelings for our progeny and for the future. Social domination can create the need, but it could be that we are ultimately manipulated because we accept with all credulity that story or situation which keeps and guards, beyond death, the child burning inside.

Did I write that? The child burning inside?

But what of another sort of child? The real child, at home, at school, in the

1. See "A Biological Homage to Mickey Mouse," in Stephen Jay Gould, *The Panda's Thumb: More Reflections on Natural History* (New York: Norton, 1980).

streets, in bed waiting for a story, waking up in the morning ready for another story? What about him and her and them?

This book has been filled with childhood, but not with children.

It has tried to determine the adult values and hidden interests that shape and infect fiction for young readers. It has also explored the infantilization that the mass media seem to radiate onto adults. It has searched for the reasons why these forms are pernicious and why they are popular.

But it has not answered the basic question, a question that lingers.

Not: What is the relationship between ideology and entertainment? Not: How do empire and childhood go together? Not: What is the secret history of these forms?

Another question.

At the end of *Diary of a Madman*, Gogol's protagonist screams, as his last warning to mankind and the audience, "Save the children."

That is the basic question.

How do we save the children?

It is a question that cannot be postponed, and yet I would have liked to avoid it. The opening of practical, immediate issues that have no easy answers threatens to spoil the unity of this book, and I've always been obsessed with the need for coherence, confident that each loose end may be fit into an overview that will dispel problems and present a context for gratifying explanations. Faced with such an omnipotent and tentacular adversary, there is no little comfort in the act of denunciation and analysis, the feeling that, by disclosing all these secrets, we have at least dealt the enemy a stunning intellectual blow.

But reality—may the *Reader's Digest* forgive me—is not a puzzle that carries with it the guarantee, before we buy it, that every last piece we need to complete our picture is in the box. There can be no certainty that once we have performed all the jigsaw operations the final product will look anything like the sunny panorama on the cover.

After I have written the essays, after the reader has read them, we are still left with the messy, sticky, hauntingly unconvincible world—the real one. We lift our eyes from the words upon words and the children are still there.

Quite frankly, I do not know what to do with them.

Just because I am able to dissect these works, just because I am persuaded that they are detrimental to our well-being, just because I have spent years trying to put them in a framework that makes their origins comprehensible, does not mean that I am any closer than other readers may be to solving the bewildering problems posed by their very existence.

It is good to admit this confusion. I have the right to be, the need to be, perplexed. This is not a superbook, a Junior Woodchucks Manual, full of hints on how to do this or that. I refuse to consider my readers, or for that matter my children, as if they had to be saved by the sort of heroic act of wisdom on my part or that of their parents that would cast us in the role of the *Reader's Digest* or the Lone Ranger. Our young ones are at this very moment assimilating fiction that, under its pert and smiling guise, turns them into competitors, teaches them to see domination as the only alternative to subjection. They are learning sex roles, perverse and deformed visions of history, how to grow up, adapt, and succeed in the world as it presently is. They are learning not to ask questions.

The solution is neither to retire from the world nor to prohibit those reading or viewing activities. I have never (I hope I haven't ever) forbidden any sort of cultural wares in our house. My children buy, and will probably continue to buy if they feel like it, the very same dreams that I have so vigorously denounced. In one sense, this is mere realism. What else can they do? Turn their backs on what are the prevalent channels for reality in these times? Feel isolated from what is popular, from the ways in which society has enacted its conflicts, the destruction of inner fears, the feelings of love, the survival of nightmares? Are they to transform themselves into little geniuses, critical at every step, uneasy with their own emotions and friends, unable to speak the language with which their peers communicate? Are they to be so critical of society that they will be unable to live within its limits and limitations? Are they to parrot views that have not sprung from their own experience, that are simply repeated to make their elders feel more comfortable, less corrupted by the world?

Are they to live their lives or ours?

We cannot treat the children, or the adults who were once children and are still treated by the media as though they were underage, as lost souls who have been cannibalized, eaten up, devoured by the fiction they enjoy. The mere act of entering into contact with all these visions has not made them, has not made any of us, suspect forever or contaminated beyond relief.

People are never "lost," as the mass media would have us believe.

I once proclaimed—it was at the Russell Tribunal on Latin America in Rome, and I was trying to impart the reasons why I thought the Chilean people had the means to defend their culture—that if the black magic of the television screen or the comic book is everywhere, invading every outlet of reality, there also persisted the white magic of people, waves made out of the capacity of thousands to renovate, rebel, criticize. Such a statement smacks today of oversimplification. The enemy is inside, and we find it hard to distinguish him from some of our innermost thoughts and nurturings. We have been produced by the same world that produced the *Digest*, Babar, Superman, Mampato, and Donald Duck. We have grown accustomed to the way they whisper to us, dawning in our eyes as a second nature does, a second and secondary humanity of which we become aware only when we try to change it. But that does not mean that my initial, oversimplified statement holds no value. Because people *are* everywhere, this is also true, and there is in them a decency, a humanness that is always on the verge of getting out of hand, a dangerous addiction to humor and sanity and—if I can rescue this term—common sense. There is in men and women a deep refusal to be manipulated. We have in ourselves intimations of another humanity, and from it we can build, we have been building since there has been memory.

We do not have to wait for tomorrow to launch this small, modest crusade.

Of course, if far-reaching and radical modifications were to occur in society and in art, the media as we now know them would be unrecognizable. More democratic societies would automatically limit or perhaps even cancel the sway that these pseudoimaginings have on us. Not only would people be better able to control the sources of the power that generates what is being served to them and their children as entertainment, but they would also find that the experience of being in command of their own existence shows up the dominant myths, makes those myths foreign and alien instead of familiar and comforting. If such a change in the social situation were accompanied, or anticipated, by changes in the ways of making art, there would also exist an alternative vision, created by teams and individuals in an elite or by millions elaborating their own participatory, multiple, plural counterimages. People who are aware of their identity, or who have come to learn it in the process of growing out of the colors and habits defined for them by others, do not have to escape their grim circumstances through dreams; like that woman from the slums, they can dream reality.

But let us insist that such long-range alterations, such a blueprint for the future, the practicality and availability of which will depend on the real choices each person must make, do not have to be waited for. It is precisely in the prolonged, confused, stuttering attempt to reach that other humanity that we discover the means, the platform, the vision, the strength by which we can differentiate ourselves from what we have been assured we are by those who seek to control our beliefs and emotions.

In a sense, every action we take each day can be of assistance on the long road toward the transformation of those dominant messages. The very way in which we live our lives, in which we judge, or love, or pardon, or understand, or stand up for what we believe in, the ways in which we try to model our own private worlds, can introduce, for the receptive child and anybody else, in the damnable middle of our web of tangled visions, a different, defiant point of view. This sort of influence may encourage more independence than can the directing of solemn attention, through intellectual arguments, to each trick or pitfall in mass media culture. The very popularity, the very innocence that such entertainment has fostered, representing itself as a fun-filled and secluded oasis, far from the everyday swamps of boredom, makes all raids seem a form of proselytizing or propaganda. This does not mean that we must renounce our right to read along with our children. Anybody can break into the closed bunkers and place the seeds of doubt, laughter, justice, rage. We can return to the accumulated treasures of our species, the artistic wonders that stir mysteries and crack conformism. And just in case anybody is suggesting that I am against the use of reason, certain structures can be gently pointed out; they can be countered; they can be brought into the open and discussed.

But above all, and without blushing, without sounding like one of the products I have been analyzing, I say that we must have faith in our children. They have to be able—with the challenge of our assistance, with our respect for the pain it entails, with our own fuzzy limits between what is true and what is false, with the mutual patience that comes from building together a future for which no insurance policy can be bought—stubbornly to reinterpret reality.

We have told many stories in this book.

Most of them have not been to our liking.

Maybe there is time, before we finish, for one more. It comes from the Greeks and advises us, thousands of years after it was first conceived, on how to slay monsters.

The dominant media and their fictions are somewhat like the Medusa that Perseus had to destroy.

The Medusa had once been a wondrous maiden, but the gods had made her so hideous that she could turn into stone anyone who looked her in the face. To kill her, remember, you must not look her in the eyes. She will convince you to chain yourself to her body, convert your heart to rock and your mind to sand. But also remember that you cannot be rid of her if you are not prepared to see her, to guide the sword hand with the eyes. If you live outside her scope and the influence of her overwhelming enchantment and horror, of "the loveliness like a shadow" that Shelley gave her in his verse, you will certainly fail.

You cannot kill her if you look; and if you do not look, you will not kill her.

Perseus solved this riddle by watching the monster's reflection in the shield that Athena, the goddess of wisdom, had conferred on him. Then he cut off the Gorgon's head.

We, too, have shields that can be used as mirrors.

Reflect the head in the mirror; accept and understand it; cut it off. Carry it with you all your life, because even after death the Medusa can still exercise that frightening power. Your actions and the art you enjoy can be mirrors; your children, your loves, your friends, your causes are mirrors that allow you to see the head obliquely, with your back turned, fully within the hissing breath, advancing crablike so as not to be destroyed.

I hope, in fact, that this book could be used as one of our mirrors, a fragment of glass to help us on our way.

But this is not the only story.

For what is a tale in a book like this one without children, without descendants? . . . Many years later, decades later, the great-grandson of Perseus was born. His name was Hercules. One of his specialties seems to have been the slaughtering of monsters.

The second of the twelve tasks he was commanded to perform was to kill the Hydra, a colossal serpent with nine heads, the middle one of which was immortal.

It was deemed impossible.

Each time he clubbed one of the heads, two more grew in its place. Assisted, however, by his nephew Iolaus (I hope the Disney corporation is satisfied that we have somehow managed to smuggle a nephew into this legend), he was able to burn all the heads but one with a red-hot sword. That final, immortal one was cut off and buried under a rock.

So this is a story in which we use our mirrors today and in which our children's children draw their swords tomorrow.

It is a story that should alarm us. The struggle that is offered is almost endless, and not easy. Heads multiply and blossom forth. To attack them is to help them gain strength. Even after they have been cut off, they continue to harden people and make them weary. And there is something in the monster that will not die, that will threaten underfoot no matter how deeply it is buried.

But listen. Listen closely.

Is there any place in that story where it is said that the heads of the monster are infinite? Is there any place where it says that the monster is invincible?

Part III
Moments of Historical Consciousness

INTRODUCTION

Left studies of particular works in various moments of American history reveal a sequence of adaptations of the basic mythology outlined in the previous section relative to the changing times. Indeed, American cultural and intellectual history, as well as scholarship about them, can be viewed as one long series of variations in what Marxist historian William Appleman Williams calls the Great Evasion of direct criticism of the ideology that equates democracy with a capitalist economy and its attendant rapacious individualism. Recent critics have traced these variations back to the nineteenth-century roots of American mass culture; our survey, though, begins with Charles Eckert's essay "Shirley Temple and the House of Rockefeller," in which he contrasts the financial and social bases of the film industry with the ideology purveyed by the Hollywood dream factory in its classic period of the thirties, a theme that at the time of his death in 1976 Eckert was developing into a book to be called *Hollywood and the Great Depression: Studies in Class, Style, and Ideology*.

Leonard Quart's article "Frank Capra and the Popular Front" sums up the present left perspective on the Popular Front liberalism of the late thirties and World War II years. In the Popular Front mentality, whether as a product of the general consciousness of the period or as the calculated line of Communist party writers in Hollywood and elsewhere, the values of mass culture shifted from middle-class consumerism toward working-class (or, more often, petit bourgeois) populism. Big businessmen and politicians were now at least sometimes portrayed as greedy, corrupt, or even fascistic. Yet, the capitalist system itself was rarely questioned, and the typical Popular Front dénouement affirmed its basic soundness in spite of its flaws and abusers—as did Roosevelt's New Deal. The honest businessman or political leader, Mr. Deeds or Mr. Smith, prevails over the evil ones, just as in the eighties good Bobby Ewing prevails over wicked J. R. on "Dallas." In *The Devil and Miss Jones* (1941), a hard-nosed department store owner, played by Charles Coburn, infiltrates his employees in disguise to ferret out union organizers but ends up being won over to their cause and turning into a benevolent paternalist. Preston Sturges, Hollywood's sharpest political satirist, was a Menckenian conservative chiding the "booboisie"; his filmmaker hero in *Sullivan's Travels* (1941) disguises himself as a hobo to explore proletarian America as research for a documentary of social significance, but he concludes that he can better serve the downtrodden masses by providing them with the escapist comedy they crave. Films with international themes, such as *Mission to Moscow* (1943), might have grotesquely sentimentalized Uncle Joe Stalin, but on the domestic front none went so far as to advocate socialism or revolution.[1] The outer limit of Popular Front leftism was what Russell Campbell calls the "wishy-washy class solidarity" of *The Grapes of Wrath*, which vaguely stands up for "the people" without envisioning their organizing politically and which creates in Tom Joad another version of the American monomythic hero, this time a kind of working-class Lone Ranger.[2] Ironically, even the most wishy-washy Popular

Front producers and products were branded subversive during the McCarthy period.

In the fifties the House Un-American Activities Committee hearings and Hollywood and television blacklists obliterated even the most equivocal Popular Front leftism. The cultural cold war restored uncontested hegemony to the traditional mythology of capitalism, whether in the crude propaganda of the *I Married a Communist* genre or in the coded versions of the monster movies, westerns, and family psychodramas analyzed in two excellent recent books on the period, Nora Sayre's *Running Time* and Peter Biskind's *Seeing is Believing*. Biskind's definitive essay "The Politics of Power in *On the Waterfront*," included here, finds in that movie a paradigm of the period's themes: the disappearance of businessmen and politicians as villains—or in any capacity (as Biskind notes, the Mr. Big central to Popular Front films makes such a brief appearance in *Waterfront* as to be missed if one blinks); the identification of organized labor with crime and Communism; the domestication and integration into bourgeois life of the rebellious working-class male under the auspices of a good woman; the reversion from collective to individual problems and solutions, reiterated in Marlon Brando's interiorized acting style, which itself became one of the symbols of the fifties. *On the Waterfront* depoliticized overtly political subject matter, but the more common pattern was avoidance of political subjects altogether. Sayre's chapter "The Private Sector" in *Running Time* traces the reduction of social conflict in fifties films to unhappy family life and the inability to love or communicate, establishing the climate to be described by Phillip Rieff as the triumph of the therapeutic and by Christopher Lasch as a culture of narcissism.[3]

In the sixties, the New Left (as distinguished from the counterculture) made little direct impact on mass entertainment media, aside from folk and rock music (see Simon Frith's evaluation of the politics of rock in Part 4); the media made the predictable accommodations to and containments of the civil rights and feminist movements, in ways such as those discussed here by Kate Ellis in "Gimme Shelter: Feminism, Fantasy, and Women's Popular Fiction." And in retrospect there appears to be far more continuity than difference between the youth-oriented sixties counterculture and the mass culture of the preceding and succeeding decades. In the seventies, Terry Malloy of *On the Waterfront* became Tony Manero of *Saturday Night Fever* or Rocky, but as Biskind and Barbara Ehrenreich note here in "Machismo and Hollywood's Working Class," these ever more depoliticized incarnations of the working-class hero continued to be viewed through middle-class lenses as noble savages of purely individual defiance. *Saturday Night Fever* hinted at a leftist theme in its hero's realization of the way various segments of the urban lumpenproletariat are set hierarchically against each other: "Everyone's dumping on someone else"—men and women, ethnic whites, blacks, and latinos. But rather than draw a conclusion with even the vague class solidarity of the heroes in *The Grapes of Wrath* or *On the Waterfront*, Tony Manero seeks only personal escape from Bay Ridge parochialism to Manhattan cosmopolitanism. Biskind and Ehrenreich claim ironically that in the climate of lowered economic expectations in the seventies the John Travolta character had less chance for upward mobility than Terry Malloy did and that only personal growth could be his goal in the Me Generation—"Werner Erhard replaces Horatio Alger." They fail to foresee the obvious solution developed in the sequel: Tony Manero becomes a John Travolta–like dancing star.

By the eighties, the old formulas were wearing out under the strain of general socioeconomic atrophy and the overproduction demanded by omnivorous commercial media. This development had some progressive consequences, such as the attempt on some television programs, "Hill Street Blues" and "Cagney and Lacey" for example, to work against stereotypical conventions—the liberal tendency that so bothered conservatives may have been more attributable to producers' desperate quest for novelty than to their political bias. But the dominant mood in television and other media—as in the national economy—was stagnation, a mood that Todd Gitlin, in an *Inside Prime Time* chapter called "The Triumph of the Synthetic: Spinoffs, Copies, Recombinant Culture," has related to the exhaustion of modernist high culture in this literally *fin de siècle* period.

The undeniable liberalizing trend in the seventies and eighties has occurred simultaneously with conflicting tendencies charted by left critics toward authoritarianism, vigilantism, every-man-for-himself survivalism, and the steady militarizing of everyday culture that mirrors the nuclear arms race and the anarchic spread of domestic crime.[4] (To be sure, a sense of proportion must be retained toward alarmist inclinations on both left and right in what has been, since Vietnam and Watergate, a relatively tranquil, unrepressive period in America—at least on the surface of public events.) Philip Wander finds a protofascist sensibility in the aesthetic motifs of bloodshed and of supernal individual fortitude in films like *Patton, The Deer Hunter*, and even the ostensibly antiwar *Apocalypse Now*.[5] Similarly, beneath the liberal intergalactic benevolence of Steven Spielberg's *Close Encounters of the Third Kind* and *E. T.*, left critics have seen reactionary antirationalism and reversion to the will to believe in superhuman sources of both evil and salvation.[6] In their forthcoming book on ideology in recent Hollywood films, Douglas Kellner and Michael Ryan trace the confused mix of disapproval and approval toward the military in films such as *Sergeant Benjamin, An Officer and a Gentleman, War Games*, and *The Killing Fields*.

Likewise, Dan Rubey sees George Lucas's *Star Wars* films as trying to have it both ways: "The good guys are supporters of a hierarchical, Imperial system with kings and princesses on the level of patriarchal fantasy, but supporters of the Republic and democracy on the level of the literal plot, a way to have your authoritarian cake and eat it too."[7] About the climax of *Star Wars*, in which Luke Skywalker calls on a combination of scientific expertise and the mystical Force to place the shot that destroys the Empire's space station, Rubey notes:

> By placing such an apocalyptic weight on the actions of one individual, the film demonstrates both the importance of individualism to the fantasy system and the difficulty in the late 1970's of creating a plot in which individual action can have convincing consequences for the society as a whole. Laser swords and guns and one-man fighters are the weapons of *Star Wars* because they are the weapons of individual combat, the equipment of fantasies in which things can be changed, outcomes significantly affected by one per-

son. . . . By setting things up this way, Lucas denies that people need to work collectively, or long, or even very hard for change. Individual heroism, at one spot, in one heroic moment, can win the war.[8]

The same faith in an individual savior projected into the future in *Star Wars* was projected into the immediate past of Vietnam in *Rambo* and into the present in Charles Bronson's *Death Wish* and Clint Eastwood's "Dirty Harry" films.

"Post-Watergate morality" saw greater cynicism toward authority portrayed in media than in any period since the thirties; by now the CIA or big business turned up occasionally as the stock villain in film or TV dramas rather than the KGB. In a 1982 film remake of Mickey Spillane's *I the Jury*, Mike Hammer has become an urban-ethnic Vietnam veteran whose former combat buddy is murdered as part of a nefarious CIA-Mafia operation. The rabid anticommunism of some of Spillane's original books has been replaced by universal paranoia: the 1980s-model Mike Hammer is the jury and avenger against anyone and everyone and has moved from the fringes of vigilante fantasy far closer to the American mainstream in the age of survivalism. Similar anarchism has been visible in films like *Alien*, *Blade Runner*, *Videodrome*, and *The Terminator* about killer androids in the service of any and all political interests but inclined to assert their independence by going free-lance in killing. Such is the endpoint of a culture that has systematically precluded consideration of any alternative solutions to social problems other than unrestrained individualism.

R. G. Davis's "Rethinking Guerrilla Theater, 1971, 1985" (Part 8) laments the political vacuousness of American oppositional theater and other performing arts in the eighties. One might add that the decline of Broadway theater into overpriced distraction for affluent suburbanites has only been compounded by putative recent alternatives like Lincoln Center in New York, the Kennedy Center for the Performing Arts in Washington, and the Los Angeles Music Center, which, with the exception of a few lively productions, have proved to be mausoleums of a moribund theatrical tradition. Their architectural opulence only spotlights the urban squalor amid which they are set and the political and intellectual poverty of the productions they mount. Meanwhile, servile media critics continue to hail each new mediocrity as a masterpiece.

Composer-lyricist Stephen Sondheim can be considered an emblematic artist of the American eighties. Sondheim's Broadway musical comedies are audacious but sterile efforts at pumping life into a genre whose vitality died with the great generation of George and Ira Gershwin, Cole Porter, Irving Berlin, Jerome Kern, Richard Rodgers, Lorenz Hart, Oscar Hammerstein, Harold Arlen, and E. Y. Harburg. Sondheim's coldly aestheticized retelling of *Sweeney Todd*, the demon barber who takes his revenge against social injustice by cutting his customers up to sell them in meat pies, holds the mirror up to the American *fin de siècle*; it is Jacobean melodrama trying futilely to be Shakespearean tragedy, Brechtian epic theater purged of political meaning for a Broadway audience that will presumably be less offended by the sight of throats being slit than by the mention of the words *class society*. John Lahr aptly sums up Sondheim and the eighties:

From My-Lai to El Salvador, the American public has become casual about absorbing catastrophe. And Sondheim has turned this numbed anguish into a mass product. His musicals claim victory for themselves as new departures, but they are the end of the musical's glorious tradition of trivialization. Sondheim's cold elegance matches the spiritual pall that has settled over American life. His musicals are chronicles in song of the society's growing decrepitude. They foreshadow the newest barbarism—a nation that has no faith in the peace it seeks or the pleasure it finds.[9]

Notes

1. See John Cogley, ed. *Report on Blacklisting*, vol. 1: *The Movies* (New York: Fund for the Republic, 1956).

2. Russell Campbell, "The Ideology of the Social Consciousness Movie: Three Films by Darryl F. Zanuck," *Quarterly Review of Film Studies* 3, no. 1 (1978): 49–71. See also the other articles in this special issue entitled "The Material History of Movies," including Charles Eckert's "The Carole Lombard in Macy's Window."

3. On the narcissism of the fifties in the United States and in Europe, especially as criticized by Camus in *The Fall*, see "Camus and the American Reader," in Donald Lazere, *The Unique Creation of Albert Camus* (New Haven, Conn.: Yale University Press, 1973), pp. 236–242.

4. See "The Militarization of Everyday Life," *Tabloid*, no. 4 (1981): 3–17; "Militarization Update," *Tabloid*, no. 7 (1983): 1–13; and Stan Takahashi, "G.I. Joe Comes Back," *In These Times*, 31 March 1982, p. 16.

5. Philip Wander, "The Aesthetics of Fascism," *Journal of Communication* 33, no. 2 (1983): 70–78.

6. Robert Entman and Francis Seymour, "Close Encounters with the Third Reich," *Jump Cut*, no. 18 (1978): 9–14.

7. Dan Rubey, "*Star Wars*: Not So Far Away," *Jump Cut*, no. 18 (1978): 12.

8. Ibid., p. 11.

9. John Lahr, *Automatic Vaudeville* (New York: Knopf, 1984), p. 21.

Further Readings

Early Twentieth Century

Alexander, William. *Film on the Left: American Documentary Film from 1931 to 1942*. Princeton, N.J.: Princeton University Press, 1981.

Bergman, Andrew. *We're In The Money—Depression America and Its Films*. New York: Harper & Row, 1971.

Campbell, Russell. *Cinema Strikes Back: Radical Filmmaking in the United States, 1930–1942*. Ann Arbor, Mich.: UMI Research Press, 1983.

Covert, Catherine L., and John P. Stevens, eds. *Mass Media Between the Wars: Perceptions of Cultural Tensions, 1918–1941*. Syracuse, N.Y.: Syracuse University Press, 1984.

Ewen, Elizabeth. *Immigrant Women in the Land of Dollars: Life and Culture on the Lower East Side*. New York: Monthly Review Press, 1985.

Lears, T. J. Jackson. *No Place of Grace: Anti-Modernism and the Transformation of American Culture, 1880–1920*. New York: Pantheon Books, 1982.

Marchand, Roland. *Advertising the American Dream: Making Way for Modernity, 1920–1940*. Berkeley and Los Angeles: University of California Press, 1985.

May, Lary. *Screening Out the Past: The Birth of Mass Culture and the Motion Picture Industry*. New York: Oxford University Press, 1980.

The Forties and Fifties

Aronson, James. *The Press and the Cold War*. Indianapolis: Bobbs-Merrill, 1970.

Bentley, Eric. *Are You Now or Have You Ever Been?* New York: Harper & Row, 1972.

Biskind, Peter. *Seeing Is Believing*. New York: Pantheon Books, 1983.

Blum, John Morton. *"V" Was for Victory: Politics and American Culture During World War II*. New York: Harcourt Brace Jovanovich, 1976.

Bogart, Leo. *Premises for Propaganda: The U.S. Information Agency's Operating Assumptions in the Cold War*. New York: Free Press, 1976.

Dowdy, Andrew. *The Films of the Fifties—The American State of Mind*. New York: Morrow, 1973.

French, Brandon. *On the Verge of Revolt—Women in American Films of the Fifties*. New York: Ungar, 1978.

Hellman, Lillian. *Scoundrel Time*. Boston: Little, Brown, 1976.

Honey, Maureen. *Creating Rosie the Riveter: Class, Gender and Propaganda During World War II*. Amherst: University of Massachusetts Press, 1984.

Jezer, Marty. *The Dark Ages: Life in the United States 1945–1960*. Boston: South End Press, 1982.

Lasch, Christopher. "The Cultural Cold War." In *The Agony of the American Left*. New York: Knopf, 1968.

Lipsitz, George. *Class and Culture in Cold War America—"A Rainbow at Midnight."* South Hadley, Mass.: Bergin, 1982.

MacDonald, J. Fred. *Television and the Red Menace: The Video Road to Vietnam*. New York: Praeger, 1985.

Murry, Lawrence. "Monsters, Spies, and Subversives: The Film Industry Responds to the Cold War, 1945–1955." *Jump Cut*, no. 9 (October–December 1975): 14–76.

Navasky, Victor S. *Naming Names*. New York: Viking, 1980.

Quart, Leonard, and Albert Auster. *American Film and Society Since 1945*. New York: Praeger, 1984.

Rogin, Michael. "Ronald Reagan's American Gothic." *democracy* 1, no. 1 (1981): 51–59.

———. "Kiss Me Deadly: Communism, Motherhood, and Cold War Movies." *Representations*, no. 6 (Spring 1984): 1–36.

Sayre, Nora. *Running Time: Films of the Cold War*. New York: Dial Press, 1982.

Trumbo, Dalton. *Time of the Toad: Study of Inquisition in America*. New York: Harper & Row, 1972.

Wolf, Allen L. *The Hollywood Musical Goes to War*. Chicago: Nelson-Hall, 1983.

The Sixties to the Present

Dickstein, Morris. *Gates of Eden: American Culture in the Sixties*. New York: Basic Books, 1977.

Greifinger, Joel. "Midflight Cowboy: Review of 'Empire Strikes Back.'" *Socialist Review*, no. 53 (September–October 1980): 132–144.

"The House of Mirrors: American Women as Reflected in the Magazines They Read" (symposium). *In These Times*, 8 March 1978.

Kellner, Douglas, and Michael Ryan. *Camera Politica: The Politics and Ideology of Contemporary Hollywood Film*. Bloomington: Indiana University Press, 1987.

Rogin, Michael. *Ronald Reagan the Movie and Other Episodes in Political Demonology*. Berkeley and Los Angeles: University of California Press, 1987.

Sayres, Sonya, Anders Stephanson, Stanley Aronowitz, and Fredric Jameson, eds. *The 60s Without Apology*. Minneapolis: University of Minnesota Press, 1984.

Willis, Ellen. *Beginning to See the Light—Pieces of a Decade*. New York: Knopf, 1981.

General Historical Surveys

Czitrom, Daniel J. *Media and the American Mind*. Chapel Hill: University of North Carolina Press, 1982.

Fox, Richard Wightman, and T. J. Jackson Lears, eds. *The Culture of Consumption: Critical Essays in American History 1880–1980*. New York: Pantheon Books, 1983.

MacDonald, J. Fred. *Don't Touch That Dial: Radio Programming in American Life from 1920 to 1960*. Chicago: Nelson-Hall, 1979.

Ray, Robert B. *A Certain Tendency of the Hollywood Cinema, 1930–1980*. Princeton, N.J.: Princeton University Press, 1985.

Roffman, Peter, and Jim Purdy. *The Hollywood Social Problem Film: Madness, Despair, and Politics from the Depression to the Fifties*. Bloomington: Indiana University Press, 1981.

Susman, Warren I. *Culture as History: The Transformation of American Society in the Twentieth Century*. New York: Pantheon Books, 1985.

Williams, William Appleman. *The Great Evasion*. Chicago: Quadrangle Books, 1964.

SHIRLEY TEMPLE AND THE HOUSE OF ROCKEFELLER

CHARLES ECKERT

Through the mid-Depression years of 1934 to 1938, Shirley Temple was a phenomenon of the first magnitude: she led in box office grosses, single-handedly revived Fox and influenced its merger with Twentieth Century, had more products named after her than any other star, and became as intimately experienced here and abroad as President Roosevelt. Her significance was then, and has been ever since, accounted for by an appeal to universals—to her cuteness, her precocious talents, her appeal to parental love, and so forth. But one can no more imagine her having precisely the same effect on audiences of any other decade of this century than one can imagine Clint Eastwood and William S. Hart exchanging personas.

One would not feel impelled to state so tawdry a truism if it were not for the resistance one anticipates to a serious study of Shirley Temple, and especially to a study that regards her, in part, as a kind of artifact thrown up by a unique concatenation of social and economic forces. One anticipates resistance because, first of all, Shirley was a child (and therefore uncomplex, innocent of history) and, second, the sense of the numinous that surrounds her is unlike that which surrounds cultural heroes or political leaders in that it is deeply sentimental and somehow purified.

But this very numinosity, this sense of transcendental and irrational significance, if we measure it only by its degree, should alert us to the fact that we are dealing with a highly overdetermined object (in the Freudian sense of an object affected by more than one determinant). A search for external determinants, however, initially faces a difficult paradox: there is no evidence in any of Shirley's films or in anything contemporaneously written about her that she was touched by the realities of the Depression. For instance, in the mid-thirties, when twenty million were on relief, Shirley woke in the morning singing a song entitled "Early Bird"; in the brutally demanding business of filmmaking, she thought everyone was playing games; and as for economics, Shirley thought a nickel was worth more than a dollar.

All of this would be intimidating if it were not that external determinants often cannot be perceived in a finished object, whether that determinant be the repression that produces a pun or the sweated labor that produces a shirt. And Shirley in film and story was as highly finished an object as a Christmas tree ornament. Some contemporary libels against her, which depicted her as a thirty-year-old dwarf or as bald-headed, and the irreverences of critics who called her a "pint-size Duse" or the moppet with the "slightly sinister repertoire of tricks" show that the surface was often too perfect to be accepted and that deceit was

From *Jump Cut*, no. 2 (July–August 1974).

suspected. But libels are not theories, and everything written about Shirley was ultimately helpless to explain her—or to exorcise her.

We might begin to chip at her surface (analytically, not iconoclastically) by noting that the industry she worked in was possibly more exposed to influences emanating from society, in particular from its economic base, than any other. To the disruption of production, distribution, and consumption shared by all industries one must add the intense economically determined ideological pressures that bore upon an industry whose commodities were emotions and ideas. Politicians directly charged Hollywood with the task of "cheering Americans up"; and such studio ideologues as Jack Warner and Louis B. Mayer gloried in their new roles as shapers of public attitudes. But far more significant pressures arose out of the grim economic histories of the major studios, all of which by 1936 had come under the financial control of either Morgan or Rockefeller financial interests (F. D. Klingender, *Money Behind the Screen*, 1937). In addition to rendering films more formulaic and innocuous, this domination drew Hollywood into a lackeying relation to the most conservative canons of capitalist ideology.

It is not my intention to recount this history, but rather to assess its effects on the content of Shirley's films and her public persona. To do this systematically I must first survey a portion of the economic history for the period 1930–1934 and describe the ideology it gave rise to. At this point my study will move synchronically, from the economic base through the ideology to Shirley Temple (her first feature films were made in 1934). I will then hedge on the synchrony by including films from 1935 and 1936 (on the pretext that Shirley's films conservatively repeated situations and themes).

ECONOMICS AND IDEOLOGY

The most persistent specter that the Depression offered to those who had come through the crash with some or most of their fortunes intact was not, as it turned out, that of Lenin or of Mussolini, although articles on communism and fascism filled the magazines, but that of a small child dressed in welfare clothing, looking, as he was usually depicted, like a gaunt Jackie Coogan, but unsmiling, unresponsive, pausing to stare through the windows of cafeterias or grocery stores— his legs noticeably thin and his stomach slightly swollen. This specter had thousands of incarnations. "We were practicing for a chorus and a little boy about twelve years old was in the front line. He was clean in his overalls, but didn't have very much on under them. He was standing in the line when all at once he pitched forward in a dead faint. This was two o'clock in the afternoon . . . He had not had anything to eat since the day before." "Mrs. Schmidt took her son Albert, five years old, into the kitchen and turned on the gas. . . . 'I don't know what I am going to give the children to eat,' said a note she had written for her husband. 'They are already half starved. I think it best to go into eternity and take little Albert along.'" "Five hundred school children, most with haggard faces and in tattered clothes, paraded through Chicago's downtown section . . . to demand that the school system provide them with food." "I love children and have often wanted to have children of my own. But to have one now, as I am going to, is almost more than I can stand. . . . I have four step-children, so there are six in my family. I have suffered so much in the past few years, and have seen my family suffer for even enough food. . . . I need fruit and milk and vegetables. I need rest. I need yards of material for shirts and gowns. I have no blankets. I need baby clothes. . . . I hate charity . . . but my condition now forces me not only to take charity but even to ask for it."

These children are, of course, symbolic, in the context of both the Depression and this article. What they symbolized was the flashpoint of the millions on relief who showed themselves, early on in the Depression, largely immune to acts of revolt and willing to tough out the hard times if their children's minimal needs for food and clothing could be met. In November 1930, Hoover was forced to reply to the observation by the White House Conference on Child Health and Protection that six million American children were chronically undernourished. "But that we not be discouraged," he said, "let us bear in mind that there are thirty-five million reasonably normal, cheerful human electrons, radiating joy and mischief and hope and faith. Their faces are turned toward the light— theirs is the life of great adventure. These are the vivid, romping everyday children, our own and our neighbors'." This may have washed with some at this early stage of the Depression, but later on the tactics had to be more frontal. "No One Is Starving," the *New York Times* and *Herald Tribune* announced in front page headlines on March 17, 1932. This was the substance of telegrams from thirty-nine governors. The issue of starvation was debated, and many cases of death by starvation were adduced by newspapers; but the statement, which begged the issues of chronic malnutrition and near-starvation, was essentially true—and it was vitally important for those in positions of wealth and power that it remain so.

To this end, the most minimal subsistence needs had to be provided. As the estimate of those needing help rose, reaching about twenty million on the eve of the election in 1932, it became increasingly likely that a federal relief program would have to be inaugurated. But to the captains of industry and the traditionally wealthy who made up Hoover's official and private entourages, the prospect of massive federal relief was dismaying. All of the initial reactions of Hoover and the class he so steadfastly represented had been self-serving. Tariffs were placed on foreign imports, absurdly low income taxes on the wealthy were reduced even further, and federal reserves were hoarded in a miserly fashion or loaned at reduced rates to select banks and industries. The remedy for the Depression, the country was told, lay in the protection and, where possible, the augmentation of the capital resources of the wealthy, for these resources were the key to renewed economic growth and revived employment.

Such naked opportunism at so desperate an hour had to be dressed in emperor's clothes of the finest make—and Hoover and his supporters spent most of their time spinning and sewing. What they fashioned was a formidable ideological garment constructed of the following materials. The economy of the country was fueled, not by labor, but by money: those who possessed money would bring the country out of the Depression as their confidence was restored by a protective and solicitous government. If the needy millions were served instead, a double blow would be struck at the nation's strength. First of all, the capital resources of the government and of the wealthy (who would have to be taxed) would be depleted; second, the moral fiber of those who received relief would be weakened—perhaps beyond repair.

The latter argument, less amenable to mystification because it was not couched in financial terms, needed more than simple assertion to give it weight. Recourse was therefore made to the deities who dwelled in the deepest recesses of the capitalist ethos. Initiative, Work, and Thrift were summoned forth, blinking at the light. An accusing finger was pointed at England, where the dole had robbed thousands of any interest in self-help. Hoover's attacks on the evils of relief were echoed at the state and local levels, and it became common to insist that those who received relief, even a single meal, do some work in compensation, such as sweeping streets. This demeaning, utterly alienating "work" became one of the most common experiences of the Depression—and one of its scandals.

Early in the Depression William Green, president of the American Federation of Labor, led organized labor in denouncing the dole and unemployment insurance as "paternalistic, demoralizing and destructive." Governor Roosevelt of New York, thinking of the votes he would need to get in the White House, asked in fall 1931 for an increase in state taxes to give "necessary food, clothing and shelter" but noted that "under no circumstances shall any actual money be paid in the form of a dole." "What an incredible absurdity," observed a writer in *The Nation.* "What is there about cold cash that makes a man like Governor Roosevelt think that giving dollar bills to a starving man or woman is worse for his character than presenting him with a suit of clothes which he might buy for himself?" Indeed, the only ones who seemed to be taken in by the argument that relief destroyed character were reactionary governors and grim county relief agents.

Clearly some other ideological weapon was needed, one that could effect material changes in conditions rather than merely mask the hardened indifference of the Hoover administration. And one was found, calculatedly developed, and financed with some of the cold cash that was anathema to the poor. Declaring that "no one with a spark of sympathy can contemplate unmoved the possibilities of suffering," Hoover, late in 1931, appointed Walter S. Gifford director of the President's Organization on Unemployment Relief and Owen D. Young chairman of the Committee on Mobilization of Relief Resources. In their official capacities they took out a series of full page advertisements in major magazines.

> Tonight, Say This to Your Wife,
> Then Look into Her Eyes!
>
> "I gave a lot more than we had planned. Are you angry?"
>
> If you should tell her that you merely "contributed"—that you gave no more than you really felt obligated to—her eyes will tell you nothing. But deep down in her woman's heart she will feel just a little disappointed—a tiny bit ashamed.
>
> But tonight—*confess* to her that you have dug into the very bottom of your pocket— that you gave perhaps a little *more* than you could afford—that you opened not just your purse, but your heart as well.
>
> In her eyes you'll see neither reproach nor anger. *Trust* her to understand. . . .

It is true—the world *respects* the man who lives within his income. But the world *adores* the man who *gives* BEYOND his income.

No—when you tell her that you have given somewhat *more* than you had planned, you will see no censure in her eyes. But *love*!

> *The President's Organization on Unemployment Relief*
> *Walter S. Gifford, Director*
> *Committee on Mobilization of Relief Resources*
> *Owen D. Young, Chairman*

The vulgarity of this charade can be more fully appreciated if we know that Gifford was president of AT & T and Young chairman of the board of directors of General Electric. This attempt to shift the burden of charitable work to the middle class and the poor was, ironically, unnecessary. As a reporter observed at a later date, "In Philadelphia, as in most other cities, the poor are taking care of the poor." But face-saving was the order of the day, and to the advertisements and the repeated appeals to local charities by Hoover one must add the many charity balls, at one of which debutantes wore hobo clothes and dined at red-and-white-checkered tables on cornbread and hotdogs.

Then there were, of course, the publicized, and the modestly unpublicized, donations to charity of the wealthy. In March 1933 when the income tax statistics for 1931 were finally published, a *Nation* reporter noted: "The results are startling, even to those who never had much faith in the philanthropy of the wealthy." The figures "destroy completely the myth of the generosity of America's millionaires." What they specifically showed was that contributions were usually of an order that reduced net taxable income to a favorable level—and no more.

In fact, the endorsement of charity by those in power served to increase the attacks on the concept of welfare. Early in 1932 the Costigan–La Follette Bill, which would have allocated $350 million for aid to local welfare agencies, was voted down by both parties. A critic noted: "The Democrats want to win the next election. . . . They are constantly currying favor with big business and entrenched wealth. They will do nothing to offend Wall Street. . . . In the words of the Washington correspondent of the Federated Press, the Democrats are 'buying the next election with the lives of the children of the unemployed.'"

If the Democrats hoped to buy it by actively demonstrating their conservatism, Hoover made his bid by requesting and getting federal relief grants of $300 million just before the 1932 election. Since the number of needy was about twenty million, the grant provided fifteen dollars per person per year, or about four cents per day. But it was doubtful that many were listening to Hoover, because shortly before he made the request, Roosevelt had accepted the nomination for President with these words:

What do the people of America want more than anything else? In my mind, two things: Work; work, with all the moral and spiritual values that go with work. And with work, a reasonable measure of security. . . . I say that the whole primary responsibility for relief rests with localities now, as ever, yet the Federal Government has always had and still has a continuing responsibility for the broader public welfare. It will soon fulfill that responsibility.

The ominous sound of the whole passage seemed to be drowned out in the resonating final line, "It will soon fulfill that responsibility."

Roosevelt did, of course, act on the issue of unemployment. The National Recovery Administration, the Works Progress Administration, and the Civilian Conservation Corps produced jobs—at rather pathetic wages—for some. But a distinction must be made between the creation of a few hundred thousand jobs and the vast needs of twenty million destitute. When Roosevelt addressed the first CCC men by radio in July 1933, he said, "You are evidence that we are seeking to get away, as fast as we possibly can, from the dole, from soup kitchens and from free lodging. . . ." And when, a few months later, he signed the Federal Emergency Relief Act, which allocated a token $500 million for grants to states, he implored citizens to "voluntarily contribute to the pressing needs of welfare services." A sense of foreboding gripped at least one reporter: "Just why this note should have been sounded when it was hoped the federal government was about to initiate a bold, vigorous and constructive policy in relief . . . is not easy to understand."

But it soon became easier. In October 1933, Roosevelt addressed the Conference of Catholic Charities: "It is for us to redouble our efforts to care for those who must still depend upon relief. . . . Many times I have insisted that every community and every state must first do their share." In January 1934, he addressed Congress on the budget: "The cornerstone of the foundation is the good credit of the government. If we maintain the course I have outlined we can look forward to . . . increased volume of business, more general profit, greater employment, a diminution of relief expenditures . . . and greater human happiness." And finally, in an address to NRA authorities in March 1934: "The aim of this whole effort is to restore our rich domestic market by raising the vast consuming capacity." By degrees, in a purely rhetorical process, relief was demoted in importance, then mentioned in passing, then forgotten.

But Roosevelt was not only more politically expedient than Hoover, he was more culpable. Hoover was insulated from, and insensitive to, mass thought and feeling. He could call children "cheerful human electrons" and think he would be understood. Roosevelt was a common sentimentalist. At Warm Springs, Georgia, he helped maintain a hospital for crippled children (he had suffered from polio himself), which he loved to visit. He also liked to lecture the children, on one occasion anticipating the thesis of this article with a bedtime exploration of the relation of economics to society. "We hear much these days of two adjectives—social and economic. . . . Here at Warm Springs we have proved that they go hand in hand." The proof, to summarize Roosevelt's prolix demonstration, lay in the fact that almost every crippled child required the care of an adult; rehabilitation made the child a "useful member of society" and released the adult "to be an economically useful unit in the community."

In another address on the occasion of his birthday and the holding of over six thousand birthday balls to raise funds for Warm Springs, Roosevelt said, "Let us well remember that every child and indeed every person who is restored to useful citizenship is an asset to the country and is enabled to 'pull his own weight in the boat.' In the long run, by helping this work we are not contributing to charity, but we are contributing to the building of a sound nation." The image of crippled children compelled to heave at the oars would be monstrous if it were not so ingenuously political.

One final anecdote. Roosevelt, a former boy scout, was asked to address the scouts on the occasion of their twenty-fifth birthday in February 1934. He asked Harry Hopkins, his relief administrator, for ideas. Hopkins suggested that the scouts be asked to collect furnishings, bedding, and clothes for those on relief. Roosevelt liked the idea and announced it, adding: "Already I have received offers of co-operation from Governors of States, from Mayors and other community leaders. . . . I ask you to join with me and the Eagle Scouts and our President and Chief Scout Executive who are here with me in the White House in giving again the Scout oath. All stand! Give the Scout sign! Repeat with me the Scout oath! 'On my honor . . .'" and so forth.

As the second year of Roosevelt's administration drew to a close in the winter of 1934, sufficient federal relief was no longer a serious possibility. Commentators noted that the impression that the Democrats would act had utterly demoralized charity efforts. And yet in New York alone there were 354,000 on relief, 77,000 more than a year before. Relief applications were coming in at the rate of fifteen hundred a day. One reporter passing through Ohio discovered families receiving one and a half cents per person. The *Nation* noted: "Within the greatest anthill of the Western Hemisphere the machinery has slowed down. One out of six New Yorkers depends on the dole. One out of three of the city's working population is out of work." As the days grew shorter and grayer it became obvious that for millions the hardest times were still ahead. Those already mentally and physically stunted by years of malnutrition would know many more years of diminished existence before the economic boom of World War II would turn the Depression around. And a few parents, broken by the responsibility of caring for hungry, ill, and constantly irritable children, would kill one or more of them— and sometimes themselves.

But then there was Shirley Temple.

SHIRLEY

Since birth, Shirley had never awakened at night. She had never been ill, although her mother seemed to remember "a little cold once." She refused to take a bottle and had to be fed with a spoon at three months. She spoke at six months and walked at thirteen. She arose every morning either singing or reciting the lines she had memorized for her day's work. She was a genius with an IQ of 155. She did not mark her books, scrawl on wallpaper, or break her toys. She did not cry, even when physically injured during the shooting of a scene. Doctors and dentists wrote her mother asking for the secrets of her diet and hygiene: her mother responded that there weren't any. Her relations with her parents were totally loving and natural. She had no concern for, or sense of, herself, and she was consequently unspoilable.

If her mother were not so straightforward a woman, and if there were not independent corroborators for some of these facts, one would have to presume that Shirley was not real—that she was a rosy image of childhood projected like a dialectical adumbration from the pallid bodies and distressed psyches of millions of Depression-era children. But she was real. Her biographies are not, as they are with most Hollywood stars, cosmeticized myths, but something on the order of fundamentalist "witnessings." "The cameraman tells me that she went through this emotional scene in such a miraculous way that the crew was spellbound, and when she finished they just stared fascinated. 'I wanted to reach out and touch her as she went by,' said Tony Ugrin who makes her still pictures. 'I could hardly believe she was real.'" Or, Adolphe Menjou speaking: "That Temple kid. She scares me. She's . . . She's . . ."—he finally settled for "She's an Ethel Barrymore at four."

Shirley's relation to the Depression history I have outlined goes far beyond this dialectical play between her biographies and the real childhoods of many Depression-era children, however. It is at once easy and difficult to conceptualize. There is a felt resonance between the persona she assumed in her films and the ideology of charity that no one can miss. But to state *why* it exists demands a theory for her studio's conscious or unconscious ideological bias, and the making of distinctions between intended ideology (propaganda of the Gifford-Young sort), opportunistic seizing on current ideas and issues (the "topical" film syndrome), and a more diffuse attunement to the movie audience's moods and concerns. When one takes into account Fox's financial difficulties in 1934, its resurgence with Shirley Temple, and its merger with Twentieth Century under the guidance of Rockefeller banking interests, one feels that the *least* that should be anticipated is a lackeying to the same interests that dominated Hoover and Roosevelt.

But such lackeying need not appear as a message or the espousal of a class view; it can as well operate (and more freely) as a principle of suppression and obfuscation. Shirley's films and her biographies do contain messages of the Gifford-Young sort—one should care for the unfortunate, work is a happy activity—but they seem more remarkable for what they do not contain, or contain only in the form of displaced and distorted contents.

I will assume that this contention is a viable one and rest the case for it on the analysis that follows. But before beginning, a few biographical facts are needed to place Shirley relative to the history already outlined. Shirley was born April 28, 1928, six months before the crash. She was discovered at a dance studio in 1933, given bit parts in shorts, then graduated to a musical number in Fox's *Stand Up and Cheer* early in 1934. During the number she pauses for a moment, puckers, leans forward, and blows a little marshmallow kiss past the camera. Audiences emerged from the experience disoriented and possessive. After another minor role in *Change of Heart*, Shirley was moved up to feature roles in *Little Miss Marker* (Paramount), *Baby, Take a Bow* (Fox), *Now and Forever* (Paramount), and *Bright Eyes* (Fox), all produced in 1934. The box-office grosses made both studios incredulous. No star of the thirties had affected audiences so. Fox tied up its property with major contracts and produced nine more films in the next two years, the period of our concern.

Shirley's most intimate connections with the Depression history I have traced are those found in her films. I will deal opportunistically with the details of these films: what I shall principally omit are Shirley's functions as an entertainer—her many dances, songs, exchanges with other cute children, and so forth. In any given film the sheer quantity of sequences in which Shirley entertains may make her other functions seem peripheral. But in the eleven films made between 1934 and 1936 the sequences devoted to plot and to the development of a persona predominate.

In these films Shirley is often an orphan or motherless (*Little Miss Marker*, *Bright Eyes*, *Curly Top*, *Dimples*, and *Captain January*) or unwanted (*Our Little Girl*). She is usually identified with a nonworking proletariat made up of the dispossessed and the outcast (clearly in *Baby, Take a Bow*, *Little Miss Marker*, and *Dimples*; more covertly in *Our Little Girl*, *Now and Forever*, and *Poor Little Rich Girl*). And when she is of well-to-do origins (*The Little Colonel*, *Poor Little Rich Girl*, and *The Littlest Rebel*), she shows affinities for servants, blacks, and itinerants. Her principal functions in virtually all of these films are to soften hard hearts (especially of the wealthy), to intercede on the behalf of others, to effect liaisons between members of opposed social classes, and occasionally to regenerate.

We can detect some very obvious forms of repression, displacement, and condensation at work within this complex. Although proletarian in association, Shirley is seldom the daughter of a worker, much less an unemployed one. In the two films in which her parents are workers (*Little Miss Marker* and *Bright Eyes*), they are killed before the film begins or during it. Therefore the fact that the proletariat *works* is generally suppressed in the films. What proletarians do to get money is to con people, beg, or steal. This libelous class portrait is softened by comedy and irony, which function, as they usually do, as displaced attitudes of superiority and prejudice. A comical proletariat is also a lovable one, opening the way to identification, and even to charitable feeling.

Shirley's acts of softening, interceding, and the rest are spontaneous ones, originating in her love of others. Not only do they function as condensations of all of the mid-Depression schemes for the care of the needy, but they repress the concepts of a *duty* to give or of a responsibility to *share* (income tax, federal spending). The solution Shirley offers is natural: one opens one's heart, à la Gifford and Young, and the most implacable realities alter or disperse. We should also note that Shirley's love is of a special order. It is not, like God's, a universal manna flowing through all things, but a love that is elicited by *need*. Shirley turns like a lodestone toward the flintiest characters in her films—the wizened wealthy, the defensive unloved, figures of cold authority like army officers, and tough criminals. She assaults, penetrates, and opens them, making it possible for them to *give* of themselves. All of this returns on her at times, forcing her into situations where she must decide who *needs* her most. It is her agon, her calvary, and it brings her to her most despairing moments. This confluence of needing and giving, of deciding whose need is greatest, also obviously suggests the relief experience.

So strongly overdetermined is Shirley's capacity for love that she virtually exists within it. In Freudian terms she has no id, ego, or superego. She is an unstructured reification of the libido, much as Einstein in popular myth reified the capacity for thought. Einstein's brain bulged his forehead, dwarfed his body, and stood his hair on end. Shirley's capacity for love drew her into a small, warm ball, curled her hair, dimpled her cheeks and knees, and set her in perpetual motion—dancing, strutting, beaming, wheedling, chiding, radiating, kissing. And since her love was indiscriminate, extending to pinched misers and common hobos alike, it was a social, even a political, force on a par with the idea of democracy or the Constitution. That all of this has great ideological potential scarcely needs arguing; but it would be naive to trace Shirley's film persona exclusively to an origin in the policies of the Hoover and Roosevelt administrations. One senses, rather, that Shirley is a locus at which this and other forces intersect, including those of the mitigation of reality through fantasy, the exacerbated emotions relating to insufficiently cared for children, the commonly stated philosophy of pulling together to whip the Depression, and others. Yet it would seem equally naive to discount the fact that Shirley and her burden of love appeared at a moment when the official ideology of charity had reached a final and unyielding form and when the public sources of charitable support were drying up.

But Depression-era attitudes toward charity, as we saw earlier, must be understood in terms of forces emanating from the economic base; and I have so far said nothing of Shirley's relation to economics. Here we must move between her films and her biographies. For our purposes, all of this material has the same status: it simply tells us everything people knew about Shirley. We have already noted that one of her functions was to pass between needy people—to be orphaned, exchanged, adopted. She always wound up in the possession of the person who needed her most. And he who possessed her owned the unique philosopher's stone of a depressed economy, the stone whose touch transmuted poverty to abundance, harsh reality to effulgent fantasy, sadness to vertiginous joy. All of this works as a displacement of the social uses and efficacy of money.

If the argument needs strengthening, we need not go far. Shirley's absolute value was a constant subject of speculation. The usual figure quoted is $10 million—in Depression dollars, an almost inconceivable sum. As a writer in the *Ladies' Home Journal* put it in a symptomatic passage, "When she was born the doctor had no way of knowing that the celestial script called for him to say, not 'It's a girl' but 'It's a gold mine.' " Her father was a bank clerk at the time of her discovery in 1932, but through his fame (which could attract deposits) he soon became manager of a posh branch of the California Bank. This conjunction of a banker and an inestimably valuable property is in itself suggestive, especially for an era when bankers like J. P. Morgan symbolized the capitalist system.

It would take too much space to repeat even a sampling of the stories that concern other white, middle class parents' hopes that their child might prove to be a financial bonanza like Shirley Temple. The following passage from the *Saturday Evening Post* will have to epitomize them: "The other studios would like a Shirley too. Her name could be Millicent, for all they care. They test her. They test little Gertie, too, and Annabelle. Hundreds of them, thousands of them. No fields are drilled for oil, no hills are mined for gold with more desperation, more persistence, more prayers, more hopes. So far, no dice. Maybe you have a little Shirley in your home. Maybe you don't suspect it. Mr. and Mrs. George Temple didn't."

If we add to all of this Shirley's function as an asset to the Fox studios, her golden locks, and the value of her name to the producers of Shirley Temple dolls and other products, the imagery closes in. She is subsumed by that class of objects that symbolize capitalism's false democracy: the Comstock Lode, the Irish Sweepstakes, the legacy from a distant relative. And if we join her inestimable value with her inability to be shared, we discover a deep resonance with the Depression-era notion of what capital was: a vital force whose efficacy would be destroyed if it was shared. Even Shirley's capacity for love is rendered economic by our awareness that Fox duplicated the Hoover-Roosevelt tactic of espousing compassion for anterior economic motives (specifically, by making a profit from the spectacle of compassion). And because of the unique nature of the star-centered movie industry of the thirties, Shirley was a power for monopoly control of film distribution.

This intricate nexus of functions and meanings contains enough material for a major study of how capitalism simultaneously asserts and denies its fetishistic attachment to money and embeds these attitudes in the metaphoric surfaces of the commodities it creates. Shirley, orphaned, often in poor clothes, with nothing to give but her love, was paradoxically specular with the idea of money. And the paradox could as easily be perceived as an oxymoron in which the terms *need* and *abundance* were indissolubly fused. Of course, paradoxes and oxymorons are classical devices for the creation of numinous effects of the sort I referred to at the beginning of this article. By the time she had made her first eleven films Shirley's name alone radiated energy, like a saint's head in a religious woodcut. A blind man came to the studio and asked to run his hands over her face. A woman wrote, asking George Temple to conceive a second Shirley upon her. Eleven industries paid Shirley to produce commodities bearing her name, and several of them grew rich. And Shirley's mother drew $1,000 a week just to keep her daughter healthy and functioning and primed for work.

And it is Shirley's relation to her work that we must next, and finally, consider, both because it received constant attention in her biographies and because it may lead us to fresh insights into her relations to love and to money. The commonplace that most work under capitalism is alienated never seems more valid than during those crisis moments known as depressions. Work during such periods is more affected not only by feelings of personal insecurity but also by a very real harshening of work conditions. For instance, millions of workers during the early thirties suffered from one or more of the following conditions: speed-up, reduced work hours, reduced salaries, the firing of high-salaried employees and the employing of those willing to work for much less, exposure to deteriorated and dangerous machinery and a general reduction of safety standards, thought and speech control so intense in some plants that workers never spoke except to ask or give instructions, inability to question deductions from paychecks, beatings by strike-breaking Pinkertons and thugs, and compelled acquiescence to the searches of their homes by company men looking for stolen articles. And there were the ultimate forms of alienated work—street cleaning, mopping a floor, painting a wall in exchange for a meal, often a bowl of soup and a piece of stale bread: this was the work that saved one from the loss of initiative and character. One cannot read far in the records of any class of workers during the Depression without discovering how abrasive and anxiety-ridden most working experiences were.

None of the biographical articles on Shirley failed to describe her attitudes toward her work. I will give just two samples. First, from *Time*: "Her work entails no effort. She plays at acting as other small girls play at dolls. Her training began so long ago that she now absorbs instruction almost subconsciously. While her director explains how he wants a scene played, Shirley looks at her feet, apparently thinking of more important matters. When the take starts, she not only knows her own function but frequently that of the other actors. . . . She is not sensitive when criticized. . . . In one morning, Shirley Temple's crony and hero, Tap Dancer Bill Robinson . . . , taught her a soft-shoe number, a waltz clog and three tap routines. She learned them without looking at him, by listening to his feet." Second, from an article written by her mother: "I never urged Shirley to go to the studio with me. She wanted to go then, as she wants to go now. Motion-picture acting is simply part of her play life. It is untinged with worry about tomorrow or fear of failure. A few times when we have left the studio together, she has looked up at me and said, 'Mommy, did I do all right?' Since there is no right or wrong about it, but only Shirley playing, I have replied, noncommittally, 'All right.' That was the end of it. . . . I do not know whether Shirley understands the plays in which she appears. We do not discuss plots or characters, or, indeed, any phase of her motion-picture work. Her playing is really play. She learns her lines rapidly, just as any child learns nursery rhymes or stories. . . . We usually go over the script the first time with enthusiasm. Sometimes, when it is issued, Shirley cannot wait until we get home to hear her lines read, 'Turn on the dashboard lights,' she said one night, 'and read my lines while you drive.' "

And for this work, accomplished with joy and ease, Shirley received $10,000 per week and over thirty-five hundred letters thanking her for the pleasure she gave. The disparity between Shirley's work and the reality of most Depression-era work experiences was ludicrous; and the frequency and consistency of descriptions of the sort just quoted indicates that the disparity was also mesmerizing, much like the disclosure in 1932 that J. P. Morgan paid no income taxes.

Shirley's relation to work adds a further counter to the set already made up of her relations to love and to money; but does it also establish interrelationships with them? One is reminded of Marx's acute observation that money, considered in its relation to the work that produces it, has a repressive and censoring role. It shares this role with most commodities, which are designed and finished so as to conceal traces of the labor that has gone into them. To clarify the point by example, the lace produced by child labor in Nottingham in the 1860s was finished under very exacting standards of quality and cleanliness, effectively effacing evidence of the handwork that produced it. The well-to-do who bought it could in no palpable way be reminded of work, or workers, or the exploitative class structure of their society, much less be led to inquire into the circumstances that saw up to twenty children crowded into an airless, fetid, twelve-foot-square room, working under the whip of a mistress for from twelve to sixteen hours a day, with their shoes removed, even in winter, so the lace would not be soiled.

One might say, then, that Shirley stands in the same relation to work as does a piece of Nottingham lace or a dollar bill: she censors or conceals work. The relation is not exact, for millions knew that she was awakened every morning by a mother who started her reciting her lines and kept her at it all the way to the studio. It was just that Shirley's work was self-obliterating—a whole deck of cards vanished into the air, or rather, magically transmuted into prepubescent games worth $10,000 a week.

But there is an exact correspondence to Marx's insight in the relation between Shirley's films and work. One probably could not find a Depression-era commodity more like a piece of Nottingham lace than a Shirley Temple film. Her directors, writers, cameramen, composers, and the rest were never written about, never mentioned, except as witnesses to something Shirley said or did. And the films they produced obliterate all traces of their craft. They are consummate examples of minimal direction, invisible editing, unobtrusive camerawork and musical scoring, and characterless dialogue. Every burr or edge has been honed away, and the whole buffed to a high finish.

There are other relations between love, money, and work that I do not have space to develop, and in some instances am not certain that I have grasped. Let me, however, attempt to give some rigor to the analysis made so far. I have argued that the ideology of charity was the creation of a class intent on motivating others to absorb the economic burdens imposed by the Depression. This privileged class regarded itself as possessed of initiative, as self-made through hard work; and it saw in all governmental plans for aid a potential subversion of the doctrine of initiative. Charity, then, came to be characterized as the bulwark of initiative. Money was a censored topic (for obvious reasons—Nelson Rockefeller today will not allow reporters to question him about his wealth); but there were clear implications that money as a charitable gift was benevolent, whereas money in the form of a dole was destructive. Money, then, was ambivalent and repressed, whereas charity and initiative were univalent and foregrounded.

In Shirley Temple's films and biographies, through a slight but very important displacement, charity appears as love and initiative as work. Both love and work are abstracted from all social and psychological realities. They have no causes; they are unmotivated. They appear in Shirley merely as prodigious innate capacities, something like Merlin's wisdom or Lancelot's strength; and they are magical in their powers—they can transform reality and spontaneously create well-being and happiness. Money, in keeping with its ambivalent nature, is subjected to two opposing operations. In Shirley's films and the depictions of real life attitudes toward money, it is censored out of existence. It is less than destructive: it is nothing. But in an opposing movement, found largely in Shirley's biographies, money breaks free and induces an inebriated fantasy that a Caliban would embrace, a vision of gold descending from the heavens, a treasure produced from a little girl's joy and curls and laughter. This fantasy is removed from all thought of effort or anxiety; one can simply sit back in his chair and, like a lotus-eater, let the drugged vision possess him.

But any attempt to further clarify these relations would probably be wrongheaded, since it would argue for coherence where there is often only a muddled interplay of the forces of censorship and obfuscation. It seems more appropriate to let the whole discourse dissolve back into the existential mass of Depression history and Shirley and her films.

I will start it on its way by attacking the last point I made. I said that Shirley's films have no creators. This is untrue. The advertising copy for her films tells us that Shirley Temple made them—sometime, we must presume, between playing with her pet rabbits and eating her favorite dish, canned peaches and ice cream. I also implied that many workers and their children suffered in material ways during the Depression. But President Hoover wisely observed that the Depression was "only a state of mind," and Shirley's life and work provide exemplary proof that Hoover was right. And I hinted that cold cash might have been more desirable to a starving man than a child's warm touch. There is a perverse logic to this; but the thought is materialistic and, above all, dehumanizing. Shirley's films never get into such Jesuitical quandaries; they keep the only authentic solution constantly before our eyes: the transforming power of love.

And with those props knocked from beneath the specious edifice of my argument, it shatters, expires, and sinks beneath the dark tarn of history from which it was fallaciously raised. But at the point where the last bubbles appear, something bobs to the surface. It begins to rise in the air and to glow, assuming the shape of a luminous being. And now, having attained full power, it begins to flash off and on like a theater marquee, and its feet begin to do little tap dance routines. It is Shirley Temple! Reborn! Released from the rational spell cast upon her by those sorcerers, Freud and Marx! And now we hear her voice announcing that the Depression is over, that it never existed, that it is ending endlessly in each and every one of her films, that these films are playing at our neighborhood theaters and that we should come and see them, and that we must learn to love children and to weep for them and open our hearts to them, that we mustn't hate rich people because most of them are old and unhappy and unloved, that we should learn to sing at our work and dance away our weariness, that anyone can be an old sourpuss about rickets and protein deficiency but only a Shirley Temple fan can laugh his pathology away.

And now that we have immersed ourselves in these egregious irrationalities and utterly clogged the processes of thought, we should once again be in the proper state of mind to see Shirley's films, and perhaps to accept her as simply and naively as she accepted her labors in Hollywood's expedient vineyards.

FRANK CAPRA AND THE POPULAR FRONT

LEONARD QUART

In the thirties and early forties, Frank Capra was a master at manipulating an audience's feelings and fantasies, at constructing archetypal characters and images guaranteed to make them feel that it was their own lives, selves, and dreams that appeared before them on the screen. His films insinuated themselves into the audience's emotional lives, sometimes sacrificing the mind's integrity in the process. Capra could convince an audience that America was a nation filled with small towns radiating Christmas cheer and harmony; of heroic ordinary men whose characters were blessed with courage, compassion, and intelligence; and of icons—historic monuments, the flag, the Constitution—that were still capable of stirring the most profound patriotic and reverential emotions. In fact, at the height of his powers Capra could make John Cassavetes's remark ring powerfully true: "Maybe there really wasn't an America, maybe there was only Frank Capra."

In his heyday, Capra's films were both great commercial and great artistic successes. His films were nominated for best picture six times, and Capra himself won three Academy Awards for best director. He was a power in Hollywood, a self-conscious and independent auteur at a time when almost all Hollywood directors worked according to studio dictates; he was committed to the maxim "one man—one film" and important enough to have his name placed above the titles of his films.

Capra's fables were perfectly suited for the thirties. He geared his films to his audience's need to find some hope of social change, and he did this by embracing the role of mass entertainer without submerging his personal vision while doing it. He genuinely believed in making films that were "songs of the working stiffs, of the short-changed Joes, the born poor and the afflicted," works that were self-admittedly sentimental but radiated an idealism based on Christian, humanitarian, nationalist, individualist, and vaguely egalitarian principles.

Capra's films were permeated with ideals but contained few ideas and lacked a coherent political and social perspective. They were also interested not in the texture of social reality but rather in fantasies and fables of American possibility and unity. His films carried messages like "No man is a failure" and "Each man's life touches so many other lives," sentiments he artfully and movingly weaved into the body of his work. These sentiments provided consolation and comfort for his audience—a sense that good neighborliness and Christian charity would suffice to purge injustice and inequity from American society.

Capra's notions of social change were folksy and simple ones. If such a notion as class struggle could be discovered in his films, it was viewed in moral rather than economic or political terms—a conflict between the caring and the humane

From *Cineaste* 8, no. 1 (1977).

and the greedy and the cynical. His villains were snobs, cynics, and those so corrupt they were beyond redemption—like the power-hungry figures played by Edward Arnold. Though his villains were often wealthy, characters like Mr. Deeds, played by a soft, vulnerable Gary Cooper, had no difficulty being both wealthy and humane at the same time. And the evil of his corrupt characters never rubbed off on the institutions they controlled or the social and economic system that shaped their behavior and allowed them to succeed. For Capra personalized social evil so an audience could leave the theater after watching *Mr. Smith Goes to Washington* (1939) believing that the Senate would be transformed once the rascals were thrown out and decent, just men replaced them.

Nobody, including Capra, would confuse his critique of American society with Alexis de Tocqueville's or Rexford Tugwell's. Nevertheless, although his thinking was breezy and facile, he was serious about indicting the inhumanities of the age and routing the "mass predators." If his critique left the core of American social myth and tradition intact, he still struggled to grant American individualism ("the only true revolutionary is the free man") a populist and social conscience. His films often faced the fact that a depression was taking place outside the theater, with images of worn, unemployed farmers, fascistic business tycoons, hapless politicians, and a spoiled upper class. There even lurked in his work a sense of the dangers inherent in the power of the mass media and of the ominous potential for ordinary individuals to turn into a conforming, howling mob. But despite the spark of vision in Capra's films of both the painful underbelly of American society and the dark, destructive elements in human nature, he never suggested that there could be an enduring sense of human tragedy. For both Capra and his audience desired fables of hope and harmony, and films like *Mr. Deeds* and *Mr. Smith* succeeded, with their Capracorn climaxes, in leaving a luminous glow.

The apogee of Capra's career took place during the middle and late thirties, a period in American cultural history when Capra's vision coincided with much of left thought. In 1935 the Communist Party moved from the sectarian militancy of the early thirties into its Popular Front phase. The Party submerged both its devotion to the proletariat and its opposition to FDR and committed itself to reform, vaporous humanitarian ideals (e.g., "unity, democracy, and peace"), and antifascist solidarity. The political struggle was no longer viewed in class terms, but as a vaguely defined conflict between the forces of "progress and reaction." The Party's strategy was to divest itself of revolutionary polemics and project a "just folks" image to the general public. It would no longer be a hard-nosed revolutionary organization, but a neighborly group, holding picnics and outings and sharing the tastes and life-styles of other Americans.

The Party publicly chose to pursue political goals that did not veer far from those of the New Deal. They eschewed sectarianism and revolutionary action for a broad democratic consensus—embracing liberals, mythologizing Franklin, Jefferson, and Lincoln ("he carried the fight against reaction to the American masses"), and sanctifying the common man. The Party embraced "Americanism," rejecting the exotic, theoretical, and deviant. As Carl Carmer wrote in the *New Masses* of 1938: "It is time that artists recognize in the figments of the

American dream the opportunity for the expression of that beauty which is distinctly a part of the land and its people." The "people" were turned into an amorphous cardboard mass, constantly invoked as the ultimate arbiters of all cultural and political activity; and the intellectuals were to be domesticated—they were no longer expected to transform the values and consciousness of the larger society but to reinforce what was already in the "American mind."

The Popular Front was both a cultural and a political phenomenon. As a political tactic it helped the Communist Party make inroads into the middle class, liberal organizations, and the labor unions and gain a degree of influence and acceptance it never held as a revolutionary group. In fact, the period of the Popular Front was the heyday of Communism in America, with Party membership rising to one hundred thousand. Of course, these gains were not accomplished without cost. For in their quest to enlist as many groups as possible into antifascist coalitions, formal unity became confused with a social program: tactics became ends in themselves. (Though given the continued failures of the American left to enlist a sustained response and support from the general public, it seems absurd to breezily and puritanically dismiss the Popular Front strategy.) The Party's new line, however, had much more effect on the culture than on the political and economic structure.

In the years 1935–1939, the Popular Front's perspective shaped the thought and creative work of many intellectuals and demi-intellectuals. The Popular Front viewed liberals as acceptable coalition partners and by 1938 gave direct support to the New Deal. Liberals in turn were attracted to the Popular Front as a bastion against fascism and as a movement committed to evolutionary change. Just as the Communist Party had begun to exult in American mores and myths ("Communism Is Twentieth-Century Americanism" being one of the prime slogans of the Popular Front), liberal intellectuals like Gilbert Seldes and Archibald MacLeish made their own contributions to this new fusion of populism and nationalism. Gilbert Seldes, who in the past had been an aggressive critic of American values, now wrote in his book *Mainland* that "the intellectuals have made no effort to understand and preserve the variety and excellence of life in America." Seldes advocated a capital-letter Democracy, attacking formal intellectualism, pitting the "average" against the "exception," maintaining that the "happy ending" may be America's prime contribution to the world. MacLeish, once a defender of the artist as independent critic, now called for a "constructive literature" committed to the American tradition. MacLeish had rediscovered America and, with the fervor of a convert, exulted in a people "who had the luck to be born on this continent where the heat was hotter and the cold was colder and the mornings were more like mornings than anywhere else on earth."

Of course, Seldes and MacLeish's embrace of America was somewhat more intense and hyperbolic than that of many of the artists and intellectuals who shared this new nationalism. For the first time, however, a large number of artists and intellectuals had found that through the Popular Front they could simultaneously belong to a "radical" mass movement and be good Americans. The past was now awaiting reconstruction. Old legends like Davy Crockett, Mike Fink, and Paul Bunyan were resurrected—gargantuan figures who represented an

American comic-heroic tradition. Uncritical biographies of Franklin, Washington, Jackson, and Lincoln were produced, works that were primarily lyric odes to past greatness. John Dos Passos, in *The Ground We Stand On*, discovered in eighteenth-century America images of human grandeur and repose that never appeared in, or could have survived the pessimism of, the *U.S.A.* trilogy. The apotheosis of the Popular Front culture was achieved when a pseudo–folk song, "A Ballad for Americans," written by a leftist, Earl Robinson, was performed at the 1940 Republican National Convention.

The Popular Front culture sought to soften and sentimentalize reality, reduce ambiguity, and project folksiness as a style and ideology. It was an aggressively egalitarian culture, although the egalitarianism often seemed self-conscious and inauthentic, like advertising copy permeated with virtuous moralizing. The Popular Front packaged and patronized "the people," and consequently Hollywood became a natural outlet for some of its energies. In fact, the Communist Party, which in the early thirties had showered contempt on Hollywood for its manufacturing of destructive, capitalist fantasies, now viewed it as a reservoir of antifascist strength.

In 1937, the Party chose Hollywood scriptwriter Donald Ogden Stewart (*Philadelphia Story*) to replace radical and avant-garde novelist Waldo Frank as head of the League of American Writers. It was an act that expressed perfectly the culture of the Popular Front: the rejection of high and avant-garde culture for those "folk arts" that came closest to popular American taste. For Hollywood, in turn, the Popular Front was the perfect embodiment of left-wing ideals. As Murray Kempton has written, "The slogans, the sweeping formulae, the superficial clangors of Communist culture had a certain fashion in Hollywood because they were two-dimensional appeals to a two-dimensional community." Kempton's witty treatment of the Hollywood left was a bit too facilely contemptuous, too smugly highbrow and arch, to be a truly accurate portrait. Nevertheless, it was true that Hollywood leftism was for the most part shallow and conventional. The Hollywood leftists may have given large sums of money to front organizations and signed innumerable petitions, but when it came to the industry, they served it obediently and well. Their politics had little practical effect on the films they worked on—either being submerged in the genre conventions or, in ostensibly political films like *Juarez*, merely affirming democratic ideals and condemning dictatorship; indeed, political films such as *Blockade*, written by John Howard Lawson (a long-time leftist) about the Spanish Civil War, ended up being acceptable even to the DAR, who viewed it as a basically nonpartisan suspense film.

In fact, given the calculating vagueness of Popular Front rhetoric, it would have been difficult to distinguish radical films from the rest. Even a film like Warner Brothers' *Mission to Moscow* (1943), which justifies the Moscow purge trials and the Hitler-Stalin pact, has no radical edge. Based on a book by FDR's ambassador to the Soviet Union, Joseph E. Davies, the film was made to introduce the American public to their new World War II ally, Russia. In the film the Soviet Union is turned into a near-double of the United States: the Russian people live in neat, studio-constructed suburban landscapes, sing folk songs, and the women are interested in cosmetics and fashion. They are a wholesome, hard-working, practical people—just like ordinary Americans. Their leaders are also given a Popular Front interpretation: Stalin is viewed as a kindly Slavic grandpa, and Foreign Minister Litvinov speaks softly of collective security. The script does try to ensure that the audience understands that the two systems differ, but the film's imagery makes these differences hard to perceive. Even the film's villains—comic Japanese, vicious, thin-lipped Germans, and, most fiendish of all, traitorous Trotskyites—fit the Popular Front line. The Trotskyites are seen as intellectuals and writers—Marxist theoreticians like Bukharin (never a Trotskyite)—who are alien and dangerous to both the Russian and the American way of life, and of course to the folksy egalitarian vision of the Popular Front.

Of course one can ask, What do Joseph Stalin and the Popular Front have in common with Frank Capra? Capra was a devout Catholic who was never a member of the Party (in fact, he was anticommunist), never a member of a front organization, never even a liberal intellectual in good standing. He never had to move, as Seldes and other liberal intellectuals did, from a past position of alienation from and contempt for American values toward a passionate embrace of our traditions. Capra always instinctively believed in America's spirit and freedom and wanted to make films that would be his "way of saying, 'Thanks, America.'"

Without denying the philosophic and political differences that existed between Capra and the Popular Front, they shared a rhetoric and imagery. His heroes, Smith and Deeds, were ordinary men with whom the public could identify, and also men of superior talents, courage, and leadership whom the public could admire—true democratic and egalitarian heroes. They were heroes in the Lincolnesque mold, and Capra actually envisioned his Jefferson Smith as "a young Abe Lincoln, tailored to the railsplitter's simplicity." Capra created men who were not elegant, cynical, or intellectual, but they were intelligent and were further humanized by their mild eccentricities (Deeds's fire engine chasing, for example). Nevertheless, none of them were bold nonconformists or revolutionaries; they attacked corrupt politicians, urban shysters, and journalists, but always in order to reinforce what was best in the American tradition. They invoked the innocence of boyhood, the mythic mores of the small town, and the redemptive quality of chaste, romantic love. They also loved their neighbors, and in common with Earl Browder (the U.S. Communist Party leader during the Popular Front phase), they believed in "a progressive, free, prosperous, and happy America."

Capra's heroes, of course, did not share the Popular Front's commitment to government intervention in the country's economic and social life, believing that individual initiative, tempered by a good measure of Christian benevolence, was the best way out of the Depression. Capra was committed to both voluntarism and individualism (as evidenced in the scene that has Deeds doling out his fortune to the dispossessed), and he was suspicious of large institutions like big business and big labor. If Capra's individualism did not fit into the Popular Front tradition, his folksy definition of class conflict as a struggle between "a bankful of money against a houseful of love" did. And if his crowd of ordinary folks—"a collection of free individuals"—could never be organized into a political group or collective (for Capra, "the masses is a herd term—unacceptable, insulting, and degrading"), their shining, ultimately benign presence could still be projected onto the screen. Capra believed in "We the people," and even if the "people" were fickle and destructive, they were preferable to all the fat cats, stuffed shirts, and power wielders in the country. They were the ones who, led by a just, homely leader, would humanize the world.

Capra's heroes—Smith, Deeds, Doe, et al.—had to struggle against patronizing literati, pompous academics, and sophisticated, slimy politicos (Claude Rains's "Silver Knight"), as well as brutal power figures. Capra was suspicious of experts and intellectuals, and he armed his heroes with only a homespun, intuitive sense of what was good and just. Smith and Doe waged their struggles without a political organization, a theoretical framework, or a body of knowledge to provide refuge and support. Of course, a man like Jefferson Smith had the sublime decency and the gift for conjuring up idyllic American dream imagery that could transform cynical reporters—like the one played by Jean Arthur and, ultimately, countless others—into dewy-eyed believers. Capra's heroes may not have been men of ideas, but they were charismatic figures who could, like Capra himself, capture the public's emotions and imagination. And in American life and myth, the politics of personality and moral regeneration have usually had more resonance than the politics of programmatic reform or revolution.

If the ultimate ends of the Popular Front differed markedly from Capra's, there existed a true meshing of sensibilities. The *Daily Worker* loved his films, calling him a "genius" and praising *Mr. Deeds* for its "magnificent trial scene," in which mass pressure in the courtroom helps bring a favorable verdict. It also applauded *Mr. Smith* (written by blacklisted screenwriter Sidney Buchman) as a "ringing indictment of the political machine" and for its creation of an "honest, uncorruptible, and sincere" character. Other left publications, such as *New Masses* and *New Theatre*, also praised Capra's social conscience and his capacity to recognize "that the world is a place of sorrow where the great multitudes of men suffer for the excesses of the few."

It didn't matter to these publications that Capra was committed to the petit bourgeois capitalism of America's past, for Capra was an optimist who believed in the "power of morality, of courage, of beauty," and had an antipathy to the brute, violent, and dark in human nature. These and other similar sentiments that ran through his films made him an artist in good standing with the Popular Front. In fact, in a recent *New York Times* interview, Yip Harburg, the urbane, left-leaning lyricist of such films as *The Wizard of Oz* and *Finian's Rainbow* and writer of such songs as "Brother, Can You Spare a Dime," attacked the music of Dylan and others as characterized by "grim" songs and "shrieks" and, in Capra-esque fashion, yearned for the "laughter, humor, courage, and hope of the songwriters of the thirties and forties." While reading Harburg's words, I sometimes feel, in opposition to all political and historical logic, that while inventing America, Frank Capra may also have created the Popular Front.

THE POLITICS OF POWER IN
ON THE WATERFRONT

PETER BISKIND

The Kazan revival has begun. Initiated in 1972 by the British journal *Movie*,[1] expedited in 1973 by Jim Kitses writing in *Cinema*,[2] and further assisted by the recent publication of a book-length interview edited by Michel Ciment of *Positif*,[3] it promises a long overdue reassessment of an unjustly neglected director. Whatever one's attitude toward either Kazan's political behavior in the fifties or the politics embedded in his films, it can no longer be denied that he is an important figure. He directed a half dozen major films of the fifties, and the Actors Studio, which he founded, left an indelible stamp on American screen acting. Marlon Brando, Lee Remick, James Dean, Julie Harris, Montgomery Clift, Shelley Winters, Paul Newman, Kim Hunter, Lee J. Cobb, Karl Malden, Rod Steiger, and many, many others cannot be understood apart from its influence.

A focusing on Kazan's work makes it no longer possible to evade the central question of film and ideology that auteurists and the more sophisticated auteur-structuralists have thus far largely obscured or ignored. This is so because Kazan, more than most directors of the fifties, was overtly concerned with political themes, while at the same time his own life was crucially affected by his appearance before the House Un-American Activities Committee (HUAC) as a "friendly witness" in 1952. It was just this proximity to the storm center of American culture in the fifties that made his reputation so vulnerable to changes in the political climate. Kazan, in a sense, has been doubly unlucky. After selling out his friends on the left and enthusiastically joining the fifties crusade against communism, he was cast out of the mainstream of American film history by auteur critics who, like himself, were cultural fellow travelers of the postwar corporate consensus but who, even more than he, turned against the aesthetics of social realism. They disliked the residue of the social seriousness of the thirties that was still evident in his work. Even left-wing auteurists who have not hesitated to paint such right-wing action directors as Fuller, Siegel, and Aldrick in various shades of red, have drawn back from Kazan.[4]

Despite the fact that Kazan's work as a whole is now being regarded with greater interest, it is his later, more "personal" films like *America, America* and *The Arrangement*, made outside his longtime collaboration with major writers, that are gaining ground over the films of the high fifties like *On the Waterfront*. In other words, the reassessment is proceeding along typically auteurist lines, putting a premium on the expression of personality.

The new stress on the later films (not unlike previous auteurist rescue operations on Ford's westerns and late Renoir) depends on a confusion of personal and private, itself a product of the fifties attempt to cauterize ideology and valorize private life. The notion that *The Arrangement* is a more personal film than *On*

From *Film Quarterly*, Fall 1975.

the Waterfront is certainly an odd one. It would be hard to think of a film that more strongly suggests an autobiographical reading than *On the Waterfront* which, after all, concerns informing, an issue that in reality marked Kazan's own life profoundly. Distinguishing early and late Kazan in this way can only proceed from a position like auteurism, which seeks to expel politics from the area of legitimate artistic discourse with the aid of threadbare romantic notions of the artist, genius, personal vision, and so on.

Kazan, of course, was engaged in precisely the same effort. *On the Waterfront* is one of the earliest and most effective attempts to suppress politics with morality and private values that the fifties produced. It takes an important first step in detaching the self from a larger social context so that the idea of self can be redefined in narrower, safer terms. *Splendor in the Grass*, *America, America*, and *The Arrangement* merely develop the notion of personality presented initially in *On the Waterfront*.

The congruence between the ideological projects of Kazan and auteurism, both firmly rooted in the necessities of the fifties consensus, suggest another reason for the critical antipathy toward Kazan. It is not that Kazan was too much a product of the thirties for fifties auteurists, too unlike them in political stance and emotional tone, but rather the opposite. He was too much *like* them. Kazan's were *les mains sales*, executing the deeds at which their eyes dared not look. His films performed the ideological dirty work of the fifties and thus had to be rejected in favor of the films of a director like Nicholas Ray, where the same process is not so embarrassingly obvious. But Kazan and Ray are two sides of the same coin. Kazan screwed others, and is therefore bad; Ray screwed himself, and is therefore good. His films have an overlay of romantic pessimism that allows liberals to weep their bad conscience away.

In the seventies, Kazan has received the benefit of an altered cultural climate. He has profited by a new catholicity on the part of auteur critics, whose major battles seem won and who are now casting about to find new tenants for the Pantheon, and by the interest of European left and American New Left critics who find in Kazan's cold war anti-Stalinism a confirmation of their own antipathy toward the old left.

Times do change, and each generation sees the film classics with its own eyes. Wounds heal, memory falters, present needs require of the past different lessons than those drawn by our predecessors. One would not wish to deny Kazan the consolations of history. Yet the social situations within which films are made continue to live, in turn, within them. Films like *Viva Zapata!* and *On the Waterfront* bear the marks, the *inscription*, as the French would say, of their historical context. They cannot be fully understood outside the passionate political controversies of which they were part. This essay is an attempt to make this inscription clear. It is intended as a contribution to the reassessment of Kazan and, beyond that, a contribution to the larger question of how Hollywood films respond to the requirements of the ideological context in which they are situated. Implicit in its approach is a critique of auteurism. While it cannot be denied that Kazan is an auteur, at the same time, like any other director, he must be seen as mediating conflicting cultural and aesthetic demands. Examining the cultural soil from which films grow does not impoverish them, as conservative critics often charge, but rather enriches them by restoring to them their original nourishment.

On the Waterfront falls in the middle of the seismic shift from the thirties to the fifties. By the time it was begun, in 1954, Kazan had long since abandoned the passionate commitment of the thirties. On the other hand, he had not yet attained the Fordian distance revealed in such later films as *Baby Doll* (1956), *Wild River* (1960), and *Splendor in the Grass* (1961). *On the Waterfront* harnesses the methods of the thirties to the ideology of the fifties. It is political allegory cast in the form of a morality play. This requires a particularly skillful form of aesthetic footwork, since its success requires that the political allegory be simultaneously admitted and refused. To deny the allegorical level runs the risk that the message of the film will go unrecorded. To acknowledge the allegorical level runs the risk that the ideological project of the film will be unmasked. Films like *On the Waterfront* walk a tightrope between revelation and concealment, between clarity and mystification.

In *Viva Zapata!* (1952), the first part of Kazan's anticommunist trilogy, he had shown that the exercise of individual power is either perverse or tragic. Zapata had to renounce state power to avoid being corrupted by it, but even so he found that the requirements of leadership poisoned his relations with his wife, led indirectly to his brother's death, and forced him to execute a trusted lieutenant. The exercise of power, in other words, entails the violation of the intimate personal bonds we hold most dear. Although the commonplace that power corrupts is a staple of Hollywood political wisdom, finding classic expression in the comedies of Frank Capra, in the fifties, and especially in the hands of Kazan, it became a weapon in the cold war struggle against the left in general, and Stalinism in particular. According to sociologists like Daniel Bell, it was the millennial, ideological movements, the Nazis and the Soviets, who exercised power; democrats did not. Liberal democracy was regarded as an ideal form of government because everybody and nobody exercises power. In America, remarks one of Zapata's band, "the government governs, but with the consent of the people. The people have a voice." In *On the Waterfront*, two years later, we see how power manifests itself in a democracy.

Where *Viva Zapata!* has aged quickly, *On the Waterfront* remains, after two decades, a tremendously powerful film, one of the best films of the fifties. In many ways, it was a child of the HUAC investigations, a blow struck in the ideological and artistic battle between those who talked and those who didn't. Many of its personnel, including Kazan, Budd Schulberg, who wrote the script, Lee J. Cobb, who played John Friendly, and Leif Erickson, who played one of the Waterfront Crime Commission investigators, had gone before the HUAC, confessed their past sins, and implicated close friends and associates. One of Kazan's closest friends (whom he did not name) was Arthur Miller, with whom he had worked on *All My Sons* and *Death of a Salesman*. In 1953, Miller's play *The Crucible*, a thinly veiled attack on the witch hunt, opened on Broadway. In it, Miller has his central character go to his death rather than inform against his friends. Asked for names, he replies: "I speak my own sins; I cannot judge another. I have no tongue for it . . . . I have three children—how may I teach them to walk like men in the world, and I sold my friends." [5]

On the Waterfront is Kazan's answer. It presents a situation in which informing on criminal associates is the only honorable course of action for a just man. The injunction against informing on friends and colleagues is axiomatic in most societies where the state does not exercise overwhelming moral authority, but the film's dialogue repeatedly defines squealing not as an absolute but as a relative matter. It depends on where you stand. Father Barry (Karl Malden) expresses this nicely: "What's ratting on them, is telling the truth for you." On the other hand, Charlie-the-Gent ("a butcher in a camel's hair coat") becomes the spokesman for the discredited principle of loyalty: "Stooling is when you rat on your friends."

By ratting on John Friendly and his boys, Terry Malloy (Marlon Brando) helps the Crime Commission destroy a corrupt union, wins the lady, Edie Doyle (Eva Marie Saint), and redeems himself in his own eyes and in those of the honest rank and file. He is the informer as hero.[6] Thus, American society may not be perfect, its institutions may be fallible, but they contain the mechanisms for their own regeneration. Although corrupt unions run the docks, the regulatory and investigatory (HUAC included?) agencies of government—the open hearings covered by the free press, the benign investigators—are more than a match for the forces of darkness. Justice prevails. As the opening title says, "It has always been in the American tradition not to hide our shortcomings, but on the contrary, to spotlight them and to correct them. The incidents portrayed in this picture were true of a particular area of the waterfront. They exemplify the way self-appointed tyrants can be fought and defeated by right-thinking men in a vital democracy."

This optimism regarding the democratic process is not so much a betrayal of the thirties as a fulfillment of certain attitudes toward the state implicit in thirties radicalism. Both the New Deal, with its stress on activist big government, and the Communist party, with its admiration for the Soviet Union, contributed to a generally positive attitude toward state power on the part of the left. A 1938 film, *Racket Busters*, scripted by Robert Rossen who himself later informed before HUAC, applauds state coercion of reluctant witnesses. The Popular Front film *Native Land* also portrays the state as an effective instrument of the people. If the state was indeed as benevolent as these films would have it, it is perhaps not so surprising that the state could later, under different circumstances, command the loyalty of its citizens against its enemies. The ex-Communist friendly witnesses of the fifties were still Stalinists at heart—only Truman and Eisenhower had become their Stalin. The U.S.A had replaced the U.S.S.R.

The submerged analogy between the criminally corrupt waterfront unions and the "crime" of membership in the Communist party reflected a belief dear to the hearts of cold war liberals—that the American Communist Party was a criminal conspiracy falling outside the traditional guarantees of civil liberties. As Sidney Hook put it, "Heresy, yes, conspiracy, no." The inadequacy of this model, obvious at the time and certainly obvious now, does not need extended discussion. Suffice it to say, the equation of overt acts of violence and "crimes" of belief that is used to justify informing against Communists and fellow travelers doesn't hold up. As Murray Kempton pointed out in 1963, "Our laws deal with what a man has done, not what he might have done given the chance."[7]

Nor is the film's portrayal of union corruption very convincing. Although it is quite faithful to the texture of East Coast waterfront life, it falsifies the overall picture. Just as Kazan conveniently overlooks the larger social and political implications of the class structure of Mexico in *Viva Zapata!*, attributing the dependent position of the dispossessed peasants solely to the venal generals and politicians, so here he is careful to circumscribe the tumor of corruption so that it may be neatly excised without undue injury or embarrassment to the body politic.[8] Despite one rhetorical gesture toward generality (a single shot shows "Mr. Upstairs" watching the Crime Commission hearings on television), Kazan emphasizes the limited and exceptional nature of his subject. He even goes so far as to have one of his dockers exclaim, "The waterfront . . . ain't part of America."

If, as Daniel Bell, Seymour Martin Lipset, and their followers maintained, the problems of the fifties were those of "piecemeal technology," amenable to technological solutions applied by an elite of experts, connections between the particular and the general that might suggest structural contradictions in society had to be suppressed.[9] The notion that racketeering might be endemic rather than incidental, that it was a natural expression of a capitalist system that concentrated power and money in the hands of a few and employed graft to lubricate and stabilize the system, was unthinkable. Corruption was exclusively regarded as a moral evil, a sin perpetrated by bad men (the theological frame of reference is enforced by the prominent place occupied by the priest Father Barry), rather than a form of mutually beneficial and politically expedient collusion between unions, management, and the Tammany Hall machine. Joseph P. Ryan, the International Longshoreman's Association (ILA) boss who could have served as a model for John Friendly, held notorious annual dinners, attendance at which was obligatory for every politician in the city, the mayor and police commissioner included.[10] Management purchased "protection" from the crooked union, freedom from strikes, disruptions over pay, and workplace grievances: "Industrial racketeering . . . performs the function . . . of stabilizing a chaotic market and establishing an order and structure in the industry." [11] Yet *On the Waterfront* portrays the shipper, a major beneficiary of this arrangement, as neutral, as a bystander above the factional fight within the union. He doesn't care who runs the docks, so long as he gets his ships loaded and unloaded.

We can now turn to the critical question of the film's conception of power. What immediately becomes clear is that the film doesn't seem to deal with power at all. The arena of conflict in *On the Waterfront*—which is, after all, a film about labor and unions—is not class but self. It is not without but within. It is Terry Malloy's interior struggle, his struggle to come to moral awareness and to act on his new perception of right and wrong.

The agent of Terry's awakening is the waterfront priest, Father Barry. Father Barry intervenes decisively at crucial moments to change the course of events: he precipitates the struggle against the mob; he persuades Terry Malloy to confess to Edie Doyle that he helped set up her brother Joey to be pushed off a roof; he prevents Terry from using his gun to avenge the death of his brother at the hands of John Friendly; he urges Terry to testify before the Crime Commission; and he prevents the dockers from aiding the badly injured Malloy so that he can make his heroic walk leading the men back to work in defiance of the mob. Kazan apparently approves of this kind of moral agency, since all these interventions turn out for the best, but they could easily have been catastrophic. What emerges is an alarming picture of a ruthless crusader who manipulates others like chess pieces in the name of a higher good for which no price is too high, no sacrifice too great.

That manipulation is not too strong a word for Father Barry's behavior is clear from the authority with which he employs his carrot-and-stick strategy to guide Terry through the intricate moral maze Kazan has constructed for him. Although his interventions in the course of action are frequently direct and forceful (at one point he knocks Terry down in order to prevent him from going gunning for Friendly), just as frequently this coercion is coyly denied or disguised. On the several occasions when Terry asks Father Barry or Edie (an ancillary manipulator) what course of action he should adopt, they insist that it is up to him, to his conscience, that they cannot tell him what to do. Invariably, this disavowal is contradicted by a moral imperative that immediately follows: do this or do that, as in this exchange in which Father Barry forcefully but obliquely urges Terry to reveal his part in Joey's death to Edie:

Father Barry:	What are you gonna do about it? . . . about telling her, the Commission, the subpoena? . . .
Terry:	I don't know . . .
Father Barry:	Listen, if I were you I would walk right—never mind. I'm not asking you to do anything . . . It's your own conscience that's gotta do the askin'—Edie's . . . coming here. . . . Come on, why don't you tell her.

Father Barry's method of persuasion is successful. Terry indeed perceives his choices as issuing from his own "conscience," his own deepest desires, when in fact they are elicited by a powerful, albeit disguised, form of psychological and moral pressure. It appears, in fact, that Charlie-the-Gent is correct when he tells John Friendly later, "This girl and the Father—they got the hooks in the kid so deep he don't know which end is up anymore."

Father Barry is doing no more than applying manipulative methods of social control that have deep roots in the American past—in the Progressive movement in general and in the philosophy of John Dewey in particular. Dewey's stress on social control and collectivism had a radical ring in the thirties, when it was intended as a counterweight to the chaotic conditions created by what seemed like an uncontrolled, irrational capitalist economy, but by the fifties Dewey's methods had become useful tools for constructing the new consensus. Christopher Lasch, in *The Agony of the American Left*, identifies the role of this manipulative liberal ideology in easing social conflict: "Even when it originated in humanitarian impulses, progressive ideas led not to a philosophy of liberation but to a blueprint for control. The task of the social reformer came to be seen as that of 'enlisting the person's own participating disposition in getting the result desired, and thereby developing within him an intrinsic and persisting direction in the right way.'" [12]

In choosing to use persuasion rather than coercion, Barry is doing no more than acting in accord with the democratic ethos as defined, for example, in 1949

by Arthur Schlesinger, Jr.: "The thrust of the democratic faith is away from fanaticism: it is towards compromise, persuasion, and consent in politics." [13] Force
was not used because it was not needed. As Schlesinger pointed out in the course
of arguing against some of the harsher measures of the witch hunt: "If we can
defeat Communism as a political force within the framework of civil liberties,
why abandon that framework?" Using the Church as a disguised instrument of
social control, as Kazan does, was characteristic of the disingenuous approach of
one strain of fifties liberalism toward problems of power. Reactionaries like Leo
McCarey were a good deal more forthright: his film *My Son John* clearly identifies the FBI as the locus of moral authority and power; the priest, in comparison,
is a severely diminished figure. [14]

What is the significance of such a ruthless and powerful but apparently moral
figure as Father Barry when Kazan has shown us in *Viva Zapata!* that power
corrupts? Although the power-to-the-people moral of *Viva Zapata!* would lead
us to expect that in a democracy, where power is shared by the *demos* (in America, "the people have a voice"), such a figure should be either evil or unnecessary. But in *On the Waterfront*, the people are incapable of exercising power.
They are a passive herd who invariably fail to act when put to the test. At best,
they can follow the leader or exercise their power in a negative refusal to act:
"How 'bout Terry? He don't work, we don't work." The conclusion that inescapably emerges from the contradiction between the two films is that when Kazan
wishes to show the self-regenerative capacities of liberal capitalist society through
mass political action, effective yet circumscribed, leaders are OK. But when he
is faced with a real social upheaval, as he is in *Viva Zapata!*, which threatens to
exceed the bounds of decorous reform, he enforces the self-serving moral that
leadership will always become corrupt.

Rather than the egalitarian society we might have expected after *Viva Zapata!*,
On the Waterfront, like many other films of the fifties, offers an elitist model of
society in which power is the prerogative of experts in the law and its enforcement (police, judges, lawyers) in alliance with social engineers (priests, psychia-
trists, social workers) and family (usually the hero's wife or girlfriend) to perform an essential task of social control. Acting in concert, the official and
unofficial agents of society curb the hero's cynical, self-interested, asocial behavior by awakening in him, at the very most, a higher moral awareness (as in *On
the Waterfront*) or, at the very least, a recognition that his own self-interest coincides with the larger purposes of the state (as in the films of Samuel Fuller). The
control exercised by these figures is indirect rather than direct, manipulative
rather than coercive. The hero perceives his commitment to family and a steady
job, and his consequent acknowledgment of the legitimacy of the established
order is a voluntary choice. Social directives are internalized. But Terry is in no
sense free; he has merely exchanged one type of bondage for another. Authoritarian coercion exercised by the mob (he had to take a fall in a fixed fight) gives way
to authoritarian manipulation exercised by the society.

Even though Terry rises bravely on his own two feet at the end, having successfully beaten Friendly in hand-to-hand combat, inspiring the men to defy the
mob, his stance is an uncertain one; we have the feeling that Terry is still at the

mercy of forces he cannot understand, forces much more subtle and dangerous than the ones he has overcome—an alliance of Wilsonian moral ferocity, Progressive institutions, the family, and management. As the film closes and the great iron door of the shed crashes shut, we feel that Malloy is not so much liberated as trapped by the shadowy figure of the shipping boss, who is the ultimate beneficiary of the action and who has (almost) the last word: "All right, let's get to work." Once power abused (again, as in *Viva Zapata!*, concentrated in the hands of one man) has been eliminated, the ships can be loaded, and the happy collaboration between capital and labor that cemented the fifties consensus can prevail.

Kazan's view of reform is as elitist as his conception of democracy. Both social reform and individual salvation are top-down affairs, conducted by experts—the Crime Commission in one case, the priest in the other. The initiative in both instances comes from the experts, from above. This becomes clear if we look at a similar situation in Fuller's *Underworld USA*, a much more populist film: in the alliance between the special prosecutor and Tolly Devlin against the syndicate, the initiative comes from Tolly, from below.

Experts were seen by many political commentators of the fifties as the logical agents for social change. As Arthur Schlesinger, Jr., wrote: "The experience of a century has shown that neither the capitalists nor the workers are so tough and purposeful as Marx anticipated: that their mutual bewilderment and inertia leave the way open for some other group to serve as the instrument of change; that when the politician-manager-intellectual type is intelligent and decisive, he can usually get society to move fast enough to escape breaking up under the weight of its own contradictions." [15]

Robert Wise's liberal science fiction film *The Day the Earth Stood Still* (1951) envisioned scientists and intellectuals alone as receptive to the message of peace on earth delivered by the interplanetary emissary Klaatu. The average man on the street was fearful, suspicious, or narrowly self-interested, like Patricia Neal's boyfriend, an insurance salesman. Confidently basing their analysis on a "post"-Marxist perspective that relegated class conflict to the dustbin of history, liberals like Kazan and Schlesinger could imagine evolutionary social change engineered by neutral managers without class affiliation on behalf of a state apparatus that was itself above class.

Although it is true that Kazan is ambivalent toward intellectuals, his "bad ones" are ineffectual; they cannot get the job done.

Even though the main thrust of *On the Waterfront* is toward the socialization of Terry, it is necessary to pay close attention to the way this operation is carried out. It occurs through an apparently contradictory process of individuation. Terry is divested of old-world ethnic ties to immediate family ("they're asking me to put the finger on my own brother"), to the extended family of the union local ("Uncle" Johnny Friendly "used to take me to the ball games when I was a kid"), and to neighborhood. He is systematically detached from the social tissue that forms his natural habitat and gathered into a larger notion of community-as-nation, associated with ahistorical absolutes like "democracy," "truth," "right and wrong," and anchored in the upwardly mobile nuclear family that provides its institutional base. For his blood brother Charlie he substitutes the claims of the Christian brotherhood of Father Barry ("you've got some other brothers") and the democratic brotherhood of America ("the people have a right to know").

This transition is facilitated in several ways. First, it is rendered as a process of growth. Terry's testimony before the Crime Commission is an indication of self-knowledge ("I was ratting on myself all them years, and I didn't even know it") and the assumption of adulthood. The measure of his maturity is his decision to inform, to transcend local loyalties for larger and presumably higher ones. Loyalty to friends is regarded as an adolescent virtue, the province of his protégé in the Golden Warriors, Tommy, who spurns him after he testifies. Although Tommy's reaction is experienced as a painful repudiation, it is somewhat undermined by being given a Freudian dimension. The sullen and hostile attitude he displays toward Edie earlier in the film suggests adolescent jealousy of the as yet latent adult relationship between Edie and Terry. Second, the mob, although in one sense Terry's family, is in another sense a false family. After all, it is an all-male group like the Golden Warriors, and it frequently acts to destroy family ties. It is responsible for Joey Doyle's death (Joey is defined in the film principally as Edie's brother); the core of Terry's accusation against his brother Charlie is that Charlie let his loyalty to Friendly take priority over his natural blood ties to his own brother. (Charlie later redeems himself by reasserting familial bonds in defiance of the mob.) Since the mob is exposed as a false family, it is not too difficult to convince Terry that they do not deserve his allegiance. Third, Terry's private goals, like his boxing career that the mob frustrated, are legitimized. And finally, all these strands are gathered up in the nuclear family, represented by Edie. It offers maturity and responsibility, adult sexuality, upward mobility (Edie has been educated in a suburb, Tarrytown, and her father has labored so that she will enjoy the advantages of which he was deprived), and satisfaction of "private" goals. If Terry's boxing career is over, he can at least experience the pleasures of romantic love, the peculiar province and strength of the nuclear family in a society where emotional gratification cannot be found outside the home. In terms of social control, society has successfully identified the "responsible" leadership (the family) within the community and forged an alliance with it in order to destroy autonomous (and thus subversive) groups outside its control.

Submerged in the valorization of romantic love, family, and "feminine" virtues is a new definition of what it meant to be a man in fifties America. The old-style immigrant morality of John Friendly, and the character structure that accompanied it, were obsolete. The ethnic ghettoes were being dispersed by assimilation and upward mobility; the protective reflexes based on fierce individual and ethnic loyalties were no longer necessary. New access to economic opportunity and suburban life-styles, along with constitutional guarantees like due process and habeas corpus, afforded first-generation Americans all the protection formerly provided by ethnic protective associations, ethnic enclaves within unions, and tight, close-knit neighborhoods. Changed social circumstances required a new, softer, more pliable and trusting version of the male role. And if Terry had to move toward Edie, Edie had to move toward him, away from old-fashioned European notions of the woman's role that were pressed upon her by her father toward a superficially more equal and activist stance. It is a comment on the distance between the fifties and the seventies that the immigrant ethos discarded in *On the Waterfront* as "un-American" is sentimentalized by the more radical film *The Godfather*, with Brando now playing what could easily be the aging John Friendly.

In the fifties, the process by which Terry is detached from his old loyalties and incorporated into an abstract community was called "massification" by social critics when it occurred in totalitarian societies. It signified the emergence of "mass" man. Groups that mediated between the individual and the state, which might have competed with the state for the loyalty of the individual, were destroyed. By means of mass culture (television, the press, and the movies), schooling, and work, all of which reproduced prescriptive hierarchical relationships, the state impinged directly on the individual. The only institution that remained intact was the nuclear family. Although it was the locus of a less authoritarian set of habits than those instilled by school and factory, it was expected to generate goals of personal gratification through consumerism and emotional relationships, which in turn were to motivate and guarantee the dichotomy between public life and private life.

It is worth noting that in the course of Terry's pilgrimage, he and Edie, who is initially a spokeswoman for the right-at-any-cost position of Father Barry, change places. As soon as she falls in love with Terry, she urges him to flee, to avoid the confrontation with Friendly that Father Barry demands and for which he is ready to sacrifice Terry, Edie, and everyone else. It's just not worth it, she feels. Although the film fails to give credence to her point of view, she comes to represent a perspective from which Barry's manipulative morality can be challenged. Within the limited terms that the film presents, it isn't worth it. In the absence of a more profound insight into the politics of corruption, Malloy is being asked to sacrifice himself for nothing. As Pauline Kael pointed out at the time, John Dwyer, one of the real-life prototypes of Terry Malloy, defied the ILA but lost the support of AFL officials who abandoned him in the crunch. His attempts to challenge the ILA ended in failure; in fact, the ILA gained even tighter control of the waterfront through a union shop. "For a happy ending," Kael wrote, wryly quoting *Time*, "dockers could go to the movies."

Although, as we have seen, Kazan falsifies the larger picture in the interests of his own political position, it is important to come to terms with the reasons the film works as well as it does. Part of the answer to this question lies in the kind of world Kazan presents. Nicholas Ray, close to Kazan in many respects, offers a Rousseauist vision; his heroes are sentimentalized innocents, noble savages inhabiting a benevolent natural world. They are presumably destroyed by the corrupt institutions of the civilized society, but since Ray's films are without a dimension of significant social criticism, they fail to dramatize this process. His films consequently lack a sense of real conflict, and issue, all too often, in saccharine happy endings in which previously antagonistic characters kiss and make up. Kazan's world, on the other hand, is entirely different. The state of nature is not innocent, it's a Hobbesian jungle. As Terry tells Edie, "You know this city's full of hawks . . . they hang around on top of the big hotels and they spot a pigeon in the park—right down on them." This predatory morality informs the ethics of the mob and makes strong claims on Terry as well. "Down here, it's every man for himself. Do you wanna hear my philosophy of life? Do it to him before he does it to you," Terry tells Edie. Opposed to this philosophy in which the strong (hawks) consume the weak (the pigeons) is Edie's morality ("Isn't everyone part of everybody else?") and Father Barry's Christianity with its promise that the meek shall inherit the earth. The battleground on which these two conceptions of man's fate contend is American democracy, and when Terry decides to become a stool pigeon, he fuses the spiritual and secular realms. Terry's protégé, Tommy, calls attention to this when he throws a dead pigeon at Terry's feet: "A pigeon for a pigeon." In Christian terms, Terry voluntarily assumes the role of the meek (the dove); in secular terms, he assumes the role of the stool pigeon (the informer), and the one transfigures the other. The political informer as Christian saint.

Terry is well on his way to crucifixion before he testifies. He puts his hand through a plate-glass window (stigmata), and later when his friends avoid him after his testimony, he experiences the abandonment of Christ on the Cross. More important for the theme of power is the subsequent beating Terry undergoes at the hands of John Friendly and company. If power in the hands of one man is always abused, as Kazan emphasized in *Viva Zapata!* and reminded us again in *On the Waterfront* (Friendly), it has to be disguised (Father Barry) or, as manifest in a character like Terry Malloy, a potentially more explosive figure than Barry, domesticated.

Marlon Brando was the ideal vehicle for the theme of power in the fifties. As the quintessential expression of the brooding, inarticulate, violent lumpen or laborer, his menacing strength with its lower-class overtones had to be transformed into negative power, the capacity to endure the aggressions inflicted upon him by others. Thus the beating or humiliation became an essential part of the Brando character, occurring not only in *Viva Zapata!* and *On the Waterfront*, but in such diverse films as *The Wild One*, *One-Eyed Jacks*, *The Chase*, and *The Appaloosa*. The significance of Terry's final walk down the pier to the shed is that his power has been chastened, transfigured, and spiritualized into the endurance of the martyr.

In a democracy, then, power is confronted not with power, but with Christian virtue. Liberal institutions (the Crime Commission) hand in hand with the Christian soldier (Terry) will ensure the reign of the meek. Like Leo McCarey and other anticommunist directors of the period, Kazan made the implicit claim not only that those who named names before HUAC were Christian saints, but indeed, that fifties America was the secular City of God on earth. A booming consumer economy offered ample proof that the God who had abandoned twentieth-century Europe to physical and spiritual destruction had come to roost in America. Father Barry's assertion that "Christ is down here, on the waterfront," is not a metaphorical or rhetorical device, but literal truth, expressing a worldview peculiar to the fifties. I know nothing about Kazan's religious convictions, but *On the Waterfront* suggests that he shared with most Americans a belief in a providence that had saved America from the ravages of war, had given her the atomic bomb, and had delivered into her reluctant hands the responsibility for world leadership. This belief in the special destiny of America was responsible in part for the suppression of transcendence (or "negation," in Marcuse's sense) in films of the fifties and for the ridiculing of utopianism as childish or unrealistic as well as the attempt to show that utopian aspirations could be realized within American institutions: thus the incarnation of the Christian (and transcendent) dove in the secular (and political) role of the stool pigeon.

Not only does the physical world incarnate spirit, but also it is transformed and redeemed by spirit. The extraordinary scene between Charlie and Terry in the back of the car is an example of this process. Its effectiveness derives in part from the tension between the confined space on the one hand and the potentially explosive nature of the interchange between the two men on the other. A shallow and constricting physical space is converted into a deep spiritual space through a series of recognitions that clarify and transform their relationship, finally freeing Terry from the lies and bad faith that had clouded his relationship with his brother and himself. In the same way, physical falling is transformed into spiritual resurrection: Joey must fall from the roof so that Terry may rise; Father Barry must descend into the hold of the ship where Dugan lies dead before he can rise with the body, hoisted aloft in the sling.

Although the physical world is violent and menacing, like the fiercely percussive sound track that deafens Edie as she listens to Terry's confession, it is the presence of spirit that facilitates the creation of a moral geography, making the physical world an expression, almost an allegory, of spirit. The moral isolation of the neighborhood is enforced by an iron picket fence that separates it from the river and the New York skyline beyond. Terry's confession to Edie appropriately takes place outside the fence. This exposed ground becomes an index of the extent to which his relationship with Edie draws Terry away from safe rationalizations and familiar relationships toward the shadowy world on the other side of the river. The fog that perpetually shrouds the park in front of the church must be seen as an emblem of Terry's confusion, while the camera movements and shot compositions insistently reinforce the vertical orientation of the film, itself the physical analogue to the verbal play on falling and rising, going down and coming up, and an iteration in physical terms of the theological framework of fall and resurrection. One example of this is the scene of Dugan's death, where the characters are inversely arranged on a vertical axis according to their moral positions, an arrangement that at the same time directly reflects their secular power: Friendly at the top, Father Barry at the bottom, and Terry in between. By the end of the film, this layering has been reversed, and we take leave of a Friendly (who has just emerged from a precipitous descent into the water) diminished by an overhead crane shot.

Despite the redemptive immanence of spirit in the physical world, Kazan's vision, unlike Nicholas Ray's, includes real conflict. Terry's cynicism about the promises of democracy expresses a real contradiction within postwar America, one that eventually generated the opposite of fifties consensus: the radicalism of the sixties. Despite Kazan's efforts to the contrary, the line from Brando's Terry Malloy and Emiliano Zapata to the sixties is a direct one, indicated by the sympathy with which young New Leftists viewed Kazan's anticommunism. That *On the Waterfront* finally produced its mirror image in *The Godfather* suggests that American popular culture is indeed dialectical in nature, contrary to the views of critics like Noel Burch who practice a mechanistic and undialectical Marxism that barely disguises their essential formalism.[16]

The seriousness of the contradiction Terry reflects is suggested by the fact that his socialization and redemption require real effort; the most sophisticated resources of church and state must be brought to bear on him. And this is not only because Kazan's vision includes a world of darkness, but because he gives this negation free expression. Despite the final harmonization of conflicting interests, the dissident voices are not hushed. Edie's anguished cries of protest are heard above Father Barry's efforts to propel Terry on his final walk. She is still opposed to his manipulation, even this close to the end of the film. Likewise, the scene of the dead pigeons is extremely effective, and its power is not entirely dispelled by its Christ-abandoned overtones. There is real loss in this world, and its complexity is reflected in the richness of characterization and acting. Even John Friendly is sympathetic, as Cobb's villains usually are, through the tremendous impact of his screen presence. He usually overwhelms everyone else in his films; if he doesn't here, it is a tribute to the brilliance of Brando's performance, probably the finest of his career. Finally, the film succeeds because of the immensely powerful grip on the American psyche exercised by the myth of individual action and redemption that lies at its heart. Especially as embodied by Brando, this myth allows us to express the fantasy of antisocial rebellion at the same time that it allows us to submerge it in an even more compelling vision of social inclusion, wholeness, and renewal.

One is tempted by a satanist reading of *On the Waterfront*, always the last resort of the hard-pressed Marxist critic faced with the excellence of reactionary art. Pauline Kael (no Marxist) has argued that "it is not Terry as a candidate for redemption who excites [the audience], but Terry the tough. . . . Terry is credible until he becomes a social hero."[17] Much as I would like to agree with her, I can't. Terry is credible to the end. However deluded, he has paid his dues; he has earned his victory. By the time he staggers to the shed, we no longer care whether Kazan has falsified the power relations in fifties America or not. There is a fitness, a completeness to the film that defies criticism.[18] Meretricious as Kazan's politics are, they are deeply felt and in some sense true to the experience of significant groups of people in the early fifties.[19]

Finally, some conclusions. Kazan twists and turns to avoid confronting the implications of American power and of power in America. He presents a picture of an ideal democratic society in which power, as such, does not exist. It is only the enemy that exercises (and abuses) power, the John Friendlys of the world. Nevertheless, since power is in fact exercised by agents with whom Kazan is sympathetic, it must be disguised in order to maintain the fiction of its absence. Power struggles in the public sphere are displaced into moral struggles in the private sphere. Manipulation replaces coercion, and power, to the extent that it cannot be denied, is transformed into the negative power of the martyr.

This is the portrait of America that the film intends to present. But the picture of America that actually emerges from the film is quite different. Power, rather than being dispersed throughout the whole society, is concentrated in the hands of an elite of experts, both official and unofficial, who wield it with a ruthless singleness of purpose for their own ends. These ends include the socialization, if possible, of dissident individuals and groups or, if necessary, their destruction. Socialization is achieved by redefining individual allegiances and goals so that they conform to those sanctioned by society.

The two antagonistic portraits of America (egalitarian and elitist) offered by *On the Waterfront* are not entirely contradictory. A view of society as run by technical elites is one way of achieving the making of power required by the egalitarian fiction. The state is viewed as a politically neutral organization of administrators standing above the petty quarrels of competing interest groups: a servant of the people.

The reasons for the felt necessity to disguise and deny the realities of power in America are not entirely clear, but they do invite speculation. Attitudes toward power distinguished and divided the various political factions during the postwar period. The older, liberal anticommunists who came of age in the thirties felt uneasy about power. They associated it with the abuses of Stalinism. The new breed of cold war liberals who came of age in the forties, on whom the experience of exercise of just power in World War II had a profound effect, felt it necessary to come to terms with power. Arthur Schlesinger, Jr., in his attempt to carve out a "vital center," a hard-headed "democratic left," denounced totalitarian communists on the one hand and scolded soft-hearted progressives on the other for their common failure to employ power effectively. The Stalinists used their power not for the general good but to create a monolithic totalitarian state that served the interests of a new class of bureaucrats and state managers. Progressives, in contrast, were afraid of power. Politics for them became merely the self-indulgence of private neuroses and guilts. The denizens of Schlesinger's vital center, however, were able to make a realistic appraisal of the potentials and limits of power. Unlike the progressives, they were not afraid to use it. Unlike the Stalinists, their power was "accountable" or "responsible" power, limited by the restraints inherent in the democratic system. For Schlesinger, as for most liberal intellectuals of the postwar period, the defining characteristic of a democracy such as America was that it was "pluralistic," that is, power was shared by a large number of different interest groups who competed on a more or less equal basis for a part of the pie. Social critics like C. Wright Mills who questioned this model, who suggested that power in America was concentrated in the hands of a ruling elite, were dismissed as cranks, communists, or both.

Kazan was considerably less frank than Schlesinger in his attitude toward power. Of an earlier generation than Schlesinger, a generation which had itself tasted the mixed fruits of Communist Party politics, he revealed some of the special bitterness and engaged in much of the special pleading that characterized ex-Communists who collaborated in the cold war witch-hunt. Schlesinger, after all, was somewhat nearer to the actual seat of power than was Kazan (by the time he wrote *The Vital Center* he had worked on the Marshall Plan as a special assistant to Averell Harriman); he was as much concerned with refurbishing liberalism for the purpose of providing a cloak of respectability for the new American hegemony as he was with scarifying the Soviet Union and the Stalinist left. While Kazan was satisfied to discredit the whole idea of political power and deny the existence of power in America, Schlesinger had, at the same time, to relegitimize power so that it could be used without scruple in the interests of American foreign policy. Kazan fought on one front, Schlesinger fought on two.

The reluctance to acknowledge or specify centers of power at a time of vast American military and economic strength may also be taken as an indication of guilt or bad conscience, a refusal to accept responsibility for the uses to which American power had already been put, not only at home in the witch-hunt, but in Hiroshima and Nagasaki as well. As Michael Wood has pointed out, many American films of the fifties, *The Gunfighter* (1950) for example, express a wish to relinquish power. Nevertheless, it would be another decade or so before these contradictions would surface. In the meantime, Kazan's longshoremen learned their lessons well. Ten years later, they would be loading weapons bound for Vietnam and their sons would be going off to fight.

Notes

1. *Movie*, no. 19 (Winter 1971/-1972).
2. Jim Kitses, "Elia Kazan: A Structural Analysis," *Cinema* 7, no. 3 (1973): 25–36.
3. Michel Ciment, ed., *Kazan on Kazan* (New York, 1974).
4. There is certainly precedent in Marxist criticism for championing an artist who on the face of it seems to be reactionary. Engels defended Balzac (see his letter to Margaret Harkness) and other critics, most notably Lukács, have followed suit. Yet in the case of Hollywood directors of the fifties, this claim seems to me highly dubious.
5. Arthur Miller, *The Crucible* (New York, 1971). It is interesting to note that Kazan could have worked with Miller on *On the Waterfront*. The idea, according to Miller, was originally his; he had done a considerable amount of work on a script before Schulberg came on the film. Schulberg's ultimate authorship of the shooting script represents, if nothing else, a symbolic shift to the right. See Arthur Miller, "The Year It Came Apart," *New York Magazine*, 30 December 1974/-6 January 1975. Miller's account also throws light on the relationship between overt and covert anticommunist films. *On the Waterfront* could have been made as an overtly anticommunist film dealing with party, not mob, control of unions. In fact, it was only under these conditions that Harry Cohn would agree to produce the film. Kazan chose to remain faithful to his original conception and produce it independently. The film is still anticommunist, but much more effective because it displaces and partially conceals its anticommunism. Liberal anticommunists like Dorothy Jones clearly saw the advantages of subtlety. She criticized Hollywood's anticommunist productions for doing more harm than good in their vulgar lack of sophistication. See her "Communism and the Movies," in *Report on Blacklisting*, vol. 1: *The Movies*, ed. John Cogley (New York: Fund for the Republic, 1956). Liberal critics often point to the poor box office returns on anticommunist films of the fifties to argue against the idea that Hollywood films are ideological; Hollywood's infrequent forays into politics, they say, have been disastrous. In fact, the evidence merely shows that Americans are allergic to overt propaganda. Covert propaganda, like *On the Waterfront*, does very well.

6. For a different perspective on informing, note the treatment accorded stool pigeons in Jules Dassin's prison film *Brute Force*, made just a few years earlier.

7. Murray Kempton, *America Comes of Middle Age* (New York, 1963).

8. Compare Kazan's sanguine treatment of corruption-as-tumor to Lang's pessimistic view in *The Big Heat* of corruption as a gradually spreading stain that eventually blackens almost the entire society.

9. In *The End of Ideology* (New York, 1961), Daniel Bell argued that New York waterfront racketeering not only took the shape it did as a result of the antiquated physical condition of the docks but was in fact caused in large measure by the fact that the port facilities were inadequate to handle modern trucks. Dockside congestion gave rise to the occupation of "loading" (goods had to be picked up off the docks and loaded onto trucks), which came to be a major source of graft. The solution, in other words, was wider streets.

10. The intimate relationship between the mob, big labor, city officials, and business can be glimpsed from the following facts. "Since the port is a municipal enterprise, a businessman had to negotiate pier leases from the city, get various licenses, and learn his way around the Office of Marine and Aviation. . . . In 1947, during the [Mayor] O'Dwyer regime, an ex-bootlegger who sought to rent a pier was told to see Clarence Neal, a power in Tammany Hall, and to engage his services for $100,000. As a result of these disclosures, Mr. O'Dwyer's Commissioner of Marine and Aviation and his two chief deputies retired. . . . From 1928 to 1938, Joe Ryan was chairman of the AFL Central Trades and Labor Council, and in that post spoke for 'labor' in the political campaigns. . . . Another hidden source of ILA influence was the . . . friendship between Joe Ryan and a prominent New York businessman . . . William J. McCormack. He was . . . executive vice-president of the powerful U.S. Trucking Corporation, whose board chairman was Alfred E. Smith. . . . His Morania Oil Company supplies fuel oil to the city. His largest enterprise, Penn Stevedore Company, unloads all the freight brought into the city by the Pennsylvania Railroad. . . . Jarka, a stevedoring concern, had paid $89,582 in 'petty cash' to steamship company officials over a five year period to earn 'good-will'; $20,000 had gone to Walter Wells, the president of Isthmian Lines (owned by U.S. Steel)" (Bell, *End of Ideology*, p. 176).

11. Ibid.

12. Christopher Lasch, *The Agony of the American Left* (New York, 1969), pp. 9, 10; quotation is from John Dewey, *Democracy and Education* (New York, 1961), pp. 26–27.

13. All quotes here from Arthur Schlesinger, Jr., *The Vital Center* (London, 1970), pp. 245, 210, 218.

14. By way of contrast, compare the role of the priest in Hitchcock's *I Confess* (1952) with that in *My Son John* and *On the Waterfront*. As Leo Braudy has pointed out, the moral authority of the priest (Montgomery Clift) runs counter to the demands of the state voiced by the police inspector—played, curiously enough, by Karl Malden. Although the film eventually reconciles the claims of conscience with the demands of society, an authentic conservative like Hitchcock still comes off as a libertarian in the fifties, while a liberal like Kazan comes off as a totalitarian.

15. Schlesinger, *The Vital Center*, p. 155.

16. See especially Noël Burch and Jorge Dana, "Propositions," *Afterimage*, no. 5 (Spring 1974).

17. Pauline Kael, *I Lost It At The Movies* (New York, 1966), p. 47.

18. Nevertheless, the ending has always been puzzling. Lindsay Anderson, in a famous and controversial piece (*Sight and Sound* 24, no. 3 [1955]: 127–130), said: "It is a conclusion that can only be taken in two ways: as hopeless, savagely ironic; or as fundamentally contemptuous, pretending to idealism, but in reality without either grace, or joy,

or love." Anderson called the film fascist because it implies the necessity of strong leadership over the rank and file, who are portrayed as children. This is certainly an important element in the film, but to call it fascist obscures more than it reveals. The ideology of the film is precisely *not* fascist, if by that term we mean authoritarian; rather, it can best be described by Marcuse's notion of manipulative repressive tolerance. Raymond Durgnat (*Films and Feelings* [Cambridge, 1971], p. 74) disagrees with Anderson, citing Bell's article as a rebuttal, but without particularizing. I would say, if anything, that Bell contradicts Kazan. On the one hand, he stresses much more rank-and-file militancy than Kazan portrays. The frequent and vigorous wildcat strikes of the late forties hardly bear out Kazan's picture of docile, sheeplike dockers. On the other hand, Bell speculates that there was not as much resistance to the ILA as these walkouts seemed to indicate (as suggested by the results of two National Labor Relations Board elections won by the ILA) and that they were largely provoked by rival mobs on the outside seeking a piece of the action. If this is true, it contradicts Kazan's picture of reform issuing from an apocalyptic confrontation of good and evil. Kazan himself has some odd comments on the ending in the Ciment interview, while Kael simply considers the end ("the shipowner, an oddly ambiguous abstraction") not "thought out." I think this is closest to the truth.

19. One place the film does ring false is in its portrait of the Crime Commission. Kazan is at pains to underscore the scrupulous solicitude with which witnesses were treated by the Crime Commission: "You have every right not to talk if that's what you choose to do"; "You can bring a lawyer if you wish; you're privileged under the Constitution to protect yourself against questions which might implicate you in any crime." This kind of special pleading is particularly offensive and hypocritical in view of the actual treatment accorded witnesses during this period; it is hardly the place of an informer like Kazan to recommend the virtue of prosecutors to defendants who were not so cooperative as he and who risked careers in the interest of principle.

Acknowledgment

I am indebted to Leo Braudy, Al LaValley, William Rothman, and Michael Wood for valuable suggestions which I have incorporated in this article.

MACHISMO AND HOLLYWOOD'S WORKING CLASS

PETER BISKIND AND BARBARA EHRENREICH

Whenever we cast our eyes up to the silver screen, wherever we look—at figures riding tall in the saddle, crouched in foxholes, careening down mountain roads in fast cars, or even cowering in the kitchen—we see men. One urgent and consistent theme that stretches through Hollywood films from Rudolph Valentino to Al Pacino has been masculinity. In the movies, masculinity is presented as an agonizing, unresolved *problem*. Will Sean Connery ever settle down? What would it have meant for James Dean to grow up? The problem that Hollywood addresses is not too different from that which Freud laid out in *Civilization and Its Discontents*: can man, that is, the male gender, find happiness in a world of nine-to-five jobs, the Little League, and aluminum siding sales?

In the real world, the seventies were a particularly trying decade for men and, not surprisingly, it is the trials of upper-middle-class men that are most poignantly recounted in best-sellers (*The World According to Garp*) and TV sitcoms. Safe, tame domesticity faded as a social ideal, and its traditional antithesis—untamed machismo—came back from Vietnam with a castration complex. At the same time a reborn feminist movement undercut the moral authority of male paternalism. And that far-reaching social upheaval known to liberals as the "life-styles revolution," and to conservatives as "the breakdown of the family," left men as well as women adrift in a shifting landscape of "relationships." Woody Allen, more than anyone, articulated the sense of victimization men felt in the grip of the mid-seventies masculinity crisis: looking plaintive as Diane Keaton reads *The Second Sex* in bed (*Annie Hall*) or trying to "rescue" his son from Meryl Streep, his lesbian ex-wife (*Manhattan*). Dustin Hoffman and Richard Gere in *Kramer vs. Kramer* and *American Gigolo* tried to beat women at some of their own games: nurturance in the one and prostitution in the other.

In the late 1970s, the movies introduced a new, and politically intriguing, perspective on the male condition. After decades of cowboys, detectives, spies, and earnest young scientists, the cameras turned—long enough to establish a genre—on working-class men, in particular the white, ethnic variety. Previously encountered in the postwar period mainly as enlisted men in World War II films, working-class males now zoomed to individual prominence as the heroes of *Saturday Night Fever*, *Blue Collar*, *Bloodbrothers*, *Rocky I* and *II*, *Paradise Alley*, *FIST*, and a handful of others. Left critics have by and large viewed this new genre as Hollywood's latest experiment in social realism, judging the films on the basis of their accuracy in portraying working-class life. Here, we will not take them quite so literally. On the whole (and with some exceptions) these films are

From *Socialist Review*, nos. 50–51 (May–June 1980).

not about the working class any more than westerns are about the West. They use the working class as little more than a backdrop for Hollywood's latest exploration of the "man question." If they do reveal anything about class in America, it is not the working class, but the middle class. These films are, in a sense, middle-class male anxiety dreams in which class is no more than a metaphor for conflicting masculine possibilities. Violence and machismo, along with male bonding and obsessive determination, are allocated to the working class. Maturity and self-mastery are allocated to the middle class. The masculine dialectic between machismo and maturity is externalized; class struggle is internalized.

FLASHBACK

The films of the fifties were generally confident in their projection of a stable, moderate social order. Male mayhem was corralled into the playworld of cowboy pictures. Grownup (and out of cowboys and Indians) men found themselves in the heterosexual middle-class married couple; any other social affinity was extremist or deviant. Films as disparate as *Marty*, *Blackboard Jungle*, *On the Waterfront*, and *Seven Brides for Seven Brothers* portrayed men in groups as either immature or criminal. In films like Ford's *My Darling Clementine*, Zinnemann's *High Noon*, Mann's *Tin Star*, and Hawks's *Rio Bravo*, the villains were the male clan, brothers without women. Male groups, whether united by class, family ties, or mere derring-do, were doomed to death or marriage.

Outside the movies, domesticity was also held up as the model for male adjustment. In an economy based on plenty, not scarcity (where, as David Riesman put it, the glad hand replaced the invisible hand), people flocked to shopping centers, not savings banks, and heterosexual "togetherness" was the hallmark of maturity. Men made their last stand in the hardware store, not the bar. The dominant ideology of the center, pluralism, viewed politics as the give-and-take among a multiplicity of interest groups competing on a more or less equal basis for a part of the pie. For this process to work, men (women were not even in the game) had to be willing to compromise. "The thrust of the democratic faith is away from fanaticism; it is towards persuasion and consent in politics, towards tolerance and diversity in society," wrote Arthur Schlesinger, Jr., in 1949. Pluralism, therefore, required a psychology, a character structure. Men were supposed to be "other-directed," not "inner-directed," "organization men," not individualists; they were supposed to be flexible, softer, more willing to give in and make the compromises that would keep the pluralist machine running smoothly. According to the conventional ideology of gender identity, the sex that embodied these traits was, of course, female. Pluralist men were thus "feminized" men, whereas old-style "masculine" men—heroic, rigid, moralistic—were derogated as "extremist" or "totalitarian." The hard-boiled male roles of the thirties and forties, and the actors who played them, became psychopaths in the late forties and fifties. Cagney played the gangster as psycho in *White Heat*. Wayne played the cowboy as an obsessive neurotic in Ford's *The Searchers*. Bogart played an unbalanced, violence-prone writer in Nicholas Ray's *In a Lonely Place*. Cooper played a neurotic capitalist in *Bright Leaf*. Meanwhile, in films as different from one another as *Red River*, *Rebel Without a Cause*, *On the Waterfront*, *Giant*, and *Creature from the Black Lagoon*, men were shown learning to be sensitive. A whole generation of male actors, like Montgomery Clift, Tony Perkins, James Dean, and Paul Newman, embodied pluralist psychology.

But there was a contradiction in the fifties construction of masculinity. Conservatives had never bought the feminized male in the first place, and even liberals like Schlesinger realized that the kind of character structure appropriate at home, for family barbecues and two-martini lunches, was not appropriate abroad. When it came to dealing with the Russians, compromise was foolhardy, flexibility fatal. As the mid-fifties Eisenhower thaw gave way to the tensions of the Berlin Wall and the Cuban Missile Crisis, the domesticated male began to be seen as one of America's greatest strategic weaknesses. The Korean War showed that American boys were too soft to stand up to enemy brainwashing; Sputnik showed that they were too dumb to compete with Soviet whiz kids. When U-2 pilot Francis Gary Powers ended up on Russian television instead of dead from cyanide, too chicken to have been a martyr for the CIA and the Free World, it was the last straw. In the late fifties and early sixties, American culture took a right turn away from permissiveness in child raising and "softness" in males. Films, so long preoccupied with the problem of how to tame men, took up the problem of the too-tame man. In 1960, Hitchcock put Tony Perkins, fresh from a bout of mental illness in *Fear Strikes Out* and one of the leading sensitive male actors, in *Psycho*. When Perkins killed white-collar thief Janet Leigh, he showed that women who rip off men go down the drain, and men who take women as role models go off their rockers.

The "man question" had been reopened. Films of the sixties took it up with a vengeance—so much so that, by the early seventies, actress Talia Shire complained in the *New York Times* that Hollywood no longer had roles for women. But in the sixties, the old masculine dialectic (feminized domesticity versus male anarchy) was drastically rewritten. For one thing, domesticity, the bedrock of the cultural consensus of the fifties, was losing its postwar, post-Depression allure. Men in the fifties had joked about being "trapped" (presumably by their wives); now the same wives were getting jobs, going to night school, and reading *The Feminine Mystique*. There was no one left at home to do the trapping; Faye Dunaway had replaced Doris Day, the dishes were piling up in the kitchen, and weeds were growing in the front yard. Where there before had been only marriage, there were now "life-styles" featuring a bewildering multiplicity of relationships, all shored up by the seemingly inexhaustible affluence of the sixties. Babies were postponed, and the manufacturers of hula hoops and lawnmowers began to lose out to the purveyors of stereo components and sports cars. *Playboy* chased the *Saturday Evening Post* off the newsstands, and a youthful, glamorous president once again gave old-fashioned male intransigence a good name. Jack Kennedy could face down Khrushchev with a single glance, while ordinary mortals cowered in their backyard bomb shelters.

In the sixties, Hollywood's strongest appeal to the public id was the spectacle of exuberant, light-hearted male violence. As the center polarized into right and left under the pressure of the Vietnam War, the liberal conventions of fair play that had always governed male combat on the screen fell into disuse. In the sixties James Bond and male-bonding films, such as *Dr. No* and *The Wild Bunch*, the heroes no longer saved themselves for one final, decisive moment of truth at the end (although there was that too); they came out shooting and continued shooting until the last frame. Marlon Brando, in *On the Waterfront*, *The Wild One*, and *One-Eyed Jacks*, earned the right to violence only after a terrible but purifying beating; for Sean Connery and Clint Eastwood, mayhem was routine. And, breaking another taboo of fifties centrist films, positive images of men in groups and couples could now be found; women could hardly be found at all. The male bonds that united Borgnine and Holden in *The Wild Bunch*, or Newman and Redford in *Butch Cassidy and the Sundance Kid* and again in *The Sting*, could never be undone by matrimony, only by death.

THE SEVENTIES: A TOUCH OF CLASS

We are getting ahead of our story. By the mid-seventies, the sixties had already been rewritten as a time of "excess." Vietnam and Watergate settled into mass consciousness as two "mistakes" of roughly the same magnitude, parallel cases of federal hubris. Carter ascended to the presidency in 1976 with the announced political project of *healing*: reuniting the generations, restoring the family, rebuilding trust in government, recreating the center, and relegitimating the old pluralist ideology. Meanwhile, the economy stagnated.* The ebbing of affluence reinforced the rising back-to-basics mentality as Americans groped for a new cultural consensus.

Films by and large took a liberal approach to the problem of reconstructing some sort of cultural unity. If the family could not be restored, as Carter had somewhat rashly promised, then at least we could learn to live with the various emerging life-styles. Refreshingly, in the films of the late seventies, people could be single parents, never married, or occasionally, though at some risk, gay; they could even, sometimes, be women. Feminism undercut the age-old equation of masculinity and adventure. Women, too, could act up, walk out (even though they were punished for it, as in *Kramer vs. Kramer*), or even (like the woman in the TV perfume commercial) drive off into the sunset—alone. But the rise of women (in *Julia*, *Alice Doesn't Live Here Anymore*, *An Unmarried Woman*) by no means drove "real men" from the screen. Instead, they reappeared in a new setting—the white ethnic working class—a world so far removed from Hollywood, so hopelessly parochial by the standards of Malibu or Beverly Hills, that it became on film a new realm of fantasy and glamor.

Before it could star in the movies, the working class had first to be "discovered." In the fifties and sixties, studios had, perhaps wisely, concluded that the

*Ironically, throughout the fifties, when leftists were daily predicting that the terminal crash of capitalism was just around the corner, the economy refused to oblige. But when leftists in the sixties and seventies finally explained why "postindustrial," "postscarcity," "one-dimensional" society refused to roll over and die, suddenly it began to decline. The energy crisis, stagflation, and the decline of the dollar were upon us, making "postscarcity" analysis as obsolescent as last year's car used to be, and forcing leftists to scramble for a post-postscarcity model of the fall of the West.

blue-collar world was not a setting for a profitable movie. No one could be expected to go out to a theater and pay money to see interiors that were drabber and more claustrophobic than the ones they had left at home. Technicolor and Vista-Vision would be wasted on faded upholstery and peeling wallpaper; who wanted to see an assembly line in 3-D or hear it in Sensurround? But for all its cinematic disadvantages, by the late seventies the blue-collar world had replaced the Old West as the mythical homeland of masculinity. Fifties pluralists acknowledged no class divisions; the working class, if it existed, only provided raw material for "upward mobility"; it was a stepping stone on the way up to the all-inclusive middle class. Then, in the early sixties, middle-class America discovered Michael Harrington's "other America," and by the mid-sixties, the poor—at least the black poor—had become a political force to reckon with. The liberal middle-class imagination divided society into "the white middle class" on the one hand and "poor people," seen as overwhelmingly black, on the other.

It wasn't until the "backlash" against the black and antiwar movements in the late sixties and early seventies that a new, previously unsuspected group emerged: people who were not black and yet were palpably not middle class either. (The black working class never gained cultural visibility, we suspect because of the continuing association of blackness with poverty and the "working class" with antiblack backlash.) This new group, the "working class," as it was soon labeled, entered middle-class consciousness in the form of hard hats: men who were well enough paid to be middle class but inexplicably liked Nixon and resented hippies, blacks, and student antiwar demonstrators.

Sociologists, anthropologists, psychologists, and student leftists hastened to make amends to this neglected group. The Department of Labor commissioned studies of "blue-collar alienation"; foundations that had funded civil rights activities began to promote the development of urban white working-class organizations; urban anthropologists turned away from "the culture of poverty" to explore exotic white ethnic enclaves. It was as if, in the early seventies, a kind of fossil culture was being excavated—people who had been curiously bypassed by the sexual revolution and the human potential movement, and had somehow managed to preserve their quaintly distinctive way of life.*

For a majority of the viewing public, this development was long overdue. Most people do not, after all, live in the well-furnished world of fifties and sixties sitcoms. So long as they had some hope of getting there, the media focus on the middle to upper middle class was pleasantly diverting, a promise of things to come. But the economic crisis of 1973–1974 dashed expectations of unlimited upward mobility—even sociologists couldn't find jobs. Visions of affluence became a reminder of mortgaged dreams, while the working-class world—or its media representations—became for the first time a commercially viable setting.

---

*Only two of the "working class" films of the late seventies address head-on the tensions at the interface of the middle class and the blue-collar working class. In Blue Collar, the auto workers fight the smooth-talking middle-class union bureaucrats rather than the bosses (the script preferred by most left critics) or just one another (the anticommunist script of the fifties). In Breaking Away, working-class youths battle pampered college boys, for reasons that are made to appear compelling and reasonable. We are amazed in the end not only that the sons of workers win against overwhelming odds, but also that the combat has been allowed to take place at all. A taboo has been broken.

Still, the working-class world might not have become a subject for major Hollywood films if its "discovery" had not coincided with the middle-class "masculinity crisis" of the seventies. On the home front, there was the inexorable spread of battlefield stretching from the kitchen, through the den, to the bedroom. On the job front, the economic downturn was limiting middle-class opportunities. Careers offering relative autonomy from corporate domination—in academia, many of the service professions, the public sector—began to decline relative to careers requiring direct subordination to corporate priorities. The young man who might, in the sixties, have studied history or philosophy now swallowed his curiosity and took up accounting. In the fifties, sociologists had bewailed the "man in the gray flannel suit," the middle-class male swallowed up by the corporate behemoth; in the seventies, their sons were glad to find a white-collar job at all. They chase after their lost autonomy, away from work or home, on the edges of highways, in Adidas sneakers.

It was in this context that the working-class male emerged, briefly, as a culture hero. In the films of the late seventies, the (previously invisible) working class becomes a screen on which to project "old-fashioned" male virtues that are no longer socially acceptable or professionally useful within the middle class—physical courage and endurance, stubborn determination, deep loyalty among men. The working-class films of the seventies draw their glamor from nostalgic images of male strength, male beauty, and nonsexual male passion.

THE GODFATHER AND ITS GODCHILDREN

The Godfather cleared the way for the late seventies genre of ethnic working-class films. *The Godfather* was, of course, about gangsters, not workers, but it introduced the social setting that would become familiar in *Mean Streets*, *Rocky I* and *II*, *Paradise Alley*, *Saturday Night Fever*, and the others: the working-class world as refracted through middle-class imagination. This world is intensely parochial, ethnically defined, and inward-looking. The great dramatic value of this new cinematic world lay in what it had to offer in redefining the masculine experience. The sixties genre of reckless-buddy films had burned out. Defiant machismo, cut loose from community or convention, was ultimately self-destructive; its exemplars ended up dead (like Butch Cassidy and the Sundance Kid) or lonely (like Little Fauss and Big Halsey). *The Godfather* retained the male bonding of the buddy films, but placed it in a *family* setting. It was a bridge between the old buddies and the new ethnic families, showing that masculinity and the family were not mutually exclusive.

The Godfather revives the ancient possibility of *patriarchy*: the family restored, the community recreated. It is still a man's world, not because women are excluded this time, but because men are secure enough to rule. It is a world where authority is vested in strong men, and young men must test their strength. But at the same time, *The Godfather* introduces Hollywood's fundamental ambivalence toward the patriarchal/ethnic setting and the masculine possibilities it represents. On the one hand, ethnic life was romanticized and celebrated over and against society at large. The ethnic enclave, the neighborhood, was the locus of community, and was used as the ground from which to criticize society. On the other hand, as the Corleone saga unfolds, the violent inwardness of the old-world community destroys its distinctive values, so that the larger society ultimately critiques the ethnic community. These changes are played out in the fortunes of the Corleone men.

Don Corleone (Marlon Brando) represents the bright side of patriarchy. He is commanding, but also nurturant, at home with drastic violence and at peace with his wife and kids. After decades of domesticated "dads," here at last is a *father* in the biblical sense. A few flashbacks to the ancestral home in Sicily remind us that we are only a generation and a steamship ticket away from a true patriarchal, agrarian society. Underneath their pinstripe suits and shoulder holsters, the Corleones are good-hearted peasants, and the wedding scene that opens *Godfather I* is suffused with rustic *gemeinschaft*. But none of this can last. Don Corleone is too befuddled by principle to keep up with modern business practices (he refuses to diversify into heroin). His eldest son, Sonny (James Caan), is too macho, emotional, "Italian," to manage the mob, or even survive. His second son, Fredo (John Cazale), is too weak and "feminine" to fill his shoes. His youngest, Dartmouth-educated son Michael (Al Pacino) is a whiz at business and does succeed his father, but he can't keep the family together. He represents authority without love, power unchecked by feudal restraints, and he ends up as desolate as any sixties loner, having killed his brother and banished his wife. When he slams the door in Diane Keaton's face at the end of *Godfather I*, we know this patriarchy has gone too far. In Don Corleone's three sons, patriarchy has deteriorated into three alternative male styles, and none of them will do. Here was the crisis in masculinity with a vengeance.

The heroes of the films we will look at in more detail occupy the same ethnic community, the same network of kin and male bonding connections first glamorized in *The Godfather*. Like the Corleones, most of them are Italian—an ethnic choice that (thanks to the prevailing stereotypes) not only evokes patriarchy but also seems to give artistic license to a level of emotional intensity that would be unlikely, if not unseemly, among, say, Finns or Norwegians. Locating the working class in an intensely ethnic scene reflects the persistent middle-class view that anyone still trapped in the working class must have just gotten off the boat. The working class is a residual category, a cul-de-sac for those who couldn't climb up and out.

Politically, these films fall into three categories: liberal, conservative, and ambivalent. The ambivalent films, such as *Breaking Away*, romanticize the neighborhood, or in this case the town, but give it up anyway to go on to something better. The liberal films, such as *Saturday Night Fever*, *Bloodbrothers*, and *The Wanderers*, embody a frank middle-class attack on working-class life, a "modern" attack on ethnic enclaves, and a "feminist" attack on machismo. Although they contain a strain of romanticism and nostalgia, the ethnic world of the neighborhood is seen as narrow and parochial compared to the liberal and humane values of the world-out-there. The extended family is either ridiculed or patronized as a hotbed of social pathology. Domesticated women are bad, while career-oriented, upwardly mobile, "liberated" women are good. Working-class men are basically pigs, and must learn to become more sensitive.

Conservative films romanticize the ethnic working-class community and the traditional masculine values it nurtures. Far from attacking the family, the neighborhood, the working class, and machismo as narrow, parochial, and stultifying, films like *Rocky I* and *II*, *Paradise Alley*, *Moment by Moment*, and *The Deer Hunter* cherish them and use romanticized images of them as a standpoint from which to assail society for being decadent and corrupt. They value traditionalism and attack "modern," melting-pot values, often in frankly racist and sexist terms.

In the following pages, we will discuss two liberal films, *Bloodbrothers* and *Saturday Night Fever*, and two conservative films, *Rocky I* and *Rocky II*, that offer contrasting attitudes toward class and ethnicity and suggest alternative approaches to the crisis of masculinity.

BLOODBROTHERS: FAMILY FEUD

In Robert Mulligan's *Bloodbrothers* (1979), the masculine alternatives are laid out with stark clarity: Stony De Coco (Richard Gere) can either be a "man," like his father, Tommy (Tony LoBianco), and his uncle (Paul Servino), or he can—in the film's terms—"grow up." In practical terms, Stony has to decide between following in his father's footsteps as a construction worker or defying his father to work as a children's recreation assistant in a hospital. It's a choice between two worlds. On the one side are the union and the family—patriarchal, parochial, but able to command the loyalty of blood: "The blood that runs in your veins—that's De Coco blood. You're ours!" Tommy De Coco bellows at his son. And the attractions of the blue-collar world are real: the barroom camaraderie, the joy of a job well done, the loving ties between the older men. When Stony goes to work with his father for the first time, the hard-hitting score reaches a crescendo as the camera pans dizzily upward at the shell of the half-constructed building. There is no particular dramatic point to this sudden surge of adrenalin (after all, people go to work every day)—the drumbeats celebrate masculinity itself, father and son united in a world of men.

On the other side is the unfamiliar middle-class world of social service, which allows a more nurturing, softer side of Stony's personality to emerge. Anticipating Dustin Hoffman's Kramer (of *Kramer vs. Kramer*), Stony finds that he likes nothing better than being with kids, hard as that is to explain to dad. "A recreation assistant? That's woman's work," Tommy scornfully tells his son. As in *Breaking Away*, the conflict between father and son centers on what is acceptable male behavior. Dave's (Dennis Christopher) father in *Breaking Away* shudders at his son's affinity for opera and draws the line when Dave (in imitation of Italian bicycle racers) shaves his legs. In both films, traditional masculinity—for all its allure—is constrictive. Feminization opens up a broader world.

In *Bloodbrothers*, as in other films of this genre, this message is articulated by a young supporting actress. Stony's girlfriend, Annette (Marylu Henner), was a social flop in high school because she "put out," but what was regarded as promiscuity a few years ago is now regarded as sexual liberation and defiance of hypocrisy. She makes Stony treat her like a human being, not a sex object, and tells him that she likes him because "you know there's something more out there besides playing cool, macho and getting laid. You could even go to college, get a degree." Against the ties of family and class she pits self-interest. "Worry about your own ass," she tells Stony, " 'cause your dad's is way outta reach."

A similar female figure passes through *The Wanderers*. She is herself middle class, inexplicably slumming among the film's ethnic youth gangs. At the end of the film, the hero is forced into an engagement with a neighborhood girl, but he bolts from his own party when he catches a glimpse of his true love walking outside. He follows her for two blocks and suddenly he's out of the Bronx and into Greenwich Village. She vanishes into a dimly lit club where a Dylan clone is singing "The Times They Are A-Changing." But not our hero, who knows he will never fit into his lost love's faintly androgynous, bohemian world. It's back to the trattoria under the wing of his Hawaiian-shirted, mafioso father-in-law.

But *Bloodbrothers*'s Stony *will* make it out. For him it's not the attraction of the middle-class world (represented by the hospital) that tips the balance, but the horrors of the ethnic enclave, particularly dad's macho madness. The world that was romanticized in *The Godfather* is condemned in *Bloodbrothers*. Underneath the expansive male solidarity of the barroom and construction site lies the family-as-nightmare. Stony's mother is a hysteric who has managed to induce anorexia nervosa in his frail younger brother. If the mother-son dining scenes are hard to take, the wife-beating scene is the last straw. Stony's father beats his wife senseless for a suspected infidelity. With this, Stony begins to see his family (and class) from the perspective of the doctor who has befriended him at the hospital: the people he has grown up with are little more than emergency-room regulars, professional outpatients. This was also the judgment of *A Woman Under the Influence* (1974) and *The Wanderers*: the working class may be a refuge for uninhibited masculinity but, viewed "objectively" by a professional (doctor or filmmaker), it's sick. Stony grabs his little brother and runs for it, taking a cab to the "feminized" middle class.

SATURDAY NIGHT FEVER: BREAKING AWAY

Saturday Night Fever passes the same judgment, but with fewer second thoughts. *Bloodbrothers* gave at least equal time to the strengths of the male-bonded, ethnic working-class world it portrayed; *Saturday Night Fever* is almost uninterrupted critique. Tony Manero (John Travolta) lives out a nocturnal male-fantasy life in Bay Ridge, a white, mostly Italian community trapped between the glamor of Manhattan and the just out-of-reach prosperity of the suburbs beyond. At home, there's not even a towering patriarch to give zest to family life; Tony's parents are dreary, bickering, beaten-down souls. Work—as a clerk in a paint store—is even duller. All the music and color in the film are reserved for Tony's leisure life as the local disco king. Out on the dance floor, with the big beat and the pulsing lights, he struts out a stunning pantomime of male transcendence. Surrounded by his male buddies, followed by adoring girls, and buoyed up by the BeeGees, Tony Manero is *somebody*.

But Saturday night fever is followed by Monday morning blues. Almost conscientiously, the film shows us the ugly, "real" side of life in Bay Ridge. When Tony's not working or dancing, he's gang-fighting Puerto Ricans or gang-banging the girls on the block. In *Saturday Night Fever*'s version of working-class teen life, sex roles are tediously traditional: boys will be boys and girls will go down—or get lost. The only exception is Stephanie Mangano (Karen Gorney), a Bay Ridge girl who's had a whiff of "culture." She takes ballet lessons, reads books, and wants a career in the big city. Like Annette in *Bloodbrothers*, Stephanie articulates the film's critique of the dead-end, working-class setting. From her point of view, Tony may be good enough to work out with on the disco floor, but he has no more lasting appeal than a cold pizza.

Gradually Tony comes to share Stephanie's judgment of Bay Ridge. First he has to find out that his special world of disco is corrupt. The moment of truth comes when Tony realizes that the dance contest he and Stephanie have won was fixed by the club's Italian owners because they didn't want the prize to go to a Puerto Rican couple. The purity of Tony's disco world—where all that seemed to matter was grace and skill—has been infected with the neighborhood's ethnic parochialism. Indignantly, he crosses the club's color line and hands the trophy over to the couple who, regardless of race-color-or-creed, were the best dancers. The next jolt is not so easy to handle, even symbolically. Tensions among Tony's gang erupt into drunken high-jinks on the Verrazano Narrows Bridge. When a friend falls to his death, Tony finally realizes that life in Bay Ridge—his nothing job, sitcom family, and dumb friends—is a dead end. Even disco dancers have feet of clay.

But Tony has one more lesson to learn. In the tradition of Bay Ridge courtship, he tries to rape Stephanie in the backseat of a car. To Tony's surprise, she is not grateful, but furious, and vanishes back to Manhattan. Bleary-eyed and repentant, he crosses the Brooklyn Bridge to find her and apologize. Thanks to Stephanie, his first glimpse of a "liberated" woman, he now understands that what was boyish in Bay Ridge is boorish in the borough of Manhattan. When Stephanie forgives him and lets him know that they will be friends, not lovers, he meekly accepts a role that would have been unthinkable only weeks earlier. Machismo was fun, but it's passé. If Tony is going to get anywhere, he'll have to drop the stud role and develop a more sensitive, "feminine" personality.

But for Tony, as for Stony De Coco, it's hard to see which way is up. We left Stony with the possibility of a low-paid social service job *if* he gets a college degree. *Saturday Night Fever* takes its hero to Manhattan but then doesn't know what to do with him. The film rehearses the melody of success, but, in the economy of 1978, it sounds flat. Since Tony can't do anything except dance and sell paint, it's hard to know how he'll make a living in the big city—short of a lucky opening at Arthur Murray's. But by not solving Tony's practical problem, the film gives its own kind of answer. Social mobility is redefined as personal growth, material success as self-actualization and human development. Tony must triumph over himself (at least over the unruly male parts of himself), because he cannot triumph over the world. Werner Erhard replaces Horatio Alger.

In both *Saturday Night Fever* and *Bloodbrothers*, the spokespeople for upward mobility and feminized masculinity are women, Annette and Stephanie. They are single women on the make, the kind who are punished for their independence by death in a conservative film like *Looking for Mr. Goodbar*. But they still play woman's perennial role in American folklore, as the tamer of men. In the films of the 1950s, domesticated women showed alienated or defiant men the way to adjustment. In these films of the 1970s, the "liberated" woman takes on the same task, chiding the men for their boyish machismo and prodding them to accede to the "realities" middle-class men have already accepted.

ROCKY I AND *II*: THE SAME OLD SONG

If Tony Manero has to get "softer," Rocky Balboa has the opposite project; as the score tells us, he's "getting stronger." Where *Bloodbrothers* and *Saturday Night Fever* repudiate the working-class, ethnic world, *Rocky I and II* romanticize it. Rocky himself, a thirty-year-old, over-the-hill fighter, is a noble savage, a natural man—Truffaut's Wild Child plopped down in south Philadelphia. Images of nature abound. Rocky keeps two turtles, whimsically named Cuff and Link, and a goldfish, and in *Rocky II* he buys a dog. He meets his wife in a pet store and proposes to her in a zoo. Even the fact that Rocky's employer (in *Rocky I*) is a gangster and Rocky's job is collecting bad debts doesn't taint the idyll one bit. The gangster is a benign, Runyonesque character, and Rocky doesn't have it in him to break any legs. In fact, Rocky's problem is that he's too sweet. If he wants to get anywhere in the cruel, cynical world beyond the neighborhood, he'll have to toughen up, get into shape, and learn what it means to be a man.

Rocky's neighborhood is used to judge society in the same way that the Ukrainian Catholic world of western Pennsylvania, with its vitality, quaint customs, and strong loyalties, is used to judge society in *The Deer Hunter* and Travolta's world is used to judge Lily Tomlin's world in *Moment by Moment*.* Tomlin's world is dominated by I. Magnin snobs who think Travolta is a delivery boy; the world into which the boys in *The Deer Hunter* are thrust is dominated by Vietnamese portrayed as savages; the world Rocky enters is dominated by blacks.

The heavyweight champion of the world is Apollo Creed, a black man. Where Rocky is all innocence, Creed is all cynicism and greed. (Not all ethnic groups are equal.) Their first match is a bicentennial-year publicity stunt concocted by Creed, who likes the idea of dressing up like Uncle Sam and messing up an un-

---

Moment by Moment could be a conservative sequel to *Saturday Night Fever*. Six months after the first film ends, Stephanie has fallen in love with an up-and-coming ACLU lawyer or an East Side gynecologist, and Travolta, unable to dance fast enough to make ends meet in Manhattan, has split to California where food stamps grow on every tree. There he becomes a beach bum and parlays the sensitivity training he picked up from Stephanie and his working-class background into an exotic attraction for bored, upper-middle-class divorcées. The slum he comes from is not the dead end it was in *Saturday Night Fever*, but a romantic world of drug dealing and petty crime. It is not Travolta who is corrupt, but Tomlin. Although she has enough credit cards to stretch from Malibu to Montecito, her life is bankrupt.

known who calls himself the "Italian Stallion." It's the white underdog against the black champ: as Michael Gallantz argued in *Jump Cut*, it is, or was, Bakke backlash time. In an early scene in *Rocky I*, Rocky finds that his locker at the gym has been given to a black fighter. "I wanna know how come I been put outta my locker," Rocky says angrily. "Because the Dipper needed it," Mickey the manager replies. "He's a contender. Know what you are? A tomato." The film's implicit statement, that blacks have gone too far, that they've unmanned decent, ordinary white guys like Rocky, is at least part of the reason for its box office success. For white audiences, racism gives the *Rocky*s an illicit thrill.*

What it means to be a man in *Rocky II* is first to establish some authority at home. Unlike the protomanagerial Stephanie in *Saturday Night Fever*, Adrian has no ambitions of her own. She's not a habituée of singles bars; she's not trying to make it to the Mainline and get away from bums like Rocky. She's so shy and overwhelmed when Rocky first drops by the pet store to buy turtle food that she can hardly speak. After a few dates, her glasses disappear, the dark circles under the eyes evaporate, and her sallow complexion gives way to a rosy glow. Rocky is her first and only love, and although they make a premarital bed-stop, it leads directly to marriage and a baby. But pregnancy brings a fleeting assertiveness. They're out of money and she wants to go back to work at the pet store. Rocky doesn't want any wife of his working, so he puts his foot down, but she does it anyway. Worse, she decides in *Rocky II* that she won't let Rocky fight Creed in a rematch. "It's all I know!" Rocky protests. "I never asked you to stop being a woman. Please don't ask me to stop being a man." During Adrian's nearly fatal childbirth, the doctor tells Rocky that the complications are probably due to Adrian's job. Rocky was right. After the due intervention of her brother and the Almighty, she changes her mind and decides to let Rocky fight. Rocky wins both bouts, but it's clear that the real battle is the one between the sexes.

In his training, too, it becomes clear that his real opponent is not Creed, but himself. Early on in *Rocky I*, Mickey (Burgess Meredith) tells Rocky that he had the makings of a champ but just didn't try hard enough. Unlike, say, *On the Waterfront*, where the mob prevents Brando's Terry Malloy from becoming a contender, here it's Rocky's own fault. He has a morale problem (and by implication, white men in general have let themselves go to seed, trading in their heritage for a mess of mortgages and Saturday night six-packs, while leaner, hungrier blacks crept into positions of power). In Rocky's struggle with himself, success is measured by the number of laps and push-ups he can do. The sporting action in *Rocky I* is not so much boxing as running, not Rocky versus Creed, but Rocky versus Rocky panting through the streets of Philadelphia. The real high point of *Rocky I* occurs not in the ring but when Rocky bounds up the grand steps of the

---

*In *Rocky II*, a black man lays Rocky off from his job in a meatpacking plant. He's not a bad guy, but white paranoia dictates that, in both *Rocky*s, blacks have power over whites. With the exception of *Blue Collar*, blacks are strikingly absent from all these films; they just don't exist. Racism is most overt in *The Deer Hunter*, where Vietnamese play the role that Turks play in *Midnight Express*, or, to a lesser degree, Puerto Ricans in *Saturday Night Fever*. The only recent film with a black hero that makes a point of his blackness (as opposed, say, to Yaphet Koto in *Alien*) is *Dawn of the Dead*, a liberal film in which the hero helps defend the melting pot from the hungry diners at the other end of the table.

Philadelphia Museum of Art, faces the city sprawled out before him, and triumphantly throws up his arms to the sky. The climax at the museum comes across as a working-class victory; the high-culture types may step on his toes, but he walks all over their steps. Ironically, though, Rocky's triumph is still cast in middle-class terms—he's not so much a boxer as a jogger.

The *Rocky*s are success stories, showing that anyone can make it if he runs far enough. The vision of success they present is radically scaled down to meet the reduced aspirations of the 1970s. In the prosperous late forties and fifties, films just *assumed* that their heroes would succeed. The problem in films like *The Sweet Smell of Success* and *Will Success Spoil Rock Hunter?* was whether the heroes really wanted to succeed. In the great forties fight films *Body and Soul* and *Champion*, the heroes won as a matter of course. The catch was that on the way up they lost their humanity. But in the *Rocky*s, success is so problematic that there's no room left to nitpick about morality. After all, it takes Rocky two films to beat Apollo Creed, and when he does, his victory is one of endurance and attrition rather than dazzling skill. There's no dramatic KO in the last round; instead, both fighters fall to the canvas exhausted. Rocky is the winner because only he is able to drag himself to his feet. Success, in Rocky's world as in *The Deer Hunter*, is not so much winning as surviving.

MASCULINITY AND CLASS

There are two, already well-worn, critical approaches to these films (and others of the genre). One is to look at them as attempts at social realism. Then the question is one of accuracy or, more precisely, correspondence: to what extent does the working class presented in these films correspond to that of the critic's experience—or imagination? what groups have been left out? what is likely or unlikely to have really happened? The goal of this line of criticism is to find, or apprehend, the "real" working class, and thus to outdo Hollywood at its presumed project of *representation*.

A second approach is to look at them as attempts at social control, messages beamed from Hollywood's corporate owners to, presumably, the working class. For this approach, the movies themselves are barely necessary; the screenplay is an adequate text. "Read" in this way, the films offer nothing more surprising than the ambient clichés: self-mastery is preferable to or necessary for success in the world; happiness can only be achieved through personal "growth"; and so forth. But these messages reveal nothing new about bourgeois strategy for social control. In a culture already permeated by evangelical pop psychology, the textual messages of the films are barely audible above the background noise.

We have tried to take another approach, concentrating on the central metaphor that runs through these films. It is in most cases really a double metaphor, first linking traditional ideals of masculinity with the blue-collar working class, then identifying that class with a parochial, ethnic subculture. By calling this equation a metaphor, we deliberately wave away questions of "accuracy" (are working-class men really more macho, more parochial, et cetera?). But we do so with no apologies, for what the metaphor has to reveal is not about the class presumably portrayed in the films, but about the portrayers themselves—and the social group, neither working class nor ruling class, that they belong to. To look at the *metaphor* is to look through the screen, past the compelling images of blue-collar men, into the mind of the *middle-class* male.

In a metaphor, each term modifies the other and is transformed by the mutual association. Consider first what happens to the idea of class. The metaphor linking class to certain styles of masculine exhibitionism and ethnicized tastes obviously takes us a long way from the almost mythic conceptions of Marxism: the working class as the agent of revolution, class struggle as the motor force of history, and so on. If any term is diminished by the metaphor these films present us with, it is this one. Class differences do not reflect conflict and exploitation, only different sets of possibilities the characters can opt for or against, as individuals. The differences are "interesting," even—by virtue of being so long suppressed—faintly shocking, but they are no cause for indignation. Some people stand on assembly lines, others sit behind executive desks; some like Perrier, some like Bud. In the ultimate middle-class judgment of the seventies, the concept of class is politically void: class is *life-style*.

But as quickly as class is depoliticized, it is sexualized, and if any term is enhanced by the metaphor, it is masculinity. When masculinity is located in the working class of these films, it takes on new properties—a touch of violence, glimpses of brawn, an aura of primitivism. If class is trivialized, masculinity achieves mythic proportions. The films' *texts* may hand down negative judgments on the versions of maleness they present, but the camera rests lovingly on naked biceps, strained and sweating male faces, macho tantrums. It is not the apologetic Tony Manero of the final scene who captures our imagination, but the wonderfully vain Tony of the dance floor. Whatever emotive power resided in the notion of the working class as a whole (strength, or perhaps the threat of violence) has now been concentrated, in this middle-class metaphor, into the individual male. Even when the film's prescription is sensitivity and gentleness, the spectacle is raw, "old-fashioned" masculinity.

What makes men—or this particular male possibility—so spectacular? We have already talked about the displacement of "unacceptable" male impulses—homoerotic, misogynistic, violent—to the collective fantasy world of the screen. But the pull of the "tough guy" is not simply sexual (in whatever sense these various impulses could be considered sexual). If the middle-class male imagination returns again and again, with anxiety and fascination, to images of men who are neither domesticated nor "sensitized," it is not only because they offer a pleasant break from repression. The seductive power of masculine imagery—for women as well as men—lies in its evocation of *defiance*: the underdog who beats incredible odds, the sullen adolescent who kicks beer cans (and clingy girls) out of his path, the tough guy who doesn't take shit from anyone. It is, in almost all the film versions, a defiance that falls far short of resistance—it is a politics of gesture and tone of voice. In real life women may be the rebels (including such unlikely subjects for Hollywood as elderly black women), but women lack the conventional mannerisms of defiance. They are attractive when they simper, not when they swagger.

To return to the metaphor presented by the "working-class" films: if class has been depoliticized, masculinity has, in an odd sense, been politicized. Defiant masculinity is the only subversive force left on this cinematic landscape. Linked to the working class, it gains a special cachet. In a curious inversion of reality, the working-class male seems to possess the autonomy the middle class feels it has lost. He gives "only" his body to the corporate endeavor, not (unlike the adman, executive, or even filmmaker) his mind and talent. And he leaves work for a world that is not yet penetrated and defined by the market—the neighborhood bar, the extended family, the women supposedly still innocent of feminist ambition. The "working-class" genre of films gives us the seventies' most powerful cultural image of defiance—the young working-class male, jacket slung over his shoulder, cigarette drooping from one corner of his mouth, arrogantly beautiful.

But the final term in the metaphor—ethnicity—qualifies even this limited image of defiance. White ethnic identity, no matter how relentlessly romanticized, has a vestigial quality. These are people who, from the camera's cosmopolitan vantage point, have not *yet* been fully assimilated, not *yet* left the urban neighborhoods for the mass anonymity of the suburbs or high-rise apartments downtown. Hollywood's defiant working-class male occupies a world whose time has gone by. It is the historical past, before the factories had run away and the parish churches had given up on Sunday morning attendance. And it is, at a subconscious level, the personal past: the world of early childhood, with its narrow boundaries, intense frustrations, towering male figures. If Hollywood was drawn to its glamorized working-class male out of a kind of secret admiration, it draws back with a sigh of nostalgia. In the end, middle-class smugness triumphs over male anxiety: the working-class male, so alluring in his small gestures of defiance, is ultimately an anachronism. Some boys, the films tell us, just never grow up.

GIMME SHELTER: FEMINISM, FANTASY, AND WOMEN'S POPULAR FICTION

KATE ELLIS

Economic predictions are grim, the ERA has been defeated, and the paperback romance market is achieving record sales and profits.[1] In the face of a strong antifeminist backlash, feminists have been concerned that the reading of romances may be feeding that backlash. These are books, after all, where a man is the sole object of the heroine's quest, and where the rules under which she completes that quest are the very ones that have historically divided "good" from "bad" women in the service of patriarchal control of both categories. Ann Snitow discusses Harlequin romances as "pornography for women" and concludes that the mystification of the hero's feelings, while titillating to the reader, keeps her in a state of expectation that cannot be fulfilled except through communication of a sort that romances cannot admit.[2] Tania Modleski is even more pessimistic: although she sees some progressive elements in Harlequins, their readers, she believes, are actually encouraged to participate in and actively desire feminine self-betrayal.[3]

Janice Radway is more optimistic about the "romance habit." She uses the framework of reader-response theory to examine what a particular group of romance readers get from their sometimes consuming habit. She finds that, though the romantic story "reaffirms the perfection of romance and marriage, . . . the constant need for such an assertion derives not from a sense of security and complete faith in the status quo, but from a deep dissatisfaction with the meagre benefits apportioned to women by the very institutions legitimated in the narrative."[4] She therefore urges feminists to build on this dissatisfaction, and not to write off readers of romances as hopelessly reactionary. But is the woman who reads these novels less or more likely to challenge her society and her family with respect to their expectations and her wishes? One way to approach this question is to look at popular literature written for women as a historical phenomenon. That is to say, if we look at the changing forms of mass market romances over their twenty-year history, and set them against changes in cultural definitions of womanhood, especially in the areas of work and sexuality, I believe we can find a strand of autonomy that pulls variously but insistently against the passivity that has been ascribed to female "nature."

What interests me about the development of a female paperback market is that, beginning as it did in the late 1950s, it preceded by only a few years the beginning of a self-conscious grouping of women into the political movement we call the second wave of feminism. It would seem logical that the Gothic romance, with its virgin heroines and its exclusive focus on heterosexual love as *the* solution to all of women's problems, would not be viewed positively by feminist critics, even though its heroines are, like their eighteenth- and nineteenth-century predecessors, quite feisty and willing to take the initiative. The continued popularity of female virginity in an age of sexual permissiveness is, for anyone studying the relationship between popular culture and social change, puzzling and perhaps discouraging. More disturbing, though, is the motif of rape that appeared with a vengeance in the novels of the seventies, while at the same time the heroine is invariably described as "indomitable," "determined to prevail," a woman who "would conquer them all—if she could subdue the hot, unruly passions of her heart."

This language is part of the back-cover advertising for the "spectacular," the subgenre that succeeded the Gothic novel in the early seventies, a longer, more openly sexual product in which an obligatory rape occurred after a hundred or so pages. "By setting this element in an historical background," commented one senior editor of a house that publishes these novels, "the ladies can indulge themselves in this rape-wish without any guilt." The author "must naturally make it seem," she adds, "that the heroine resists at the time and hates her rapist afterwards." [5] Her point, to which much of our culture still subscribes, is that women "escape" to what they want, and what they want is to be raped, to have sex without "responsibility." Of course, this mainstream view of women's fiction is tied into a host of other cultural assumptions about what women want as "escape" and what women's search for gratification in this form means.

The feminist critique of the objectification of women in the mass media was formulated, in part, to counter the negative view of women and of female sexuality from which these assumptions arise. Concentrating on their effects rather than trying to explain their appeal, feminist media criticism has tended to see romances not through the lens of Freudian wish-fulfillment but rather as a source of patriarchal indoctrination by which women learn to see themselves as objects for men. [6] What is needed to connect the truth of these two perspectives is a third: that of social history. This third term would connect media-induced fantasy to the historical milieu in which it is being created and consumed, and would explain its appeal in terms of how it helps those consumers interpret what is actually going on in their lives. By this I mean not only their individual lives, but also their lives as part of a particular culture at a particular time. In this sense romances do resemble dreams, plumbing the secrets of the waking world. It is important, then, to explore the world of romance readers as they themselves see it, and to connect the interpretation of women's reading with this part of the feminist project.

Ernst Bloch made the point in the thirties that fascist ideology was not simply an instrument of deception but "a fragment of an old and romantic antagonism to capitalism, derived from deprivations in contemporary life, with a longing for a vague 'other.'" [7] He criticized his fellow Marxists for refusing to address the irrational aspects of behavior and thought, such as dreams, religion, and fantasy, thus abdicating this entire terrain to the right. The success of the fascists, he thought, was due to the fact that people do not live only in the rational now but carry within them "remnants" of a preindustrial mode of production that persists in consciousness, and to some extent in their lives as well. For Bloch, these "remnants" were obstacles to class consciousness and impediments to political action; more important, they were also the seeds of a positive vision whose development had been thwarted by the rise of industrial capitalism. He therefore concluded that, although the appeal to a "purer" past untouched by bureaucracy and alienated labor had, in the twentieth century, become the property of the right, it need not necessarily be so.

The Gothic castle, the pillared antebellum or Regency mansion, the home that has been in the family for generations and is taken care of by a "family" of loyal servants: all these standard features of popular romances are "remnants" of the sort Bloch is talking about. These pockets of aspiration do not automatically house progressive political views, as the German experience demonstrates so graphically. But a "longing for a vague 'other'" that drives a woman to spend as much as $150 a month on romances does not necessarily indicate that "the family" is the name of the haven they are seeking. Romances are about childhood, about hierarchical households and mysterious passages; but they are also about adventure, about going somewhere new, different, and (sometimes despite appearances to the contrary) dangerous. This is less true of Harlequin romances, where foreign settings are seen as if from safely behind a tour guide. But since the appearance of the first Gothic in the late eighteenth century, popular fiction for women has taken up the theme of *getting out*. Of course the family is important to women, but the attempts of the feminist movement to widen the terrain of women's experience find strong, if muffled, resonances in their "escapist" reading.

I would like to develop an analysis of women's popular fiction in the last two decades that would help us to deepen our analysis of women's aspirations without jettisoning our critique of the institutions that support inequality between the sexes. Part of this project demands more space than is possible here: situating contemporary Gothics in a historical context, seeing them as recent representatives of a tradition that uses the past not as an ideal to be recovered or a haven into which to escape from a dreary present but as a point from which to criticize and struggle against that present. The Gothic novel from Ann Radcliffe to Charlotte Brontë contained what Michael Sadleir has called a "deep subversive impulse," [8] in that it pitted a mercenary older generation against the heroine and let her win the husband of her choice. These novels were popular in a stage of patriarchy in which the right of women to choose their husbands, and of poor gentlewomen like Jane Eyre and Lucy Snowe to find husbands at all, was a struggle in which women had very few cards in their hands.

What then are we to make of the reappearance of this genre—modeled roughly on *Jane Eyre* and on an updating in the thirties of Brontë's material and Daphne DuMaurier's *Rebecca*—in a period of such intense political activism as the 1960s? By placing these novels in their historical context, I will argue that issues critical to their female readers were being raised within the rather rigid formula that characterizes the genre. I will then examine these contemporary drugstore Gothics as articulations of Ernst Bloch's "remnants," in order to draw out elements that function to subvert patriarchal gender arrangements—elements existing alongside other, blatantly reactionary motifs in these works. My intention is not to show that the subversive elements are truer than the reactionary ones: artifacts of a sexist culture are invariably saturated with sexism. Rather, I hope to show, in placing current romances first in a historical context and then in a context of changing social conditions for women's lives, that such a literature has nourished radical politics and might still serve ends not intended by their publishers.

In *The Mistress of Mellyn*, a 1960 Gothic by Victoria Holt, the heroine says of herself: "My eyes were large, in some lights the color of amber, and were my best feature; but they were too bold—so said Aunt Adelaide; which meant that they had learned none of the feminine graces which were so becoming to a woman." [9] This failure to conform to the prevailing stereotype connects Holt's heroine with Jane Eyre, whom Brontë created "as plain and small as myself." [10] This means that the Gothic heroine tends to be older than her late adolescent counterparts in other romances. *The Mistress of Mellyn* is set in the nineteenth century, but the Gothic writer could count on resonances from readers who had learned the meaning of "feminine graces" in the fifties.

A related, and even more important, feature of *Jane Eyre* taken over by the drugstore Gothic is the fact that the heroine is a woman who needs to work. Martha Leigh, the heroine of *The Mistress of Mellyn*, for instance, is twenty-four when we first meet her. Orphaned, but blessed with a kinder aunt than Jane Eyre's Mrs. Reed, she was given a debut at the age of twenty along with her more conventionally attractive sister. But unlike this sister, she did not achieve the purpose for which her debut had been planned, and four years later she is still husbandless. Therefore, says her aunt, in her best ersatz nineteenth-century manner, she must take the second of the "two courses open to a gentlewoman when she finds herself in penurious circumstances." She must find herself "a post in keeping with her gentility." In twentieth-century terms, "gentility" meant being raised without the expectation of working. In the fifties it meant becoming, on graduation from high school, the year when a debut takes place, a nonworking prospective mistress of a household. The message of the Gothic, then, is the message of *Jane Eyre*: the outwardly mousy young woman who is forced out of the marriage market and into the job market will make thereby a better match for herself than will her more conventionally attractive peers.

Not all Gothics bring their heroine to a large house as an employee. Some simply follow the strand of *Jane Eyre*, in which a hostile Mrs. Reed figure, because of some mystery in the past, tries to deny the heroine the inheritance she finally gets. But the need to work in one's middle twenties indicates that the heroine has moved outside the structures that protect women from the necessity of being on their own: marriage, home, and family. And the kind of work that is "in keeping with their gentility" is social service work: looking after or teaching a young or an old person, sometimes with light secretarial work thrown in. To perform these tasks is to become a surrogate wife, more wifely than a wife, in fact. This is the kind of job that is waiting for the heroine in the Gothic house, and it is the dedication with which she performs her work that captures the heart of her employer, the owner of the house. Other women (shades of Blanche Ingram) try to win him through their beauty and seductiveness, and the heroine may feel pangs of jealousy because of her perceived inability to compete in this area. But she has developed qualities to compensate for what her aunt perceived to be a lack in her makeup. She takes initiative on her job and is not deterred by obstacles: traits which lead to unravel the secret of the house and its wifeless owner.

In *The Mistress of Mellyn*, the large house is named Mount Mellyn, and its secret devolves around the death of Alice Tremellyn, wife of Connan, who owns the house and is Martha's employer. The official story is that Alice was killed in a train wreck while running away with her lover, Geoffrey Nansellock. But Martha, intrepid investigator, finds an appointment book of Alice's that leads her to suspect that this was not the case. She then learns from Alice's aunt that Geoffrey was the father of Alvean, the child she has come to Mount Mellyn to look after, and that her employer's marriage to the faithless Alice was an arranged one. Guidelines for romance writers indicate that a romance hero may appear to have strayed from the path that leads him, finally, to the heroine, but a divorce, for instance, must have been instigated by his former wife. Since he must be about ten years older than the heroine, such a past is necessitated not only by the Gothic need for a mystery but also by the same rules that require an unmarried romance heroine to have no past, at least until recently.[11] Connan is thus particularly clean in this regard. Not only did he not instigate the end of his marriage, he did not initiate the beginning of it either. Alice's murderer turns out to be Celestine Nansellock, the sister of Geoffrey. Her motive is a lust for property, a desire to be the mistress of Mellyn. But that honor goes, finally, to Martha.

Here we see the central feature of the Gothic genre that has persisted from its beginning: a large interior space in which some violation of familial bonds is rumored to have taken place, a house that "is not a home." But whereas in the Gothic up through *Rebecca* the rumor proves true, the villain in this piece is not a part of the house. Thus Victoria Holt, who reigns over the modern Gothic world along with Phyllis Whitney and Dorothy Eden, does for the modern Gothic house what Charlotte Brontë did for its owner. It does not have to be destroyed or abandoned the way Otranto and Udolpho, Thornfield Hall and Manderlay, were. The heroine wants the luxury that the house displays. "How I wanted it!" exclaims Martha, watching the guests arrive for a ball. It is a remark Jane Eyre could never have made. She has a "leveling" spirit of contempt for the members of Rochester's class, and retires from what she views as its empty displays to a small dwelling, as did Ann Radcliffe's Emily and Horace Walpole's Isabella before her. In the drugstore Gothic, on the other hand, marrying up is what it's all about.

One way to read the recurring symbol of the large house in these novels is to see it as the house of one's childhood. To a small person all houses, no matter how humble in actuality, seem immense and fraught with secrets and secret places. The social order of the Gothic household, too, seems clear and immutable, with those who give orders (the family) above and those who receive them (the servants) below, and no way for the child/governess, who is right in the middle, to move up. Yet as the story develops, the heroine encompasses both spheres. Indeed, the task she is brought to the house to perform is so defined. The name of this task is mothering, and it is by performing it adequately that the heroine redeems the once-haunted house of her employer. In doing so she finds out that the man who at first seemed cold and distant, whose attentions had seemed to be taken up with a woman more beautiful and more highly placed on the social ladder than she, turns out to want no one but her for his wife. In short, she marries Daddy.

In the novel we are discussing, Martha Leigh perceives her small charge to be suffering from a lack of paternal attention. Learning that Connan Tremellyn wants his daughter to ride, but that little Alvean is terrified of horses, Martha dons a riding habit belonging to the dead Alice and teaches Alvean to be what her father wants and what she, Martha, already is: a good horsewoman. Simultaneously a sibling playing "dress-up" in mother's clothes and a good mother conspiring with Alvean to win a love they both want, Martha then gets a chance to lecture Connan on his parental duties when Alvean, attempting a feat beyond her ability in order to impress her (supposed) father, is injured at a horse show. In addition, Martha befriends another child of Geoffrey Nansellock, whose mother has committed suicide. This child, whose marginality takes the form of craziness, shows Martha where Alice was murdered. The lesson of all this is that, by being a good "little mama" to two fellow orphans, Martha is then (but only then) allowed to assume the adult version of that role, the one that involves getting married and having children of one's own.

But a novel about coming to the fantasy house of one's childhood, where servants act the part of fantasy parents whose sole purpose in life is to look after you and where your virtues are truly appreciated by a man much richer and more powerful than you are, is not a novel about growing up. One difference between Jane Eyre and her contemporary variants is that staying at Thornfield Hall became for Jane, in the period before as well as after her aborted marriage, a way of *not* growing up, of being her master's "little elf" in perpetuity. Before her wedding day, she has two dreams in which she is carrying and then drops a child, who represents an infant part of her that Rochester's love has nurtured. The dream tells her what she senses but is too needy to act on: that even without the impediment of Bertha Mason, this marriage to this fascinating, lonely aristocrat would keep her from ever becoming an adult woman. That this same man, trained by his culture to require a plaything for a wife, might have driven Bertha Mason crazy is a possibility that hovers below the surface of this novel but never rises above it. Needless to say, it never appears in the drugstore Gothic.

This is why the old covers of Gothics are somewhat deceiving. The heroine might feel, and often rightly, that someone is trying to kill her, but flight in a flowing white dress is not part of the fictional paradigm. This, too, makes a contrast with Jane's enunciated desire for self-determined activity and freedom, which she articulates during one of her habitual visits to the attic of Thornfield to look longingly at the world beyond her reach. Later she is offered a chance to see that world, but merely as a toy that had charmed her master and to which he had no legal obligations. She rejects this offer, not just because it is immoral, but because it would not offer the "exercise of their faculties" that women need: she would remain the pampered little girl Rochester was making of her during the preparations for their wedding, and he would tire of her as he had tired of his previous "playthings."

It follows, therefore, that the crucial phase of Jane's development takes place away from Thornfield Hall. Interestingly, both film versions of the novel leave this phase out, and so does the contemporary Gothic.[12] In these books the heroine invariably senses that she is at the mercy of someone who has a vested interest in keeping her from learning the secret past concealed in the house. In the eighteenth-century Gothic it is the villain/owner of the castle who plays this role, which in *Jane Eyre* is taken up by Rochester. But since the contemporary owner of the house has had all the stains removed from his character, it must be an outsider who brings evil into the Gothic world, as it is in *The Mistress of Mellyn*. And since it is the mission of the heroine to discover the source of this evil, she manages to outwit this outsider. Her reward thus comes not because she leaves the castle, but because she does not. Imagining herself trapped in a fantasy parental home, she literally works her way out of the powerlessness of childhood by importing into her situation a newer ideology of self-affirmation through work.

One of the functions of popular culture is to mediate experience for its audience, particularly when that experience comes into conflict with what one has been implicitly or explicitly taught. But like other commodities, it also creates a need, whose gratification it depicts. One thinks of Emma Bovary, who might have died of old age had not cheap novels and fashion magazines filled her mind with the arsenic of romantic love. Yet it was not just a mode of lovemaking foreign to her husband, the country doctor, that Emma's reading revealed to her. Pictures of the latest styles suggest a multitude of social pleasures available to the wearers of high fashion. In popular fiction, love is the eternally open doorway to this world, transcending the barriers of class. The discovery that love does not have this power may lead, at worst, to suicide, or at best, in times of political ferment, to action directed toward social change. Emma's tragedy was not that she read cheap literature but that the "longing for a vague 'other'" it engendered in her consciousness could attach itself to no more durable a source of sustenance.

But the fact that a novel raises expectations that cannot be satisfied within the prevailing structure of class and family relations is not a reason to dismiss it as "mere escapism." Raised expectations are one precondition for the development of a social movement, though not the only one, as the case of Emma Bovary makes clear. But if we see "escape" fiction as one way of giving shape to these expectations, however conventional, we may be able to see in contemporary romances a common interest in expanding women's proper sphere, thus linking them with the novels of Ann Radcliffe, the Brontës, Mary Shelley, and many less well known practitioners of the genre.

To do this we must first take note of the fact that the marketing success of the paperback romance generally, and of the sixties Gothic in particular, grew out of a specific historical situation: the exodus to the suburbs of over a third of the American population. Moreover, this migration did more than provide publishers with a market. In the 1960s home ownership and higher education came within the reach of an unprecedented number of people, and with the latter came the promise of work that was socially honored and socially useful. *The Mistress of Mellyn* was published in 1960, three years before *The Feminine Mystique* and right at the beginning of the Kennedy era. The pressures on women to stay out of the workplace, of which Friedan speaks, were thus still in effect. But in the early sixties college graduates who had grown up in the suburbs were urged to ask not what their country could do for them but what they could do for their country. In addition, women's participation in the paid labor force had been expanding steadily since World War II in the face of an ideology that posited full-time wife-and-motherhood as the true expression of a woman's nature.

But the jobs to which the postwar female labor force was being relegated, in the expanding service sector, had in them a rationale quite compatible with traditional definitions of womanhood: taking care of the needs of others. Nor was it only in the marketplace that women as nurturers were in demand. The Peace Corps, the civil rights movement, and the New Left gave women opportunities to act the role of "good mother" in siding with society's oppressed. Women's desires for a larger sphere of endeavor—the very aspirations to which Jane Eyre had given voice over a hundred years earlier—were thus given a tangible outlet, at least for middle-class women. That this role too often took the form of typing and making coffee is, of course, another story.

By conflating work and mothering, the contemporary Gothic resolved an ideological conflict in the definition of women's role, just as the earlier Gothic did for its time period. This conflict was between the "feminine mystique" of the fifties, which stressed passivity as the key to womanly fulfillment, and the lure of "adventure" outside the home that appeared in the next decade. These calls to the cause of human betterment were directed to women whose expectations were higher than those of the less-educated women for whom the romance market was developed. But romance readers were certainly not immune from the conflict between work and domesticity, which the Gothic novel solved by placing the heroine's work within the confines of the home. If postwar propaganda warned women that working outside the home would deprive them of their femininity, the situation of the "genteel" but "impecunious" heroine lets her have her cake and eat it too.

But by making home the place of woman's work, it also makes the workplace an extension of home. One of the goals of nineteenth-century feminists was to feminize the public sphere, to bring to it the qualities that women had developed in their role as mothers. But the transformation of service work, and secretarial work especially, has in reality meant the extension of patriarchal relationships into the office. The relationship between an executive and his secretary is similar in many ways to that between Jane Eyre and Rochester, or between Martha Leigh and her handsome, seemingly unattainable employer. Just as a governess might hope to find a situation in which her employer was single, so might a secretary. The way to his heart, the Gothic novel is saying, is not through the usual stratagem of wearing a low-cut dress and leaning over his shoulder at just the right angle. Rather, it has to do with competence, translated into good mothering in the form of neat typing, good coffee, careful attention to his engagements, and taste in ties. There is here a hope of egalitarianism, however structurally inhibited, an ideal of redeeming work time by connecting it, through love, to the sphere of domestic relations. This is the appeal of the Gothic, as it is of office romances.

In the spectacular, the large house is not present from the beginning, as it is in the Gothic; it is the heroine's final destination but may, however, appear at various points along the way. The back jacket of *The Flame and the Flower*, the Kathleen Woodiwiss novel that in 1972 launched the spectacular as a new category of women's fiction, sums up the scenario thus:

In an age of great turmoil, the breathtaking romance of Heather Simmons and Captain Brandon Birmingham spans oceans and continents! Their stormy saga reaches the limits of human passion as we follow Heather's tumultuous journey from poverty . . . to her kidnapping at a squalid London dockside . . . to the splendour of Harthaven, the Carolina plantation where Brandon finally probes the depths of Heather's full womanhood!

The obligatory rape that sets off the spectacular from its predecessors occurs on page forty-four, after which there is a marriage (at her father's insistence) and a birth, but no actual sex for three hundred more pages. This is because it takes that long for Heather to get over her rage at Brandon, and because Brandon reveals his finer nature in refusing to exercise his marital prerogative until he finds her a willing woman. But by the end, of course, she is smiling at her husband "with something close to worship in her eyes," her full womanhood having been, as the jacket says, probed.

The heroines of these novels live in the age of Defoe: the early eighteenth century. One pattern, which *The Flame and the Flower* exemplifies, involves early marriage and a heroine who sleeps with only one man. But another pattern, pioneered by Warner paperbacks under Jerry Gross and now taken up by other houses, has a heroine who does not marry her rapist. Sometimes, after her initial violation, she enjoys sex with a series of men, sometimes to her great surprise, and marries in the end one whose arrogance she initially found distasteful. In *Love's Tender Fury* by Jennifer Wilde, the heroine begins as a governess who is raped by her employer. In this and several similar novels, the lovers, and even the future husbands, of the heroines buy them at auctions and are, for a while, their literal owners. The message about men is thus the same in both patterns, and it has something in common with that of other romances. First impressions are not reliable, particularly if the man is cold or violent or both. Male domination is what these novels are all about.

But to say that their heroines only pretend to struggle against it, as the editor I quoted earlier implies, gives too little credit to the women who read these books, and concludes that the women's movement has had no impact on their thinking. An alternative explanation for the popularity of these books among women begins with the thesis that the women's movement has made women more conscious of the meaning and frequency of rape. The rise in reported rapes may mean that women are being raped more often, but in fact violence against women is falling as a percentage of an increasing total.[13] Then, too, the women's movement has opened up for discussion the area of sexual pleasure as defined by women. We hear much about the confusion of men in response to this, but the conflicting demands it places on women are equally difficult to resolve. They must straddle the old and the new orders, take responsibility for birth control but not for sex itself, acknowledge desire but not act on it. Is it any wonder that rape becomes appealing *as a fantasy* resolution to conflicts between permissible lust and potential rejection?

The women's movement did not give women permission to enjoy sex, but it did make them aware that a lot of what they felt they ought to be enjoying was the product of myths equating force with sexual prowess. By breaking down these myths, feminist ideology has helped women to define their own pleasure, and thus (I would venture to guess) has increased it. But at the same time, women are apparently becoming increasingly aware that their experience of male sexuality has at least elements of rape in it, especially on the occasion of losing their virginity. Finally, it is the women's movement that has focused public attention on the problems of male brutality within the family, in the form not only of wife-beating but also of father-daughter incest. If male violence and how to deal with it has become a dominant theme in romance fiction over the last decade, it has become equally prominent in the women's movement itself.

Thus, women are more aware of the prevalence of rape and of the possibility of their experiencing it. To read a spectacular is to read about a woman who has had that dreaded and shame-producing experience and gone on to become a whole person in a satisfying relationship. The preindustrial settings of these novels do for their heroines what the Middle Ages did for the heroines of the first Gothics: it frees them to go out into the world in pursuit of the happiness to which they feel they have a right, and to escape the countervailing messages about "nice girls" that are still transmitted to women along with the newer ideology of assertiveness training. Colonial America, where most of the spectacular heroines end up, did not require passivity as a mark of "full womanhood." The shift backward in time is thus a displacement by means of which present behavior is given a history and a validity. It is, however, a fantasy shift to a world where the problems that so plagued real Colonial America no longer threaten people's lives. The sex is entirely recreational in these books. There are no unwanted pregnancies, no outbreaks of disease, no deaths due to starvation, no crop failures. Above all, there is no God keeping his flock in line with the hope of heaven and the fear of hell.

Viewed in this way, the spectacular offers a woman reader not the vicarious experience of rape she really wants but a framework through which she can view her sexual history, involving, in all probability, more than one man. Forced to steer a course between the Scylla of the double standard and the Charybdis of the sexual revolution, the reader encounters in its five or six hundred pages a heroine men assume they can have for the taking, and who says yes to some and no to others. Given a situation in which sex outside of marriage has not the dire physiological and social consequences for women that it has had for most of our history, and given that not all men demand virgins as brides, though some still say they prefer them, women need to develop new ways of protecting themselves from the sexism that still surrounds them. In presenting heroines who can face harassment, humiliation, and danger and still come out winning what *they* want, the spectacular does help its readers to do this.

Yet there remains the problem that the heroine gets what she wants not just because she is tough but also because she is "breathtakingly beautiful." Moreover, what she wants just happens to be an aristocrat with an immense house and a fortune to match. Clearly, this continues the mystification of class relations we saw in the Gothic. At the same time, the stability and order of the large servanted house have inherent appeal to contemporary women readers, over and above the general fascination with wealth, which is not confined to women, or to this country, or to this decade. This stability is brought out in frequent references, in the novels, to the fact that the large house has been in the owner's family for several generations. Outside of the use made by Marxist and feminist historians of oral histories, family history has been the prerogative of the rich, who could leave durable memorials to themselves in the places where they settled. The frequent relocations that have characterized the lives of the postwar working class, often in the service of real or illusory upward mobility, have made the experience of raising one's children in the old family house virtually unthinkable for most of us. The much-discussed breakdown of the family has entailed a geographical scattering of generations and an atomization of communities and the kin networks they encompassed. The centrifugal pressure on the contracting American household has created the space in which feminism could develop, but at the same time has brought hardship and deprivation to many women.

The right is now capitalizing on the failure of the promise the suburban migration of the forties, fifties, and early sixties held. Home ownership did not provide, for those middle-class Americans who took advantage of FHA loans and tax incentives, the same material base for ties between generations that inherited property provides for the affluent. Houses in working-class developments are as interchangeable as the jobs their owners perform and are subject to constantly increasing taxes, deterioration due to negligent construction, and so forth. The romance house, on the other hand, is a fantasy creation that does provide a material base for family life extending through time. In the Gothic novel, its continuity is gravely threatened for a while, but through the detective work of the heroine it is rescued and redeemed. In the spectacular, it is often the owner of the house who is endangered: the swashbuckling male world is a dangerous place. But his marriage to the heroine brings her into a family that has been known in the community for generations. In both forms, transformation of the house into a home is a metaphor for the domestication of the man.

I would like to return, at this point, to Ernst Bloch's conception of fascist ideology as "a fragment of an old and romantic antagonism to capitalism, derived from deprivations in contemporary life, with a longing for a vague 'other.'" The part of his theory that is useful in drawing out the connection between the "romantic antagonism to capitalism" evident in women's popular fiction, on the one hand, and the current success of the antifeminist right's crusade to preserve the family, on the other, is his concept of nonsynchronism. Bloch sees the simultaneous existence, in consciousness, of a present shaped by a rational, technological mode of production and a dying past constituted by precapitalist "remnants" to be a source of contradictions vital to the process of politicization, as vital, indeed, as the contradictions in the present between socialized labor and private profit that Marxists use to account for the genesis of a revolution. Since remnants in consciousness derive from continuing, though obsolete, modes of production, Bloch's theory is best applied to the German peasantry and petite bourgeoisie. Its weakness lies in its inability to explain the attraction of the urban working class to the fascist movement of the thirties. But perhaps this might be rectified, and made more applicable to our present political situation, if we see the increasingly isolated nuclear family, whose chief economic function is to reproduce labor power, as every bit as "backward" as the isolated rural household or the independent small business.

There has been fairly wide agreement among feminists about the necessity to capitalism of the unpaid labor involved in laundering, defrosting the refrigerator, mediating conflict, looking good for a husband, supervising homework, arranging trips to the dentist, and all the other physical and psychological tasks that go into "the reproduction of labor power." But granting that free labor in the sphere of reproduction is as essential to capitalist profit as the extraction of surplus in the sphere of production, it seems to me that the individual units in which labor power is reproduced have more in common with the combined home-and-work-place of a precapitalist economy than with the efficiency-oriented capitalist workplace. For, setting aside the idea of the husband as owner and the wife as worker, this place is, ideally, privately owned, as are the washing machine, refrigerator, car, and other "tools" used in the reproduction of labor power. Not all homes conform to this model, of course, but this is the ideal. It is therefore a logical source of Bloch's nonsynchronous contradictions, that is, the continued existence of the past in the present and of wishes and needs associated with that past which cannot be met in the present. In the sphere of the home, these unmet wishes and needs have fueled the demand of the right for the preservation of a precapitalist set of social relations: the patriarchal family.

I mean by this term an ideological as well as an actual construct: one that gives the father absolute economic control over the other members of his family, whether or not he chooses to exercise it, and in which these other members know they are supposed to look up to him, however they actually feel. Now, however, as Christopher Lasch has so brilliantly demonstrated,[14] this construct has been dismembered, primarily by the state acting as the agent of monopoly capitalism. The counterattacks of the right are directed partly at the state, but their most vulnerable targets are those whom patriarchal ideology has most victimized: homosexuals, feminists, and women with children but no visible means of support.

Essentially, for the right today, the appeal of the past is not the nineteenth-century vision of a world unfragmented by wage labor, but rather the ideal of a world not held together by an impersonal, all-embracing state. In fact, the right wants the state to be more patriarchal, to deny public funds to those who do what a strict father would punish: conceiving an unwed or unwanted child, performing a homosexual act, losing a job and accepting "public charity." The left has not been able to counter the right in this area because it has not given sufficient thought to the scale of state power. Much has been written about seizing power or, more recently, appropriating it democratically. But popular distaste for the notion of state power has to do with the scale on which it exists in bourgeois society. Conversely, the growing popularity of novels with large houses in them on the one hand, and the ease with which the right has organized around the home on the other, come from the fact that, battered or not, the home is at present the only antidote to capitalist alienation, the last relatively small, manageable unit in an economic order whose sources of control are centralized and remote. Given the fact that a socialist economy might have to be highly centralized also, it seems to me that feminists and Marxists need to reassess, in the light of changes that have taken place in the almost one hundred years since Engels gave us his analysis of patriarchy, the role of the home in that famous trinity: the family, private property, and the state.

For Engels, the sexual division of labor became prototypical of oppressive class relations only when the institution of private property required the control of women's reproductive powers in order to ensure patrilineal inheritance. Yet the obsession with male heirs, female chastity, and family names that Engels rightly perceived to be the driving force behind patriarchal rule has been considerably undermined, over the last hundred years, by both technology and the law. Some feminists have argued that these developments, along with the entrance of women in large numbers into the paid labor force, has brought about a withering away of patriarchy.[15] I am more convinced, however, by the arguments of Jessica Benjamin, who draws on the work of Horkheimer, Adorno, Marcuse, and Lasch to show that the authority formerly vested in the father has simply become diffused into distant, faceless institutions.[16] And if this is the case, then feminists, women, and people in general have less reason to rejoice at the demise of classical patriarchy than might at first appear.

But the danger is not, I think, the one that Lasch and his predecessors set forth, that is, the idea that in the absence of a strong father the capacity to rebel does not develop. This conclusion grows out of the equation of strength with distance that is so much a part of the masculine ideology of our culture, and it leads in turn to another danger: nostalgia for fathers whose word was law but who were rarely home. The problem with this nostalgia, in my view, is that it does not go back far enough: it goes back, that is, only to the father thrust upon us by capitalism, who worked outside the home and whose contact with his children was minimal. Perhaps these fathers did create in their children the repressive superego described by Freud, but it is not clear that they thereby provided the necessary catalyst for rebellion. In the more distant past, in contrast, fathers worked on land that was in some measure theirs, and remnants of this past mode of production may persist in the consciousness of those segments of our present society with reputedly high right-wing sentiments: in rural areas and among the petite bourgeoisie, or at least in their televised counterparts.

They certainly persist in the novels we have been examining. Here we find, in an overwhelming number of cases, a fantasy that counters the reality of the contemporary home with its absent father and its (theoretically or actually) omnipresent mother. This is the home, pillared or gabled, where the father turns out to be the benevolent presence, however unpromising he may have seemed at first, whereas the "good mothers" are mysteriously absent, leaving only "bad mothers" who see themselves as the heroine's rivals and who try to keep her from getting close to Daddy. Surely this means that the parent who is always available functions in fact mainly as a target for blame and resentment, unlike the absent parent, whose presence is mystified by its relative rarity.

Nevertheless, the depersonalization of paternal authority, which the right and

the male left have deplored and feminists have greeted with appropriate but debilitating ambiguity, presents a real danger for a feminist anticapitalist movement. That danger is that feminists will not take sufficiently seriously, in theory
or in practice, the popular protest against institutional facelessness that the forces
of reaction are again directing against the present government and, even more
fiercely, against a left they fear. But the wish for a home, some privacy, and a
caring father have no special affinity with an antifeminist right; indeed, its incorporation into a socialist feminist vision would have far-reaching ramifications,
not only in personal life but in the workplace and at the state level as well. In
constructing this future, we need to select elements from the present and also
from our precapitalist past. Such a society would, of course, have to include a
good deal more than a concept of home that does not enshrine patriarchal relations. As we work toward its realization, then, we have not only past socialist
uprisings but also our own thwarted radical heritage to draw upon, thus grounding the next revolution in the completion of a previous one.

Notes

1. "Special Report on Romance Fiction," *Publishers Weekly* 220, no. 20 (1981),
claims that "upwards of $200 million of paperback publishers' annual sales are repre-
sented by romance fiction. Readership is estimated at 20 million." Noting that "figures are
generally difficult to gather from publishing firms," *PW* reported that "outside of Harlequin, where 100% of the title output is romance fiction, the rest of the paperback houses
claim an 8% to 40% range of annual title output is romance fiction."

2. Ann Snitow, "Mass Market Romances," *Radical History Review* 20 (Spring–
Summer 1979), reprinted in *The Powers of Desire*, ed. Ann Snitow, Christine Stansell,
and Sharon Thompson (New York: Monthly Review Press, 1983), pp. 245–263.

3. Tania Modleski, "The Disappearing Act: A Study of Harlequin Romances," *Signs*
5, no. 3 (1980): 435–448. See also her *Loving with a Vengeance: Mass-Produced Fantasies for Women* (Hamden, Conn.: Shoestring Press, 1982).

4. Janice Radway, "Women Read the Romance: The Interaction of Text and Context,"
Feminist Studies 9, no. 1 (1983): 72.

5. Yvonne McManus, quoted in "Editor's Report: The Paperback Historical Romance," *The Writer*, April 1977, p. 34.

6. This criticism has focused on the issue of pornography. See especially *Take Back
the Night: Women on Pornography*, ed. Laura Lederer (New York: Morrow, 1980).

7. Ernst Bloch, *Erbschaft*, quoted in Anson Rabinbach, "Ernst Bloch's *Heritage of
Our Time* and the Theory of Fascism," *New German Critique*, no. 11 (Spring 1977): 7.

8. Michael Sadleir, "The Northanger Novels: A Footnote to Jane Austen," *English Association Pamphlet*, no. 68 (November 1927): 4.

9. Victoria Holt, *The Mistress of Mellyn* (New York: Fawcett, 1960), p. 5.

10. Elizabeth Gaskell, *The Life of Charlotte Brontë* (London: Dent, 1960), p. 216.

11. "With two publishers, Harlequin and Silhouette, having a firm hold on the mostly
female market, others are joining in the fray, offering the romance reader something new
by shifting away from the classical [read: virginal] heroine to the experienced woman in a
more modern world" (*New York Times*, 8 March 1982, pt. 4, p. 1).

12. See Kate Ellis and Ann Kaplan, "Feminism in the Brontë Novel and Its Film Versions," in *The English Novel and the Movies*, ed. Gillian Parker and Michael Klein (New
York: Ungar, 1981).

13. See Jean Bethke Elshtain, "The Victim Syndrome: An Unfortunate Turn in Feminism," *The Progressive*, June 1982, pp. 42–47. Elshtain cites FBI and Justice Department statistics to make the point that "the chief targets of male crime are other males, not women."

14. Christopher Lasch, *The Culture of Narcissism* (New York: Norton, 1978).

15. See, for instance, Barbara Easton, "Feminism and the Contemporary Family," *Socialist Review*, no. 39 (April 1978): 11–36.

16. Jessica Benjamin, "Authority and the Family Revisited; or, A World Without Fathers?" *New German Critique*, no. 13 (Winter 1978): 35–57.

Part IV
The Mass-Mediation of Popular and Oppositional Culture

INTRODUCTION

The writings in this section indicate the extent to which left critics have moved away from the Frankfurt School's wholly disapproving view of mass culture. The consensus today is that even the most commercial productions can provide many pleasures, in spite of the negative features of the system as a whole. In recent decades highbrows and leftists have come to recognize the merit of works like "The Mary Tyler Moore Show," with its perfectly knit ensemble acting and gentle comedy of character, or "The Cosby Show," with its rare view of upper-middle-class family life through a black center of consciousness (though the latter show can be criticized for its implication that the attainment of middle class status by a minority among minorities has effectively ended racial discrimination). The native genius of the composers and performers of American popular music and musical comedy—crassly commercial media—in the period spanning roughly the second quarter of this century has become increasingly apparent as that extraordinary generation has died off and the forms they worked in have declined. George Gershwin's *Porgy and Bess*, which has come to rank with the classic European operas, was written under the financial pressures of Broadway, although its initial production was not a box office success. Economic and historical factors in the rise and decline of creativity in rock music since the sixties have been intelligently studied by such Marxists as Simon Frith, Steve Chapple, and Reebee Garofalo, and economic studies of Tin Pan Alley and Broadway are equally instructive. Such studies, however, can never wholly account for cycles of creativity, which remain largely fortuitous. To paraphrase Freud, before the mystery of artistic creation Marxism can only lay down its arms in admiration.

Nevertheless, as anyone who has worked in mass media knows, the creator's quest for artistic or political integrity constantly runs up against corporate pressures to water the product down for mass consumption; thus, quality emerges in spite of, certainly not because of, the conditions of commercial production. On a more theoretical level, much recent left criticism has focused less on the forms of direct cultural manipulation discussed in Part 1 than on the notion of ideological hegemony, that is, on the multiplicity of ways in which dominant ideology, indirectly and unintentionally, permeates cultural consciousness—as traced here in Todd Gitlin's "Television's Screens: Hegemony in Transition." A related theme—developed by Gitlin, by Tania Modleski in her study of soap opera here ("The Search for Tomorrow in Today's Soap Operas") and of other popular literary forms in *Loving with a Vengeance: Mass-Produced Fantasies for Women*, and by other critics including Fredric Jameson, Douglas Kellner, and Paul Buhle—is that bourgeois hegemony, direct and indirect, is presently limited in many ways and that mass culture embodies a conflicted mix of progressive and regressive political tendencies; its works would not maintain their popularity if they did not to some extent fulfill authentic aesthetic needs and a utopian vision of a more humane social order.

The essays in this section, then, addressing mainly content—along with Gitlin's essay and those in Part 5, which deal with the ideological implications of the ways in which media's institutional conventions, techniques, formats, and genres structure patterns of perception—trace the stress lines between populist or oppositional tendencies and the restraints imposed by both commercial production and ideological hegemony. For example, Boggs and Pratt, in "The Blues Tradition: Poetic Revolt or Cultural Impasse?" examine the historical role the blues have played in black oppositional culture and the changes in the political meaning of blues music as it has become commercialized and redirected toward white and middle-class black audiences. Or, to take the case of sports, Louis Kampf's article in Part 8 is representative of current left critics, who express a love for participant and spectator sports equal to that of a conservative like Michael Novak in *The Joy of Sports*. They find in sports at its best a model of the utopia envisioned in Marx's early manuscripts, in which class divisions and the alienation of work from play would be overcome. But whereas Novak minimizes the degradation sports has suffered from commercialism, militarism, sexism, and racism, left critics consider this degradation integral to capitalism's social needs and document its deliberate engineering in American history, as Kampf is doing more fully in a book in progress.

As these readings and others throughout the volume indicate, mass culture manages oppositional impulses by intermingling them with conventional ones, in the effort to provide something for audience members of every persuasion. In 1983 a televised dramatization appeared of "My Life as A Man," a *Village Voice* account by Carol Lynn Mithers of her experience of being disguised for several weeks as a man and of the insights it gave her into male prerogatives. Mithers was depicted in the article as an ordinary-looking, dark-featured Greenwich Village bohemian; nothing was mentioned about the effect of the disguise on her love life or job (she only wore her disguise after working hours). In the TV fictionalization, the setting shifted from New York to Hollywood, and the heroine was portrayed by a beautiful, fair-featured *Playboy* model; she had a wealthy, chauvinistic fiancé who was outraged by her disguise, and a glamorous writing job at a sports magazine, complete with lunches at Ma Maison. The producers evidently calculated that even an equivocally feminist message would only be palatable to Middle America in a chic social milieu with WASP-ized characters and romantic interest. The TV additions did have the virtue of criticizing sexual stereotyping in employment (the heroine is turned down for a job as a sportswriter when she first applies but is hired when she presents herself as a man) and in relationships (her fiancé is rankled when her career as a man begins to take priority over his). When she finally reveals her identity to her boss, after proving her worth as a sportswriter, she is allowed to keep her job; her fiancé also learns the error of his sexist ways, and so they marry into what will now be a peer relationship. Hollywood happy ending, eighties-style.

These contradictory messages, and the ones that Modleski points out in soap opera and women's popular fiction, are instances of the master fantasy pandered to by all mass culture, that you can have your cake and eat it too: there is no contradiction between women's liberation and happy homemaking, rebellion and conformity, rugged individualism and the corporate society, adventure and safety, accumulation of expensive commodities and Christian self-denial, vicarious identification with the wealthy (as in "Dallas" and "Dynasty") or the beautiful (Bo Derek in *10*) and condemnation of their morals. The "extravagant expectations" that Daniel Boorstin speaks of primarily serve the commercial purpose of maximizing audiences, but they also contribute to susceptibility to politicians' equally facile, irreconcilable promises, such as reducing taxes and big government without raising the deficit or cutting any public programs we have a special interest in (see the Gerbner studies in Part 6).[1] All these messages assure us that there are no irreconcilable conflicts within the present social order and that those presently in power are capable of resolving every problem if we just trust them. About the accommodations of television to feminism, Kate Ellis writes:

They're still doing their patriarchal number from eight to ten (and on the news as well) telling us that clean is sexy and surrounding those elements in their programs that might be disturbing with the cotton candy of comedy so that we'll keep getting the message that *everything is just fine*. But that voice is less and less the voice of a father who knows best, and more and more the voice of a sister who is coping with her life, on a good day anyway, one day at a time.[2]

In addition to the above lines of recent criticism addressing mass culture's mediations of popular and oppositional culture, many left critics have taken the opposite tack, exploring the mediations and appropriations of mass culture by audiences. The older, simplistic stimulus-response model of media effects has been modified by several studies indicating that audiences frequently interpret media messages differently than the senders intended them to; as Stuart Hall puts it, the processes of encoding and decoding may be quite at odds.[3] According to some researchers, response to television, for example, is an interactive process rather than the purely passive one described by more pessimistic writers such as Neil Postman (Part 6); the Gerbner "cultivation analysis" studies similarly note differentials in the influence of television on the political attitudes of various control groups, although these studies indicate that heavy viewers are more apt than light ones to agree with TV messages in every control group. Sociological and psychological variables in audience response to mass media are a little-explored but much-needed area of research for literary scholars, who could make good use here of reader-response theory.

One recent left school of thought is close to the Popular Culture Association and liberal-pluralist positions in accentuating the positive inroads populist and working-class culture have made into mass media (Jackie Gleason's "The Honeymooners" and Phil Silvers's "Sergeant Bilko" are favorites of this school). The journals *Radical America* and *Cultural Correspondence* (the latter now defunct) have been strong proponents of this position, largely due to the editorial presence at both of Paul Buhle.[4] George Lipsitz's article here on country music, "Working People's Music" from *Cultural Correspondence*, typifies the position, which is further developed in the chapters "Hierarchical Culture and Popular Resistance" (dealing with film noir, roller derby, working-class vernacular speech, car customizing, and drag racing) and "The Class Origins of Rock and Roll" in his book *Class and Culture in Cold War America*.[5] Mark Naison's "Sports and the American Empire" (Part 7), from *Radical America*, is also representative in its emphasis on the way blacks have capitalized on the American sports mania to advance their own status. Along similar lines, the German New Left critic Hans Magnus Enzensberger and his American followers have applied a dialectical approach to the culture industry, emphasizing its unintentional but unavoidable generation of oppositional tendencies and opportunities for the kind of leftist interventions explored by Kellner and other media activists in Part 8.[6]

Many of the points of the *Radical America* and Enzensberger schools are well taken; with regard to racism, for example, despite its past history and present vestiges in American mass culture, through the last few decades sports, television, film, and popular music have clearly helped advance minorities (at least the stars among them, though it is less clear that their success has greatly benefited any but these elect few). By the eighties, then, Michael Jackson, a black singer-dancer with less talent than countless earlier black musicians, could become a full-fledged teenage idol of all races. Furthermore, elements from commercial culture have sometimes been appropriated by working-class and ethnic groups to create machine-age folk culture—drag racing in the fifties, low-riders in the seventies, break dancing in the eighties. Noteworthy as these vestiges of folk culture may be, however, they are at best only pockets of resistance against total control rather than substantial oppositional movements. And the critics who follow this line tend, like those of the earlier Popular Front period, to hold a sentimentalized belief in the progressive nature of all culture that is populist, like country music, or youthful, like rock music (Simon Frith, in "Rock and Popular Culture" here, admirably resists this tendency); such critics avoid facing up to the apolitical or reactionary character of much populist and youth culture. They must eventually, however, address the question of whether such "autonomous moments," to use the Marxist terminology, make much difference in the overall social system, or whether they are essentially cultural wildlife preserves allowed by grace of the benevolent dictatorship of the totally administered society.

Notes

1. Daniel Boorstin, *The Image; or, What Happened to the American Dream* (New York: Harper Colophon, 1962), pp. 3–6.

2. Kate Ellis, "Queen for One Day at a Time," *College English* 38, no. 8 (1977): 780.

3. Stuart Hall, "Encoding and Decoding," in *Culture, Media, Language*, ed. Hall et al. (London: Hutchinson, 1980).

4. See Paul Buhle, ed., "Fifteen Years of *Radical America*: An Anthology," *Radical America* 16, no. 3 (1983); and James Green, ed., *Workers' Struggles, Past and Present: A "Radical America" Reader* (Philadelphia: Temple University Press, 1983).

5. George Lipsitz, *Class and Culture in Cold War America* (South Hadley, Mass.: Bergin, 1982), pp. 173–225.

6. See Hans Magnus Enzensberger's *The Consciousness Industry: On Literature, Politics and the Media* (New York: Seabury Press, 1974), and "Television and the Politics of Liberation," in *The New Television: A Public/Private Art*, ed. Douglas Davis and Allison Simmons (Cambridge, Mass.: MIT Press, 1977).

Further Readings

Race in Mass Media

Baldwin, James. *The Devil Finds Work*. New York: Dial Press, 1976.

Bogle, Donald. *Toms, Coons, Mulattoes, Mammies, and Bucks*. New York: Viking Press, 1973.

Cantor, Milton. *Images of the Negro in American Literature*. Chicago: University of Chicago Press, 1966.

Friar, Ralph E., and Natasha A. Friar. *The Only Good Indian . . . , The Hollywood Gospel*. New York: Drama Book Specialists, 1972.

Levine, Lawrence W. *Black Culture and Black Consciousness*. New York: Oxford University Press, 1977.

MacDonald, Fred J. *Black and White On TV: Afro Americans in Television Since 1948*. Chicago: Nelson-Hall, 1983.

Manchel, Frank. "Stereotyping in Film." *Film Study—A Resource Guide*. Cranbury, N.J.: Associated University Press, 1973.

Maynard, Richard A. *The Black Man on Film: Racial Stereotyping*. Rochelle Park, N.J.: Hayden, 1971.

———. "How Dark Is a Dark Continent? Myths About Tropical Africa Created by Motion Pictures." In *The Celluloid Curriculum: How to Use Movies in the Classroom*. Rochelle Park, N.J.: Hayden, 1971.

"The News Media and the Disorders." Chapter 15 in *Report of the National Advisory Commission on Civil Disorders*. New York: Bantam Books, 1968.

Pettit, Arthur G. *Images of the Mexican American in Fiction and Film*. College Station: Texas A & M University Press, 1980.

"A Symposium on *Roots*." *The Black Scholar* 8, no. 7 (May 1977).

Gender in Mass Media

Batsleer, Janet, et al. *Rewriting English: The Politics of Gender and Class*. London: Methuen, 1986.

Edgar, Patricia, and Hilary McPhee. *Media She*. Melbourne, Australia: Heinemann, 1974.

Ehrenreich, Barbara. *The Hearts of Men*. Garden City, N.Y.: Anchor Press/Doubleday, 1983.

Gornick, Vivian, and Barbara K. Moran, eds. *Women in Sexist Society—Studies in Power and Powerlessness*. New York: Basic Books, 1971.

Janus, Noreene Z. "Research on Sex-Roles in the Mass Media: Toward a Critical Approach." *The Insurgent Sociologist* 7, no. 3 (1977): 19–32.

Kaplan, E. Ann. *Women and Film: Both Sides of the Camera*. London: Methuen, 1983.

Lakoff, Robin, and Racquel Scherr. *Face Value: The Politics of Beauty*. Boston: Routledge & Kegan Paul, 1984.

Lopate, Carol (Ascher). "Daytime Television: You'll Never Want to Leave Home." *Radical America*, January–February 1977, pp. 40–51.

Mellen, Joan. *Women and Their Sexuality in the New Film*. New York: Dell, 1973.

Miles, Betty. *Channeling Children: Sex Stereotyping in Prime Time TV*. Princeton, N.J.: Women on Words and Images, 1975.

Radway, Janice A. *Reading the Romance: Women, Patriarchy, and Popular Literature*. Chapel Hill: University of North Carolina Press, 1984.

Robinson, Lillian S. *Sex, Class and Culture*. Bloomington: Indiana University Press, 1978.

Rosaldo, Michelle Zimbalist, and Louise Lamphere, eds. *Women, Culture, and Society*. Stanford, Calif.: Stanford University Press, 1974.

Russo, Vito. *The Celluloid Closet: Homosexuality in the Movies*. New York: Harper & Row, 1981.

Signorielli, Nancy. "Marital Status in Television Drama: A Case of Reduced Options." *Journal of Communication*, 26, no. 2 (1982).

Snitow, Ann Barr. "Mass Market Romance: Pornography for Women is Different." *Radical History Review* 19 (1979): 141–161.

Strainchamps, Edith, ed. *Rooms with No View: A Woman's Guide to the Man's World of the Media*. New York: Harper & Row, 1974.

Tuchman, Gaye. "Review Essay: The Depiction of Women in the Mass Media." *Signs*, Spring 1979, pp. 538–542.

Tuchman, Gaye, Arlene K. Daniels, and James Benet, eds. *Hearth and Home: Images of Women in the Mass Media*. New York: Oxford University Press, 1978.

Van Gelber, Lindsay. "Women's Pages: You Can't Make News Out of A Silk Purse." *Ms.*, November 1974.

Weibel, Kathryn. *Mirror, Mirror: Images of Women Reflected in Popular Culture*. Garden City, N.Y.: Anchor Press, 1977.

Film and Television

Ang, Ien. *Watching Dallas: Soap Opera and the Melodramatic Imagination*. London: Methuen, 1986.

Davies, Philip John, and Brian Neve. *Cinema, Politics, and Society in America*. New York: St. Martin's Press, 1982.

Furhammar, Leif, and Folke Isaksson. *Politics and Film*. New York: Praeger, 1971.

Gitlin, Todd, ed. *Watching Television*. New York: Pantheon Books, 1987.

Kaplan, E. Ann, ed. *Regarding Television: Critical Approaches—An Anthology*. Los Angeles: University Publications of America, 1983.

MacBean, James Roy. *Films and Revolution*. Bloomington: Indiana University Press, 1975.

Nichols, Bill. *Ideology and the Image: Social Representation in the Cinema and Other Media*. Bloomington: Indiana University Press, 1984.

———, ed. *Movies and Methods*. Berkeley and Los Angeles: University of California Press, 1976.

———, ed. *Movies and Methods*, Volume II. Berkeley and Los Angeles: University of California Press, 1985.

Steven, Peter, ed. *Jump Cut. Ten Years of Radical Film and Criticism. Essays from "Jump Cut" Magazine*. New York: Praeger, 1986.

White, David Manning, and Richard Averson. *The Celluloid Weapon: Social Comment in the American Film*. Boston: Beacon Press, 1972.

Sports

Edwards, Harry. *Sociology of Sport*. Homewood, N.J.: Dorsey Press, 1973.

———. *The Revolt of the Black Athlete*. New York: Free Press, 1969.

Gruneau, Richard. *Class, Sports, and Social Development*. Amherst: University of Massachusetts Press, 1983.

Hoberman, John M. *Sport and Political Ideology*. Austin: University of Texas Press, 1985.

Hoch, Paul. *Rip Off the Big Game: The Exploitation of Sports by the Power Elite*. Garden City, N.Y.: Doubleday, 1972.

Isaacs, Neil D. *Jock Culture, U.S.A.* New York: Norton, 1978.

James, C. L. R. *Beyond the Boundary*. New York: Pantheon Books, 1984.

Lapchick, Richard E. *Broken Promises: Racism in American Sports*. New York: St. Martin's Press, 1984.

Lipsyte, Robert. *Sports World: An American Dreamland*. New York: Quadrangle, 1975.

Meggyesy, David M. *Out of Their League*. Berkeley, Calif.: Ramparts Press, 1970.

Novak, Michael. *The Joy of Sports*. New York: Basic Books, 1976.

Scott, Jack. *The Athletic Revolution*. New York: Free Press, 1970.

Popular Music

Baker, Houston A., Jr. *Blues, Ideology, and Afro-American Literature*. Chicago: University of Chicago Press, 1984.

Baraka, Amiri (LeRoi Jones), and Amina Baraka. *The Music: Reflections on Jazz and Blues*. New York: Morrow, 1987.

Chapple, Steve, and Reebee Garofalo. *Rock 'n' Roll Is Here to Pay: The History of Politics in the Music Industry*. Chicago: Nelson Hall, 1977.

Frith, Simon. *Sound Effects: Youth, Leisure, and the Politics of Rock 'n' Roll*. New York: Pantheon Books, 1981.

————. *The Sociology of Rock*. London: Constable, 1978.

Garofalo, Reebee, and Steve Chapple. "The Pre-History of Rock and Roll." *Radical America* 14, no. 4 (1980): 61–71.

Grossberg, Lawrence. "The Politics of Youth Culture: Some Observations on Rock and Roll in American Culture." *Social Text* 8 (Winter 1983–1984): 104–126.

Hebdige, Dick. "Reggae, Rastas, and Rudies." In *Mass Communication and Society*, ed. James Curran, Michael Gurevitch, and Janet Woollacott. London: Open University Press, 1979.

Keil, Charles. *Urban Blues*. Chicago: University of Chicago Press, 1979.

Rosselson, Leon. "Pop Music: Mobilizer or Opiate?" In *Media, Politics and Culture: A Socialist View*, ed. Carl Gardner. London: Macmillan, 1979.

Sinclair, John, and Robert Levin. *Music and Politics*. New York: World, 1971.

Street, John. *Rebel Rock: The Politics of Popular Music*. New York: Blackwell, 1986.

Toop, David. *The Rap Attack: African Jive to New York Hip Hop*. Boston: South End Press, 1984.

TELEVISION'S SCREENS: HEGEMONY IN TRANSITION

TODD GITLIN

In advanced capitalist societies, popular culture is the meeting ground for two linked (though not identical) social processes. (1) The cultural industry produces its goods, tailoring them to particular markets and organizing their content so that they are packaged to be compatible with the dominant values and mode of discourse, and (2), by consuming clumps of these cultural goods, distinct social groups help position themselves in the society, and work toward defining their status, their social identity. By enjoying a certain genre of music, film, television program, they take a large step toward recognizing themselves as social entities. To study popular culture fully is to study the ensemble of this complex social process. The artifacts are produced by professionals under the supervision of cultural elites themselves interlocked with corporate and, at times, state interests; meanings become encased in the artifacts, consciously and not; then the artifacts are consumed. The act of consuming appropriates and completes the work: it activates from among the work's range of possible meanings—those that are actually present in the work—those that will embody what the work means, here and now, to a given social group and to individuals within it. What requires study is the totality of this process of production, signification, and consumption. But before I break popular culture down into its component parts, I want to insist on the density of the complex interrelation of those parts. For each of these "moments" presupposes the others, and is partly determined by them. The totality of popular culture is a tense one, at once institutionalized and changing. It contains the possibility of its own transformation, and even the transformation of the society, and it contains these possibilities in two senses: it includes them, and it limits them.

The key to grasping the popular culture process of corporate capitalism, in all its dynamism and ornery self-contradiction, lies with Gramsci's concept of hegemony, and the particular version of it I have distilled (Gitlin 1980) from the British neo-Gramscian work of Raymond Williams (1973, 1977), Stuart Hall (1973, 1977), and Paul Willis (n.d., 1978). By hegemony I mean the process in which a ruling class—or, more likely, an alliance of class fractions—dominates subordinate classes and groups through the elaboration and penetration of ideology into their common sense and everyday practice. Through training and reward, the dominant social groups secure the services of cultural practitioners—producers, writers, journalists, actors, and so on. To articulate ideals and understandings, to integrate the enormous variety of social interests among elites, and between elites and less powerful groups, in a modern capitalist society, the corporate and political elites must depend on the work of skilled groups of symbolic

Excerpted from *Cultural and Economic Reproduction in Education*, ed. Michael W. Apple (London: Routledge & Kegan Paul, 1982).

adepts, what Gramsci called "organic intellectuals." In order to make their livings, these practitioners organize their production to be consonant with the values and projects of the elites; yet in crucial respects they may depart from the direct programs of the elites who hire, regulate, and finance them. (Indeed, the competitive corporate elite may not be able to formulate its common interests without the work of the symbolic adepts.) The content of the resulting cultural system is rarely cut and dried, partly because the cultural practitioners have their own values, traditions, and practices, which may differ from those of the elites, and partly because market constraints exist that keep the hegemonic ideology flexible. (The bald, uncontested affirmation of the value of corporate greed, for example, would probably fail to attract organic intellectuals, and would probably, moreover, fail to entertain the mass audience.) Ideological domination, in other words, requires an *alliance* between powerful economic and political groups on the one hand, and cultural elites on the other—alliances whose terms must, in effect, be negotiated and, as social conditions and elite dispositions shift, renegotiated.

Hegemony encompasses the terms through which the alliances of domination are cemented; it also extends to the systematic (but not necessarily, or even usually, deliberate) engineering of mass consent to the established order.[1] It is best understood as a collaborative process rather than an imposed, definitively structured order; in general, hegemony is a condition of the social system as a whole, rather than a cunning project of the ruling group. As Michael Burawoy so lucidly writes (1979, 17–18, citing Poulantzas 1975, 31),

Ideology is . . . not something manipulated at will by agencies of socialization—schools, family, church, and so on [one could easily add mass media]—in the interests of a dominant class. On the contrary, these institutions elaborate and systematize lived experience and only in this way become centers of ideological dissemination. Moreover, dominant classes are shaped by ideology more than they shape it. To the extent that they engage in active deception, they disseminate propaganda, not ideology. As a first approximation, it is lived experience that produces ideology, not the other way around. Ideology is rooted in and expresses the activities out of which it emerges.

Ideology is generally expressed as common sense—those assumptions, procedures, rules of discourse that are taken for granted. Hegemony is the suffusing of the society by ideology that sustains the powerful groups' claims to their power by rendering their preeminence natural, justifiable, and beneficent.

The decisive point is that hegemony is a collaboration. It is an unequal collaboration, in which the large-scale processes of concentrated production set limits to, and manage, the cultural expressions of dominated (and dominating) groups. Yet it is a collaboration nevertheless. Absolute power coerces; hegemony persuades, coaxes, rewards, chastises. Absolute power forbids alternatives; hegemony organizes consent and allocates a certain limited social space to tailored alternatives. Both parts of this formulation are important. Hegemony is a process of organization in which cultural elites occupy top positions and supervise the work of subordinates in such a way as to draw their activity into a discourse that supports the dominant position of the elites; at the same time, hegemony cannot operate without the consent of those subordinates. Hegemony takes place behind the backs of its operatives; it is a silent domination that is not experienced as domination at all. Hegemony is the orchestration of the wills of the subordinates into harmony with the established order of power.

The system of popular culture is one important domain through which the terms of hegemony are affirmed and negotiated. The process of renegotiation is mandatory because the hegemonic ideology in liberal capitalist society is inherently contradictory and changeable. The hegemonic ideology in the United States attempts to bridge the rival claims of freedom and equality: it propounds equality of opportunity rather than equality of results. It affirms patriarchal authority—currently embodied most successfully in the national security state—while at the same time embracing individual worth and self-determination: it accomplishes this compromise by propounding the ideal of meritocracy, promotion of the most competent, as a principle of technocratic rule within all institutions.[2] The dominant ideology of corporate capitalist society cannot for long be unbridled individualism, but must also render homage to the legitimate claims of a wider community—familial, religious, ethnic, or national or even supranational (as in the sometime internationalism of scientists). Nationalist sentiment is the most readily available.

These tensions within hegemonic ideology render it vulnerable to the demands of insurgent groups and to cultural change in general. Insurgencies press upon the hegemonic whole in the name of one of its components—against the demands of others. *And popular culture is one crucial institution where the rival claims of ideology are sometimes pressed forward, sometimes reconciled in imaginative form.* Popular culture absorbs oppositional ideology, adapts it to the contours of the core hegemonic principles, and domesticates it; at the same time, popular culture is a realm for the expression of forms of resistance and oppositional ideology. Popular culture is the expressive domain where pleasure is promised and contained, articulated and packaged. The mass culture industry of advanced capitalist society packages the representations; it organizes entertainment into terms that are, as much as possible, compatible with the hegemonic discourse.

But this does not necessarily mean that popular culture suppresses alternative or even oppositional ideology.[3] Indeed, in a *liberal* capitalist order, suppression proceeds alongside accommodation: sometimes one predominates, sometimes the other. The blandness of television entertainment in the 1950s (perhaps partly an assurance to purchasers of the new, expensive receivers) was displaced in the 1970s by a style of entertainment that takes account of social conflict and works to domesticate it—to individualize its solutions, if not its causes. Likewise, the light, innocent romance of popular music of the early 1950s ("Tennessee Waltz," "Memories Are Made of This") as recorded by singers like Patti Page, Perry Como, Dean Martin, and Frank Sinatra, and mass-distributed through radio, was supplanted by black-based rock and roll, which embodied in lyrics, but more in beat and instrument, a certain prepolitical youth revolt and carried a certain stylized anger and collective passion. The visible hand of the market rewards those corporate cultural ventures that succeed in attracting public attention: mass market imperatives dictate that the culture industry respond, however partially, sluggishly, and reductively, to public moods and tastes.[4] Diverse cultural enterprises respond differently to their markets. They all take account of hegemonic ideology in the ways they package their contents. But the degree to which they are incorporated into hegemonic ideology depends on several features of their industrial organization, as well as the particular historical situation: it depends on the degree of economic concentration in the industry, the amount of capital required to enter the field, and the ideology of cultural producers. In popular music, for example, the ideological range is relatively small (a few hundred dollars suffice to press a record in a garage), and market segmentation sets the tune. (Of course distribution to stores and through radio is much more highly controlled by oligopolistic companies.) In contrast, network and syndicated television, with their vast markets dictated by a combination of oligopoly and high capitalization, are less open to genuinely independent entries. Yet television, too, as I shall argue below, must strive for audiences that cut across class, race, and ideological lines. Thus the commercial core of the culture industry aims for middle-of-the-road (MOR) productions, the stylistic center of gravity shifting in response to certain (not all) cultural changes. Mass-cultural elites and gatekeepers do not simply manipulate popular taste; they do not write on tabulae rasae. Rather, they shape and channel sentiment and taste, which churn and simmer in the larger society, and express popular desires in one form or another.

The genius of Marx's critique of capitalism, as opposed to the romantic protest against it, began with his insistence that the capitalist's exploitation of labor was the exploitation of something socially desirable and full of potential for enlarging the scope of human existence. Let the analysis of popular culture proceed in a similar spirit. The production and promotion of cultural meanings is also a necessity: in a diverse society, it is in popular culture that groups can declare themselves, converse with each other, consolidate their identities, and enact—on the symbolic level—their deepest aspirations, fears, and conflicts. The genius of the cultural industry, if that is the right word, lies in its ability to take account of popular aspirations, fears, and conflicts, and to address them in ways that assimilate popular values into terms compatible with the hegemonic ideology. The cultural industry packages values and beliefs, relays and reproduces and focuses them, distorting and adjusting elements of ideology that are constantly arising both from social elites and from social groups throughout the society, including, not least, media practices and their social worlds. The culture industry does not invent ideology from scratch. To paraphrase the old saying about hypocrisy, the forms of commercial culture amount to the tribute that hegemony pays to popular feeling. The executives who sit uneasily at the commanding heights of the cultural industry, desperately holding on to their tenuous positions, are not so much managers of the mind as orchestrators of its projects and desires.[5] Likewise, their products are commodities, but not commodities only. They are always containers of works that appeal to popular aesthetics and beliefs, containers that work to smooth out the rough edges, to tame the intractable feelings, and to reconcile emotions and images that may well be irreconcilable, at least in the established society.

One further note of prologue: My discussion of popular culture centers on entertainment, not news. Yet the workings and functions of the hegemonic news-selecting and -distributing industry are not essentially different from those of entertainment. (On news, see Gans 1979; Gitlin 1980; Tuchman 1978.) In news, as in entertainment, hegemony is the product of a chain of assumptions, concretely embedded in work procedures, that rarely require directorial intervention from executives or political elites in order to produce a view of the world that at key points confirms the core hegemonic principles: individualism, technocracy, private control of the economy, the national security state. Hegemony in news as in entertainment takes notice of alternatives to the dominant values, descriptions, and ideals, and frames them so that some alternative features get assimilated into the dominant ideological system, while most of that which is potentially subversive of the dominant value system is driven to the ideological margins.

Indeed, in important respects, news and entertainment are converging. News borrows from entertainment important conventions of structure and content. In *structure*, television news stories are ordinarily organized as little narratives (Epstein 1973; Gitlin 1977a). A problem is set forth, and the action proceeds in a standard curve. Conflict takes place between rival actors. At least one solution is set forth (generally by duly sanctioned authority, the main protagonist of the tale). The disinterested narrator stands for the viewer, certifying either that the problem is being taken care of or else that the problem is beyond human agency altogether. The narrative curve now descends to earth with a certain closure: an action will be taken; or, if not, the narrator supplies an artificial rhetorical closure, in the easily mocked empty formula of "It remains to be seen. . . ." And in content, as already mentioned, television news stories are built around images of particular personages and dramatic conflict (Gitlin 1977a, 1980). Stories are personified; they issue forth from sanctioned politicians and certified authorities. Stories include visual images that will secure the flickering attention of the mass audience. Other things being equal, the dramatic image—a burning flag, a raging fire, a battle—gets priority, especially the image that lies on the surface, immediately available to the camera. These devices are borrowed from the theater, and from ancient and modern myths, trickster myths, homecoming myths, and all manner of others, refurbished to encompass the concerns of the hour. The story about the Vietnam veteran returning home draws on, and plays against, the Odyssey; a story about the war, or about devastation in the South Bronx, draws on imagery from the Indian wars.[6]

As for entertainment, it borrows liberally from the conventions of news—that is, from realism. As Ian Watt (1957) has argued, the English novel, from its emergence in the eighteenth century, has always insisted that it represents reality. The recent trend toward the "nonfictional novel" (Mailer) or the fictional appropriation of actual historical personages (Capote, Doctorow) only continues a longer tradition: the novel indulges in the artifice that it describes something that actually happened, and readers suspend disbelief. Photography obviously traded on its claim to transparency (see Benjamin 1978; Sontag 1977), and so did the fiction film, capitalizing on its appearance of permitting direct representation of some sort of actual life, even as the viewer is at another level aware that "it's only a movie." The recent vogue of the television "docudrama," in which actors "re-create" the lives of great individuals at great moments in history (the Cuban Missile Crisis, Truman firing MacArthur, the travails of Eleanor and Franklin Roosevelt), simply continues the grand tradition; as defenders of the nonfiction novel enjoy pointing out, Tolstoy put lines into Napoleon's mouth in *War and Peace*. One need not endorse Georg Lukács's (1964) dismissal of modernist heresies to acknowledge the truth of his larger claim: that realism is the distinctly bourgeois literary mode.

In short, only a misguided formalism would draw a hard and fast line between news and entertainment; their mythic and realistic conventions touch, and influence each other. And just as the news organizations process reports of reality into packages of information and imagery that help reconfirm the legitimacy and completeness of the hegemonic worldview, so do the organizations of entertainment production selectively absorb elements of discrepant ideology, ensuring that the hegemonic ideology remains up to date, encompassing, sufficiently pluralistic in accent to attract different audiences, while transposing social conflicts into a key where the hegemonic ideology is re-legitimated. Both news and entertainment thus reinforce each other to reproduce the dominant ideology—*in all its contradiction and sometime instability*. It is one paradox of the culture of liberal capitalism that its reproduction takes place through partial and limited transformations. It stands still, in a sense, by moving.

[In the next section, cut here, Gitlin sketches out an analysis, developed more fully in his book *Inside Prime Time*, of the processes of network television production, including organizational structures, market strategies, creators' personal values, conventional corporate practices, and the perception of audience wants.]

. . . .

Consider some of the conventions in which ideological hegemony is embedded: format; plot formula; genre; setting; character type; images of social and psychological conflict and its solution; images of authority, the state, family, work, and social movements; images of emotion, its texture and legitimacy.

FORMAT

Until recently at least, the TV schedule has been dominated by standard lengths and cadences, standardized packages of TV entertainment appearing, as the announcers used to say, "same time, same station." This week-to-weekness—or, in the case of soap operas, day-to-dayness—obstructed the development of characters; the primary characters had to be preserved intact for next week's show. Perry Mason was Perry Mason, once and for all; watching the reruns, only devotees could know from character or set whether they were watching the first or the last in the series. For commercial and production reasons, which are in practice inseparable—and this is why ideological hegemony is not directly reducible to the economic interests of elites—the regular schedule prefers the repeatable formula: it is far easier for production companies to hire writers to write for standardized, static characters than for characters who develop. Assembly-line production works through regularity of time slot, of duration, and of character to convey images of social steadiness: come what may, "Gunsmoke" or "Kojak" will occupy a certain time on a certain evening. Should they lose ratings (at least at the "upscale" reaches of the demographics, where ratings translate into disposable dollars),[7] their replacements would be—for a time, at least!—equally reliable. Moreover, the standard curve of narrative action—stock characters show their standard stuff; the plot resolves—over twenty-two or fifty minutes is itself a source of rigidity and forced regularity.

In these ways, the usual programs are performances that rehearse social fixity: they express and cement the obduracy of a social world impervious to substantial change. Yet at the same time there are signs of routine obsolescence, as hunks of last year's regular schedule drop from sight only to be supplanted by this season's attractions. (The very concept of "season"—in TV as in fashion, and in the opera, ballet, and theater of high culture—claims the authority and normality of nature's cycles for man-made products.) Standardization and the likelihood of evanescence are curiously linked: they match the intertwined processes of commodity production, predictability, and obsolescence in a high-consumption capitalist society. I speculate that they help confirm audiences in their sense of the rightness and naturalness of a world that, in only apparent paradox, regularly requires an irregularity, an unreliability, which it calls progress. In this way, the regular model changes in TV programs, like the regular changes in auto design and the regular elections of public officials, seem to affirm the sovereignty of the audience while keeping deep alternatives off the agenda. Elite authority and the illusion of consumer choice are affirmed at once—this is one of the central operations of the hegemonic liberal capitalist ideology.

Then, too, by organizing the "free time" of persons into end-to-end interchangeable units, broadcasting extends, and harmonizes with, the industrialization of time. Media time and school time, with their equivalent units and curves of action, mirror the time of clocked labor and reinforce the seeming naturalness of clock time. Anyone who reads Harry Braverman's *Labor and Monopoly Capital* can trace the steady degradation of the work process, both white and blue collar, through the twentieth century, even if Braverman has exaggerated the extent of the process by focusing on managerial *strategies* more than on actual work *processes*. Something similar has happened in other life-sectors. Leisure is industrialized, duration is homogenized, even excitement is routinized, and the standard repeated TV format is an important component of the process. And typically, too, capitalism provides relief from these confines for its more favored citizens, those who can afford to buy their way out of the standardized social reality that capitalism produces. Beginning in the late 1970s, the home videocassette recorder enabled upscale consumers to tape programs they would otherwise have missed; by 1984 there were ten million in American homes. The widely felt need to overcome assembly-line "leisure" time thus became the source of a new market—to sell the means for private, commoditized solutions to the time jam.

Commercials, of course, are also major features of the regular TV format. There can be no question but that commercials have a good deal to do with shaping and maintaining markets—no advertiser dreams of cutting advertising costs as long as the competition is still on the air. But commercials also have important *indirect* consequences on the contours of consciousness overall: they get us accustomed to thinking of ourselves and behaving as a market rather than a public, as consumers rather than producers or citizens. Public problems (like air pollution) are to be understood as susceptible to private commodity solutions (like eyedrops). In the process, whether or not we are offended or annoyed by commercials, they acculturate us to interruption through the rest of our lives. Time and attention are not one's own; the corporations in effect advertise their own dominion along with their products. Regardless of the commercial's effect on our behavior, we consent to its domination of the public space. Yet we should note that this colonizing process does not actually require commercials, as long as it can form discrete packages of ideological content that call forth discontinuous responses in the audience. Even public broadcasting's children's shows take over the commercial forms by herky-jerky bustle. The producers of "Sesame Street," in likening knowledge to commercial products ("and now a message from the letter B"), may well be legitimizing the commercial form in its discontinuity and its invasiveness. Again, regularity and discontinuity, superficially discrepant, may be linked at a deep level of meaning. And perhaps the deepest privatizing function of television, its most powerful impact on public life, may lie in the most obvious thing about it: we receive the images in the privacy of our living rooms, making public discourse and response difficult. At the same time, the paradox is that at any given time many viewers are receiving images that do not accord with many of their beliefs, thus challenging their received opinions.

Television routines have been built into the broadcast schedule since its inception. But arguably their regularity has been waning since Norman Lear's first comedy, "All in the Family," made its network debut in 1971. Lear's contribution to TV content was obvious: where previous shows might have made passing reference to social conflicts, Lear brought wrenching social issues into the center of his plots. Lear also let his characters develop. (Previously, only the children in family series had been permitted to change—a forced maturation.) Edith Bunker grew less sappy and more feminist and commonsensical; Gloria and Mike moved next door, and finally to California. On the threshold of this generational rupture, Mike broke through his stereotype by expressing affection for Archie, and Archie, oh-so-reluctantly, but definitely for all that, hugged back and broke through his own. Other Lear characters, the Jeffersons and Maude, had earlier been spun off into their own shows. (Since Lear's success with spin-offs, popular actors on other shows have been able to bargain themselves into their own series— "Rhoda" from "The Mary Tyler Moore Show," "Flo" from "Alice," ad infinitum.) Lear's precedents have flourished; they were built on intelligent business perceptions that an audience did exist for situation comedies that directly addressed racism, sexism, and the instability of conventional families. But there is no such thing as a strictly economic explanation for production choice, since the success of a show—despite market research—is not foreordained. In the context of my argument, the importance of such developments lies in their partial break with the established, static formulae of prime-time television.

Daytime soap operas and their prime-time variants have also been sliding into character development and a direct exploitation of divisive social issues, rather than going on constructing a race-free, class-free, feminism-free world. And more conspicuously, the "miniseries" has now occasionally disrupted the taken-for-granted repetitiveness of the prime-time format. Both content and form mattered to the commercial success of "Roots"; certainly the industry, speaking through trade journals, was convinced that the phenomenon was rooted in the break the series made with the week-to-week format. When the programming wizards at ABC decided to put the show on for eight straight nights, they were also, inadvertently, making it possible for characters to develop within the bounds of a single show. And of course they were rendering the whole sequence immensely more powerful than if it had been diffused over eight weeks. The very format was testimony to the fact that history takes place as a continuing process in which people grow up, have children, die; that people experience their lives within the domain of social institutions. This is no small achievement in a country that routinely denies the continuity and directionality of history.

PLOT FORMULA AND GENRE[8]

The conventions of television entertainment are flexible precisely because they operate under limited but real market constraints: they enable popular forms to express and manage shifts in the available stock of ideology. In the 1950s, the networks tended to reproduce the image of a society at one with itself, without significant social tensions—though even then, the shows sometimes did register a muted sense of the routine frustrations caused women by male supremacy ("I Love Lucy") and the routine psychic injuries done to workers ("The Honeymooners"). For the most part, the world of television was what Herbert Gold called a world of "happy people with happy problems." Then, after social conflict grew explosive in the 1960s, television began, gingerly and selectively, to incorporate certain symbols of dissonance and changing "life-styles"—racial and ethnic consciousness, hip professionalism, new living arrangements, ecological awareness, and sanitized middle-class versions of feminism. Where the family dramas and sitcoms of the 1950s usually denied the existence of deep social problems in the world outside the set, or sublimated them into obscurity, programs of the 1970s much more often acknowledged that the world is troubled and problematic, and then proceeded to show how the troubles could be domesticated. From "Ozzie and Harriet" and "Father Knows Best" to "All in the Family" and "The Jeffersons" marks a distinct shift in formula, character, and slant: a shift, among other things, in the image of what the larger social world amounts to, how stable it is, and how a family copes with it.

Some shows become popular by speaking directly to a compact, socially homogeneous public. But more likely—or so it seems on the near side of systematic research—the most popular shows are those that succeed in speaking simultaneously to audiences that diverge in social class, race, gender, region, and ideology: and this because of the mass market imperative of network television. To package the largest possible audience, the networks must offer entertainment that is literally broadcast: appealing to a multiplicity of social types at once. It may embody its values directly or indirectly, overtly or covertly, but it will do best if it embodies them ambiguously enough to attract a variety of audiences at once. The "socially relevant" situation comedies produced by Norman Lear, beginning with "All in the Family" in 1971, may well have broken through to ratings success precisely because they directly and ingeniously broached the divisive social issues of race and political culture. Some studies of audience response have suggested that "All in the Family" permitted audiences on both sides of the generational and political chasms to feel confirmed in their attitudes: older conservatives rooted for Archie, younger liberals for Mike (Vidmar and Rokeach 1974). (One aspect of the show's hegemonic framing was that most of the divisive issues were represented as matters of generation, not class or power.)

Why the great success of Lear's new genre? A brief excursus may suggest more general explanations for shifts in program formula. For one thing, the historical timing of a show bears heavily on its commercial prospects. ABC rejected "All in the Family" before CBS bought it. In contrast, consider an earlier attempt to bring problems of class, race, and poverty into the heart of television: CBS's 1963–1964 "East Side, West Side," in which George C. Scott played a caring social worker who was consistently unable to accomplish much for his clients however hard he tried. As time went on, the Scott character came to the conclusion that politics might accomplish what social work could not, and went to work as the assistant to a liberal Congressman. It was rumored that the hero was going to discover there, too, the limits of reformism—but the show was then canceled, presumably because of low ratings. In the middle and late 1960s social conflict had been too inflammatory, too divisive, to permit network television to indulge in Lear's formula for accommodation through ambiguity. And Lear's shows, by contrast to "East Side, West Side," have lasted partly *because they are comedies*. Audiences will partake of comedy's ready-made defenses to cope with threatening impulses, especially when the characters are, like Archie Bunker, ambiguous normative symbols. The comedy form allowed white racists to indulge themselves in Archie's rationalizations without seeing that the joke was on them. And finally, as Michael J. Arlen once pointed out, Lear was further inspired to unite his characters in a harshly funny *ressentiment* that was peculiarly appealing to audiences of the Nixon era and its cynical, disabused sequel. One alluring subtext of the show was that a family could hold together despite everything pressing on it from outside; the family could encompass the social conflicts that had seemed to be tearing the country apart.

So here we see the range of textual features that an interpretation can take into account. But how was the show possible in the first place? Structural and organizational explanations for the show's origins and success begin on the shoulders of the interpretive reading. Lear was in a position to shatter conventions, first of all, because producers had gained in the power to initiate. In the 1950s, sponsors directly developed their shows and were thus better able to control and sanitize content. When the networks took much of that power away in 1960, in the wake of the quiz show scandal, they began to make decisions in the interest, as it were, of advertisers in the aggregate. By the late 1960s, television had become so important an advertising medium that advertisers were standing in line to buy scarce commercial time. Thus networks were somewhat more willing to take chances with risky shows, knowing that if a few advertisers were offended there would likely be others eager to replace them, unless the content were in flagrant violation of hegemonic norms (the adventures of a union organizer, say, or a fundamentalist preacher).

Changes in content also flow from changes in social values and sensibilities—changes among producers, writers, and other practitioners, but also changes they are aware of in the audiences that are most salient to them. Lear's own political position—he is a major contributor to liberal causes—was mostly beside the point: it mattered only insofar as it attuned him to a new marketing strategy. Lear was aware that there was, in the 1970s, a large audience nurtured ideologically in the opposition movements and counterculture of the 1960s and now preferring to acknowledge and domesticate social problems, hoping to reconcile contraries in imagination rather than to ignore or deflect them. The whole texture of social life had changed: where the official mythology of the 1950s had stressed cultural consensus, the consensus had cracked in the 1960s and ideological divisions had surged into the open. And crucially, there were now writers available who had ideological roots in the opposition movements of the 1960s, though by themselves they could not account for content or success; there was also, after all, such a supply in the 1950s, but it was cut off by the blacklist, which exercised a chilling effect on subject matter and plot formula.

That chill had been produced by the networks, which accorded veto power to police agencies and professional associations (notably the American Medical Association), thus acting instrumentally in behalf of a hegemonic interest originating on the outside. ABC, for example, gave routine veto power to the FBI over its long-running series of the same name. On one occasion, the TV writer David W. Rintels was asked to write an episode of "The FBI" on a subject of his choosing. Rintels proposed a fictionalized version of the 1963 bombing of a Birmingham church, in which four black girls were killed. Rintels wrote later (1974a: 389–390):

The producer checked with the sponsor, the Ford Motor Company, and with the FBI—every proposed show is cleared sequentially through the producing company, QM; the Federal Bureau of Investigation; the network, ABC; and the sponsor, Ford, and any of the four can veto any show for any reason, which it need not disclose—and reported back that they would be delighted to have me write about a church bombing subject only to these stipulations: the church must be in the North, there could be no Negroes involved, and the bombing could have nothing at all to do with civil rights.

After I said I wouldn't write that program, I asked if I could do a show on police brutality, also in the news at that time. Certainly, the answer came back, as long as the charge was trumped up, the policeman vindicated, and the man who brought the specious charge prosecuted.

On another occasion, a network acted as direct guardian of the hegemonic limits: NBC refused to permit "Dr. Kildare" to run a show about venereal disease, this time despite clearance from the AMA, the National Education Association, and the surgeon general of the United States (Rintels 1974b: 391).

But times have changed. Medical shows on venereal disease have been aired. The FBI is no longer exalted. From 1977 through 1982 "Lou Grant" took account of contemporary issues from a muckraking point of view. The networks now arrogate to themselves the right and the power to legitimize the respectable framing of social problems, and they yield less authority than before to agencies of the State. Now, when a specific show slants to the right (see my discussion of "The Six Million Dollar Man," below), it is most likely because the producers anticipate an audience in that direction; direct state intervention is not necessary. By the 1970s, in short, the cocky, commercially booming networks had eclipsed specific advertisers and government agencies; they had made themselves the direct shapers of hegemonic content. And they had devised a new formula to coexist with some older ones and to displace others. Observing shifts in the tolerances and potential enthusiasms of the market—especially the younger, more liberal, more "permissive" upscale market—they had downplayed crude censorship, and preferred to take account of shifts in social ideology by domesticating them, by offering hegemonic solutions (as we shall see below) to real problems.

This active processing of deviance and lifestyle seems automatic, the sum of innumerable production decisions played out as if by reflex and commercial instinct. Yet this hegemonic strategy at times surfaces into the thinking of culture industry elites: it may be quite sophisticated, quite precise in its implications for television content. In a March 1960 speech (*Broadcasting* 1980a) to the Southeast and Southwest councils of the American Association of Advertising Agencies, held at St. Thomas, Virgin Islands, Jane Fitzgibbon, senior vice-president of the research firm of Yankelovich, Skelly & White, told advertising executives that television's role has been "to legitimize new life styles after they have emerged," rather than to inaugurate them. "I think we can honestly say," she went on, "that the television medium has speeded up what you might call the filtration of new values and new life styles throughout the population. Television does this simply by *documenting* new life styles, particularly through its news service." She took account of cultural conflict:

We now have at least two audiences to appeal to if we talk in *grosso modo* terms: traditional values—and they are still around—and new values. But within the new values segment there are two groups. There's the self-fulfillment, quality-of-life, self-improvement segment; and there's the experience and the escapist-oriented new values segment. What I see this leading to is more and more audience fragmentation, probably smaller market shares, smaller rating shares and probably few blockbuster shows.

And finally, she nicely articulated the hegemonic managerial task for program developers:

Television must be consistently attuned and alert to life-style changes (this goes for the advertisers as well as the writers), so that it can accurately and responsibly portray them at a point in time when the public will neither be bored because they are too outdated, nor outraged because they are too far out on the fringes. Instead, television's portrayal of societal change can insure that the public be stimulated, informed, sensitized, reassured about what is happening in their own personal lives and the lives of other people in the world at large.

The "accurate and responsible portrayal" that forswears both the outdated and the far-out; the combination of stimulation, information, sensitization, and reassurance—these are the terms with which the strategy of domestication is accomplished.

Another example suggests both the subtlety and the possible intentionality of this process. The popularity of "Charlie's Angels," beginning in 1976, suggests that television producers have learned how to appeal to elements of the new feminism and to its opposition at the same time. The Angels are highly skilled, motivated, working women; they show a certain amount of initiative. How else would they appeal to a certain female audience, toward whom many of the show's ads are beamed? (They represent, paradoxically, the subordinated side of Mary Tyler Moore, the progenitor of the single-woman show, who signals that some sort of feminism is here to stay as a "new life style" for the single career woman.)[9] At the same time, plainly the Angels are sex objects for men, as the cults of Farrah Fawcett-Majors and Cheryl Ladd attest. And they are subordinated: they usually rely on Charlie's aid to bail them out of the dangers to which their spunk has exposed them. It is no small element of the show's appeal to men that Charlie, the detective boss, is never seen. Male authority is invisible, and the "girls" are kept free of romance. Thus, in the male viewer's fantasies, the Angels remain available—to him and him alone. He, in unconscious fantasy, *is* Charlie, ever supervising, ever needed, ever jovial, ever returned to. The show thus caters simultaneously to feminism and to backlash against it; it permits men to indulge prurience while psychologically admitting women's importance to the workforce. (I must add that I had thought this for months, marveling at the impersonal ingenuity of television production process, when I came upon a quotation from an anonymous "top television executive of one of America's big three networks [who] said quite seriously, 'A series like *Charlie's Angels* performs a very important and valuable public service. Not only does it show women how to look beautiful and lead very exciting lives, but they still take their orders from a man' " (quoted in Lewin 1980). This is not to say that such thinking preceded the show and its popularity. A post hoc theory of function is not a program for strategy. But it is interesting that savvy network executives may become conscious theorists of hegemony, may recognize it when they see it.

In general, then, genre is necessarily sensitive; in its rough outlines, if not in detail, it brews a blend of popular sentiments.[10] Sometimes genre runs in advance of hegemonic ideology; more often it lags. A fine analysis of its themes will probably reveal elements of both in any given case. New genres coexist for a time with old ones, which may themselves be rooted in traditional forms: the western, the detective story, the variety show. New genres sometimes transpose old ones: the ever-popular "Star Trek," for example, was essentially a western whose team of professional lawkeepers operated in space.

Without attempting here a thorough account of the metamorphoses of TV genre, I can suggest by way of hypothesis a few other signs of network sensitivity to actually *and potentially* shifting moods and group identities in the audience. One decisive clump of questions to be asked of television entertainment is: What is its attitude toward authority? Where does it locate legitimate and illegitimate sources of authority? How does authority cope with transgression? To take one example, the adult western of the middle and late 1950s, with its drama of solitary righteousness and suppressed libidinousness, can be seen in retrospect to have played on a subterranean casualness about authority that was at odds with the dominant hierarchical motif of the Eisenhower years: TV drama here was vaguely premonitory of a counterculture that had not yet crystallized into social action. Richard Boone's Paladin in "Have Gun, Will Travel" and James Garner's Bart Maverick in the series of the same name were lone heroes standing solidly within the tradition of frontier insouciance. Like classical good-guy western moralists, they took official law-and-order wryly.[11] And yet, unlike the Lone Ranger and his puritanical ilk, they mixed their pursuit of outlaws with a pursuit of pleasure; they were hedonists. In the meantime, Matt Dillon of "Gunsmoke" was a decent Eisenhower-like public official, affirming the necessity of paternalistic law and order against the temptations of worldly pleasure (Kitty, the saloonkeeper? madam?) and the depredations of unaccountably wicked outlaws. In the early 1960s the western declined, and with the rise of Camelot counterinsurgency and the vigorous "long twilight struggle" of John F. Kennedy, its values were taken over into spy-adventure drama. Series like "Mission: Impossible" and "The Man from UNCLE" capitalized on the CIA's mystique and reined individualism into teamwork; such shows were more or less synchronized with official government policy. "Star Trek," launched in 1966, continued the teamwork and processed the cast's internationalism (intergalacticism, rather, if we allow for Spock) into a benign interstellar imperialism: the disordered universe, full of misguided utopians and deceitful aliens, needed a continuing United Nations police action operating under the cool white American head of Captain Kirk.

Police shows also display a metamorphosis that matches the decomposition of the dominant view of crime and punishment. In Jack Webb's "Dragnet," beginning in 1952, the police are in harmony with society's values; they detect according to the book; they are pure technicians ("Just the facts, ma'am"), representing the coincidence of technical and political capacities in the state. Organization is strictly hierarchical: Sergeant Friday's authority is undisputed. Crime never pays; each installment ended by telling the audience that the criminal was convicted and sentenced to a definite term in prison (see Knutson 1974). But by the late 1960s, the social consensus about the decency and the effectiveness of the state has unraveled, and the next generation of police shows displays uncertainty about the legitimacy and consequence of the law, and of the police within it, and about the organization of authority within the police. Into the 1980s, one continuing message is the practical futility of liberalism, a sense imported from the larger political culture.

In cop and detective shows, there are a variety of hybrid mixtures of authority and outlawry, elaborating, in turn, a range of popular ambivalences toward bureaucracy, law, and the state. Hierarchy is no longer taken for granted and is no longer harmonized with effective law enforcement. Insider official authority and outsider cowboy integrity and restlessness have been combined and condensed into the character of the private detective, halfway between the police force (which continually gets in his way and must be outfoxed) and the criminal (who shares his resistance to corporate norms, yet testifies to the permanence of evil). The ex-cop private detective, from fiction's Lew Archer to TV's Harry O, is the anarchist as refugee from the organization. He shares the goal of the police but disdains the standard rules. He is the classic American frontier individualist, but in the service of a law and order whose primary institutional embodiment, the police force, he scorns. He is half anarchist, half vigilante. He represents the individualist's partial resistance, partial accommodation to a bureaucratic order that conditions his own ideals and yet cannot contain his spirit. Through his persona, scriptwriters who are confined to the organized strictures, however remunerative, of series formulae pay tribute to the glimmering image of the autonomous writer they want to be. This imago, straining at the social leash, speaks to the frustrated aspirations of employees in living rooms. So, in a different way, does Kojak, the antibureaucratic cop trapped in red tape, scornful of criminal-coddling officials who are pushed around by the courts and let legal niceties stand in the way of rough justice (see Alley 1979: 138–139; Sage 1979). In still different ways, so do the various disillusioned officers of "Hill Street Blues" (Gitlin 1981b, 1983) and the corner-cutting heroes of "Miami Vice."

The transformations in other genres also register shifts and variations in the condition of hegemonic ideology. The technologically enhanced superhero, for example, has metamorphosed over the course of four decades, as Thomas Andrae's study of Superman [this volume, Part 2] delineates. In the 1960s, the straight-arrow Superman was supplemented by the whimsical, self-parodying Batman and the Marvel Comics heroes, symbols of power gone slightly silly, no longer prepossessing. In playing against the conventions, their producers were doubtless affected by the modernist self-consciousness so popular in high culture at the time. Thus do shifts in genre presuppose the changing mentality of critical masses of writers and cultural entrepreneurs; yet these changes would not take root commercially without corresponding changes in the disposition (even the self-consciousness) of large audiences. Changes in cultural ideals and in audience sensibilities must be harmonized to make for shifts in genre or formula.

If I have left the impression that television entertainment ordinarily tilts toward liberal variants of the hegemonic worldview, this is an apt moment to correct the picture. Although at this writing technological superheroes are missing from prime-time television, their most recent incarnations, in the 1970s, corresponded to militarist tendencies in the American polity. The Six-Million-Dollar Man and the Bionic Woman were not only obediently patriotic, they were organizational products through and through. Such team players had no private lives from which they were recruited task by task, as in "Mission: Impossible"; they were not fortuitous arrivals from another planet, nurtured by sturdy farm folk, like Superman; they were rescued by the state and equipped by it. They owed their very existence to the state's fusion of moral right and technological know-how. And occasional topical slants anchored these shows' general support of military solutions to international problems. One 1977 episode of "The Six-Million-Dollar Man," for example, told the story of a Russian–East German plot to stop the testing of the Air Force's new B-1 bomber; by implication, it linked the domestic movement against the B-1 to the foreign red menace.

SETTING AND CHARACTER TYPES

Just as prevailing television genres shift in historical time, so do the settings and character types associated with them. Shifting market tolerances and producer interests make for noticeable changes, some of which we have already discussed. Even in the formulaic 1950s, a few comedies were able to represent discrepant settings, permitting viewers both to identify and to indulge their sense of superiority through comic distance. Jackie Gleason's "The Honeymooners" and "The Phil Silvers Show" (Sergeant Bilko) capitalized on their stars' enormous personal popularity and theatrical experience, and were able to confer dignity on working-class and deviant characters in situations the opposite of glamorous (see Czitrom 1977).

Indeed, these examples point to the general importance of stars *as such* in binding the audience to the show. Stars who exude sexual auras are, of course, especially alluring, although talent scouts are notoriously unable to predict which auras are going to work. The audience is in part, then, psychologically involved with the actor, who is perceived beneath the momentary mask of the character (Holland 1975, 97). But all television (like film) rests on libidinal identifications with characters, whether explicitly sexual or not (Metz 1976). Audiences invest stars with powers that descend from residues of infantile experience, experience that comes back into play during the provisional regressions of viewing. It is a nice fantasy that particular stars embody particular aspects of hegemonic ideology, particular dimensions of the audience's structures of feeling, most likely in transposed forms; but how this embodiment takes place concretely, in particular stars at particular times, requires a full-blown analysis of its own.

Suffice it to say, for the moment, that two uniformities of setting and character underlie almost all the variation. For one, the set itself almost always propounds a vision of consumer happiness. Living rooms and kitchens usually display what David Riesman has called the standard package of consumer goods. Even where the set is ratty, as in "Sanford and Son," or working class, as in "All in the Family," the bright color of the TV tube almost always glamorizes the surroundings so that there will be no sharp break between the glorious color of the program and the glorious color of the commercial. In the more primitive 1950s, by contrast, it was still possible for a series like "The Honeymooners" or "The Phil Silvers Show" to get by with one or two simple sets per show: the life of a good skit was in its accomplished acting. But that series, in its sympathetic treatment of working-class mores, was exceptional. Color broadcasting accomplishes the glamorous ideal willy-nilly.

Second, the major characters are winners. Most of the time, networks and sponsors want to convey images of glamor and fun; the settings and characters must be showcases not just for commercials but for an entire fantasy world that will entice the mass audience. Although program control has shifted from sponsors to networks—with certain implications for settings and character types, as we shall see below—what has not changed is television's preference for winners. In 1954, for example, one advertising agency wrote to the playwright Elmer Rice explaining why his *Street Scene*, with its "lower class social level," would be unsuitable for telecasting (quoted in Barnouw 1970, 33):

We know of no advertiser or advertising agency of any importance in this country who would knowingly allow the products which he is trying to advertise to the public to become associated with the squalor . . . and general "down" character . . . of *Street Scene*. . . .
    On the contrary it is the general policy of advertisers to glamorize their products, the people who buy them, and the whole American social and economic scene. . . . The American consuming public as presented by the advertising industry today is middle class, not lower class; happy in general, not miserable and frustrated.

Twenty-five years later, it is the networks that are directly enforcing this cheer. Television's professionals must get results; they must return each week, like fixed stars, to embody the upbeat.[12] Bob Shanks, an ABC vice-president who has written a revealing insider's book about television, explains bluntly why he would advise against a series about a black ex-convict: "Perry Mason must win every week. So must Dr. Welby." Shanks's (1977, 149) rationale reveals the mentality of television executives, if not necessarily the whole audience:

Comedians and social critics may scoff; we ourselves know life is not like that. So what? People, masses of people, do not watch television to learn what life is like, but rather to escape it. Defeat and dreariness are what happen to you during the day. At night, in front of the box, most people want to share in victories, associate with winners, be transferred from reality.

For dramatic purposes, victory should be hard won. There is nothing more boring than the inevitable. Therefore, week after week, the hero should confront forces that are convincingly wicked, whether social (the cop's "bad elements") or natural (the doctor's diseases). In either case, wickedness usually erupts outside social contexts; it has no deep cause. It happens, it needs to be fixed, period. The melodramatic need for the service justifies the hero's power in the situation. Clients, fools that they are, often start out recalcitrant, then turn out cooperative as they discover what is good for them. The patient is part of that intractable material world that makes the professional's job so difficult—yet, in the end, so rewarding, so necessary, so worthy of the prestige that attends it.

And yet knowledge is not the decisive attribute of the hero's status; he (or, rarely, she) deserves respect by virtue of his personality. Dr. Marcus Welby was not just any doctor; he was the persona created by the paternal Robert Young we already knew best for his crinkly smile and moral excellence. Even if gruff, he was warmhearted, dedicated to keeping families together. "Father Knows Best" . . . Welby Knows Best. Many of the most successful shows were adept at fusing skill and character in the same hero. In the highest form of this fusion the actor succeeds in investing himself with the character's prowess, carries his aura from character to character, and also exploits it commercially. Karl Malden (playing his "Streets of San Francisco" character) advertises American Express Travelers Checks to foil crooks; Robert Young heaps praise on decaffeinated coffee to ease tension. As I have pointed out above, it is in the nature of the viewing process that some portion of the audience-clientele will respond to this blurring of fact and fiction: during the years that "Marcus Welby" enjoyed such popularity,

Robert Young got five thousand letters a week asking for medical advice (Real 1977, 118).

The senior professional hero is also a man fixed in the present. Whatever he knows, he always knew. He did not arrive; he was not recruited; he was not trained; he did not come from this or that class; he did not go to these or those schools. We know him almost entirely by his works and his personality.[13] Except for an occasional origin myth, which tells a story about how the man got where he is, he is never a man in formation. Thus his prowess is presented as something magical. Only his understudy, the stereotypic up-and-coming young acolyte, can hope to learn what the older man knows. As for clients, they are lucky to be flattered with his attention. But lower-status professionals, though they too have come out of nowhere, are less competent. According to Michael Real (1977, 119, citing Schorr 1963) many real-life nurses wrote letters to the producer of "The Nurses" "complaining of the ineptness of the student nurse in the program, failure to show her in a student role, overly dramatic presentations of hospital life and the nurse's role, and portrayals of nurses as alcoholics, reactionaries, and neurotics."

Above all, the televised professional is an idealist and an individualist. His motives are pure: to restore a warm, decent status quo ante, the symptom-free family or the crime-free neighborhood. The fee is never much of an issue, if it is mentioned at all. Perry Mason accepted a retainer with a quick flat grin, the impersonal gesture of a cash register, before getting on with the job he was born to do. Doctors have been even more exempt from the marketplace. As David W. Rintels (1974b) has said, "Anyone who watches *Marcus Welby, M.D.*, *Medical Center*, and *The Doctors* . . . must of necessity believe . . . no doctor ever charges for his services; no hospital ever bills a patient; no one ever has to go on charity, or do without care." A good deal of the reason is that the great majority of the patients can afford to pay their own way handsomely; Michael Real (1977, 119) has shown, for example, that almost all Welby's patients were well-to-do. Cops may occasionally grumble about their salaries: this is in keeping with the more realistic tone of the cop show. But, cops and teachers aside, the televised professional is generally a *free* professional.

We have, then, what seems at first glance distortion pure and simple. While the actual professions have become more bureaucratized and specialized, the television hero upholds the traditional image of the self-sufficient practitioner. The doctor has been either an omnicompetent general practitioner or a surgeon, that most prestigious of medical specialists, embodying a power of life and death that lends itself easily to melodrama. In either case, he does not condescend to bureaucratic relations with Medicaid or Medicare or Blue Shield or the hospital administration; he is not hedged about by insurance companies; he does not politic through professional organizations because he does not need to. His hands are not dirtied by the complicated structures of his everyday world. He is free to be a household god: he is a romantic figure. Even the cop, forced to work within the confines of bureaucracy, as we have seen, is the romantic as organization man, his rebellion always incipient, always stylistic, always idealistic, always solitary. In the real America, the professional carries forward an older tradition: the frontiersman, the sawbones, the Lone Ranger. Almost everyone in the audience works for someone else; only about 2 percent of the working population are unsalaried professionals (*Statistical Abstract*, 1979). But television conventions allow the audience its free-standing heroes: repositories of freedom and nurturance united, and dreams of independence for the kids.

For if television is untrue to the reality of society, it is true to a dream; it pays tribute to popular fantasy. The televised image both anchors and reinforces the prevailing aspiration toward professional status. In 1962, less than 2 percent of the sons of manual laborers had entered the professions; but the aspiration persists, the luminous hope that the child will be a successful and respectable professional, will be able, as Richard Sennett (1972: 229) writes, "to unite love and power." So it is fair to criticize television images for lacking naturalistic accuracy, for racist and sexist and class-biased stereotyping; yet in one crucial respect the criticism misses the point. Television, like much popular culture through the ages, embodies fantasy images that speak to real aspirations. It does not simply reflect the social world; it is no mirror. The hegemonic image is an active shaping of what actually exists, but it would not take hold if it did not correspond, one way or another, to strong popular desires—as well as to defenses against them (Holland 1975, chap. 4). "False consciousness" always contains its truth: the truth of wish, the truth of illusion that is embraced with a quiet passion made possible, even necessary, by actual frustration and subordination.

But to say that the hero corresponds to a popular wish is not to say that the wish constructs the image. It is the culture industry that generates the image, often enough tailoring it to the public relations desires of the actual profession. The networks guarantee that the professional image will not be too starkly, consistently, "controversially" idealistic by setting up direct and indirect systems of censorship. After self-censorship has had its chance, most of the work of censorship is done in-house, by the networks' own censorship bureaus. Earlier, some of this work was farmed out to professional associations such as the American Medical Association, which had first crack at approving the televised images of their professions. We have already noted the case of the FBI. And as for medicine, we have the testimony of Norman Felton (quoted in Rintels 1974b, 391), the executive producer of "Dr. Kildare," "The Eleventh Hour," and "The Psychiatrist," that

on the *Dr. Kildare* series we were asked by NBC to get the approval and seal of the AMA. This meant that we submitted scripts for approval to the AMA. Although the organization gave us technical help, it goes without saying that we did not present an accurate picture of the practice of medicine, or the difficulties many people had in obtaining medical care.

But in the end it is the networks that confer censorship power. They operate within a web of hegemonic institutions; their oligopoly is interlinked with the prestigious monopolies, where power and knowledge interpenetrate; and the networks act in behalf of their conception of the whole. They may well relax censorship over dirty words and sexual innuendo in order to keep up with the changing standards of their younger, hipper audiences (and of Hollywood); but they work to secure a complexly articulated version of legitimate social authority—

which needs to be traced out in detail. The *NBC Radio and Television Broadcast Standards and Practices* manual reads: "Respect for lawyers, police, teachers and clergy should not be diminished by undue and unnecessary emphasis on unfavorable aspects of members of these professions" (Rintels 1974b, 392). Bob Shanks of ABC writes (1977, 79) that "all three networks have similar policy guidelines and adhere to the same industry and government codes." (See also Gitlin 1983.)

Again, although most hegemonic constancies remain, shifting market structures make variation possible. The near universality of television set ownership (in 1960, 87 percent of American households had a TV set; in 1965, 92.6 percent; in 1970, 95.2 percent; in 1975, 97.1 percent) creates the possibility of a wider range of audiences than existed in the 1950s. Minority-group, working-class, age-segmented, and subculturally compact audiences have proliferated. Since more than half of American households own two or more television sets, it becomes possible to target relatively narrow bands of the population. Programming becomes more centrifugal. Cable and pay television multiply, and the market becomes more segmented. The glamor standards can slacken off at times. The industry noted that the miniseries "Roots" reached people who don't normally watch TV, with the homes-using-television levels during the week "Roots" was aired up from 6 to 12 percent over the comparable week a year earlier (*Broadcasting*, 31 January 1977). Untapped markets can only be brought in by unusual sorts of programming. There is room in the schedule for rebellious human slaves, just as there is room for hard-hitting technological superheroes. Movies made for single showings on television also may veer toward counterhegemonic political positions: they may sympathize with homosexuals, or they may criticize Senator Joseph McCarthy and the blacklist of the 1950s. ABC's 1980 version of Attica, based on Tom Wicker's *A Time to Die*, focused its first half on the grievances of prisoners and construed subsequent events in that light; ABC did insist that the producer splice in new footage at the last moment, showing prisoners' knives at the throats of their hostage guards, but the power of the show's reformist sympathy for the prisoners remained powerful. Such shows have prestige value and help deflect critical opinion from the networks. Network elites do not, however, invest in regular heroes who will challenge, from left, right, or elsewhere, the core values of corporate capitalist society—who are, say, union organizers or explicit socialists or, for that matter, born-again evangelists. And the emergence of independently syndicated programs for independent stations does not necessarily translate into increased diversity of substance. The everyday settings and character types of television entertainment go on confirming the essential soundness of commercial values, the prerogatives of individualism, the authority of professionals (though not political leaders or business executives),[14] and the legitimacy of the national security state.

CONFLICT AND SOLUTION

All narratives set out problems and point to solutions. High art works its problems through with absorbing thoroughness, toward genuine resolutions; much commercial art, slapped together under pressure by formula, fails to justify its own feeble, jerry-built passes at solutions. But solutions, in either case, there must be. For it is in solution that the tensions provoked in the audience by the shaping and disguising of their desires and fears get resolved; it is through solution that the work finally produces its psychological effect. Through *happy* ending, that harmonious result which reality denies may be granted by fantasy; the irreconcilable may be reconciled.

But to say that solution is important is not to say *how* a given cultural form will frame its solutions. There must be conventions; but which will prevail? The essence of the dominant television convention is that, whatever social and psychological problems come up, they are susceptible to successful individual resolutions. However grave the problems, however rich the imbroglio, the episodes regularly end with the click of closure: an arrest, a defiant smile (now held with freeze-frame technology), an I-told-you-so explanation before the credits. As we have already seen in the discussion of character types, the convention of the star-based series requires that preserving solutions be found; it would hardly do for the hero to fail week after week, or to be killed in the line of duty. The characters with which the audience identifies must stay alive and well, ready for next week's imbroglio. (Only when there is a contract dispute or an actor departs for more alluring horizons or dies, does a character get written out of the script. The more sympathetic the character, the more gentle the departure.) However deeply the problem may be located within society, it will be solved among a few persons: the heroes must attain a solution that leaves the rest of society untouched. Crime is solved by arrests; citizens never organize against it. Meanness is resolved by changes of heart or the bad guy's "come-uppance."

Again, there are variations alongside the normal convention. There was the short-lived "East Side, West Side," and Norman Lear's independently syndicated "Mary Hartman, Mary Hartman," which extended soap opera conventions in the process of parodying them. (The networks would not buy it.) Beginning in 1978, CBS's successful "Dallas" signaled that the convention of daytime serial continuity—the rolling plot in which one damn thing leads to another—had become acceptable in prime time. Earlier, Norman Lear's archetypal "All in the Family" was unusual among network broadcasts in sometimes ending obliquely, softly, or ironically, on the curvature of a question mark, thus acknowledging that the Bunkers could not solve a problem whose genesis was outside their household. "Lou Grant" was even more unusual: for a time it specialized in open rather than closed endings. One show, for example, revolves around Lou's encounter with several young black men who hang out on the street corner. Learning that one outspokenly cynical one is unemployed, Lou, the humane liberal, urges him to apply for a job at the *Tribune*. The young man, by the end of the show, has failed to get a job, and when Lou returns to the street corner and asks about him, his buddies report that he's left town. His story is still open. The problem remains; individual action cannot eliminate unemployment. According to one of the show's writers, the censors of CBS Standards and Practices, who had not objected to any of the antiestablishment politics implicit in many "Lou Grant" shows, had objected to the show's open form and were trying to regear it to orthodoxy. An even more startling variation from type was ABC's 1983 "The Day After," in which personal action was utterly unavailing.

Form as well as manifest content—to the extent they can be distinguished—are matters of concern for the television elite. "Roots," for example, represented both the cruelty of slavery and the possibilities of resistance; it humanized blacks and romanticized the possibility of a class alliance between slaves and poor whites. Yet the series also pointed to the chance for upward mobility; the upshot of travail was freedom. Where Alex Haley's book was subtitled "The Saga of an American Family," ABC's version carried the label—and the patriotic and institutional self-congratulation—"The *Triumph* of an American Family." Who could say categorically whether the prevailing impression was that of the collective agony or that of the family's triumph? Both themes were there, to be taken seriously in different proportions by different audiences. Those elements conflicted within a complex whole and helped renew the hegemonic understanding of right relations among nation, family, and individual. The friction between agony and triumph reproduced a larger friction. Cultural bargains of this sort keep the hegemonic ideology in motion and in equilibrium at the same time.

CONCLUSION

The technologies of mass culture do not stand still, and they are imprinted by the structure and strategies of the political-economic system at the moment (see Williams 1975, 14–41). Radio, developed by private capital in the context of expanding consumer production, made for considerable changes in the volume of image-manufacture, and helped reconstruct the meanings of other cultural forms. Motion pictures and the form of the fiction film narrative together amounted to a historically specific social institution, with the star system anchoring a form of audience worship that reproduced the social relations of political dependency. Television broadcasting brought the spectacular image into the home, helping to undermine the family's ability to withstand the fragmenting powers of the consumer economy. And the development of technology—always to be understood within the strategy of social institutions—does not stop there.

New television distribution systems loom. Cable television already enters about forty million American homes, pay cable about twenty-three million. Satellites make possible low-cost production and syndication of alternative programming.[15] A fourth network becomes imaginable. Videocassette recorders open up the range of consumer choice and make it easy for viewers to skip past commercials—which prospect sends advertisers into a tizzy. But what do these possibilities augur for ideological content or consequence? The most successful satellite channels specialize in sports, current and recycled feature films, the self-improvement routines of health and fitness, religious programs, and, to a lesser extent, news. Most of the new national channels are owned by entertainment conglomerates looking to maximize the mass audience. For the most part, the cable-distributed shows are ruled by the conventions marked out by the networks. Entertainment is upbeat, slick, glamorous. News is dominated by nationalist and individualist ideology, although the Cable News Network, operated by

Turner Broadcasting in Atlanta, has somewhat widened the ideological range toward the liberal and conservative ends of the American political spectrum. Any more deviant programming will have to finance itself through advertising: a risky proposition. Public television remains the most vital and open sector of American broadcasting, though even there the shrinkage of public funds, the growing involvement of giant corporate sponsors, and the dependence on affluent subscribers set real limits on what can be said and shown. These margins are nothing to sneer at, to be sure: the range of political outlooks evident in public television's "MacNeil-Lehrer News Hour" and National Public Radio's "All Things Considered" is sometimes impressive, especially given the cramped condition of American culture.

But in a larger sense, the future of American popular culture depends on larger currents in our political culture and sensibility. There are ideological rhythms in popular culture. Periods of diversity and competition alternate with periods of consolidation and market concentration (Peterson and Berger 1975). The market may serve for a while to amplify an oppositional style, as with rock music in the middle and late 1960s; oligopoly then regroups to assimilate the new forms, to flatten them and reduce them to formulae. New marginal forms, like New Wave music, spring up when the older ones have calcified. One cannot say in advance where the screw will stop turning, where a given content will prove to have gone out of bounds. Artists find out where the limits are by stepping over them.

By themselves, new forms of distribution signify nothing momentous. By no means do they guarantee that substantive alternatives will emerge; they might simply circulate new assortments of the standard ingredients. Genuine innovation can never be reduced to a technological fix. What develops in popular culture depends on the practitioners, on the degree to which they generate culture that matches the desires of publics in distinguished ways—and not least, on the texture of political life and the quality of demands that social groups make on the political-economic system and the culture industry within it. The sway of the culture industry presupposes two elements: audiences that it satisfies—by packaging their desires and dissatisfactions, then retailing them back—and cultural producers who are willing to work within the going conventions, under oligopolistic constraints. To reverse Plato's formula: When the mode of the city changes, the walls of the music shake. And Plato's original tribute to the power of culture is not defunct either. The hegemonic walls can be relocated. What does not change is the existence of those walls, or the existence of art and mind battering against them.

Notes

1. These sentences partly paraphrase, partly revise, the similar statement in Gitlin 1980, 253. See also Hall 1977, 332.

2. On the psychological consequences of the meritocratic principle for the working class, see Sennett and Cobb 1972; for a defense of meritocracy's central tenets, see Bell 1973.

3. The distinction is Raymond Williams's (1973, 10), and needs to be made more subtly and sharply. What exactly is alternative, what oppositional? It does not suffice to say that "alternative senses of the world" are those "which can be accommodated and tolerated within a particular effective and dominant culture," since the limits of toleration may not be plain before the fact of their testing, and since even the oppositional may be "accommodated and tolerated" through encapsulation in subcultural ghettoes. Refining the distinction, as Silvia Bizio has pointed out to me, is one of the outstanding theoretical tasks in the sociology of popular culture.

4. This is emphatically not to say that the industry "gives people what they want." As an oligopoly, its choices are limited to the most easily packaged commodities, and they are contained within the hegemonic forms.

5. This argument was informed by Leiss (1976).

6. On the striking continuities in American mythology, especially the myth of the hunter-hero, see Slotkin 1973.

7. In 1975, CBS canceled "Gunsmoke" although it had ranked eighth and fifteenth in Nielsen ratings over the previous two seasons. The audience was primarily older and disproportionately rural, and thus not worth as much to advertisers as its numbers might have suggested. So much for the network's democratic rationale.

8. I use "genre" loosely to refer to general categories of entertainment, like adult western, police show, black show. Genre is not an objective feature of the cultural universe, but a conventional name for a convention that exists and shifts in history, and should not be reified—as both cultural analysis and practice often do—into a cultural essence.

9. Mary Tyler Moore's "Rhoda" illustrates the sensitivity of a show to audience veto. "Rhoda" built its audience when the protagonist married in 1974 and lost millions when she got separated in 1976.

10. Indeed, since there are only three networks, the oligopoly is oversensitive to success. For example, "Charlie's Angels" engendered "Flying High" and "American Girls," about stewardesses and female reporters respectively, each on a long leash under male authority. But clones usually fail, since they replicate formula without aura; and these sank without a trace.

11. This discussion of western and spy shows is indebted to Wright's (1975) structuralist analysis of movie westerns and their transformations.

12. The following discussion draws heavily on Gitlin 1977b.

13. Occasionally we see a bit of family life, or even a lot, as in "Police Story" or the more recent and startling breakthrough series "Hill Street Blues." I haven't the space here to discuss variations in TV treatment of the professional archetype. On styles of police show, see Alley 1979, Sage 1970, and Schneider 1977. On stylistic and structural innovations in "Hill Street Blues," see Gitlin 1981b, 1983.

14. For an impressionistic, exaggerated, but provocative argument about television's hostility to business, see Stein 1979. Stein fails to see that television can be hostile to individual businessmen and friendly to business values at the same time. See also Gitlin 1983, chap. 13.

15. With the federal government subsidizing ground stations for the reception of signals bounced off satellites, it becomes technically possible for independent producers to broadcast to ad hoc syndicates of local stations. Thus, in May 1979, independent producers broadcast three hours of live coverage of a Washington demonstration against nuclear power; their program was broadcast live by fifteen stations and taped for later broadcast by seven others. The satellite time cost $1,200, and a hundred people donated their

services. In July 1979, this Public Interest Video Network broadcast for ninety minutes, live, from the national Right-to-Life convention in Cincinnati.

References

Adorno, T. W. 1954. "How to Look at Television." *Hollywood Quarterly of Film, Radio and Television*, Spring. Reprinted in *Mass Culture: The Popular Arts in America*, ed. Bernard Rosenberg and David Manning White, pp. 474–488. New York: Free Press, 1957.

Alley, Robert S. 1979. "Television Drama." In *Television: The Critical View*, 2d ed., ed. Horace Newcomb, pp. 118–150. New York: Oxford University Press.

Barnouw, Erik. 1978. *The Sponsor*. New York: Oxford University Press.

Bell, Daniel. 1973. *The Coming of Post-Industrial Society*. New York: Basic Books.

Benjamin, Walter. [1934] 1978. "The Author as Producer." In *Reflections*. New York: Harcourt Brace Jovanovich.

Blum, Alan F. 1964. "Lower-Class Negro Television Spectators: The Concept of Pseudo-Jovial Scepticism." In *Blue-Collar World*, ed. Arthur B. Shostak and William Gomberg, pp. 429–435. Englewood Cliffs, N.J.: Prentice-Hall.

Brenkman, John. 1979. "Mass Media: From Collective Experience to the Culture of Privatization." *Social Text*, no. 1 (Winter): 94–109.

Broadcasting. 1980a. "Researcher Fitzgibbon Tells AAAA Audience It Will Have to Deal with Changing Social Values." March 24, pp. 56–57.

Burawoy, Michael. 1979. *Manufacturing Consent*. Chicago: University of Chicago Press.

Czitrom, Danny. 1977. "Bilko: A Sitcom for All Seasons." *Cultural Correspondence*, no. 4 (Spring): 16–19.

Epstein, Edward Jay. 1973. *News from Nowhere: Television and the News*. New York: Random House.

Fiske, John, and John Hartley. 1978. *Reading Television*. London: Methuen.

Gans, Herbert J. 1974. *Popular Culture and High Culture*. New York: Basic Books.

———. 1979. *Deciding What's News*. New York: Pantheon Books.

Gitlin, Todd. 1977a. "Spotlights and Shadows: Television and the Culture of Politics." *College English* 38 (April): 789–801.

———. 1977b. "The Televised Professional." *Social Policy*. November–December, pp. 93–99.

———. 1979. "Prime Time Ideology: The Hegemonic Process in Television Entertainment." *Social Problems* 26 (February): 251–266.

———. 1980. *The Whole World Is Watching: Mass Media in the Making and Unmaking of the New Left*. Berkeley and Los Angeles: University of California Press.

———. 1981a. Review-essay of Erving Goffman, *Gender Advertisements*; John Fiske and John Hartley, *Reading Television*; and Judith Williamson, *Decoding Advertisements*. *Theory and Society* (January).

———. 1981b. "Make it Look Messy." *American Film* (September).

———. 1983. *Inside Prime Time*. New York: Pantheon Books.

Haight, Timothy R., and Christopher H. Sterling. 1978. *The Mass Media: Aspen Institute Guide to Communication Industry Trends*. New York: Praeger.

Hall, Stuart. 1973. "Encoding and Decoding in the Television Discourse." Centre for Contemporary Cultural Studies, University of Birmingham. Mimeo.

———. 1977. "Culture, the Media, and the 'Ideological Effect.'" In *Mass Communication and Society*, ed. James Curran, Michael Gurevitch, and Janet Woollacott, pp. 315–348. London: Edward Arnold.

Holland, Norman N. 1975. *The Dynamics of Literary Response*. New York: Norton.

Knutson, Pete. 1974. "Dragnet: The Perfect Crime?" *Liberation*, May, pp. 28–31.

Leiss, William. 1976. *The Limits to Satisfaction*. Toronto: University of Toronto Press.

Lewin, David. 1980. "The Hidden Persuaders: The American Producers with the Powerful Punch." *San Francisco Sunday Examiner and Chronicle*, April 20.

Lukács, Georg. 1964. *Studies in European Realism*. New York: Grosset & Dunlap.

Metz, Christian. 1976. "The Fiction Film and Its Spectator: A Metapsychological Study." *New Literary History*, Autumn, pp. 75–103.

Peterson, Richard A., and David G. Berger. 1975. "Cycles in Symbol Production: The Case of Popular Music." *American Sociological Review* 40: 158–173.

Poulantzas, Nicos. 1975. *Classes in Contemporary Capitalism*. London: New Left Books.

Real, Michael R. 1977. *Mass-Mediated Culture*. Englewood Cliffs, N.J.: Prentice-Hall.

Rintels, David W. 1974a. "How Much Truth Does 'The FBI' Tell about the FBI?" *The New York Times*, 5 March 1972. Reprinted in *The Age of Communication*, ed. William Lutz. Pacific Palisades, Calif.: Goodyear.

———. 1974b. "Will Marcus Welby Always Make You Well?" *The New York Times*, 12 March 1972. Reprinted in *The Age of Communication*, ed. William Lutz. Pacific Palisades, Calif.: Goodyear.

Sage, Lorna. 1979. "Kojak and Co." In *Television: The Critical View*, 2d ed., ed. Horace Newcomb, pp. 151–159. New York: Oxford University Press.

Schneider, Bob. 1979. "Spelling's Salvation Armies." *Cultural Correspondence*, no. 4 (Spring): 27–36.

Schorr, Thelma. 1963. "Nursing's TV Image." *American Journal of Nursing* 63.

Sennett, Richard, and Jonathan Cobb. 1972. *The Hidden Injuries of Class*. New York: Knopf.

Shanks, Bob. 1977. *The Cool Fire: How to Make It in Television*. New York: Vintage.

Slotkin, Richard. 1973. *Regeneration Through Violence: The Mythology of the American Frontier, 1600–1860*. Middletown, Conn.: Wesleyan University Press.

Sontag, Susan. 1977. *On Photography*. New York: Farrar, Straus & Giroux.

Stein, Ben. 1979. *The View From Sunset Boulevard*. New York: Basic Books.

Tuchman, Gaye. 1978. *Making News*. New York: Free Press.

Vidmar, Neil, and Milton Rokeach. 1974. "Archie Bunker's Bigotry: A Study in Selective Perception and Exposure." *Journal of Communication* 24 (Winter): 36–47.

Watt, Ian. 1957. *The Rise of the Novel*. Berkeley and Los Angeles, Calif.: University of California Press.

Williams, Raymond. 1973. "Base and Superstructure in Marxist Cultural Theory." *New Left Review*, no. 82: 3–16.

———. 1975. *Television: Technology and Cultural Form*. New York: Schocken Books.

———. 1977. *Marxism and Literature*. New York: Oxford University Press.

Willis, Paul E. (n.d.) "Symbolism and Practice: A Theory for the Social Meaning of Pop Music." Centre for Contemporary Cultural Studies, University of Birmingham. Mimeo.

———. 1978. *Profane Culture*. London: Routledge & Kegan Paul.

Wright, Will. 1975. *Sixguns and Society*. Berkeley and Los Angeles, Calif.: University of California Press.

THE SEARCH FOR TOMORROW IN TODAY'S SOAP OPERAS

In soap operas, the hermeneutic code predominates: "Will Bill find out that his wife's sister's baby is really his by artificial insemination? Will his wife submit to her sister's blackmail attempts, or will she finally let Bill know the truth? If he discovers the truth, will this lead to another nervous breakdown, causing him to go back to Springfield General where his ex-wife and his illegitimate daughter are both doctors and sworn enemies?" Tune in tomorrow, not in order to find out the answers, but to see what further complications will defer the resolutions and introduce new questions. Thus the narrative, by placing ever more complex obstacles between desire and its fulfillment, makes anticipation of an end, an end in itself. Soap operas invest exquisite pleasure in the central condition of a woman's life: waiting—whether for her phone to ring, for the baby to take its nap, or for the family to be reunited shortly after the day's final soap opera has left *its* family still struggling against dissolution.

According to Roland Barthes, the hermeneutic code functions by making "expectation . . . the basic condition for truth: truth, these narratives tell us, is what is *at the end* of expectation. This design implies a return to order, for expectation is disorder."[1] But, as several critics have observed, soap operas do not end. Consequently, truth for women is seen to lie not "at the end of expectation" but *in* expectation, not in the "return to order" but in (familial) disorder.

As one critic of soap opera remarks, "If . . . as Aristotle so reasonably claimed, drama is the imitation of a human action that has a beginning, a middle, and an end, soap opera belongs to a separate genus that is entirely composed of an indefinitely expandable middle."[2] The importance of this difference between classical drama and soaps cannot be stressed enough. It is not only that successful soap operas do not end, it is also that they cannot end. In *The Complete Soap Opera Book*, an interesting and lively work on the subject, the authors show how a radio serial forced off the air by television tried to wrap up its story.[3] It was an impossible task. Most of the storyline had to be discarded, and only one element could be followed through to its end—an important example of a situation in which what Barthes calls the "discourse's instinct for preservation"[4] has virtually triumphed over authorial control. Furthermore, it is not simply that the story's completion would have taken too long for the amount of time allotted by the producers. More importantly, I believe it would have been impossible to resolve the contradiction between the imperatives of melodrama—i.e., the good must be

From *Film Quarterly* 32, no. 1 (Fall 1979). A longer version appears in Modleski's book *Loving with a Vengeance: Mass-Produced Fantasies for Women* (Hamden, Conn.: Archon Books, 1982), which also studies contemporary American Gothic novels and Harlequin romances. The afterword is taken from the book and alludes to its other chapters.

rewarded and the wicked punished—and the latent message of soaps—i.e., everyone cannot be happy at the same time, no matter how deserving they are. The claims of any two people, especially in love matters, are often simply mutually exclusive.

John Cawelti defines melodrama as having

at its center the moral fantasy of showing forth the essential "rightness" of the world order. . . . Because of this, melodramas are usually rather complicated in plot and character; instead of identifying with a single protagonist through his line of action, the melodrama typically makes us intersect imaginatively with many lives. Subplots multiply, and the point of view continually shifts in order to involve us in a complex of destinies. Through this complex of characters and plots we see not so much the working of individual fates but the underlying moral process of the world.[5]

It is scarcely an accident that this essentially nineteenth-century form continues to appeal strongly to women, whereas the classic (male) narrative film is, as Laura Mulvey points out, structured "around a main controlling figure with whom the spectator can identify."[6] Soaps continually insist on the insignificance of the individual life. A viewer might at one moment be asked to identify with a woman finally reunited with her lover, only to have that identification broken in a moment of intensity and attention focused on the sufferings of the woman's rival.

If, as Mulvey claims, the identification of the spectator with "a main male protagonist" results in the spectator's becoming "the representative of power,"[7] the multiple identification that occurs in soap opera results in the spectator's being divested of power. For the spectator is never permitted to identify with a character completing an entire action: instead of giving us one "powerful ideal ego . . . who can make things happen and control events better than the subject/spectator can,"[8] soaps present us with numerous limited egos, each in conflict with one another and continually thwarted in its attempts to "control events" because of inadequate knowledge of other peoples' plans, motivations, and schemes. Sometimes, indeed, the spectator, frustrated by the sense of powerlessness induced by soaps, will, like an interfering mother, try to control events directly: "Thousands and thousands of letters [from soap fans to actors] give advice, warn the heroine of impending doom, caution the innocent to beware of the nasties ('Can't you see that your brother-in-law is up to no good?'), inform one character of another's doings, or reprimand a character for unseemly behavior."[9] Presumably this intervention is ineffectual, and feminine powerlessness is reinforced on yet another level.

The subject/spectator of soaps, it could be said, is constituted as a sort of ideal mother: a person who possesses greater wisdom than all her children, whose sympathy is large enough to encompass the conflicting claims of her family (she identifies with them all) and who has no demands or claims of her own (she identifies with no one character exclusively). The connection between melodrama and mothers is an old one. Harriet Beecher Stowe, of course, made it explicit in *Uncle Tom's Cabin*, believing that if her book could bring its female readers to see the world as one extended family, the world would be vastly improved. But in Stowe's novel, the frequent shifting of perspective identifies the reader with a variety of characters in order ultimately to create an alliance with the mother/author and with God, who, in their higher wisdom and understanding, can make all the hurts of the world go away, thus insuring the "essential 'rightness' of the world order." Soap opera, however, denies the "mother" this extremely flattering illusion of her power. On the one hand, it plays on the spectator's expectations of the melodramatic form, continually stimulating (by means of the hermeneutic code) the desire for a just conclusion to the story, and, on the other hand, it constantly presents the desire as unrealizable, by showing that conclusions only lead to further tension and suffering. Thus soaps convince women that their highest goal is to see their families united and happy and at the same time console them for their inability to bring about familial harmony.

This is reinforced by the image of the good mother on soap operas. In contrast to the manipulating mother who tries to interfere with her children's lives, the good mother must sit helplessly by as her children's lives disintegrate; her advice, which she gives only when asked, is temporarily soothing, but usually ineffectual. Her primary function is to be sympathetic, to tolerate the foibles and errors of others.

It is important to recognize that soap operas serve to affirm the primacy of the family, not by presenting an ideal family, but by portraying a family in constant turmoil and appealing to the spectator to be understanding and tolerant of the many evils that go on within that family. The spectator/mother, identifying with each character in turn, is made to see "the larger picture" and extend her sympathy to both the sinner and the victim. She is thus in a position to forgive most of the crimes against the family: to know all is to forgive all. As a rule, only those issues that can be tolerated and ultimately pardoned are introduced on soaps. The list includes careers for women, abortions, premarital and extramarital sex, alcoholism, divorce, mental and even physical cruelty. An issue like homosexuality, which, perhaps, threatens to explode the family structure rather than temporarily disrupt it, is simply ignored. Soaps, contrary to many people's conception of them, are not conservative but liberal, and the mother is the liberal *par excellence*. By constantly presenting her with the many-sidedness of any question, by never reaching a permanent conclusion, soaps undermine her capacity to form unambiguous judgments.

These remarks must be qualified. If soaps refuse to allow us to condemn most characters and actions until all the evidence is in (and of course it never is), there is one character whom we are allowed to hate unreservedly: the villainess,[10] the negative image of the spectator's ideal self. Although much of the suffering on soap operas is presented as unavoidable, the surplus suffering is often the fault of the villainess, who tries to "make things happen and control events better than the subject/spectator can." The villainess might very possibly be a mother, trying to manipulate her children's lives or ruin their marriages. Or perhaps she is avenging herself on her husband's family because it has never fully accepted her.

This character cannot be dismissed as easily as many critics seem to think.[11] The extreme delight viewers apparently take in despising the villainess[12] testifies to the enormous amount of energy involved in the spectator's repression and to her (albeit unconscious) resentment at being constituted as an egoless receptacle for the suffering of others. This aspect of melodrama can be traced back to the middle of the nineteenth century when *Lady Audley's Secret*, a drama about a governess turned bigamist and murderess, became one of the most popular stage melodramas of all time.[13] Discussing the novel on which the stage drama was based, Elaine Showalter shows how the author, while paying lip service to conventional notions about the feminine role, managed to appeal to "thwarted female energy":

> The brilliance of *Lady Audley's Secret* is that Braddon makes her would-be murderess the fragile blond angel of domestic realism. . . . The dangerous woman is not the rebel or the blue-stocking, but the "pretty little girl" whose indoctrination in the female role has taught her secrecy and deceitfulness, almost as secondary sex characteristics.[14]

Thus the villainess is able to transform traditional feminine weaknesses into the sources of her strength.

Similarly, on soap operas, the villainess seizes those aspects of a woman's life that normally render her most helpless and tries to turn them into weapons for manipulating other characters. She is, for instance, especially good at manipulating pregnancy, unlike most women, who, as Mary Ellmann wittily points out, tend to feel manipulated by it:

> At the same time, women cannot help observing that conception (their highest virtue, by all reports) simply happens or doesn't. It lacks the style of enterprise. It can be prevented by foresight and device (though success here, as abortion rates show, is exaggerated), but it is accomplished by luck (good or bad). Purpose often seems, if anything, a deterrent. A devious business benefitting by indirection, by pretending not to care, as though the self must trick the body. In the regrettable conception, the body instead tricks the self—much as it does in illness or death.[15]

In contrast to the numerous women on soap operas who either are trying unsuccessfully to become pregnant or have become pregnant as a consequence of a single unguarded moment in their lives, the villainess manages, for a time at least, to make pregnancy work for her. She gives it "the style of enterprise." If she decides she wants to marry a man, she will take advantage of him one night when he is feeling especially vulnerable and seduce him. And if she doesn't achieve the hoped-for pregnancy, undaunted, she simply lies about being pregnant. The villainess thus reverses male/female roles: anxiety about conception is transferred to the male. He is the one who had better watch his step and curb any promiscuous desires or he will find himself saddled with an unwanted child.

Moreover, the villainess, far from allowing her children to rule her life, often uses them to further her own selfish ambitions. One of her typical ploys is to threaten the father or the woman possessing custody of the child with the deprivation of that child. She is the opposite of the woman at home, who at first is forced to have her children constantly with her, and later is forced to let them go—for a time on a daily recurring basis and then permanently. The villainess enacts for the spectator a kind of reverse *fort-da* game,[16] in which the mother is the one who attempts to send the child away and bring it back at will, striving to overcome feminine passivity in the process of the child's appearance and loss. Into the bargain, she also tries to manipulate the man's disappearance and return by keeping the fate of his child always hanging in the balance. And again, male and female roles tend to get reversed: the male suffers the typically feminine anxiety over the threatened absence of his children.

The villainess thus continually works to make the most out of events that render other characters totally helpless. Literal paralysis turns out, for one villainess, to be an active blessing, since it prevents her husband from carrying out his plans to leave her; when she gets back the use of her legs, therefore, she doesn't tell anyone. And even death doesn't stop another villainess from wreaking havoc; she returns to haunt her husband and convince him to try to kill his new wife.

The popularity of the villainess would seem to be explained in part by the theory of repetition compulsion, which Freud saw as resulting from the individual's attempt to become an active manipulator of her or his own powerlessness.[17] The spectator, it might be thought, continually tunes in to soap operas to watch the villainess as she tries to gain control over her feminine passivity, thereby acting out the spectator's fantasies of power. Of course, most formula stories (like the western) appeal to the spectator or reader's compulsion to repeat: the spectator constantly returns to the same story in order to identify with the main character and achieve, temporarily, the illusion of mastery denied him in real life. But soap operas refuse the spectator even this temporary illusion of mastery. The villainess's painstaking attempts to turn her powerlessness to her own advantage are always thwarted just when victory seems most assured, and she must begin her machinations all over again. Moreover, the spectator does not comfortably identify with the villainess. Since the spectator despises the villainess as the negative image of her ideal self, as she watches the villainess act out her own hidden wishes, she simultaneously sides with the forces conspiring against fulfillment of those wishes. As a result of this "internal contestation," the spectator comes to enjoy repetition for its own sake and takes her pleasure in the building up and tearing down of the plot. In this way, perhaps, soaps help reconcile her to the meaningless, repetitive nature of much of her life and work within the home.

Soap operas, then, while constituting the spectator as a "good mother," provide in the person of the villainess an outlet for feminine anger: in particular, as we have seen, the spectator has the satisfaction of seeing men suffer the same anxieties and guilt that women usually experience and of seeing them receive similar kinds of punishment for their transgressions. But that anger is neutralized at every moment in that it is the special object of the spectator's hatred. The spectator, encouraged to sympathize with almost everyone, can vent her frustration on the one character who refuses to accept her own powerlessness, who is unashamedly self-seeking. Woman's anger is directed at woman's anger, and an eternal cycle is created.

And yet . . . if the villainess never succeeds, if, in accordance with the spectator's conflicting desires, she is doomed to eternal repetition, then she obviously never permanently fails either. When, as occasionally happens, a villainess reforms, a new one immediately supplants her. Generally, however, a popular villainess will remain true to her character for most or all of the soap opera's duration. And if the villainess constantly suffers because she is always foiled, we should remember that she suffers no more than the good characters, who don't even try to interfere with their fates. Again, this may be contrasted to the usual imperatives of melodrama, which demands an ending to justify the suffering of the good and to punish the wicked. As long as soap operas thrive, they present a continual reminder that woman's anger is alive, if not exactly well.

We must therefore view with ambivalence the fact that soap operas never come to a full conclusion. One critic, Dennis Porter, who is interested in narrative structures and ideology, completely condemns soap operas for their failure to resolve all problems:

Unlike all traditionally end-oriented fiction and drama, soap opera offers process without progression, not a climax and a resolution, but mini-climaxes and provisional denouements that must never be presented in such a way as to eclipse the suspense experienced for associated plot lines. Thus soap opera is the drama of perepetia without anagnorisis. It deals forever in reversals but never portrays the irreversible change which traditionally marks the passage out of ignorance into true knowledge. For actors and audience alike, no action ever stands revealed in the terrible light of its consequences.[18]

These are strange words indeed, coming from one who purports to be analyzing the ideology of narrative form! They are a perfect illustration of how a high-art bias, an eagerness to demonstrate the utter worthlessness of "low" art, can lead us to make claims for high art that we would ordinarily be wary of professing. Terms like "progression," "climax," "resolution," "irreversible change," "true knowledge," and "consequences" are certainly tied to an ideology; they are "linked to classical metaphysics," as Barthes observes. "The hermeneutic narrative, in which truth predicates an incomplete subject, based on expectation and desire for its imminent closure, is . . . linked to the kerygmatic civilization of meaning and truth, appeal and fulfillment."[19] To criticize classical narrative because, for example, it is based on a suspect notion of progress and then criticize soap opera because it *isn't* will never get us anywhere—certainly not "out of ignorance into true knowledge." A different approach is needed.

This approach might also help us to formulate strategies for developing a feminist art. Claire Johnston has suggested that such a strategy should embrace "both the notion of films as a political tool and film as entertainment":

For too long these have been regarded as two opposing poles with little common ground. In order to counter our objectification in the cinema, our collective fantasies must be released: women's cinema must embody the working through of desire: such an objective demands the use of the entertainment film. Ideas derived from the entertainment film, then, should inform the political film, and political ideas should inform the entertainment cinema: a two-way process.[20]

Clearly, women find soap operas eminently entertaining, and an analysis of the pleasure that soaps afford can provide clues not only about how feminists can challenge this pleasure, but also how they can incorporate it. For, outrageous as this assertion may at first appear, I would suggest that soap operas are not altogether at odds with a possible feminist aesthetics.

"Deep in the very nature of soaps is the implied promise that they will last forever."[21] This being the case, a great deal of interest necessarily becomes focused on those events that retard or impede the flow of the narrative. The importance of interruptions on soap operas cannot be overemphasized. A single five-minute sequence on a soap opera will contain numerous interruptions from both within and without the diegesis. To give an example from a recent soap opera: a woman tries to reach her lover by telephone one last time before she elopes with someone else. The call is interrupted by the man's current wife. Meanwhile, he prepares to leave the house to prevent the elopement, but his ex-wife chooses that moment to say she has something crucial to tell him about their son. Immediately there is a cut to another couple embroiled in an entirely different set of problems. The man speaks in an ominous tone: "Don't you think it's time you told me what's going on?" Cut to a commercial. When we return, the woman responds to the man's question in an evasive manner. And so it goes.

If on the one hand these constant interruptions and deflections provide consolation for the housewife's sense of missed opportunities by illustrating for her the enormous difficulty of getting from desire to fulfillment, on the other hand the notion of what Porter contemptuously calls "process without progression" is one endorsed by many innovative women artists. In praising Nathalie Sarraute, for example, Mary Ellmann observes that she is not

interested in the explicit speed of which the novel is capable, only in the nuances which must tend to delay it. In her own discussions of the novel, Nathalie Sarraute is entirely antiprogressive. In criticizing ordinary dialogue, she dislikes its haste: there not being "time" for the person to consider a remark's ramifications, his having to speak and to listen frugally, his having to rush ahead toward his object—which is of course "to order his own conduct." [22]

Soap opera is similarly antiprogressive. Just as Sarraute's work is opposed to the traditional novel form, soap opera is opposed to the classic (male) film narrative, which, with maximum action and minimum, always pertinent, dialogue, speeds its way to the restoration of order.

In soaps, the important thing is that there always be time for a person to consider a remark's ramifications, time for people to speak and listen lavishly. Action and climaxes are of only secondary importance. I may be accused of wilfully misrepresenting soaps. Certainly they appear to contain a ludicrous number of climaxes and actions: people are always getting blackmailed, having major operations, dying, conducting extramarital affairs, being kidnapped, going mad, and losing their memories. The list goes on and on. But just as in real life (one constantly hears it said) it takes a wedding or a funeral to reunite scattered families, so soap opera catastrophes provide convenient occasions for people to come together, confront one another, and explore intense emotions. Thus, in direct contrast to the male narrative film, in which the climax functions to resolve difficulties, the "mini-climaxes" of soap opera function to introduce difficulties and to complicate rather than simplify characters' lives.*

---

* In a provocative review of *Scenes from a Marriage*, Marsha Kinder points out the parallels between Bergman's work and soap operas. She speculates that the "open-ended, slow-paced, multiclimaxed structure" of soap operas is "in tune with patterns of female sexuality" and thus perhaps lends itself more readily than other forms to the portrayal of feminine growth and developing self-awareness (*Film Quarterly* [Winter 1974–1975], p. 51). It would be interesting to consider Kinder's observation in the light of other works utilizing the soap opera format. Many segments of "Upstairs

Furthermore, as with much women's narrative (such as the fiction of Ivy Compton-Burnett, who strongly influenced Sarraute), dialogue in soap operas is an enormously tricky business. Again, I must take issue with Porter, who says, "Language here is of a kind that takes itself for granted and assumes it is always possible to mean no more and no less than what one intends." [23] More accurately, in soaps the gap between what is intended and what is actually spoken is often very wide. Secrets better left buried may be blurted out in moments of intensity, or they are withheld just when a character most desires to tell all. This is very different from nighttime television programs and classic Hollywood films, with their particularly naive belief in the beneficence of communication. The full revelation of a secret on these shows usually begins or proclaims the restoration of order. Marcus Welby can then get his patient to agree to treatment; Perry Mason can exonerate the innocent and punish the guilty. The necessity of confession, the means through which, according to Michel Foucault, we gladly submit to power, [24] is wholeheartedly endorsed. In soap operas, on the other hand, the effects of confession are often ambiguous, providing relief for some of the characters and dreadful complications for others. Moreover, it is remarkable how seldom in soaps a character can talk another into changing his or her ways. Ordinarily, it takes a major disaster to bring about self-awareness—whereas all Marcus Welby has to do is give his stop-feeling-sorry-for-yourself speech and the character undergoes a drastic personality change. Perhaps more than men, women in our society are aware of the pleasures of language—though less sanguine about its potential as an instrument of power.

An analysis of soap operas reveals that "narrative pleasure" can mean very different things to men and women. This is an important point. Too often feminist criticism implies that there is only one kind of pleasure to be derived from narrative and that it is essentially a masculine one. Hence, it is further implied, feminist artists must first of all challenge this pleasure and then out of nothing begin to construct a feminist aesthetics and a feminist form. This is a mistaken position, in my view, for it keeps us constantly in an adversary role, always on the defensive, always, as it were, complaining about the family but never leaving home. Feminist artists *don't* have to start from nothing; rather, they can look for ways to rechannel and make explicit the criticisms of masculine power and masculine pleasure implied in the narrative form of soap operas.

One further point: feminists must also seek ways, as Johnston puts it, of releasing "our collective fantasies." To the dismay of many feminist critics, the

Downstairs," for instance, were written by extremely creative and interesting women (Fay Weldon, for one). The only disagreement I have with Kinder is over her contention that "the primary distinction between *Scenes from a Marriage* and soap opera is the way it affects us emotionally. . . . Instead of leading us to forget about our own lives and to get caught up vicariously in the intrigues of others, it throws us back on our own experience" (p. 53). But soap opera viewers constantly claim that their favorite shows lead them to reflect upon their own problems and relationships. Psychologists, recognizing the tendency of viewers to make comparisons between screen life and real life, have begun to use soap operas in therapy sessions (see Dan Wakefield, *All Her Children* [Garden City, N.Y.: Doubleday, 1976], pp. 140–143). We may not like what soap operas have to teach us about our lives, but that they *do* teach and encourage self-reflection appears indisputable.

most powerful fantasy embodied in soap operas appears to be the fantasy of a fully self-sufficient family. Carol Lopate complains:

Daytime television . . . promises that the family can be everything, if only one is willing to stay inside it. For the woman confined to her house, daytime television fills out the empty spaces of the long day when she is home alone, channels her fantasies toward love and family dramas, and promises her that the life she is in can fulfill her needs. But it does not call to her attention her aloneness and isolation, and it does not suggest to her that it is precisely in her solitude that she has a possibility for gaining a self.[25]

This statement merits close consideration. It implies that the family in soap operas is a mirror image of the viewer's own family. But for most viewers, this is definitely not the case. What the spectator is looking at and perhaps longing for is a kind of *extended* family, the direct opposite of her own isolated nuclear family. Most soap operas follow the lives of several generations of a large family, all living in the same town and all intimately involved in one another's lives. The fantasy here is truly a "collective fantasy"—a fantasy of community, but put in terms with which the viewer can be comfortable. Lopate is wrong, I believe, to end her peroration with a call to feminine solitude. For too long women have had too much solitude, and—quite rightly—they resent it. In a thought-provoking essay on the family, Barbara Easton persuasively argues the insufficiency of feminist attacks on the family: "With the geographical mobility and breakdown of communities of the twentieth century, women's support networks outside the family have weakened, and they are likely to turn to their husbands for intimacy that earlier generations would have found elsewhere."[26] If women are abandoned to solitude by feminists eager to undermine this last support network, they are apt to turn to the right. People like Anita Bryant and Mirabel Morgan, says Easton, "feed on fears of social isolation that have a basis in reality."[27] So do soap operas.

For it is crucial to recognize that soap opera allays *real* anxieties, satisfies *real* needs and desires, even while it may distort them.[28] The fantasy of community is not only a real desire (as opposed to the "false" ones mass culture is always accused of trumping up), it is a salutary one. As feminists, we have a responsibility to devise ways of meeting these needs that are more creative, honest, and interesting than the ones mass culture has come up with. Otherwise, the search for tomorrow threatens to go on, endlessly.

AFTERWORD

Criticism of mass art can often be a tedious affair. Periodically, a champion of high culture will deplore at great length the decline of taste and sensibility on the part of the reading or viewing public. At least since the publication of Q. D. Leavis's *Fiction and the Reading Public* in 1932 many "high art" critics have assumed that mass art dulls the mind and renders its consumers unfit to appreciate the beauties of great works. Contrary to what one might expect, Marxist-oriented critics have not taken an entirely different tack. To be sure, they tend to complain of mass art's imposition of "false consciousness" upon the masses, rather than decrying its tendency to debase taste. However, both groups have usually found it necessary when studying mass art to oppose it to high art, thereby demonstrating the political or aesthetic superiority of the latter.

Recent Continental theory places us in an excellent position to reevaluate the ideas of Leavis and her followers as well as those of the Frankfurt School. Although contemporary theorists have not always drawn out the full implications of their work for the study of mass culture, much of their writing actually contains forceful challenges to commonplace assumptions about the nature of high art and mass art. The Althusserian Pierre Macherey, for example, repudiates the search for structural unity, for "concealed order," in the work of art, arguing instead that

the order which [the work of art] professes is merely an imagined order, projected on to disorder, the fictive resolution of ideological conflicts, a resolution so precarious that it is obvious in the very letter of the text where incoherence and incompleteness burst forth. It is no longer a question of defects but of indispensable informers. . . . The work derives its form from this incompleteness which enables us to identify the active presence of a conflict at its borders. In the defect of the work is articulated a new truth.

Macherey's reasoning, taken to its logical conclusion, leads to an extreme position. For when defects are accorded such privileged status, the work of mass art, defective by any traditional aesthetic standard, assumes a kind of superiority to the work of high art. Nevertheless, the new emphasis provides the political critic with what Macherey calls "the revealing form of a knowledge" about the mass cultural text and its consumers.[29]

In this book, for example, I have repeatedly shown the precariousness of the resolutions that are nevertheless so crucial to Harlequin romances and Gothic novels. In both texts, the transformation of brutal (or, indeed, murderous) men into tender lovers and the insistent denial of the reality of male hostility toward women point to ideological conflicts so profound that readers must constantly return to the same text (to texts that are virtually the same) in order to be reconvinced. In the chapter on soap operas we saw what amounts to a literal application of Macherey's thesis that "the work derives its form from . . . incompleteness," for in soap operas no attempt is made to project, once and for all, an imagined order onto disorder. The disorder of the form conveys a structure of feeling appropriate to the experience of the woman in the home whose activities and concerns are dispersed and lacking a center. But precisely because of its decentered nature this most discredited genre can be aligned with advanced feminist aesthetics and advanced critical theory as a whole.

Throughout the book I have tended to regard "defects" (that is, what a realist aesthetic would judge to be defects) as "indispensable informers" that reveal the contradictions in women's lives under patriarchy. Textual absences, or the "incompleteness" of which Macherey speaks, have frequently pointed to the active presence of conflicts at the borders of the works. For instance, some critics have castigated Harlequin romances for portraying heroines as unbelievably naive, passive, and confused, thus denying the strength and intelligence possessed by many women in real life. However, we saw in this "defect" evidence of various painful psychological dilemmas: for example, women are supposed to be unconscious of themselves if they are not to incur the charge of narcissism, and yet they are continually forced to look at themselves being looked at. In Gothics, the absence of the mother, and the displacement of this figure by various surrogates, spoke of the difficulty women experience in coping with their ambivalence toward the first important person in their lives. And in soap operas, what concerned us was not the way the television family "mirrored" the modern nuclear family but the way it necessarily deviated from the norm in order to appear fulfilling. The isolation, solitude, and drudgery of the housewife's world are denied in the creation of a very different world: "Another World."

The idea of contradiction has been crucial to this study—has, in fact, been an informing principle. The concept helps us to understand how certain critics can insist, with some plausibility, on the purely escapist nature of mass art, while others persuasively argue the opposing view, that mass art legitimates the status quo. Both sides are partly right; where they err is in regarding the phenomenon as a simple one. Rather than endorsing either of these views, each of my analyses has been predicated on the assumption that mass art not only contains contradictions, it also *functions* in a highly contradictory manner: while appearing to be merely escapist, such art simultaneously challenges and reaffirms traditional values, behavior, and attitudes.

As Richard Dyer points out in his excellent article "Entertainment and Utopia," mass art appears to be escapist because it "offers the image of 'something better' to escape into, or something we want deeply that our day-to-day lives don't provide."[30] This is the utopian function of entertainment. Dyer lists several aspects of the utopian sensibility most commonly found in mass culture: energy, abundance, intensity, transparency, and community. These terms have obvious relevance to popular narratives for women. The wish for "transparency"—for open, honest, direct, and unambivalent relationship—is perhaps the most urgently expressed desire in all the texts under consideration. I have placed great emphasis throughout this study on the "enigmas" that stimulate questions about people's motives, thoughts, and intentions. I related this emphasis to the dependency of women on men and to the situation of the housewife, who must continually be attuned to the moods of her family. Of the other aspects of the utopian sensibility enumerated by Dyer, the wish for community is most strongly evoked by soap operas. I would add to his list the desire for "transcendence" (self-forgetfulness), which is a major current in Harlequin romances, and the desire for female autonomy, a constant preoccupation of Gothic novels.

However, the utopia envisioned by mass culture is by no means a complete one. As Dyer points out, "the ideals of entertainment imply wants that capitalism itself [and, we might add, patriarchy itself] promises to meet."[31] Therefore, only certain aspirations are admitted by mass art to be valid, while others are ignored or even ridiculed. For example, in Harlequin romances, the need of women to find meaning and pleasure in activities that are not wholly male-centered, such as work or artistic creation, is generally scoffed at. Soap operas also undercut, although in subtler fashion, the idea that a woman might obtain satisfaction from these activities. A soap opera woman might very well be engaged in important work such as law or medicine, but even on the job she is likely to be obsessed with her love life, or perhaps actually carrying on her love life, simultaneously weeping over and operating on the weak heart of her intended. Thus, while popular feminine texts provide outlets for women's dissatisfaction with male-female relationships, they never question the primacy of these relationships. Nor do they overtly question the myth of male superiority or the institutions of marriage and the family. Indeed, patriarchal myths and institutions are, on the manifest level, wholeheartedly embraced, although the anxieties and tensions they give rise to may be said to provoke the need for the texts in the first place.

It is useless to deplore the texts for their omissions, distortions, and conservative affirmations. On the contrary, it is crucial to understand them: to let their very omissions and distortions speak, informing us of the contradictions they are meant to conceal and, equally important, of the fears that lie behind them. For the texts often do speak profoundly to us, even those of us who like to think we have shed our "false consciousness" and are actively engaged in challenging patriarchal authority. We cannot rest content with theories that would attribute the popularity of the texts to the successful conspiracy of a group of patriarchal capitalists plotting to keep women so happy at home that they remain unwilling to make demands that would greatly restructure the workplace and the family. Such changes are frightening to *most* of us, for they involve an entire reorganization, not just of our social lives, but of our psychic lives as well. Given the radical nature of the feminist task, it is no wonder that college students occasionally cut their women's studies classes to find out what is going on in their favorite soap opera. When this happens, it is time for us to stop merely opposing soap operas and to start incorporating them, and other mass-produced feminine fantasies, into our study of women.

Notes

1. Roland Barthes, *S/Z*, trans. Richard Miller (New York: Hill & Wang, 1974), p. 76.

2. Dennis Porter, "Soap Time: Thoughts on a Commodity Art Form," *College English* 38, no. 8 (1977): 783.

3. Madeleine Edmondson and David Rounds, *From Mary Noble to Mary Hartman: The Complete Soap Opera Book* (New York: Stein & Day, 1976), pp. 104–110.

4. Barthes, *S/Z*, p. 135.

5. John Cawelti, *Adventure, Mystery, and Romance* (Chicago: University of Chicago Press, 1976), pp. 45–46.

6. Laura Mulvey, "Visual Pleasure and Narrative Cinema," in *Women and the Cinema*, ed. Karyn Kay and Gerald Peary (New York: Dutton, 1977), p. 420.

7. Ibid.

8. Ibid.

9. Edmondson and Rounds, *Mary Noble to Mary Hartman*, p. 193.

10. There are still villains in soap operas, but their numbers have declined considerably since radio days—to the point where they are no longer indispensable to the formula. "The Young and the Restless," for example, does without them.

11. See, for example, Kathryn Weibel, *Mirror, Mirror: Images of Women Reflected in Popular Culture* (New York: Anchor Books, 1977), p. 62. According to Weibel, we quite simply "deplore" the victimizers and totally identify with the victims.

12. "A soap opera without a bitch is a soap opera that doesn't get watched. The more hateful the bitch the better. Erica of 'All My Children' is a classic. If you want to hear some hairy rap, just listen to a bunch of women discussing Erica."

'Girl, that Erica needs her tail whipped.'

'I wish she'd try to steal my man and plant some marijuana in my purse. I'd be mopping up the street with her new hairdo'" (Bebe Moore Campbell, "Hooked on Soaps," *Essence*, November 1978, p. 103).

13. "The author, Mary Elizabeth Braddon, belonged to the class of writers called by Charles Reade 'obstacles to domestic industry'" (Frank Rahill, *The World of Melodrama* [University Park: Pennsylvania University Press, 1967], p. 204).

14. Elaine Showalter, *A Literature of Their Own* (Princeton, N.J.: Princeton University Press, 1977), p. 165.

15. Mary Ellmann, *Thinking About Women* (New York: Harvest Books, 1968), p. 181.

16. *Fort-da* is a game, observed by Freud, in which the child plays "disappearance and return" with a wooden reel tied to a string. "What he did was to hold the reel by the string and very skillfully throw it over the edge of his curtained cot, so that it disappeared into it, at the same time uttering his expressive 'o-o-o-o.' [Freud speculates that this represents the German word *fort*, or gone.] He then pulled the reel out of the cot again by the string and hailed its reappearing with a joyful '*da*' [there]." According to Freud, "Throwing away the object so that it was 'gone' might satisfy an impulse of the child's, which was suppressed in his actual life, to revenge himself on his mother for going away from him. In that case it would have a defiant meaning: 'All right, then go away! I don't need you. I'm sending you away myself'" (Sigmund Freud, *Beyond the Pleasure Principle*, trans. James Strachey [New York: Norton, 1961], pp. 10–11).

17. Speaking of the child's *fort-da* game, Freud notes, "At the outset he was in a *passive* situation—he was overpowered by experience; but by repeating it, unpleasurable though it was, as a game, he took on an *active* part. These efforts might be put down to an instinct for mastery that was acting independently of whether the memory was in itself pleasurable or not" (Ibid., p. 10).

18. Porter, "Soap Time," pp. 783–784.

19. Barthes, *S/Z*, p. 76.

20. Claire Johnston, "Women's Cinema as Counter-Cinema," in *Movies and Methods*, ed. Bill Nichols (Berkeley and Los Angeles: University of California Press, 1976), p. 217.

21. Edmondson and Rounds, *Mary Noble to Mary Hartman*, p. 112.

22. Ellmann, *Thinking About Women*, pp. 222–223.

23. Porter, "Soap Time," p. 788.

24. Michel Foucault, *La Volonté de savoir* (Paris: Editions Gallimard, 1976), esp. pp. 78–84.

25. Carol Lopate, "Daytime Television: You'll Never Want to Leave Home," *Radical America*, January–February 1977, p. 51.

26. Barbara Easton, "Feminism and the Contemporary Family," *Socialist Review*, May–June 1978, p. 30.

27. Ibid., p. 34.

28. Hans Magnus Enzensberger makes this point about mass consumption in general. See his *The Consciousness Industry* (New York: Continuum Books, 1974), p. 110.

29. Pierre Macherey, *A Theory of Literary Production*, trans. Geoffrey Wall (London: Routledge & Kegan Paul, 1978), pp. 155–156.

30. Richard Dyer, "Entertainment and Utopia," in *Genre: The Musical—A Reader*, ed. Rick Altman (London: Routledge & Kegan Paul, 1981), p. 177.

31. Dyer, *Genre*, pp. 184–185.

THE BLUES TRADITION: POETIC REVOLT OR CULTURAL IMPASSE?

CARL BOGGS AND RAY PRATT

What has been the social and political significance of blues music in the United States? To what extent has this tradition given rise to a culture of resistance, or poetry of revolt, directed against the dominant forms of ideology—against those components of the mass culture industry (commodification, passivity, individualism) that continue to reinforce bourgeois values and social relations? That blues grew out of the oppression of blacks is generally recognized, but its historical impact on collective consciousness (black as well as white) has scarcely been explored. In this essay we set out to analyze the broad political legacy of blues in contemporary American society as part of a dialogue with a number of significant recent contributions to the blues literature.[1]

Blues music in the United States evolved as perhaps the most dynamic and popular expression of Afro-American culture over a period that extended from the Civil War to the 1950s. In the past two decades, however, it has given way to a variety of more commercialized forms that originally appeared as offshoots of the blues: rhythm and blues, soul, rock, and, more recently, disco. With the emergence of technologically elaborate styles of popular music designed to be sold to a mass market, the blues tradition has been dismissed by many critics as a cultural relic appropriate to the black experience in the pre–World War II rural South. Yet somehow blues has found creative space and managed to persist beneath the surface of corporate-dominated music;[2] it survives and maintains a lively presence, even if today it is becoming increasingly detached from its social origins. There is without question a "living blues," as the Chicago-based magazine of that name reaffirms, although it is a blues profoundly transformed since the days of Leadbelly, Robert Johnson, and Bessie Smith. Although the creative forces that inspired the music during its heyday of the thirties, forties, and fifties are gone, there is ironically now a greater *awareness* of the music in the society as a whole, as measured by the number of blues record albums being released, the proliferation of blues clubs and festivals, and the broadening circulation of books and magazines devoted at least in part to blues.[3]

Blues originally developed out of several types of traditional folk music in the slave life of the plantation South—gospel music, spirituals, popular ballads, work songs, shouts. Having grown into a cohesive music following the Civil War, it became probably the most distinct expression of the black struggle for survival and cultural identity. To the extent that the social conditions that shaped blues were agrarian, precapitalist, and racially defined, the music existed primarily outside the dominant economic system and social relations. The prevailing white attitude was that blacks were too "dehumanized" to build their own cultural forms. What Afro-American traditions in fact did, as Herbert Gutman, Eugene

Genovese, and Lawrence Levine have shown,[4] was to help shield blacks from the incursions of white capitalist ideology and enable them to withstand the crippling effects of racial and class oppression. Simultaneously, blues developed into a personal and secularized expression of the religious experience: it mobilized black creativity. If enslavement had its spiritual and cultural dimension, so too did the rebellion against it. When, toward the end of the century, blues was popularized among blacks in the Delta, it did not merely extend, it *transformed* its religious heritage: blues occupied and redefined the public realm in what was still very much a "separate society." As secularization advanced, the theme of work—on the plantations, in the river ports, in the cotton mills—became more integral to the music, although it never became the sole impetus. Classical blues embodied the totality of black social reality, including religion, community, racial identity, and personal/sexual life, as well as work.

When blues spread from the Delta to other areas of the South and then to Northern cities after 1900, it retained these early characteristics even as its structure changed. Northward migration threw blacks up against even more insidious forms of racism, not to mention a depressed social and economic situation that offered mainly disillusionment to an entire generation of job-seekers. The Northern ghettoes perpetuated in a new setting the marginal status of blacks. The post–World War I migration was accompanied by drastically high levels of unemployment—at least 50 percent in Chicago and Detroit, for example. Blacks were largely excluded from skilled jobs in the industrial sector and restricted to "Negro" work (e.g., domestic and personal service) involving essentially unskilled, seasonal, and part-time labor. To the extent blacks constituted a "reserve army" of unemployed, their proletarianization was more uneven than that of white workers; they remained a racially oppressed stratum both within and outside the labor force. This condition produced even more direct and violent racial conflict than was typical of the South. In turn, the black community was subjected to ever more elaborate modes of social and ideological control.[5]

This subproletarian, racially embattled dimension of black life, then, furnished the driving force behind urban blues culture. Once transplanted into the cities, blues emerged as part of an underground social life world concentrated around bars, cafés, and street corners. It both reflected the tension and alienation of ghetto life and carried over the spirit of resistance from the South. With its relocation in the North, blues underwent change; it took on a more aggressive, rhythmic, group-defined, and (later) more electronic quality. By the twenties and thirties, with the emergence of radio and the "race" recording business, blues had expanded geographically and socially, but still retaining its Delta base. After Mamie Smith made the first commercial blues recording in 1920, blues took on the character of an entertainment medium rooted in leisure culture; this gave rise to the professional musician.[6] Once implanted in cities like Memphis, Kansas City, St. Louis, Chicago, and Detroit, this pattern continued into the forties and the postwar period, laying the basis for a new urban life-style.

For blacks, blues was a major cultural resource in their struggle to resist racism and other forms of oppression. Pain, suffering, broken love affairs, and loneliness produced a music not only of survival but also of self-affirmation, revolt, even joy. It was largely preoccupied with the *psychological* element of everyday life. Even in a context of overburdening poverty, blues singers generally stressed the personal (and sexual) side of social struggles.

In defining blues as a poetry of revolt, Paul Garon, in his *Blues and the Poetic Spirit*, sees the emergence of an urban black subculture as a force subversive of capitalist economic and social relations. It is the secularization of Afro-American culture, the celebration of everything that is repressed and denied by capitalist morality: desire, imagination, the erotic impulse, community, equality. Such revolt cannot be grasped simply through a content analysis of lyrics—although Garon does plenty of that; it can only be understood by exploring the underlying themes and social framework of the music. Blues is subversive not merely in its implicit attack on racism, but in its activation, through a spontaneity, intensity, and proximity to everyday life, of deep instinctual needs and impulses. In contrast to mass pop culture, which has a pacifying effect, blues generates a "psychology of enjoyment" that inspires a creative drive toward freedom and solidarity. The passion of performers and audience is stimulated by the physical and sensual quality of the music. Garon is correct in dispelling the common illusion that blues is strictly a music of pain and sadness, since it is precisely in the *overcoming* of such experience that the music affirms joy, optimism, and excitement.

From the surrealist perspective, Garon suggests that blues can be seen as a "cry" of people opposing exploitation and estrangement. Music, in this sense, embodies a language of popular resistance and struggle. While lacking explicit political content, it is still "political" insofar as it creates autonomous currents that oppose both the commodification of popular art and the inaccessibility of "high" culture. Imagery, dreams, fantasy—these are the critical and rebellious forces motivating blues. Garon writes that "fantasy alone enables us to envision the real possibilities of human existence, no longer tied securely to the historical effluvia passed off as everyday life; fantasy remains our most preemptive critical faculty, for it alone tells us what *can be*. Herein lies the revolutionary nature of the blues: through its fidelity to fantasy and desire, it generates an irreducible and, so to speak, *habit-forming* demand for freedom." [7]

Garon's treatment of blues culture parallels Ben Sidran's thesis in *Black Talk*, [8] which remains probably the most coherent theoretical presentation of blues as a subculture that is in essential opposition to the literary modes of thinking characteristic of white American society. Sidran introduces the concept of "oral" culture, in contrast to the conventional bourgeois notion of "literate" culture. As "modes of perceptual orientation," oral and literate culture have radically different views of what constitutes "practically useful information." Thus, oral cultures employ only the spoken word and its oral derivatives (including musical representations of basic vocal styles). As Sidran puts it: "To paraphrase [Marshall] McLuhan, the message is the medium." The oral tradition encourages a greater degree of emotional, and perhaps even physical, involvement in the environment, which in turn allows for a more developed sense of community, as well as a heightened collective awareness and even "collective unconsciousness." [9]

The advantages of the oral mode are manifest in the "ability to carry out spontaneous, often improvised acts of a group nature." In this cultural motif, music is one of the most legitimate outlets for blacks—indeed, in some periods it has constituted virtually the *only* outlet. It is this concept of music as a larger cultural expression that makes it so powerful. The vocalized tone and rhythmic approach "allow for communication of a nonverbal nature, often at an unconscious level." This African and black cultural tradition thus constitutes a negation of the entire European tradition rooted in a pattern of structure and regularity.[10] Ernest Borneman has conceptualized this phenomenon in technical terms:

While the whole European tradition strives for regularity—of pitch, of time, of timbre and of vibration—the African tradition strives for precisely the *negation* of these elements. In language, the African tradition aims at circumlocution rather than at exact definition. The direct statement is considered crude and unimaginative; the veiling of all contents in ever-changing paraphrases is considered the criterion of intelligence and personality. In music, the same tendency towards obliquity and ellipsis is noticeable: no note is attacked straight; the voice or instrument always approaches it from above or below, plays around the implied pitch without ever remaining on it for any length of time, and departs from it without ever having committed itself to a single meaning. The timbre is veiled and paraphrased by constantly changing vibrato, tremolo, and overtone effects. The timing and accentuation, finally, are not *stated*, but *implied* or *suggested*.[11]

In oral culture, music is created by the group as a whole, and the individual is integrated into the society at such a basic level of experience that individuality in fact "flourishes in a group context." Rhythm plays a major role in this process; it not only creates and resolves tension but also conveys information. Whereas the literate culture stores information through writing, oral culture stores through physical assimilation, thus *itself* constituting a matrix of information. Within the music, therefore, the subject/object dichotomy is eventually transcended so that performer and listener enter into the same process. In Sidran's words, "The idea and act are one: the process of communication is in fact the process of community."[12] Within the blues motif, according to Sidran, we especially see "the semantic value of intonation contouring." Hence the "blue" notes, the melisma or vocal smears, the cries and moans of field hollers and gospel songs and, later, the unique sound of the great saxophonists, all carry a "nonverbal kind of information." There is a certain "*galvanization of meaning and pitch* into a single vocalization," which is musically expressed through the unique "voice" of each instrument or vocalist, culminating in an individualized "sound."

This form of blues, moreover, is inseparable from a specific *context*. As Sidran describes it,

the message carried by this vocalized approach was perhaps initially one of resignation. Although there must have been a longing for escape and freedom, as well as resistance and revenge . . . , this communication through intonation operated at an emotional level, more basic than that of verbal interchange. The use of cries and melismatic approach was also a means of bringing out the individualism in an otherwise destroyed personality. . . . It began with slaves who were able to express themselves fully as individuals through the act of music.[13]

Herein lies part of the "revolutionary" character of black music. Sidran suggests that "the development of cries was thus more than a mere stylization; it became the foundation on which a group of people could join together, commit a social act, and remain individuals throughout, and this in the face of overt oppression.

. . . The social act of music was at all times more than it seemed within the black culture." Hence, to the extent people as individuals were involved in the music, they were involved in a process of social change. From Sidran's viewpoint, "black music was in itself revolutionary if only because it maintained a non-western orientation in the realm of perception and communication." Beginning with work songs and spirituals, black music took on a countercultural meaning; slaves created an immense culture of resistance under the very eyes of their masters.[14]

The result was that

in an otherwise decimated society . . . [these musical forms] provided some outlet for group activity which was not wholly controlled by the white man's influence. The revolutionary aspects of vocalization, which were expressed by a leader and encouraged by the responses of a chorus—the basic antiphonal (call-and-response) pattern of almost all Afro-American music—were central to these songs . . . [which] constituted a social act, committed en masse by the black culture during a period when mass activity was outlawed.

Thus music became for black people not simply a leisure activity, but a way of life. "For the black culture, particularly during times of great cultural suppression, it was an act of physical, emotional, and social *commitment*. Black music was therefore hardly escapist in nature, but was a direct reflection of the combined experiences of many individuals, all of them grounded in reality. The communal nature of black music never lost its impact."[15]

The blues has been the wellspring of all subsequent black music and most white popular music over the past century. Jazz in its various forms is "a result of the combination of the circus and minstrel bands with the blues tradition . . . a product of a peculiarly black voice (blues) in a peculiarly white context (Western harmony)." Sidran suggests that the blues tradition, first and foremost, has been an idiom of individual expression and social activity. It has been, and remains today, a music of freedom insofar as "its structure is perfectly suited to improvisation and spontaneous composition. It employs a minimum number of Western chords, and even these are in such a relation to one another as to allow the imposition of almost any note upon any chord."[16]

The creative persistence of blues, linked in part no doubt to its ability to evade strict definition, attests to its immense strength and survival power. Perhaps the most compelling definition is the one ventured by Leadbelly: "The blues is a feeling and when it hits you, it's the real news."[17]

In what sense, then, can we refer to blues as a "revolutionary" form of music? This question is of particular importance given the way the social audience for blues has changed in recent decades. Where the constituency was once largely black and poor, it is now largely white, college-educated, and middle class. What factors have contributed to such a profound transformation? We believe the answer lies in the form and content of the music itself—for example, in the synthesis of meaning and pitch indicated above—which in the end constitute the very "message" of the music. But this does not exhaust the explanation.

As we have noted, black music was from the outset subversive, if only because it sustained a non-Western "oral" orientation in the realms of perception and communication. These basic elements have remained central to the music. Its appeal can be felt by anyone seeking emotional release from the tension, frustration, and alienation that are the natural outgrowth of contemporary social conditions. Whites can and do feel its message, and they can and do preserve, play, and create it; whites, too, have entered into the dialectic of individuality and community, which blues uniquely expresses. Hence, if blues emerged originally from the alienation experienced by blacks in white bourgeois society, it not only reflects this condition, it goes beyond it. As Sidran points out, "black musicians have not only given voice to frustration . . . , they have created a channel for its release. Therein lies their great importance. Black music can resolve as well as generate tension of a specifically social nature." [18] The blues as a kind of secular "devil's music" has functioned through the years as "both a catharsis for the anxieties caused by irrational suppression, and, finally, a healthy, if cynical, assertion of the black ego." Yet the white ego too can experience "the pain of catharsis and the joy of assertion which are not inconsistent and [which are] both resolved in the blues." [19] For the creative musician, this resolution may be characterized as the effort to carve out an "area of freedom" where before none had existed.

A further subversive component of the blues can be located in the economic sphere. In *Black Rage*, Grier and Cobbs suggest that "in capitalist society, economic wealth is interwoven with manhood (personality). . . . Closely allied is power to contest and direct . . . , power to influence the course of one's own and other's lives." [20] This led to the emergence of a "peculiarly black economic system" comprising gamblers, musicians, hustlers, and street people. Here Charles Keil's insights in *Urban Blues* are relevant. Seeing black music as "ritual drama, or dialectical catharsis," Keil understands black underworld figures and musicians as vital cultural stereotypes—people clever enough not to have to work (at least in the conventional sense), for, in the case of the musician, work *is* play. A more extensive analysis of who benefits from the black underground economy is beyond the scope of this essay, but in many areas the fruits have probably been reaped not by black people but by the white corporate music industry. The history of blues and jazz is one of rip-off and economic rape from the 1920s to the present, as the frustration of hundreds of blues musicians living and dead has reflected. [21]

Well into the 1950s, blues (and the various jazz currents derived from it) persisted as the most influential cultural force in the black community. Despite its popularity and the success of the "race" music industry, it was largely able to resist commercialization; the productive sphere of blues was still centered in the clubs, taverns, and other places of daily gathering and in this sense was still "local." Hence, it did not suffer real erosion of identity in its transplantation from the Delta to the cities but simply added new dimensions (amplification, electronic instruments, rhythm sections, urban-flavored lyrics, and so on). Because blues did not become integrated into the capitalist mass culture industry in the way other forms of pop music did, it was relatively free of promotional gimmicks, slick packaging, and commercial fads. For blacks, it remained a living culture.

In the fifties and sixties, however, blues began to lose its special status among blacks and yielded its popularity to the more commercialized forms that evolved into big business: rhythm and blues, rock, Motown, and soul. Whereas blues had never become a mass-marketed commodity, its derivatives thrived on lucrative recording contracts, constant radio exposure, and big live audiences. But this new music, with some exceptions, became less subversive as it became more "successful" (according to the criteria of pop culture); although it often carried over the drive and excitement of blues, generally it lacked the characteristically sharp edge and social thrust. And the audiences were as much white as black. One aspect of this change was articulated by Muddy Waters when he said, "The boogaloo ain't gonna make no history."

The real dilemma for blues has been how to respond to the process of cultural centralization and media standardization—what Jim DeKoster calls the "nationalization" of music[22]—that accompanies the expansion of the commodity structure in advanced capitalism. To the extent that blues was always a "local" culture that depended for its creativity on a strong grassroots identity, any compromise with mainstream norms would probably destroy its cultural base and transform it into a bland, stylized replica of the authentic music. Yet the alternative seemed equally depressing: resist "nationalization," and thereby lose visibility as a dynamic musical form that could compete with the "modern" currents, since the marketing of cultural products tends to emphasize the *general* audience. Blues went in the second direction—even if not by choice of the musicians themselves—but it, too, wound up adapting to the pressures of media and the recording industry, which enabled it to gain a white clientele at the very time it was losing popularity among blacks. One of the great effects of cultural standardization has been to undercut the appeal of distinctly racial, or "black," music,[23] a process that is no doubt reinforced by the loss of cohesiveness in black communities in both the North and the South.

The recent commercialized offshoots of blues seem more appropriate to the "modern," assimilationist tendencies among blacks. Blues itself now commonly appears as an archaic and even "primitive" culture associated with a history of oppression that blacks want to escape. Over the past twenty years blues performers have found themselves playing before fewer blacks and more whites. KoKo Taylor expresses this predicament:

My favorite audience is any one which digs blues. This is usually a white audience with a few blacks. I've worked in strictly black clubs for many years and always had to play a lot of soul, rock, and pop stuff to get it over—you know, Aretha Franklin and Tina Turner. Let's face it, they don't want to hear the blues. That's why I like doing concerts, festivals, college crowds and things. I think it's a conforming thing with blacks. A lot of them deny the blues because they're ashamed of the past.[24]

Oddly, the single most important thing keeping blues alive today is white patronage, which resulted from the discovery of blues by young whites in the sixties, partly through the influence of the "rock revolution." Today, with the exception of southside Chicago and a few other blues enclaves, the music—though still performed mostly by blacks—is supported overwhelmingly by whites.

All of this poses embarrassing problems for Garon and the surrealists, who contend that "the spectre of Afro-American music continues to haunt the white power structure" [25] and who argue that white involvement in blues can only be a source of degeneration. Garon, of course, is not oblivious to the decline of blues (and of subversive cultural forms generally) within the black community; nor is he unaware of the recent popularization of blues among whites. But his analysis of these developments is, in our opinion, both short-sighted and contradictory.

The erosion of blues as a poetic inspiration for blacks can be traced, in Garon's view, to the social integration of blacks into the structure of advanced capitalism since World War II and, more significantly, to the cultural hegemony of a small but influential black bourgeoisie. The material and ideological basis for challenging the dominant culture diminished with the fading away of the lumpen stratum that, since emancipation, was the social underpinning of the black "outsider." The extension of white bourgeois hegemony throughout the black community, via the mass culture industry and the mediation of a rising black bourgeoisie, has meant the decline of Afro-American traditions and, ultimately, a certain alienation of blacks from their own history. Once this history became repressed, the eclipse of the blues singer was a foregone conclusion. As Garon puts it, the idea of a cultural "free agent" attacking bourgeois conventions and values was now obsolete within the black frame of reference; predictably, "the lyric of earlier decades tended to be imaginative while the lyric of today tends to be vapid." [26] Garon's general perspective leads to a final note of pessimism: under conditions of advanced capitalism, where white assimilationist techniques are highly effective, "the poetic assault on consciousness becomes neutralized." [27] In other words, blues—or any other subversive culture, for that matter—has no future.

On the first point, Garon is simply incorrect: although a black bourgeoisie has certainly developed since World War II, and although the absolute number of blacks in the work force has substantially increased, the black population *as a whole* is no more integrated into the dominant structures today than it was in the twenties and thirties. There is still a large subproletarian stratum among blacks, fueled by massive unemployment; as Wilhelm and others have shown, [28] blacks are no more integral to the functioning of capitalism today than they were in previous periods, since racism has operated *within* the working class to confine blacks to a marginal status. Yet, even if we accept Garon's argument, its logic is to locate subversive potential only *outside* the work force and to negate the possibility of any revolutionary tendency arising from working class struggles. We are left with a choice between a hopeless fatalism and faith in the cultural resurgence of a black lumpen community. Garon does make a compelling point about the hegemonic role of the black bourgeoisie—a stratum that has always rejected the blues tradition—but it is much too one-dimensional. In reality, the power of the black bourgeoisie is far more limited than Garon suggests, and the cultural tendencies emanating from the black population are more diverse than he seems willing to admit. For example, some contemporary jazz currents are as close to Afro-American culture (and as self-consciously subversive) as blues was at its peak; moreover, rhythm and blues, soul, and rock, although predominantly mainstream music, have produced strains that carry over the blues motif of poetic revolt. [29] Capitalist hegemony (white *or* black) is not as universalized as Garon argues.

But the crucial question remains: what can we say about the future of blues? Ironically, in Garon's scheme of things, we are left with an analysis that relegates blues to the realm of historical nostalgia—a poetic tradition that has finally been obliterated by the repressive apparatus of late capitalism. Its decline over the past two decades is presented as more or less inevitable, with little prospect of revival. Garon is trapped by his own fatalism, which negates the very premise of his book—namely, that blues has a subversive poetic continuity that makes it viable today.

If blues has lost its centrality to the black experience, then what are the prospects of revitalization through white engagement in (and redefinition of) the music? White blues—not to mention the fusion of blues and rock—has been a reality in the United States for at least a decade, but Garon finds it nothing short of scandalous: it represents not the extension but the actual *denial* of the spirit of poetic revolt.

Garon's critique of white blues is that the music is primarily imitative rather than creative or original. In the hands of whites, blues tends to degenerate into rock; it is loud, too fast, repetitive, and slick—a music that rarely exceeds the bounds of "stupefying mediocrity." Whites, according to Garon, want a blues that is not too nasty or objectionable: it must be palatable enough to be sold to middle-class audiences as a commodity. Whites who perform blues—and, to a lesser extent, those who consume it—do so out of a desire to *reproduce* the interests and life-styles of blacks, and thus wind up detaching themselves from their own alienation and creative potential. "In exceedingly few cases do we find fresh, inventive, creative, poetic, original work which could, without the most irresponsible generalizations, be still considered blues." [30] The goal is "faultless imitation." Thus: "Removed from their historical base and their socio-economic setting, these songs as purveyed by white adolescents are sickly, pale, and offensive." [31] The reasons for this bankruptcy of white blues, aside from the inexorable process of commercialization, are in Garon's mind largely subconscious, "whereby the black blues man comes to represent the father or brother of the white" (instilling a drive toward emulation), and through this process of identification "the 'white bluesman' gains enormously in self-esteem, thus reaffirming his masculinity, etc." [32]

Garon's point, in effect, is that white blues can never have any validity; it is the music of impostors. As for rock, it is even further removed from the poetic tradition, having sacrificed any semblance of creativity for the sake of technique and raw power. Of all present-day musical forms, the only one to embellish the blues spirit is jazz, which, however, Garon has very little to say about.

Garon's critique of white blues contains a kernel of truth: it is largely an imitative phenomenon. [33] But the critique is much too facile, in that it overlooks the creative energy many whites have brought to blues and, by extension, slights its potential as a medium of cultural revolt for whites. In defining white blues by its worst tendencies, Garon can then go ahead and dismiss it completely. For every white who seeks to imitate or rip off black music, there are many talented musicians who have made powerful contributions to blues and who, consequently, have the support of members of the black blues community itself: Paul Butterfield, Mike Bloomfield, Ry Cooder, John Hammond, Bonnie Raitt, Tracy Nelson, David Bromberg, Charlie Musselwhite, and Janis Joplin, to name just a few. In many cases whites have expropriated blues as part of their own poetic strivings and injected new meaning into the tradition. Although white involvement in blues actually started in the twenties, and at that time was largely imitative, it received its main impetus during the cultural and political rebellion of the sixties, when musical forms emerged as catalyzing forces in youth culture and produced, within the confines of the rock explosion, the white rediscovery of blues as an antimainstream music. Future inspiration for the development of white blues could emanate from feminism and other social movements that focus on the psychological aspects of oppression.

Such potential ought to be encouraged, for both musical and political reasons, as the possible basis of a rejuvenated blues culture that cuts across racial lines. It emphatically should *not* be opposed on the flimsy grounds that blues somehow "belongs" to blacks or that whites are congenitally incapable of building upon it according to their own definition of poetic revolt. The historical flow and merger of diverse intellectual and cultural forces has always transcended any fixed point of creative origins. If not, opera would be the strict possession of the Italians, and surrealism would belong to the French alone. Garon's conception of culture is rigidly insular, and his fears of commodification, although well founded, ignore the fact that many creative and even subversive "products" manage to slip through the capitalist market mechanism.[34] The very appearance of Garon's book makes this point quite effectively.

The special merit of efforts by Sidran and Garon, then, lies in their illumination of the poetic beauty and subversive power of blues through the lens of a radical perspective. They cover the thematic universe of blues with imagination and breadth.[35] Their analysis further dispels the simplistic notion prevalent in left cultural criticism that blues is mainly "escapist" or "down" music; they show, on the contrary, how it evolved within Afro-American culture as a counter hegemonic tradition. The *vision* of blues that emerges from these books, even allowing for certain excesses, captures what is best in this fusion of Western and Afro-American poetry and music. Their enthusiasm is validated by history: the dynamism of blues is reflected in the fact that virtually every form of contemporary popular music in the United States, from jazz to country-and-western, has been profoundly shaped by it.

Yet neither Sidran nor Garon effectively demonstrates that blues is still a living and subversive culture. Nor do they indicate how the rebellious poetic elements of the music (fantasy, desire, imagination) lead to or support any broader political or revolutionary tendency. In the absence of any such demonstration, creativity alone seems to constitute a revolutionary virtue. Lacking from Garon's schema is the important distinction between culture of revolt (which blues certainly is) and revolutionary force or movement (in which blues has never really been involved). Without this political linkage, blues remains a self-conscious underground culture that expresses its identity through a sense of separateness, only rarely merging with some larger process of social struggle.

Garon argues that the political isolation of blues was the result of the "anti-black cultural chauvinism" of the Communist party and the "contradictory nationalism" of black organizations. "Thus, as poets with spontaneous radical inclinations the blues singers did not have the advantages of even the slightest fraternal climate in the avowedly 'revolutionary' milieu: they were forced to 'go it alone.' The question to be considered is not the blues singer's isolation from the revolutionary movement but the 'revolutionary' movement's isolation from the blues singer."

We see here a dilemma of all critical and potentially liberating forms of culture: is it possible for them to assist in decisively *transforming* oppressive structures, values, and social relations? Do they not run the risk, at the same time, of being neutralized by the integrative power of the mass culture industrial complex? Or worse, of suffering an oblivion corresponding to defeated political movements with which they might be allied?

Where, then, does the "revolutionary" power of the blues lie? As we suggested above, following Sidran's analysis, we can understand the "oral" motif of blues (the "poetic," in Garon's terms) as antagonistic to capitalist ideology in a way that goes beyond the issue of racism itself (a theme, incidentally, that is rarely explicit in the lyrics). It incorporates a *general* assault on the system of capitalist culture and social relations and a critical orientation toward traditional values (patriotism, religion) that are often glorified in other forms of popular music. That the assault never became linked to concrete political objectives does not contradict this, nor does it deny the expressive power of the blues.

The leap from a "subversive" cultural form to an organized sociopolitical movement is an enormous and complicated one, and blues historically has exercised little, if any, radicalizing influence on the black community or on American politics in general. Sidran is sensitive to this problematic relationship between culture and politics and draws back from making global assertions of the sort abundantly found in *Blues and the Poetic Spirit*. Lawrence Levine, in *Black Culture and Black Consciousness*, explicitly notes that "group consciousness and a firm sense of self have been confused with *political* consciousness and organization" in conventional analysis of the blues.[36] For Garon, this essential distinction between "subversive" or "revolutionary" culture and political movement is collapsed within an all-encompassing surrealist framework that blinds him to the limits of blues culture, which, in turn, stem from the contradictions of black consciousness. One might argue that blues mystifies and distorts the very spirit of revolt it advances. From a political standpoint, the music contains a number of potentially destructive elements. Thus, Garon never mentions the fatalism, cynicism, sexism, and self-indulgent hedonism that are consistent themes in blues. These features are by no means dominant, but they cannot be dismissed completely in favor of the ascribed underlying motif of poetic revolt. Both coexist as part of the conflicting impulses within society as a whole, shaped by the capitalist cultural hegemony that Garon largely ignores.

In some ways, *Blues and the Poetic Spirit* affirms a vision of blues much like that held by radical enthusiasts of rock in the sixties, the idea that an emotionally charged and progressive music, created out of cultural alienation and part of an emerging counterculture, would mobilize human commitments and serve the goals of political emancipation. The decline of both forms—the transformation of rock into a cultural commodity, the decline of blues as a *mass* cultural form—surely undermined the credibility of such visions. We cannot assume that a political translation of subversive cultural movements will in fact occur. At the same time, of course, the failure of blues to inspire or merge with any organized political tendency—in the way that reggae has done in Jamaica, for example [37]—does not detract from its *cultural* integrity and expressive power. When it hits you, it's still, as Leadbelly says, "really the news."

Notes

1. We were especially inspired by Paul Garon's volume *Blues and the Poetic Spirit* (London: Edison Books, 1975). Very few writers have approached blues (or jazz, since it is often linked with blues as a cultural development) from as explicitly radical a perspective as Garon. See also Leroi Jones's *Blues People* (New York: Morrow, 1963) and his *Black Music* (New York: Morrow, 1969); Charles Keil's *Urban Blues* (Chicago: University of Chicago Press, 1966); and Mike Rowe's *Chicago Blues* (New York: Da Capo Press, 1975), which present sympathetic treatments of the black struggle to create a separate cultural identity in white society, but which rarely address explicitly political themes. Ben Sidran's *Black Talk* (New York: Holt, Rinehart & Winston, 1971) is one of the few attempts to analyze black music from a critical or left perspective, but it does not systematically address blues (as distinct from jazz). Earlier Marxist efforts worth noting are Francis Newton (pseudonym of E. J. Hobsbawm), *The Jazz Scene* (London, 1960; reprinted, New York: Da Capo Press, 1978); and Sidney Finkelstein, *Jazz: A People's Music* (New York: Citadel, 1948; reprinted, New York: Da Capo Press, 1975). For Marxist jazz criticism and analysis, see Frank Kofsky, *Black Nationalism and the Revolution in Music* (New York: Merit Books-Pathfinder Press, 1970); see also Kofsky's effort to express the essentials of Marxist musical analysis in "The Jazz Tradition: Black Music and its White Critics," *Journal of Black Studies* 1, no. 14 (1971): 402–433. Ortiz Walton, in *Music: Black, White, and Blues* (New York: Morrow, 1972), presents a number of significant insights. James M. Cone, *Spirituals and the Blues* (New York: Seabury Press, 1972), makes a strong case for the culturally critical and even revolutionary aspects of spirituals and blues.

2. Simon Frith, in *Sound Effects: Youth, Leisure, and the Politics of Rock 'n' Roll* (New York: Pantheon Books, 1981), notes in his discussion of rock music and mass culture that capitalist cultural forms have been seen by some as generating "creative space" in spite of the corporate music system's effort to generate a commercial product. As he puts it, "Rock was 'squeezed out' of the conflict between commercial machinations and youthful aspirations. If the industry was seeking to exploit a new market, the youthful audience was seeking a medium through which to express its experience, and musicians, who were at the center of this conflict, were able to develop their own creative space" (p. 47). This insight probably applies directly to the blues tradition during the first wave of recording in the 1920s, when companies sent out talent scouts to find musicians in the South. On this period, see John Godich and Robert Dixon, *Recording the Blues* (London: Studio Vista, 1970).

3. The major U.S. blues publication is *Living Blues* (Chicago). There has been a proliferation of U.S. and European reissue labels in the seventies and eighties, as well as the spectacular growth of two independent labels, Alligator and Rounder. The vitality of both

blues and jazz recording may be seen in the growth of large mail order businesses to sell the products of small labels. Perusal of the pages of *Living Blues* and *Downbeat* indicates how significant this trend is. The vitality of blues scholarship can be seen by examining the extended bibliography in Robert Palmer's *Deep Blues* (New York: Penguin Books, 1982) and David Evans's *Big Road Blues* (Berkeley and Los Angeles: University of California Press, 1982). Both of these works focus on the Mississippi Delta as a regional culture but contain valuable theoretical insights; Palmer's work is one of the most accessible and exciting works on any American musical form.

4. Eugene D. Genovese, *Roll, Jordan, Roll: The World the Slaves Made* (New York: Pantheon Books, 1974); Herbert G. Gutman, *The Black Family in Slavery and Freedom, 1750–1925* (New York: Pantheon Books, 1976); Lawrence W. Levine, *Black Culture and Black Consciousness* (New York: Oxford University Press, 1977).

5. For elaboration of this point, see Sidney Wilhelm, *Who Needs the Negro?* (Cambridge, Mass.: Shenkman, 1970); and William H. Harris, *The Harder We Run: Black Workers Since the Civil War* (New York: Oxford University Press, 1982).

6. See Jones, *Blues People*, p. 98. Ross Russell, in *Jazz Style in Kansas City and the Southwest* (Berkeley and Los Angeles: University of California Press, 1971), describes the development of a whole style—a fusion of blues and jazz—that grew out of the underworld of leisure in Kansas City and affected most subsequent strains of jazz and the rhythm and blues tradition.

7. Garon, *Blues*, p. 64.

8. Sidran is an interesting combination of scholar (he holds a Ph.D. in American Studies) and musician (he is the author of several jazz-influenced popular albums). In recent years he has served as host of the National Public Radio "Jazz Alive" series.

9. Sidran, *Black Talk*, pp. 2–3.

10. Ibid., pp. 3, 6.

11. Ernest Borneman, "The Roots of Jazz" (1959), in *Jazz*, ed. Nat Hentoff and Albert J. McCarthy (New York: Da Capo Press, 1978), p. 17.

12. Sidran, *Black Talk*, pp. 8, 11.

13. Ibid., pp. 13–14.

14. Ibid., pp. 14–16. See also Alan Lomax's illuminating discussion in his notes to the New World Records collection *Roots of the Blues*.

15. Sidran, *Black Talk*, pp. 16–17.

16. Ibid., p. 34.

17. Quoted in ibid., pp. 34–35.

18. Ibid., p. 87.

19. Ibid., p. 36.

20. William Grier and Price Cobbs, *Black Rage* (New York: Bantam Books, 1968), p. 50.

21. On the white rip-off of black music, see especially Steven Chapple and Reebee Garofalo, *Rock 'n' Roll Is Here to Pay: The History and Politics of the Music Industry* (Chicago: Nelson-Hall, 1977), esp. chap. 7, "Black Roots, White Fruits."

22. Quoted from Jim DeKoster's review of Rowe's *Chicago Breakdown* in *Living Blues*, no. 24 (November–December, 1975): 46.

23. Disco and soul are especially noteworthy because they are not black music in the same sense that earlier "race" music was, having sold largely to black audiences. Their audience is much more national, and probably more white than black. In terms of the music's social content, it is much more affirmative than subversive. For a discussion of the manufacturing of "Motown" music, see the excellent treatment in the *Rolling Stone Illustrated History of Rock 'n' Roll* (New York: Vintage, 1980).

24. Quoted in Robert Neff and Anthony Connor, *Blues* (Boston: Godine, 1975), p. 122.

25. From Franklin Rosemont's preface to Garon's *Blues and the Poetic Spirit*, p. 14.

26. Garon, *Blues*, p. 50.

27. Ibid., p. 51.

28. Harris, *The Harder We Run*; and Wilhelm, *Who Needs the Negro?*

29. Here the boundaries between the different traditions are not so clearly established or rigid as Garon suggests. Where should we situate performers such as Chuck Berry, Ray Charles, Dinah Washington, Sam Cooke, or Jimi Hendrix? Though none would be considered, strictly speaking, blues singers, they were all influenced by blues, played it as part of their repertoire, and identified with rebellious tendencies in black culture.

30. Garon, *Blues*, p. 57.

31. Ibid., p. 60.

32. Ibid., pp. 57–58.

33. For discussion of white-black cultural cross fertilization, see Tony Russell, *Blacks, Whites and Blues* (London: Studio Vista, 1970; New York: Stein & Day, 1970). Of particular interest is Muddy Waters's view that the Rolling Stones and similar groups played a significant role in developing a consciousness of the blues among American whites. See Robert Palmer, *Deep Blues*, p. 259. On this question see also Bob Groom, *The Blues Revival* (London: Studio Vista, 1970).

34. Frith makes this point about rock in *Sound Effects*, p. 47.

35. Paul Oliver's *The Meaning of the Blues* (New York: Collier Books, 1963) also provides an extensive thematic analysis based on hundreds of recorded examples and remains an essential basic reference.

36. Levine, *Black Culture*, p. 239.

37. The "advanced" development of Jamaican reggae in comparison with blues in terms of political linkages is rather striking, although it is itself not without contradictions. See Linton Kwesi Johnson's textual analysis, "Jamaican Rebel Music," *Race and Class* 17, no. 4 (1976).

WORKING PEOPLE'S MUSIC

GEORGE LIPSITZ

The singular contribution of the New Left has been its understanding of the importance of culture in the struggle to change society. Having experienced the impact of youth culture, black nationalism, and radical feminism, New Leftists have been delving into the works of Marcuse, Gramsci, Lukács, and others to try to formulate a strategy for producing what Bruce Brown has called a subversive yet therapeutic culture.

It is indispensable to the discussion to understand exactly what cultural forms exist now and what people see in them. This article is an attempt to study country music and blues from that perspective: to see what they are, where they come from, and what their possibilities are for the future. I intend to show that blues and country music reflect the working-class experience in America, that they originated as folk arts and retain some collectivity from that origin, and that they contain the seeds for the kind of liberating culture that can be produced in this country.

Now I realize that at a time when Richard Nixon appears on the stage of the Grand Ole Opry and Johnny Cash tells us to beat the energy shortage by slipping on a sweater, a lot of people are not kindly disposed to looking at the positive aspects of country music. And at a time when B. B. King owns his own plane, motel, radio station, and who knows what else, some are going to think that what's left of blues must personify neocapitalist ideology. In fact, I recently corresponded with the editors of a socialist publication who contended that country music is "right-wing and racist" and that blues are "defeatist."

Yet we would do well to remember Gramsci's admonition that only the truth is revolutionary if we are to be able to see exactly what this music is and why people like it. This of course does not mean that we should close our eyes to whatever we don't like and proclaim the rest as "revolutionary"; it does mean that we should try to analyze what the music is about and why.

WORKING-CLASS CULTURE

Most workers recognize the qualitative and material injustices of this society; the problem is in turning that awareness into action. One of the biggest barriers to political activity for workers is a feeling of powerlessness, self-hatred, and lack of trust in others. It is of course no accident that they feel this way; all of the significant institutions in their lives have instilled and reinforced those feelings.

Bourgeois culture reinforces those attitudes: this culture is produced by "artists" because ordinary people are considered too stupid to create culture; it is bought and sold, which turns potential creators into passive consumers; it talks in romantic and idealized terms to foster classless illusions, which act as barriers

From *Cultural Correspondence*, August 1976.

against perceiving real material conditions. Yet these tendencies do not exist unchallenged.

Blues and country music were created from the collective wisdom and experience of millions of people who translated their feelings about work and life into their music. This music was not designed primarily to be bought and sold; it served social purposes such as making work seem to go faster, creating a background for dancing, or simply expressing collective views about life. Nor was this music composed entirely of ethereal metaphors and romantic ideals, as was popular music; it often used the language and events of everyday life—real sorrow, real love, and real sexuality. It did not represent a vague universal worldview but rather was created by people from a particular class experience, and its content reflected that experience. Even when country music and blues eventually reached a mass audience, its identification with the working class was an important part of its appeal.

This music played an important part in the totality of the working-class consciousness. While it often carried the self-denying ideals of bourgeois ideology, it also conveyed a self-affirming and progressive message. The forms of this music, while ultimately not escaping the definitions of bourgeois culture, nonetheless pointed toward a collective, active, and participatory art rooted in the material conditions of everyday life. Although country music and blues are not and could not have been "revolutionary" or "socialist" music, and although working class culture has never been autonomous from bourgeois culture, in both form and content this music contains the seeds of a more liberating culture.

. . . .

CLASS ORIGINS OF COUNTRY MUSIC AND BLUES

It is possible to see how country music and blues have been used as an escape, how they reinforce bourgeois values, and how they prefigure more liberated forms. However, it is also helpful to see how this music grew out of a class situation, how it reflects the dilemmas and experiences of that class, and how it exists today and what functions it serves.

What justification is there for calling country music and blues "working people's music"? Certainly people from different social classes like this music, and it does not represent an uncompromisingly consistent class view. Yet support for the idea is solid enough to make it a useful concept.

The people who have created this music have overwhelmingly been of working-class (defined to include agricultural workers before 1945) origins, with industrial workers especially prominent. Not only did those who became recording artists generally come from working-class backgrounds, but also the workplace and the working-class community have always served as important focal points for the creation of this music.

Then there is the worldview expressed in country music and blues. In contrast to the commercial bourgeois notion of culture and artists, the people who saw themselves and other workers as producing the wealth of this country logically saw culture as part of a collective and shared process created by ordinary people. The collective nature of the music, its ability to cross racial lines, and its deep sources in the events of everyday life grew naturally out of the worldview and experiences of the American working class.

The third confirmation of this music as belonging to the "working people" lies in the audience it has attracted. This music may have started out as a regional art of one segment of the working class, but it has grown in direct relation to the proletarianization of large numbers of people. If you look at who makes up the audience for this music, what is on the juke boxes in working-class neighborhoods, and the location of country and blues nightclubs, the class nature of this music's audience becomes clear.

Finally, the topics of the songs clearly reflect the experience of the working class. From Darby and Tarlton's "Weaver's Blues" and Jimmie Rodgers's "Brakeman's Blues" to Lightnin' Hopkins's "Tom Moore Blues" and Chuck Berry's "Too Much Monkey Business," work has always played a prominent role in song lyrics, and in all cases the work is discussed from the worker's point of view.

COLLECTIVITY AS REPRESENTED IN
WORKING PEOPLE'S MUSIC

One important part of the modern bourgeois idea of culture is that "great culture" is produced by "great artists" who presumably have a special line to the muses and who go off to a corner somewhere and come up with great art. Although this was not always the case, even for the bourgeoisie, in modern-day capitalism culture itself has become more alienated from life than ever before. Country music and blues represent an alternative idea of how great culture is created.

The names of most of the people who originated this music are unknown to us today. Growing out of earlier forms of both black and white music, this art was created by families singing on their back porches, by people singing while working, by congregations in churches, and by musicians at Saturday night dances. The music was spread around by individuals who took their music on their travels, particularly by those whose work took them to different areas.

Because so much of our current knowledge of the early development of this music is limited to the people who were recorded, it is important to make a special effort to examine the structure of the music; only by doing so can the contributions of individuals be placed in perspective. Many of the musical forms that exist in country music and blues are so widespread, and appeared so early in so many different places, that they give eloquent testimony to the idea that this art is the product of the creativity of a lot of different people drawing on common traditions.

Until World War II, blues and country music existed as a mass art among Southern whites and blacks. The increasing commercialization of this music after that time, coupled with other social and political developments, paved the way for the extension and growth of this music into a big business. But at the same time, it also became the music of working people all over the country, unleashing new energies and cultural forms that in themselves had a great social and political effect.

The combination of an urban industrial boom and the failure of small agriculture throughout the South caused massive migration of rural blacks and white into the cities of the North in the late 1940s. They brought their music with them, but the change in their circumstances changed the music as well.

Alienated by their jobs in heavy industry, by the housing that was available to them, by the impersonal nature of the cities, and by the postwar disillusionment (the war hadn't made things any better), they responded in a variety of ways. The most important cultural manifestation of this sense of alienation was the proliferation of nightclubs, small record companies, and groups of musicians, all centered around traditional music. One refuge (real or imagined) from the rigors of industrial society is small business, and in the late 1940s and early 1950s, a number of blacks and whites opened small nightclubs or record companies. The move to the cities had disrupted old ties, but it also created the possibility for a new group identity, which, thanks to the concentrated population, had a much greater potential than had existed in the rural South.

One form of music created in this context was called rhythm and blues, a synthesis of blues and country music that became popular in urban areas. Musically, R & B combined the boogie-woogie rhythms Bob Wills had taken from black dance bands with an older blues vocal tradition, and pioneered the screaming saxophones of people like Red Prysock and Illinois Jacquet. R & B also developed the twelve-to-the-bar sound (12/8 time), with triplets being used to create an undercurrent of tension in the music. (Although this sound already existed in blues, it was popularized by rhythm and blues.)

This music was played by young blacks who had recently been exposed to the blues singers in the cities of the North and the West—T-Bone Walker in Los Angeles, Elmore James in Chicago, John Lee Hooker in Detroit, Joe Turner in New York. It was recorded by new small record companies—Aladdin, King, Chess, Atlantic, Cameo. Some of these companies were owned by blacks, some were owned by whites seeking to make a profit off the interests of the new market of blacks in their cities. Rhythm and blues was a mass art-form, created by hundreds of small groups who performed at dances and parties and cut the records that became hits in the black community.

A substantial number of whites, particularly the younger ones, began picking up on the rhythm and blues artists, as well as on country artists like Lefty Frizell and Hank Williams. In 1952 a disc jockey in Cleveland, Alan Freed, decided to put on a concert featuring some of the big R & B acts of the day, including Fats Domino, the Moonglows, the Drifters, and the Harptones. Freed's concert was an enormous success, and it firmly established that there was a market among young whites for black music.

To capture this market, record companies resorted to their traditional practice of issuing "cover" records (records by white pop artists that stole their material from blues, jazz, or country by copying the melody and lyrics but smoothing out all the "rough" edges). For example, the McGuire Sisters covered the Moonglows' version of "Sincerely," and George Gibbs turned Etta James's "Rock With Me Henry" into "Dance With Me Henry."

Some companies, however, found that if country singers performed in an R & B style, the result could be even more effective than "cover" records. Sam Phillips of Sun Records in Memphis said, "If I could find someone who looks white and sings black I could make a million dollars." The importance of finding whites to sell rhythm and blues was an outgrowth of the traditional racism of bourgeois culture, which dictated that whites would not buy music made by blacks. Although black music provided the technical base for almost all pop music, it was always sold by having whites do the music in a white style. This practice continued in pop music until Sam Cooke's version of "You Send Me" not only outsold Theresa Brewer's version but actually got more radio airplay as well.

Yet, while the motivation for finding whites to do rhythm and blues was racist, the music that was produced was not always a rip-off. The white country singers who recorded for Sun came to an R & B style naturally—they had been directly or indirectly influenced by black music all their lives. One of these was Elvis Presley, a truck driver from Mississippi, who had been a promising country singer (he had toured with Roy Acuff) before he recorded such R & B numbers as Joe Turner's "Shake Rattle and Roll" and Big Mama Thornton's "Hound Dog." Presley always named Arthur "Big Boy" Crudup and Bill Broonzy as having been important influences on him.

Other country singers who preserved that music's integrity when they turned to rock 'n' roll were Jerry Lee Lewis, Carl Perkins, and Eddie Cochran. Some of the blacks most successful in rock 'n' roll owed as much to the influence of country music as they did to blues. Chuck Berry, the St. Louis cosmetologist, recorded "Maybelline" for Chess Records, and it became the top seller on the pop, R & B, and country charts. Fats Domino, Sam Cooke, and Sonny Til were other black singers with a lot of country influence in their music.

By the mid-fifties, rock 'n' roll was established as the most popular commercial music, but it was also part of a mass culture and helped in creating and reflecting new attitudes and life-styles. This music was not just something you listened to, it was something that was constantly being created. Every playground, street corner, cafeteria, locker room, and classroom echoed the sounds of rock 'n' roll. Kids gathered together and would sing the latest hits or make up their own songs. The recording stars of this era were not press agent and record company hypes, they were young people like their audience. The music came from groups of kids like the Dubs, the Chantels, the Flamingos, the Crests, and Frankie Lymon and the Teenagers.

The success of rock and roll was an important cultural milestone in American history. (Yes, Danny and the Juniors were right, it will go down in history.) Its success extended, on a massive scale, the black-white interaction of the rural South to millions in the North, and it created a common culture for young people from diverse ethnic backgrounds—not the packaged culture of Madison Avenue, but a culture that grew out of real-life experience and spoke in real terms about everyday events.

Rock 'n' roll was the first music heard on a wide scale that talked in specific terms about sex, adolescence, school, jobs, and love. Of course, this was possible because of its roots in country music and blues, which pioneered the use of the language of real life. In the 1930s pop singers could only say things like

> We two could be a couple of hot tomatoes
> but you're as cold as yesterday's mashed potatoes

whereas in rock 'n' roll they could use lyrics like

> Over the hill and way down underneath
> you make me roll my eyes and then I grit my teeth.

The ability to speak frankly about sex was an important part of the music's appeal to young people—it talked about what was on their minds, defying the sexual repression that dominated society. Rock 'n' roll also dealt with alienation from school, parents, and work. Much of the creative energy of country music and blues came out in rock 'n' roll at this time, further developing the interactions between the two, interactions that continue to this day.

PICTURES FROM LIFE'S OTHER SIDE

Most of the "interactions" between country music and blues came in the form of whites adapting black styles to their own folk music. In popular culture, this was a totally oppressive process by which white musicians stole black music and made it "respectable" by stripping it of its social meaning and watering down its key components. Coupled with the rigid exclusion of blacks from access to white audiences, the use of black music in popular culture has been an accurate micro-cosm of the racism of the society at large.

The experience in country music was significantly different. The incorpora-tion of black music into country was done in a spirit of respect rather than of rip-off; the integrity of blues was thus largely maintained. While of course racism was still a prevalent facet of the lives of people who made country music, it was significantly less so in the music itself, especially in contrast with pop music.

More than any other kind of music, black music represents a view of culture opposite to that held by the ruling class. Just as the lives of black people from slavery through lynchings and segregation represent the negation of the idea that this is a free country, black music represents the negation of the culture that has been used to keep people passive and dependent.

The popular culture of bourgeois America has been largely passive, imitative of European culture, and idealized in that it never talked about the day-to-day life of real people. By contrast, black music has been active, original, and deeply rooted in the lives of the people who created it. As the negation of the prevailing ideology, it is no accident that the whites who did the hardest work and got the least reward would pattern their music after black music.

Jimmie Rodgers didn't just sing in a black style. He used to upset his friends because, as one put it, "Jimmie talks like a black man, sings like a black man, he even sits like a black man." This is not to overrate Rodgers's thinking on the sub-ject. He still sang about "when the pickaninnies pick the cotton," but this, too, only indicates that Rodgers was dealing within the limits and values of his time and culture.

Rodgers recorded with Louis Armstrong at a time when whites and blacks did not generally record together. The Carter family worked closely with Leslie

Riddles in the 1930s, and Jimmie Tarlton has described recent troubles in the South as a "punishment" for the treatment given to blacks.

Despite segregation, many blacks and whites did work together, or at least close to each other, and in this manner different kinds of music as well as different philosophies and attitudes were exchanged. Moreover, the social function of music was similar for people of similar class experience—it was an opportunity to get together, to create, to provide a commentary on day-to-day life and to make work go faster.

What did whites see in black music? Bill Monroe, the father of bluegrass music, played at dances with a black man named Arnold Schulze; he once explained his own lonesome tenor singing by recalling, "I remember in Rosine, this colored man would haul freight from the train station to six or seven stores bringing each man what he wanted. And he would be riding his mule on those muddy roads just whistling the blues. And you could tell by the way he whistled that he was the bluest man in the world."

Again, it should be emphasized that what was true for these artists must have been true on a broader level. The widely favorable reception given to blues and blues forms by whites in country music represents an identification with another view of the world than the one promulgated by bourgeois culture. And as people moved into the cities and became factory workers, this feeling increased.

The period after World War II marked the beginning of a great upsurge in black consciousness. The beginnings of the civil rights movement, successful anticolonialist revolutions in the Third World, and greater participation in the work force all increased the consciousness of black people. Together with the disillusionment and cynicism brought on by World War II and Korea in the population as a whole, the beginnings of a youth revolt (juvenile delinquency), and the demise of the trade unions as instruments of social struggle, the acceptance of black-oriented music by large numbers of young people indicated in a certain sense rebellion and alienation—and that rebellion and alienation best found expression in the culture of America's most alienated group.

THE CULTURE AS A COMMODITY

The Music

Commercialization of music on records and on the radio played a great role in encouraging the cultural interactions between country music and blues. It also provided the opportunity for millions of people to enjoy and empathize with the artistry of people like Bessie Smith and Hank Williams. But just as that process changed the lives of the artists performing the music, commercialism altered the music as well.

This music grew up as part of an active creative process, but when it was transformed into a commodity to be sold, the music became less active and creative and more alienated from its previous roles. The prevailing values of commercial music revolve around the music that will sell, not the music that might be important or serve socially and culturally useful functions.

This tendency can be seen clearly in the way record companies and publishers dealt with black music. Blues and jazz constitute some of the finest original culture in this country, yet the record industry turned a blind eye because it disapproved of the class origins and content of the music. "Good" culture—meaning white, passive, idealized, and commercial—was almost all that was available for people to hear. In addition, the kinds of working people's music that were recorded remained artificially separate. By segregating country music from blues, the record industry tried to disrupt the interactions that had been going on. Joint efforts like "Blue Yodel #9" were extremely rare, and many evidences of cross cultural influences were edited out of records by producers.

When the Skillet Lickers began recording in the 1920s, they wanted to record such popular tunes of the day as "Royal Garden Blues," a song made famous by Louis Armstrong. But because they were a white country string band, the record company insisted that they do fiddle tunes that to them were "old-fashioned stuff." Their recordings were of tunes their grandparents played—a valuable cultural heritage, but far different from the active and creative music they played live.

When Bob Wills and the Texas Playboys got their first recording date in Chicago, the record company man objected to Wills's blues-based verbal patter during the music. When the man told Wills to stop, Wills didn't say a word to him, he just turned to the band and said, "Pack up boys, we're going home." They left, and they didn't record until two years later. Few artists had that much integrity, though, and undoubtedly much was lost in the music that was recorded.

Popular music also depends on gimmicks or fads, since it has no real social base of its own. The music doesn't grow out of a consistent social situation, so artificial cultural needs and contexts must constantly be created. Those artists who wanted to record were always pushed into styles designed to catch the ear—and the pocketbook—of the listener, not to appeal to the listener's worldview. The blacks who recorded in the thirties had to do white dance band–style numbers, and the big push in country music in the forties was to do Gene Autry–type western music.

The popularity of rock 'n' roll in the fifties was in some ways set up by the contrivances of bourgeois culture. Music capitalists know capitalism better than they know music, and they are willing to go almost anywhere to pick out a "gimmicky" sound that will sell. But, although they can create profits, they can't create music, so they have to draw on other sources for their material. Since their concept of culture is totally contrived, their music is by nature derivative.

In the early 1950s the pop music industry started a fad by ripping off country music and rhythm and blues, just as in the 1920s it had started a fad by ripping off jazz. Rhythm and blues songs were slowed down and given string-section accompaniment, and their words were changed so that pop artists such as the Hilltoppers, the McGuire Sisters, and Perry Como could sing them. The same thing happened with country songs, which were "interpreted" by Frankie Laine, Guy Mitchell, and Patti Page.

This manipulation only succeeded in better preparing a mass audience for the real thing, though. The explosion in the number of small record companies and the social needs of people in the cities broke through this system of contrivance and made a commercial success out of a mass music based in country music and blues.

Later in the fifties, three major changes came about as the big record companies began to adapt to and ultimately co-opt the new trends in music. The big record companies bought up smaller ones and attempted to record the kind of music that had proven so successful. These companies depended on extensive marketing and, because of their larger investment, tended to go for music that would be a sure thing. So, rather than gambling with unknown talent as the smaller labels had done, they tried to "manufacture" rock 'n' roll stars. Movie stars like Tab Hunter and Annette Funicello became recording artists, there was a great increase in the number of "novelty" songs, and "pop" singers on the big labels incorporated some of the superficial mannerisms of rock 'n' roll into their music.

The smooth sounds produced by this process sold well, but not as well as the wilder and more exciting kinds of music it was trying to replace. It took a wave of censorship and repression of rock 'n' roll to really turn the tide. Radio stations stopped playing music that sounded too black or too country or too "wild," and the music of particular artists, including Chuck Berry and Jerry Lee Lewis, was blacklisted for reasons having to do with their personal lives. The music was associated with all sorts of immorality and juvenile delinquency (a correct association, but only because it grew out of the same roots, not because the music was in any way a mystical cause).

This censorship produced a lot of sterile and uninteresting rock 'n' roll, but it also left a vacuum that created a taste for newer and more exciting forms. In the early 1960s Motown became the first widely popular black label to gain a large share of the white market. This created the greater commercial possibilities for black music, and although the price of that success included watering down a lot of the genuine black sound (Motown's emphasis on strings, the studio sound, and pop lyrics tended to play down the gospel and blues roots of its music), Motown's success did pave the way for the more authentic black sound produced later in such places as Memphis and Muscle Shoals.

Another important change after 1958 was of course the success of groups from England, heavily influenced by blues musicians such as Muddy Waters, Howlin' Wolf, Chuck Berry, and Sonny Boy Williamson. The commercial success of these groups was due to their ability to reduplicate some of the blues feeling in their music, and in the process they sparked the beginnings of a blues revival that helped to focus attention in this country on hitherto little-known (at least among white audiences) blues artists. The appeal of the British rock 'n' roll rooted in blues stimulated a new direction, advanced by people who had been involved in the earlier "wild" rock 'n' roll but who lost interest as it became more sterile. Many of these people had become attracted to the folk tradition present in country and mountain music and had been schooled in the music of Woody Guthrie, Pete Seeger, and others. These people fused their interest in folk with British-style rock, creating folk-rock. The leading practitioner of this form was, of course, Bob Dylan, who grew up in Minnesota idolizing Hank Williams and Little Richard and listening to black blues on late-night radio shows.

The sterility of rock 'n' roll after 1958 also drove many country-oriented rock stars—including Jerry Lee Lewis, Conway Twitty, Brenda Lee, Elvis Presley, Sonny James, Marty Robbins, and Johnny Cash—back into country, and they brought with them new forms, thus reinvigorating country music and sparking a renaissance of interest in it.

Although much of the original nature of country music and blues survives in modern forms, it has nonetheless been definitely changed by the music industry. Both forms have been made to imitate what has been successful in pop music; their lyrics and music thus do not rise as directly from mass roots as they once did. This change in the music has also tended to fuel working-class self-hatred. Country music's reputation as hillbilly music and the association of the blues with the low life are both advanced by the record industry, which seeks a broader, homogenous—and therefore less black and less country—sound. The excessive use of background violins and choruses is one example of how this is done; the emphasis in lyrics on bourgeois romantic notions of love is another. These developments reflect the ways the music has become more contrived, more of a studio production and less of a mass art.

The effect of commercialism has been to alter the music, blur distinctive musical traits, and emphasize gimmicks. It has also, however, forced new alignments and combinations of music, often because of its very inability to be in touch with the roots of culture. Needs can be exploited and new needs can be created, but as long as real needs are unmet there will be a real culture expressing that fact.

The Audience

Capitalism's effect on culture cannot be ascertained solely by looking at the ways in which commercialism has affected the artists or the music itself. The crucial area to be explored is how the capitalist domination of culture has affected the consciousness of the people relating to that culture. Although the possibility of making a living from music has probably stimulated many people to become musicians, it is probably also true that the overall effect of music marketing tacks has tended to diminish the amount of live music that people hear. There is less incentive to hear your neighbor sing if you can get Hank Williams at the flick of a switch, and probably less incentive to learn to play an instrument if everybody dances to records. Passivity is also ingrained in the way music is distributed. Music is created by "artists," but the listener is expected to be just that: a listener. You pay money to hear a concert, and become a passive consumer, not a participant in an ongoing process.

The popular idea of music has also been distorted. At one time, music was something people created whenever they wanted, spontaneously or for a given social function. The emphasis on professionalism, though, has tended to mystify music; now you sit respectfully and listen, feeling inadequate to participate because you're not as "good" as a professional artist. Music is something to be purchased or produced in studios—it seems less of a human creation.

This situation leads to the star system, which creates larger-than-life heroes out of human beings who happen to make music. We have talked earlier about how this system hurts the artists, but what about the listener? First, hero worship results in making yourself look small and incapable of acting, since you are not a "great figure" like your idol. Second, it individualizes things that are social in origin. The greatest entertainers in country music and blues are interpreters of a mass art, a mass creativity; yet their interpretation alone is praised, and the social origins of it in the experience of a whole class go unrecognized. Culture is seen solely as an individual accomplishment, not as something that is collectively produced out of the common experience.

The star system is also used to reinforce objectification of sex, particularly in the person of the "sex symbol" star. Certainly country music and blues contain much frank talk about sexuality, but that frankness has been manipulated and exploited with the creation of singing sex symbols whose commercial appeal depends on their ability to manipulate the audience's anxieties and confusions about sex. The women who scream at Elvis Presley or the men who drool at Tina Turner's act are being encouraged to channel their sexuality into identification with a distant and idealized sexual figure. In this way sexuality becomes divorced from any other kind of human relationship; it is confused with power—the power to dominate an audience—and reinforces the notion of hierarchies. Valued things like sex become the property of larger-than-life stars, made more exciting by their "status," and no longer belong in common to all human beings. The dynamic of rock stars and their groupies is merely a logical extension of the pattern of human relations encouraged by the "star" system.

This notion of sexuality is of course used to reinforce capitalist attitudes about women and sexuality. As in real life, women stars are almost always judged by their "sex appeal," an image that sells with people from all backgrounds. This presents a model for other women to envy and compete with, and a fantasy image for men to dwell on and possibly attempt to make come true.

Culture under capitalism is a way to convey many other societal values as well. A historical example is the role of women and blacks in recorded music. In the folk tradition, women contributed as much as men to the development and passing along of music, yet the number of women recorded is far less. Blacks have been formally excluded from access to tools that would enable them to spread and preserve their culture; thus, the parallel between recorded black music and the music that existed on a wide scale is disproportionate and unrepresentative. And of course, those women and blacks who were recorded were virtually forced to fit the images society had of them.

Other bourgeois ideas are conveyed by the music industry. What is a "hit" song? In the folk tradition, songs were passed around among people and towns, and those songs that fit the feelings of the most people tended to survive. Capitalism has reduced the questions about the merits of a song to how much it sells and how fast. Promotion and fads mean sales, which means that Donny Osmond and Bobby Sherman have probably been heard by more people than Memphis Minnie or Sonny Boy Williamson have. But does the number of records sold indicate anything active in people's lives, or is it just a business statistic? All art is different, and the merit of any art depends on the subjective feelings it pro-vokes—which can't be rated in dollars and cents.

Thus, commercialism and the culture industry have led to a lessened self-image, passivity, dependence, sexism, racism, and acceptance of ideas in direct contradiction to the life experience of the working and poor people who listen to this music. Yet that same process has also served some positive functions.

Through commercialism, people have gained access to cultures they would not otherwise have come in contact with. Many of the young whites who have related to rhythm and blues might not even have become aware of the existence of blacks and black culture had it not been for the distribution of black music. Many children of immigrants, who found their own parents denying their ethnic culture in an attempt to assimilate, found themselves relating to the culture of rural whites and blacks, people they didn't know but whose alienations seemed famil-iar. The marketing of different kinds of music has also helped give listeners a living sense of history. People like Bessie Smith and Hank Williams open to us, through their music, a view of life in this country we might never find in the history books. Through commercial distribution of this music, moreover, people from diverse backgrounds have found a common language and common frame of cultural reference based on the concerns of everyday life.

COUNTRY MUSIC AND BLUES TODAY

By emphasizing the historical evolution of blues, country music, and rock 'n' roll, I do not mean to say that the only music worth relating to is the "pure" blues and country sounds of thirty years ago. On the contrary, I believe that the impor-tant distinguishing features of this music survive to the present day and are re-sponsible for the contemporary popularity of country music and blues and its modern hybrids.

Most of the positive features of this tradition survive, although they coexist uneasily with commercial values, of which they are the antithesis. The song forms rely on the same devices: call and response, three-line twelve-bar blues, flatting of certain notes, slide guitar sounds, and variations of 4/4, 8/8, or 12/8 rhythms. This music also preserves other traditional folk arts such as storytelling and dancing. Certain musical figures have survived as representations of non-musical ideas, for example the steel guitar riff originated by Leon McAuliff and used by Ernest Tubb and Hank Thompson, a takeoff on "Boomer Sooner," the Oklahoma fight song and a badge of regional pride in the southwest; or the sys-tem of punctuation represented by the guitar playing of Lightnin' Hopkins. This music also preserves the creative street argot of working people, as represented by Bo Diddley's "Say Man" and Jerry Reed's "When You're Hot, You're Hot."

It is the lyrics of country music and blues that pose problems for people look-ing for progressive social content. When James Brown sings that "It's a Man's Man's Man's World" and Tammy Wynette sings "Stand by Your Man," sexism seems to be the essence of this music's appeal. The aggressive posturing of Merle Haggard in "Fightin' Side" and the hopelessness of the situation described by

Lightnin' Hopkins in "Tom Moore's Blues" make country music seem right wing and the blues defeatist.

These observations, however, need to be placed in perspective. Country music and blues are basically folk arts that speak to the immediate feelings of the working class; they are therefore bound to reflect the sexism and national chauvinism that exists in that class. It would be a great disservice to the working class (as well as a betrayal of dialectical materialism), though, to conclude that those elements of bourgeois ideology exist unchallenged and wholly internalized. In fact, they exist side by side with their opposites, as part of contradictions. To the extent that they do exist, they work against people's own class interests and are thus manifestations of self-hatred and self-doubt. The goal of radical artists— and of all radicals—should be to help turn that self-denial into self-affirmation, to construct a positive class consciousness.

Let's be specific and start first with country music, since it seems to be more criticized for its lyrics than blues. When people label country music as right wing, they usually bring up Merle Haggard and "Okie from Muskogee" and "Fightin' Side." "Muskogee," released in 1969, is a defensive affirmation of traditional values under attack. Haggard defines himself and his listeners by what they are not: they don't wear long hair, they don't burn draft cards, and they don't take drugs. The only positive, nonreactive statements are that "We still wave Old Glory down at the courthouse, and white lightnin's still the biggest thrill of all." In "Fightin' Side," released early in 1970, he says that people who criticize the war or the American way of life are just running down this country and better be prepared to fight him. Although the pride expressed in "Muskogee" in being an "Okie" and a "square" is laudable, that pride is based on obedience to authority, making the song generally reactionary. "Fightin' Side" has no redeeming values, and if it were the totality of Haggard's work or country music all the criticisms branding it right wing would be justified. But placed in the context of the rest of Haggard's work and the rest of country music, "Fightin' Side" is an exception, not the norm.

The same Merle Haggard who wrote those songs wrote "Hungry Eyes," a beautiful song about growing up poor and seeing the sadness in his mother's eyes because she never got the things she wanted, for "another class of people, put us somewhere down below." "Hungry Eyes" was number one for seventeen weeks in 1969 (longer than "Muskogee" or "Fightin' Side"). Another Haggard song, "Irma Jackson," tells the story of a white man who falls in love with a black woman and condemns society for not leaving them alone. Haggard spent some time in San Quentin as a prisoner, and his prison songs, such as "Mama Tried," "Sing Me Back Home," and "Huntsville," deal beautifully with the feelings of prisoners. In "Big Time Annie's Square" Haggard falls in love with one of the hippies he was so afraid of in "Muskogee"; and his recent "If We Make It Through December" captured the feelings of workers facing layoffs and hard times.

Haggard's music shows no trace of racism, little sexism (except in "If You've Got Time," where he doesn't want to cry because "a man should never show his feelings"), and some national chauvinism ("Fightin' Side"), but its outstanding characteristics are vulnerability and self-doubt. In "Mama Tried" he blames himself for being in prison; in "Working Man's Blues" his only mark of self-respect is that he's not on welfare. In this respect, it is instructive to compare Haggard's music with that of self-affirming country singers—who consequently have much better politics.

Compare "Mama Tried" with "I Never Picked Cotton," by Roy Clark. Unlike Haggard's self-blaming prisoner, Clark's tells about watching his family slave picking cotton, and about his father dying young as a coal miner. In this song, crime is juxtaposed favorably to alienating work: at the end the singer says that even though they're going to hang him he looks back with pride on the fact that he never picked cotton; he never accepted the conditions he was born into.

Compare "Muskogee" with John Cash's "What Is Truth?" and "Man in Black." In "Truth," Cash points to social ills—the Vietnam War, the hypocrisy of adults—and concludes that you can't blame kids for questioning society. In "Man in Black," he talks about "the poor and beaten down," "the prisoner who is a victim of the time," and "the lives that could have been" of those killed in Vietnam, and pledges "to make a move to make a few things right."

Or compare "Fightin' Side" to such antiwar songs as Henson Cargill's "Pencil Marks," Mel Tillis's "Ruby," Skeeter Davis's "When You Gonna Bring Our Soldiers Home," Bobby Bond's "Six White Horses," and Tom T. Hall's "Mama Bake a Pie."

The same kind of comparison can be made with Tammy Wynette's music. Ever since *Five Easy Pieces*, many people have considered her "Stand by Your Man" representative of the sexism of country music. Wynette's songs describe very well the feelings of many women, particularly the self-hatred a woman suffers from always blaming herself when things go wrong and from judging her worth by her ability to fulfill her female role. Yet women have been important in country music, and that importance has been reflected by a series of self-affirming, self-conscious women's songs, dating back to Kitty Wells's "It Wasn't God Who Made Honky Tonk Angels" in 1952, an answer to Hank Thompson's "Wild Side of Life," and continuing to the present and Dolly Parton's "Just Because I'm a Woman" and "Washday Blues," Loretta Lynn's "One's on the Way," and Norma Jean's "Heaven Help the Working Girl." These songs express the many facets of the oppression women have felt; they may not give any easy solutions, but they do give the women facing those problems a greater sense of self-respect.

Some other lyrically significant songs are "Oney" by Johnny Cash, "Singer" by Jeannie C. Riley, "California Cottonfields" by Dallas Frazier, "America the Ugly," "Hang Them All," "Morning Dew," "One Hundred Children," "Subdivision Blues," "Coot's Blues," and "Clayton Delaney" (and just about everything else) by Tom T. Hall, "Six Days on the Road" by Dave Dudley, "Forty Acres" by the Willis Brothers, "Do You Believe This Town" by Roy Clark, "Dark As A Dungeon," "Ira Hayes," "Mississippi Delta Land," "As Long as the Grass Shall Grow," and "San Quentin" by Johnny Cash, "Saginaw Michigan" by Lefty Frizell, and many many others. . . . The lyrics of these songs capture the ways in which society affects individuals on the most immediate level. Their greatest weakness is their frequent inability to tie the oppressions of everyday life to any larger causes or to point the way toward collective political solutions.

This weakness hardly indicates ideological integration with the system, however. These lyrics reflect a social reality, and if they do not express a collective vision it is because that vision is not sufficiently a part of people's lives to show up in their music. As it becomes more so, the music will respond and reflect that change. Furthermore, although it is important that both the immediate and the long-range nature of oppressions and aspirations be discussed, a political analysis will most likely grow out of an understanding of the dynamics of day-to-day life, not the other way around.

This music has no built-in political dynamic separate from the political future of the people who make it. The future of this music will depend on the future of the working class. To the extent that the future includes self-affirming cooperative experiences and aspirations, we will get more songs like "Oney" and "Little Brother." To the extent that people's experiences reaffirm the self-denying divisiveness of the system and the romantic illusions of sexism, we will get more songs like "Muskogee" and "Love Jones." It is up to us to further the positive trends and combat the negative ones in both cultural and social practice.

SOME CULTURAL PRACTICE

For those of us who are not musicians or artists, it is sometimes difficult to see how cultural questions can be dealt with in practice. An artist can simply create something consistent with the progressive social forces to be drawn upon, but what can the rest of us do to help integrate politics and art, and to further both?

We can, for a start, discuss these questions so that they become open, conscious, and public arguments, and not subliminal private forces. Pamphlets, newspapers, and conversations with friends can focus on these questions in a way that politicizes art and brings aesthetic breadth to the political questions of day-to-day life.

Recently, some of us here in St. Louis put together some tapes entitled "Working People's Music" to demonstrate the points made in this article. We wanted to make public the culture working people have created in spite of tremendous obstacles, and we wanted to focus on the positive self-affirming aspects of that culture as something to be proud of. We also wanted to deal with the self-denying aspects of it, to show that they are a product of social relationships and can be changed.

We tried to give proper respect to the antiracist implications of this music and at the same time deal with the racism that did and still does exist. We tried to show the ways in which the values of capitalism have conflicted with the worldviews that originated this music.

Most important, we tried to demonstrate the relationship between the music and the social issues, that music can point the way toward good things, but only by changing society can we make those things a reality. But we also tried to show that part of changing society means dealing with the ideas and attitudes that are culturally transmitted and maintained. We tried to identify the positive trends in modern country music and blues that still represent its origins as a mass art that crossed racial lines and reflected a class experience. We also tried to examine the music that demonstrated co-optation and bourgeois values, as well as a lot of the music in between that just expresses the dilemmas many people feel.

These tapes were played on Sunday afternoons over listener-supported KDNA-FM for thirteen weeks. While of course we don't know the total effect they had, we are encouraged by the feedback we have received. Many workers told us that they liked the music we were playing and that what we said about it coincided with their own experiences. People who previously couldn't stand country music told us they saw a lot more in it, and a lot of people from different backgrounds have told us that we helped them put a lot of ideas together. We were invited to speak to classes at two local high schools with very satisfying results, and we found that we had generally stimulated a lot of interest in these concerns and topics.

ROCK AND POPULAR CULTURE

SIMON FRITH

Robert Christgau, *Any Old Way You Choose It: Rock and Other Pop Music, 1967–1973*; Penguin, 330 pp., $2.50

Jon Landau, *It's Too Late to Stop Now: A Rock and Roll Journal*; Straight Arrow, 228 pp., $3.95

Greil Marcus, *Mystery Train: Images of America in Rock 'n' Roll Music*; E. P. Dutton, 276 pp., $8.95

> *Q.: Why is rock like the revolution?*
> *A.: Because they're both groovy.*
> (CHRISTGAU, p. 94)

In the 1960s, rock 'n' revolution wasn't such a joke. Bob Dylan infiltrated left-wing organizations as slyly as the FBI, political solidarity was sustained by record collections, and ideologues like Tom Hayden and Eldridge Cleaver were agreed that the "liberation" of white youth could be rooted in rock 'n' roll. Rock music was, in fact, central to the claims of the counterculture.

In this review I don't want to examine these claims or rock's contribution to them. My interest is not in rock as counterculture but in rock as popular culture. The questions I want to raise concern the analysis of rock music as a form of mass communication—questions that are begged in the numerous attempts to assess the political significance of the counterculture. The books by Christgau, Landau, and Marcus provide the necessary way in to these questions—their writers are not only intelligent and incisive, they also function as rock ideologists, teaching their readers how to listen and respond to the music. Landau and Marcus in their work for *Rolling Stone* and Christgau in his for *Village Voice* not only record the values and assumptions of rock culture, they also help to form them.

More words are written about rock than about any other mass medium (in Britain, for example, there are four newspapers devoted to the subject, with sales ranging from 80,000 to 180,000 per week), but most of them are part of the phenomenon itself, central to the process of music promotion and advertisement and publicity. Christgau, Landau, and Marcus are important because, in contrast to the usual hack pros of the record business, they seek to establish rock as a serious area for both artistic and social criticism. It is this combination that makes them interesting. Other critics have treated rock as art (see R. Melzer's *Aesthetics of Rock*, for example, or Paul Williams's pioneering reviews in *Crawdaddy*), and numerous commentators have asserted rock's importance for the "youth movement." Few, however, have tried to grasp rock's "relative autonomy" or to relate

From *Socialist Revolution*, no. 31, January 1978.

its social meanings to its artistic form. (I should mention Lester Bangs and Dave Marsh and their work for *Creem*, but this has not been systematized or collected in book form.) The three authors I want to consider here are certainly not Marxists (though they have radical concerns of various sorts), nor are they spokesmen for the counterculture. Their concern is to uncover and clarify the positive aspects of rock while remaining critically conscious of its negative ones, and their arguments must be taken seriously by Marxists, whose analyses of mass cultural products tend to be wholly negative. In this review I shall stress the (1960s-based) affirmations of rock criticism and neglect discussion of the apparent decline of rock's artistic and social power in the 1970s. Discussion must begin with the correctives made by these rock critics to the negative Marxist treatment of mass culture.

I

A Chilean socialist, in exile from Pinochet, told me that the most disturbing thing about living in England was that he couldn't see the class struggle. He reads about it in the newspapers, politicians pronounce that British capitalism is in its worst crisis ever, but all he can see is a complacent and conservative people taking care of business. Except in Northern Ireland, there are few signs of struggle or repression—after the last decade in Chile, Britain seems to be in a state of suspended animation. "Where is the working class?" he asks; "When is something going to *happen?*"

When ideological forces are working well, as they are still in Britain, they are difficult to observe. The same problem faced another group of socialist exiles forty years ago in the United States: the Frankfurt scholars fled a repressive state for a more advanced capitalist society and found a shadowy working class and the least developed socialist movement anywhere. Little wonder that one of the obsessions of the Frankfurt School became mass culture, how it was created, how it worked.[1]

Their arguments were remarkably influential. In the thirties, when American intellectuals agonized over joining the Communist party and the New Deal sponsored "people's art," the dominant left ideology was a populism that found authenticity in mass culture and attacked the elitism of high art. The debates about socialist realism and proletarian literature brought aesthetic values, political truths, and mass popularity into an uneasy unity, and for committed artists the problem was not the control of the means of ideological production but, more directly, the correctness of their work, and this was to be judged not against bourgeois or traditional cultural standards but by the spontaneous response of the masses themselves. Antimass arguments came from the right.

By the 1950s the position was reversed. It was the left, led by the Frankfurters, who denounced the mind-numbing trivia, the philistinism, the debilitating political effects of mass culture, and the right, pluralists and defenders of America's cold war honor, who proclaimed the democracy of popular culture, its wealth of choice, its enriching and educational effects. (*Encounter*, as Conor Cruise O'Brien once pointed out, even felt obliged to explain to the world the noble purpose of horror comics.) The left argument (and variations of it can be found in all Marxist analyses of ideology, those of Gramsci and Althusser as well as Marcuse) was a straightforward combination of social and artistic judgments. The sociological effect of the mass media was an alienated, depoliticized, passive working class; aesthetically, mass art was worthless, but politically it was of great significance, a crucial mechanism by which the capitalist system instilled a habit of thought and life and ensured its reproduction.[2]

It was the very negativity of this argument that made the experience of the counterculture of the 1960s so exhilaratingly positive. Christgau parodies the result: "Rock and roll, as we all know, was instrumental in opening up the generation gap and fertilizing the largely sexual energy that has flowered into the youth life-style, and this life-style, as we all know, is going to revolutionize the world" (p. 95). The terms of the previous argument were reversed. If straight mass culture was of crucial political significance, then counterculture must be of crucial revolutionary significance. Its art objects, notably rock music, must be of great aesthetic value, and this value must come from the liberating effects of those objects, their ability to politicize, collectivize, and arouse an audience.

This argument doesn't have much credibility for anyone anymore, although different reasons are given for this. The rather supercilious post hoc Marxist point is that it never was credible. A cultural community cannot form a real power base, and anyway, the class basis of the counterculture made it politically suspect from the beginning. But this argument leaves open the question of what sort of social forces do operate in the superstructure. The strength of the counterculture's political claims derived, after all, from the orthodox left view of the power of ideology in American society.

This is evident in the subsequent suggestions of the countercultural radicals themselves. They claim that their position was once credible, but their ideological force was, by various means (including direct repression), diluted and fragmented and then absorbed into the dominant mode of mass cultural production, with fatal results. It is common for rock people to present the history of their music as a continual battle between Rock and Commerce. In the sixties, Rock won; in the seventies, Commerce came storming back and the fight goes on. Listen to Landau, for example:

Rock, the music of the Sixties, was a music of spontaneity. It was a folk music—it was listened to and made by the same group of people. It did not come out of a New York office building where people sit and write what they think other people want to hear. It came from the life experiences of the artists and their interaction with an audience that was roughly the same age. As that spontaneity and creativity have become more stylized and analyzed and structured, it has become easier for businessmen and behind-the-scenes manipulators to structure their approach to merchandising music. The process of creating stars has become a routine and a formula as dry as an equation. (p. 40)

The implication is that the usual negative judgment of mass culture is correct, but rock is, or can be, a special case.

II

The most popular way of distinguishing rock from the rest of mass culture is to claim it as a high art form. The art/mass culture distinction is common in cultural criticism and rests on a series of oppositions: individual sensibility versus lowest-common-denominator consciousness, moral enrichment versus escapism, self-conscious creation versus alienated consumption.[3] To claim rock as art means to claim that rock songs and records are demanding individual creations. This raises two problems.

First, rock music, like other works of mass art in "the age of mechanical reproduction," is not made by an individual creator communicating directly to an audience. The basic means of rock expression is the phonograph record, and record making (as opposed to music making) depends on a complex structure of people and machines. Rock critics have had to establish their own version of auteur theory. Landau is most explicit about this: "To me the criterion of art in rock is the capacity of the musician to create a personal, almost private, universe and to express it fully" (p. 15).

The rock auteur (who may be writer, singer, instrumentalist, band, and even, on occasion, record producer or engineer) creates the music with his or her unique experience, skill, and vision. Everyone else engaged in record making is simply part of the means of communication. For many fans it is this process of individual artistic creation that distinguishes rock from other forms of mass music—the Beatles wrote their own songs!—and, as Marcus points out, one result has been the equation in the singer/songwriter genre of art and personal confession: honesty is all.

The second problem is rock's entertainment function. Entertainment, in this account of culture, is neither improving nor instructive; it takes its audience nowhere and comes easy. Art, in contrast, makes people work. (It is this sort of distinction between art and entertainment that Brecht was determined to deny.) One solution to this sort of distinction has been to make rock work, too, to complicate its structure (usually by aping classical music or jazz) and move it (both literally and metaphorically) from the dance hall to the concert hall. But the more subtle response (again echoing film criticism) has been to deny that the immediate reaction to rock exhausts its meaning: formal analysis, the hard work of decoding, is also necessary. Rock can't just be consumed; it must be responded to like any other form of art, its tensions and contradictions engaged and reinterpreted into the listener's experience. Such engagement is intellectual and moral; the results are enriching and can be disturbing. Landau, Christgau, and Marcus are all involved in this process of decoding (if without the formal techniques of structuralism that are beginning to be used by film critics), and, like literary critics, they experience their task as a demanding and responsible one. (The literary analogy is the correct one. Although no rock critic has the simple-minded notion that content can be reduced to lyrics, few—Landau is the exception—seem to have the ability or interest to provide the technical musical analysis of a classical critic.)

But, with their profession firmly established as an honorable one, all these critics are uneasy. Landau, for example, suddenly declares that "rock is not primarily poetry or art . . . ; rock and roll may be the new music, but rock musicians are not the new prophets" (p. 134). His uneasiness has two sources. First, auteurism is often unconvincing—the image of the individual creator, the Genius, is too obviously part of the process by which a Star is born. Even worse, in the very distinction of rock from other mass art, the baby seems to have been flung out with the bath water. As Christgau admits:

I came to understand that popular art was not inferior to high art, and decided that popular art achieved a vitality of both integrity and outreach that high art had unfortunately abandoned. Popular art dealt with common realities and fantasies in forms that provided immediate pleasure—and it was vital aesthetically, as work. And because it moved and was moved by the great audience, it was also vital culturally, as relationship. (p. 3)

From this perspective, the power of rock depends on it *not* being high art. A new distinction is made—between mass culture and folk culture.

III

A distinction between mass and folk culture has always been essential for left theories of art. The oppositions here are community versus mass, collective creation versus fragmented consumption, solidarity versus alienation, activity versus passivity. The argument is that folk art is created directly out of a communal experience. There is no distance between artist and audience, no separation between the production and consumption of art. The cultural basis of folk art is destroyed by the means and relations of artistic production under capitalism. Cultural products become commodities, produced and sold for profit, alienated from both their producers and their users. The resulting processes of taste manipulation and artistic exploitation are made possible by the available technologies of art, the recording techniques that enable cultural objects to be mass produced and individually consumed.[4]

This argument was, in the fifties, central to the ideology of folk music, and placed it in a tradition of live performance in which the performer was not even distanced from the listeners by electric amplification. Pop music was condemned not just for being embedded in the relationships of commercial profit making, but for using the technology of mass production; Bob Dylan, for instance, was booed at the Newport Folk Festival simply for playing with electrified instruments.[5]

Undaunted by the commercial and technological trappings of their music, rock critics assert that it is, despite everything, a folk music, the genuine expression of a collective experience. Landau writes of classic rock 'n' roll: "It was unmistakably a folk-music form. Within the confines of the media, these musicians articulated attitudes, styles and feelings that were genuine reflections of their own experience and of the social situation which had helped to produce that experience" (p. 130). Marcus uses the image of rock as a "secret" that bound a generation and made it culturally independent of its elders. Christgau emphasizes that rock is a source of solidarity and a potential source of action: "If rock and roll is to continue to function politically, it must continue to liberate its audience—to broaden fellow-feeling, direct energy, and focus analysis" (p. 279).

All three writers suggest that it is not so much the lyrical content of rock 'n' roll that makes it relevant to youth as its physicality. Rock's entertainment function—as dance music—is essential to its folk function of giving form to the energy and needs of its users. Critical attention thus moves away from the producers of rock to its consumers, the rock audience. Landau stresses that, anyway, the rock artist is part of this audience: "There existed a strong bond between performer and audience, a natural kinship, a sense that the stars weren't being imposed from above but had sprung up from out of our ranks. We could identify with them without hesitation" (p. 21). Christgau and Marcus both argue that it is the technology of rock, particularly radio, that enables it to provide a disparate audience with a shared experience:

We fight our way through the massed and leveled collective safe taste of Top 40, just looking for a little something we can call our own. But when we find it and jam the radio to hear it again it isn't just ours—it is a link to thousands of others who are sharing it with us. As a matter of a single song this might mean very little, as culture, as a way of life, you can't beat it. (Marcus, p. 115)

Rock music is not confined to ceremonial occasions but enters people's lives without "aura" and takes on a meaning there independent of the intentions of its original creators. The rock audience is seen not as a passive mass, consuming records like cornflakes, but as an active community, making music into a symbol of solidarity and an inspiration for action.[6]

The work of criticizing rock as folk resembles anthropology rather than literary criticism: rock carries collective meanings, and it is these that must be interpreted. In Christgau's account of the 1967 Monterey Festival, for example, the musicians and audience are treated as one, equal participants in a folk event:

No one stopped to wonder how soul and rock and blues and funk meshed with the "peace and acceptance" (*Newsweek*) of Monterey. The new rock has no more peace and acceptance about it than the old. To the adolescent defiance of the fifties has been added not only whimsy and occasional loveliness but also social consciousness and the ironic grit of the blues. The big beat has been augmented by dissonance, total volume, and a scientific panoply of electronic effects. But the paradox is on the surface. The music isn't peace itself; it is a means to peace. It is how the love crowd mediates with an unfriendly environment. (p. 33)

Aesthetic and sociological judgments are, here, fused.

The assumption of the rock-as-folk argument is that rock's mass audience is not manipulated but has real needs and makes real choices. The music doesn't impose an ideology, but, in Marcus's phrase, "absorbs" events, absorbs its listeners' concerns and values. The problem of this assumption is its circularity—the music is folk music because its audience is a real community, but this community is recognized by its common use of the music.

The way out of the circle is via an independent measure of the rock community, and it is at this point of the argument that the idealism of the rock ideologues becomes evident. Little attempt is made to investigate the material conditions of the rock audience; class is not a concept of much use in rock criticism. For Landau the rock community is youth, plain and simple. He doesn't (except in terms of immediate, ad hoc, situations) explain why the young in America—or elsewhere, for that matter—should have generated a set of values that crossed class lines but distinguished generations. Christgau is aware of this problem but veers uneasily between a vanguard theory in which the counterculture is seen as the result of hard political thought and organization, and a populist theory in which the people are always right. In the former argument, rock is heard as the music of youth but not, therefore, as carrying any particular message. Musicians make political choices, too, and our judgment of their music must depend on the choices they make. In the latter argument, all popular art must, by definition, touch on real popular concerns, and real people are rarely concerned with politics but usually with tomorrow's date or yesterday's fight with the spouse. Popular art, including rock, can only tell people what they already want to hear, otherwise they wouldn't listen. And the questions thus raised concern rock not as art or folk music but as ideology.[7]

IV

Christgau's and Landau's books are both collections of articles and reviews written for a variety of magazines between 1967 and 1973; the primary concern of both writers was to establish rock's significance as a cultural force. Marcus takes that significance for granted. His book is "an attempt to broaden the context in which the music is heard; to deal with rock'n'roll not as youth culture, or counter culture, but simply as American culture" (p. 4). In doing this, Marcus shifts attention back to the music makers; his concern is the relationship of rock artists' visions and the ideological structures within which they work. He analyzes the music of six artists—Harmonica Frank, a Southern white street singer (born in 1908) who claims to have invented rock 'n' roll; the blues singer Robert Johnson; the Band; Sly Stone; Randy Newman; and Elvis Presley. What appears at first sight a perverse selection enables Marcus to cover every base: blues and country music, the South and rural America, California and the city streets.

Marcus's assumption is that his musicians, disparate in background and interests, are equally patriotic: their visions are visions of America. Rock 'n' roll is a metaphor for politics, a form of self-expression and a source of democracy. The form/content distinction is dissolved: rock carries collective meanings, but it does more than simply communicate them—in its role as a mass art it symbolizes them. Rock's vision of America as a political community is symbolized by its creation of the rock audience as a cultural community. Marcus measures the importance of rock 'n' roll by the numbers of boundaries it crosses: black music for white folk, white music for black folk, city music for the country, country music for the city. It is precisely the "massness" of its audience that gives rock its ideological force.

All popular art in America functions to provide a sense of community for people fragmented by the reality of competitive capitalism; all popular art involves an ideology of what it is to be "American" (and, by implication, un-American). Marcus distinguishes good and bad popular art by reference to the ideas of American involved. Most mass culture plays safe—American-ness is a bland and shallow acceptance of a lie, that the way things are is just dandy. Mass culture—rock—becomes art when its creator's visions are so individual, so powerful, that they can't be denied, even by mass consumption. The problem for all popular artists is that "if you get what you have to say across to a mass audience, that means what you have to say is not deep enough, or strong enough, to really matter" (p. 132), but, Marcus argues, popular art can communicate even disturbing truths if, in doing so, it exploits the contradictions that are already powerful and disturbing in popular ideology. In doing this, rock becomes a folk music.

The central contradiction of American ideology lies in the concept of equality. In its most immediate form the problem is that the assertion of equality is denied by everyday experience—American society is profoundly unequal in terms of both wealth and power. But, Marcus suggests, there are contradictions even in the American vision of equality: it opposes an individualistic ambition and a sense of private worth to an ideology of community, to the collective values and prejudices that support the unequal in their individual failure. It is this contradiction that Marcus finds expressed in the best rock music: on the one hand, ambition and risk-taking, a sense of style and adventure, a refusal to be satisfied, and on the other hand, a feeling for roots and history, a dependence on community and tradition, an acceptance of one's lot.

Rock 'n' roll music is rooted in the ideology of the American poor, black and white. As the central image of black music, Marcus takes the story of Staggerlee, the gambler who shook off the chains of religion and racism and cautious survival and in his freedom shot a man and became a myth—admired, feared, fated. The central image of white popular music is Elvis Presley, demanding good times and getting them, and finding them all too easy. And as rock 'n' roll music became rock, forced its way into a much wider community of white middle-class youth, its tense combination of dissatisfaction and guilt took meaning as a looser contradiction, between utopianism—California as the promised land—and cynicism—California as the final dead resting place of alien souls.

In many ways, *Mystery Train* reads like an old-fashioned text for an American Studies course. Marcus's America is an ideological place, a product of ideas, not material forces, and his rock 'n' roll is placed in a tradition of idealist political theory inspired by Tocqueville. Like his fellow critics, Marcus is uninterested in the material conditions of the production or consumption of popular art and confines analysis to the superstructural level. If he is hip to the problem of equality as an American ideal, he avoids the problem of fraternity—exploitation, like class, does not feature much in the rock critic's vocabulary. In the end, Marcus's vision of America is of a society not without capitalism or capitalists but without labor. He dreams not of a classless but of a one-class society, in which people are their own producers, meet in the marketplace, and make politics together.

The ideology of the petite bourgeoisie has always been central to American popular culture, with its individualism and fears of organized labor and big capital and state power; what Marcus makes clear is how far this ideology permeates rock culture, too. Rock even draws its rebellious element from bohemianism, and bohemians are petit bourgeois standing on their heads—the same individualism, the same paranoias, and a rejection of the social conditions of capitalism that is entirely aesthetic and moral and utopian.[8]

V

What are we to conclude about rock music? The first point to stress (because it is mostly ignored by rock ideologists) is that all rock records, whatever their artistic or folk or ideological status, are commodities, produced, marketed, and sold in the pursuit of profit. But the second point, the point made by all three of these critics, is that while its commodity status may constrain rock's meanings, it does not (*pace* the Frankfurt analysis) determine them. Certainly rock records are churned out, like all mass cultural products, for instant gratification, but it is at least possible for artists to use the forms of mass communication to disturb rather than comfort: mass art can carry critical ideological force, it can expose and work with the contradictions of popular ideology—hence the role of rock music in the counterculture.

In the face of the sophisticated idealism of the best rock critics (and Marcus's book is an astonishing tour de force), socialists have two immediate tasks. The first is to provide a materialist account of leisure. Popular culture is leisure culture, and our understanding of the mass media of entertainment depends on our understanding of leisure. The problem of most current understandings lies in their assumption that people work in order to enjoy leisure. The values expressed in leisure are then treated as independent of work—they are the result of ideological conditions, the product of the manipulation of the leisure industries. But the point that Marx made long ago was that under capitalism, people enjoy leisure in order to work. The function of leisure, its possibilities, is determined by relations of production, and it is this determination that now needs attention. Only by treating leisure as an aspect of production (and not just as an aspect of consumption) will we be able to provide the materialist analysis of the audience that is so obviously missing from the accounts of rock as youth/counter/popular culture.

The second task is to take seriously the argument that mass culture is an expression of popular ideology and not just a means of manipulation. The left has a tendency to be both crude and contemptuous in its treatment of mass culture. Assertions are made about the "meaning" of mass cultural products which are both ignorant and arrogant: the complexity of both the products and their audience's use of them is ignored when, for example, rock music is dismissed by reference to the banality of its lyrics, or when it is assumed (in good positivist social-scientific fashion) that "systematic content analysis" tells us all we need to know about the effects of television or film. More disturbingly, socialists veer alarmingly between believing the best of working-class culture and the worst. One day workers are spontaneously class-conscious and assertive and unfoolable, the next day they are irredeemably racist and reactionary. The truth, of course, is that working-class culture is made up of contradictions and tensions and competing tendencies; it is articulated in fits and starts and fragments. Mass culture is a source of clues to these contradictions, and we must use it as such. (We need to explain, for example, the dominance of petit bourgeois values in so much of popular art.) And here I am in total agreement with these three rock critics. For the past twenty years I have enjoyed rock music as the most vital form of mass culture, and its vitality has come precisely from its contrary effects—a form of self-indulgence and escape on the one hand, a source of solidarity and dissatisfaction on the other. At one point in the *Grundrisse*, Marx comments that the capitalist, needing purchasers for his products, "searches for means to spur workers on to consumption, to give his wares new charms, to inspire them with new needs by constant chatter, etc. It is precisely this side of the relation of capital and labor which is an essentially civilizing moment, and on which the historic justification, but also the contemporary power of capital rests." [9]

Cultural commodities may support the contemporary power of capital, but they have their civilizing moments, too.

Notes

1. Obviously the members of the Frankfurt School were interested in popular culture before their arrival in the United States, but it was as a result of their American experience that they made clear the political implications of their cultural theories: "Increasingly, the Institut came to feel that the culture industry enslaved men in far more subtle and effective ways than the crude methods of domination practiced in earlier eras." See Martin Jay, *The Dialectical Imagination* (Boston: Little, Brown, 1973), pp. 212–218.

2. For American intellectuals and "the popular arts" in the 1930s, see Robert Warshow, "The Legacy of the '30s," in *The Immediate Experience* (New York: Atheneum, 1961). For the fifties, see Bernard Rosenberg and David M. White, eds., *Mass Culture* (New York: Free Press, 1965). The Frankfurt analysis was eventually popularized by Herbert Marcuse, particularly by his *One-Dimensional Man* (Boston: Beacon Press, 1964). Structuralist Marxism, in most respects an alternative version of Marx to that of Frankfurt, is in basic agreement with the Frankfurt School's assessment of the mass media. See, for example, Althusser's "Ideology and Ideological State Apparatus," in *Lenin and Philosophy* (New York: Monthly Review Press, 1971). There are significant differences between the various Marxist schools as to how best to read mass cultural objects, but not about their manipulative purposes and negative political effects.

3. These distinctions were bequeathed to cultural criticism by the Leavisite school of literary criticism. See Q. D. Leavis, *Fiction and the Reading Public* (1932), and F. R. Leavis and D. Thompson, *Culture and Environment* (1933), and more recently, Richard Hoggart, *The Uses of Literacy* (Oxford: Oxford University Press, 1957); Dwight Macdonald, *Against the American Grain* (1962); and Raymond Williams, *Communications* (1962). These days the distinctions are not argued but assumed. See, for example, Pauline Kael, "Art, Trash, and the Movies," in her *Going Steady* (Boston: Little, Brown, 1970).

4. These distinctions are present in both the Leavisite and Frankfurt analyses of culture (cf. Marcuse's famous comment to the effect that it's better to fuck in a field than in the back of a car), and on them rest the cultural practices of most Marxist political parties—hence, for example, the close connection of folk singers and the Communist party in both Europe and America.

5. The ideology of the folk song movement in the 1950s and 1960s was recorded in the magazine *Sing Out!*; see also A. L. Lloyd, *Folk Song in England* (New York: International Publishers, 1968).

6. The only "classical" Marxist critic for whom this argument would have made sense is Walter Benjamin. See his essay "The Work of Art in the Age of Mechanical Reproduction," in *Illuminations* (New York: Schocken Books, 1969).

7. The problems of reading texts as ideological products have been most elaborately discussed by structural critics; for their analyses of films, see recent issues of *Screen* or *Film Quarterly*. The only attempt I know at any kind of structural analysis of rock is Andrew Chester, "For a Rock Aesthetic," *New Left Review* 59 (1970).

8. Several people have discussed the petit bourgeois character of the counterculture and the American new left (e.g., R. Jacoby, "The Politics of Subjectivity," *New Left Review* 79 [1973]), but without relating this to the general character of American popular culture. One question that this raises for the analysis of rock is its relationship to its source musics—blues on the one hand, country music on the other. How do their values enter into rock? I can only raise such questions here, and point to a fruitful area for future cultural and historical analysis.

9. Karl Marx, *Grundrisse* (London: Penguin Books, 1973), p. 287.

Part V:
Ideology in Perception, Structure, and Genre

INTRODUCTION

Much of the most interesting recent left criticism has examined the way ideology is embodied in the regularizing and controlling effects of the technology of media, their structuring of perceptions of time and space, their formats, formulas, and genres. The authoritarian tendencies implicit in routinized artistic forms and technologies were perceived with extraordinary foresight by Walter Benjamin in "The Work of Art in the Age of Mechanical Reproduction" (1936) and T. W. Adorno in "Television and the Patterns of Mass Culture" (1954), on which many of the critics in this section and elsewhere in the collection have built.

All humans need a sense of order and control over the hazards of existence; all social organization, culture, and communication fulfill this need, and few left critics deny the progress bourgeois society has made in stabilizing the human condition. But the rage for order can become excessive in various ways: one is totalitarianism, another the boundless drive in a democratic, free-enterprise society to "give the people what they want." Mass culture's ever-increasing promises of control and regularization are enormously conservative, rendering people simultaneously fearful of any possible disruption of social routine and in awe of those who hold the mystery of establishing order. As Adorno observed about stereotyped media subjects and formats, "The more stereotypes become reified and rigid in the present setup of cultural industry, the less people are likely to change their preconceived ideas with the progress of their experience. The more opaque and complicated modern life becomes, the more people are tempted to cling desperately to cliches which seem to bring some order into the otherwise ununderstandable." [1] Marx said about the dynamic force of capitalism that everything solid melts into air; today he might have said that everything solid—all reality—becomes plastic, recombinable, subject to atomizing and compressing as in newscasts or *Reader's Digest*. Our conditioning to believe in the unlimited malleability of the world prepares us for extravagant claims of control over political reality by government and corporate authorities. If Walter Cronkite says, "And that's the way it is," then that's the way it is.

Gaye Tuchman's book *Making News*, excerpted here in "Representation and the News Narrative," suggests some of the many ways ideological assumptions may consciously or unconsciously influence camerawork in film or television, through the judgments implicit in choices of close-ups and long shots, angles of vision, foregrounding and backgrounding, body language and positioning between people (men and women, for example), and so forth. Tuchman's approach is similar to Gitlin's study of the ways the news media ideologically frame protest movements in *The Whole World Is Watching*, and to Erving Goffman's insightful, though less expressly political, studies in *Frame Analysis* and *Gender Advertisements*. The ideology of spatial relations in painting and still photography, especially the controlling power of freezing and framing experience, has been analyzed by John Berger, Roland Barthes, Susan Sontag, and Judith Williamson (who, in *Decoding Advertisements*, draws from the psychoanalytic theory of Jacques Lacan emphasizing the psychic determinants of visual perception).

The theoretical approach to the apparatus of film and television deriving from Continental semiology, Althusserian Marxism, and Lacanian psychoanalysis is summarized and sensibly criticized here by Dana Polan ("Bertolt Brecht and Daffy Duck: Toward a Politics of Self-Reflexive Cinema?") and Jane Gaines ("Women and Representation"). The opaque language in which this purportedly demystifying, deconstructive approach is often couched itself needs to be demystified and deconstructed, but its most salient points seem to be the following. The film spectator's instinctive identity with the camera eye's viewpoint and framing and the editor's cutting fosters a sense of being a "subject" in control of the filmic world rather than an "object" whose responses are controlled by the filmmaker. This aesthetic experience reinforces the social experience of the working class and petite bourgeoisie, who in reality are the objects of social manipulation but who through false consciousness identify with their rulers, thereby perceiving themselves as the controllers, not the controlled. Moreover, a gratifying sense of omnipotence in film viewing comes from the illusion that the order enunciated within the film is natural and inevitable rather than arbitrarily constructed, contrived and simulated through the artistic apparatus. "Realism," as the dominant genre of film and modern literature, depends on this illusion. (Resnais's and Robbe-Grillet's *Last Year at Marienbad* is often cited as a breakthrough film in its suggestions that the events narrated and the camera's viewpoint on them might have been different in any number of ways.) Again, the aesthetic illusion reinforces the illusion of the naturalness and inevitability of capitalist society and its products.

In psychoanalytic terms, according to semiotic theory, the capacity for language and symbolic representation develops at the same stage of childhood as does the awareness of gender differences—especially the male child's awareness of anatomical and existential differentiation from his mother, the phallus coming to symbolize differentiation in general. Hence, development of the power to make linguistic or pictorial representations and differentiations between objects of signification comes to be associated in every phase of culture with masculinity—giving rise, so to speak, to Jacques Derrida's yoking of *phallus* and *logos* into "phallogocentrism." In any social order such as capitalism, in which patriarchy coincides with class domination, the dominant political ideology is bound to be reproduced in the sex bias structured into all "signifying practices." In the context of semiotic-feminist film theory, the conventional filmic viewpoint and presumed spectator identity are invariably male; thus women viewers (and even filmmakers) are conditioned to identify with male norms here as everywhere else in the patriarchal social order. The very act of constituting a film image of women implies phallic domination of them, both in the voyeuristic gaze of the camera/spectator and in the male privileges of symbol making and objectification of the Other. (A favorite subject for this line of criticism is Alfred Hitchcock's work, particularly *Vertigo*, *Marnie*, *Rear Window*, and *Psycho*, in which these themes form an all-but-explicit subtext.)

Obviously, semiotic theory has important cultural implications and possible applications, especially in feminist criticism. These have been limited, however, by the coterie mentality of many of its proponents, who fancy themselves a political as well as cultural vanguard and who believe they are preparing the Revolution by writing deconstructive articles for obscure journals and making deconstructive films seen by a minute audience of initiates. They tend to dismiss any critical approach not based on their predicates and to display puritanic disapproval of all conventional aesthetic pleasures in high or mass culture, wanting instead (it sometimes seems) to inflict audiences with the dreary didacticism of Jean-Luc Godard's worst films.

One point on which the diverse schools of contemporary left criticism converge is the regularizing effect of mass media's structuring of time. As Rose K. Goldsen sums it up, "The power to control the way in which people experience time is a fundamental power, convertible into political and economic control and domination." [2] Gitlin says, "Media time and school time, with their equivalent units and curves of action, mirror the time of clocked labor and reinforce the seeming naturalness of clock time. . . . Even excitement is routinized, and the standard repeated TV format is an important component of the process." Goldsen develops the same theme:

Television is introducing massive changes in the way this whole country—especially children—experiences time, even though they are so ever present and widespread that most people hardly have a chance to notice how these rhythms are changing. "Sesame Street" teaches children the fragmented hour and the fifty-four-minute hour. . . . In my town, Ithaca, some of the schools now pace the periods in the lower grades in such a way that a twenty-minute lesson period is interrupted by a ten-minute break. This rhythm, reminiscent of the television half-hour, continues throughout the day. [3]

Tuchman, Goldsen, and Gitlin, along with Raymond Williams, John Fiske, and John Hartley in England, have also analyzed the tempo of television's "flow" through the broadcast day, bringing out the continuity in theme and structure between program content and commercials within individual shows and in the totality of the day's programs and commercials—continuity that once again reproduces the shape of dominant ideological assumptions. Gitlin's "Television Screens" (Part 4) explained how the drive for temporal constancy is reconciled with the contradictory drive for novelty and obsolescence, through the regularity of irregularity and programmed turnover within unchanging formats.

Roland Barthes says that capitalism's structuring of our perceptions reifies and commodifies historical time, just as it does spatial representation and organization (cf. Jeffrey Schrank's discussion of supermarkets and shopping malls [cited in introduction to Part 1] or Gitlin's study of the Hyatt Regency Hotel in Part 2), nature, dissent, industrial production, and on and on. History, along with every other aspect of the external world, becomes perceived as an immaculately conceived, completed entity, rather than as an uncertain, dialectical flux, with a direction that is contestable because it must be determined by will and labor.

Myth deprives the object of which it speaks of all History. In it, history evaporates. It is a kind of ideal servant: It prepares all things, brings them, lays them out, the master arrives, it silently disappears: all that is left for one to do is to enjoy this beautiful object without wondering where it comes from. Or even better: it can only come from eternity: since the beginning of time, it has been made for bourgeois man, the Spain of the *Blue Guide* has been made for the tourist, and "primitives" have prepared their dances with a view to an exotic festivity. We can see all the disturbing things which this felicitous figure removes from sight: both determinism and freedom. Nothing is produced, nothing is chosen: all one has to do is to possess these new objects from which all soiling trace of origin or choice has been removed. This miraculous evaporation of history is another form of a concept common to most bourgeois myths: the irresponsibility of man.[4]

Recent left critics have brought an increasingly refined political focus to genre studies such as those done in the forties and fifties by Robert Warshow and James Agee of the gangster, western, and comedy film. Genres that have come under study include realism, melodrama, serials, science fiction, detective stories, pornography, musical comedy, comic books and strips, fairy tales and other children's culture, and the various forms oriented toward female audiences in print and television. (Popular fiction with contemporary settings is one genre that calls for much more attention than it has received, along the lines of Umberto Eco's study of the James Bond books.)[5] The most fruitful approach has been to assume that any genre, like any technology or form, will adapt not only to different ideologies but also to different times and places; that is, genre should not be considered as intrinsic to one ideology, in the way semiologists have treated the realistic mode and the conventions of film and the novel as intractably bourgeois forms, regardless of their political content. In the dispute over realism between Georg Lukács and Bertolt Brecht (somewhat oversimplified here by Polan), both theorists envisioned the possibility of socialist versions of realism that maintain artistic integrity—as opposed to the propagandistic socialist realism of the Stalinist era—although they disagreed over the particular nature of authentic socialist realism.[6] Similarly, Dorfman and some other left critics writing about melodrama have defined its ideological function as sublimating the irresolvable conflicts in capitalist society into simply resolved, apolitical plots giving the audience a comforting illusion of control over events.[7] This assessment is largely an accurate one in the context of our present social order, but melodrama can also be and has been used in socialist culture (with varying degrees of artistic quality), where the danger is that issues that are not political *will* be politicized, rather than the reverse. Jane Gaines surveys recent explorations in female erotica as liberatory alternatives to pornography; Greg Blachford has similarly envisioned the possibility of nonexploitative pornography for homosexuals as well as heterosexuals.[8]

The potential ideological implications in genres, then, are multiple and conflicted rather than monolithic. But, as with the other conflicted elements in mass culture discussed in Part 4, those implications in any genre that can be turned to support the dominant ideology are apt to overshadow the ones that challenge it. Timothy Brennan demonstrates this tendency in "Masterpiece Theatre and the Uses of Tradition," an analysis of PBS's televised adaptations of middlebrow-to-highbrow fiction. He traces a recurrent motif celebrating the marriage of British imperial rule to American bourgeois entrepreneurship that is both congenial to the corporate sponsors of PBS and counteractive to the surface liberalism that is more frequently identified in PBS fare—especially by conservatives when they lobby to cut government funding for public broadcasting. A similar case of relatively deliberate ideological engineering in the genre of televised drama was Mobil Oil's presentation of the Royal Shakespeare Company's *Nicholas Nickleby* on syndicated TV. Mobil selflessly replaced its usual commercials with public service announcements in support of various charitable causes. These announcements were neatly juxtaposed with the storyline telling how the Cheryble brothers, a pair of charitable businessmen, save Nicholas and his family from poverty by setting him up in business. Thus the Dickens novel was turned into one long commercial for President Reagan's economic program to defund government spending on poverty programs in the faith that private enterprise would pick up the slack.

Or consider open versus closed genres. Critics such as Modleski, Laura Mulvey, and Jane Feuer have suggested that closed forms with definitive resolutions of conflict, defeat of evil forces, and completed time sequences endorse the bourgeois status quo and the patriarchal will to power, whereas serial forms— especially soap opera—are more dialectical, true to life, and female in their unending permutations of conflict and relationships. Feuer says, for example, "It might be argued that prime time family dynasty serials in particular offer a criticism of the institution of bourgeois marriage and romantic love, since marital happiness is never shown as a final state. (Nor is marriage seen as the symbol of narrative closure, as it is in so many comic forms. Indeed, to be happily married on a serial is to be on the periphery of the narrative.)" [9]

These are valid points, but it can also be argued that keeping the main characters in serials intact works against the kind of portrayal of dialectical processes needed to demystify bourgeois ideology. In contrast to Modleski's emphasis on the progressive aspects of soap opera's portrayal of time, Dennis Porter asserts that soap opera "mystifies everything it touches, including time. It represents the latter as a succession of frozen moments. The time of soap opera is merely incremental. Nothing grows or ripens in soap time and nothing is corroded or scattered." [10] Blondie, Dagwood, their children and little dog, too, have been fixed in the same vague moment of history and block of suburbia for half a century. This convention in serial forms not to allow characters to age contributes to the myths of ahistoricity and the immutability of capitalist society criticized by Barthes and Dorfman and Mattelart. (The convention has broken down somewhat in recent years, as Andrae notes about the Superman films.) Any definitive social change, such as revolution or peaceful conversion to socialism, is likely to be most effectively portrayed in a closed form—although an ingenious socialist artist might devise a good serial based on the problems of a revolutionary regime or life in a classless society. Similarly, unemployment and labor conflict, chronic ills of capitalism, do not lend themselves to episodic treatment, though Chaplin managed it in *Modern Times* within the limits of an eighty-five-minute film. In the seven years of "The Mary Tyler Moore Show," the only irrevocable firing occurred on the final episode; one earlier show has Murray getting fired after standing up to the boss, with conflict arising over whether his fellow workers will side with him—but he ends up groveling and being returned to the fold in time for the final commercial. Similarly, in a sequence of "All in the Family" episodes, Archie Bunker is first laid off and then laid up in a hospital where he is dependent on black and latino medical workers; his reactionary views are shaken, leading to a promise of real character development and "situation" comedy—in the Marxist sense of having a precise historical and socioeconomic site—but again a deus ex machina resolution restores his job, health, and prior attitudes so the series can go on unchanged.

Kate Ellis's study (Part 3) of the history of gothic romances is exemplary in its perceptions of the adaptations of a genre to changes in political economy and sex roles. Equally exemplary are Jack Zipes's Marxist studies of fairy tales, in which he applies developmental psychology, sociolinguistics, and reader-response criticism to the writing and reception of fairy tales in different historical moments and class situations; Zipes's analyses correct approaches such as Bruno Bettleheim's psychoanalytic studies of fairy tales that do not take adequate account of such variables. The progressive fairy tales that Zipes surveys here in "The Liberating Potential of the Fantastic in Contemporary Fairy Tales for Children" provide a model for the task of left critics to envision alternative themes and structures that might transcend the shaping of genres to capitalist ideology.

Notes

1. T. W. Adorno, "Television and the Patterns of Mass Culture," in *Mass Culture: The Popular Arts in America*, ed. Bernard Rosenberg and David Manning White (New York: Free Press, 1957), p. 484.

2. Rose K. Goldsen, *The Show and Tell Machine: How Television Works and Works You Over* (New York: Dial Press, 1977), p. 350.

3. Ibid., p. 250.

4. Roland Barthes, *Mythologies* (New York: Hill & Wang, 1972), p. 151.

5. Umberto Eco, "Narrative Structures in Fleming," *The Role of the Reader* (Bloomington: Indiana University Press, 1979), pp. 144–172.

6. Polan has further refined the analysis presented here in his book *The Politics of Film and the Avant-Garde* (Ann Arbor, Mich.: UMI Press, 1985). Also see Werner Mittenzwei, "The Brecht-Lukács Debate," in *Preserve and Create: Essays in Marxist Literary Criticism*, ed. Gaylord C. LeRoy and Ursula Beitz (New York: Humanities Press, 1973), pp. 199–230; and Georg Lukács, "Critical Realism and Socialist Realism," in *Realism in Our Time* (New York: Harper & Row, 1971), pp. 93–135. Among many recent works on Marxist theory and criticism of literary realism in general, see Stanley Aronowitz's *The Crisis in Historical Materialism* (New York: Praeger-Bergin, 1981); and Fredric Jameson's *Marxism and Form* (Princeton, N.J.: Princeton University Press, 1971) and *The Political Unconscious: Narrative as a Socially Symbolic Act* (Ithaca, N.Y.: Cornell University Press, 1981).

7. Ariel Dorfman, *The Empire's Old Clothes* (New York: Pantheon Books, 1983), pp. 91–107; Chuck Kleinhans, "Notes on Melodrama and the Family Under Capitalism," *Film Reader* 3 (1978): 40–48.

8. Greg Blachford, "Looking at Pornography: Erotica and the Socialist Morality," *Radical America* 13, no. 1 (1979): 7–17.

9. Jane Feuer, "Melodrama, Serial Form, and Television Today," *Screen* 25, no. 1 (1984): 4–17.

10. Dennis Porter, "Soap Time: Thoughts on a Commodity Art Form," *College En-*

glish 38, no. 8 (1977): 782–788; reprinted in Horace Newcomb, ed., *Television: The Critical View*, 2d ed. (New York: Oxford University Press, 1979), pp. 87–96.

Further Readings

Adorno, T. W. "Television and the Patterns of Mass Culture." In *Mass Culture: The Popular Arts in America*, ed. Bernard Rosenberg and David Manning White, pp. 474–478. New York: Free Press, 1957.

Altman, Rick, ed. *Genre: The Musical*. London: Routledge & Kegan Paul, 1981.

Angenot, Marc, and Darko Suvin. "Not Only But Also: Reflections on Cognition and Ideology in Science Fiction and SF Criticism." *Science Fiction Studies* 6, no. 2 (July 1979).

Auster, Al. "Gotta Sing! Gotta Dance! New Theory and Criticism on the Musical." *Cineaste* 12, no. 4 (1983): 30–39.

Barthes, Roland. *Image Music Text*. Trans. Steven Heath. New York: Hill & Wang, 1977.

Baum, L. Frank. *The Wizard of Oz*. Ed. Michael Patrick Hearn. New York: Schocken Books, 1983.

Benjamin, Walter. "The Work of Art In The Age Of Mechanical Reproduction." In *Illuminations*. New York: Harcourt Brace Jovanovich, 1968.

Berger, Arthur Asa. *The Comic-Stripped American*. Baltimore: Penguin Books, 1974.

Berger, John, and Jean Mohr. *Another Way of Telling*. New York: Pantheon, 1982.

Berger, John. *About Looking*. New York: Pantheon Books, 1980.

————. *And Our Faces, My Heart, Brief as Photos*. New York: Pantheon Books, 1984.

————. *Ways of Seeing*. London: British Broadcasting Company/Penguin Press, 1972.

Bloch, Ernst. "A Philosophical View of the Detective Novel." *Discourse*, no. 2 (Summer 1980): pp. 32–52.

Buhle, Paul. "Dystopia as Utopia: Howard Phillips Lovecraft and the Unknown Content of American Horror Literature." *Minnesota Review*, no. 6 (Spring 1976): pp. 118–131.

————. "The New Comics and American Culture." In *Literature in Revolution*, ed. Abbott White and Charles Newman. New York: Holt, Rinehart & Winston, 1972.

Cawelti, John. *Adventure, Mystery, and Romance*. Chicago: University of Chicago Press, 1976.

————. *The Six-Gun Mystique*. Bowling Green, Ohio: Bowling Green University Popular Press, 1973.

deLauretis, Teresa. *Alice Doesn't: Feminism, Semiotics, Cinema*. Bloomington: Indiana University Press, 1984.

Elkins, Charles. "An Approach to the Social Functions of American Science Fiction." *Science Fiction Studies* 4, no. 3 (1977): 228–232.

Ellis, Kate. "I'm Black and Blue from the Rolling Stones and I'm Not Sure How I Feel About It: Pornography and the Feminist Imagination." *Socialist Review*, nos. 75–76 (May–August 1984): 103–126.

Elsaessar, Thomas. "Tales of Sound and Fury." *Monogram*, no. 4 (1973): 3.

Feuer, Jane. *The Hollywood Musical*. Bloomington: Indiana University Press, 1984.

Goffman, Erving. *Frame Analysis*. New York: Harper & Row, 1974.

Griffin, Susan. *Pornography and Silence: Culture's Revenge Against Nature*. New York: Harper & Row, 1981.

Jameson, Fredric. "Ideology, Narrative Analysis, and Popular Culture." *Theory and Society*, no. 4 (1977): 543–559.

————. "On Raymond Chandler." *Southern Review* 6, no. 3 (1970): 642–650.

Kleinhans, Chuck, and Julia Lesage. "Marxism and Film Criticism: The Current Situation." *Minnesota Review*, no. 8 (Spring 1977): 146–149.

Knight, Stephen. *Form and Ideology in Crime Fiction*. Bloomington: Indiana University Press, 1981.

Long, Elizabeth. *The American Dream and the Popular Novel*. Boston: Routledge & Kegan Paul, 1985.

Lowe, Donald M. *History of Bourgeois Perception*. Chicago: University of Chicago Press, 1982.

Mandel, Ernest. *Delightful Murder: A Social History of the Crime Story*. Minneapolis: University of Minnesota Press, 1984.

Metz, Christian. *Language and Cinema*. The Hague: Mouton, 1974.

———. *Film Language*. London: Oxford University Press, 1974.

Nichols, Bill. *Ideology and the Image: Social Representation in the Cinema and Other Media*. Bloomington: Indiana University Press, 1984.

Perelman, Les. "Teaching Science Fiction." *The Radical Teacher*, no. 15 (December 1979): 31–34.

Porter, Dennis. *The Pursuit of Crime: Art and Ideology in Detective Fiction*. New Haven, Conn.: Yale University Press, 1982.

Radway, Janice A. *Reading the Romance: Women, Patriarchy, and Popular Literature*. Chapel Hill: University of North Carolina Press, 1984.

Renault, Gregory. "Science Fiction as Cognitive Estrangement: Darko Suvin and the Marxist Critique of Mass Culture." *Discourse*, no. 2 (Summer 1980): 113–141.

Soble, Alan. *Pornography: Marxism, Feminism, and the Future of Sexuality*. New Haven, Conn.: Yale University Press, 1986.

Sontag, Susan. *On Photography*. New York: Dell, 1977.

Suvin, Darko. *Metamorphoses of Science Fiction: On the Poetics and History of a Literary Genre*. New Haven, Conn.: Yale University Press, 1979.

———. "The State of the Art in Science Fiction Theory: Determining and Delimiting the Genre." *Science Fiction Studies* 6, no. 1 (1979).

Williams, Raymond. *Television: Technology and Cultural Form*. New York: Schocken Books, 1975.

Williamson, Judith. *Decoding Advertisements*. London: Boyars, 1978.

Wood, Robin. "Never Never Change, Always Gonna Dance." *Film Comment*, September–October 1979, pp. 29–31.

Wright, Will. *Sixguns and Society: A Structural Study of the Western*. Berkeley and Los Angeles: University of California Press, 1975.

Zipes, Jack. *Breaking the Magic Spell: Radical Theories of Folk and Fairy Tales*. Austin: University of Texas Press, 1979.

———. *Don't Bet on the Prince: Contemporary Feminist Fairy Tales in North America and England*. New York: Methuen, 1986.

———. *The Trials and Tribulations of Little Red Riding Hood*. South Hadley, Mass.: Bergin & Garvey, 1985.

REPRESENTATION AND THE NEWS NARRATIVE: THE WEB OF FACTICITY

GAYE TUCHMAN

The language of television news film is a recently evolved foreign tongue that we have all learned to translate but few of us speak. Precisely because that language is quickly grasped, it makes accessible some presuppositions of news. The visual rendition of the web of facticity, it also serves the interests of news organizations in controlling work by decreasing the variability of raw materials, and it serves the newsworker's professional interests by enabling autonomy and protecting his or her intent.

Unlike written copy, film and videotape maximize the reporters' and cameramen's intent. One can change the written word but cannot easily alter the recorded spoken word to insert a new phrase. Nor can one change the distance between camera and speaker, the framing of the picture, short of filming again. Some alteration, of course, is possible. One can reorder sequences of film to create an argument unintended by the person filmed or the one filming. But there are distinct limits to the alternatives possible without refilming. Those limits mean that the rules governing the visual language of news film must be more explicit and hence more accessible than the rules governing the written and spoken word.

Unfortunately, analysts of news do not customarily treat news film as a visual language. Rather, they naively suppose that news film captures reality without imposing its own rules. To be sure, echoing an early essay by Lang and Lang (1953), analysts may ask what has been omitted from the camera's frame. But since news film is a moving picture, critics give in to what might be called the "representational temptation." Worth describes that temptation this way:

It would, of course, be tempting to argue that pictorial events—at least those on a "representational" level—are meaningful because they are signs that have an iconic relation to the "real world"; that, in contrast to verbal events . . . recognition of pictures is physiologically easier; and that, therefore, assumptions of existence are more reasonably made. Given this tempting argument, one can then continue by saying that when we look at pictures, meaning is developed by . . . a simple "natural" process of recognition without codes, conventions, and social schemata. (1978, 19, 20)

However, as Worth points out, the term *representational*, whether applied to drawing, photographs, or news film, must refer to codes, conventions, and social schemata, identified as representational by members of a specific culture.

Anthropological work on conventions of documentary filmmaking in nonindustrial cultures suggests that television news film builds upon conventions of

Adapted from sections of Tuchman, *Making News: A Study in the Construction of Reality* (New York: Free Press, 1978), and "The Technology of Objectivity," *Urban Life and Culture* 2, no. 1 (1973): 3–26.

representation. Adair, Worth, and their students have instructed Navajos, deaf-mutes, and ghetto adolescents on the operation of cameras and editing devices. Left on their own to discover shots and sequences, the filmmakers produced cinematic variations of their verbal languages and storytelling traditions. For instance, Navajo silent films contain a plethora of walking sequences, recreating the role of walking as a connective between two activities, as in Navajo oral narratives. The makers of these films go out of their way to avoid close-ups of faces. And, interestingly, the films are far more accessible to Navajo speakers than to English speakers. Worth and Adair (1970, 22) report the reaction of a monolingual Navajo to a *silent* film made by a bilingual Navajo artist. She said, "I cannot understand English. It was telling all about [the subject of the film] in English, which I couldn't understand."

This Navajo's reaction to the silent film warns us to avoid the representational temptation, and suggests that we should regard television news film as professionally and organizationally produced patterns of news culture. To be sure, news film presents itself to us as actual representations, not as symbols and signs manipulated by set conventions. This self-presentation is specifically contained in the word used by newsworkers and filmmakers to indicate film taken of events in progress. Applied to demonstrations, wars, public meetings, and other sorts of seemingly nonstaged gatherings, that term is *actuality*. Following the Navajo's warning, though, one must understand the claim to actuality and actual representation as a claim to facticity and as a visual rendition of the web of facticity. To paraphrase Goffman (1974, 450), the acceptance of representational conventions as facticity makes reality vulnerable to manipulation. Identifying those conventions as artful manipulations enables one to regard filmed events as social accomplishments—the product of newswork.

NEWS FILM AND CULTURAL
DEFINITIONS OF FACTICITY

News film casts an aura of representation by its explicit refusal to give the appearance of manipulating time and space. Instead, its use of time and space announces that the tempo of events and spatial arrangements have *not* been tampered with to tell this story. By seeming *not* to arrange time and space, news film claims to present facts, not interpretations. That is, the web of facticity is embedded in a supposedly neutral—not distorted—synchronization of film with the rhythm of everyday life. Like the construction of a newspaper story, the structure of news film claims neutrality and credibility by avoiding conventions associated with fiction. To associate distortion (lack of neutrality) with the conventions of fiction both limits the filmic vocabulary and defines fact by contrast, much as the label "news analysis" on a specific newspaper article reinforces the facticity of stories presented without that label.

·   ·   ·   ·   ·   ·   ·   ·   ·   ·   ·   ·   ·   ·   ·   ·   ·   ·   ·

News film's arrangement of space eschews dramatic conventions to create an aura of facticity. In cinema various angles are used to forward the dramatic action. For instance, low camera placement may emphasize suspense. This technique, common in the 1930s, was used in *The Maltese Falcon* to intensify Sidney Greenstreet's forbidding girth. The camera may be placed above an action to suggest danger, as often is the case in the perennial police chase across rooftops. This type of wide-angle shot may also be used to emphasize the physical distance of one event from another.[1]

Television news film is rarely shot from above when recording *animate* objects, but towns, forests, escape routes of bank robbers, tornado paths, and battlefields are often filmed from a helicopter. For a news cameraworker, facticity is produced by meeting an event "head on," with camera placement fixed to simulate the angle of a person of average height confronting another person eye to eye. All else is condemned as "distortion," and the team responsible for the affronting footage is likely to receive an official reprimand.

Cameramen see little variation in the way stories are photographed. As the head cameraman at NEWS [a pseudonym for the television station used in this study] explained, one sets up the camera, lines up the reporter and the persons to be interviewed, and then shoots. Although prodded, he saw no variation on this simple procedure, and I never observed a significant variation in either an interview or a press conference. On the contrary, public relations officers arranged the typical press conference to facilitate this procedure, and the room in which the governor held his press conferences was constructed to enable the head-on, fixed-point perspective.[2]

Significant variations on this procedure are found only when unscheduled events of a noninterview nature are being filmed. Then the cameraperson must battle to maintain control of the allocation of space. This may occur at a fire, a demonstration, a riot. Dan Rather (1977) reports that when covering a demonstration, one seeks the safety of height; in war one may shoot while crawling on the ground, or from helicopters entering or leaving battle areas.

Significantly, since "bird's-eye" and "worm's-eye" perspectives are generally reserved for inanimate objects, shooting participants in demonstrations, fires, and riots from these perspectives symbolically converts the participants into objects. Rather than individuals, they appear as components of some quantitatively portrayed mass. That is, just as statistics on crime are presented as independent phenomena (in news accounts the murder rate increases or decreases for unanalyzed reasons, as though having a life of its own [Dahlgren, 1977]), the mass-as-thing comes alive. Like a tornado or crime rate, the mass seems independent of its individual components.

This view of the conversion of numbers of citizens into a mass is supported by other professional preferences for the representation of neutral renditions of space. Film that is jumpy is dramatic; it captures a feeling of tumult. News reporting supposedly avoids rendering feeling by its use of time and space. Accordingly, as Dan Rather (1977) mentions, at a demonstration, where a jostled camera might result in jumpy film, the camera is placed on a nearby roof or in a suitable window. There, the otherwise-avoided bird's-eye view provides steady film and a wider angle. Significantly, in this situation, the cameramen working at NEWS frequently had to explain to editors why this camera placement was used. Typically, one cameraman said, "I had to go upstairs to shoot it; there was so much pushing." However, cameramen never search out a high spot when other shoving newsworkers interfere with their shooting a single individual, as is frequently the case when dignitaries arrive at an airport or courtroom. In filming one person, the head-on perspective is maintained. Neither the dignitary nor the newsworkers are transformed into a tornadolike mass. Filming the newsworkers-as-mass would show that newsworkers (not the flow of occurrences) create views, and so would challenge the credibility of news. Such an overview would reveal that much of the excitement of the event has been generated by newsworkers. And just as newspaper reporters use quotation marks to claim impartiality and credibility, so, too, news footage must avoid implying that newsworkers and organizations generate both occurrences and their rendition as events. Supposedly, to imply involvement is to undermine the web of facticity.

NEWS FILM AND SOCIAL ROLES

Cameramen use the head-on perspective for individuals, and in news footage those individuals are generally legitimated and quasi-legitimated officials. Those whose activities break the social order—rioters and demonstrators, like tornadoes and floods—are filmed from a different perspective. In general, news film's adaptations of social roles stress neutrality. By neutrality I do not mean the refusal to take sides in a dispute, for the anchoring of the news net in time and space necessarily involves the news organization in the process of legitimation. Rather, I mean that the visual portrayal of roles stresses noninvolvement: reporters filmed at the scene of a story are clearly portrayed as being removed from, and uninvolved in, the action sequences. Both reporters and newsmakers are framed as officials and professionals, as one would see them if one sat in front of their desks. These social meanings—seeming representations—are achieved by filmic conventions regarding camera range. The framings are designed to be neither intimate nor distant.

Drawing on the work of Grosser, a portrait painter, Hall (1966) attributes social meaning to the use of height, width, and depth on a horizontal and vertical plane, applicable to a painting or a frame of film. Hall describes four categories of space and their social meanings. One of these is public space, defined by Grosser's statement that bodies perceived from a distance of more than thirteen feet are seen "as something having little connection with ourselves." Hall's other classifications are social distance (four to twelve feet) and intimate distance (zero to eighteen inches). Each is divided into a "close" and "far" phase, whose cultural usage Hall describes.[3]

Hall (1966, 112–115) suggests that at close personal distance "one can hold or grasp the other person. . . . A wife can stay inside the circle of her husband's personal zone with impunity. For another woman to do so is an entirely different story." Hall goes on to discuss "keeping someone at arm's length away." That far personal distance "extends from a point that is just outside easy touching distance by one person to a point where two people can touch fingers if they extend both arms. . . . Subjects of personal interest and involvement can be discussed

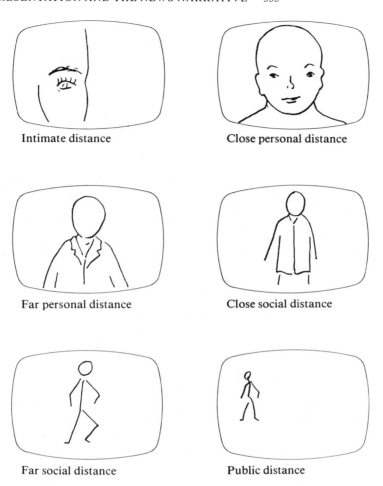

Figure 1

at this distance." Far personal distance melts into close social distance: "Impersonal business occurs at this distance, and in the close phase there is more involvement than in the far phase. People who work together tend to use close social distance." Far social distance is, according to Hall, "the distance to which people move when someone says, 'stand away so I can look at you.' Business and social discourse conducted at the far end of social distance has a more formal character than if it occurs inside the close phase [of social distance]." In sum, Hall suggests that different distances have different social meanings; more specifically, he implies that patterned role relationships are expressed through physical distance.

Newsworkers' use of social distance conforms to Hall's descriptions, sketched in figure 1 as they would appear on a television screen. Of these six possible framings, three are commonly found in television news film. These are far per-

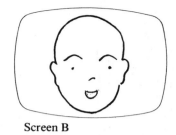

Screen A   Screen B

Figure 2

sonal distance, close social distance, and far social distance, all of which, according to Hall, are used in our culture for discussions ranging from "personal interest and involvement" to more formal "business and social talks." I refer to these three as "talking distance," and to close personal distance and intimate distance as "touching distance."

The meanings that newsmen attribute to talking and touching distance are demonstrated by considering frame arrangements rarely found on television news presentations. On screen A of figure 2, the subject is framed as in the customary television close-up technique. On screen B, the subject is framed as in a dramatic close-up technique. Both screens present a "talking head," the newsworker's term for film showing someone speaking in the studio or at least removed from any action. By providing a greater distance between the camera lens (viewer) and the subject, screen A is supposedly more impartial; being farther away, it literally seems more detached. "Coming in tight" on the talking head, as screen B does, is not seen as neutral. The framing sketched in screen B is used to capture moments of drama, which newsmen do not associate with "straight, hard news." As one cameraman-informant explained, screen B is used for dramatic impact when someone with an "interesting face" is expressing emotion. An example he cited was Rose Kennedy discussing her dead sons. Here, the camera would come in on her face and try to capture a tear. Again, the exception is interesting. As the NEWS cameraman noted, Rose Kennedy "occupies a special place" in the "hearts of Americans." Rendering her in an involved manner can still connote neutrality, since that framing captures her particular role in American society. Supposedly, admiration for her is "above politics."

Significantly, the cameraman volunteered that he would *absolutely* never use that range technique on the talking heads of reporters. Indeed, when one unfortunate cameraman framed a TV reporter in touching distance (to compensate for a previous error in the filming), the work was scornfully disparaged by colleagues. As newsworkers, television reporters must be shown as nonparticipants whose role is to comment and describe neutrally. The camera may not suggest that the TV workers have emotions or ideas about the story they are reporting, that the reporters get "too close." [4]

Public distance is all but forbidden in recording events involving "individuals," even though those events may normally be seen from a public distance. One might suppose that television news film would use public distance to give viewers the illusion of having attended an event or speech. This may be called neutral because, theoretically, it would decrease the emotional involvement between viewer and speaker. However, public distance precludes the personal and social contact that is the hallmark of television news. Public distance *de*personalizes and is used only to show masses, not individuals. (Conversely, intimate distance is said to capture emotion at the cost of objectivity.) Since news portrays individuals (as participants in or symbols of events) and individuals' opinions about events, the use of public distance is "unnewslike." Furthermore, public distance greatly limits the ability of news film to capture emotions. As Hall (1966, 117) points out, "Most actors know that at thirty or more feet, the subtle shades of meaning conveyed by the normal voice are lost, as are the details of facial expression and movement." Recording at public distance, the film might gain exaggerated neutrality, but it would lose the other central characteristic of television news film, emotional impact.

Usage of talking distance depends on who is talking. Anchorpersons and commentators appear in standard torso shots, emphasizing their head and shoulders and initially including their hands holding the program script. The camera operators attempt to project friendliness to the audience through this framing, and to maintain neutrality by keeping the torso framing standard throughout a sequence of stories. The consistency of the camera work serves as the visual correlative of the newspaper's news-speak, symbolically proclaiming neutrality by announcing, "We treat one event the same way we treat any other."

The head and shoulders of a talking head, whether that of a mayor, senator, or secretary, may be similarly framed or presented at a greater distance from the camera lens (varying between Hall's far personal and close social distance). All newsmakers are presented from this same distance or combination of distances, again connoting neutral presentation.[5] The anchorperson, commentators, and newsmakers may be portrayed in a tighter (closer) shot than the TV reporter at the scene of a story, who appears in close-social or far-social distance. When a reporter is shot interviewing a newsmaker, at least the reporter's torso appears on-screen. More frequently, and as a general rule, the reporter is portrayed standing in front of the scene of a story, the camera moving in, eventually focusing on the reporter from the waist up; the event in the background is shown at "depersonalizing" public distance. But the reporter is "farther" from the camera lens and viewer than either an anchorperson or newsmaker. This technique includes the events in the background and shows the reporter detached from the event and not part of it.[6]

The distinction between cinematic detachment and participation connotes neutrality. A movie actor would be shown acting in a crowd, despite the extent to which such a shot might initially block the viewer's clear identification of him. The movie director would want to portray the hero acting with others to show his involvement, in contrast to the intentional portrayal of the uninvolved reporter. A newspaper reporter, hired by NEWS despite his lack of television experience, quickly learned his "role" in on-film reporting. Editing his footage, the technicians told him before the editors could, "Next time you cover a story like this, stand in *front* of the picketers."

To state that television newsworkers customarily use certain framings to convey social roles is to suggest that television news film employs a lexicon of standard shots. Compiling that lexicon, the Glasgow Media Group (1980) has reduced television news images to about fifty shots and variations. Such limitation strongly suggests that television news speaks through codes. The visual detachment of reporters from the phenomena placed in the background may be seen as a code for detachment. Additionally, news film codifies places and events.

STANDARD SHOTS OF PEOPLE, PLACES, AND EVENTS

Consider some standard shots commonly used in television footage to claim representational facticity. First, by framing reporters in front of easily identified symbolic locations, news film informs viewers that the reporter is actually *at* the scene of the story. For instance, a White House correspondent is framed against the portico of the White House; a London reporter, in front of Big Ben; a Soviet correspondent, against Red Square; a reporter in Prague, on a bridge overlooking the Old Town. Alternately, as in the last example, if a story concerns general activities in a city, news film may show a slow panorama of the skyline, sometimes drawn from files or, if the film library is so disordered that retrieval is expensive or if construction has made old footage "inaccurate," the skyline may be shot again. Similarly, exteriors of buildings set the stage for interviews and "actuality" once the reporter is inside the building.

Second, events are coded by the supposed essence of the ongoing activity. For instance, a union strike is symbolized by picketers milling outside an uncrossed plant gate. Or, if access to the plant is made available by the management, the film may show shut-down machines, or simply a locked gate (see Glasgow Media Group, 1980). Similarly, strikes by farm workers are symbolized by pictures of unpeopled fields, unused machinery, and crops described as growing too ripe. Jungle wars, such as in Southeast Asia, are symbolized by soldiers cutting their way through dense growth, helicopters removing the wounded, and shots of trenches, fortifications, and of soldiers resting, crawling, or throwing themselves on their bellies to avoid the enemy's fire. Murders are symbolized by blood on sidewalks and by car windshields sprayed with bullets. Drug busts result in film of piles of packets, displayed on a table in the room where they were found or in the locked storeroom of the police property clerk. Police stakeouts are symbolized by officers on roofs, in windows, and crouching in doorways or behind cars.[7] In all these examples, one quick look tells American viewers what the story is.

Third, people are presented symbolically. Not only are they garbed in the clothing appropriate to their occupation, but also nonlegitimated individuals are made to typify all members of their particular group or class. NBC's coverage of a strike at an automobile plant during the Vietnam War provided a particularly apt example of this phenomenon, especially since Detroit had experienced racial violence. A correspondent interviewed a black striker, his wife beside him, in his home, and asked about their financial problems due to the strike and their feelings about their son, then on combat duty in Vietnam. Similarly, stories about fluctuations in agricultural prices feature an "average farmer." Stories about rising homicide rates in small cities and towns are set in a "typical American small town," where a "typical citizen" (or alternatively, a local official) tells of his or her life-style and fears.

Said to lend drama and human meaning to the news (Epstein 1973), symbols accomplish two factors associated with the web of facticity. They provide "actual" supplementary evidence: people as symbols tell of the impact of news events on their lives so that the reporter need not present interpretations. The symbols thus "protect" reporters from presenting themselves as being involved in the story. And the use of symbols strengthens the distinction between legitimated newsmakers and "just plain folks." The talking heads of congresspersons and senators, mayors and chairpersons, cabinet members and generals, offer their own opinions and demonstrate their own expertise (unless, of course, the story concerns the daily routines of an "average" member of Congress or other official). Although they are said to be representatives of the people by dint of their legitimated positions and power, they speak for themselves. But symbols are only symbols: people whose ideas and opinions are not news in and of themselves. They are not representatives but are assumed to be *representations* of others who are coping with a mutual dilemma. When the dilemma has passed—the strike has ended or the town has started to recover from the hurricane—the symbol loses all news value and once again is merely an ordinary person undifferentiated from the mass of ordinary people, a member of the public.

When someone is a symbol, he or she is framed at talking distance but is rarely shown seated behind a desk or conference table.[8] More likely settings are the home, supermarket, a blue-collar worksite, or some scene of common recreational activity. Again, the use of such settings sets the symbol off from other persons interviewed on the news. Occasional variations in camerawork also serve to differentiate the symbol from legitimated newsmakers. If the symbol is speaking about a particularly emotional topic, the film may sometimes approximate touching distance; tears and other displays of emotion are welcomed by the now more intimate camera. These displays do not function as an attribute of the individual. They are social indicators of the plight of a group, whether the group is parents with incurably ill children, wives of soldiers missing in action, or families made homeless by a natural disaster. Similarly, the joy of returning prisoners of war and their families, whether captured at touching or talking distance, symbolizes the joy of all in that situation.

Why does television news use such symbols and framings? Identifying these devices as professional skills that lend an aura of neutrality to the web of facticity does not suffice. For by serving as basic components of news-film narratives, these frames also place professionalism in the service of organizational flexibility.

. . . .

The news media's bureaucratic organization of time and space is reified in the news narrative's organization of frames of film. And the use of filmic conventions and narrative forms enables reporters to ensure that their rendition of stories will not be mauled by editors. It facilitates the news organization's ability to be flexible, to move reporters from story to story during the day. It enables film crews to cover any assignment, to be generalists who can transform any idiosyncratic occurrence into a conventional news event.

. . . .

INTERPRETING SURVEY FINDINGS

The association of camera techniques with cultural definitions and patterned role relationships has at least one implication for research on mass communications. With a consistency almost unnerving to the sociologist aware of the extent to which television cameras construct a reality, national surveys continue to report that Americans, faced with conflicting media reports of the same event, are "most inclined to believe" television news reports (Roper Organization, Inc., 1971).

The question, asked in 1959, 1961, 1963, 1964, 1967, 1968, and 1971, was, "If you got conflicting or different reports of the same news story from radio, television, the magazines and the newspapers, which of the four versions would you be most inclined to believe—the one on radio or television or magazines or newspapers?" Except for 1959, when 32 percent responded "newspapers," the modal answer was "television." The percentage of people answering "television" increased from 29 percent in 1959 to 49 percent in 1971, while the answer "newspapers" decreased from 32 percent in 1959 to 20 percent in 1971. Throughout the entire period, television was cited least often in the response to the converse question, "Which of the four versions would you be least inclined to believe?" The percentage answering "television" varied from 5 to 9 percent; "newspapers," from 24 to 30 percent.

A *Time*–Louis Harris poll in 1969 (*Time* 1969, 39) found that "while a majority believes that newspapers are 'sometimes unfair and slanted in news coverage,' only a minority of one in three sees television news this way." According to *Newsweek* (1970: 59), a Gallup poll found, two months after Agnew's attack on the media, that 40 percent of the respondents believed television news "deals fairly with all sides in presenting news dealing with political and social issues," and 35 percent believed this to be true of newspapers. Slightly more people believed that newspapers "tend to favor one side" (45 percent) than believed this of television (42 percent), although respondents made "apparently no distinction between news and editorial pages of newspapers."

Two polls taken by the Opinion Research Center (ORC) for *TV Guide* (Hickey 1972; Youman 1972) support the Roper data. The question asked was, "Which of these media do you think is the fairest and most objective in its political reporting and coverage?" and included the same four media as options. Forty-seven percent answered "television" on the first survey; 53 percent on the second. The percentage answering "newspapers" was 18 percent and 15 percent, respectively. However, ORC qualified the results (Hickey 1972, 8), finding "waning confidence in TV news the further one departs from simple life-styles. College-trained, professional people, big-city dwellers, Easterners, and higher-wage earners are far less convinced of television's preeminent right to be called 'the fairest and most objective' news medium." In both the ORC and Roper studies, the percentage answering either "magazines" or "radio" was appreciably smaller than those expressing confidence in either television or newspapers.

Apparently, and frequently mistakenly, "seeing is believing." Television news presentations lend themselves to acceptance of this everyday dictum, because a television presentation entails more dimensions of perception than either newspapers relegated to the written word, radio programs bound to spoken presentations, or magazine formats wedded to the written word and the still photograph. On television, the viewer can "judge" most or all of these dimensions at the same time, with the added benefit of moving films. A man's facial expressions as he makes a statement may seem to serve as a check on his commitment to his views. Furthermore, some television viewers, who regularly watch a specific news program, identify as a friend the news announcer who enters their home and insist that "Tom Jones of Channel 1" tells the truth. It is certainly not surprising, then, that television news presentations are held up to be more credible than news presentations of other media. Nor is it surprising that viewers ignore the sociological dictum that "the facts never speak for themselves."

However, these explanations do not suffice. In the last few years, television news has been under repeated attack from both governmental and nonofficial sources, particularly radical and reactionary political groups. The Presidential Commission on Civil Disorders scored some media practices; Agnew launched an attack on television news in the name of "middle America"; mass media magazines pointed to television's ability to construct the news in the cutting room. Others, picking up on Lang and Lang's (1953) early suggestion that live newscasts may not "accurately" telecast an event, pointed to the ability of television personnel to decide which parts of an event might be excluded from the film frame.

Given these criticisms, why do more Americans place greater faith in television news reports than in the reports of other news media? Certainly one explanation is that many citizens reject the criticisms and attacks on television news. Another and more powerful explanation is inherent in the very techniques used in television news film. As previously discussed, whenever possible—and it is almost always possible—television news film records events and interviews in a manner consistent with "visual objectivity," and it arranges space to give the impression of a business conversation between colleagues. That is, the frames of film telecast more than closely resemble the visual perceptions of an American in a specific type of everyday interaction. It is possible that by recreating these conditions of everyday life, television news film masks from the viewer the extent to which newsmen may and must manipulate film.

One may hypothesize that Americans "trust" television news more than news disseminated by other media, not because "seeing is believing," but rather because viewers are seeing events and interviews filmed in a specific way, a way that draws upon taken-for-granted cultural definitions of visual perception and patterned role expectations concerning the use of space. One might even suppose that television news film constructs reality to match everyday conditions of multidimensional perception and so maintains greater credibility than other media restricted to reproducing events through one or two dimensions of perception. However, such a possibility is highly speculative. It requires confirmation from carefully controlled studies of viewers' reactions to news stories filmed by both objective and nonobjective techniques.

. . . .

NEWS AND THE CONSTRUCTION OF REALITY

Americans take as given that news presentations are ahistorical, atheoretical accounts of daily happenings in specific institutions, employing the logic of the concrete. We take for granted the daily production of news as a consumer commodity without noting its historic association with the development of advertising by the penny press. We take for granted the embeddedness of the news net in legitimated institutions and the existence of centralized news gathering, as handed down to us from the nineteenth century. And we fail to realize how that embeddedness militates against the emergence of new forms of news. For so long as hard news continues to be associated with the activities of legitimated institutions and the spatial and temporal organization of newswork remains embedded in their activities, news reproduces itself as a historical given. It not only defines and redefines, constitutes and reconstitutes, social meanings; it also defines and redefines, constitutes and reconstitutes, ways of doing things—existing processes in existing institutions.

Notes

1. The camera may also be placed so as to give a limited view of the action. Clearly, news film eschews a limited view of an action, for it aims "to capture accurately" an event. Although it has been suggested that TV news film may show a limited view of an action, giving the "wrong" impression of what happened, as in the telecasting of MacArthur Day (a 1953 Chicago parade in honor of Gen. Douglas MacArthur; Lang and Lang 1953) or of riots (National Advisory Commission on Civil Disorders 1968, 363), newsworkers claim to have recorded the crucial events.

2. The governor sat behind a desk on a raised podium. A platform near the back of the room was provided for television news cameras. From the platform, cameramen could shoot over the heads of reporters and record the governor from a head-on perspective. Designing a room suitable for all newsworkers presupposes a familiarity with newswork not yet available to most radical social movements.

One might counter that a film frame of a man sitting behind a desk represents a variation on this perspective, because the desk is in fixed space and thereby influences camera placement. However, the cameraworkers retain the power to rearrange space for their own purposes, including use of the appropriate perspective. They may alter the spatial relationship between desk and desk chair, rearrange items on the desk top, or choose to film the newsmaker sitting in an armchair rather than at his desk. They may suggest the angle at which the newsmaker faces the camera and the point toward which the newsmaker directs his or her eyes. Having exercised this power, a cameraperson frequently lowers the tripod to make sure the sitting person will be filmed in a head-on perspective.

3. According to Grosser, "At more than thirteen feet away . . . the human figure can be seen in its entirety as a single whole. At this distance . . . we are chiefly aware of its outlines and proportions. . . . The painter can look at his model as if he were a tree in a landscape or an apple in a still life. But four to eight feet is the portrait distance. . . . The painter is near enough so that his eyes have no trouble in understanding the sitter's solid forms, yet he is far enough away so that the foreshortening of the forms presents no real problem. Here, at the normal distance of social intimacy and easy conversation, the sitter's soul begins to appear. . . . Nearer than three feet, within touching distance, the soul is far too much in evidence for any sort of disinterested observation" (in Hall 1966, 71–72).

4. Occasions prompting newsworkers to show emotion become professional gossip and sometimes cause conversation among audience members. One example of this break in emotional distance was Walter Cronkite's self-presentation during reports on President John Kennedy's assassination. The reporter's ability to contain emotions and so create social distance may be particularly striking to his or her intimates. Rather (1977) recalls his wife's amazement that he reported on that presidential assassination without showing sorrow or grief.

5. Sometimes I witnessed the filming of exceptions to these generalizations. On every observed occasion, though, the affronting footage was the only available method of filming, and the crew was quick to tell the managing editor why they had filmed the way they did.

6. When reporters break the association between patterned role relationships and camera range by getting involved in an event, other newsworkers consider it newsworthy. One example of this is John Chancellor's hasty exit from the 1968 Democratic Convention. He spoke on the air as he was being carried out of the hall.

7. Jay Ruby (personal communication) speaks of what he terms "the Kissinger plane ritual," footage of diplomats arriving at and leaving airports. The viewer assumes that each airport is in a different city, but airports are so similar that they could all be the same stage set. Such footage seems designed to provide reassurance that American diplomacy is actively seeking solutions to impasses.

8. In a recent documentary shown at the 1977 independent film seminar sponsored by the Public Broadcasting System and Film Seminars, Inc., at Arden House, Alfonso Beato framed a peasant analyzing the economic history of Puerto Rico as though he were a reporter. After the viewing, the first question asked by seminar participants was, "Who was that guy that you framed him like Dan Rather?"

References

Dahlgren, Peter. "Network TV News and the Corporate State: The Subordinate Consciousness of the Citizen-Viewer." Ph.D. diss., City University of New York, 1977.

Epstein, Edward Jay. *News from Nowhere: Television and the News*. New York: Random House, 1973.

Glasgow University Media Group. "Bad News." *Theory and Society* 3 (Fall 1976).

———. *More Bad News*. London: Routledge & Kegan Paul, 1980.

Goffman, Erving. *Making the Papers*. Lexington, Mass.: Heath, 1974.

Hall, Edward. *The Hidden Dimension*. Garden City, N.Y.: Doubleday, 1966.

Hickey, N. "What America Thinks of TV's Political Coverage." *TV Guide*, 8–14 April 1972.

Lang, Kurt, and Gladys Engel Lang. "The Unique Perspective of Television and Its Effects: A Pilot Study." In *Mass Communications*, ed. Wilbur Schramm. Urbana: University of Illinois Press, 1953. Reprinted 1960.

National Advisory Commission on Civil Disorders. *Report*. New York: Bantam Books, 1968.

Newsweek. "Divided Opinion." 19 January 1970.

Rather, Dan. *The Camera Never Blinks: Adventures of a TV Journalist*. New York: Morrow, 1977.

Roper Organization, Inc. *An Extended View of Public Attitudes Toward Television and Other Mass Media*. New York: Television Information Office, 1971.

Time. "Judging the Fourth Estate: A *Time*-Louis Harris Poll." 5 September 1969.

Worth, Sol. "Man Is Not a Bird." *Semiotica: The International Journal of Semiotics* 23, nos. 1–2 (1978).

Worth, Sol, and John Adair. "Navajo Film-Makers." *American Anthropologist* 72 (1970).

Youman, R. "What Does America Think Now?" *TV Guide*, 3 September–6 October 1972.

BERTOLT BRECHT AND DAFFY DUCK: TOWARD A POLITICS OF SELF-REFLEXIVE CINEMA?

DANA B. POLAN

In a 1940s Bugs Bunny cartoon, Elmer Fudd, once again forced by destiny and by narrative to chase Bugs, fires several times at his fleeing nemesis. The bullets fail to have their desired effect. Of course, the lack of deadliness is a typical quality of Warner cartoon bullets, but this time Bugs stops and comments to the audience: "Folks, those bullets are fake; we're saving the real ones for the boys overseas."

For me, this moment aptly demonstrates the attitudes an artwork can adopt toward the material world and the dynamics of history. First, there is a distance from worldly reality, a distance inherent in art and that makes it art. This is a distance of codes and of constructions—a distance that, if it allows the work to be a form of knowledge, does so only in a mediated or a nonscientific fashion.[1] The cartoon is first of all a cartoon and not something else. Second, there is a distance in which the work turns in on itself and speaks about its own artistic conventions and presuppositions. This is an attitude of self-reflexivity, of the text calling attention to the artificiality of its own formal devices, as in this case when the cartoon explicitly signals its own cartoon-ness. Finally, there is a third attitude, which the cartoon brings to the foreground at this moment: a movement out of the self-enclosed world of the artwork toward a real world usually left behind by the mediations of art. The cartoon reminds us of an activity—killing—which cartoons normally distort. These attitudes—the inherent one, which makes art art and not something else, and the forced ones, which appear as a conjunction of or a conflict between self-reflexivity and social awareness—form the primary concerns of this essay.

To me, the two most important signs, if we may call them that, in my title are the question mark and the word "toward." For a skepticism motivates this paper, a discontent that manifests itself as a set of tentative forays into an *over*charted region. To raise the question of the politics—intrinsic or otherwise—of self-reflexive film is to reinvoke issues of central importance in the history of film theory, if not art theory in general. How does film relate to a reality? to an audience? What is form? What is content? How are they political? If they are not political, how can they be made so? Here I don't pretend to be able to answer such awesome questions; I merely propose some movements toward their investigation, movements toward a politics of self-reflexive film.

Originally presented as a paper for a panel on self-reflexive films at the annual conference of the Society for Cinema Studies in March 1977; modified somewhat for publication.

In their recent manifestation, debates on these issues have generally come to revolve around a single object of inquiry: viewing. What does it mean to view a film? What happens ideologically when we view a world on a screen before us? At first glance, the activity of viewing may seem to be simple, both in its workings and in its ability to be understood. Yet the surface simplicity obscures a deeper intricacy. In *Reading Capital*, French philosopher Louis Althusser suggests that the great achievement of the modern age—an achievement that describes that age's break with the past—has been the "discovery and training in the meaning of the 'simplest' acts of existence: seeing, listening, speaking, reading. . . ." Freud, he suggests, pinpointed the dimensions of speaking; Marx, those of reading. Similarly, recent criticism of the visual arts—such as that of painting by Pierre Francastel and John Berger or of film by recent writers in *Screen*—is attempting, I would suggest, to understand ways of seeing.

Indeed, recent film theory's "critique of illusionism" derives from the same theoretical impulse as the critique of empiricism put forward by Althusser and others. To these theorists, empiricism or illusionism depends on a conception of the subject/object duality as easily bridged.[2] The world manifests truth, and all one has to do is contemplate the world or its identical embodiment in human activity—texts—to gain insights into that meaning.

Clearly, André Bazin epitomizes the film version of this optimistic theory of the possibilities of meaning. With such notions as the close-up as window to the soul, the destructiveness of conscious artistic intervention, and film as the revelation of the spiritual life (*la vie intérieure*) of the world, Bazin becomes the target for many, if not most, newer theories that see film as a production of meaning, as a site of work in the viewer's consciousness.

Narrative, and its ostensible canonization in Hollywood, also becomes a target. In *S/Z*, Roland Barthes clearly sees the hermeneutic and the proairetic codes (the codes of suspense and of the logic of actions, respectively) as the most determined and determining codes of fiction. Similarly, Noel Burch, in an interview in *Women and Film* (nos. 5–6), declares linearity—that is, narrative—to be an inherent code of what he calls the "dominant cinema." Against narrative and against transparency, critics and artists suggest a whole range of deconstructive devices. Many of these strategies are based on a notion of work. Empiricism, it is claimed, invites passivity; all one has to do is contemplate and texts will deliver up their meaning. Subjects—be they viewing subjects, reading subjects, or historical subjects—will unite automatically with objects and with the knowledge of objects. To counter the encouragement of passivity, many recent critics push for a difficult art, an art that forces its audience into an active interpretive response. The problem of passivity further provides the impetus for a rediscovery of Brecht, who, for recent critics, has become the master of deconstruction, the champion of formal subversion. Burch, for example, in *Theory of Film Practice*, adopts Brecht's theory, but only after declaring it necessary to eliminate Brecht's concern for content. A new Brecht—Brecht the formalist—arises.

But there is also, and foremost, Brecht the realist. And it is this Brecht who will provide my perspective here. I believe that radical aesthetics—including film aesthetics—is falling prey to the rise of a new ahistorical formalism. This formalism is present in attacks on particular types of cinema practice and cinema structure—the practices, as I have mentioned, of narrative and of representation.

But more recently, with the French and British rediscovery of Freud through Jacques Lacan, the attack on representation has become even more pronounced. Whereas formerly a certain type of film practice, which was alone in effecting a particular audience response (namely, passivity), was singled out for attack, now the very practice of representation undergoes criticism as being ideologically reactionary. In this view, the very structure of film viewing (audiences sitting before a screen and watching from a particular viewpoint or perspective) contributes to the constitution of the subject as a viewing subject—that is, a subject safely elevated by self-confidence to a privileged, unchallenged position vis-à-vis the screen world. Thus, in an article on television in a recent issue of *Screen* (Summer 1977), Gillian Skirrow and Stephen Heath go so far as to declare that "there is a generality of ideological position." Certainly, the recent critics often differ as to the sorts of films that contribute most to this nonchallenge to the supposed passivity of viewing. But at its limit, this psychological model suggests that the very (f)act of seeing a film, regardless of the film story, turns spectators into nonacting subjects. In his essay "Diderot, Brecht, Eisenstein" (*Screen*, Summer 1974), Roland Barthes banishes content from art and declares that "representation is not defined directly by imitation: even if one gets rid of notions of the 'real,' of the '*vraisemblable*,' of the copy, there will still be representation for so long as a subject casts his gaze towards a horizon on which he cuts out an apex. . . ." Barthes is thereby able to declare that Brecht and Eisenstein are prepolitical artists since they don't break out of a presentational model. Jean-Pierre Oudart's examination of the influence of classical perspective on film and Jean-Louis Baudry's description of the ideological effects of the basic cinematographic apparatus also move in the same direction.[3] This rejection of representation suggests a subversion not only from within but also from without. Critics and artists push for new artistic experiences that will call the traditional boundaries of the arts into question. But the overriding question remains: is this sort of aesthetic undermining the political?

In part, an answer depends on what we mean by "political." To give a definition (obviously open to disagreement), I would suggest that the political concerns itself with analyzing and then proposing answers to the contradictions of a particular historical situation. The recent formalist critics, of course, might contend that the formal innovations of works that challenge viewing experiences serve as such an investigation of historical contradictions. For example, in the 1972 postscript to *Signs and Meaning in the Cinema*, Peter Wollen declares that a new art would cause the spectator to "produce fissures and gaps in the space of his own consciousness (*fissures and gaps which exist in reality but which are repressed by an ideology, characteristic of bourgeois society*, which insists on the 'wholeness' and integrity of each individual consciousness)" (p. 162, my emphasis). Wollen partially covers his own tracks by declaring that such a repression is *characteristic* of, and not intrinsic to, bourgeois society, but that disclaimer is itself uncharacteristic of the radical formalist approach, where a rigid either/or divides the progressive from the reactionary. The new aesthetic, if I may reductively sum it up, bases itself on a belief that texts repress, that they lead to a domination of their subjects by placing those subjects in a particular position, physically, formally, perhaps ideologically. A text, in this sense, is an ensemble of codes that rationalize a particular way of relating to the world, and they make this rationalization attractive by not interfering with the fetishistic or voyeuristic perspective of the viewing subject. In his essay "The Politics of Separation" (*Screen*, Winter 1975–1976), Colin McCabe goes so far as to call this seduction "the bribe of identity," thereby situating textual persuasion in the realm of crime.

It seems, though, that his sort of position leaves a lot of points unanswered, or at least ambiguous. Before we can examine the validity of certain subversive strategies as answers, we need to make sure that the problem has been correctly understood. We need to examine the notion of textual domination.

Such a notion, especially as a critique of representation, rests on a great number of assumptions. I would like to concentrate on two of these: that texts confirm the world and blind us to contradictions, and that submission to a text means submission to its ideology. The belief in a bribe of identity sees the texts as a complicity of codes, a rhetoric that hides its own rhetorical nature. Thus critics like McCabe see the text as a force of domination over spectators. However, we need to rigorously investigate such an argument. What does domination, in terms of a work of art, mean?

All texts dominate. Without a degree of code sharing between art makers and art receivers, the artwork becomes a noise. To alter McCabe's economic metaphor (which he obviously does not mean as a metaphor), texts aren't bribes; they are contracts in which spectators or readers willingly agree to relate to codes in a certain way and usually, I would contend, with knowledge of the workings of many of these codes. The signs of the contract appear throughout the texts; they may become familiar to us, but, precisely because they are signs, we have to learn them to be able to read or to view. And yet submission to a contractual promise is only one side of the working of a text. Information theory emphasizes not only that information ceases without a common code but also that it ceases if a transgression of codes does not appear, a transgression actually inherent in the system and that expands it. Art—all art—bases itself not just on confirmation but also on contradiction. Literary critic Frank Kermode has alternatively described this interplay as one between credulity and skepticism (in *The Sense of an Ending*) or between recognition and deception ("Novels: Recognition and Deception," *Critical Inquiry*, no. 1). To a large extent, what we refer to as self-reflexivity represents one more strategy in the interplay of a technique intrinsic to and actually defining the process of art. One sort of pleasure comes from precisely this interplay of credulity and skepticism (which may explain why detective fiction— which in many ways ideally embodies many of the workings of the code of suspense—is so popular). Self-reflexive art appeals in part because it heightens this intrinsic interplay.

If we survey the development of the literary and dramatic arts, we continually come across examples of art that signal awareness of their own artifice. Literary critics often point to Laurence Sterne's eighteenth-century novel *Tristram Shandy* as a special high point of conscious artistic artifice; in a revealing comment, Russian formalist critic Viktor Shklovsky called it "the most typical novel in world literature." Yet in the same literary period, Henry Fielding's *Tom Jones* goes as far as Sterne's book in uncovering the codes a reading of literature depends upon. Fielding, for example, explicitly invokes the model of a contract by comparing the novel to a meal where there is a certain interplay between the fixed order of courses and the changing identities of the foods within that order. But the difference between *Tristram Shandy* and *Tom Jones* is one of degree, not a break. Similarly, both texts are no more than a *logical* culmination of a tendency and a characteristic of art. But the recent formal aesthetic has little awareness of degrees. Roland Barthes, for example, has declared that modernism was not really a possibility for art until 1850; he thereby ignores the fact that every artistic period is an interplay between tradition and artistic revolution. We need to examine different types and degrees of artifice and relate them to the history both of their production and of their reception.

Standard humanist literary and art criticism has long been able to accommodate transgressions of the rules. The usual schema is to see such transgressions as necessary to a progress that otherwise would stultify. Obviously this accommodation could be considered an instance of co-opting, but only that which can be co-opted will be co-opted. Critics have long been able to situate modernism in a nonrevolutionary aesthetic. One could cite many examples of this accommodation. Recently two books of literary criticism (Robert Alter's *Partial Magic* and Albert Guerard's *The Triumph of the Novel*) have celebrated what both authors call "the Great Other Tradition," thereby expanding the establishment, the canon, the Great Books of the Western world, beyond the limits proscribed by F. R. Leavis.[4] Both critics (and there are many others) turn aesthetic disturbances into positive, humanist values. To be more precise, they recognize literary, formal innovation for what it is: a nonthreatening, typical component of art. Guerard, for example, refers to the novel's powers of "illuminating and imaginative distortion": literature can introduce an imbalance for the precise purpose of establishing a higher balance. Today's revolution is tomorrow's handservant of the established order. In its literal sense, the term avant-garde suggests nothing more than an advance force, a forward branch of the establishment.

Viktor Shklovsky argued for art as *ostranenie*: a "making strange" of the world. And indeed, if art confirms, it also makes strange the normal order of things. Suspension of disbelief is accompanied by suspension of belief. But recent criticism would like to obscure this condition. Hollywood has been declared a paradigm of a fundamental lack of irony, of a celebration of art as transparency. The heritage of recent film critics from literary critical models with their high art/popular art distinction is obvious. Recent radical literary criticism has committed historical and theoretical errors by adhering to a conception of the novel based on nineteenth-century forms. In fact, the nineteenth-century novel is only one type of literature—and one that is itself not without its ironies and formal subversions. Similarly, there is no one type of Hollywood film; indeed, very few actual Hollywood productions would fit the abstract category of transparency that recent criticism has instituted as the Hollywood paradigm.

With the new formalistic critics, a particular conception of Hollywood cinema is made to monolithically serve as the type of all classical films. A few exceptions crop up, such as the nonconformist auteurs Nick Ray or Sam Fuller. But Hollywood itself is defined as conformist, as the ultimate briber, the ultimate concealer of codes.

All art is distanced. This is as true of Hollywood as of Laurence Sterne or Aristophanes. We learn to read through this distance from material reality, but we also learn to want new distances. Hollywood not only presents unreality as reality, it also openly acknowledges its unreality. In his book *America in the Movies*, Michael Wood even suggests that unreality can become formulaic. Campiness is not merely a subgenre of films but a tendency of most if not all Hollywood films, and Wood suggests that this distance represents one cause of Hollywood's appeal. As he exclaims, Hollywood is "the only place in the world where anyone says, 'Santa Maria, it had slipped my mind.'"

For example, the Hollywood cartoon—a staple of Hollywood production— embodies many of the formal techniques claimed to be deconstructive. And yet, if any *political* concern can be attributed to these cartoons, that is so only in the etymological sense of political: that which deals with the *polis*, with the universal relations of people to each other and to the world. To modify my initial comments, films demonstrate not three attitudes but *two*. Films differ significantly not so much in their degrees of formal complexity as in their political attitude, their sense of the changing and changeable nature of the world. I would suggest that what I initially described as a separate category of attitude—namely, conscious and deliberate self-reflexivity—may be nothing other than an expansion and making manifest of inherent qualities of art.

This difference of attitude—between textual artifice (forced or not) and social attitude—is the difference between art and political art. Let's take a closer look at a Hollywood cartoon for an example. *Duck Amuck* (1953) is a virtual culmination of the experimental possibilities of the Hollywood cartoon.[5] The subject of the cartoon is the nature of animation technique itself. In *Duck Amuck*, Daffy Duck undergoes victimization at the hand of his animator, ultimately revealed to be none other than Bugs Bunny. Bugs tortures Daffy by playing with such film coordinates as framing, background, sound, and color. In an article on *Duck Amuck* in *Film Comment*, Richard Thompson rightly notes that the film manifests a high degree of emphasized formal complexity: "The film is extremely conscious of itself as an act of cinema, as is much of Jones's work. . . . *Duck Amuck* is a good example of Noel Burch's dialectic idea of film elements: foreground and background, space and action, character and environment, image and soundtrack are all in conflict with one another. . . ." Yet Burch's dialectic idea, as he himself notes, is far from political, and so is *Duck Amuck*. If *Duck Amuck* is a metaphor for the confusions of life (as Thompson suggests), it is a disengaged metaphor at best, for it fails to examine confusion through a politicized perspective. Indeed, the source of Daffy Duck's angst reveals itself to be none of the agents of social domination in the real world, but merely Bugs Bunny—another fictive character, whose power is tautological in origin. The film opens up a formal space, not a political one in viewer consciousness. *Duck*

Amuck closes in on itself, fiction leads to and springs from fiction, the text becomes a loop that effaces social analysis. This is the project of all nonpolitical art, realist or modernist.

We may approach this issue from another direction if we examine those theories that deal with classical or traditional art's supposed function vis-à-vis the daily workings of the material world. The recent critics contend, as the earlier quote from Peter Wollen suggests, that bourgeois art works to instill a complacency in the viewer, a complacency both about the art object itself *and* about the world outside of art. But there is nothing necessarily consoling or optimistic about conventional art. Similarly, bourgeois life is not necessarily one of complacency and isolation from an awareness of contradiction. It depends on what kind of contradiction we're talking about. That our day-to-day expectations can be thwarted is a normal and accepted possibility of everyday life. The conventional work of art does not banish contradiction; rather, it works by divorcing contradiction from its social causes. Bourgeois existence is often little more than a continual succession of disappointments, of subversions, all of which fissure our self-unity and social unity as acting subjects. Art doesn't deny this malaise; it merely hides and denies its bases in historical forces. This is why contemporary culture can accommodate formally subversive art; as long as such art does not connect its formal subversion to an analysis of social situations, it becomes little more than a further example of the disturbances that go on as we live through a day. And a work of art that defeats formal expectations does not lead to protest against a culture that itself deals continually in defeating expectations.

This accommodation of contradictions, I would suggest, explains much of the appeal of "Mary Hartman, Mary Hartman." It may also help to explain the morbid underside of fan fascination with Hollywood—an underside of scandal magazines and, ultimately, of the elevation of such trashy books as Kenneth Anger's *Hollywood Babylon* into coffee table respectability. We are used to having our realities deconstructed; thus it does not bother us to see the reality of the movie screen world deconstructed as well. In an article on "Mary Hartman, Mary Hartman" in *Socialist Revolution* (no. 30), Barbara Ehrenreich suggests that the TV series represents the triumph of contradiction: a show that attacks the consumer world is sponsored to sell the very sort of products its content disdains. And it succeeds. Ehrenreich presents this plenitude of contradictions as a stumbling block to socialist theories of popular culture. If it were merely a question of art inspiring blind optimism, criticism would be easy. Shows like "Mary Hartman, Mary Hartman" have made pessimism, discontent, and irony marketable. We need to deal with this realm of contradiction that obscures political contradiction.

And here we return to Brecht. Brecht, too, sees a distance between art and political art. Art automatically embodies a distancing, a making strange. But there's nothing political about that yet: to be political, art has to be made so. In his essay "The Modern Theatre is the Epic Theatre," Brecht uses the example of opera to present his conception of art as possessing *intrinsic* qualities of distance from reality, to which the artist can add a sense of political engagement. As is well known, Brecht's theory of art reception emphasizes conscious knowledge over intuition. So does his theory of art creation. Like his teacher, Erwin Piscator, Brecht sees art as filling a *programmed* function. This implies conscious attention to form and content.

This emphasis on conscious intention is probably what most separates Brecht from the Hungarian Marxist critic Georg Lukács. Lukács's approach to literary creation seems to fall quite often into an intuitionist theory of creation: "Lasting typologies based on a perspective of this sort [i.e., based on the "selection of the essential and the subtraction of the inessential"] owe their effectiveness not to the artist's understanding of day-to-day events but to his *unconscious* possession of a perspective independent of and reaching beyond his understanding of the contemporary scene" (*Realism in Our Time*, my emphasis). This belief on Lukács's part in unconscious awareness leads Brecht to call him a formalist, for it is precisely a belief such as Lukács's—that the nineteenth-century masters had the answers *and* that these answers are still relevant to the twentieth century—that signals a refusal to situate literary production within the actual workings of history.

In fact, Brecht's aesthetic suggests that we need to expand and clarify the notion of realism. Significantly, Brecht referred to his own artistic project as realism. Realism is no more (and no less) than a type of attitude to the world and to art. Realism is not a natural quality; it is a social quality. Brecht's theory most significantly distinguishes between realism—which he saw as the overriding impulse of his art—and unrealism, the setting up of false or limited or reified attitudes toward the world and worldly possibilities. In "Against Gyorg Lukács," he defines realism as "discovering the causal complexes of society/unmasking the prevailing view of things as the view of those who rule it." Realism, thus, is a form of knowledge, a picturing of reality. To judge the efficacy of a particular realism, "one must compare the depiction of life in a work with the life that is being depicted." Like the Lacanian theories of the subject that critics today draw upon, Brecht's theory depends on a notion of positioning, of the subject's place in the circuit of communication. But Brecht diverges from these critics in an essential way. For Brecht, the attitudinal position of the viewing subject springs from an attitudinal position in the work—the political artwork embodies a difference between the way things are and the way they can be.

Brecht's formal experimentation depends on content in two ways. First, form must change to reflect changing realities; otherwise, the formalism of a Lukács may result. Second, Brecht's political theater is a theater of possibility—a theater showing that life doesn't have to take on only the forms it generally does. Political art compares an image of human beings as "unalterable" to one of them as "alterable and able to alter" (quoted from "The Modern Theatre is the Epic Theatre"). As such, the new theater shows that formal arrangements of life can change. We can do things we never thought possible. But the partial grounding in Brecht of groups like the Living Theater—groups that disconnect the potentials of activism from its social(ist) responsibility—suggests that qualifications need to be placed on the sorts of possibilities a Brechtian political art would encourage. Not all possibilities are equally valid; Brecht chooses validity on the basis of a socialist perspective. Hence, content once again makes its entrance. It is what the work says about the real world that matters. Artists must pay close attention to the world of possibility their work promises.[6]

For Brecht, political art plays off a political redefinition of credulity and skepticism. To prevent the new world of possibility from appearing as nothing but noise, the artwork must also make use of the old world as a standard. Meaning, and its realization in action, come from the differences between the two worldviews. Political art defamiliarizes the world. But it does so by playing off our connections to that world.

This reading of Brecht has two important implications for our discussion. First of all, if the political text invites production from the spectators, this production is a source of pleasure. Obviously, Brecht sees the theater as a site of learning, but that learning—that accession to knowledge—brings and is immersed in pleasure. The spectators find joy in comparing a worldview that they now realize is a strangling one to a worldview of possibilities. Pleasure comes from knowing the world can be remade. Pleasure, as Brecht says in note 2 of "A Short Organum for the Theatre," is "the noblest function that we have found for the 'theatre.'" Or as he says later in the Organum, the audience "must be entertained with the wisdom that comes from the solution of problems, with the anger that is a practical expression of sympathy with the underdog, with the respect due to those who respect humanity . . . *in short, with whatever delights those who are producing something*" (my emphasis).

Second, insofar as Brecht's political art includes the presence of the familiar world and yet presents a more attractive world as well, Brechtian art is an art of identification. In examining Brecht's theories, critics have too often declared that the theories allow no place for identification. In fact, Brecht's theory of art embodies two identifications: one empathetic and unquestioning—the one connected to the reified vision of the world—and one critical—a new perspective of knowledge from which the old way is scrutinized. In his essay "Alienation Effects in Chinese Acting," Brecht is emphatic about the need for identification in political theater: "the audience identifies itself with the actor as being an observer, and accordingly develops his attitude of observing or looking on."

We need to carefully examine questions of art's relation to an audience and to the production of pleasure. Pleasure and the importance of artistic popularity come under attack in much of the new radical criticism. I would suggest that we are witnessing the rise of a break or gap between criticism and popular reception. This trend has several causes, among them the growth of a new, difficult art demanding strenuous audience participation. The emphasis in recent criticism on theory rather than practice (as in Althusser's elevation of philosophizing into a sort of practice), and the resulting romanticism of the intellectual, also contribute to this new aesthete-ism. Aesthetic theory thus seems to be falling prey to an elitism in which a select group of critics claim for themselves exclusive knowledge of the workings of literary production. In his review of Charles Grivel's *Production de l'intérêt romanesque* (in *Diacritics* 6, no. 1), Jean Alter calls this new totalitarian approach "terrorist semiotics," and he pinpoints many of its strategies of clique inclusion and popular exclusion: a scientistic mode of writing, neologisms, haughtiness, and an obscure range of references. A similar charge is being argued in what we might call "the *Screen* resignation debate," in which several editors resigned from *Screen* because of its intellectual elitism and subsequent disdain for the day-to-day needs of screen education.

Paradoxically, although the new critics situate themselves in opposition to humanist criticism, they invoke a division of taste parallel to the high culture/mass culture distinction so beloved in humanist criticism. From Ortega y Gasset's dehumanization of art through Susan Sontag's erotics of art to Roland Barthes's distinction between pleasure and bliss, there is little change in the elitism of the critical endeavor. Recent critics see themselves as possessing a heightened approach to literary appreciation (an approach which Barthes and others refer to as the "freeing of the signifier"), while mass audiences supposedly stumble along in realist naiveté. At worst, this approach refuses history; it regards a certain popular sort of viewing practice as debased, quotidian, and so dismisses it, refusing to examine its social dimensions: how texts have been received, how they have mattered. When, for example, Peter Wollen suggests in "Semiotics and *Citizen Kane*" that "it is now possible to read there [in the film] an entirely different film, one which Welles probably never intended," I believe he blurs the more important issue: to analyze how the film *has* been read, to examine its influence on audiences who *don't* see an entirely different *Kane*.

Terrorist aesthetics feeds both into and on the precise sort of formalism that turns Brecht's theory into a theory of work, that downgrades realism, disdains identification, and condemns pleasure. In fact, we need to pay more open attention to *degrees* of identification and pleasure.

At the very least, we can distinguish three possible forms of pleasure in a work of art. There is the pleasure of familiarity—this is the pleasure of uncritical, reified realism. Then there is the pleasure that comes from art's dehumanization or from forced self-reflexivity—this is the pleasure of art as form, as aesthetic emotion, as Kant suggested. This is a pleasure that, as Barthes contends in *The Pleasure of the Text*, derives its force by shying away from history, by trying to be outside ideology (although such an attempt is itself ideological). Then there is the pleasure elaborated by Brecht, the pleasure of an art that finally realizes the dream of the Roman poet Horace in his *Ars poetica* (which Brecht continually refers to): to please and instruct; to please through instruction; to instruct through pleasure—an art whose content is a combination of the world and a better version of the world.

We also need to examine instances of defamiliarization in popular art. In a valuable article on audience response in *Jump Cut* (no. 4), Chuck Kleinhans distinguishes between self-reflexive and self-critical films, the latter being films that directly examine both their form and their content. If, as I have claimed, all films embody a self-reflexivity, then we need to go on to examine differing uses and degrees of self-criticism. Of course, such self-criticism is not necessarily in itself political. We need to go back to Brecht's notion of conscious political criticism, but we also need to be more receptive to the *possibility* that such a critical mode may be operative in films of the so-called "dominant cinema." This whole realm of investigation seems a promising one, but only if we can get beyond the dismissive attitude currently in fashion and move toward a knowledge important not only because it is knowledge but also because it matters.

Notes

1. Coming from Kant, who saw practical reason and imagination as distinct regions of the human mind, nineteenth-century Romanticism tended to privilege the artwork as a special and superior activity of the creative portion of the intellect. In contrast, a politically aware criticism places an emphasis on seeing artworks as results of practical human activity rather than a transcendent creative talent above and beyond social responsibility. Thus, the use of terms like *code* and *text* to refer to aspects of an artwork has a deliberate and polemical intent. Such usage stresses that artworks are constructions, that they are objects produced by people and for people in particular social situations.

The text is the configuration of elements in a single work of art. Unlike the Romantic theory of Organicism, which treats the artwork as a unified (organic) whole, the notion of the text concentrates on the individual elements and how they go together. For example, *Cahier du Cinéma*'s famous analysis of *Young Mr. Lincoln* extracts two elements from the text—sexuality and politics—to examine how the film's ostensible unity actually conceals a set of divergent and even contradictory impulses.

Codes are rules of communication whose application appears from text to text. Effective communication can occur only when senders and receivers share knowledge of the codes. The notion of the code is important in the examination of artistic media because it raises questions about the very extent to which we can consider an artistic text as an act of communication, and about the extent to which convention and rules govern the traditions and transgressions in art production and reception.

2. The subject/object distinction has been one of the central concerns of philosophy throughout its history. The distinction concerns human beings (conscious subjects) and the possible ways in which they can come to know about and perhaps understand the world around them. Marx, for example, suggests that people can best live in the world not as passive observers but as active participants. Those film critics who attack film illusionism and its notion of film as a window on the world generally direct their attack against two targets: first, the passivity that illusionist film seems to force spectators into; and second, the impression illusionist film seems to convey of a world one can understand simply by viewing it.

3. Oudart and Baudry are two French critics who argue that the very technology of filmmaking—for example, the lens used—reproduces the ideological perspective of Western civilization. A useful introduction to this argument is Baudry's essay "Ideological Effects of the Basic Cinematographic Apparatus," *Film Quarterly* 28, no. 2 (1974–1975).

4. In his study of English literature, *The Great Tradition*, moralist literary critic F. R. Leavis declared that the privilege of being part of *the* great tradition belonged exclusively to Jane Austen, George Eliot, Henry James, and Joseph Conrad. Thus he excluded writers ranging from Dickens, who he felt was too popular in appeal, to James Joyce, whose experiments he believed represented a "dead end." Many of the literary scholars who have criticized Leavis have done so simply to argue for the writers he leaves out rather than to question the very notion of a great tradition, no matter who its members might be.

5. The screenplay for *Duck Amuck* appeared in Richard Thompson's article on the film in *Film Comment* 11, no. 1 (1975): 42–43.

6. Brecht's qualification here is an important one. In suggesting the need to awaken people to new life possibilities, so many works of art fail to distinguish adequately between valid and invalid experiences, and so they promote an art that holds valuable as-

pects of human life in contempt. For example, the cult of cruelty in art often glorifies the violation of the human body. The ostensible suggestion is that this opens up new artistic experiences: violence is a source of heightened aesthetic pleasure. That such art (which ranges from *A Clockwork Orange* to *The Story of O* to "punk rock") often singles out women as the target of violence suggests one (and only one) of the dangers of such an approach. For an example (there are many!) of this defense of violence as a source of higher consciousness, see Susan Sontag, "The Pornographic Imagination," in *Styles of Radical Will* (New York: Delta Books, 1969). Sontag calls for an "erotics of art"; given the fascism this can lead to, Brecht would not have favored such an art.

WOMEN AND REPRESENTATION: CAN WE ENJOY ALTERNATIVE PLEASURE?

JANE GAINES

Feminist analysis of pornography's industry, image, and "effect," has overlapped at times with issues in contemporary film theory: the marketing of diversion and pleasure, the institutionalization of voyeurism, and the relationship between violent acts and representations of violence.[1] Debates around pornography in the first half of the 1980s have had a familiar resonance for those who follow feminist film criticism. At the time of the 1982 Conference on the Politics of Sexuality at Barnard College, the paradigm evoked in the discussions of pornography bore an uncanny resemblance to the dominant cinema/countercinema model introduced into feminist film theory in the mid-seventies. That paradigm is now, however, undergoing some change. In the struggle against the monoliths that serve male desire, feminist critics are asking if woman's pleasure as counterpleasure can be a viable oppositional practice. The serious interest in women's sexuality—in fantasy and in practice—marked by the Barnard pro-sex conference and the publication of the proceedings, is a bold new tack for American feminism. *Pleasure and Danger*, the collection that contains the conference papers, suggests the way women's desire is inextricably linked with the prohibitions against it. In her introduction to the book, editor Carol Vance lines up those perils that historically have mitigated women's pleasure. "When unwanted pregnancy, street harassment, stigma, unemployment, queerbashing, rape, and arrest are arrayed on the side of caution and inaction," she says, "passion doesn't have a chance."[2] In Vance's analysis, women's passion is tentative and easily intimidated by antipornography rhetoric, which classifies all sexual expression as male.[3]

Until recently, the U.S. feminist stand on pornography appeared to be consistent with the toughest line of the most visible antipornography activist group, Women Against Pornography.[4] Some of the first signs of falling away from the hard line on pornography can be seen in the *Heresies* "Sex Issue." This issue, published in 1981, contains a variety of arguments for challenging the watchdog position on porn, among them that pornography is not a *cause* of violence against women but rather a symptom of patriarchal power relations, that concentration on the extreme and exotic can eclipse or even excuse the more common acts of degradation related to the requirements of heterosexuality, and even that pornography may have a subversive potential in a sexually repressive society.[5] One of the articles in the issue turns a critique of the antipornography

An earlier version of this essay served as the introduction to a special section on Women and Representation, *Jump Cut*, no. 29 (February 1984).

movement into a statement of feminist strategy based on shifting our emphasis from men's pleasure to women's. "In placing the gratification of men above our own," says Paula Webster, "we pose absolutely no danger to male-dominated society"; the "active pursuit of our own gratification," then, is a political act. Webster acknowledges, however, that this pursuit will finally need to address the more difficult sexuality and power issue: What if women are aroused by the imagery designed exclusively for male satisfaction?[6]

This development finds its parallel in feminist film criticism, which has reached the point of exasperation with the cataloging and analysis of male pleasure. The use of the extreme to condemn the ordinary, as seen in the comparison between male voyeurism and cinema viewing (which has its equivalent in the comparison between pornography and sexual images of women), seems to have lost its original potency. Also, new work on popular fiction and film directs interest away from forms now established as "male" to forms marketed for female audiences. Since the mid-seventies, it has been the critical vogue to study the cinematic construction of male pleasure in the classic realist text—the ways in which the masculine "gaze" controls viewing within the film, sets up the spectator's "looking position," and coincides with the "look" of the camera. Analysis in this tradition has considered "sexual difference" to be the eroticizing hinge on which classical Hollywood cinema turns. For the female, there are two places in this construct—either as overvalued "fetishized" star image (Mae West or Marlene Dietrich), exhibited and displayed, no more than a sign in a "patriarchal exchange," or as audience, but occupying the point of view reserved for the male.[7]

The source of this method and the inspiration for so much of the current work on woman as spectacle is Laura Mulvey's 1975 essay "Visual Pleasure and Narrative Cinema," which marks the first attempt to use Lacanian psychoanalysis to develop a coherent feminist theory of narrative film as signifying system.[8] Claire Johnston's "Women's Cinema as Counter-Cinema,"[9] published two years before, had already analyzed the fetishized female image as substitute for phallic sexuality, following Freud's theory of symbolic displacement and male narcissism.* Both articles extend the combination of Freud and Lacan suggestively used in *Cahiers du Cinéma*'s collective analysis of *Morocco*, originally published in 1970, but not translated into English until 1980.[10] With the publication of "Visual Pleasure and Narrative Cinema" in the issue following the translation of Christian Metz's "The Imaginary Signifier," the British journal *Screen* had thoroughly committed itself to an integration of Lacanian psychoanalysis into film theory.[11] For roughly ten years, terms such as "mirror phase," the "imaginary," "desire," and the "look," introduced in these two issues, seemed to be the favored critical currency of the exchange on women and cinema.

Editor's note: That is, the idealized film image of the woman becomes the object of infantile fantasy as a substitute for adult, genital sexuality, a regression to the image of the mother in the mind of the pre-oedipal male child, not yet a symbol or threat of castration. Even as a "sex symbol," she remains precisely a *symbol*, whose unattainability as a real-life sex partner and nonexistence as an autonomous individual relieve the male of the anxieties of phallic potency, castration fears, and mature personal relationships. Mulvey suggests in addition a second pattern of female representation in which women are viewed from an adult male sexual viewpoint but with their threatening aspects overcome by portrayals of male control or punishment of them.

The connection between the Freudian notions of fetishism and voyeurism and the distinctly male spectator was not made immediately. In the United States, one of the earliest attempts to theorize the eroticized female image, Maureen Turim's "Gentlemen Consume Blondes," analyzes *Gentlemen Prefer Blondes* in Marxist terms of commodity exchange. Although men are implicated in the title, Turim makes no gender distinctions in her discussion of the way cinema makes voyeurs and fetishists of us all while at the same time excusing our tendencies.[12] Soon after, Lucy Fisher, in her examination of Busby Berkeley's decorative uses of the showgirl, made a tentative connection between fetishism and male, as opposed to female, eroticism.[13] The *Cahiers du Cinéma* analysis of Marlene Dietrich in *Morocco*, which clearly influenced both Mulvey and Johnston, assumes a phallocentric society and is interested in both the economic and the erotic functions of the fetish.

Feminist analysis, however, has not pursued the Marxist notion of fetishism (that is, the attribution of magical qualities) to the commodity in capitalist economic relations or to the converse, commodification of noncommodities, for instance, the reification of the female body. I will suggest some of the reasons why the Freudian notion of the fetish has been preferred.[14] First, we have to consider the immediate appeal of the feminist argument, which links social practices with perversion. This argument often starts with a study of the exotic; through analogy, the more common practice is then implicated. Mulvey's theory of the female image as a phallic replacement that eases male fear of phallic loss was developed in an analysis of explicitly fetishist imagery. Just before the publication of "Visual Pleasure and Narrative Cinema," she undertook an attack on one of the most notorious exploiters of the female form in the British art world in an encyclopedic review of Allan Jones's visions of female body contortion and torture.[15] Fettered in the classic imagery of the private fetishist—belts, spike heels, rubber corsets, brassieres, and garters—Jones's models confirm feminists' worst fears about male fantasies. As the basis for an analysis of the onscreen image of woman, fetishism makes a stunning connection between aberrant eroticism and "normal" male sexual behavior.

However, this potent metaphor for cinema spectatorship has too quickly become a comprehensive explanation for all representation of the female form. Joanna Russ criticizes rhetorical use of the exotic to damn the ordinary as characteristic of feminist debates. Once the commonplace is likened to the extraordinary—as corset-wearing is compared with the fetishist's tight-lacing—or heterosexuality is equated with rape, we still have not explained the more routine acts, says Russ.[16] Feminists should be careful not to confuse the specialized sexual eroticism or the brutal crime with widespread practice, particularly since, she concludes, "nobody has decided what relation exists between rape, rape fantasies, clinical masochism, and ordinary behavior. And what are we to understand by 'ordinary behavior'?"[17]

Recent psychoanalytic theory hypothesizes that all conventional language and pictorial representation is male-biased, for reasons rooted in the psychology of infantile sexuality. To understand the dominant cinema as thoroughly voyeuristic and to identify all sexual representation of women within it as phallic substitution implies a definite political analysis. If even everyday viewing is organized along these lines, with patriarchal power relations being reproduced in every depiction of woman on a magazine page or billboard, then we are all ideological captives. Moreover, if we are ideologically "surrounded," if all language and every image produced in bourgeois society is steeped in patriarchal ideology—the female body always being a vehicle for something other than itself—then there is a definite advantage for feminists in borrowing a Freudian analysis that theorizes femininity as silence. Always discussing the image of woman in its negation, we are constantly qualifying representational practices and reminding ourselves of the impossibility of female expression in male-dominated culture. In their introduction to the most recent collection of feminist film criticism, Mary Ann Doane, Patricia Mellencamp, and Linda Williams defend this theoretical stance for its tactical avoidance of essentialism.[18] By shifting emphasis to the negative spaces—or, following the French feminists, to the linguistic in-between—the feminist critic sidesteps the assertion that any imagery could be naturally or essentially female.[19] But these authors find neither critical option satisfactory as a theoretical basis; hence the kind of crisis we find in feminist film criticism:

The feminist theoretist is . . . confronted with something of a double bind: she can continue to analyze and interpret various instances of the repression of woman, of her radical absence in the discourses of men—a pose which necessitates remaining within that very problematic herself, always repeating its terms; or she can attempt to delineate a feminine specificity, always risking a recapitulation of patriarchal constructions and a naturalization of "woman."[20]

A theory based on the exclusion of women poses a special challenge to the feminist filmmaker who would create alternative representations or political commentary on the photographic uses of the female body. How can the feminist artist speak out or act to shape culture from a position of absence?

On this basis, some feminists have opposed all uses of Freud in criticism. Why borrow a method based on describing woman's repressed place in language and society? they argue. What new understanding of oppression can it yield? To be fair, the British feminist use of psychoanalysis follows Juliet Mitchell's rereading of Freudian theory, which she takes as a kind of description of the ideological, or an illumination of the site of gender construction.[21] In this analysis, Freudian theory is not taken to be anything more than social diagnosis. Jacqueline Rose further defends the feminist use of Freud: "The description of feminine sexuality is . . . an exposure of the terms of its definition, the very opposite of a demand as to what that sexuality should be."[22] Yet although it offers a social explanation of oppression, Freudian theory concentrates causality in a depository of its own invention that is characterized by its detachment from social conditions.[23]

For Marxists, the use of psychoanalysis is especially problematic both because it privileges an autonomous realm and because it poses a subject that is undifferentiated by either social class or history.[24] Although Marxist feminists have been able to compensate with Freud for what was missing in Marx—gender distinctions—the theoretical advantage of gender specificity is outweighed by the political disadvantage of expecting an already completely constituted subject to come to class consciousness. Terry Lovell sees the psychoanalytic notion of subject as having "deeply pessimistic" implications for women, because "an account of sexed identity which locates the constitution of women in processes so massively concentrated in the first few years of life more or less completed with the resolution of the Oedipus complex, is to place women . . . under a crippling burden of determination in an epoch of their lives in which they have the least possibility of control and change." [25] Following Althusser's introduction of Lacan into the Marxist theory of ideology, the apparent shift of emphasis from class struggle to ideological struggle seemed to concentrate effectivity in cultural products and to forgo political movement in favor of critical activity. Christine Gledhill, another British feminist who, like Lovell, has been critical of the incorporation of Lacan via Althusser into Marxist cultural studies, asks how this theory translates into political strategy. In her critique of feminist film criticism, Gledhill argues that if feminists are up against the "ideologically positioned" subject, political change begins to look like an impossible task. As she puts it, "We are clearly in a very weak political position if rupturing the place of the subject in representation is our chief point of entry." With no clear means of connecting gender construction to historically shifting economic conditions, she says, feminists may have difficulty formulating and implementing programs for social change. [26]

One of the related dangers of using Freudian theory is the ease with which it can be recuperated for a totally reactionary position. Since Freud strikes a mean between the biological and the social, and can often be interpreted both ways, a feminist case for understanding sexuality as a social construct may sound like a case for biological determinism. Ann Kaplan's definition of cinematic voyeurism, based on that of Mulvey, for instance, could lend itself to the analysis that viewers, especially biological males, are hopelessly doomed by instinct and cannot help their proclivity to look in a sexual context. "Pleasure in the cinema," she says, "is created through the inherently voyeuristic mechanism that comes into play here more strongly than in the other arts." [27] Implying that pleasure in looking is innate rather than learned, feminists back down from their best argument: that gender differences are socially constructed. But Freud is slippery, and an extra step makes this theory seem to serve a materialist position. Kaplan is thus able to justify her use of psychoanalysis because she will force it to "unlock the secrets of our socialization within (capitalist) patriarchy." [28] A similar stance may have been taken by other film theorists who depend heavily on psychoanalysis, but this would be difficult to tell from their work. Until recently, those feminist film theorists who recruited psychoanalysis into a Marxist analysis did not feel the need to answer the charge that Freudian concepts are ahistorical. [29]

Certainly the historical coincidence of the invention of a storytelling machine on the one hand and Freud's discovery of the unconscious within the bourgeois epoch on the other is remarkable, but this one fortuitous connection has too easily satisfied the need for historic specificity in Marxist-psychoanalytic film criticism. Although some of the post-1968 French film theory, which introduced Lacanian psychoanalytic concepts into cinema studies, was also interested in locating the historical moment of the construction of ideology in the invention of cinema technology, these historical reference points have dropped out in psycho-analytic discussions of the way the text positions its subject.[30] Early theorizations of the cinema subject began by citing the historical continuity between the perspective rendered by the camera lens and the Renaissance code of pictorial space. What had been considered a "scientific" instrument, the camera, re-produced ideology in its model of the idealist worldview, which organized vision around the human eye, flattering it with a godlike vantage point. This spectator eye, implied in the convergence of light rays and referred to by the vanishing lines, also defined a particular conception of the self.[31] Freud's analogy between photographic instrument and psychic process, each described as an *apparatus* in *The Interpretation of Dreams*, inspired and encouraged comparisons between the two.[32] Finally, in the notion of "the apparatus" and its operations, motion picture technology (a culmination of nineteenth-century invention) and the human psyche have become interchangeable. Here, then, the provocative play with metaphor, which in psychoanalytic theory teases out correspondences, seems to have provided a shortcut for theorists. Certainly there *are* connections among Freud's "dream economy," narrative economy, and the economy characterized by commodity production, just as there is a relationship between the projection mechanism and the mechanism of the unconscious, but in the way Marxist theory has borrowed Freud, it has still only suggested these links.[33]

Finally, other Marxist feminists have been critical of British feminist film theory because its specialized knowledge fosters an elite position. On this point, Kaplan was originally one of the clearest and strongest critics of the British. In an early review of "Women's Cinema as Counter-Cinema" and Pam Cook and Claire Johnston's work on Raoul Walsh and Dorothy Arzner, she noted that not only was a background in psychoanalytic theory a prerequisite to these discussions, but in order to follow the arguments the reader had to accept the Freudian premises without question. At the time, Kaplan asked what might be valuable about the Freudian interpretations already established in literary criticism, since "the predictable nature of such interpretations takes away from their interest . . . ; given the premises, everything else follows like clockwork."[34] Kaplan's remark describes much of the criticism that followed in this tradition, and here I refer to the bulk of the academic work extending feminist film theory in the United States from the mid-1970s into the present. To the insider, the appeal of this criticism explicating the "look" and unraveling the oedipal is that it *does* come off "like clockwork." To the outsider, this analysis is often as impenetrable as the patriarchal unconscious it hopes to unlock.

Analyzing patriarchal forms has only been half of the feminist project outlined by the dominant cinema/countercinema paradigm. "Breaking down" mainstream film has also meant constructing new forms that directly oppose classical conventions in order to withhold its two indulgent pleasures: voyeuristic "looking" and narrative closure. Again, echoing a strategy in women's movement politics, the creation of a new language of desire was made contingent on the destruction of male pleasure. Women's cinematic forms were not imaginable as long as illusionistic narrative cinema (the patriarchal favorite) retained its fascination for us. In theory, the feminist countercinema proposed by Mulvey and Johnston is a continuation of Godard's goals for a revolutionary cinema—to combat form with form. The disruptive fragmentation of continuity editing and point-of-view construction and the frustration of narrative unity pioneered a new aesthetic based on refusal. Theoretically, the inventive interruption of classical narrative is meant to destroy the codes of mainstream entertainment and ultimately replace them with a cinema that provokes thought and encourages analysis. Counter-cinema here borrows from Brecht the idea that critical distance, and ultimately consciousness-change, can be effected in the theatrical audience by annihilating the pleasure of identification. It also has in common with Brecht a bias against ease and satisfaction, which cannot be expected to serve the goals of political education. Recent reevaluation of these issues from a Marxist mass-culture per-spective, however, reminds us that Brecht may not have intended such austerity.[35] People's pleasures (popular music, television, cinema, and other amusements) might serve politics after all if the fantasies they inspire help to feed an under-nourished utopian imagination.[36]

Leftists have raised strong objections to a cinema that snubs popular ap-peal and that would spurn the more accessible pleasures for the "passionate de-tachment" of an intellectual experience. *Riddles of the Sphinx*, Laura Mulvey's high-theory film, for instance, austerely avoids continuity editing and withholds narrative resolution to such an extreme that women viewers have found it dis-orienting. The subversion of sexual looking, although compelling as a concept, is not so riveting in its translation to the screen. Finally, the "test" of counter-cinema implies a very difficult standard: the work must show that what we are seeing is shaped by cinematic form; at the same time, it must not give the im-pression (usually encouraged by conventions of cinematic realism) that there is any final reality that can be known outside the linguistic forms that access it. Does this political aesthetic make impossible demands on audiences—and on film texts? Those of us who eat, sleep, and breathe political theories of represen-tation, who have made the politics of meaning our life's work, are not always aware of the ways our own consciousness is shaped by words, images, or other signifying material. Are we, in expecting a film text to effect change on its own, asking too much of it, especially if it is screened out of the context of political organizing and education efforts? Why should a film that considers its own sig-nification process necessarily require its audience to know advanced film theory in order for them to enjoy, appreciate, and, ideally, reflect upon what they see? The futility of sharing this new cinema with a theoretically uninitiated audience is dramatized by this admission from a scholar in an adjacent field:

An innovatory piece of work may be experienced as such, or as startling, shocking, dis-turbing, if the audience is sufficiently familiar with the conventions it seeks to challenge and subvert. . . . I am aware, for example, that, while I can see for myself a departure from tradition in a contemporary novel, I have to be told by others that such and such a camera angle or style of shot constitutes a rejection of bourgeois practice in film-making.[37]

The feminist case for countercinema is an argument for modernism, which undeniably offers rarefied pleasures and is a taste acquired through educational and cultural privilege.[38] Black women filmmakers, sensitive to the class bias of aesthetic preference, have as a whole chosen not to produce any media work that diverges from standard formats and calls attention to its own formal devices. Interviews with this new group of film and video makers—whose work is still unevenly available in the United States even through alternative distribution channels—suggest agreement on the question of aesthetic style: It is more important to make comprehensible and accessible films than it is to experiment with subverting classical Hollywood narrative.[39] The films these women have produced deal with black body language and image, skin color consciousness, child custody, childbirth, single parenting, prostitution as survival, rape, and women's retaliation against sexual abuse, and their messages are an intentional affront to white male society. Do these films, then, constitute any less of a political challenge because they use conventional forms?

For all the interest in countercinema as theory, feminist film and video making in the United States seem to have been influenced relatively little by the original British models such as *Nightcleaners* (Berwick St. Collective, 1975) and *Riddles of the Sphinx* (Laura Mulvey and Peter Wollen, 1977). The small number of U.S. and British feminist works following in this tradition have received a disproportionate amount of critical attention. This response is evidence of the symbiotic relationship between these "avant-garde theory films," as Ann Kaplan calls them, and an evolving feminist criticism, which certainly has its significance; but the attention has also created an instant canon in a very new field of inquiry. Too quickly, a hierarchy of works has been organized, which has meant that many women's productions have been relegated to the periphery, and many others remain undiscovered. Those feminist works that may have been overlooked by theorists have been found by women's groups, however, particularly in the United States, where several traditions of radical filmmaking coexist. Documentaries in the style of *Union Maids* (Julia Reichert and Jim Klein, 1976) have been strong with unions and community groups. These documentaries use the rhetoric of archival footage or testimonial interview and thus employ realist conventions without question; but they are also effective as organizing tools, and in this sense they pose a challenge to the countercinema corollary that change cannot be effected by "revealing" the photographic "truth" of woman's oppression.[40] Third World film and video makers have consistently made their more radical statements in the documentary mode, a choice that indicates the power of politics to determine representational priorities. Leftist media workers cannot afford to undertake an abstract analysis or make an educational statement *about* representation if it is politically imperative that they make a representational reference to a "brutal actuality" in order to counteract its ideological version.[41]

For feminists, investigating women's pleasure as counterpleasure has become politically imperative. We have already produced a potent analysis of patriarchal culture as oppressive monolith, but we are still determining the relation of woman's culture to the dominant. Is this culture excluded or "muted"? Does it modify or resist?[42] Annette Kolodny recently remarked that while sexual difference absorbed us in the first two decades of the Second Wave of Feminism, the issue of the next decade will have to be how difference "interacts with the dominant." [43] The equation between mainstream cinema and male privilege set up by "Visual Pleasure and Narrative Cinema" may have diverted the attention of feminist scholars, but it seems also to have provided an "out" for them—by introducing interest in the gendered spectator into contemporary film theory. [44] The very questions that Mulvey did *not* address have become the most compelling: Is the spectator restricted to viewing the female body on the screen from the male point of view? Is narrative pleasure always male pleasure? Theoretical solutions to the enigma of female spectatorship range from the more pessimistic and dubious psychoanalytic analyses to the spirited reversal of the lesbian readings and the renewed expectations of the soap opera studies. Psychoanalytic analyses of the horror film show agreement on one point—that the female vision, whether perception or discernment, is jeopardized in this genre. [45] Punishments inflicted on female characters, as Marcia Landy and Lucy Fisher show in their analysis of *The Eyes of Laura Mars* (Irvin Kershner, 1978), may serve as a warning against female occupation of male points of view. [46]

Mary Ann Doane has theorized female spectatorship as a psychoanalytic and semiotic impossibility. For one thing, the female cannot assume a voyeuristic position in regard to the cinema spectacle, because she is semiotically too close to that image which is ultimately her own. Neither does she have the power to transform her own castrated figure in the same way the male spectator is thought to use his ability to "fetishize." [47] Following this line of thought, with sexual difference determining the construction and operation of classical narrative cinema *in all genres*, even those films centered on a female protagonist and directed toward a woman's audience will renounce female looking. Doane's study of the Hollywood woman's picture shows that the prohibition against female sight is so strong that some films must integrate this renunciation into the narrative. For example, one could understand Joan Crawford's dilemma, as patron and lover to concert violinist John Garfield in *Humoresque* (Jean Negulesco, 1946), as the denial of her control over him, worked out in terms of her surveillance of his performances and emphasized by the habitual removal of her glasses. Following Doane's suggestion, Crawford's tragic suicide (she walks into the surf to the strains of her lover's violin, broadcast from the concert hall) could be seen as resolving the tension between the desire to be viewed as a love object and the need to scrutinize an investment. [48] If even women's forms frustrate the spectator, what are we to make of women's attraction to melodrama? Do these entertainments offer a privileged point of view and the possibility of female desire—and then withhold the enjoyment of them? [49] Is the viewer tricked into a masochistic pleasure?

In contrast to psychoanalytic film theory, lesbian studies assign more power to the spectator than to the text. These analyses show that the female "look" cancels the male point of view and that active reading resists the flow of classical narrative. In one of the most convincing challenges to work on male pleasure to date, Lucie Arbuthnot and Gail Seneca argue that in *Gentlemen Prefer Blondes* (Howard Hawks, 1953), Jane Russell and Marilyn Monroe "resist objectification" and project an intimacy with each other that invites both identification and a kind of female voyeurism.[50] In this tradition, Chris Straayer and Liz Ellsworth have considered the feminist and lesbian reception of *Personal Best* (Robert Towne, 1982), demonstrating in two different studies that the power and force of the female "look" has been underestimated. Based on her observations that oppositional communities build their own interpretations and construct social pleasures to complement their fantasies, Ellsworth recommends that feminists work out strategies to maximize their "illicit" viewing pleasure.[51] Straayer's discovery of lesbian respondents' ingenious viewing strategies, which allow for the "clever co-existence of pleasure and displeasure," is an important opening in the study of the double consciousness of oppressed groups.[52] In contrast with formal analysis, these more sociological studies may seem relatively "messy," in the way they deal with "gut" feelings, inarticulate responses, and ordinary opinions; they are significant, however, because they remind us that meaning is always social and that hothouse studies of film language alone cannot construct a semiotics of the cinema.

An approach that considers the lesbian as spectator causes all the premises of feminist film theory centered on male voyeurism to shift. In the introduction to the *Jump Cut* "Lesbian Special Section," Edith Becker, Michelle Citron, Julia Lesage, and B. Ruby Rich describe how the exclusion of a lesbian perspective has seriously "warped" contemporary film theory:

A true recognition of lesbianism would seriously challenge the concept of women as inevitable objects of exchange between men, or as fixed in an eternal trap of "sexual difference" based on heterosexuality. Feminist theory that sees all women on the screen only as objects of male desire—including by implication, lesbians—is inadequate.[53]

To consider the exquisitely fit female-fantasy bodies in *Flashdance* (Adrian Lyne, 1983) only in terms of male desire, one has to ignore women's responses to the film.

Likewise, to analyze the lesbian sexual awakening in *Lianna* (John Sayles, 1983) in terms of the male "look" negates the film's premises. Visually, *Lianna* is not the film that either a straight woman or a lesbian would have made in celebration of women loving women.[54] *Lianna* is not just cautious, it is apologetic about photographing women. The tentative representation of lesbian love-making, for instance, is an attempt not to intrude voyeuristically or shape salaciously, and clichés of sexual gazing are reversed in a female-body montage Lianna sees just after she has first made love with Ruth. Showing wholesome lesbian bodies with restraint neither withdraws the image entirely from male view nor subtracts the "to-be-looked-at" connotations from the female body. But finally, as a film about female desire *Lianna* is incredibly pallid. *Flashdance*, in contrast, is an alluring inducement to give oneself over to watching gorgeous women dance. Judging from the film's reception, women audiences have enthusiastically taken up the invitation to look. My informal poll of friends shows that both lesbians and straight women have claimed this film. Some women said that *Flashdance* was the first film in years that they had gone back to see a second time. Does its "fantasy of control" explain why women, after seeing the film, are dancing along with *Flashdance* videocassettes in their living rooms and signing up for classes in jazz dance?[55]

Do responses to *Personal Best* and *Flashdance* suggest that women are suddenly "ready" for an eroticized imagery of their own? Will they no longer have to steal their glancing pleasure in the cinema or reroute their own plots? It is not as though women's sexual fantasies have never been served. Feminist work on women's traditional fiction such as Harlequin and gothic novels, melodrama and soap operas, shows that women have historically turned to these forms, which direct their readers through familiar conflicts with loved ones and provide releases and gratifications women probably won't find in conventional marriage.[56] Ann Barr Snitow's consideration of mass market romance as women's pornography suggests that feminists should take a second look at forms so often dismissed as reactionary if we would define the rhythms and emphases of women's sexual imagination. "The romantic intensity of Harlequins—the waiting, fearing, speculating—is as much a part of their functioning as pornography for women as are the more overtly sexual scenes," she says.[57] Similarly, Tania Modleski identifies distinctive narrative forms in women's television programming and suggests that these forms derive from those experiences that are thought to be woman's "lot in life"—waiting, anticipating, and the state of being constantly distracted and interrupted. Modleski concludes her analysis of soap operas with the assertion that new forms of women's pleasure won't necessarily be "made from scratch."[58] These traditional female forms promise a model for an emerging feminist aesthetic, and ideally, this aesthetic would even be compelling to those Harlequin readers who finish a novel every other day.[59] The political countermove here is in the reclamation of narrative gratifications for ourselves, for, as Modleski says, "this pleasure is currently placed at the service of the patriarchy."[60]

What could be new or liberating about an aesthetic based on woman's plight? Again, one of the crucial concerns of feminist film theory intersects with a burning issue in women's movement politics—correct pleasure. To replicate the dominant/subordinate power relation in either sexual practice or fantasy life has been considered a political taboo for feminists. In the turnabout in feminist discussions of sexuality I have described, women are daring to say that politically correct practices and proper fantasies do not necessarily fuel their passion. The alternative imagery of a radical pornography for women may leave us cold. "If pornography is to arouse," says Ellen Willis, "it must appeal to the feelings we have, not those that by some utopian standard we ought to have."[61] Of course, erotic tastes, just as preferences for romantic narrative resolutions, may be understood as the residue of oppression, but what if reactionary tastes are ingenious compensations? The woman's fiction studies to which I have referred point out that romance fantasies are a means of symbolic conflict management. Also, we have yet to understand the connection between fantasy and erotic acts. As Chuck Kleinhans and Julia Lesage remind us, "Fantasy is precisely what people desire but do not necessarily want to act on. It is an imaginative substitution and not necessarily a model for overt behavior."[62] Pointing out the discrepancies between feminist egalitarian ideals of desire and what women report they like is not an argument for indifference to the imagery of power imbalance or the industries that profit from reproducing this imagery. Women's erotic daydreams are clues to structures of sustenance and release, and are due for the same serious consideration that women's diversions have begun to receive from feminists.

Finally, for academics, I suggest that in our critical studies of the next wave of feminist media—women's video productions, the heirs of the countercinema tradition—we be clearer about the source of our own fascination with aesthetic "play," off and against the dominant structures of prime-time television and mainstream cinema. The "correct" formula for alternative feminist film practice, the rearrangement of the "relations of looking," and the rejection of closure offer feminists a rather tight-lipped satisfaction. Restrained intellectual pursuits have a specialized recompense that bear little resemblance to the absorbing delight that means "pleasure" to so many women. Correct pleasure is a very privileged pleasure.

Notes

1. For further discussion of these similarities, see Julia Lesage, "Women and Pornography," *Jump Cut*, no. 26 (December 1981): 46–47; also see, in the same issue, Gina Marchetti's bibliography "Readings on Women and Pornography," pp. 56–60.

2. Carol Vance, "Pleasure and Danger: Towards a Politics of Sexuality," in *Pleasure and Danger*, ed. Carol Vance (Boston: Routledge & Kegan Paul, 1984), p. 4.

3. Vance, "Pleasure and Danger," p. 6.

4. For more of this history, see the introduction to Ann Snitow, Christine Stansell, and Sharon Thompson, eds., *Powers of Desire* (New York: Monthly Review Press, 1983).

5. Ellen Willis has argued that women's enjoyment of pornography could be seen as a "form of resistance in a culture that would allow [them] no sexual pleasure at all" ("Who is a Feminist?: A Letter to Robin Morgan," *Village Voice*, 21 December 1981, p. 17).

6. Paula Webster, "Pornography and Pleasure," *Heresies* 3, no. 4 (1981): 50.

7. The majority of books published as feminist film theory would suggest the psychoanalytic vogue, if nothing else. After the first two collections of articles published in the United States—Karyn Kay and Gerald Peary's *Women and Cinema* (New York: Dutton, 1977), and Patricia Erens's *Sexual Stratagems* (New York: Horizon, 1979)—the basic texts have privileged the earliest work of the British feminist film theorists, which has been so solidly grounded in Freud. Here I refer to Annette Kuhn, *Women's Pictures* (London: Routledge & Kegan Paul, 1982), and E. Ann Kaplan, *Women and Film* (New York: Methuen, 1983), as well as E. Ann Kaplan, ed., *Women in Film Noir* (London: British Film Institute, 1978). More recent attempts to creatively extend this theory can be found in Mary Ann Doane, Patricia Mellencamp, and Linda Williams, eds., *Re-Vision* (Frederick, Md.: University Publications of America, 1984), and Teresa de Lauretis, *Alice Doesn't* (Bloomington: Indiana University Press, 1984), which proposes a bridge between psychoanalytic semiotics and cultural semiotics.

8. Laura Mulvey, "Visual Pleasure and Narrative Cinema," *Screen* 16, no. 3 (1975): 6–18 (reprinted in Kay and Peary, *Women and Cinema*, pp. 412–428); and Gerald Mast and Marshall Cohen, eds., *Film Theory and Criticism*, 3d ed. (New York: Oxford University Press, 1985). Also see Laura Mulvey and Colin MacCabe's "Images of Woman, Im-

ages of Sexuality," chap. 4 in Colin MacCabe, *Godard: Images, Sounds, Politics* (Bloomington: Indiana University Press, 1980); Dee Dee Glass, Laura Mulvey, Griselda Pollock, and Judith Williamson, "Feminist Film Practice and Pleasure: A Discussion," in Fredric Jameson et al., *Formations of Pleasure* (London: Routledge & Kegan Paul, 1983), pp. 156–160.

9. Claire Johnston, "Women's Cinema as Counter-Cinema," in *Notes on Women's Cinema*, ed. Claire Johnston (London: Society for Education in Film and Television, 1973) (reprinted in Erens, *Sexual Stratagems*, pp. 133–143); Bill Nichols, ed., *Movies and Methods* (Berkeley and Los Angeles: University of California Press, 1976), pp. 208–217.

10. "*Morocco*," *Cahiers du Cinéma*, no. 225 (November–December 1970) (reprinted in Peter Baxter, ed., *Sternberg*, trans. Diana Matias [London: British Film Institute, 1980], pp. 81–93). I am indebted to Chuck Kleinhans for pointing out this correspondence to me.

11. Christian Metz, "The Imaginary Signifier," *Screen* 16, no. 2 (1975): 14–76; Julia Lesage's "The Human Subject—You, He, or Me?" which challenged the editors of *Screen* on their incorporation of psychoanalytic terms into film theory, appeared in this same issue.

12. Maureen Turim, "Gentlemen Consume Blondes," *Wide Angle*, Spring 1976, p. 71.

13. Lucy Fisher, "The Image of Woman as Image: The Optical Politics of *Dames*," *Film Quarterly* 30 (Fall 1976): 8 (reprinted in Erens, *Sexual Stratagems*, pp. 41–61); and Rick Altman, ed., *Genre: The Musical* (London: Routledge & Kegan Paul, 1981), pp. 70–84.

14. I refer here to Karl Marx's theory of commodity fetishism, in *Capital*, vol. 1.

15. Laura Mulvey, "You Don't Know What Is Happening, Do You, Mr. Jones?" *Spare Rib* 8 (February 1973) (reprinted in *Spare Rib Reader*, ed. Marsha Rowe [London: Penguin Books, 1982], pp. 48–57).

16. Joanna Russ, "Comment on Helene E. Roberts's 'The Exquisite Slave: The Role of Clothes in the Making of the Victorian Woman' and David Kunzle's 'Dress Reform as Antifeminism,'" *Signs* 2, no. 3 (1977): 521. Gayle Rubin ("Thinking Sex: Notes for a Radical Theory of the Politics of Sexuality," in Vance, *Pleasure and Danger*, p. 306) is critical of the way the antipornography movement focuses on "non-routine acts of love rather than routine acts of oppression, exploitation, or violence."

17. Russ, p. 521.

18. Mary Ann Doane, Patricia Mellencamp, and Linda Williams, "Feminist Film Criticism: An Introduction," in Doane, Mellencamp, and Williams, *Re-Vision*, p. 8.

19. Hélène Cixous ("The Laugh of the Medusa," in *The Signs Reader*, trans. Keith Cohen and Paula Cohen, ed. Elizabeth Abel and Emily K. Abel [Chicago: University of Chicago Press, 1983], p. 291) describes the way creativity might take place from the cultural "in-between":

If woman has always functioned "within" the discourse of man, a signifier that has always referred back to the opposite signifier which annihilates its specific energy and diminishes or stifles its very different sounds, it is time for her to dislocate this "within," to explode it, turn it around, and seize it; to make it hers, containing it, taking it in her own mouth, biting that tongue with her very own teeth to invent for herself a language to get inside of.

20. Doane, Mellencamp, and Williams, "Feminist Film Criticism," p. 9.

21. Juliet Mitchell, *Psychoanalysis and Feminism* (London: Lane, 1974).

22. Jacqueline Rose, quoted in de Lauretis, *Alice Doesn't*, p. 165.

23. Griselda Pollock ("Report on the Weekend School," *Screen* 18, no. 2 [1977]: 112) cautions feminists about the use of Freud:

Furthermore, in so far as Freudian theory correctly describes the laws by which we are placed as subjects within a particular social formation, it also posits an inevitable resistance outside clinical or quite specific situations to the very knowledge that psychoanalysis offers. Thus, even within a film theory that uses the concerns of psychoanalysis, these resistances operate to counter the radical possibilities offered by the use of the theory. There is therefore every likelihood that the repression of the feminine is doubly ensured even at the point of potential exposure in theoretical analysis of film.

24. I refer here to larger debates within Marxist cultural studies, focused around the British journal *Screen*'s introduction of Lacanian psychoanalysis into film theory. See, for instance, Anthony Easthope, "The Trajectory of *Screen*, 1971–79," in *The Politics of Theory*, ed. Francis Barker et al. (Colchester, Eng.: University of Essex, 1983), pp. 121–133; Kevin Robins, "Althusserian Marxism and Media Studies: The Case of *Screen*," *Media, Culture and Society* 1, no. 4 (1979): 355–370; Iain Chambers et al., "Marxism and Culture," and Rosalind Coward, "Response," *Screen* 18, no. 4 (1977): 109–122.

25. Terry Lovell, "The Social Relations of Cultural Production: Absent Centre of a New Discourse," in *One-Dimensional Marxism*, ed. Simon Clarke, Victor Jeleniewski Seidler, Kevin McDonnell, Kevin Robins, and Terry Lovell (London: Allison & Busby, 1980), p. 243.

26. Christine Gledhill, "Recent Developments in Feminist Criticism," *Quarterly Review of Film Studies* 3, no. 4 (1978): 483 (reprinted in Doane, Mellencamp, and Williams, *Re-Vision*, pp. 18–45).

27. Kaplan, *Women and Film*, p. 14.

28. Ibid., p. 24.

29. For examples of the Marxist feminist reconsideration of psychoanalytic theory in response to this criticism, see Annette Kuhn, "Women's Genres," *Screen* 25, no. 1 (1984): 19–27; and Claire Johnston, "The Subject of Feminist Film Theory/Practice," *Screen* 23, no. 1 (1982): 27–34.

30. Jean-Louis Baudry ("Ideological Effects of the Basic Cinematographic Apparatus," *Film Quarterly* 28, no. 2 [1974–1975]: 46n) gives the reader some help with the concept of "subject," at a time when the term was used more tentatively than it is now: "We understand the term 'subject' here in its function as vehicle and place of intersection of ideological implications which we are attempting progressively to make clear, and not as the structural function which analytic discourse attempts to locate. It would rather take partially the place of the ego, of whose deviations little is known in the analytic field." The editors also thought it necessary to make it clear to readers that "the term 'subject' is used by Baudry and others not to mean the topic of discourse, but rather the perceiving and ordering self, as in our term 'subjective'" (p. 40).

31. One of the most comprehensive discussions of this "spectator eye" appears in another post-1968 French work on technology and ideology, Jean-Louis Comolli, "Technique and Ideology: Camera, Perspective, Depth of Field," *Film Reader*, no. 2 (February 1977): 128–140; reprinted in Bill Nichols, ed., *Movies and Methods*, vol. 2 (Berkeley and Los Angeles: University of California Press, 1985), pp. 40–57.

32. This analogy is fully explored in Jean-Louis Baudry, "The Apparatus," *Camera Obscura* 1 (Fall 1976): 104–123.

33. My complaint here is that concepts which originally were forged within the terms of a materialist analysis have gradually become removed from the Marxist theoretical structures that first defined them. Another example of this is the way *signifying practice* has come to stand for nothing more than the construction of meaning. Originally, as theorized by Julia Kristeva (see her "Signifying Practice and Mode of Production," *Edinburgh '76 Magazine*, no. 1, pp. 64–76), *signifying practice* included both the social maintenance function and the subversive possibilities of linguistic practices, with meaning-making activities always relative to the mode of production in a society.

34. E. Ann Kaplan, "Aspects of British Feminist Film Theory: A Critical Evaluation of Texts by Claire Johnston and Pam Cook," *Jump Cut*, nos. 12–13 (December 1976): 54.

35. See Terry Lovell, *Pictures of Reality* (London: British Film Institute, 1980), p. 94, for more on Brecht and pleasure.

36. For example, see Fredric Jameson, "Pleasure: A Political Issue," in Jameson et al., *Formations of Pleasure* (London: Routledge & Kegan Paul, 1983); and Richard Dyer, "Entertainment and Utopia," *Movie*, no. 24 (Spring 1977): 2–13 (reprinted in Altman, *Genre*, pp. 175–189).

37. Michèle Barrett, "Feminism and the Definition of Cultural Politics," in *Feminism, Culture, and Politics*, ed. Rosalind Brunt and Caroline Rowan (London: Lawrence & Wishart, 1982), p. 54.

38. See Terry Lovell, *Pictures of Reality*, pp. 87 and 95.

39. Claudia Springer, "Black Women Filmmakers," *Jump Cut*, no. 29 (February 1984): 34–38.

40. Claire Johnston, in "Women's Cinema as Counter-Cinema," p. 28, first articulated this in relation to feminist film theory: "The sign is always a product. What the camera in fact grasps is the 'natural' world of the dominant ideology. Women's cinema cannot afford such idealism; the 'truth' of our oppression cannot be 'captured' on celluloid with the 'innocence' of the camera: it has to be constructed/manufactured."

41. Kimberly Safford, in "*La Operación*: Forced Sterilization" (her review of the film, in *Jump Cut*, no. 29 [February 1984]: 37–38), says that for the filmmakers, the most direct way to demystify sterilization for Puerto Rican women is to demonstrate using documentary realism that since women's tubes are always severed in surgery, the sterilization operation is not as easily reversible as many women continue to believe. *La Operación* makes this argument with a conventional journalistic technique—graphic detailing of the surgery itself, the theory being that photographic "reality" that directly contradicts viewers' conceptions has the power to reverse those conceptions.

42. The idea of women's culture as "muted" is Elaine Showalter's; see, for instance, "Feminist Criticism in the Wilderness," in *Writing and Sexual Difference*, ed. Elizabeth Abel (Chicago: University of Chicago Press, 1982), pp. 9–35.

43. Annette Kolodny, informal talk at Duke University, 1 March 1985.

44. Mulvey has since modified her provocative position that spectator point of view in the cinema is consistently the male point of view. In "Afterthoughts on 'Visual Pleasure and Narrative Cinema' Inspired by *Duel in the Sun*" (*Framework*, nos. 15–17 [1981]), she admits that her "masculinized" spectator-screen image relation was a calculated irony and that the actual gender of the viewer was not a consideration here.

45. See, for instance, Linda Williams, "When the Woman Looks," in Doane, Mellencamp, and Williams, *Re-Vision*, pp. 83–99.

46. Marcia Landy and Lucy Fisher, "*The Eyes of Laura Mars*: A Binocular Critique," *Screen* 23, nos. 3–4 (1982): 4–19.

47. Mary Ann Doane, "Film and the Masquerade—Theorizing the Female Spectator," *Screen* 23, nos. 3–4 (1982): 74–87.

48. Ibid., p. 83; see also Mary Ann Doane, "The 'Woman's Film': Possession and Address," in Doane, Mellencamp, and Williams, *Re-Vision*, pp. 67–82.

49. Pam Cook ("Melodrama and the Women's Picture," in *Gainsborough Melodrama*, ed. Sue Aspinall and Robert Murphy [London: British Film Institute, 1983], pp. 14–28) takes the position that female desire is conceivable in these genres but that the films themselves register this possibility as contradiction.

50. Lucie Arbuthnot and Gail Seneca, "Pre-Text and Text in *Gentlemen Prefer Blondes*," *Film Reader* 5 (Winter 1981–1982): 14.

51. Liz Ellsworth, "The Power of Interpretative Communities: Feminist Appropriations of *Personal Best*" (paper delivered at Society for Cinema Studies Conference, University of Wisconsin-Madison, March 1984).

52. Chris Straayer, "*Personal Best*: Lesbian/Feminist Audience," *Jump Cut*, no. 29 (February 1984): 40–44; for another viewpoint, see Linda Williams, "*Personal Best*: Women in Love," *Jump Cut*, no. 27 (July 1982): 11–12.

53. Edith Becker, Michelle Citron, Julia Lesage, and B. Ruby Rich, "Lesbians and Film: Introduction to Special Section," *Jump Cut*, nos. 24–25 (March 1981): 17.

54. See Lisa DiCaprio, "*Lianna*: Liberal Lesbianism," *Jump Cut*, no. 29 (February 1984): 45–47.

55. See Kathryn Kalinak, "*Flashdance*: The Dead-End Kid," *Jump Cut*, no. 29 (February 1984): 3–5.

56. See, for instance, Janice Radway, *Reading the Romance* (Chapel Hill: University of North Carolina Press, 1984).

57. Ann Barr Snitow, "Mass Market Romance: Pornography for Women is Different," *Radical History Review* 20 (Spring–Summer 1979): 157 (reprinted in Snitow, Stansell, and Thompson, *Powers of Desire*, pp. 245–263).

58. Tania Modleski, *Loving with a Vengeance* (Hamden, Conn.: Archon Books), p. 103.

59. Pat Aufderheide, "What Are Romances Telling Us?" *In These Times*, 6–12 February 1985, p. 20.

60. Modleski, *Loving with a Vengeance*, p. 104.

61. Ellen Willis, "Feminism, Moralism, and Pornography," in Snitow, Stansell, and Thompson, *Powers of Desire*, p. 463.

62. Chuck Kleinhans and Julia Lesage, "The Politics of Sexual Representation" (introduction to special section on Pornography and Sexual Images), *Jump Cut*, no. 30 (March 1986): 24–26.

MASTERPIECE THEATRE AND THE USES OF TRADITION

TIMOTHY BRENNAN

Masterpiece Theatre could easily have had a short run after its debut in 1970 or become a show of "specials" like Great Performances and American Playhouse. Instead, it led a wave of British programming on American public television that has lasted ever since. This success is related to the fact that the show is not a masterpiece, or a theater, or even a collection of individual programs, but a "literary" tradition.

Masterpiece Theatre's popularization of literary "classics" is familiar in many earlier forms—for example, it is found in the British magazine *Titbits* at the turn of the century, in the American journal *Blackwood's* in the 1830s, and in some of the railway bookstall offerings of the same period. Popularizations with a high cultural veneer inevitably accompany mass literacy as a mediating agent for the professional, upwardly mobile classes. That is why the sudden discovery by angry media critics of Masterpiece Theatre's ludicrous snobbery and ersatz culture is misplaced. Snobbery was the target of *National Lampoon's* 1981 spoof on the "PBS Anything British Theatre" and of Michael Arlen's early articles on Masterpiece Theatre in the *New Yorker*. More recently Eric Mankin, in *In These Times*, made the same points, but he also found a new angle when he complained of the show's "second-rate up-the-empire hokum." [1]

These reactions are unsatisfactory. Masterpiece Theatre stands at the center of a much more tangled web of conflicts than that between fine art and imitations. There is, for example, the issue of the commercialization of public television, over which Masterpiece Theatre has presided for more than a decade. There is also Masterpiece Theatre's unusual success in carving out a role for "literature" in a culture of pop videos and variety shows. It has to be emphasized that Masterpiece Theatre is probably the only PBS program to produce spin-offs on the commercial networks, for this is precisely what *The Thorn Birds*, *The Far Pavilions*, and *A.D.* (among others) are. In fact, these rehashes often employ the very same British faces as Masterpiece Theatre, faces that can be seen in gala balls at New York nightclubs or in the celebrity photos of the next day's *New York Post*.

And this brings us to the most obvious and important conflict of all, one that strangely suggests the earlier conflict between "literature" and television—that is, the conflict between Britain and the United States, embodied in the congenial presence of the Americanized Englishman, Alistair Cooke, the show's host.

From *Social Text*, no. 12 (Fall 1985).

Author's Note: Research was conducted for the most part at the Museum of Broadcasting in New York, and at Frank Goodman Associates, distributors for the BBC in the New York area. Thanks to *Channels* magazine for commissioning an earlier version of this article.

Lingering behind the complaints of snobbery is the feeling that American culture is more democratic, more rough-edged than the pretentious one imported from England. But this view actually reinforces a central Masterpiece Theatre dogma about the irrepressible *class* nature of nationality itself—at least as nationalities are commonly perceived. On the one side, we find powdered wigs, crown jewels, and buckled shoes; on the other, log cabins, rolled-up sleeves, and six-shooters. In Masterpiece Theatre, national cultures are playing roles in a political melodrama: England plays the role of gentry; America, the entrepreneurial class; and others—very many others—play proletarians pure and simple.

Masterpiece Theatre would not have had this success if it were only a launching pad for TV novels, although this is exactly how it began. We expect shows produced by the "Petroleum Broadcasting Company" to promote conservative views, but we are underestimating Mobil if we assume that these views are passive products of a corporate outlook. The mastermind behind Masterpiece Theatre is after all Herb Schmertz, the same Mobil Public Affairs executive responsible for a notoriously aggressive procorporate publicity posture best exemplified by its paid columns on the *New York Times* op-ed pages.

I am suggesting that Masterpiece Theatre's snobbery—its supposedly offensive popularization of classic novels (or, depending on your point of view, its supposedly wonderful representation of them)—is only an instrument of a larger, sometimes very conscious, corporate strategy. Masterpiece Theatre is a cultural colonization in the heart of empire, an attempt to fuse together the apparently incompatible national myths of England and the United States in order to strengthen imperial attitudes in an era of European and North American decline. The commercialization of public television has been an important adjunct to this process, and the popularization of high art has been an important source of appeal to an audience being asked to buy an ideological commodity. I want to show first how Masterpiece Theatre works, then examine what it is saying.

THE BUSINESS OF CULTURE

Richard Hoggart once observed about postwar Britain that "great numbers of people simply assume that the BBC is 'them.'" By contrast, commercial television is—or seems more truly to be—"us."[2] But America's PBS, more dependent on corporate funding than the BBC, has correspondingly sought to become "us" for greater numbers of people.

Not only does Masterpiece Theatre bear the marks of a newly commercialized product of educational television, it has actually been instrumental in bringing about the change to corporate sponsorship. The connections are only circumstantial, and there are other factors involved (including a decline in federal support), but the rise of Masterpiece Theatre has coincided with the victory of privately funded "public" television. In some ways, Masterpiece Theatre is the model for an entire generation of programs whose selling point, "artistic quality," is the very feature that allows them to compete with the commercial networks.[3]

The mass appeal of elitism seems less likely to succeed on television than it did in the pages of *Titbits* or *Blackwood's*. The pretense of highbrow literature is difficult to maintain in a medium that draws attention to its own wide accessibility. Although consumed like books, in private spaces, television is also "broadcast"—it is viewing for the "crowds."

At first Mobil did not know which combination of myths to use. Mobil Public Affairs chief Herb Schmertz, along with Joan Wilson of WGBH Boston (the two forces behind the show), appear to have decided slowly on the proper mix. Their paradoxical task can be traced in the transformation of Masterpiece Theatre from a show of adaptations to a show of "instant classics." Images of England and the United States united by empire are metaphorically inscribed in most Masterpiece Theatre programs. But the motivations behind the alliance also help explain the evolution of that programming. The first three seasons dedicated themselves to the high bourgeois novel, reproducing as closely as possible the masterpieces of Balzac, Dostoevsky, and James. It was from this stage that Masterpiece Theatre directly grew.

In recent seasons, however, the emphasis has been on original dramas based on schemata from the nineteenth-century British novel. My argument is that this shift to original screenplays has been neither an inevitable outcome of the adaptation process nor a predictable relaxation of high television standards after years of vigilance. The shift has two motivations, both of which revolve around Masterpiece Theatre's increased ability to control content when using the original screenplays of the "instant classic." These motivations are (1) ensuring entertainment levels (since now PBS was beginning to compete with commercial networks) and (2) underlining the central message of British and American unity. Of the seventy-four separate programs aired by Masterpiece Theatre in the first thirteen years, the small number of original screenplays all happen to be among the show's greatest successes—*The First Churchills*; *The Six Wives of Henry VIII*; *Upstairs, Downstairs*; *Flickers*; and *The Duchess of Duke Street*.

According to Schmertz, Mobil "has no idea who watches Masterpiece Theatre. We [are] simply looking to support quality television."[4] Some background details suggest that this is not so. Several years ago, Schmertz single-handedly fought his advisors to include *Upstairs, Downstairs* in the Masterpiece Theatre curriculum. *Upstairs, Downstairs*—a look at the fading hierarchies of an Edwardian household—deviated from the former adaptation of classics in that it was not taken from a novel. Moreover, unlike earlier original screenplays, it wasn't closely modeled on a well-known classic, as, for example, *Elizabeth R* had been in the early days when it was made to look like a Shakespearean history play. When *Upstairs, Downstairs* was first aired, Alistair Cooke actually apologized, and later he hedged: "This show is a departure from our practice of dramatizing literature. . . . But you could call it . . . the *Forsyte Saga* upside down." This all seems silly in retrospect, since the show was given a whole new run with original episodes two years later and has been repeated several times since. Masterpiece Theatre's literariness, while still very important, was being driven to the limits of tenuousness.

Again, the commercialization of public television and the alliance between England and America went hand in hand. Despite Schmertz's pretended indifference to the kind of audience watching the show, the question of the PBS audi-

ence as a whole was loudly disputed during the very years of Masterpiece Theatre's ascendance. The Corporation for Public Broadcasting president, Jay Iselin,
under fire for programming that had been called "WASP-oriented and Anglo-
philiac," cited a Roper report of 1976 revealing that 59 percent of PBS viewers
had a high school education or less. In fact, according to the report, the demographic character of public television viewers paralleled that of the total adult
population, with the exception of blue-collar workers. Iselin was later to distinguish himself as a major proponent of private funding.

Says Schmertz, "If you go by the mail that comes in here unsolicited, you
would be led to believe that the Masterpiece Theatre audience is pretty much a
cross segment of the population. I think people who watch it or know a lot about
it would like to think that they're somehow elite. That's nonsense." [5]

But it is nonsense that ensures Mobil's continued support. For the relatively
small cost of $7 million, Mobil receives the use of about fifty hours of public
television time, a much lower rate than that paid by advertisers on commercial
channels.[6] Obviously, the greater the audience, the larger the bargain. The myth
of selectivity helps to depress the market value of advertising time on PBS—
hence the need to forge a group that is open to the blandishments of high culture
and secretly thankful that there are corporations to save them from the entertainment of the "masses." [7]

On the British side, the manipulation of nationalities as classes is good business. The gap that British television aspires to fill in the American market for
"quality television" is continually made to appear wider than it is. Instead of
seeing Masterpiece Theatre as a tawdry fabrication of BBC education, we are
made to see it as an opportunity for Americans to enrich their cultural life. British polish and American crudity are offset by British fadedness and American
wealth. They need one another.

The commercialization of public television may not be the result only of appeals for private funding by a financially endangered network facing waning federal subsidies. The eagerness may be coming from the corporations themselves
that seek the complacent atmosphere of PBS to peddle their wares. On cultural
programming, the wares are less commercial than ideological. The object, of
course, is not always to sell a dirty little commodity. It is just as important to set
the tone within which many commodities can be sold efficiently. An empire is a
feel-good community.

A COCKNEY IN A SMOKING JACKET

In one program called *Flickers*, about the early days of the British film industry,
cockney filmmaker Arnie Cole refuses to cut a hokey scene from one of his films
by pointing to its literary merits. His skeptical wife, knowing his lack of education asks, "And you know about literature, I suppose?" He answers, "Well, I
read the synopses, didn't I? If their stories is any good, I been nickin' 'em."

Scenes like this—and they occur throughout Masterpiece Theatre—show just
how aware Masterpiece Theatre is of its own function. The regulation of content
through original screenplays allows the show to bring to the surface these moral-

ity plays of good business sense and the respectability of "literature," always allowing the audience a comfortable space within which to play Arnie's wife— both politely aghast and also amused by his mercenary instrumentalization of "literature." In the spirit of the cinema remake, two seasons later we get *Pictures*, where the identifications are made clearer still. Arnie (cockney, crude, mercantile) is now found in the form of an American film tycoon (brash, slovenly, rich) who makes an English working girl into a star, relying on the advice of an English "novelist" who happens to be mucking about writing film scripts between moments of "serious" writing. All the essential elements are here: England and the United States married in a film enterprise dependent on an inspiration that is primarily literary. On a more self-conscious level, these particular shows are mimicking the British and American collaboration being literally acted out in the offices of New York Mobil and the British Networks.[8] Like so much prime time, the show becomes a commercial for itself.

The usual criticisms of Masterpiece Theatre waver between resentment of English upper-class airs and (conversely) an elitist scorn for Masterpiece Theatre's watering-down of the classics for mass consumption. As I said, these criticisms are wholly a part of the same outlook Masterpiece Theatre thrives on. Arguments of taste do not go far enough here. The show's popularizing of classics, although it strips away the subtleties that separate the two sides of class-divided art, still desperately holds on to a literary aura—the paraphernalia and the atmosphere of literary life.

Any melodramatic prop is permissible as long as the subject is an author or a literary event. The titillation and scandal promised by the title of the original screenplay *Notorious Woman* gives way to a story based on the life of the French author George Sand. A figure like Beatrix Potter not only provides the story for another show, but she is herself the story, clipping roses in her garden, arguing with her publisher, and taking up camera time by turning the pages of her books. While Hardy's *Jude the Obscure* is a good example of the show's early emphasis on the classics, it is common to see something like *Cakes and Ale* later, Somerset Maugham's satire on Hardy and the best-selling society novelist Hugh Walpole.

For an almost unbroken three-year stretch from 1973 through 1976, these experiments with such middlebrow figures as Potter and Walpole become an open embrace in which high literary gestures are temporarily set aside. In this period, the popular genres come into their own with the mystery story of Dorothy Sayers's *Murder Must Advertise*, popular history and adventure in Major Bill Hartley's *Danger UXB*, and romance in H. E. Bates's *Love for Lydia*. But middlebrow entertainment was not the primary mission. Soon afterward, the authority and the appeal that the classics and the lower genres respectively provide once again become Masterpiece Theatre's trademark.

In the eighties, the popular genres served as the basis for an increasing number of Masterpiece Theatre and other English-produced PBS dramas with anti-communist themes, undoubtedly prompted in part by conservative charges of a leftist bias on PBS. The Mystery series presented *Reilly: Ace of Spies*, based on the biography of a White Russian counterrevolutionary, anglicized in the TV version into a dashing real-life James Bond. Great Performances was the rubric used for dramatizations of Englishmen spying for Russia in *Man from Moscow* and *An Englishman Abroad*, the latter a play by Alan Bennett presenting a half-sympathetic, half-caustic portrait of the Oxbridge culture that produced turncoat Guy Burgess.

The real issue is to see how this literary aura is functioning. The Oxbridge education that was so important a part of the Masterpiece Theatre fiction (especially before 1973) had to be scaled for television in the form of *manners*. For manners are the outward sign of a literary education as well as of English upper-class power, and, unlike the vast training of classical education, can be communicated in a weekly television program. Masterpiece Theatre's literary trappings and its political message merge. One episode from *The Flame Trees of Thika* illustrates this. The program documents the hardships of the British pioneers in Kenya. In it, we hear homesteader Robin Huxley exclaim about a new English arrival, "His manners were so perfect he made me feel like a boy born to serve." When later he is told by a neighbor that he needs a "really good headman," he answers, "Is there such a thing?"

Snobbery is a defense of class; the popularization of snobbery is, however, only possible in an imperial context, where it is something every white Englishman or American can hope to exercise over the unruly blacks of Kenya. At the same time, the tension between Oxford don and city merchant, or between toff and bumpkin (expressions of the tension between the English and American national stereotypes), is relieved, submerged, and blended.

The arrogance and racism of colonialism as they appear in this *Flame Trees of Thika* episode are unusual for Masterpiece Theatre, which prefers to play out the same fables of domination on a more metaphoric plane, and in more civilized surroundings. The alliance between England and America, however, is brilliantly codified here. Just as Arnie Cole was a cockney (hence vulgar, mercenary), Robin Huxley is a "pioneer." Although there are occasionally American characters, the American presence is much more commonly suggested only obliquely. These pioneers speak with British accents, are excessively punctual and well groomed, and record their journey in memoirs under the name of a reputed English literary family, Huxley.

These motifs are present in various guises in almost all of Masterpiece Theatre's individual programs—ruggedness and delicacy, frontier and Oxford, philistinism and good breeding. America and England combine forces in allegories of power designed to please both sides, always related to, if not present at, the colonial nexus. In this program, Africa is both itself and a proxy American wilderness—the same role Australia played in another program, *A Town Like Alice*. Both satisfy the vaguely American criteria of having frontiers, entrepreneurial settler types, settlers already removed from their English origins, and a nonwhite population ready for domination.

Masterpiece Theatre is a kind of training in the manners necessary for running an empire with dignity. The British have had more practice, and the Americans need their legitimacy and their cultural expertise.

THE NATIONAL AND THE POPULAR

Masterpiece Theatre is more a part of British culture than it appears from a look at its corporate history. One obvious influence, for example, is the well-known British literary celebrity F. R. Leavis, whose populist elitism can be seen in all the features of the Masterpiece Theatre pose: the strong sense of an exclusive English literary tradition, the role of literature in preserving the values of the preindustrial English village, and the hatred of mass art (which Leavis called "de-creation").

Leavis's tortured awareness of popular culture in such books as *Mass Civilization and Minority Culture* prefigures Masterpiece Theatre's awareness of the meeting place of high and low art in a national context. But although Masterpiece Theatre suggests Leavis, it does not really repeat him. It is a terrible business proposition, for instance, to believe, as Leavis did, that the ills of modernity come from the participation of the people. Leavis spent volumes reviling the culture of the machine, whereas Masterpiece Theatre creates its literary coterie by using one.

But the case of Leavis is actually very useful in understanding how Masterpiece Theatre works. Although Leavis fought both the middle class and the people, his apotheosis of "literature" and his position that it could be used to preserve and sanctify a tradition are essential to Masterpiece Theatre. For Leavis, the bourgeois cheapens literature by making it entertainment; for PBS, the vulgar local concerns (especially among the minorities) obscure the purity of the English imagination.[9]

Masterpiece Theatre's popularity should have intrigued media critics trained in the Leavis school, as so many postwar English critics were. As Orwell pointed out in his essay on Boys' Weeklies in 1939, the left has been slow to challenge the relentless, mostly conservative political messages of media culture. That high art, or its auspices, could also play a role in reactionary politics is an idea that has not really come of age in a generation schooled in the aesthetic opinions of Marx, Marcuse, and Lukács.

The media criticism of Stuart Hall, Richard Hoggart, and Raymond Williams in postwar England has tried to go beyond Leavis in ways that now resemble the efforts of Antonio Gramsci (although they began their critique long before Gramsci's work came on the English scene). Unfortunately, Gramsci's influence, while it has been pronounced in political science and sociology, has not been strong in culture, except in terms of the concepts of "hegemony" and "organic intellectual." For example, the specific and detailed criticism Gramsci produced on theater between 1916 and 1920 for *Avanti* has only now been translated.

This work on theater could offer valuable ways to assess Masterpiece Theatre. It conceived of bourgeois drama in two forms: the *Commedia 'Per Bene,'* which reflected a "petty bourgeois worldview of simplicity, superficiality, facile dialogue and sentimentality"; and the *Commedia 'dell'uomo Spiritoso,'* which reflected the "tastes and platitudes of the middle and haute bourgeois's socially gratifying Weltschmertz."[10]

Because little work has been done on the way television takes over earlier forms of popular and middle-class drama, the relevance of this research is easy to miss. Williams did, however, note in his book on television that "in most parts of the world, since the spread of television, there has been a scale and intensity of dramatic performance which is without precedent in the history of human culture."[11] Clearly, the roles played by these Italian dramas and the current role of Masterpiece Theatre are similar. Both present the same banalities of today's prime time in the formidable guise of "taste," designed to exclude groups on the basis of class and nationality and having no absolute value as such.

I bring up Gramsci here because he in many ways represents Leavis's alter ego and also because he has been influential on media critics of the Masterpiece Theatre generation. The fact is, arguments over "taste" are very hard to shake in media criticism, and often lead to a populist reverie most fully realized by Leavis himself.[12] Gramsci's emphasis on culture's functionalism, specifically on its nation-forming function, is on the contrary a fruitful and rarely used alternative. It seems especially useful in regard to Masterpiece Theatre's Anglo-American chauvinism.

One of the unlikely objects of Gramsci's studies was the playwright Pirandello, whose highly intellectual studies of identity fascinated Gramsci, not only because of drama's ability to reach the broad public, but specifically because Pirandello's philosophical skepticism weakened the mystifying powers of the Catholic clergy. It was this same clergy, with its Holy Roman Imperial vestiges, that Gramsci felt retarded Italy's nationhood.

Gramsci felt that Italy's inability to produce a viable popular literature, as France had in the popular romance and England had in the detective story, was an important factor in its national disunity. Italy could produce a "refined" author like Manzoni, but not a Conan Doyle or Dumas *fils*. His ideal continued to be the popular novel that was also the great epic novel—in short, the "national-popular" novel as produced in Russia by Tolstoy.[13]

My point is that because Gramsci was able to view literary hybrids from the perspective of national function rather than "taste," he equips us to understand Masterpiece Theatre, which is really a distorted version of the national-popular. The magic of Masterpiece Theatre is its ability to convince the critical community that it is raising the cultural level of the public, when it is really creating the illusion of mass elitism. As I've said, mass elitism is in one sense not an illusion at all—that is, when one is talking about "our" nation over other nations. The same applies even when it is the provisional, tacked-together nation of England and United States. This is the show's imperial function.

Such provisional cultural nationalisms are more common in the atmosphere of clamoring Third World polities articulating their cultural demands in UNESCO position papers. The retrenchments of Europe are evident all the way from the European Common Market to what E. P. Thompson ingeniously called "Natopolitan culture."[14] Tom Nairn has also shown how in many ways the European community has made efforts "to reconcile and somehow fuse together a collection of nation-states and nationalisms."[15] Mobil's collaboration with English television is an expression of these European developments and is intensified by the common language and the joint dominance which the English and American empires have consecutively enjoyed for over two centuries.[16]

THE NEW NOVEL

If Masterpiece Theatre's programs based themselves on the model of nineteenth-century bourgeois novels, they did not make extraordinary efforts to reproduce them (even within the obvious constraints of a televised format).[17] The sharp class tensions, the historical details, and the psychological realism of the nineteenth-century novel were all useful for describing the conflicts of British and American culture; however, in order to be free of rancor, these conflicts had to be smoothed over, domesticated into polite class struggle. The conflicts between the aristocratic and the bourgeois in Masterpiece Theatre's *Pride and Prejudice* or *Madame Bovary* are therefore subdued, while the critique of bourgeois accumulation (*Père Goriot*) and patriarchal marriage laws (*Anna Karenina*) are privatized into a scandalous contest of wills. With the help of its instant classics, the show sometimes parodied these class tensions, as in *The Duchess of Duke Street*, in which an imperious cockney matron operates an aristocratic hotel. Such programs presented a recurrent parable of bourgeois revolutions in miniature, epitomized in the courting by American society lady Wallis Simpson of King Edward VI in *Edward and Mrs. Simpson*—the literal fulfillment of Masterpiece Theatre's ideal of the marriage of American bourgeois entrepreneurship to British imperial rulership, and a confirmation of the ultimate victory of the middle-class usurper, since the marriage forces Edward to abdicate.

The real British and American working classes, white and nonwhite, domestic and colonial, are rarely the center of dramatic attention in themselves, least of all if they are acting in militant solidarity; instead, the focus is on upward mobility to bourgeois success. The figure of the admirable upstart is repeated over and over again, not only in types like Arnie Cole, the Duchess of Duke Street, and Nancy Astor, but also in those like Australian cowboy Joe Harmon (*A Town Like Alice*), referred to at one point by Alistair Cooke as "Gary Cooper with an Australian accent," who marries a British heiress against the wishes of her protective London solicitor. In a climactic episode of *Upstairs, Downstairs*, the Bellamys' former parlor maid, Sarah, arrives victoriously in the Bellamys' sitting room on the arm of her husband, Thomas Watkins—formerly the valet to their impotent son-in-law. Thomas had adroitly used his knowledge of Bellamy family scandals to extort money from Lord Bellamy with which to start his own auto repair shop and is now a thriving entrepreneur; his success is set off against the failures of the Bellamys' son and heir James, who had impregnated and abandoned Sarah and whose feckless life eventually ends in suicide. (The mixture here of nostalgic affection for the aristocracy and acceptance of its superannuation by the more vital bourgeoisie was later reiterated in one of PBS's most popular literary dramatizations, Evelyn Waugh's *Brideshead Revisited*, in the paralleled decline into alcoholism of Sebastian Flyte and rise of his friend Charles Ryder, a sensitive but successful artist and level-headed bourgeois.)

The enormously successful *Jewel in the Crown* extends the pattern of adapting middlebrow literature (in this case, Paul Scott's *Raj Quartet*) and continues to suggest the classics by alluding to Forster's *A Passage to India*, repeating its central plot device of a controversial rape case set against the background of British excesses and cultural misunderstandings. Here the figure of the deserving upstart is ambiguously codified in the story's principal villain, the ruthless colonial police chief Ronald Merrick, whose inferior status in the English class system embitters him toward the local officials, who lack the will to accept the necessary cruelties of imperial rule. In this variation, the image of efficiency is not a pretty one; it recalls that of the *Poldark* series, in which good-hearted mining magnate Ross Poldark (who has just returned from fighting on the colonial side in the American revolution!) does battle with the unscrupulous but vastly more successful Warleggan bankers. Despite *Jewel in the Crown*'s critique of the British role in India, British fair play prevails in the sensitive accounts of Edwina Crane and Daphne Manners, who realize that the racialist premises of people like Merrick are now outdated. That kind of Empire is no longer viable.

When mass literacy in eighteenth-century England reached significant proportions, the English rulers were obliged to make it a form of training in bourgeois norms and values. In a modest and limited way, Masterpiece Theatre is training us to read the "literary" in a TV culture—to see in America the recurring parable of rugged American success; to see in England the continued value of good breeding; and to imagine, as is only possible in the confines of a living room, that a TV literature can raise select groups above the thousands of others who simply aren't tuned to the right channel.

But we are also being asked to believe that the great English novel of the nineteenth century is naturally fulfilled in the great American TV novel of the twentieth, and that both prove Anglo-American superiority—nearly two centuries of uninterrupted domination over the minor characters and bit parts that inhabit the rest of the world.

Notes

1. Michael Arlen, "Pervasive Albion," in *The View from Highway 1* (New York: McGraw-Hill, 1976); and Eric Mankin, "Mobil and the Masterclass," *In These Times*, 22 February 1984.
2. Robert Hewison, *In Anger: Culture in the Cold War 1945–60* (London: Weidenfeld & Nicolson, 1980), p. 171.
3. I am simply assuming here that most will agree that "artistic quality" is what Masterpiece Theatre pretends to offer. My purpose is not to define what art or "quality" is, or to tarnish Masterpiece Theatre's reputation by proving it doesn't have it. When I mention "popular art," I am referring to cultural objects produced for those who are not necessarily intellectuals, academics, bureaucrats, or artists—in short, for the lower classes, the "broad public." It does *not* necessarily mean the appeal is not also and simultaneously to intellectuals.
4. Interview with Herb Schmertz, Fall 1981, New York.
5. Schmertz interview. [*Editor's Note*: Such statements show a distinct change of tune in the rhetoric of conservatives, who fifteen years ago were successfully campaigning for government defunding of public broadcasting in order to gain financial and ideological

control of it themselves. At that time, for instance, Benjamin Stein wrote in that voice of the common people, the *Wall Street Journal*: " 'Public' television represents a subsidy by the lower-middle-class people, who pay the bulk of federal taxes, to the upper-income groups, and a subsidy of the many to the few. It is income transfer from the poor to the rich." Heads I win, tails you lose.]

6. Mankin, "Mobil and the Masterclass."

7. Under the euphemism "enhanced underwriting," commercials have now entered public television with full force. At present, they are still restricted from mentioning price or product superiority, but they may talk about services and locations. According to Sally Bedell Smith in the *New York Times* (1 April 1985), "Corporate contributions to PBS's national program service in 1984 were $57.1 million versus $38.1 million in 1983."

8. Mobil has not only done business with the BBC; its first several seasons were dominated by BBC programs. According to John Stringer, the chief executive of BBC's Commercial Operations at the time, "Just about everything we produced was eventually picked up by PBS." As the taste for more expensive on-location shootings rose, Masterpiece Theatre increasingly made deals with Grenada TV, Thames TV, and London Weekend TV.

9. This particular distaste for the nationalist fragmentation of minorities within the British isles (a miniature version of the crumbling empire) is not limited to conservative social theorists like Leavis. See Orwell's 1945 essay "Notes on Nationalism" or Tom Nairn's *The Break-up of Britain* (New York: Schocken, 1977). It should be said, however, that all three arrive at their views in different ways.

10. See Wallace Sillanpoa's discussion (rare in English) in "Cultural Theory and Literary Criticism in the Prison Notebooks of Antonio Gramsci" (Ph.D. diss., University of Connecticut, 1980), pp. 336–337.

11. Raymond Williams, *Television: Technology and Cultural Form* (New York: Schocken Books, 1975), p. 59.

12. Unless, that is, one counts such postwar English left writing as Hoggart's *The Uses of Literacy* or sections of Wiliams's *The Long Revolution*.

13. "National-Popular" (sometimes translated "people-nation") is Gramsci's own phrase, and recurs throughout the Prison Notebooks.

14. E. P. Thompson, "Outside the Whale," in *The Poverty of Theory and Other Essays* (New York: Monthly Review Press, 1978), pp. 213 ff.

15. Nairn, *Break-up of Britain*, p. 312.

16. With the uneventful temporary rifts of Grenada and the Falklands, this unity is stronger than ever. It is particularly noticeable in three areas: in the U.S. nuclear strategy for Europe; in the active rehabilitation of South Africa's international status; and (most pertinent of all) in the attempts to undercut UNESCO by promising to withhold funds (collectively making up 33 percent of UNESCO's budget) unless the organization cease its attacks on "Western values." Information of a specifically cultural type has been among those things Third World representatives of UNESCO have wanted more power over. See Jeremy Tunstall's *The Media Are American* (New York: Columbia University Press, 1977).

17. In this, Masterpiece Theatre differs from its British prototype, Classic Serials, which was the explicit model for Masterpiece Theatre in the early days. Now defunct, Classic Serials never strayed from straight reproductions of the literary canon.

THE LIBERATING POTENTIAL OF THE FANTASTIC IN CONTEMPORARY FAIRY TALES FOR CHILDREN

JACK ZIPES

> *The point is that we have not formed that ancient world—it has formed us. We ingested it as children whole, had its values and consciousness imprinted on our minds as cultural absolutes long before we were in fact men and women. We have taken the fairy tales of childhood with us into maturity, chewed but still lying in the stomach, as real identity. Between Snow-White and her heroic prince, our two great fictions, we never did have much of a chance. At some point, the Great Divide took place: they (the boys) dreamed of mounting the Greta Steed and buying Snow-White from the dwarfs; we (the girls) aspired to become that object of every necrophiliac's lust—the innocent, victimized* Sleeping Beauty, *beauteous lump of ultimate, sleeping good. Despite ourselves, sometimes knowing, unwilling, unable to do otherwise, we act out the roles we were taught.*
>
> ANDREA DWORKIN, *WOMAN HATING* (1974)

Our views of child-rearing, socialization, technology, and politics have changed to such a great extent since World War II that the classical folk and fairy tales appear too backward-looking to many progressive-minded critics and creative writers. Not only are the tales considered to be too sexist, racist, and authoritarian, but the general contents are said to reflect the concerns of semi-feudal, patriarchal societies.[1] What may have engendered hope for better living conditions centuries ago has become more inhibiting for today's children in the Western world. The discourse of classical fairy tales, its end effect, cannot be considered enlightening and emancipatory in the face of possible nuclear warfare, ecological destruction, growing governmental and industrial regimentation, and intense economic crisis.

Of course, there are numerous classical folk and fairy tales that still speak to the needs of children and illuminate possibilities for attaining personal autonomy and social freedom, and it would be foolish to reject the entire classical canon as socially useless or aesthetically outmoded. Moreover, as we know, the classical fairy tale as genre has not been static. Such nineteenth-century writers as Charles Dickens, George MacDonald, John Ruskin, George Sand, Oscar Wilde, Andrew Lang, L. Frank Baum, and others, designated now as "classical," opposed the authoritarian tendencies of the civilization process and expanded the horizons of

From Jack Zipes, *Fairy Tales and The Art of Subversion* (London: Heinemann, 1981).

the fairy tale discourse for children. They prepared the way for utopian and sub-versive experiments that altered the fairy tale discourse at the beginning of the twentieth century. Hope for liberating changes in social relations and political structures was conveyed through symbolic acts of writers who criticized abusive treatment of children and the repressive methods of sexual pedagogy.

Still, the innovative tales for children produced during the first three decades of the twentieth century did not successfully re-utilize fantastic projections and configurations of the classical fairy tales to gain wide acceptance among children and adults. If anything, the fantastic was used to compensate for the growing rationalization of culture, work, and family life in Western society—to defend the imagination of children. Thus, the fantastic was really on the defensive while appearing to be offensive. Something else was on the march in the name of prog-ress and civilization. The Taylorization of factory and office life, the panoptic organization of schools, hospitals, and prisons, the technical synchronization of art to create formations such as chorus lines and choreography resembling con-veyor belts, the celebration of uniform military power in parade and warfare—these were the real sociopolitical tendencies against which the progressive and experimental fairy tales for children reacted at the beginning of the twentieth century. These were the forces that confined and subdued the protest elements in the fairy tale discourse during the thirties, forties, and fifties.

Since then, the fantastic in fairy tales for children has been forced to take the offensive. This situation has not arisen because the fantastic is assuming a more liberating role but because it is in the throes of a last-ditch battle against what many writers have described as technologically instrumental and manipulative forces that operate largely for commercial interests and cast a "totalitarian" gloom over society by making people feel helpless and ineffectual in their at-tempts to reform and determine their own lives. "Brave new world," "1984," "one-dimensional society"—these have become key words in critiques of social development in both the West and the East. In commenting on the fairy tale in the postwar world, Marion Lochhead has asserted that the near victory of fascism was of utmost concern to such writers as C. S. Lewis and J. R. R. Tolkien: "Myth-making continues. The renaissance of wonder has reached maturity. And we need it. The conflict between good and evil—absolute evil—in which the child heroes of fantasy are caught up and taxed to the limit of their endurance has become a common theme."[2] Yet it is not merely the survival of good that is re-flected in contemporary fairy tales but the fantastic projection of possibilities for nonalienating living conditions. Hope for such a future follows on the struggles of the 1960s, which were marked by civil rights movements, antiwar protests, the rise of feminism, and demands for autonomy by minority groups and small de-prived nations throughout the world.

Since it would be too difficult to cover the entire development of the literary fairy tale for children in response to these struggles since 1945 and to demon-strate how and why fairy tale writers have sought to use fantastic projections in a liberating manner, I want to limit myself to a small number of representative writers in England, the United States, Italy, Germany, and France who have ex-pressly tried to make their tales more emancipatory in light of the restrictiveness of advanced industrial countries. My concern is twofold: I want to depict the motifs, ideas, styles, and methods used by these writers to make the fantastic projections within the fairy tales more liberating, and I want to question whether the intentions of a liberating fairy tale can actually have the effect desired by the writer in societies where socialization is concerned most with control, discipline, and rationalization.

Before I address these two points, though, it is crucial to discuss the "power" of the literary fairy tale—both classical and the innovative—in general, to clarify the meanings of such terms as "progressive" and "regressive," "liberating" and "inhibiting." Certainly the classical fairy tales have not retained their appeal among children and adults simply because they comply with the norms of the civilizing process. No, they have an extraordinary power, a power that Georges Jean locates, on a conscious level, in the way all good fairy tales aesthetically structure and use fantastic and miraculous elements to prepare us for our everyday life.[3] Magic is used paradoxically not to deceive us but to enlighten us. On an unconscious level, Jean believes that the best fairy tales bring together subjective and assimilatory impulses with objective intimations of a social setting that intrigue readers and allow for different interpretations according to one's ideology and belief.[4] Ultimately, Jean argues that the fantastic power of fairy tales consists in the uncanny way they provide a conduit into social reality.

Yet, given the proscription of fairy tale discourse within a historically prescribed civilizing process, a more careful distinction must be made between regressive and progressive aspects of the power of fairy tales in general if we are to understand the liberating potential of contemporary tales for children. Here I want to discuss Sigmund Freud's concept of the "uncanny" and Ernst Bloch's concept of "home" as constitutive elements of the liberating impulse behind the fantastic projections in fairy tales, whether they be classical or experimental. Their ideas will be related to Jean Piaget's notions of how children view and adapt to the world so that we can grasp the regressive and progressive features of contemporary fairy tales as politically symbolic acts seeking to make their mark on history.

I

In his essay on the uncanny, Freud remarks that the word *heimlich* means that which is familiar and agreeable *and also* that which is concealed and kept out of sight, and he concludes that *heimlich* is a word the meaning of which develops in the direction of ambivalence, until it finally coincides with its opposite, *unheimlich* or uncanny.[5] Through a close study of E. T. A. Hoffmann's fairy tale *The Sandman*, Freud argues that the uncanny or unfamiliar (*unheimlich*) brings us in closer touch with the familiar (*heimlich*) because it touches on emotional disturbances and returns us to repressed phases in our evolution:

If psychoanalytic theory is correct in maintaining that every effect belonging to an emotional impulse, whatever its kind, is transformed, if it is repressed, into anxiety, then among instances of frightening things there must be one class in which the frightening element can be shown to be something repressed which *recurs*. This class of frightening things would then constitute the uncanny; and it must be a matter of indifference whether what is uncanny was itself originally frightening or whether it carried some *other* affect. In the second place, if this is indeed the secret nature of the uncanny, we can understand why linguistic usage has extended *das Heimliche* ("homely") into its opposite, *das Unheimliche*; for this uncanny is in reality nothing new or alien but something which is familiar and old-established in the mind and which has become alienated from it only through the process of repression. This reference to the factor of repression enables us, furthermore, to understand Schelling's definition of the uncanny as something which ought to have remained hidden but has come to light.[6]

Freud insists that one must be extremely careful in using the category of the uncanny, since not everything that recalls repressed desires and surmounted modes of thinking belongs to the prehistory of the individual and the race and so can be considered uncanny. In particular, Freud mentions fairy tales as excluding the uncanny.

In fairy tales, for instance, the world of reality is left behind from the very start, and the animistic system of beliefs is frankly adopted. Wish-fulfillments, secret powers, omnipotence of thoughts, animation of inanimate objects, all the elements so common in fairy stories, can exert no uncanny influence here; for, as we have learnt, that feeling cannot arise unless there is a conflict of judgment as to whether things which have been "surmounted" and are regarded as incredible may not, after all, be possible; and this problem is eliminated from the outset by the postulates of the world of fairy tales.[7]

Although it is true that the uncanny becomes the familiar and the norm in the fairy tale because the narrative perspective accepts it so totally, there is still room for *another kind of uncanny experience* within the postulates and constructs of the fairy tale. That is, Freud's argument must be qualified regarding the machinations of the fairy tale. I do not, however, want to concern myself with this point at the moment but would simply like to suggest that the uncanny plays a significant role in the act of reading or listening to a fairy tale. Using and modifying Freud's category of the uncanny, I want to argue that *the very act of reading a fairy tale is an uncanny experience* in that it separates the reader from the restrictions of reality from the onset and makes the repressed unfamiliar familiar once again. Bruno Bettelheim has mentioned that the fairy tale estranges the child from the real world and allows him or her to deal with deep-rooted psychological problems and anxiety-provoking incidents to achieve autonomy.[8] Whether this is true or not, that is, whether a fairy tale can actually provide the means for coping with ego disturbance, as Bettelheim argues, remains to be seen.[9] It is true, however, that once we begin listening to or reading a fairy tale, there is estrangement or separation from a familiar world, inducing an uncanny feeling that is both frightening and comforting.

Actually, the complete reversal of the real world has already taken place on the part of the writer before we begin reading a fairy tale, and the writer invites the reader to repeat this uncanny experience. The process of reading involves dislocating the reader from a familiar setting and then identifying with the dislocated protagonist so that a quest for the *Heimische*, or real home, can begin. The fairy tale ignites a double quest for home: one occurs in the reader's mind and is psychological and difficult to interpret, since the reception of an individual tale varies according to the background and experience of the reader; the second occurs within the tale itself and indicates a socialization process and acquisition of values for participation in a society where the protagonist has more power of determination. This second quest for home can be regressive *or* progressive, depending on the narrator's stance *vis-à-vis* society. In both quests, the notion of home or *Heimat* (closely related etymologically to *heimlich* and *unheimlich*) retains a powerful progressive attraction for readers of fairy tales. The uncanny setting and motifs of the fairy tale already open us up to the recurrence of primal experiences, and we can move forward at the same time because it opens us up to what Freud calls "unfulfilled but possible futures to which we still like to cling in fantasy, all the strivings of the ego which adverse external circumstances have crushed, and all our suppressed acts of volition which nourish in us the illusion of Free Will." [10]

Obviously, Freud would not condone clinging to our fantasies in reality. Yet Ernst Bloch would argue that *some* are important to cultivate and defend, since they represent our radical or revolutionary urge to restructure society so that we can finally achieve home. Dreaming that stands still bodes no good.

But if it becomes a dreaming ahead, then its cause appears quite differently and excitingly alive. The dim and weakening features, which may be characteristic of mere yearning, disappear; and then yearning can show what it really is able to accomplish. It is the way of the world to counsel men to adjust to the world's pressures, and they have learned this lesson; only their wishes and dreams will not hearken to it. In this respect virtually all human beings are futuristic; they transcend their past life, and to the degree that they are satisfied, they think they deserve a better life (even though this may be pictured in a banal and egotistic way), and regard the inadequacy of their lot as a barrier, and not just as the way of the world.

To this extent, the most private and ignorant wishful thinking is to be preferred to any mindless goose-stepping; for wishful thinking is capable of revolutionary awareness, and can enter the chariot of history without necessarily abandoning in the process the good content of dreams. [11]

What Bloch means by "the good content of dreams" is often the projected fantasy and action of fairy tales with a forward and liberating look: human beings in an upright posture who strive for an autonomous existence and nonalienating setting, which allows for democratic cooperation and humane consideration. Real history that involves independent human self-determination cannot begin as long as there is exploitation and enslavement of humans by other humans. The active struggle against unjust and barbaric conditions in the world leads to home, or utopia, a place nobody has known but which represents humankind coming into its own:

The true genesis is not at the beginning, but at the end, and it starts to begin only when society and existence become radical: that is, comprehend their own roots. But the root of history is the working, creating man, who rebuilds and transforms the given circumstances of the world. Once man has comprehended himself and has established his own domain in real democracy, without depersonalization and alienation, something arises in the world which all men have glimpsed in childhood: a place and a state in which no one has yet been. And the name of this something is home or homeland. [12]

Philosophically speaking, then, the real return home or recurrence of the uncanny *is* a move forward to what has been repressed and never fulfilled. The pattern in most fairy tales involves the reconstitution of home on a new plane, and this accounts for the power of its appeal to both children and adults.

In Bloch's two major essays on fairy tales, "Das Märchen geht selber in Zeit" (The Fairy Tale Moves on its Own in Time) and "Bessere Luftschlösser in Jahrmarkt und Zirkus, in Märchen und Kolportage" (Better Castles in the Air in Fair and Circus, in Fairy Tale and Sensationalist Literature),[13] Bloch is concerned with the manner in which the hero and the aesthetic constructs of the tale illuminate the way to overcome oppression. He focuses on the way the underdog, the small person, uses his or her wits not simply to survive but to live a better life. Bloch insists that there is good reason for the timelessness of traditional fairy tales. "Not only does the fairy tale remain as fresh as longing and love, but the demonically evil, which is abundant in the fairy tale, is still seen at work here in the present, and the happiness of 'once upon a time,' which is even more abundant, still affects our visions of the future."[14]

It is not only the timeless aspect of traditional fairy tales that interests Bloch, but also the way they are modernized and appeal to all classes and age groups in society. Instead of demeaning popular culture and common appeal, Bloch endeavors to explore the adventure novels, modern romances, comics, circuses, country fairs, and the like. He refuses to make simplistic qualitative judgments of high and low art forms; rather, he seeks to grasp the driving utopian impulse in the production and reception of artworks for mass audiences. Time and again he focuses on fairy tales as indications of paths to be taken in reality.

What is significant about such kinds of "modern fairy tales" is that it is reason itself which leads to the wish projections of the old fairy tale and serves them. Again what proves itself is a harmony with courage and cunning, as that earliest kind of enlightenment which already characterizes *Hansel and Gretel*: consider yourself as born free and entitled to be totally happy, dare to make use of your power of reasoning, look upon the outcome of things as friendly. These are the genuine maxims of fairy tales, and fortunately for us they not only appear in the past but in the now.[15]

If Bloch and Freud set the general parameters for helping us understand how our longing for home, which is discomforting *and* comforting, draws us to folk and fairy tales, we must now become more specific and focus on the interest of children in fairy tales. In fact, we already know from sociological and psychological studies that originated after World War I that children between the ages of five and ten are the first prime audience of fairy tales of all kinds.[16] Given this common knowledge and research, which have been variously interpreted, we must ask whether the interest of children in fairy tales can be related to their desire for an ideal home, that is, a world or state in which they come into their own.

In *Child and Tale: The Origins of Interest*, André Favat explores the usefulness of Jean Piaget's theories to explain why children are drawn to fairy tales.[17] By concentrating on the age group between six and eight, Favat demonstrates that the content and form of the "classical" fairy tales (Perrault, Grimm, and Andersen) correspond to the way a child of this age, according to Piaget, conceives of the world. During this particular phase of development, children believe in the magical relationship between thought and things, regard inanimate objects as animate, respect authority in the form of retributive justice and expiatory punishment, see causality as paratactic, do not distinguish the self from the external world, and believe that objects can be moved in continual response to their desires. Favat maintains that such a child's conception of the world is generally affirmed by the fairy tale, even though the tale may not have been created precisely to meet the needs of children.

Between the ages of six and eight the child perceives his or her world as being tested more and more by outside forces, and it is for this reason that Favat makes careful differentiations when he talks about the response of children and their need for stability. Following Piaget, Favat also stresses that the relative development of children and their conception of the world have to be qualified by the specific cultural socialization children undergo. Thus, as their animism and egocentrism give way to socialization and greater conscious interaction in society, children come by age ten generally to reject the fairy tale. By this time they have become more acclimated to the real world and view the fairy tale as an impediment to further adjustment. Only later, after adolescence is completed, do young people and adults return to fairy tales and fantasy literature, quite often to recapture the child in themselves.

To recapture the child is not a frivolous project but a serious undertaking for self-gratification and self-realization. Such earnestness can be seen in the initial attraction of children to fairy tales. As Favat maintains:

Children's turning to the tale is no casual recreation or pleasant diversion; instead, it is an insistent search for an ordered world more satisfying than the real one, a sober striving to deal with the crisis of experience they are undergoing. In such a view, it is even possible, regardless of one's attitude toward bibliotherapy, to see the child's turning to the tale as a salutary utilization of an implicit device of the culture. It would appear, moreover, that after reading a fairy tale, the reader invests the real world with the constructs of the tale.[18]

If we synthesize Freud, Bloch, and Favat's notions of Piaget in regard to home as liberation, we can now grasp the liberating potential of the fantastic in fairy tales. On a psychological level, the fairy tale, through the use of unfamiliar (*unheimlich*) symbols, liberates readers of different age groups to return to repressed ego-disturbances, that is, to return to familiar (*heimlich*) primal moments in their lives. But the fairy tale cannot be liberating ultimately unless it projects on a conscious, literary, and philosophical level the objectification of home as real democracy under nonalienating conditions. This does not mean that the liberating fairy tale must have a moral, doctrinaire resolution; rather, to be liberating it must reflect a *process of struggle* against all types of suppression and authoritarianism and posit various possibilities for the concrete realization of utopia. Otherwise, the words "liberating" and "emancipatory" have no aesthetic categorical substance.

Piaget notes that from age six to age twelve, the sense children have of morality and justice changes from a belief in retributive justice through expiatory punishment to distributive justice with equality. Corresponding to the early phase of development, the traditional folk tales and classical fairy tales tend to reinforce a regressive notion of home by centering on arbitrary authority (generally in the form of monarchs or monarchs-in-the-making) as the last instance of justice.

Raw power is used to right wrongs or uphold a mixture of feudal and bourgeois patriarchal norms constituting a "happy end" (which is not be confused with utopia). It is exactly this configuration in the classical tales—and there are many exceptions [19]—that caused numerous authors in the course of the last two centuries to experiment with the fairy tale discourse. And as our own conception of what constitutes the substance of liberation in Western culture has changed, the revised literary fairy tales for children have steadily evinced a more radical and sophisticated tendency. The question we must now ask is how some contemporary writers, whom I shall designate as "countercultural," endeavor to make their tales more liberating and conducive to the progressive pursuit of home, in contrast to the regressive pursuits in the tales of yesteryear.

II

In examining the unique narrative modes developed by "countercultural" fairy tale writers, it will become apparent that their experimentation is connected to their endeavors to transform the civilizing process. They interject themselves into the fairy tale discourse on civilization first by distancing themselves from conventional regressive forms of writing, thinking, and illustration: the familiar is made unfamiliar only to regain a sense of what authenticity might be on a psycho- and sociogenetic level. Or, to put it another way, by seeking what "unadulterated" home might mean under nonalienating conditions, the fairy tale writers transfigure classical narratives and distinguish their final constellations of home by provoking the reader to reflect critically upon the conditions and limits of socialization. The countercultural intention is made manifest through alienating techniques that no longer rely on seductive, charming illusions of a happy end as legitimation of the present civilizing process but rather make use of jarring symbols that demand an end to superimposed illusions. The aim is to make readers perceive the actual limits and possibilities of their deep personal wishes in a social context.

The narrative voice probes and tries to uncover the disturbing, repressed sociopsychological conflicts so that the young reader might imagine more clearly what forces operate in reality to curtail freedom of action. Uncomfortable questions about arbitrary authoritarianism, sexual domination, and social oppression are raised to show situations that call for change and can be changed. In contrast to the classical fairy tales of the civilizing process, the fantastic projections of the liberating tales are used not for rationalistic purposes to instrumentalize the imagination of readers but rather to subvert the controls of rationalization, enabling readers to reflect more freely upon ego disturbances and perhaps draw parallels to the social situation of others, which will allow them to conceive of work and play in a collective sense.

Needless to say, there are a multitude of ways one can write a liberating tale. Here I want to concentrate on just two major types of experimentation that have direct bearing on cultural patterns in the West. One type is the transfiguration of the classical fairy tale. Generally the author assumes that the young reader is already familiar with the classical tale and so depicts the familiar in an estranging fashion. Consequently, the reader is compelled to consider the negative aspects of anachronistic forms and perhaps transcend them. The tendency is to break, shift, debunk, or rearrange the traditional motifs to liberate the reader from the contrived and programmed mode of literary reception. Transfiguration does not obliterate the recognizable features or values of the classical fairy tale but cancels their negativity by showing how a different aesthetic and social setting relativizes all values. To this extent, the act of creative transfiguration by the author and the final artistic product as transfiguration are geared to make readers aware that civilization and life itself are processes that can be shaped to fulfill the basic needs of the readers. Although the liberating and classical fairy tales may contain some of the same features and values, the emphasis placed on transfiguration as process, both as narrative form and as substance, makes for a qualitative difference.

The second type of experimentation is similar to transfiguration; it involves the fusion of traditional configurations with contemporary references within settings and plot lines unfamiliar to readers yet designed to arouse their curiosity and interest. Fantastic projections are used here to demonstrate the changeability of contemporary social relations, and the fusion brings together all possible means for illuminating a concrete utopia. In effect, the narrative techniques of both fusion and transfiguration are aimed at disturbing and jarring readers so that they lose their complacent attitude toward the status quo of society and envision ways to realize their individuality within collective and democratic contexts. What distinguishes the contemporary writers of liberating tales, however, is their strident antisexist and antiauthoritarian perspective.

For instance, Harriet Herman's "The Forest Princess" varies the traditional Rapunzel fairy tale to question male domination and sexual stereotypes. Her story concerns "a princess who lived alone in a tall tower deep in the woods. An invisible spirit had brought her there when she was just a little girl. The spirit watched over her bringing her food and clothing and giving her special gifts on her birthday." [20] One day after a storm she saves a prince who had been shipwrecked. At first she thinks that she, too, is a prince, since she looks very much like him and does not know that there are differences in sex. They begin living together and teaching each other their respective skills. But the prince misses his home, and the princess agrees to go to the golden castle if he will teach her the secrets of that place. However, the princess is compelled to change at the golden castle—to wear fancy clothes and makeup and to restrict her activities to the company of other girls. Against the orders of the king, she teaches them how to read, and, since the prince does not want to go riding with her, she practices riding by herself. On the prince's fourteenth birthday she exhibits her astonishing riding skills to the entire court. The king decides to reward her with one wish, and she replies: "Your majesty, what I have done today could have been done by any of the boys and girls in your land. As my reward I would like the boys and girls to ride horses together, to read books together and to play together." [21] But the king refuses to grant this wish, saying that the boys and girls are happy the way they are—despite their protests. The princess realizes that she must leave the golden castle, and nobody knows where she is today. We are told by the narrator, though, that after her departure her wish came to be fulfilled, because fairy tales *must* end happily.[22]

The irony of the ending suggests a contrast: though fairy tales must end happily, life itself must not, and thus the reader is compelled to consider the reasons for a lack of happiness or home in reality. Moreover, the possibility for a comparison with the traditional "Rapunzel" allows the authoritarian quality of the older tale to become visible.

In a project similar to Herman's, four women of the Merseyside Women's Liberation Movement in Liverpool, England, began publishing fairy tales to counter the values carried by the traditional fairy tales—acquisitive aggression in men and dutiful nurturing of this aggression by women. They argued that "fairy tales are political. They help to form children's values and teach them to accept our society and their roles in it. Central to this society is the assumption that domination and submission are the natural basis of all our relationships."[23] In response they rewrote such well-known classics as "The Prince and the Swineherd," "Rapunzel," "Little Red Riding Hood," and "Snow White." In "The Prince and the Swineherd," a gluttonous prince is made into the laughing stock of the people by Samia the swineherd. In "Red Riding Hood," the setting is a timbermill town in the North, and the shy little girl Nadia learns to overcome her fear of the woods in order to save her great-grandmother from the wolf, whom she kills. His fur is used as the lining for Red Riding Hood's cloak, and the great-grandmother tells her: "This cloak now has special powers. Whenever you meet another child who is shy and timid, lend that child the cloak to wear as you play together in the forest, and then, like you, they will grow brave."[24] From then on Red Riding Hood explores, going deeper and deeper into the forest.

In both these tales the small, oppressed protagonists learn to use their powers to free themselves from parasitic creatures. Life is depicted as an ongoing struggle and process; the "happy" end is thus not an illusion, that is, it is depicted not as an end in itself but as the actual beginning of a development. The emancipatory element comes about when the fantasy (imagination) of the protagonists themselves is projected within the tale as a means by which they can come into their own and help others in similar situations.

Like the Merseyside Group, Tomi Ungerer has been drawn to rewriting "Little Red Riding Hood," which he entitled "a reruminated tale." Though his perspective is emancipatory, it is much different from that of the Merseyside group. As in his revision of Andersen's "The Little Match Girl," which he entitled "Alumette," he is irreverent, sly, and anarchistic. His wolf, dressed like a classy baron, is much different from the devious wolf in the traditional tale, and his Red Riding Hood is "the real no-nonsense one"—she is not gullible or afraid to voice her opinion. We learn that her grandmother is mean and cranky and even beats her sometimes. So she stops to pick berries to delay her visit. When the wolf appears, he states candidly: "I know of your grandmother and all I can say is that her reputation is worse than mine."[25] He offers to take her to his castle and treat her like a princess in a fairy tale. Red Riding Hood is suspicious. She begins to ask questions about the wolf's jowls and tongue, and he insists that she stop asking foolish questions. He overcomes her objections and tells her that her parents and grandmother will be able to care for themselves. So the wolf and Red Riding Hood marry, have children, and live happily, and the nasty grandmother shrinks in size and remains mean as ever.

Ungerer's tale uses irony and clever reversals to break the sexual taboos of the traditional tale. The "uncanny" wolf becomes identified with familiar sexual longings of childhood pleasure instincts, and the transformations in the tale are calculated liberating effects, measured against the superego function of the parents and grandmother. The wolf allows Red Riding Hood to grow and enter into a mature sexual relationship. What becomes "home" in this fairy tale is in implications less social than in other liberating tales, but it does make a claim for the autonomy of the young girl and wolf, who demonstrate that "reputations" spread through the rumors of old tales no longer hold true and should not be taken at surface value today.

For the most part, the post-1945 tales of "Little Red Riding Hood" transfigure and criticize the traditional transgression perpetuated against the girl as a helpless, naive, and sweet thing and against the wolf as evil predator and troublesome male rapist. In "Little Polly Riding Hood," [26] Catherine Storr depicted a clever and independent girl, whom a bumbling wolf would like to eat. Time and again she outwits the comical wolf, who uses the old Red Riding Hood tale as a manual on how one should behave. Naturally his announced expectations are never fulfilled. In a more serious vein, Max von der Grün rewrote the tale to comment on prejudice and conformity. [27] His Red Riding Hood is ostracized by the community because of her red cap, which is strongly suggestive of the anti-Semitic and anti-communist feelings that existed in Germany at one time. There have also been tales written in defense of the wolf, such as Iring Fetscher's "Little Redhead and the Wolf" and Philippe Dumas and Boris Moissard's "Little Acqua Riding Hood." [28] Fetscher gives a wry, mock-psychological interpretation that depicts the father killing the wolf because the beast had befriended Red Riding Hood's brother, whom the neurotic father disliked. In the story by Dumas and Moissard there is another ironic portrayal; this time it is Red Riding Hood's granddaughter who frees the grandnephew of the wolf from the zoo in the Jardin des Plantes because she wants to relive the classical story and become a star in Parisian society. However, the wolf is wise, for he has learned a lesson from the tragedies that have occurred in his family. He flees to Siberia and warns young wolves about the dangers of "civilization" in France.

The reversal of the classical fairy tales is at the center of the other stories in Dumas and Moissard's book *Contes à l'envers* as well, and it is the basis of such other collections as Jay Williams's *The Practical Princess and Other Liberating Tales*, Jane Yolen's *Dream Weaver*, and Hans-Joachim Gelberg's *Neues vom Rumpelstilzchen*. [29] The traditional stories are transfigured so that their repressive substance is subverted. The reversal of form, characters, and motifs is intended to expand the possibilities to question the fairy tale discourse within the civilizing process.

Aside from the transfiguration of fairy tales, the second most common manner in which writers of fairy tales have endeavored to suggest options to dominant cultural patterns is through the fusion of actual references to disturbing social occurrences in contemporary society. Here I want to focus on four remarkable fairy tale experiments in Italy, Germany, France, and England. The *international* quest for liberation and a new sense of home manifested in different fairy tales is clearly a reaction against *international* trends of domination, standardization, and exploitation.

In Italy, we find a consistent protest for freedom in the creative work of Adela Turin, Francesca Cantarellis, Nella Bosnia, Margherita Soccaro, and Sylvie Selig. Seven of their books have been translated and distributed by the Writers and Readers Publishing Cooperative in London.[30] Significant here is the tale entitled *Of Cannons and Caterpillars*. The very first paragraph sets the dramatic predicament of modern society:

No one in the palace of King Valour any longer remembered the first war. Not the ministers or the privy councillors, or the secretaries, observers, or the directors, or the reporters, the strategists or the diplomats; not even the generals, the colonels, the sergeants, the majors or the lieutenants. Not even Terence Wild, the very oldest soldier alive, stitched and restitched, with one glass eye, one wooden leg, and a hook in place of a hand. Because after the first war, there had been a second war, then a third, a fourth, a fifth, and then a twentieth and a twenty-first too, which was still going on. And no one in the palace of King Valour could remember anything about peaches or sparrows, or tortoise-shell cats, or bilberry marmalade, or radishes, or bed-sheets spread out to dry on green meadows. Besides, King Valour had become enthusiastic about his plans for a twenty-second war: "Not a single tree will be left standing, not a blade of grass will survive; no, not one solitary shamrock or grasshopper," so he predicted, "because we have the ultimate weapon, diabolical defoliants, death-rays, paralysing gas and cannons of perfect accuracy."[31]

Grotesque and comically exaggerated as King Valour may seem, his manner of thinking is not unlike that of some of our contemporary statesmen. His menace and madness are sadly recognized by his own wife, Queen Delphina, who is sentenced to live in the modern skyscraper castle behind bullet-proof windows with her daughter, Princess Philippina, and 174 widows and war orphans, both boys and girls. Confronted with a synthetic, suffocating technological life, Delphina endeavors to teach her daughter about nature, including caterpillars, flowers, animals, and vegetables, by writing illustrated stories for her. As her storybook expands, Philippina and all the widows and orphans of the skyscraper become less sad. Then one evening "King Valour returned in excellent humour: a new war had just been declared, and it promised to be the longest most homicidal ever. . . . So he decided that the Queen, the Princess, widows, and orphans were to leave on a Saturday morning for the Castle of King Copious, which stood further away from the battlefields."[32]

This decision turns out to be fortunate for the queen and her entourage. Along the way they stop at an abandoned castle ruined by wars, and because it is so beautifully situated in the country, they decide to renovate the buildings and cultivate the land. So they unpack the big Book, and all the dreams that had been pictured in the Book they now endeavor to realize in their surroundings. Many years pass, and we learn that King Valour and his wars are all but forgotten. The transformed castle, however, flourishes in the middle of a busy, densely populated village, and everyone knows the name of Delphina, the legendary writer of the beautifully illustrated Book.

This extraordinary antiwar fairy tale is uniquely illustrated with pictures projecting a critique of authoritarianism and the possibility for collective democratic life: the entire concept of the fairy tale encourages the creative realization of peaceful coexistence. Moreover, it is a fairy tale in praise of the utopian power of fairy tales. Delphina manages to retain the principle of hope and humanism in the prison-castle of her husband by writing the illustrated Book for her compatriots. Given the opportunity to escape a sick situation, they become joyful and creative. Their sterile existence is exchanged for a life without fear and oppression. Thus, finally, they can come into touch with their own skills and harness technology to serve their collective needs in peace.

The dangerous potential of technology and bureaucracy to create means for enslaving humankind is portrayed with even greater insight and originality in Michael Ende's 270-page fairy-tale novel *Momo*.[33] This work, published in 1973, won the German Youth Book Prize, and it has been translated into seventeen different languages. It recalls the struggles of a little Italian orphan, a wiry, ingenuous girl named Momo, somewhere between the ages of eight and twelve, who makes her home in the ruins of an ancient Roman amphitheater. Momo has an amazing gift: by merely listening in her own special way to people telling their problems, she provides them with the power to discover their own solutions; she is thus regarded as somewhat of a saint and is protected by everyone in the neighborhood. Surrounded by all sorts of children who play in the amphitheater, including her two special friends, Beppo the street cleaner and Gigi the young con artist, she lacks nothing and prospers through her wit and creativity.

In general, all the people in the district are poor, but they try to share and enjoy what they have with one another and struggle to improve the quality of their lives at their own pace and time. Unknown to them, however, their manner of living and playing is being threatened by the time-savers, men dressed in gray whose ash colored faces match their suits. They wear stiff round hats, smoke gray cigars, and carry blue-gray briefcases. Nobody knows who these men are, and everyone forgets them once they enter their lives and influence them to conduct themselves according to such principles as "time is money," "time is costly," or "saved time is double time." So great is their clandestine impact that the city gradually begins to transform itself into a smooth-functioning machine. Buildings and streets are torn down to make way for modern technology and automatization. Everyone rushes around seeking ways to save time and make more money. The total architecture of the city informs the psyche of people's minds, which are now geared to work for work's sake. The gray men gain control over everyone and succeed in isolating Momo. Only after she finds her way to the "nowhere house" of Master Secundius Minitus Hora is she safe from the threat of the gray men, for it is Master Hora, a wizened and humane guardian of time, who can explain the essence of time to Momo—that it resides in the heart of each individual and can become as beautiful as the individual decides. Given this realization, Momo seeks to struggle against the gray men, and, with the help of Master Hora and a magic turtle, she eventually undermines the nefarious plans of the gray men: time is liberated so that human beings can determine their destiny.

Ende's colorful fairy-tale novel is told in such a fashion that the events could seemingly take place in the past, present, or future. In unusual symbolic form he incorporates a critique of instrumental rationalization, making it comprehensible for readers between the ages of eight and fifteen. As is the case in most contemporary fairy tales with liberating potential, Ende has a female protagonist bring about or point a way to change: Momo comes into her own as an individual, and social relations appear to be reconstituted such that time will blossom for everyone. Nevertheless, there are problems with the ending of *Momo*, which is deceptively emancipatory. That is, Ende employs the fantastic to celebrate individualistic action or the privatization of the imagination.

Such individualism is supposed to be the answer to the growing rationalization of everyday life, and it is celebrated in Ende's second best-seller, *The Neverending Story (Die unendliche Geschichte)*,[34] in which a fat, fearful boy named Bastian discovers that he can use his imagination to invent a never-ending story that helps him adjust to reality. Ende has Bastian steal a book, and, as the boy reads it in a secluded place, he feels summoned by the troubled realm of Phantásien, where he has numerous adventures. Aided by his devoted friend Atréju and magical animals, he prevents Phantásien from being destroyed. Upon returning to reality, he has a reconciliation with his father and feels strong and courageous enough to take on the world. In contrast to *Momo*, *The Neverending Story* depicts a pursuit of home as a form of regression and compromise. Moreover, there are too many traditional clichés and stereotypes in Ende's endeavor to endorse the student revolt slogan "all power to the imagination"; in the final analysis, his story actually deludes readers and prevents them from seeing their potential and problems against the background of social forces that manipulate and exploit both consciousness and imagination.

Such delusion is not the case in Jean-Pierre Andrevon's remarkable fairy-tale novel *La fée et le géometre* (The Fairy and the Land Surveyor).[35] Andrevon describes an idyllic verdant country filled with fairies, dwarfs, gnomes, witches, magicians, elves, dragons, and sylphs, who live in harmony with one another without rules, money, or rationalized relations of production. Nor is nature threatened with gross exploitation. All creatures benefit from their interchange and exchange with one another, and sexual discrimination does not exist. Each individual works and plays according to his or her own need—until, that is, Arthur Livingschwartz, an explorer who works for an international conglomerate, discovers this paradise. From that point on, Andrevon portrays the gradual colonization of the verdant country. Technicians, scientists, soldiers, architects, and businessmen arrive and transform the small virgin land into a tourist resort with a tiny industrial capacity. Roads, towns, and factories are built. Nature is devastated and polluted. The gnomes, dwarfs, fairies, and elves are compelled to work for money and to regulate their time and lives according to the demands of outsiders, who now control the production of the country. There are intermarriages between humans and the fairy creatures, and some, like the fairy Sibialle and the land surveyor Loïc, try to oppose the onslaught of colonization and industrialization. However, it is not until their daughter and other children from mixed marriages grow up and experience human exploitation and ecological destruction in the name of progress that a strong organized protest movement develops. There are struggles over the construction of nuclear reactors and the encroachment of nature by industry and highways—all without violence. These struggles commence as Andrevon concludes his narration:

> The country of the fairies will never be as it was before. The country of the fairies will not regress. To live does not mean to move backward but to move forward. It means to be like the shark and to advance unceasingly. And the shark is not a malicious creature. He must live like all of us. That's all.
>
> The best thing that can happen to the country of the fairies is not a return to the past, nor should it seek to model itself after the human world. It can become *different*, mixing the qualities of fairies and humans alike.[36]

Whether this can happen, whether the struggle of the people in the verdant country to change their lives can succeed, remains an open question at the end of this fairy tale. Yet, Andrevon manages to raise most of the significant social and political questions for today's youth in a discourse that provides an inkling of home. He does not paint rosy illusions by offering an individualistic solution to the instrumentalization of magic, fantasy, and natural needs the way Ende does in *The Neverending Story*. In fact, he sees the collective opposition to possible ecological and social destruction as arising out of the contradictions created by capitalist colonization itself. In this sense he views modern technology and industrialization as revolutionary, as transformative forces that can be beneficial to living creatures and nature, but only if they are *not* employed for profit and exploitation. Unlike some romantic anticapitalist writers of fairy tales, such as J. R. R. Tolkien and C. S. Lewis, who look back conservatively to the past for salvation, Andrevon knows that technology and industry are not evil per se. He assumes the viewpoint of the socialist ecologist and points with optimism to the struggle for a qualitatively new type of "homeland."

Not all progressive fairy tale writers are as optimistic as Andrevon is. For instance, Michael de Larrabeiti writes from the perspective of the urban lower class, and he draws different conclusions than Andrevon in his endeavor to subvert and satirize Tolkien's *Lord of the Rings* and Richard Adams's *Watership Down*. In his first fairy-tale novel, *The Borribles*,[37] he created fictional characters from his own childhood in Battersea who are notable for their social defiance. Borribles are outcasts or runaways who value their independence more than anything else because they take a deep delight in being what they are. They avoid adults, and especially policemen, who represent arbitrary authority. Their ears grow long and pointed, a sign of their nonconformism, and, if they are caught by the law, their ears are clipped and their will is broken. Borribles exist everywhere in the world, but de Larrabeiti writes mainly about the Borribles who inhabit London.

In his first novel he wrote about the Borribles' great struggle with the high and mighty Rumbles, representative of middle-class snobs, and the loss of a vast treasure in the River Wendle. In the sequel, *The Borribles Go for Broke*,[38] he depicted the further adventures of a small group of Borribles, who are manipulated by Spiff, the irascible Borrible chief, to search for the lost treasure in the underground territory of the treacherous Wendles. Actually, the group of Borribles (consisting of the two tough girls Chalotte and Sidney, a Bangladeshi named Twilight, Stonks from Peckham, and Vulge from Stepney) want primarily to rescue the horse Sam, who had been of immense service to them on their Great Rumble Hunt. The police, however, have created a Special Borrible Group (SBG) under the command of the fanatic Inspector Sussworth, and the Borribles are pursued with vengeance. In fact, at one point they are even captured by the SBG but then are rescued by an extraordinary tramp named Ben, who is a grown-up Borrible in his own way. Though the Borribles and Ben have no difficulty in making fools of the police, it is a different story with the Wendles in the sewers of London. Spiff has instigated everything so that the Borribles must help him search for the lost treasure and eliminate the tyrannical chieftain Flinthead, who turns out to be Spiff's brother. Ultimately, Spiff and Flinthead are both killed, the Borribles escape, and Sam is rescued. But in the end, the Borribles are still not happy unless they can continue to bicker and argue among themselves about their next step in opposition to the normal routine of an oppressive society.

It is difficult to do justice to the style and manner in which de Larrabeiti makes the unbelievable believable. His starting point is obviously the young lumpenproletariat, the down-and-out of the London lower class. In this novel he begins by focusing on the interaction between Chalotte as hard-nosed courageous girl and Twilight as sensitive and sensible Bangladeshi. His immediate concern is to establish the integrity and skills of these two characters, representative in general of females and minority groups. Thereafter, he expands the scope of his attention by depicting the relations between Ben as adult dropout and the Borribles as defiant young outsiders. At first the Borribles distrust Ben, but they learn quickly that his principles are similar to theirs: he lives from day to day contented with the waste and abundance of a wasteful society, abhors the deadliness of routine, shuns profit-making, and minds his own business. All this is proclaimed in his special song:

> Let the world roll round an' round
> Wiv its hard-worked folk in fetters:
> All'oo think themselves yer betters,
> Money-mad and dooty bound.
>
> Make yer choice, there ain't so many,
> No ambition's worth a fart;
> Freedom is a work of art—
> Take yer stand with uncle Benny![39]

Together Ben and the Borribles reveal how creative and adroit one must be to gain and protect one's independence. Not only are they surrounded by powerful social forces demanding law and order just for the sake of law and order, but they must also contend with each other's disrespectful and suspicious natures. De Larrabeiti's fantasy projection shows lower-class life more accurately than do many so-called realistic novels for young readers. He does not mince words or pull punches. His character portrayals and command of colloquial speech, especially Cockney, are remarkable. At times his plot lines are too contrived, and he lets his imagination carry him away. (Yes, even in fantasy literature this is possible.) Still, he manages to employ the fairy tale discourse to deal with themes pertaining to racial, sexual, and political struggles of the present in such a way that young readers can comprehend the importance and urgency of protest by outsiders. There is no such thing as "home" in this fairy-tale novel. It is the refusal of the Borribles to go home, to make a regular home, that demonstrates the false promises of the classical fairy tales, with their celebration of regressive notions of home in the so-called happy endings.

III

Most of the tales discussed up to this point—and there are many more one could discuss[40]—provide a social and political basis for the fantastic projection, thus instilling it with a liberating potential. The configurations of the experimental fairy tale discourse shift the perspective and meaning of socialization through reading. The active, aggressive behavior of male types in the classical fairy tales gives way to a combined activism on the part of both the males and the females who uncover those wishes, dreams, and needs that have been denied by social structures and institutions. The fantastic projections carried by the plots, characters, and motifs of the tales reflect the possibility for a transformation of constraining social conditions through major changes in social relations. The fairy tale discourse in general is confronted with a demand to transform itself and become more emancipatory and innovative. The question remains, however, as to whether the experimental tales are truly liberating and can achieve their object: that is, can they have the desired effect on young readers?

Several critics have pointed to the difficulties in predicting the effect emancipatory literature can have on children.[41] For the most part, particularly in regard to the classical fairy tales, children resist change. If they have been reared with the old tales, they do not want them altered. If their social expectations have been determined by a conservative socialization process, they find changes in fairy tales comical, but often unjust and disturbing as well, even though the tales purport to be in their interests and seek their emancipation.

Yet, it is exactly this *disturbance* that the liberating fairy tales seek on both a conscious and an unconscious level. They interfere with the civilizing process in hopes of creating change and a new awareness of social conditions. This provocation is why it is more important for critics to recognize the *upsetting* effect of emancipatory tales and to study their uncanny insinuations for old and young readers alike. The quality of emancipatory fairy tales cannot be judged by the manner in which they are accepted by readers but only by the unique ways they bring undesirable social relations into question and force readers to question themselves. In this regard, the liberating potential of the fantastic in experimental fairy tales will always be discomforting, even when concrete utopias are illuminated through the narrative perspective.

With some exceptions, the emancipatory tales are skillfully written and employ humor and artwork in original, stimulating ways to accomplish their paradoxical kind of discomforting comfort. The major difficulty facing the emancipatory fairy tales, it seems to me, lies in the system of distribution, circulation, and use of the tales, and all this is dependent on the educational views of teachers, librarians, parents, and those adults who work with children in community centers. The more regressive tales of Perrault, the Grimm Brothers, Andersen, and other conservative writers are used in schools, libraries, and homes without a blink of the eye, but the unusual, forward-looking, fantastic projections of the liberating fairy tales have not found general approval among the publishers and adults who circulate the tales.

This is not to say that there has been no headway made by the experimental fairy tales and by adults who experiment with fairy tales. Throughout the Western world, storytellers, writers, publishers, and educators have developed new methods and techniques to question and expand the classical fairy tale discourse. In Italy, Gianni Rodari,[42] a well-known writer for children, has created a series of games intended to deconstruct classical fairy tales in the hope of stimulating children to create their own modern versions. By introducing unusual elements into the fairy tale—for instance, by making Cinderella disobedient and rebellious or having Snow White meet giants instead of dwarfs and organize a band of robbers—the child is compelled to shatter a certain uniform reception of fairy tales, to reexamine the elements of the classical tales, and to reconsider their function and meaning and whether it might not be better to alter them. In France, Georges Jean has outlined various pedagogical means he has used in schools to enable children to become more creative in their use of fairy tales.[43] He describes certain card games in which children are called upon to change characters or situations of the classical fairy tales so that they relate more directly to their own lives. Jean considers the reinvention of fairy tales a means for children to become aware of traditional discourse and the necessity to modernize it.

The works of Rodari, Jean, and others make it quite clear that until progressive social ideas are set into practice among adults, the liberating fairy tales will remain restricted in their use and effect among children. In other words, until there is a more progressive shift within the civilizing process itself, the liberating potential of these tales will be confined to those social groups seeking that end. One thing, however, is certain: the writers themselves have experienced some sense of liberation in projecting their fantasies through the magic of the fairy tales. Home for them is achieved through the creative production of these tales, which allow them to regain a sense of their familiar longings through the uncanny. It is this sensory experience that they want to share with us symbolically, for their sense of liberation can only be confirmed when others, especially children, read and benefit from the subversive power of their art.

Notes

1. See Claire R. Farrer, ed., *Women and Folklore* (Austin: University of Texas Press, 1975); Madonna Kolbenschlag, *Kiss Sleeping Beauty Good-bye: Breaking the Spell of Feminine Myths and Models* (New York: Doubleday, 1979); Marcia Lieberman, " 'Some Day My Prince Will Come': Female Acculturation Through the Fairy Tale," *College English* 34 (1972): 383–395; Allison Lurie, "Fairy Tale Liberation," *New York Review of Books* 42 (17 December 1970); Heather Lyons, "Some Second Thoughts on Sexism in

Fairy Tales," in *Literature and Learning*, ed. Elizabeth Grugeon and Peter Walden (London: Ward Lock Educational, 1978), pp. 42–58; Robert Moore, "From Rags to Witches: Stereotypes, Distortions and Anti-Humanism in Fairy Tales," *Interracial Books for Children* 6 (1975): 1–3; Jane Yolen, "America's Cinderella," *Children's Literature in Education* 8 (1977): 21–29; and Heide Göttner-Abendroth, *Die Göttin und ihr Heros* (Munich: Frauenoffensive, 1981).

2. Marion Lochhead, *The Renaissance of Wonder in Children's Literature* (Edinburgh: Canongate, 1977), p. 154.

3. Georges Jean, *Le pouvoir des contes* (Paris: Casterman, 1981), pp. 153–154.

4. Ibid., pp. 206–209.

5. Sigmund Freud, "The Uncanny," reprinted in *New Literary History* 7 (Spring 1976): 619–645. See also Hélène Cixous, "Fiction and its Phantoms: A Reading of Freud's *Das Unheimliche*," *New Literary History* 7, pp. 525–548.

6. Freud, "The Uncanny," p. 634.

7. Ibid., p. 640.

8. See Bruno Bettelheim, *The Uses of Enchantment: The Meaning and Importance of Fairy Tales* (New York: Knopf, 1976).

9. See my critique of Bettelheim's book, "On the Use and Abuse of Folk and Fairy Tales with Children: Bruno Bettelheim's Moralistic Magic Wand," in *Breaking the Magic Spell: Radical Theories of Folk and Fairy Tales* (London: Heinemann, 1979), pp. 160–182.

10. Freud, "The Uncanny," p. 630.

11. Ernst Bloch, "Karl Marx and Humanity: The Material of Hope," in *On Karl Marx* (New York: Seabury Press, 1971), pp. 30–31.

12. Ibid., pp. 44–45.

13. For a detailed discussion of Bloch's essays, see my chapter "The Utopian Function of Fairy Tales and Fantasy: Ernst Bloch the Marxist and J.R.R. Tolkien the Catholic," in *Breaking the Magic Spell*, pp. 129–159.

14. Ernst Bloch, "The Fairy Tale Moves on Its Own in Time" (1930), quoted in Zipes, *Breaking the Magic Spell*, p. 133.

15. Ibid., p. 135.

16. See Charlotte Bühler, *Das Märchen und die Phantasie des Kindes* (Berlin: Springer, 1977), based on the original 1918 edition; Alois Jalkotzy, *Märchen und Gegenwart* (Vienna: Jungbrunnen und Verlagsbuchhandlung, 1930); Alois Kunzfeld, *Vom Märchenerzähler und Märchenillustrieren* (Vienna: Deutscher Verlag für Jugend und Volk, 1926); Wilhelm Ledermann, *Das Märchen in Schule und Haus* (Langensalza: Schulbuchhandlung F.G.L. Gressler, 1921); Erwin Müller, *Psychologie des deutschen Volksmärchens* (Munich: Kösel & Pustet, 1928); and Reinhard Nolte, *Analyse der freien Märchenproduktion* (Langensalza: Beyer, 1931).

17. André Favat, *Child and Tale: The Origins of Interest* (Urbana, Ill.: National Council of Teachers of English, 1977).

18. Ibid., p. 54.

19. There is a tendency to think that the patterns of folk tales and classical fairy tales do not vary much. This widespread belief, based on Vladimir Propp's *Morphology of the Folk Tale*, 2d rev. ed. (Austin: University of Texas Press, 1968), fails, however, to consider the effects of cultural differences on the contents and configurations of the tales. For a more differentiated viewpoint, see August Nitzschke, *Soziale Ordnungen im Spiegel der Märchen*, 2 vols. (Stuttgart: Frommann-Holzborg, 1976–1977).

20. Harriet Herman, *The Forest Princess* (Berkeley: Rainbow Press, 1975), pp. 1–2.

21. Ibid., p. 38.

22. Herman wrote a sequel to this story, *Return of the Forest Princess* (Berkeley:

Rainbow Press, 1975), which is, however, not as stimulating and open-ended as her first tale.

23. Merseyside Women's Liberation Movement, *Red Riding Hood* (Liverpool: Fairy Story Collective, 1972), p. 6.

24. Ibid., p. 5.

25. Tomi Ungerer, *A Storybook* (New York: Watts, 1974), p. 88.

26. Catherine Storr, *Clever Polly and the Stupid Wolf* (Harmondsworth: Puffin Books, 1967), pp. 17–23.

27. "Rotkäppchen," in *Bilderbogengeschichten, Märchen, Sagen, Abenteuer*, ed. Jochen Jung (Munich: DTV, 1976), pp. 95–100.

28. See Iring Fetscher, *Wer hat Dornröschen wachgeküßt?* (Frankfurt am Main: Fischer, 1974), pp. 28–32; and Philippe Dumas and Boris Moissard, *Contes à l'envers* (Paris: L'école des Loisirs, 1977), pp. 15–26.

29. Jay Williams, *The Practical Princess and Other Liberating Tales* (London: Chatto & Windus, 1979); Jane Yolen, *Dream Weaver* (Cleveland: Collins, 1979); and Hans-Joachim Gelberg, *Neues vom Rumpelstilzchen* (Weinheim: Beltz & Gelberg, 1976).

30. See Adela Turin and Margherita Saccaro, *The Breadtime Story*; Adela Turin, Francesca Cantarelli, and Nella Bosnia, *The Five Wives of Silverbeard*; Adela Turin and Sylvie Selig, *Of Cannons and Caterpillars*; and Adela Turin and Nella Bosnia, *Arthur and Clementine, A Fortunate Catastrophe, The Real Story of the Bonobos Who Wore Spectacles*, and *Sugarpink Rose*. All were published by the Writers and Readers Publishing Cooperative between 1975 and 1977; many have been translated into German and French.

31. Turin and Selig, *Of Cannons and Caterpillars*, p. 1.

32. Ibid., p. 17.

33. Michael Ende, *Momo* (Stuttgart: Thienemann, 1973).

34. Michael Ende, *Die unendliche Geschichte* (Stuttgart: Thienemann, 1979).

35. Jean-Pierre Andrevon, *La fée et le géometre* (Paris: Casterman, 1981).

36. Ibid., p. 264.

37. Michael de Larrabeiti, *The Borribles* (London: Bodley Head, 1978).

38. Michael de Larrabeiti, *The Borribles Go for Broke* (London: Bodley Head, 1981).

39. Ibid., p. 80.

40. For example, see Christine Nöstlinger, *Wir pfeifen auf den Gurkenkönig* (We Don't Give a Hoot for the Pickle King) (Weinheim: Beltz & Gelberg, 1972); Ursula LeGuin, *The Wizard of Earthsea* (1968) and *Orsinian Tales* (1976); John Gardner, *Dragon, Dragon and Other Tales* (1975), *Gudgekin the Thistle Girl and Other Tales* (1976), and *The King of the Hummingbirds and Other Tales* (1977); Robin McKinley, *Beauty* (1980).

41. Cf. Nicholas Tucker, "How Children Respond to Fiction," in *Writers, Critics, and Children* (New York: Agathon, 1976), pp. 177–188; and Maximilian Nutz, "Die Macht des Faktischen und die Utopie: Zur Rezeption emancipatorischen Märchen," *Diskussion Deutsch* 48 (1979): 397–410.

42. See Gianni Rodari, *Grammaire de l'imagination* (Paris: Français Réunis, 1978).

43. Jean, *Pouvoir des contes*, pp. 203–232.

Part VI
Media, Literacy, and Political Socialization

INTRODUCTION

What have been the effects of mass media, especially television, on literacy and learning, and what are the political implications of these effects? The readings in this section collectively argue that the cognitive effects of media on audiences are predominantly conservative, not in the sense of a reasoned conservative ideology but in the sense of uncritical conformity that reinforces the status quo and precludes oppositional consciousness. Many thoughtful conservatives are concerned over the moral and cognitive influence of television, video games, rock music, and so on, but their allegiance to capitalism prevents their pursuing their ad hoc criticisms of media to their logical conclusion: that many of the media's destructive effects are inextricably bound to the fact that commercial media are driven by the profit motive and are key institutions of corporate capitalism.

Neil Postman's "The Teachings of the Media Curriculum" comes from his 1979 book *Teaching as a Conserving Activity*. Although in this book Postman—who co-authored an earlier book entitled *Teaching as a Subversive Activity*—is critical of the excesses of sixties radical educators, he still agrees with most leftists that teaching needs to conserve what Alvin Gouldner called a culture of critical discourse against the stupefying effects of consumer capitalism and its mass media. The title of Postman's book, then, is one signal of a trend in the eighties, in which the left is recouping arguments previously made by conservatives and turning them against the untenable equation between conservatism—as a synonym for conservation—and modern capitalism, with its disruptive effects on the natural environment, family and community life, and individual moral and cognitive development.

There is a remarkable congruence between the cognitive patterns traced by Postman and other researchers of television-viewing among children and those discovered through research on the nature of reading and writing deficiencies in college students. Although direct cause-and-effect relationships between television-viewing in childhood and reading and writing skills, especially in college students, are difficult to verify empirically, the similarity of patterns is too striking to discount. Mina Shaughnessy, a pioneer researcher of college remedial-writing students, found the following common cognitive traits: difficulties in concentrating and sustaining an extended line of thought in reading and writing; lack of facility in analytic and synthetic reasoning; deficiencies in reasoning back and forth from the concrete to the abstract, the personal to the impersonal, the literal to the figurative, and the present to the past and future; and difficulties in perceiving irony, ambiguity, and multiplicity of meanings or points of view.

The similarity between these patterns and those induced by television viewing in children extends further to findings in several other fields of scholarship, including studies by developmental psychologists of the cognitive traits associated with immature stages of moral reasoning; historical and psychological studies of oral versus literate cultures; studies in social psychology and political socialization dealing with the authoritarian personality; sociological accounts of a "culture of poverty"; and sociolinguistic research such as that of Basil Bernstein (summarized in this section by Claus Mueller), which has found "restricted" linguistic codes and cognitive operations in lower social classes, as compared to the "elaborated" codes more common in the middle and upper classes. (The problematic definition of class involved in the last three groups of studies will be discussed later.)

In each of these groups of studies there is an association, explicit or implicit, of low levels of literacy and cognitive development with conservative political attitudes. One study, for example, conducted by a follower of Shaughnessy, Andrea Lunsford, applied cognitive-developmental stage theories to the teaching of college remedial writers. According to her results, these students tend to be fixed in Piaget's egocentric and Kohlberg's conventional stages of moral reasoning, and have political attitudes that are correspondingly authoritarian, operating on a good-guy-vs.-bad-guys understanding.

What is the link between low literacy and conservatism? People suffering from immediate, intense political oppression—the situation of the proletariat in Marx's scenario for socialist revolution—need little abstract information or sophistication in reasoning to be persuaded that change is in their interests. In a society like that of present-day America, however, the grosser forms of injustice and conflict have been greatly reduced, and the majority of the population has been socialized into a mood of at least passive assent. Outside of a still sizable but politically atomized underclass, many people today do not directly experience, or cannot understand, the social injustices that persist. In order to understand them, people must not only have access to a diversity of information sources, many of which are in print and written at an advanced level of literacy, but they must also have the reasoning capacities associated with elaborated codes and advanced stages of cognitive development, such as the ability to evaluate abstract, impersonal data. Insofar as mass media perpetuate low literacy and restricted codes, then, the status quo is shielded from the growth of opposition.

One necessary qualification to this analysis is that mass media, and particularly television in recent years, have in some ways offered linguistic codes and a worldview that are more literate, complex, and cosmopolitan than the indigenous local culture of many segments of their audience—hence the charge of fundamentalist Christians and other conservatives that TV, Hollywood films, and "the Eastern news media" are hotbeds of liberalism. Nevertheless, although television's language, for example, may promote higher cognitive development in previously illiterate sectors of the public, studies such as Postman's indicate that it may also lead to lower literacy in sectors, mainly of the middle class, in which children's cognitive development was previously structured largely through reading and writing. Furthermore, the totality of readings in this book develops a case that mass media have tended to replace the parochialism of local culture not with a substantially leftist alternative but merely with a different form of conservatism—nationally regimented culture and patterns of cognitive formation.[1] Along similar lines, Postman suggests that television undermines traditional authorities and hierarchies, as conservatives claim, but replaces them with its own, no less authoritarian hierarchies. And Joshua Meyrowitz, in *No Sense of Place:*

The Impact of Electronic Media on Social Behavior, an admirably nuanced, evenhanded analysis of the cognitive and socializing influences of television, concludes that TV's multiplication of perspectives on the world, which tends to favor left political interests, is apt to be offset by its overload effect: "Ironically, the 'liberalizing' effect of the multiple perspective view may still give a political advantage to conservatives, reactionaries, and special interest groups. After all, multiple perspectives often lead many people to an overabundance of empathy and, therefore, to political ambivalence and inaction."[2]

This general analysis is substantiated by the findings of the long-term "Cultural Indicators" study of television conducted at the Annenberg School of Communications, University of Pennsylvania, under the direction of George Gerbner (represented here in "Charting the Mainstream"). The Gerbner group has attempted to correlate empirical research on the sociopolitical content of television, audience reception among adults, and the influence of television on cognitive development and socialization in children. Their content analyses indicate that television transmits a predominantly middle-class, middle-of-the-road worldview that is both congenial to its corporate producers and effective in maximizing audiences; this "moderate" television mainstream, however, tends to run toward the political right. The studies of audience reception indicate that heavy viewers are more likely than light ones to have conservative attitudes resembling those transmitted by television. Although Gerbner's group does not assert a direct cause-and-effect relation, the similarities prompt them to surmise that television "cultivates" these attitudes in heavy viewers. This conjecture does not preclude two other likelihoods: that (1) factors other than television, for example, low level of education, contribute to the conservatism of heavy viewers, and thus the causation works both ways—conservatives watch more television, and television in turn reinforces their conservatism; and (2) market considerations by television producers and advertisers induce them to program to the conservative tastes they perceive to be dominant in heavy viewers, and so the causation is again reciprocal.

Let us look more closely at the political implications of the cognitive patterns induced by mass culture, as analyzed by our authors and many others doing related research (although some of the latter do not directly address political questions).

LACK OF ANALYTIC REASONING

Claus Mueller, in "Class as the Determinant of Political Communication," sums up a growing body of sociolinguistic research on the restricted linguistic and cognitive codes typical of mass media content and reception, keyed to class differentials in audiences. (Mueller discusses mainly television and tabloid journalism; equally significant research could undoubtedly be done on the cognitive effects of the monotonous, ear-shattering rock and disco music of the seventies and eighties.) This sociolinguistic research focuses on the deficiencies in media and audiences of the analytic and synthetic reasoning necessary to relate the concrete and the abstract, cause and effect, past, present, and future, as well as to view issues in sufficient complexity to avoid stereotyping and either/or thinking.

The mind at advanced stages of cognitive development seeks both to relate personal, specific impressions to impersonal, general truths and to ground abstract generalizations in concrete examples. American mass culture, however, lurches between excesses of concreteness and abstraction in such a way that critical analysis of sociopolitical issues is precluded. On the one hand, media ceaselessly reproduce, with tacit approval, concrete images of the status quo: commodity consumption, "Life Styles of the Rich and Famous," how-to techniques, the actions of government officials, and so on. On the other hand, when media discourse deals with abstractions, it is usually not in order to critically question the value system implicit in these concrete images but to propagate equally unexamined platitudes about the American way of life, patriotism, democracy, and the Free World. These abstractions can be reasonably concretized and defended, but all too often in our public discourse they are not.

ORAL VERSUS WRITTEN DISCOURSE

The foregoing deficiencies in analytic and abstract reasoning, along with the discontinuity in perception of time induced by heavy television viewing discussed by Postman, are also characteristics of the oral culture in preliterate societies, according to Jack Goody and Ian Watt in "The Consequences of Literacy," and in the culture of poverty according to Oscar Lewis. Studies, like those of the Gerbner group, of the class makeup of television viewers indicate that, above the level of the underclass who are too poor and alienated to own television sets, poorer and less-educated people watch the most and are most credulous about what they watch. Thus the oral culture of TV is bound to reinforce the oral culture of poverty. In their *Reading Television*, John Fiske and John Hartley analyze, with reference to England and the BBC, differences between the cognitive patterns in the encoding of TV messages by producers—as members of the dominant, literate class—and the decoding by audience members of the dominated, oral class. Goody and Watt confirm that since the beginnings of literate societies, access within them to written language has been a prime mark of dominant social classes, a form of what the French sociologist Pierre Bourdieu calls "cultural capital." There may be somewhat of a tautology here in the fact that society's recognition of literacy, or at least standard dialect, as a sign of status—or of inferiority in those who lack it—is to some extent an arbitrary matter of class bias; it is indisputable, however, that in our society's sophisticated information environment, facility in reading and writing is indispensable for either social domination or effective opposition.

In his studies of the black American language and subculture of the inner city, sociolinguist William Labov claims to have refuted Basil Bernstein by finding highly sophisticated reasoning and linguistic usage among ghetto children. Many leftists have sided with Labov against Bernstein, but Labov's studies are limited in that they are based mainly on oral rather than written discourse, on children rather than on people of more advanced stages of cognition, and on what Bernstein would categorize as the restricted code of local culture and localized experience rather than on understanding of more abstract, distant social realities as perceived through travel, education, reading, and other communications media. Thomas J. Farrell's studies of college remedial English students, black and white, confirm that Labov and his supporters may have misperceived the key issue in terms of standard English versus nonstandard dialects rather than in terms of oral versus literate cognitive patterns. In working-class blacks (far more than in middle-class ones), these patterns are those of black American oral culture; rich though that culture is in oral literary traditions, these traditions do not transfer readily into reading and writing skills. In white remedial-writing students of diverse social classes, the common denominator is often the oral patterns formed by heavy exposure to television and other electronic media. (Some empirical research has been done on the differential cognitive and socializing effects of television and other mass media on whites and minorities—see, for example, the collection *Television and the Socialization of the Minority Child*, edited by Gordon L. Berry and Claudia Mitchell-Kernan—but many important questions have not been sufficiently explored, such as the interaction between the white dialect dominant on TV and the dialect of black viewers.) Two eminent cognitive psychologists, Michael Cole and Jerome Bruner, have similarly countered Labov by concluding, in their article, "Cultural Differences and Inferences About Psychological Processes," that although there may be little intrinsic qualitative difference between various dialects and subcultures in terms of cognitive potential, exclusive socialization in black dialect and culture does amount to a "cultural deficit" in a white-dominated society. Pending a revolutionary reversal of white and black hegemonic roles in American politics and culture, then, leftists might best direct their criticisms at the forces excluding poor minorities and whites from literate culture, rather than minimizing the value of that culture as some leftists do.

Carl Boggs and Ray Pratt's "The Blues Tradition: Poetic Revolt or Cultural Impasse?" (Part 4) provides an interesting sidelight on this issue. American blacks, restricted since slavery days to oral discourse, were able to code oppositional messages in both the lyrics and musical structure of the blues; these messages were indecipherable to the writing-oriented white mind. This confirms Bernstein's point that the language of restricted codes may be quite sophisticated within a subculture though not functional in the larger culture. The significance of the complex coding in the blues is that this music was the recourse of a dominated group denied access to education or overt political communication, especially in written form.

PASSIVITY, ATOMIZATION, HYPNOSIS

The passive modes of information processing that Postman describes in television viewing in contrast to reading reinforce the absence of audience interaction with broadcasters or of control over media institutions. Postman and other researchers discuss the fragmentation of time segments and visual units in television; its lack of recursiveness, which precludes the revision process inherent in reading and writing; and the holistic manner in which children perceive television images as opposed to the linear, analytic, and synthetic patterns of reading and writing. Kate Moody asserts, "The eye and brain functions employed in TV viewing likely put demands on different parts of the brain than those used in reading, causing incalculably different kinds of cognitive development at the expense of reading and writing aptitudes."[3] Marie Winn reports research indicating that extended viewing of the contour and movement of TV images not only has a disorienting effect on vision and on bodily equilibrium similar to seasickness but also induces brainwave states similar to drug trances, hypnosis, or dreaming.[4]

EGOCENTRISM AND SOCIOCENTRISM

As Postman suggests, the substitution of the TV world for the real world impedes cognitive development from what Piaget calls the egocentric—or "narcissistic" in psychoanalytic terms—to the reciprocal stage in which mature object relations are established.[5] The ever-increasing privatizing of cultural activity—plays and films (now even pornographic ones) viewed at home rather than in a theater, music heard on radio, records, or TV rather than in a concert hall, televised sports, home computers, and so on—leads, in those not exposed to a diversity of other cultural influences, toward the solipsism of Jerzy Kosinski's "videot" in *Being There*. The resulting inhibition of normal ego formation perpetuates childlike dependency on parental and political authority. The egocentric cognitive stage is also most susceptible to ethnocentric, or what Piaget terms sociocentric, biases, hence to manipulation by chauvinistic propaganda. Moreover, the research of Gerbner's group indicates that heavy television viewers tend to develop exaggerated fears of violence in the streets and of foreign enemies, making them susceptible to simplistic appeals to law and order and the official use of force by the military and police.

Empirical research on the cognitive and socializing effects of television viewing is still in its preliminary stage; its findings are inconclusive and often conflicted. Gerbner's early studies on violence, for example, have occasioned a lengthy debate between his group and media sociologist Paul Hirsch. Some recent researchers, such as Gavriel Salomon and Patricia Marks Greenfield, cite more positive effects—modes of active audience interaction with the screen that are absent in reading; accelerated visual or mental responses; increased motivation for learning because of the nonacademic setting of television viewing, and so forth. For the most part, however, even these researchers do not deny the countervailing negative effects reported here.

Obviously, television *can* make advanced cognitive demands on viewers comparable to reading, as in televised Shakespeare or "Hill Street Blues," one of the rare commercial programs that requires viewers to synthesize a mosaic of characters, events, images, and sounds and to process nonstereotypic portrayals. But literate viewers have an obvious advantage in understanding this type of programming, and here, as in most other aspects of media reception, adults with a broader range of education, culture, and experience—that is to say, those usually in the higher social classes—tend to have the most resistance to the restricting effects of mass media, as the Gerbner studies document. Similarly, studies like those by Paul Messaris and Carla Sarett of the cognitive and socializing effects of TV on children suggest that the negative influence tends to be less in families in which the children are exposed to a diversity of cultural influences such as reading, travel, and general socialization incorporating Bernstein's elaborated codes.

LIMITED IMAGINATION

Perhaps the most profoundly conservative force in all of the cognitive patterns discussed here is their potential for inhibiting people from being able to imagine any social order different from the established one. The present reality is concrete and immediate, alternatives abstract and distant; ability to understand an alternative is further obstructed by lack of the sustained attention span necessary for analytic reasoning, of the capacity to imagine beyond the actual to the hypothetical (which semantically entails reasoning from the literal to the figurative and symbolic), and of a sense of irony, necessary if the social conditioning that endorses the status quo is to be effectively called into question.

Such widespread constriction of imagination would be a conservative force, that is, it would block fundamental change, in any social order—as it undoubtedly is in an ostensibly leftist country like the USSR, and as it would be to a lesser extent in a firmly entrenched liberal America under a sequence of charismatic Democratic presidents like Roosevelt or Kennedy or even in the most ideally realized socialist society. Nor is the point of this argument that change is always a priori beneficial; leftists can respect, to a point, the conservative position that people may show good sense in preferring to bear those ills they have rather than fly to others that they know not of. What *is* at issue is the hypothesis that people's loss of the capacity to imagine things being any different than they are could preclude their supporting changes that would in fact be strongly in their interests. Without necessarily espousing socialism, for example, can we not entertain the possibility that such a state of mind would keep socialistic policies off the American agenda no matter how demonstrably preferable they might be to capitalistic ones?

Following Bernstein, Richard Ohmann presents such a hypothesis about American workers' attitudes:

A number of studies . . . suggest that only a few people—those sharing in power or influence, by and large—have ordered and relatively abstract understandings of society. (This is not to say, of course, that their understandings are right, or that workers are not in many ways more sensible.) Workers' belief systems tend to be less conceptual, more fixed on concrete things, more centered in the local and particular. Their ideas on specific issues also tend to be more fragmented and inconsistent than the ideas of the more highly educated and privileged. Finally, the American working class as a whole lacks a consensus in beliefs and values, compared to the ruling class and the professional and managerial strata.[6]

(Ohmann's last two sentences echo Fiske and Hartley's analysis of the difference in class and power between those who program television and those who watch it.) Ohmann goes on to say that research such as Bernstein's implies that "a totalizing system of ideas such as marxism would be uncongenial, by virtue of its form, to workers."[7]

Mueller makes a similar point:

Today's working class symbolism has become so opaque that it is impossible for the worker to link his situation to an ideological framework with which he could understand, and more importantly, act upon the deprivation he experiences. . . . The concept of alienation, for example, can hardly be made operative politically because a semantic barrier built of a restricted language code excludes it from the workers' ideational world. This sort of difficulty was encountered by West German trade unions which tried to make the symbol "participation" a meaningful one for the workers.[8]

Another illuminating perspective on this problem was provided by Armand Mattelart, a Belgian sociologist of communication working in Chile with the Allende Popular Unity government during its three years of power from 1970 to 1973. Mattelart discussed the difficulties a socialist government with strong working-class participation encountered trying to improvise alternatives to the institutions and conventions of a whole system of mass culture established for capitalistic ends and projecting a middle-class world view, exemplified by the Disney productions Mattelart and Ariel Dorfman had criticized in *How to Read Donald Duck* (see Part 7). About the halting experiments in communicating the socialist experience through newspapers published by the *cordones industriales*, units of popular power founded by militant workers in the Santiago suburbs in 1972, "a kind of embryonic 'soviet,'" he observed with regret:

In this partisan political press, all the normality of daily life was absent. The not-said was considerable; in other words, new social relations were implicitly redefined but few were expressed explicitly. I remember being in a *cordón* just one month before the coup d'état, and the talk was about the changes which these men had experienced with their wives and their children, during the three years of Popular Unity. Yet never, either in the press of the *cordones*, or that of the extreme Left, or in the traditional press, had this type of fundamental change inspired a theme for mass information. All the books about the Chilean experience talk about political strategy in the strict sense of the term, but they ignore, apart from a few literary flights, the richness of this popular explosion. This is the real repression; the people live another life, a more important one, and yet can't express it, except in familiar gatherings; then they go back to the factories, unable to speak of it with their workmates, their *compañera*, their children.[9]

THE QUESTION OF CLASS

Returning now to the references to social class by several of the scholars cited here, there has been much controversy since the early sixties over the empirical validity of the studies by Bernstein and by Oscar Lewis and others on the culture of poverty, and over the possible class biases of the researchers themselves. Much of this controversy stems from the fact that although some scholars involved, such as Bernstein and Mueller, see their studies as comprising a leftist critique of class-structured society, their findings have also been appropriated by conservatives such as Seymour Martin Lipset and Arthur Jensen, who see the studies either as justifying "compensatory education" toward middle-class socialization or as providing evidence of the intractable difficulties in educating the poor and racial minorities. In both of these conservative arguments, blame has tended to be shifted from the discriminatory nature of capitalist society onto the victims of that discrimination. "The culture of poverty" was an ill-chosen phrase that provoked much controversy in the sixties because it was interpreted by some leftists as falsely implying that poor people, especially black and latino, had an impoverished culture or none at all. Perhaps "psychology of poverty" would have been a less ambiguous way of denoting the self-perpetuating internalization of external causes of poverty.

Further confusion on this issue has resulted from the ambiguous or differing definitions of class among the various scholars involved, on both the left and the right. Correlations between political attitudes and economic status, occupation, level of education, culture, and cognitive development are often not established sufficiently. Nor have many of these scholars adequately delineated particular segments within classes, between which there are apt to be significant differences in the criteria studied. It is often unclear in studies of the working class whether their subject is only the industrial proletariat or white-collar workers as well, whether it includes both organized and unorganized labor, men and women, urban and rural workers, the hardcore poor, whites and other races, and so on.

Crucial though the resolution of these disputes and ambiguities is for media scholarship, it is not essential for the concerns of this book. We need only recognize that none of the disputants would claim that the cognitive traits associated with restricted codes, exclusively oral culture, the culture of poverty, or the authoritarian personality are beneficial to either individuals or a progressive society in contemporary America—no matter what social class they appear in. To the extent that illiteracy and mass media perpetuate restricted cognitive capacities, they contribute to an impoverished, powerless mentality in millions of people who, if measured by income level and other common criteria, otherwise belong to very diverse social classes. Teachers in colleges with upper-middle-class suburban white students have been struck by the similarity in cognitive deficiencies between many of these students and the inner-city black and Hispanic students Shaughnessy studied. C. Wright Mills and the Frankfurt School theorists plausibly suggested that mass society and culture have created a new class division in which a large percentage of the proletariat and middle classes—including millions of relatively affluent people—have become homogenized in the consciousness comprised by the passive, authoritarian cognitive patterns described above. Conversely, Alvin Gouldner hypothesized in an essay called "The New Class as a Speech Community" that a "culture of critical discourse"—his term for Bernstein's elaborated codes—has become a determinant of membership in the dominant class in contemporary society, whose members include both the administrators of the status quo and, in smaller numbers, its most effective opponents.

All other things being equal, there is no denying the liberalizing effect of higher education, elaborated language codes, and the cosmopolitan outlook bred by travel and high culture. (The fact that creative literature in particular is characterized by precisely the cognitive traits in Bernstein's elaborated codes—irony, ambiguity, multiplicity of viewpoints, etc.—is a powerful reaffirmation of the value of literature and its academic study.) This is not to argue that higher education or upper social class invariably leads to liberal or socialist beliefs. Although in the contemporary American context, elaborated linguistic-cognitive codes are for many people the preconditions for such beliefs, countervailing factors such as the blandishments of prosperity, power, or the elite social milieu of high culture often make people who are born into or attain the upper social classes as conservative as, or more so than, those in lower classes. (The conservative effects of power on academic and journalistic intellectuals is the central theme of Noam Chomsky's several books attacking "the new American mandarins.") Moreover, on immediate issues such as labor disputes, unionized industrial or clerical workers are likely to be more militant than middle-class intellectuals (although the former may be less able to connect militancy on concrete issues to a broader leftist ideology). And regardless of self-interest, educated people often rationally assimilate leftist perspectives yet move beyond them to a refined conservative philosophy. Indeed, elaborated codes are necessary for the formation of *any* reasoned ideology—socialist, liberal, conservative, libertarian, or whatever. Public debate at the higher cognitive levels between the left and right would be an immense improvement over the infantile level of current American political and media discourse.

Richard Ohmann asks leftist teachers and other intellectuals, "When we try to communicate to workers a socialist understanding of things, must we think of our task as, in part, making up a cognitive and linguistic deficit? Or should we take it that the problem is more in the way *we* talk and write, and attempt somehow to translate marxism into more concrete and immediate terms than the ones we ordinarily use?" [10] It is unquestionably imperative that leftists seek more accessible modes of communication, but how far can they do so without debasing the irreducible complexities of socialist thought and duplicating the oversimplifications of right-wing propaganda or vulgar Marxism? Perhaps Ohmann's two questions, then, should be regarded as suggesting not mutually exclusive strategies but complementary ones. And perhaps they should both be preceded by a more basic question: What are the root causes in American history and present society of the separation of leftist intellectuals from the working class, which precludes the possibility of a coalition based on common interests as envisioned by such theorists as Marx and Gramsci, and what kind of political action might be most effective to address these causes directly? Insofar as our limited powers as cultural critics and educators are concerned, the thrust of this anthology—as well summed up by Stanley Aronowitz's article here, "Mass Culture and the Eclipse of Reason"—is that the most immediate responsibility of leftist intellectuals is not to impose their political persuasion on the public or students, least of all in simplistic form, but rather to struggle toward bringing about the free play of critical political thought as a means of overcoming the reflex conservatism induced by illiteracy and mass culture.

Notes

1. In an exchange between Herbert Gans and Christopher Lasch on this point, Gans presented a liberal-pluralist case for the broadening effects of mass culture, whereas Lasch's position, as in his *The Culture of Narcissism* and *The Minimal Self*, was similar to that presented here, with the added dimension that Lasch appears to be working toward an alternative to both capitalist and industrial-socialist societies: a decentralized, communitarian socialism following a tradition extending from William Morris to Paul and Percival Goodman (Herbert Gans, "Culture, Community, and Equality," *democracy* 2, no. 2

[1984]: 81–87; Christopher Lasch, "Mass Culture Reconsidered," *democracy* 1, no. 4 [1982]: 7–22; idem, "Popular Culture and the Illusion of Choice," *democracy* 2, no. 2 [1984]: 88–92).

2. Joshua Meyrowitz, *No Sense of Place: The Impact of Electronic Media on Social Behavior* (New York: Oxford University Press, 1985), p. 144.

3. Kate Moody, *Growing Up on Television—The TV Effect* (New York: Times Books, 1980), p. 67.

4. Marie Winn, *The Plug-In Drug* (New York: Viking Press, 1977), pp. 61–62.

5. Jean Piaget, "The Development in Children of the Idea of the Homeland and of Relations with Other Countries," in *Piaget Sampler*, ed. Sarah Campbell (New York: Wiley, 1976), pp. 37–58.

6. Richard Ohmann, "Questions About Literacy and Political Education," *Radical Teacher*, no. 8 (May 1978): p. 24.

7. Ibid., p. 25. Ohmann revised his position, in a direction more critical of Bernstein and Mueller on grounds of their definitions and methods, in "Reflections on Class and Language," *College English* 44, no. 1 (1982): 1–17. See also the subsequent exchange between Ohmann and two commentators in *College English* 45, no. 3 (1983): 301–307.

8. Claus Mueller, *The Politics of Communication: A Study in the Political Sociology of Language, Socialization, and Legitimation* (New York: Oxford University Press, 1973), p. 115.

9. "Cultural Imperialism, Mass Media and Class Struggle: An Interview with Armand Mattelart," *Insurgent Sociologist* 9, no. 4 (1980): 76–77.

10. Ohmann, "Questions About Literacy," p. 25.

Further Readings

English Studies in Basic Writing

Farrell, Thomas J. "Developing Literacy: Walter J. Ong and Basic Writing." *Basic Writing* 2, no. 1 (1978): 30–51.

———. "IQ and Standard English." *College Composition and Communication* 34, no. 4 (1983): 470–484. See also responses in *College Composition and Communication* 35, no. 4 (1984): 455–477.

Lunsford, Andrea. "The Content of Basic Writers' Essays." *College Composition and Communication* 31, no. 3 (1980): 278–290.

Shaughnessy, Mina P. *Errors and Expectations—A Guide for the Teacher of Basic Writing*. New York: Oxford University Press, 1977.

Sociolinguistics

Bernstein, Basil. *Class, Codes, and Control: Theoretical Studies Toward a Sociology of Language*. New York: Schocken Books, 1975.

Bourdieu, Pierre, and Jean-Claude Passeron. *Reproduction in Education, Society, and Culture*. Trans. Richard Nice. London: Sage, 1977.

Cole, Michael, and Jerome S. Bruner. "Cultural Differences and Inferences About Psychological Processes." In *Culture and Cognition: Readings in Cross Cultural Psychology*, ed. J. W. Berry and R. Dasen. London: Metheun, 1974.

Gouldner, Alvin. "The New Class as a Speech Community." In *The Future of Intellectuals and the Rise of the New Class*. New York: Seabury Press, 1979.

Gramsci, Antonio. "Notes on Language." *Telos*, no. 59 (Spring 1984): 119–150.

Labov, William. "The Logic of Nonstandard English." In *Language and Social Context*, ed. Pier Paolo Giglioli. New York: Penguin Books, 1972.

————. *The Study of Nonstandard English*. Urbana, Ill.: National Council of Teachers of English, 1978.

Lawton, Denis. *Class, Culture and the Curriculum*. Boston: Routledge & Kegan Paul, 1975.

History and Psychology of Oral Versus Literate Cultures

Disch, Robert, ed. *The Future of Literacy*. Englewood Cliffs, N.J.: Prentice-Hall, 1973.

Goody, Jack, and Ian Watt. "The Consequences of Literacy." In *Language and Social Context*, ed. Pier Paolo Giglioli. New York: Penguin Books, 1972.

Havelock, Eric A. *The Literate Revolution in Greece and Its Cultural Consequences*. Princeton, N.J.: Princeton University Press, 1982.

————. *Preface to Plato*. Cambridge, Mass.: Harvard University Press, 1963.

Luria, A. R. *Cognitive Development: Its Cultural and Social Foundation*. Cambridge, Mass.: Harvard University Press, 1976.

————. *Language and Cognition*. Somerset, N.J.: Wiley, 1981.

McLuhan, Marshall. *The Gutenberg Galaxy*. Toronto: University of Toronto Press, 1962.

————. *Understanding Media: The Extensions of Man*. New York: New American Library/McGraw-Hill, 1964.

Ong, Walter J. *Interfaces of the Word*. Ithaca, N.Y.: Cornell University Press, 1977.

————. *Orality and Literacy: The Technologizing of the Word*. London: Methuen, 1982.

————. *The Presence of the Word*. New Haven, Conn.: Yale University Press, 1967.

Scribner, Sylvia, and Michael Cole. *The Psychology of Literacy*. Cambridge, Mass.: Harvard University Press, 1981.

Vygotsky, L. S. *Mind in Society: The Development of Higher Psychological Processes*. Cambridge, Mass.: Harvard University Press, 1978.

————. *Thought and Language*. Cambridge, Mass.: MIT Press, 1962.

Political Socialization and the Culture of Poverty

Adorno, T. W., Else Frenkel-Brunswik, D. J. Levinson, and R. N. Stanford. *The Authoritarian Personality*. New York: Harper, 1950.

Allport, Gordon W. *The Nature of Prejudice, 25th Anniversary Edition*. Reading, Mass.: Addison-Wesley, 1979.

Deutsch, Martin, and Associates. *The Disadvantaged Child*. New York: Basic Books, 1967.

Deutsch, Martin, Irwin Katz, and Arthur R. Jensen, eds. *Social Class, Race, and Psychological Development*. New York: Holt, Rinehart & Winston, 1968.

Freire, Paulo. *The Politics of Education: Culture, Power, and Liberation*. South Hadley, Mass.: Bergin & Garvey, 1985.

Giroux, Henry A. *Ideology, Culture, and the Process of Schooling*. Philadelphia: Temple University Press, 1981.

Hoggart, Richard. *An English Temper: Essays on Education Culture and Communication*. New York: Oxford University Press, 1982.

————. *The Uses of Literacy: Changing Patterns in English Mass Culture*. New York: Oxford University Press, 1957.

Hoyles, Martin, ed. *The Politics of Literacy*. London: Writers and Readers Publishing Cooperative, 1977.

Kohn, Melvin L. *Class and Conformity: A Study in Values*. 2d ed. Chicago: University of Chicago Press, 1977.

Leacock, Eleanor Burke, ed. *The Culture of Poverty: A Critique*. New York: Simon & Schuster, 1971.

Lewis, Oscar. *Five Families: Mexican Case Studies in the Culture of Poverty*. New York: Basic Books, 1959.

Lipset, Seymour Martin. *Political Man: The Social Bases of Politics*. Garden City, N.Y.: Anchor Books/Doubleday, 1963.

Rokeach, Milton. *The Open and Closed Mind*. New York: Basic Books, 1960.

Valentine, C. *Culture and Poverty: Critique and Counter Proposal*. Chicago: University of Chicago Press, 1968.

Psychology of Moral Development

Gilligan, Carol. *In a Different Voice*. Cambridge, Mass.: Harvard University Press, 1982.

Habermas, Jürgen. "Moral Development and Ego Identity." In *Communication and the Evolution of Society*. Boston: Beacon Press, 1979.

Kohlberg, Lawrence. *Essays on Moral Development*. Vol. 1: *The Philosophy of Moral Development*. San Francisco: Harper & Row, 1981.

Perry, William. *Forms of Intellectual and Ethical Development in the College Years*. New York: Holt, Rinehart & Winston, 1970.

Piaget, Jean. "The Development in Children of the Idea of the Homeland and of Relations with Other Countries." *Piaget Sampler*, Sarah Campbell, ed. New York: Wiley, 1976.

———. *The Language and Thought of the Child*. New York: New American Library, 1955.

Effects of Television on Literacy and Cognition

Altheide, David L., and Robert P. Snow. *Media Logic*. Beverly Hills, Calif.: Sage, 1979.

Giroux, Henry A. "Mass Culture and the Rise of the New Illiteracy: Implications for Reading." *Interchange* 10, no. 4 (1979–1980): 89–98.

Greenfield, Patricia Marks. *Mind and Media*. Cambridge, Mass.: Harvard University Press, 1984.

Gross, Larry. "Modes of Communication and the Acquisition of Symbolic Competence." In *The Seventy-Third Yearbook of the National Society for the Study of Education*. Chicago: NSSE, 1974.

Mander, Jerry. *Four Arguments for the Elimination of Television*. New York: Morrow, 1978.

Mankiewicz, Frank, and Joel Swerdlow. *Remote Control: Television and the Manipulation of American Life*. New York: Ballantine Books, 1978.

Moody, Kate. *Growing Up on Television—The TV Effect*. New York: Times Books, 1980.

Morgan, Michael, and Larry Gross. "Television and Educational Achievement and Aspiration." *Television and Behavior: Ten Years of Scientific Progress and Implications for the Eighties*. Washington, D.C.: National Institute of Mental Health, 1982.

Postman, Neil. *Amusing Ourselves to Death*. New York: Viking Press, 1985.

Salomon, Gavriel. *Communication and Education: Social and Psychological Interactions*. Beverly Hills: Sage, 1981.

———. *Interaction of Media, Cognition, and Learning*. San Francisco: Jossey-Bass, 1979.

———. "Television Literacy and Television vs. Literacy." In *Literacy for Life: The Demand for Reading and Writing*, ed. Richard W. Bailey and Robin Melanie Fosheim. New York: Modern Language Association, 1983.

Winn, Marie. *The Plug-In Drug*. New York: Bantam Books, 1978.

Effects of Television on Socialization

Berry, Gordon L., and Claudia Mitchell-Kernan. *Television and the Socialization of the Minority Child*. New York: Academic Press, 1982.

Comstock, George, et al. *Television and Human Behavior*. New York: Columbia University Press, 1978.

Fiske, John, and John Hartley. *Reading Television*. New York: Methuen, 1978.

Gerbner, George, and Larry Gross. "The Violent Face of Television and Its Lessons." In *Children and the Faces of Television: Teaching, Violence, Selling*, ed. Edward L. Palmer and Aimee Dorr. New York: Academic Press, 1981.

Gerbner, George, Larry Gross, Michael Morgan, and Nancy Signorielli. "The Mainstreaming of America: Violence Profile Number 11." *Journal of Communication*, 30, no. 3 (1980): 10–29.

———. "A Curious Journey into the Scary World of Paul Hirsch." *Mass Communication Review Yearbook*. Beverly Hills, Calif.: Sage, 1982.

Gross, Larry, and Michael Morgan. "Television and Enculturation." In *Broadcasting Research Methods: A Reader*, ed. Joseph R. Dominich and James Fletcher. Boston: Allyn & Bacon, 1981.

Hirsch, Paul M. "On Not Learning from One's Own Mistakes: A Reanalysis of Gerbner et al.'s Findings on Cultivation Analysis, Part II." *Mass Communications Review Yearbook*. Vol. 3. Beverly Hills, Calif.: Sage, 1982.

———. "The 'Scary World' of the Nonviewer and Other Anomalies: A Reanalysis of Gerbner et al.'s Findings on Cultivation Analysis." *Mass Communications Review Yearbook*. Vol. 2. Beverly Hills, Calif.: Sage, 1981.

Messaris, P., D. Kerr, and A. Soudack. "Social Class, Family Communication Patterns, and Mothers' TV-Related Comments to Their Children." Paper presented at 32d Annual Conference of the International Communication Association, Boston, 1982.

Meyrowitz, Joshua. *No Sense of Place: The Impact of Electronic Media on Social Behavior*. New York: Oxford University Press, 1985.

Sarett, Carla J. "Social Class, Socialization, and Children's Learning from Television and Film." Unpublished paper, 1982.

———. "Socialization Patterns and Preschool Children's Television-and-Film-Related Play Behavior." Ph.D. diss., University of Pennsylvania, 1981.

THE TEACHINGS OF THE MEDIA CURRICULUM

NEIL POSTMAN

Since the television curriculum is pervasive and powerful, we can assume that it will have effects at several levels, including the physiological, the psychological, and the social. Of the physiological, we can, of course, only make conjectures. Nothing will really be known for a very long time, and not by us. But it can reasonably be imagined that excessive immersion in nonlinguistic, analogic symbols will have the effect of amplifying the functions of the right hemisphere of the brain while inhibiting the functions of the left. The left hemisphere is the source of most of our language power (at least for right-handed people). A left hemisphere lesion will lead to damage to our capacity to speak, write, count, compute, and reason (but not necessarily to our capacity to sing, a fact that Plato might have suspected had he been a brain surgeon). The right hemisphere of the brain is largely nonlinguistic and nonlogical in both its coding and decoding of information. Such language as it is capable of is underdeveloped and lacks both the syntax and semantics required for digital communication. Apparently, the right brain works through pattern recognition, which is to say it apprehends the world holistically rather than through linguistic structures. In recognizing a human face, or a picture of it, or anything that requires an "all at once" perception, such as watching TV, we are largely using the right hemisphere of the brain, the left possibly being something of a burden in the process. Thus, continuous television watching over centuries could conceivably have the effect of weakening left-brain activity and producing a population of "right-brained" people.[1]

What this would mean is difficult to say except possibly that such people would be strong on intuition and feeling but weak on reflection and analysis. The left hemisphere, being the source of our power to speak and, therefore, to categorize, name, and objectify experience, has apparently been in the ascendancy for several millennia of human development. A good case can be made, along the lines Julian Jaynes has pursued, that the gradual emergence of left-brain dominance has generated our uniquely human capacity for consciousness; that is, our capacity to reconstruct the past and project ourselves into a future.[2] A reversal of this trend is certainly imaginable as the word recedes in importance and the fast-moving, analogic image replaces it. If we imagine such a reverse trend carried to an extreme over many centuries, we might, then, have people who are "in touch with their feelings," who are spontaneous and musical, and who live in an existential world of immediate experience but, at the same time, cannot "think" in the way we customarily use that word—in other words, people whose state of mind is somewhat analogous to that of a modern-day baboon.

But one does not need to resort to millennia-wide speculation about the modifications of brain functions in order to talk about the consequences of an un-

From Neil Postman, *Teaching as a Conserving Activity* (New York: Delacorte Press, 1979).

opposed TV education. There are, even now, observable behaviors in our youth that indicate they are undergoing certain serious psychological changes, attributable at least in part to television. For example, I have suggested elsewhere that the highly compressed TV learning modules, especially those of ten- to thirty-second commercials, are affecting attention span. Many teachers have commented on the fact that students, of all ages, "turn off" when some lesson or lecture takes longer than, say, eight to ten minutes. TV conditioning leads to the expectation that there will be a new point of view or focus of interest or even subject matter every few minutes, and it is becoming increasingly difficult for the young to sustain attention in situations where there is a fixed point of view or an extended linear progression.

There is also evidence that youth are exhibiting behaviors—for example, in school—that are appropriate to television watching but not to situations requiring group attention. For instance, it is not uncommon for teachers to report that students will openly read newspapers in class or engage in other unconcealed side-involvements that are usually considered to be "rude" in the context of a lesson or lecture. My own investigation of this phenomenon suggests that these behaviors are not "rude" if by that word we mean a deliberate effort to violate the rules of a social situation; many students are not aware that they have violated any rule at all. In watching television or listening to records or the radio, they continuously engage in such side-involvements without reproach and do not always understand why these behaviors are inappropriate when carried over to other communication environments.

It has, of course, also been widely noticed that the linguistic powers of our youth appear to be diminishing. Scores on reading tests are in decline. But even more important, writing, the clearest demonstration of the power of analytical and sequential thinking, seems increasingly to be an alien form to many of our young, even to those who may be regarded as extremely intelligent. Moreover, it has been observed that oral expression has not improved as writing skills have fallen off. Many teachers, for example, have abandoned giving writing assignments altogether, but they have not found their students to be especially organized or even coherent in talking about anything of minimal complexity.

This deficiency is especially alarming because it suggests that we are in fact not moving back to a pre-Platonic oral culture in which memory, argumentation, and dialectic take command. Astonishingly, the two electronic media perfectly suited to the transmission of the human voice—the radio and the phonograph—have been given over almost entirely to the transmission of music. Such language as is heard on records is little else but comedy routines, or song lyrics at the level of Neanderthal chanting. On a radio, language is largely a commercial message, mostly a parody of human speech—disjointed, semihysterical, almost completely devoid of ideational content.

I believe this development to be only in part a consequence of the economic structure of the broadcasting and record industries. For if we say that these industries only give our youth what they will pay for, the question remains: why do our youth turn away from civilized speech? The answer, in my opinion, is that the electronic information environment, with television at its center, is fundamentally hostile to conceptual, segmented, linear modes of expression; thus, both writing and speech must lose some of their power. Language is, by its nature, slow-moving, hierarchical, logical, and continuous. Whether writing or speaking, one must maintain a fixed point of view and a continuity of content; one must move to higher or lower levels of abstraction; one must follow to a greater or lesser degree rules of syntax and logic. Even more, language is inevitably ambiguous, filled with confused notions. It is this very ambiguity that gives natural language its conceptual scope and versatility, for every word contains the possibility of multiple meanings and therefore of multiple ideas. And because words do not have closed, invariant meanings, they are our most effective instruments for changing our concepts and making them grow. The word is not just an idea: it is a small universe of ideas. Even more, every spoken sentence contains the seed of an argument, not only because of its ambiguity but also because whatever is asserted implies simultaneously its negation or opposite. Every proposition is debatable, or at least an impetus to inquiry.

The television curriculum will have none of this, though—or at least, very little. As I have argued, its imagery is fast-moving, concrete, discontinuous, and alogical, requiring emotional response, not conceptual processing. Not being propositional in form, its imagery provides no grounds for argument and contains little ambiguity. There is nothing to debate, nothing to refute, nothing to negate. There are only feelings to be felt. Thus the TV curriculum poses a serious challenge, not merely to school performance, but to civilization itself. And the challenge is not made only by the TV curriculum, for in considering what we are facing we must take into account the cumulative impact of the entire electronic information environment of which television is only an element, although a central one. Radio, the LP, audio tape, the photograph, film—each in its own way lends support to the undermining of traditional patterns of thought and response. Taken together, their "hidden curriculum" conspires against almost all of the assumptions on which the slowly disseminated, logically ordered, and cognitively processed word is based. In an environment in which nonlinguistic information is moved at the speed of light, in nonhierarchical patterns and vast, probably unassimilable quantities, the word and all it stands for must lose prestige, power, and relevance.

Our problem, then, is not how to produce higher reading scores or better school compositions but how to close the "generation gap." "Generation gap" here means the age-old tradition of a language-centered view of the world standing opposite a recently emerged image-centered view. On one side, then, there is always a historical presence with its mirror image, the future; on the other there is only an overpowering present. It is the ideal of reason versus the ideal of authenticity of feeling.

Do I overstate the case? I certainly hope so. And yet the effects to which I am alluding can be observed not simply in the fragmented, impatient speech of the young or their illogical, unsyntactical writing but in the rapid emergence of an all-instant society: instant therapy, instant religion, instant food, instant friends, even instant reading. Instancy is one of the main teachings of our present information environment. And constancy is one of the main teachings of civilization.

But constancy presupposes the relevance of historical precedence, of continuity, and above all, of complexity and the richness of ambiguity. A person trained to read a page in three seconds is being taught contempt for complexity and ambiguity. A person trained to restructure his or her life in a weekend of therapy is being taught contempt not only for complexity and ambiguity but also for the meaning of one's own past. And a person who abandons a millennia-old religious tradition to follow a fourteen-year-old messenger from God has somehow learned to value novelty more than continuity.

Where does the seeming plausibility of instancy as a way of life come from? It is at least a reasonable hypothesis that it emerges from the "worldview" advanced by our present information environment. Consider this: Every one of the one million commercials—every one—that a youngster will see or hear on TV or the radio presents a problem and a solution. The problem is rarely trivial, but the solution always is. Your anxiety about your sexual appeal gets solved with Scope—in thirty seconds. Your failure to achieve social status gets solved with a bottle of Coke and a song—in sixty seconds. Your fear of nature gets solved with Scott toilet tissue—in twenty seconds. Even the heartbreak of psoriasis can be relieved in a few seconds, not to mention the agony of hemorrhoidal tissues or, through Pan Am, the boredom of your life. These are powerful and incessant teachings, and they are not directed only at the young. They present us all with a paradigm of how to think and how to live and what to expect. We become, as Edmund Carpenter says, what we behold. The new media are more than extensions of our senses; they are ultimately metaphors for life itself, directing us to search for time-compressed experience, short-term relationships, present-oriented accomplishment, simple and immediate solutions. Thus, the teaching of the media curriculum must lead inevitably to a disbelief in long-term planning, in deferred gratification, in the relevance of tradition, and in the need for confronting complexity.

But this is far from the end of it. There are many reasonable hypotheses about the teachings of our electronic information environment for which suggestive evidence exists and against which civilization must prepare itself. For example, the nonlinear, nonsequential nature of electronic information works in powerful ways to create a frame of mind hostile to science. Science depends on linearity of thought, the step-by-step presentation of evidence and argumentation. This method of organizing information is the structural basis of scientific thought: it makes possible the refutation of evidence and argument; it permits translation into other digital forms, such as mathematics; it encourages delayed response and reflective analysis. The growth of science also depends on our ability to create increasingly sophisticated abstractions, particularly in digital modes. What happens, then, if our information environment does not encourage this mode of thinking? It is improbable that scientists will disappear, but we shall quite likely have fewer of them, and they are likely to form, even in the short run, an elite class who, like priests of the pictographic age, will be believed to possess mystical powers. The rest of the population may move rapidly toward an increasing fascination with mysticism and superstition, in other words, beliefs that are neither refutable nor comprehensible but are expressed with great feeling. There is already some evidence that this is in fact happening, as we can see in the growth of interest and belief in the occult, astrology, Eastern mysticism, levitating gurus, and English-speaking extraterrestrials.

Scientific thinking must also recede in prestige and relevance because of the discontinuity of content that characterizes much of our information environment. The fundamental assumption of science is that there is order and unity in diversity. A scientist must believe that events can be explained by reference to some organizing principle. Above all, he must believe that the world *makes sense*. But when one is immersed in a world of disconnected media presentations, it is extremely difficult to internalize this assumption. The young in particular are experiencing an acute inability to make connections, and some have given up trying. The TV curriculum, we must remember, stresses the fragmented and discrete nature of events and, indeed, is structurally unable to organize them into coherent themes or principles.

This fact must inevitably contribute to the undermining of a sense of history as well. Like science, history requires a belief in connectedness—the assumption that there are explanatory principles that account for social change or human conflict or intellectual growth. In this context, Jacob Bronowski's *The Ascent of Man* offers an instructive case of the nature of our problem, for it is about both history and science. Although the book version of his ideas was in fact a television script, it has the power, because it is a book, to explain the principles by which culture and science have developed; that is, the book has a thesis. In the TV version, the thesis disappeared. And so did history. Television is always in the present tense. There is no way to show what happened in the past. Whatever is shown appears as something that *is* happening. This is why we must be told frequently that a videotape we are watching was actually recorded at some earlier date. But even when film is used, as was the case in Bronowski's programs, it must present history as "now." In the "grammar" of both film and television, there simply is no correlate to a linguistic past tense. So, much of Bronowski's point of view was lost: he was concerned to show historical development, but the audience saw only a series of interesting events of equivalent contemporaneousness. Moreover, television or film cannot reveal a thesis. A thesis, a principle, a theme, a law, a hypothesis—these are all linguistic concepts. Pictures have no theses. They are analogues whose level of abstraction is concrete and invariable, and whose impact is immediate and existential. Bronowski *talked* his thesis as a supplement to the images, but his talk could not compete with his pictures. In the end, what the audience saw was a series of discrete, disconnected images that had no history and suggested no principles.

We must also worry about the plausible hypothesis that any decline in linguistic power will tend to increase the extent of personal maladjustment. As I write, there are reports from colleges and universities all over the country about the widespread incidence of suicide and other less definitive but serious symptoms of emotional difficulty among youth.[3] We appear to have an epidemic on our hands. Without meaning to deprecate the usefulness of either art or music therapy, I think it accurate to say that articulate language is our chief weapon against mental disturbance. Through language we are able to formulate in relatively clear terms the origins and nature of our distress, and through language we may chart the route toward resolution and relief. I seriously doubt if you can sing, dance, draw, or scream your way out of an impulse to suicide—but you can talk your way out. Of course, you can talk your way in as well, which is why knowledge of and competence in language are so essential to helping one achieve and maintain emotional balance. I have already written one book on this subject, *Crazy Talk, Stupid Talk*, and do not intend to rewrite it here. But surely it is no startling thesis to say that any decline in the resources of language is likely to be accompanied by an increase in personal maladjustment or, if you will, crazy talk.

And when we put the nonlinguistic bias of the media together with their bias toward one-way communication, the result is something more than maladjustment symptoms. We may have a near-lethal problem in social psychology. For example, there is no doubt that the new information environment provides access to knowledge about events and people all over the world. Through electronic media everyone's affairs become our business. The phrase Marshall McLuhan has used to describe this situation is "the world as global village." But if we all live in a global village, it is a strange village indeed: though we live in it, we are both mute and powerless. In fact, we do not live in it—we observe it, and can exert no influence on it. Even worse, we cannot even decide what portions of the village or aspects of its life we will see or the points of view from which we will see it. These decisions are made by the frame of a television screen, by the values of a television director, according to the biases of a television network.

What is the effect of making people aware of many things over which they have no control? I would suspect that it leads to anomie and an increasing sense of impotence. There are occasions, such as during the Vietnam War, when a large segment of the population is capable of rousing itself and responding to a grievance. There have been other occasions when similar mass responses have occurred. But the point is that these responses must be made en masse. Individuals no longer live in a context that allows them to have an impact on their environment. McLuhan himself has described the problem. "When man lives in an electric environment," he says, "his nature is transformed and his private identity is merged with a corporate whole. He becomes 'Mass Man.' Mass man is a phenomenon of electric speed, not of physical quantity. Mass man was first noticed as a phenomenon in the age of radio, but he had come into existence, unnoticed, with the electric telegraph." [4]

Mass man, as we know, can be an exceedingly dangerous animal, especially in a situation where there exists skepticism about the basis of traditional authority. [5] As I have pointed out, the electronic information environment tends to undermine hierarchies, and television in particular amplifies the appeal of personality. In such an environment, totalitarian ideas expressed by charismatic people find a congenial ground for growth. It is no accident that Reverend Moon, Werner Erhard, L. Ron Hubbard, and other messiahs with expensive tastes are especially appealing to the young.

But the undermining of hierarchies through the rapid and undifferentiated diffusion of information contains the possibility of still other undesirable consequences. I have referred to the fact that hierarchies always involve "secrets."

There are, of course, many kinds of secrets, including information that everyone knows but that is not considered suitable for public sharing. Everyone knows, for example, what one does in the bathroom, but it is part of our concept of personal dignity and civilized interaction that we do not display or discuss it. What is shared between a priest and a sinner, what happens among members of a family, what is discussed between a psychiatrist and a patient, these are secrets, too—or used to be, for the electronic environment assists in the dissolution of secrets.[6]

In the first place, some of the social structures—for example, the family and church—that are traditionally places and occasions for secret-sharing have diminished in prestige and influence. Thus, people turn to strangers, that is, public forums, including electronic forums, to reveal their secrets. The emergence of the radio phone-in show is explainable, in part, by this need. It is a form of controlled exhibitionism, and is thus both a symptom and a cause of the blurring of the difference between private life and public life. As Richard Sennett suggests in *The Fall of Public Man*, electronic communication is one means by which the distinction between private and public life is brought to an end.

But more important, the new media require a constant supply of information. Television, for example, is compelled to display novel events continuously in order to control the public's attention. Thus, any sphere of human activity is a potential source of supply. We have already seen the Loud family display every conceivable secret of their private life, a president and his wife being asked to discuss their bedroom habits, the host of a daytime TV program being analyzed by his psychiatrist, babies being born, transvestites discussing their sex-change operations, and so on. So far as I know, there has not yet been a program in which moral transgressors confess their sins to priests or physicians tell patients they are going to die, but in principle there is no reason why not.

Television and radio (and, one might add, the movies) are inherently hostile to the *idea* of privacy. But it is a hostility without vindictiveness or even emotion. There is certainly nothing conspiratorial about it. Simply, information must be moved and consumed continuously—that is the price to be paid for speed-of-light transmission. What the information may be is of no consequence, as long as it is attention-getting, and does not inhibit the flow of new information coming fast behind it. Of course, in the process, our ideas of propriety and personal identity become altered; that is to say, dangerously eroded. The Mass Man, as McLuhan describes him, is one whose private identity is merged with the corporate whole. This means, as Bruno Bettelheim described it in *The Informed Heart*, that people are stripped of their secrets and therefore of their sense of personal dignity. The relatively new "values" of openness, of letting it all hang out, of not being uptight, of saying exactly what is on one's mind, are a consequence of the present information environment. We are being moved rapidly away from the concept of a private identity by the egalitarianism of total, undifferentiated information disclosure.

There is still another consequence of this movement, described very well by C. P. Snow. He observed in 1968 at Westminster College that "the rapidity and completeness of human communications are constantly presenting us with the sight of famine, suffering, violent death. We turn away, inside our safe drawing rooms. It may be that these communications themselves help to make us callous." You will recognize in this conjecture the conventional complaint against the display of excessive violence, for example on television. It is not a complaint to be taken lightly. But there is another meaning to callousness here that is, in my opinion, even more ominous. I refer to a certain degree of immunization and therefore indifference to reality itself that may be generated by the "rapidity and completeness of human communications." That is, even if there were a reduction in the images of famine, suffering, and violent death, there would be no reduction in the amount of *symbolic* experience in which we are daily immersed. Again, what is important here is not so much the content of the media but the experience of media itself. Life on the TV screen, however it is depicted, is still seen through a twenty-one-inch flat-surfaced frame. Life on the movie screen is seen seven times life size. Even when we hear an authentic human voice on the radio, it is a voice entirely disembodied. Life, then, becomes a stylized, edited media event, and it is not inconceivable that in the "completeness" of our immersion in media, we come to prefer media-life to reality itself.

Even before the electronic revolution, we understood the role that reading itself may play in encouraging a fantasy life. There were probably many readers in the nineteenth century, for example, who preferred fictional characters and places to the real people and situations they were forced to live with. If we now multiply by a factor of ten the opportunities for experiencing life at a distance, life through the filter of a technological symbolic system, we can get some idea of the extent to which media may now be serving as a surrogate for reality, and a preferred one at that. At stadiums throughout the country, huge TV screens have been installed so that spectators can experience the game through TV, because TV is better than being there—even when you are there. Conferences and other group meetings are videotaped so that participants may look at themselves to see what "really happened." Tourists travel everywhere with still cameras so that they can document their vacations. In the end, the photographs are the reality of the experience; should they be ruined, how would one know what was really seen? or if one was really there? And we must remember that not only did "Marcus Welby" receive more than a quarter of a million letters seeking his medical advice but the American Medical Association actually invited him to be a keynote speaker at one of their annual conventions. Perhaps it is not even too much to say that the increase in what are called "senseless" crimes is part of the consequence of the replacement of reality with symbolic experience. For the "sense" in "senseless" has two meanings, one of which refers to thinking, the other to touch, smell, taste, and so on. Is it possible that a "senseless" crime has its origin in an acute deprivation of real sensory experience? Is it possible that, immersed in a world of surrogate experience, we simultaneously lose our senses and lose touch with them both?

Admittedly, this last observation, as well as some that preceded it, must be regarded as speculation. But none of it is "mere" speculation. I believe that reason, historical analogy, and observable trends within our society point to the plausibility of these observations. We can be sure that a curriculum as powerful as the electronic information environment will have powerful effects, and in suggesting what these might be, I have done nothing more than what educators do every September when they predict the effects of a school curriculum. They tell us that certain things will be taught in certain ways and within a certain context, and that certain results can be expected. I am saying the same thing, with this difference: the curriculum I am referring to has more money spent on it, commands greater attention, is more pervasive, and is less carefully monitored than the school curriculum. Moreover, in its competition with the school curriculum for the control of our young, the electronic curriculum is an ungracious—one might even say, merciless—adversary. It makes no concessions whatever to the school curriculum, unless you want to count "Sesame Street," which is, in my opinion, no concession at all, but a promiscuous flaunting of everything the TV curriculum represents and in the worst possible way—by trying to mimic the forms of the electronic curriculum and therefore to indulge its biases. School courses are reduced to twenty-minute modules so that children's attention will not wander. Required courses are eliminated and replaced with inconsequential electives. Teachers become entertainers. Programmed machines and other techniques that stress isolated learning are introduced. Audiovisual aids flood the classroom. Relevant—that is, attention-centered—topics are stressed. There even develops a widespread interest in what are called "alternative curriculums." But the school as we normally think of it (or used to think of it) is now, itself, an alternative curriculum, one whose teachings very much need to be preserved in the face of the onslaught of the First Curriculum.

The school curriculum is subject matter–centered, word-centered, reason-centered, future-centered, hierarchical, secular, socializing, segmented, and coherent. Assuming that these characteristics are maintained, and even strengthened, we may hope that the education of our youth will achieve a healthful balance, and therefore a survival-insuring direction. Marshall McLuhan wrote prophetically more than a decade ago that our education must assume a thermostatic function: "Just as we now try to control atom-bomb fallout, so we will one day try to control media fallout. Education will become recognized as civil defense against media fallout."[7]

Notes

1. I mean these remarks about the hemispheres of the brain (as well as those that follow) to be taken only half seriously. In the first place, you will notice that my comments have a distinct Lamarckian flavor to them. In the second, I know very little about neurology and brain research. I include these speculations because I find them both plausible and interesting, but I vow, here and now, to make no further comments about the structure of the brain until such a time as I have a medical degree, with a specialty in brain research.

2. See Julian Jaynes's *The Origin of Consciousness in the Breakdown of the Bicameral Mind*, (Boston: Houghton Mifflin, 1976). In contrast to me, Jaynes knows a great deal about the structure of the brain and has written the most fascinating book on the subject of consciousness I have ever read. If you are not put off by the book's discouraging title, you will enjoy a delightful intellectual adventure.

3. See the front page of the *New York Times*, 27 February 1978.

4. McLuhan has made several remarks conveying this idea. The one quoted here was

taken from *Dreadnaught Broadside*, an unusual series of pamphletlike publications produced by students at the University of Toronto.

5. For an interesting discussion of this idea, see José Ortega y Gasset's *The Revolt of the Masses* (New York: Norton, 1932), particularly chapter 13, where, among other things, he notes the astonishing growth in the number of police departments throughout the "civilized" world.

6. For a well-developed argument on this point, see Joshua Meyrowitz's *No Sense of Place: The Impact of Electronic Media on Social Behavior* (New York: Oxford University Press, 1985).

7. This quotation is found in Marshall McLuhan, *Understanding Media* (New York: McGraw-Hill, 1965), p. 305. Several others similar to it may be found throughout *Understanding Media*.

CLASS AS THE DETERMINANT OF POLITICAL COMMUNICATION

CLAUS MUELLER

Pierre Bourdieu has noted a "refusal to articulate" in the French working class, which he links to class ethnocentrism.[1] It seems that working-class groups lack the necessary "distance from language" to handle it rationally or in an instrumental way. This "distance" is an individual's consciousness of language, the awareness that language is a tool for both emotional expression and analytic description and the belief that language is a means of articulating one's individuality. Anselm Strauss, in his study of the communicative modes of adults belonging to the lower and middle classes in the United States, observed phenomena similar to those noted by Bourdieu. For the sake of brevity, the differences he observed between the two groups are summarized in the following list:[2]

	Lower Class	Middle Class
perspective	fixed perspective; rigid description	use of several standpoints and alternative interpretations
organization	lack of clear referents; few qualifications; segmented organizational framework; little grasp of context of event if more than one actor involved	frequent qualifications and illustrations; clear narrative even when narrative is complex; unitary framework of organization
classification and relation	relative inability to use categories for people and acts since the speaker tends not to think in terms of classes; imprecise use of logical connections	rich conceptual terminology; frequent classification and use of logical categories
abstractions	insensitivity to abstract information and questions	sensitivity to generalizations and patterns
use of time	discontinuous; emphasis on the particular and ephemeral	continuous; emphasis on process and development

Excerpted from Claus Mueller, *The Politics of Communication: A Study in the Political Sociology of Language, Socialization, and Legitimation* (New York: Oxford University Press, 1973).

It is apparent from Strauss's report that Bourdieu's concept of distance from language applies as well to the way adult members of the American lower and middle classes describe situations and events. Members of the lower classes provided sociocentric answers and showed little familiarity with the rituals of middle-class communication. Their socially restricted universe does not require precise statements and refined observations. Thus there is no experience of a need to "be very self-conscious about communicative techniques."[3] Members of the middle classes were comparatively detached from the content of their descriptions and were "sensitive to communication *per se* and to communication with others who may not share [their] viewpoints or frame of reference. . . . People of this stratum can, if required, handle the more complex and consciously organized discourse."[4] A well-developed language permits the individual to articulate intentions clearly and to engage in more precise communication with others. It provides the basis for analytic statements and abstractions that transcend the particular. A language that is limited in its lexical or syntactic dimensions tends to confine the speaker to emotive and concrete expressions.

An individual's language can be so constricted that communication with members of other groups not subject to an identical linguistic and social environment becomes difficult, if not impossible.[5] According to Rosalie Cohen, the language of the "hard-core poor"* is distinguished by a predominantly descriptive rather than analytic mode of abstraction, by great semantic concreteness, by a personalization of objects and groups, by a lack of subtlety and differentiation, and by a tendency to collapse logically distinct categories (for example, cause and effect, means and ends) into one dimension. Persons speaking this language respond most readily to external features of their environment rather than to abstract qualities. The individual has a discontinuous feeling of time, believes himself to be important only within his social group, is not interested in those aspects of the environment that have no immediate relevance to him, and is more attracted by the unique than by patterns and procedures.[6]

The language of the hard-core poor is a restricted speech code in the extreme and contains several of the features reported by Strauss. Since it cannot be used in an instrumental, reflective way, the language itself, spoken by a person living in starkly deprived conditions, reinforces his social location. The individual's language, cast in the immediacy of his environment, conditions his perception. The categories of his language allow for a grasp of the here and now, but they do not permit an analysis, hence a transcendence, of his social context. Seen politically, this language reinforces the cohesion of a group that shares a specific code, but it can prevent the group from relating to the society at large and to its political institutions. The individual experiences his deprivation subjectively; cognitively speaking, however, he lacks the reference points necessary to perceive the objective reasons for his condition and to relate it to the structure of the society in which he is living. The individual's language thus becomes his internal plausibility structure. In narrowing his ability to discriminate, to conceptualize, and to

---

*R. Cohen and her collaborators estimate that up to 30 percent of the permanent urban slum dwellers in ghetto areas constitute a group termed "the hard-core poor."

analyze, it renders his condition more acceptable to him. He is immune from perceiving alternatives.

Basil Bernstein, who has provided the analytic point of departure for most contemporary research on class-specific modes of speech, ascertained in his own studies the existence of restricted and elaborated codes.* After numerous testing of speech and writing samples, the linguistic form of middle-class subjects proved to be an elaborated (formal) one, since it allows for analytic perception and discrimination and for individuated expression of meaning. That of the lower class proved to be a restricted (public) one, since it, as demonstrated as well by Lawton, encourages descriptive thinking and greatly diminishes abstract reasoning.[7] The restricted code is distinguished by its high degree of predictability. Apart from the lexical limitations of this code, there are constraints on the syntactic level that reduce the possible range of verbal alternatives. These constraints, however, cause little problem for personal communication, since commonly shared interests and the individual's strong identification with the values and norms of his group reduce the restricted code speaker's need to state explicitly his intent.† Cues to indicate changes of meaning are transmitted extraverbally. Because the content of verbal messages is less important than the form they take, emphasis is placed on the latter.[8] This mode of speech is marked by grammatical simplicity, a uniform vocabulary, short and often redundant sentences, a scarcity of adjectives and adverbs, repetitive use of conjunctions, and comparatively little verbal differentiation or symbolism.[9] The capacity to formulate generalizations is therefore restricted. As already observed in the language of the hard-core poor, categorical statements express simultaneously cause and effect. Bernstein points to the strictures this mode of speech exerts on those who speak it, noting that

the short, grammatically simple, syntactically poor sentence . . . does not facilitate the communication of ideas and relationships which require a precise formulation. . . . A public [restricted] language does not permit the use of conjunctions which serve as important logical distributors of meaning and sequence. . . . The frequency of, and dependency upon, the categoric statement in *public* language reinforces the personal at the expense of the logical. . . . Traditional phrases . . . tend to operate at a low causal level of generality in which descriptive, concrete . . . symbols are employed aimed at maximizing the emotive rather than the logical impact.[10]

Bernstein specified the qualities of the elaborated code in comparison to those of the restricted one and enumerated several features, including accurate use of grammar and syntax; complexity of sentence structure and of attendant qualifying conjunctions, relative clauses, and prepositions; careful use of adjectives and adverbs; and verbal mediation of individuated meaning.[11] Since the elaborated

---

* In his early writings, Bernstein classified the dominant speech pattern of the middle class as a "formal" language and that of the lower class as a "public" language. He subsequently changed these terms to "elaborated" and "restricted" codes, respectively.
† It should be noted that the middle-class speaker's speech code can approximate a restricted code in certain situations where, prior to communication, common understandings can be assumed; for example, in a peer group he can switch to the restricted code. The reverse is not applicable to the lower-class speaker.

speaker's code does not limit his use of the syntactic and lexical dimensions of the language, his language performance is relatively unpredictable—in any case less predictable than that of the restricted code speaker. Those who share this code have to convey meaning explicitly through language. This in turn implies that language takes on an instrumental character and that the speaker engages in verbal planning. Complex conceptual hierarchies make accurate syntactical and lexical usage possible. Messages exchanged are qualified, and the established causal links are logical. Speakers do not engage in the sociocentric speech observable in the lower classes but rather try to depersonalize their speech.

Comparing children who speak the elaborated code to those who speak the restricted code, Bernstein notes that children from the middle classes "learn to scan a particular syntax, to receive and transmit a particular pattern of meaning, to develop a particular [verbal] planning process, and very early learn to orient toward the verbal channel," whereas those from the lower classes, "limited to a restricted code, will tend to develop through the regulation inherent in the code." Generalizations and concrete, descriptive statements can be transmitted in the latter code, but they involve a "relatively low order of conceptualization." [12]

Almost from birth, the individual acquires the language code specific to his group, which in turn provides the matrix for all that he can explore in speech and thought. If the available lexical and syntactic resources are underdeveloped and arrested communication persists, an individual or group will not be able to select freely among existing perceptual and cognitive alternatives. The ability to generalize and to use an abstract mode of understanding will be limited. In short, these individuals will be unable to exceed cognitively those social relationships from which the code emanates. Language thus becomes an intervening variable.

The restricted code has essentially a practical function. Speakers of this code are not, however, aware of the existence, functions, or limitations of this code and its descriptive and concrete features. Conversely, the middle-class speaker is aware of his code, of its analytic function, and of its potential for perceiving distinctions and grasping generalizations. It becomes apparent that linguistic codes are rooted in the class structure. These codes—as separated by lexical, syntactic, and conceptual boundaries—reinforce the social structure by shaping the speaker's personal and social identity.

CLASS AND POLITICAL ATTITUDES

Middle-class parents have a greater sense of independence from political institutions than lower-class parents and, according to Kohn, believe themselves "to be in control of the forces that affect their lives." Lower-class parents feel an inescapable dependency on society and its institutions, a resistance to innovation, and an "intolerance of any belief threatening the social order." [13] These orientations serve as a framework within which the political values of children develop. Given the high correlation between political attitudes of children and those of their parents, it is not surprising that lower-class children either are apathetic with regard to political symbols and institutions or tend to personalize political events. The apathy results from a feeling of powerlessness, and the tendency to personalize ensues from an inability to understand complex phenomena. The sense of powerlessness of lower-class children is probably related to their parents' lack of authority in political matters. Robert D. Hess noted as the most significant social-class difference between middle- and lower-class children "the tendency for lower class children to feel less efficacious in dealing with the political system than do children from high status homes. . . . Social class differences were large even at the third and fourth grade, and they increased with age. The differences on the efficacy items are among the most striking class discrepancies in the data of this study." [14]

Feelings of powerlessness and uncertainty mean susceptibility to influence from outside agencies. [15] Patterns of dependency and subordination, as we have seen, are more likely to occur in lower- than in middle-class homes. [16] These patterns can lead to an identification with existing political institutions which acts as a deterrent to critical examination of the political process. Thus, as Hess states, "lower class children more frequently accept authority figures as correct and rely on their trustworthiness and benign intent. There is more acquiescence to the formal structure and less tendency to question the motivations behind the behavior of the government and government officials." [17] Government is seen as needing no change. [18]

The cognitive state of lower-class children that has been demonstrated above also has a bearing on political attitudes, since cognitive simplicity and the concomitant lack of flexibility and subtlety in concepts or categories result in a narrow, stereotyped view of political reality. [19] Discussing children's understanding of politics, Hess noted that "the ability to deal with an abstract rather than personalized system is apparently related to cognitive maturity. . . . Working class children also personalize their view of the government. The social class difference may follow from the tendency of the working class parents to emphasize rules rather than offering rationales which are more impersonal and abstract guidelines for behavior." [20]

.   .   .   .

Political communication becomes distorted when symbols and interpretational rules that are contrary to official symbols and definitions cannot be used publicly without sanctions. If contrary and alternative symbols are repressed from official language, they are then confined to the private one, where for technical reasons control or manipulation cannot be exercised by those in power, for they cannot interfere directly with the primary socialization process. If language is seen as the medium for the perpetuation and generation of symbols and meanings potentially contrary to predefinitions imposed from above, a restricted code would provide only a limited basis for a private language and for resistance to official definitions of reality. Moreover, the values of children coming from families with limited linguistic and self-differentiation faculties are more likely, as has been seen, to be supportive of a political system than are the values of children from families where communication and individuation are encouraged. These predispositions would most likely express themselves in adult behavior patterns that would inhibit the articulation of conflicts and contradictions, especially if they touch on issues exceeding material needs.

To the extent that the official language, as expressed in mass media, educational institutions, and advertising, infringes on the primary socialization process, external influence over private language is exerted. For middle-class families, however, the realm of private language appears to be relatively broad, since the capacity to manipulate symbols inherent in an elaborated speech code combined with a focus on self-direction allows for a defense system against the influence of extrafamiliar socialization agencies. Possession of an elaborated code equals political as well as cultural capital. It makes it possible for an individual to understand and respond to conflicts, whether experienced in the growth process of youth and adolescence or in encounters with external agencies as an adult. The individual can reflect about his experience in society, even if external agencies try to reduce the range of symbols that may be antagonistic to dominant political interests. He is able to formulate his own interpretations.

The situation appears different for individuals from the working class. The restricted speech code shared by them, in conjunction with the stress on conformity, does not allow for a questioning of official legitimating rationales; corrosion of these rationales is thus unlikely. The possibility of neutralizing symbols that support existing modes of domination or control is absent.

THE INFLUENCE OF THE MEDIA

In most cases there is a correspondence between the sophistication of a medium—with respect to language and interpretation—and that of the audience. An analysis by James Chambers of the *Daily News* and the *New York Times* showed significant differences between the two papers in the use of syntax and vocabulary.[21] The simplified wording and sentences of the *Daily News* correlated, as would be expected, with the class background of its readership, which tends toward a restricted code, while the more complex vocabulary and syntax of the *New York Times* correspond to the generally elaborated code of its middle-class readers. Research on a German mass circulation paper, the *Bildzeitung*, corroborates Chambers's analysis. Ekkehart Mittelberg found a number of stylistic elements in this German paper that are typical of the restricted code, such as concrete metaphors, dichotomized statements, simplified sentence structures, typified formulations, an undifferentiated vocabulary, and stereotypifications.[22] The use of a restricted code by these papers results in unqualified descriptions of political reality that more often than not are conservatively slanted. Because of the style utilized, the reader's language does not inhibit comprehension, but he may be manipulated through the effective application of the very stereotypes he uses in his everyday language. As Mittelberg suggested, an appeal to emotions, strong metaphors, and superficial formulations suspend the reader's thinking.[23] The frame of reference of these papers is consistent, and it is possible to predict with a high degree of accuracy their interpretations of a given political event. Sensationalism, repetition, and a simplistic depiction of political reality contribute little to the reader's knowledge of society.

Other observers of media addressed to both lower- and middle-class groups have come up with similar findings. The French philosopher and sociologist Henri Lefebvre remarked that the "mass media form the taste and dilute judgment. They instruct and they condition. They fascinate and they debase by saturation with images, with 'news' that is not newsworthy. They proliferate communication and threaten coherence and reflection, vocabulary and verbal expression, and language itself." *[24]

Editorial policies in the mass media cannot be detached from commercial considerations, which require that the largest possible audience be reached. Interpretations that may alienate either the sponsor or the audience of a program generally will not be transmitted. In early 1972, David W. Rintels, chairman of the Committee on Censorship of the Writers Guild of America, testified before the Senate Subcommittee on Constitutional Rights that, according to a poll of the Guild, of those who responded

eighty-six per cent have found, from *personal* experience, that censorship exists in television. Many state, further, that they have never written a script, no matter how innocent, that has not been censored. Eighty-one per cent believe that television is presenting a distorted picture of what is happening in this country today—politically, economically and racially. Only eight per cent believe that current television programming is "in the public interest, convenience and necessity" as required by the Federal Communications Act of 1934.[25]

This censorship is exerted prior to and during the production of a program, not only by the sponsor but also by companies that invest heavily in television advertising. This was the case in the spring of 1972 when the National Broadcasting Company removed a section from a documentary on the conditions of migrant workers employed by a Florida subsidiary of the Coca-Cola Company because of pressures applied by the parent corporation.[26]

The "dramatic, low taste content" of entertainment is most likely to appeal to the majority of the consumers who are little educated and who do not critically evaluate the programs they watch or hear.[27] Programming corresponds for the most part to the tastes and preferences of the audience and serves to "maintain the financial equilibrium of a deeply institutionalized social system [i.e., the media] which is tightly integrated with the whole of the American economic institutions."[28] This function of the media deflects public attention from political issues and perpetuates the definition of the "good life" in strictly materialistic terms.

Although the audience may influence the type of entertainment presented in the media, it has little control over the selection of information and quality of interpretations transmitted. The flow of information is downward, as is the direction of influence.[29] Certainly, the individual can disregard a message because he deems it irrelevant or incorrect. But the validity of political messages, such as those pertaining to foreign and fiscal policies, cannot be assessed at the moment

---

*If the receiver of a message has doubts about its content, it will be repeated, since redundancy "is the simplest way of reducing the equivocation [of] the receiver." Persuasion calls for repetition and the reduction of complex matters into a limited number of typifications and their associated negative or positive connotations (Colin Cherry, *On Human Communication* [Cambridge, Mass.: MIT Press, 1966], p. 210).

of transmission, since any evaluation presupposes an acquaintance with the relevant facts most of the audience does not have.

It is precisely in this area that the stabilizing influence of the media becomes apparent. As noted earlier, individuals belonging to the lower classes are more dependent on group norms than are those coming from the middle classes. Conformity and allegiance to established authority as well as resistance to change were found to be political predispositions of individuals brought up in the lower classes. Empirical research also demonstrates that class-specific factors such as conformity, reception to one-sided arguments, and the absence of skepticism correlate with the susceptibility to persuasion and manipulation.[30] It cannot be doubted that interpretations and opinions disseminated by the media have an influence on large segments of the audience.

Governmental constraints on political communication, the mobilization of bias by powerful interests, and the commercial character of the media create a situation in which news items that would invite challenges of the status quo are either omitted or embedded in interpretations that depreciate them. If members of the audience have no counterinterpretations or alternative sources of information, they may mistake the selected messages presented by the media for the real world. In doing so they unwittingly support existing institutions and policies. Renate Mayntz has described this condition as the "half-resigned acceptance of the *status quo* [which] may well be reinforced by a fake cultural integration and feeling of participation induced by the mass media."[31]

Notes

1. Pierre Bourdieu, "Culture et transmission culturelle," (Centre de Sociologie Européenne, Paris, 1966, mimeo), p. 123.

2. A. Strauss and L. Schatzman, "Social Class and Modes of Communication," *American Journal of Sociology* 60, no. 4 (1955); and idem, "Cross Class Interviewing: An Analysis of Interaction and Communicative Styles," *Human Organization* 14, no. 2 (1955). The list is adapted from their articles. See also M. A. Straus, "Communication, Creativity and Problem Solving Ability of Middle- and Working-Class Families in Three Societies," *American Journal of Sociology* 73, no. 4 (1968).

3. Strauss and Schatzman, "Social Class and Modes," p. 337.

4. Ibid., pp. 336, 337.

5. S. Ervin-Tripp ("Language Development," in *Review of Child Development Research*, ed. M. L. Hoffman and L. W. Hoffman, vol. 2 [New York: Russell Sage, 1966]) reports that the conceptual hierarchies of children living in urban slums are retarded.

6. R. Cohen et al., "The Language of the Hard Core Poor," *Sociological Quarterly* 9, no. 1 (1968): 24ff.

7. Basil Bernstein, "A Public Language: Some Sociological Implications of a Linguistic Form," *British Journal of Sociology* 10 (1959): 311–325; idem, "Language and Social Class," *British Journal of Sociology* 11 (1960): 271–276; and idem, "Elaborated and Restricted Code: Their Social Origins and Some Consequences," *American Anthropologist* 64, no. 6 (1964), pt. 2.

8. Bernstein, "Elaborated and Restricted Code," p. 62.

9. Bernstein, "A Public Language," p. 311.

10. Ibid., pp. 315, 317.

11. Ibid., p. 312.

12. Bernstein, "Elaborated and Restricted Code," p. 65.

13. Melvin L. Kohn, *Class and Conformity* (Homewood, Ill.: Dorsey Press, 1970), p. 81.

14. Robert D. Hess and Judith V. Tournay, *The Development of Political Attitudes in Children* (Chicago: Aldine, 1967), pp. 256, 171.

15. See, for instance, Martin Deutsch and H. B. Gerard, "A Study of Normative and Informational Influence upon Individual Judgement," *Journal of Abnormal and Normal Psychology* 51, no. 3 (1955).

16. Cf. J. Davis, "The Family's Role in Political Socialization," *American Academy of Political and Social Science* 361 (1965).

17. Hess and Tournay, *Political Attitudes in Children*, p. 179.

18. Ibid., pp. 154ff.

19. See F. W. Koenig and M. B. King, "Cognitive Simplicity and Out Group Stereotyping," *Social Forces* 62, no. 3 (1964); G. M. Vaughan and K. D. White, "Conformism and Authoritarianism Reexamined," *Journal of Personality and Social Psychology* 3, no. 3 (1966); J. White et al., "Authoritarianism, Dogmatism and Usage of Conceptual Categories," *Journal of Personality and Social Psychology* 2, no. 2 (1965); and R. M. Frunkin, "Dogmatism, Social Class Values and Academic Achievement," *Journal of Educational Sociology* 34, no. 9 (1961).

20. Hess and Tournay, *Political Attitudes in Children*, pp. 151, 154.

21. James Chambers, "The Content Analysis of Two Newspapers to Determine the Existence of Class-Specificity" (master's thesis, Hunter College, 1972).

22. Ekkehart Mittelberg, *Wortschatz und Syntax der Bildzeitung* (Marburg: Ewert, 1967).

23. Ibid., p. 46.

24. Henri Lefebvre, *Critique de la vie quotidienne*, vol. 2 (Paris: Arche, 1961), p. 226.

25. *New York Times*, 5 March 1972, sec. 2, p. 1.

26. *New York Times*, 4 June 1972, p. 14.

27. See, for instance, the collection of essays "Mass Culture and Mass Media," *Daedalus* (Spring 1960).

28. Melvin L. DeFleur, *Theories of Mass Communication* (New York: McKay, 1970), pp. 169, 171. Distortions in "highbrow" media are reported in several comparative studies. See, for example, G. S. Turnbull, "Reporting of the War in Indochina," *Journalism Quarterly* 34, no. 1 (1957); E. J. Rossi, "How 50 Periodicals and the *New York Times* Interpreted the Test Ban Controversy," *Journalism Quarterly* 41, no. 4 (1964); G. Lichtheim, "All the News That's Fit to Print," *Commentary*, no. 3 (1965); and C. C. Conway, "A Comparative Analysis of the Reporting of News from China by *Le Monde* and the *New York Times*, September 1967–September 1968" (manuscript).

29. See Elihu Katz and Paul F. Lazarsfeld, *Personal Influence* (Glencoe, Ill.: Free Press, 1955). For evidence from small-group research, see O. N. Larsen and R. J. Hill, "Social Structure and Interpersonal Communication," *American Journal of Sociology* 63 (March 1958).

30. I. L. Janis, "Personality as a Factor in Susceptibility to Persuasion," in *The Science of Human Communication*, ed. Wilbur Schramm (New York: Basic Books, 1963), pp. 62ff., 58ff.; and N. Z. Medalia and O. N. Larsen, "Diffusion and Belief in a Collective Delusion," *American Sociological Review* 23, no. 2 (1958). See also H. Cantril,

"The Invasion from Mars," in *Readings in Social Psychology*, ed. G. W. Swanson (New York: Holt, 1952).

31. Renate Mayntz, "Leisure, Social Participation, and Political Activity," *International Social Science Journal* 12, no. 4 (1960): 574. For a similar argument, see W. Breed, "Mass Communication and Socio-Cultural Integration," *Social Forces* 37, no. 2 (1958).

CHARTING THE MAINSTREAM: TELEVISION'S CONTRIBUTIONS TO POLITICAL ORIENTATIONS

GEORGE GERBNER, LARRY GROSS, MICHAEL MORGAN,
AND NANCY SIGNORIELLI

Television is part and parcel of our daily life, investing it with particular meanings. This is a report of research on the political significance of these meanings. It is part of our ongoing project called Cultural Indicators [1] and develops our paradigm of "mainstreaming" first published in the *Journal of Communication* (Gerbner, Gross, Morgan, and Signorielli 1980).

We will first sketch the theoretical and research context in which we present our findings. Then we will summarize our theory of television and apply our paradigm to political orientations. We will use survey data to show television's contributions to political orientations and to attitudes on such issues as minority and civil rights, free speech, government spending, and taxes. The implications of our findings challenge conventional theories of the role of the "press" in the political process, and suggest new ways of thinking about television as well as political research.

Some conception of the role of the press has always been a central feature of modern political theory. A secular press of politics and commerce was instrumental in the rise of diverse mass publics independent of church and nobility. The press was (and is) a relatively specific and selectively used organ of the more literate of every class. Freedom of the press to advocate party and group (including class) interests and to cultivate competing and conflicting perspectives was supposed to sustain the political plurality presumably necessary for representative government in a complex society.

The decline of the party press and subsequently of political parties themselves as primary means of communication with voters limits the viability of the theory of the press as a pluralistic ideological advocate. The rise to dominance of a single, market-driven, advertiser-sponsored, and thus ideologically more coherent press system, which claims superior journalistic objectivity and invokes constitutional protection of its freedom to virtually preempt the mass marketplace of ideas, further strains the traditional concept of the role of the press in democratic political theory.

Nevertheless, the print-based and literacy-oriented culture from which our political assumptions stem still offers a possibility of a certain relative diversity of perspectives and selectivity of uses. Compared to the historic strains and stresses

From *Journal of Communication* 32, no. 2 (1982). This version omits some tabular and footnote material in the original glossing the research methodology and statistical analysis.

qualifying the applicability of theories rooted in the print era, the challenge of television, and of the telecommunications system with television at its cultural center, is of a different order of magnitude.[2]

Television is a centralized system of storytelling. Its drama, commercials, news, and other programs bring a relatively coherent world of common images and messages into every viewing home. People are now born into the symbolic environment of television and live with its repetitive lessons throughout life. Television cultivates from the outset the very predispositions that affect future cultural selections and uses. Transcending historic barriers of literacy and mobility, television has become the primary common source of everyday culture of an otherwise heterogeneous population.

Many of those now dependent on television have never before been part of a shared national political culture. Television provides, perhaps for the first time since preindustrial religion, a strong cultural link, a shared daily ritual of highly compelling and informative content, between the elites and all other publics. What is the role of this common experience in the general socialization and political orientation of Americans? That question, of such far-reaching social and political importance, has not yet been fully addressed.[3]

The reasons for the lag are financial, methodological, and conceptual. The exigencies of social science research inhibit sustained theoretical development based on abundant and varied data collected over extended periods of time. Research methodologies dealing with selective exposure and specifically targeted communication effects have been inadequate to the study of pervasive symbol systems, broad continuities in the symbolic environment, and slow but massive cultural shifts. Research concentration on individual attitude and behavior change has inhibited the investigation of aggregate transformations in the lifestyles of generations (those born before and after television, or into heavy- and light-viewing homes, for example) that remain stable for individuals. Finally, focusing political-communication research on explicitly "political" communications (or news) has obscured the complex nature of political socialization, especially in the television age, in which the entire spectrum of program types (the bulk of which is drama) plays an integral part.

Our opportunity to address the broader question comes after more than a decade of data collection and analysis mapping the world of television and tracing viewers' conceptions of reality. The Cultural Indicators project employs a two-pronged research strategy. We call the first "message system analysis" and the second "cultivation analysis." Both relate to—and help develop—a conception of television's historical and institutional position, roles, and functions.

For message system analysis we record and analyze week-long samples of network television drama and have done so for each year since 1967. We subject these sample weeks of television drama to rigorous and detailed content analysis in order to reliably delineate selected features of the television world. We consider these the potential lessons of television and use them as the source of questions for the second prong of the inquiry, cultivation analysis. Here we examine the responses of light and heavy viewers to these questions, phrased to refer to the real world. (Nonviewers are too few and demographically too scattered for serious research purposes.) We want to determine whether those who spend more of their time with television are more likely to answer the questions in ways that reflect the potential lessons of the television world (the "television answer") than are groups that watch less television but are otherwise comparable (in terms of important demographic characteristics) to the heavy viewers. We have used the concept of "cultivation" to describe the contributions of television to viewer conceptions. "Cultivation differential" is our term for the difference in the percent giving the "television answer" within comparable groups of light and heavy viewers.[4]

On issue after issue we have found that the assumptions, beliefs, and values of heavy viewers differ systematically from those of light viewers in the same demographic groups. The differences tend to reflect both what things exist and how things work in the television world. Sometimes these differences hold across the board, meaning that those who watch more television are more likely—in all or most subgroups—to give "television answers" to our questions. But in many cases the patterns are more complex. We have found that television viewing may relate in different but consistent ways to different groups' life situations and worldviews. We have named the most general of these consistent patterns "mainstreaming."

The "mainstream" can be thought of as a relative commonality of outlooks and values that exposure to features and dynamics of the television world tends to cultivate. By "mainstreaming" we mean the expression of that commonality by heavy viewers in those demographic groups whose light viewers hold divergent views. In other words, differences found in the responses of different groups of viewers, differences that can be associated with other cultural, social, and political characteristics of these groups, may be diminished or even absent from the responses of heavy viewers in the same groups.[5]

Our concept of cultivation relates the process to those features and dynamics of television content that are the most stable and repetitive parts of the ritual, cutting across different program types. The reason is that heavy viewers watch more of all kinds of programs. Viewer availability determines program ratings and viewing patterns (Barwise, Ehrenberg, and Goodhardt 1982). Furthermore, our message system analysis finds such general features as demography, action structure, and fate of characters to be similar in most program types. Therefore, it is these general features and dynamics of the world of prime time, rather than specific programs, that would be likely to cultivate the most pervasive perspectives and orientations of heavy viewers. So to understand, and even to discover, the substance of issues involved in the cultivation process, we must know something about the nature of the mainstream and the institutional context of its creation.

Living with television means growing up in a symbolic environment shaped by service to client institutions. The creation of that environment is a tightly controlled process. Commercial television is effectively insulated from public access; removed from public participation via direct consumer marketplace, box office, or ballot box; shielded from public governance by current interpretations of the First Amendment; and yet publicly licensed and protected on terms that render the medium dependent on private corporate governance.[6] The economic mechanism guiding that governance is advertising, a tax-deductible business expense, charged to all consumers regardless of their use of the medium. Sponsors pay television (and other media) for attracting and delivering customers and providing other services through news and entertainment. The occasionally unflattering portrayal of business people (probably useful for regaining credibility lost through advertising) only points up the fact that television serves its business clients through delivery, not flattery.

When many millions of dollars of revenue ride on a single ratings point, there are few degrees of freedom to indulge egos or yield to many other pressures. Competition for the largest possible audience at the least cost means striving for the broadest and most conventional appeals, blurring sharp conflicts, blending and balancing competing perspectives, and presenting divergent or deviant images as mostly to be shunned, feared, or suppressed. When a deviant viewpoint *is* presented, no matter how sensible or nonsensical it might be intrinsically, it must be "balanced" by other "extreme" manifestations, preferably on "both sides," to make its presentation appear "objective," "moderate," and otherwise suitable for mass marketing.

These institutional pressures and functions suggest the cultivation of relatively "moderate" or "middle-of-the-road" presentations and orientations. More specific hypotheses can come from the results of the analysis of those features and dynamics of the television message system that may be relevant to the cultivation of those orientations.

Our summary of results is based on the Cultural Indicators message system data bank (unless otherwise noted) and focuses on prime-time network programming. The world of prime time as seen by the average viewer is animated by vivid and intimate portrayals of over three hundred major characters a week, mostly stock dramatic types, and their weekly rounds of dramatic activities.

Conventional and "normal" though that world may appear, it is in fact far from the reality of anything but consumer values and social power. The curve of consumer spending, unlike that of income, bulges with middle-class status as well as middle age. Despite the fact that nearly half of the national income goes to the top fifth of the real population, the myth of middle class as the all-American norm dominates the world of television. Nearly seven out of every ten television characters appear in the "middle-middle" of a five-way classification system. Most of them are professionals and managers. Blue-collar and service work occupies 67 percent of all Americans but only 10 percent of television characters. These features of the world of prime-time television should cultivate a middle-class or "average" income self-designation among viewers.

Men outnumber women at least three to one. Most women attend to men or home (and appliances) and are younger (but age faster) than the men they meet. Underrepresentation in the world of television suggests the cultivation of viewers' acceptance of more limited life chances for women, a more limited range of activities, and more rigidly stereotyped images than for men.

Young people (under eighteen) comprise one-third and older people (over sixty-five) one-fifth of their true proportion in the population. Blacks on television represent three-fourths and Hispanics one-third of their share of the U.S. population, and a disproportionate number are minor rather than major characters. A single program such as "Hawaii Five-O" can result in the overrepresentation of Orientals, but again mostly as minor characters. A study by Weigel, Loomis, and Soja (1980) shows that although blacks appear in many programs and commercials, they seldom appear with whites, and actually interact with whites in only about 2 percent of total human appearance time. The prominent and stable overrepresentation of well-to-do white males in the prime of life dominates prime time. Television's general demography bears greater resemblance to the facts of consumer spending than to the U.S. Census (Gerbner, Gross, Signorielli, and Morgan 1980; Gerbner and Signorielli 1979). These facts and dynamics of life suggest the cultivation of a relatively restrictive view of women's and minority rights among viewers.

The state in the world of prime time acts mostly to fend off threats to law and order in a mean and dangerous world. Enforcing the law of that world takes nearly three times as many characters as the number of all blue-collar and service worker characters. The typical viewer of an average week's prime-time programs sees realistic and often intimate (but usually not true-to-life) representations of the life and work of thirty police officers, seven lawyers, and three judges, but only one engineer or scientist and very few blue-collar workers. Nearly everybody appears to be comfortably managing on an "average" income or as a member of a "middle class."

But threats abound. Crime in prime time is at least ten times as rampant as in the real world. An average of five to six acts of overt physical violence per hour involves over half of all major characters. Yet pain, suffering, and medical help rarely follow this mayhem. Symbolic violence demonstrates power; it shows victimization, not just aggression, hurt but not therapy; it shows who can get away with what against whom. The dominant white males in the prime of life score highest on the "safety scale": they are the most likely to be the victimizers rather than the victims. Conversely, old, young, and minority women and young boys are the most likely to be the victims rather than the victimizers in violent conflicts.

What might be the "television answers" relevant for political orientations? The warped demography of the television world cultivates some iniquitous concepts of the norms of social life. Except among the most traditional or biased, television viewing tends to go with stronger prejudices about women and old people (Gerbner, Gross, Signorielli, and Morgan 1980; Gerbner and Signorielli 1979; Morgan 1980; Signorielli 1979). Children know more about uncommon occupations frequently portrayed on television than about common jobs rarely seen on the screen (DeFleur and DeFleur 1967). Viewing boosts the confidence rating given to doctors (Volgy and Schwarz 1980) but depresses that given to scientists, especially in groups that otherwise support them most (Gerbner, Gross, Morgan, and Signorielli 1981b).

Cultivation studies continue to confirm the findings that viewing tends to heighten perceptions of danger and risk and maintain an exaggerated sense of mistrust, vulnerability, and insecurity. We have also found that the prime-time power hierarchy of relative levels of victimization cultivates similar hierarchies of fears of real-world victimization among viewers. Those minority group viewers who see themselves more often on the losing end of violent encounters on television are more apprehensive of their own victimization than are the light viewers in the same groups (Morgan 1982). Television's mean and dangerous world can thus be expected to contribute to receptivity to repressive measures and to apparently simple, tough, hard-line posturings and "solutions." At the same time, however, the overall context of conventional values and consumer gratifications, with their requirements of happy endings and material satisfaction, may suggest a sense of entitlement to goods and services, setting up a conflict of perspectives.

Thus we can expect the cultivation of preference for "middle-of-the-road" political orientations alongside different and at times contradictory assumptions. These assumptions are likely to include demographically skewed, socially rigid and mistrustful, and often excessively anxious or repressive notions, but also expansive expectations for economic services and material progress even among those who traditionally do not share such views.

As most of our discussion revolves around differences among light, medium, and heavy viewers in otherwise comparable groups in giving "television answers," it will be useful to describe these groups. The analyses presented here utilize data from the General Social Survey (GSS) of the National Opinion Research Center for 1975, 1977, 1978, and 1980. About 1,500 respondents took part in hour-long personal interviews each year, for a total of 6,020 respondents. For analysis, respondents have been divided into light viewers (24.6 percent), who said they watch a daily average of less than two hours; medium viewers (45.3 percent), who said they watch from two to three hours; and heavy viewers (30.1 percent), who said they watch four or more hours a day.

Differences in amounts of viewing are of course rooted in the way people live. The heavy-viewing segment of the population includes a disproportionate number of women, young and old people, non-college-educated, and lower-income persons (see Table 1). Conversely, relatively more men and middle-aged, college-educated, and higher-income persons tend to be light viewers.

It is evident, therefore, that simple comparisons of light, medium, and heavy viewers involve more than television. In order to isolate the independent contribution of television viewing to the cultivation of political orientations, it is necessary to control for other factors and to compare viewing-related differences in relatively homogeneous subgroups. All findings reported in this article include such controls. Subgroup differences in each viewing group enable us to specify the differential as well as the common dynamics of television viewing.

In this article we refine and apply the paradigm of mainstreaming to political orientations. We will advance and illustrate some propositions about television's contribution to class and political self-identification. We will examine the political dynamics of television through the analysis of the positions of heavy and light viewers of different political tendencies, simultaneously controlling for a wide range of other influences and factors.

Political party affiliation is traditionally related to social status. Therefore, it

Table 1. Relationship Between Amount of
          Television Viewing and
          Demographic Variables

	Television viewing [a]		
	Light %	Medium %	Heavy %
Sex			
Male	50	46	37
Female	50	54	63
Age			
18–29	24	24	31
30–54	51	46	34
55+	25	30	36
Education			
No college	54	67	82
Some college	46	33	18
Income			
Low	31	33	49
Medium	35	37	33
High	35	30	18
Region			
Urban	45	43	43
Non-urban	55	57	57

[a]TV viewing: light = 0–1 hours per day; medium = 2–3 hours
per day; heavy = over 4 hours per day.

is not surprising that among heavy viewers, who tend to have lower status, we
find more Democrats than among light viewers (45 as opposed to 35 percent),
whereas proportionately more light than heavy viewers are Independents (41 to
34 percent) and Republicans (24 to 21 percent).[7] We will see, however, that television alters the social significance and political meaning of these and other conventional labels.

An example of this transformation is the blurring of class lines and the self-
styled "averaging" of income differences. Table 2 (graphed in Figure 1) shows
that low-socioeconomic-status (SES) respondents are most likely to call themselves "working class"—but only when they are light viewers. Heavy-viewing
respondents of the same low-status group are significantly less likely than their
light-viewing counterparts to think of themselves as "working class" and more
likely to say they are "middle class." The television experience seems to counter
other circumstances in thinking of one's class. It is an especially powerful deterrent to working-class consciousness.

Middle-SES viewers show the least sense of class distinction at different viewing levels. They are already "in" the mainstream. The high SES group, however,
like the low-SES group, exhibits a response pattern that is strongly associated
with amount of television viewing. More high-SES heavy viewers consider them-

Table 2.   Relationship Between Amount of Television Viewing and Subjective Class
Identification and Perception of Family Income as Average

	Television viewing			
	Light %	Medium %	Heavy %	CD[c]
Subjective class identification[a] by actual SES[b]				
Low SES				
Working class	65	64	55	−10
Middle class	25	28	32	+7
Medium SES				
Working class	55	58	55	0
Middle class	42	39	38	−4
High SES				
Working class	25	29	36	+11
Middle class	68	66	59	−9
Percent who say their family income is "average," by actual family income				
Under $10,000	43	44	43	0
$10–$20,000	62	65	66	+4
Over $20,000	38	47	60	+22

[a] "Lower" and "upper" class responses omitted because of small number of cases.
[b] Based on trichotomization of weighted factor scores of education, income, and occupational prestige.
[c] CD = Cultivation Differential: percent of heavy viewers giving response minus percent of light viewers giving response.

selves to be "working class" than do high-SES light viewers.[8] Television viewing tends to blur class distinctions and make more affluent heavy viewers think of themselves as just working people of average income.

These processes show up clearly when we relate television viewing to labels of direct political relevance. We used a relatively general and presumably stable designation of political tendency that would be most likely to structure a range of political attitudes and positions: the self-designations "liberal," "moderate," and "conservative."[9] We are assuming that the GSS respondents, and indeed, most of us, locate political positions on a continuum ranging from liberal to conservative (if not further in either direction), owing in part to the generally accepted and commonplace use of these terms in interpersonal and mass media discourse. Consequently, unlike many things respondents might be asked about, we believe that these self-designations have a prior existence and are not created in response to the interview situation.

Table 3 shows the percentage of light viewers in each political tendency category and the percentage spread between them and heavy viewers, both by demographic classification and by party affiliation. The most general relationship between television viewing and political tendency is that significantly more heavy than light viewers in all subgroups call themselves moderates and significantly

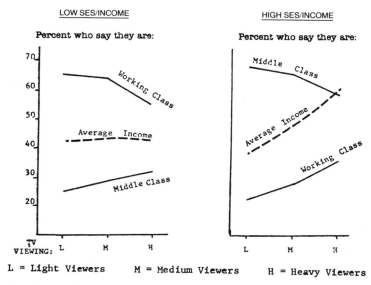

Figure 1.   Class and income self-designations by television viewing within actual SES/income groups.

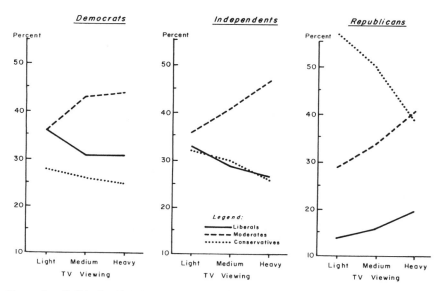

Figure 2.   Political self-designation by amount of television viewing, within party categories.

fewer call themselves conservatives. The number of liberals also declines slightly among heavy viewers, except where there are the fewest liberals (that is, among Republicans). Figure 2 illustrates the absorption of divergent tendencies and the blending of political distinctions into the "television mainstream." [10]

On the surface, mainstreaming appears to be a "centering"—even a "lib-

Table 3.   Relationship Between Amount of Television Viewing and Political
Self-Designation

| | Percentage Who Say They Are: | | | | | |
| | Liberals | | Moderates | | Conservatives | |
	%L[a]	CD[b]	%L	CD	%L	CD
Overall	31	−3	33	+12	36	−8
Controlling for:						
Sex						
Male	33	−1	30	+8	38	−8
Female	29	−3	36	+12	35	−9
Age						
Under 30	45	−7	30	+13	26	−7
30–54	29	−5	32	+14	39	−8
55+	20	+3	39	+6	41	−9
Education						
No college	24	+2	41	+6	35	−8
Some college	38	−1	25	+8	37	−7
Income						
Low	34	−4	35	+8	31	−4
Medium	29	−3	35	+13	36	−10
High	31	−5	30	+14	39	−9
Region						
Urban	36	−3	31	+9	33	−6
Non-urban	26	−2	34	+14	40	−12
Party affiliation						
Democrat	37	−6	37	+7	27	−2
Independent	34	−7	33	+14	33	−7
Republican	16	+5	29	+13	55	−18

[a] %L = percent of light viewers giving response.
[b] CD = Cultivation Differential: percent of heavy viewers giving response minus percent of light viewers giving response.

eralizing"—of political and other tendencies. After all, as viewing increases, the percentage of conservatives drops significantly within every group (except Democrats), and the relationships of amount of television viewing with the percentage of liberals are generally weaker. However, a closer look at the actual positions taken in response to questions about political issues such as minorities, civil and personal rights, free speech, and the economy shows that the mainstream does not always mean "middle-of-the-road."

Eight questions about attitudes toward blacks were asked in at least two of the four GSS years analyzed here, designed explicitly to assess respondents'desire to keep blacks and whites separate. Questions include, "Do you think that white students and black students should go to the same schools or to separate schools?" and "Do you think that there should be laws against marriages between blacks and whites?" Table 4 summarizes the relationships between amount of television viewing and these eight items, for self-designated liberals, moderates, and con-

Table 4. Summary of Relationships Between Amount of Television Viewing and Attitudes Toward Blacks, Controlling for Political Self-Designation (Whites Only)

	Liberals		Moderates		Conservatives	
	%L[a]	CD[b]	%L	CD	%L	CD
Favor laws against interracial marriage	13	+22	31	+10	32	+9
Would object if a black were brought to dinner	13	+11	22	+7	26	+7
Strongly agree: blacks shouldn't push where not wanted	25	+15	43	+7	38	+12
Strongly agree: whites have right to segregate neighborhood	10	+9	14	+8	22	+1
Are against open housing laws	43	+12	63	−1	70	−1
Are against busing	73	+6	87	−5	93	−5
Would not vote for black for president	8	+12	18	0	17	+9
Believe whites and blacks should go to separate schools	6	+11	12	+1	16	0

[a] %L = percent of light viewers giving response.
[b] CD = Cultivation Differential: percent of heavy viewers giving response minus percent of light viewers giving response.

servatives. Light-viewing liberals are always least likely to endorse segregationist statements. Light-viewing moderates and conservatives are, interestingly, often very close; in more than one instance, light-viewing moderates are slightly *more* likely to support racial segregation than are light-viewing conservatives.

More important, associations between amount of viewing and these attitudes are sharply different for liberals, moderates, and conservatives. Liberals, who are least likely to hold segregationist views, show some dramatic associations between amount of viewing and the desire to keep blacks and whites separate. Among moderates and conservatives, in contrast, the relationships between viewing and these attitudes are smaller and inconsistent. (Four of the interaction terms are significant, showing the correlates of heavy viewing to be systematically different across political categories.) On busing, moderates and conservatives even show a significant negative association, indicating *less*-segregationist attitudes among these heavy viewers; this is an instance of viewing bringing divergent groups closer together from both directions.

In general, these patterns vividly illustrate mainstreaming. There are, to be

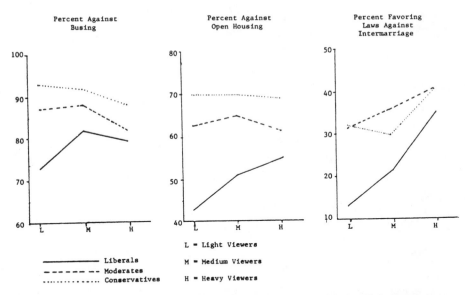

Figure 3.   Television viewing and attitudes about blacks, by political self-designation.

sure, some across-the-board relationships, but even these are markedly weaker for moderates and conservatives. Overall, these data show a convergence and homogenization of heavy viewers across political groups.

The differences between liberals and conservatives—that is, the effects of political tendency on attitudes toward blacks—decrease among heavy viewers. Among light viewers, liberals and conservatives show an average difference of 15.4 percentage points; yet among heavy viewers, liberals and conservatives differ by an average of only 4.6 percentage points.

Figure 3 shows the mainstreaming pattern for three of these items. In the first, opposition to busing, we can see that heavy-viewing conservatives are more "liberal" and heavy-viewing liberals more "conservative" than their respective light-viewing counterparts. In the second instance, opposition to open housing laws, viewing is not associated with any differences in the attitudes expressed by conservatives, but among liberals we see that heavy viewing goes with a greater likelihood of such opposition. Finally, in response to a question about laws against marriages between blacks and whites, we find that heavy viewers in all groups are more likely to favor these laws than are light viewers in the same categories, especially in the case of liberals.

In sum, the responses of heavy-viewing liberals are quite comparable to those of all moderates and conservatives, and there is not much difference between moderates and conservatives. The television mainstream, in terms of attitudes toward blacks, clearly runs to the right.[11]

Many of the fiercest political battles of the past decade have been fought on the nation's "home front"—around a group of so-called moral issues which have sharply divided liberal and conservative forces. We find liberals confronting conservatives over the propriety, morality, and even legality of personal behavior.

The fights involving reproductive freedom, the rights of sexual minorities, and the Equal Rights Amendment have become a focus of that confrontation.

Our view of television as a stabilizing force, seeking to attract the largest possible audience by celebrating the "moderation" of the mainstream, leads us to expect that heavy viewers, once again, will show a convergence of attitudes on issues of personal morality. We expect to find that self-designated moderates and conservatives are generally close together regardless of television viewing, and that heavy-viewing liberals take up positions alongside moderates and conservatives.

Table 5 supports our predictions.[12] In the case of attitudes on homosexuality, abortion, and marijuana, there is considerable spread between light-viewing liberals and light-viewing conservatives (an average of 28 percentage points); the latter are always much more likely to be opposed. And, once again, the attitudes of heavy-viewing liberals and heavy-viewing conservatives are far more similar (an average deviation of 13 percentage points), primarily because of the difference between light- and heavy-viewing liberals. In all instances, the self-designated moderates are much closer to the conservatives than they are to the liberals (see Figure 4).[13]

The narrowing of the political spectrum is also revealed in some more explicitly "political" findings. Whatever its reasons and justifications, anticommunism has been used as the principal rationale for political repression since the first red scare of 1919–1920. Responses to several GSS questions tap television's relationship to anticommunist sentiments and to the tendency to restrict free speech.[14]

Table 6 shows the familiar pattern (illustrated in Figure 5). Five out of ten light-viewing moderates and six out of ten light-viewing conservatives consider communism "the worst form [of government] of all." Heavy-viewing moderates

Table 5. Relationship Between Amount of Television Viewing and Attitudes Toward Personal Conduct, Controlling for Political Self-Designation

	Television viewing		
	Light %	Medium %	Heavy %
Saying homosexuality is always wrong			
Liberals	47	54	67
Moderates	71	79	77
Conservatives	77	81	82
Against abortion			
Liberals	32	38	44
Moderates	45	46	51
Conservatives	55	47	51
Against legalization of marijuana			
Liberals	50	56	67
Moderates	72	79	79
Conservatives	80	84	84

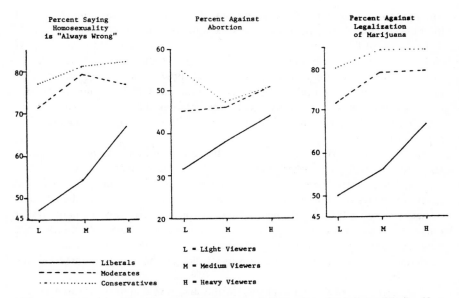

Figure 4.   Television viewing and attitudes toward personal conduct, by political self-designation.

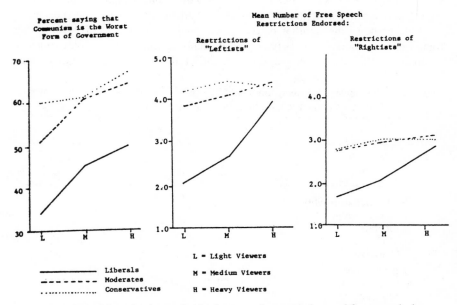

Figure 5.   Television viewing and attitudes toward communism and free speech, by political self-designation.

Table 6.   Relationship Between Amount of Television Viewing and Attitudes Toward Communism and Free Speech, Controlling for Political Self-Designation

	Television viewing		
	Light %	Medium %	Heavy %
Communism is the worst form of government			
Liberals	34	45	49
Moderates	51	61	64
Conservatives	60	61	67
Willingness to curtail freedom of speech of Left	Light	Medium	Heavy
Liberals	2.04	2.66	3.95
Moderates	3.81	4.06	4.40
Conservatives	4.24	4.42	4.29
Right			
Liberals	1.71	2.07	2.83
Moderates	2.78	2.99	3.14
Conservatives	2.79	3.01	3.03

and conservatives nearly unite in condemning communism as "worst" by even larger margins (64 and 67 percent, respectively). But viewing makes the biggest difference among liberals: only one-third of light-viewing but half of heavy-viewing liberals agree that communism is "the worst form" of government. (The interaction of amount of viewing with political self-designation is significant over and above all controls and main effects).

Responses on restricting free speech show similar patterns. Heavy viewers of all three political persuasions are more likely to agree to restrict, in various ways, the speech of "left" and "right" nonconformists than are their light-viewing counterparts. There is little difference between conservatives and moderates. But again, the most striking difference is between light- and heavy-viewing liberals.

In general, with respect to anticommunism and restrictions on political speech of the left and right, those who call themselves conservatives are in the "television mainstream." Those who consider themselves moderates join the conservatives—or exceed them—as heavy viewers. Liberals perform their traditional role of defending political plurality and freedom of speech only when they are light viewers. Mainstreaming means not only a narrowing of political differences but also a significant tilt in the political balance.[15]

But political drift to the right is not the full story. As we noted before, television has a business clientele that, although it may be politically conservative, also has a mission to perform requiring the cultivation of consumer values and gratifications that pull in a different direction.

A number of surveys have documented the tendency of respondents to support government services that benefit them while at the same time taking increasingly

Table 7.   Relationship Between Amount of Television Viewing and Attitudes Toward
Federal Spending, Controlling for Political Self-Designation

	Television viewing		
	Light %	Medium %	Heavy %
Respondents saying we spend too much on:			
Health			
Liberals	5	3	3
Moderates	9	5	4
Conservatives	17	11	8
Environment			
Liberals	7	7	8
Moderates	14	10	9
Conservatives	22	20	13
Cities			
Liberals	13	15	15
Moderates	23	20	16
Conservatives	31	28	27
Education			
Liberals	7	9	7
Moderates	10	9	8
Conservatives	20	16	14
Foreign aid			
Liberals	70	70	69
Moderates	71	75	74
Conservatives	73	74	79
Welfare			
Liberals	48	51	43
Moderates	62	61	52
Conservatives	71	66	58

hard-line positions on taxes, equality, crime, and other issues that touch deeply felt anxieties and insecurities. The media interpreted (and election results seemed to confirm, at least in the early 1980s) these inherently contradictory positions as a "conservative trend" (Entman and Paletz 1980). Television may have contributed to that trend in two ways. First, as our Violence Profiles have demonstrated, heavy viewers have a keener sense of living in a "mean world" with greater hazards and insecurities than do comparable groups of light viewers (Gerbner, Gross, Morgan, and Signorielli 1980; Morgan 1982). Second, while television does not directly sway viewers to be conservative (in fact, heavy viewers tend to shun that label), its mainstream of apparent moderation shifts political attitudes toward conservative positions.

When positions on economic issues are examined, however, a different if perhaps complementary pattern emerges. Television needs to attract a wide following to perform its principal task of delivering the buying public to its sponsors. It could afford even less than most politicians to project austerity, to denigrate

Table 7.   (*continued*)

	Television viewing		
	Light %	Medium %	Heavy %
Blacks			
Liberals	19	21	17
Moderates	30	28	22
Conservatives	35	33	29
Respondents saying we spend too little on:			
Crime			
Liberals	58	66	70
Moderates	69	74	77
Conservatives	65	70	69
Drugs			
Liberals	48	58	68
Moderates	57	64	67
Conservatives	55	56	64
Arms			
Liberals	18	27	31
Moderates	32	35	33
Conservatives	41	40	41
Space			
Liberals	20	16	10
Moderates	10	10	8
Conservatives	18	15	9

popular bread-and-butter issues, or to urge saving instead of spending for goods, services, and security. The essential mission of the television institution—mass mobilization for consumption—would seem to dictate an economically popular and even populist stance.

We examined patterns of responses to questions about government spending on eleven programs. The results are shown in Table 7. Seven are traditional "liberal" issues: health, environment, cities, education, foreign aid, welfare, and blacks. The percentages of light, medium, and heavy viewers in the three political categories who say the United States spends "too much" on health, welfare, and blacks are shown in the three topmost graphs of Figure 6.

Here, instead of heavy-viewing liberals taking positions closer to conservatives, the opposite happens: heavy-viewing conservatives, and moderates as well, converge toward the liberal position on six of the seven issues. The more they watch, the less they say the United States spends "too much." On these six issues, the average distance between liberal and conservative light viewers is 16 percentage points, whereas for heavy viewers it is only 9 percentage points, with conservatives accounting for most of the convergence. The exception is the relatively distant issue of foreign aid.

The remaining four issues are crime, drugs, defense, and space exploration.

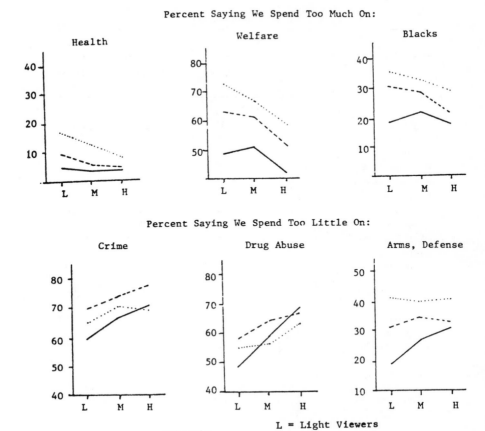

Figure 6.   Television viewing and attitudes toward federal spending, by political self-designation.

Percentages of respondents who say the United States is spending "too little" on the first three issues can be seen in the graphs at the bottom of Figure 6. Here again, with the exception of space, heavy viewers generally want to spend more. As these are somewhat more "conservative" issues, it is the moderates and conservatives who are in the "television mainstream," taking a position toward greater spending, with heavy-viewing liberals standing close to them. On these four issues, an average liberal-conservative spread of nearly 10 percentage points for light viewers compares with a gap of 4 percentage points among heavy viewers.

To investigate further the populist streak in the otherwise restrictive political mix of the typology of the heavy viewer, we looked for questions that combine outlooks on both taxes and spending. The 1980 GSS permitted us to isolate those

Table 8.   Percentage of Respondents Who Oppose Spending Cuts and Reductions in Services but Feel Their Taxes Are Too High, by Television Viewing

	Television viewing		
	Light %	Medium %	Heavy %
Overall	29	31	38
Controlling for:			
Sex			
Male	26	26	36
Female	32	35	39
Age			
Under 30	35	32	44
30–54	27	35	41
55+	26	22	29
Education			
No college	36	32	40
Some college	23	28	29
Income			
Low	31	32	37
Medium	28	29	40
High	28	30	35
Region			
Urban	29	29	40
Non-urban	29	32	36
Party affiliation			
Democrat	40	35	42
Independent	24	31	38
Republican	20	22	30
Political self-designation			
Liberal	36	32	44
Moderate	32	33	37
Conservative	20	26	30

respondents who oppose reductions in government spending and yet feel their taxes are too high.[16] As shown in Table 8, heavy viewers are more likely to express this contradictory position in every subgroup. Figure 7 illustrates the political lineup.

As on the other economic issues, liberals and moderates are close together, and heavy-viewing conservatives join the liberal-moderate mainstream; the tilt is in the liberal (if conflicted) direction. Heavy-viewing Republicans and Independents also express attitudes closer to the Democratic position than do their light-viewing political counterparts. But all heavy viewers are more likely to want a combination of more social spending *and* lower taxes.

Is "commercial populism" the new American melting pot? Certainly the cultural—and evidently political—television mainstream tends to absorb the divergent tendencies that traditionally shaped the political process and to contain its

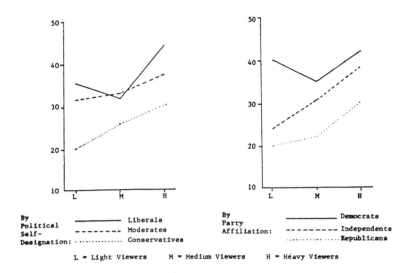

By
Political
Self-
Designation:
————— Liberals
- - - - - - - Moderates
············· Conservatives

By
Party
Affiliation:
————— Democrats
- - - - - - - Independents
··············· Republicans

L = Light Viewers   M = Medium Viewers   H = Heavy Viewers

Figure 7.   Television viewing's association with opposing spending cuts but feeling taxes are too high, by political self-designation and party affiliation.

own crosscurrents. Heavy television viewers tend more than comparable light viewers to call themselves "moderate" but take positions that are unmistakably conservative, except on economic issues.

Our analysis shows that although television viewing brings conservatives, moderates, and liberals closer together, it is the liberal position that is weakest among heavy viewers. Viewing blurs traditional differences, blends them into a more homogeneous mainstream, and bends the mainstream toward a "hard-line" position on issues dealing with minorities and personal rights. Hard-nosed commercial populism, with its mix of restrictive conservatism and pork-chop liberalism, is the paradoxical—and potentially volatile—contribution of television to political orientations.

The "television mainstream" may indeed be the true twentieth-century melting pot of the American people. The mix it creates is of central significance for the theory as well as the practice of popular self-government. If our charting of the mainstream is generally valid, basic assumptions about political orientations, the media, and the democratic process need to be reviewed and revised to fit the age of television.

Notes

1. The project began in 1967–1968 with a study for the National Commission on the Causes and Prevention of Violence. It continued under the sponsorships of the U.S. Surgeon General's Scientific Advisory Committee on Television and Social Behavior, the National Institute of Mental Health, the White House Office of Telecommunications Policy, the American Medical Association, the U.S. Administration on Aging, and the National Science Foundation.

2. New communications technologies are more likely to extend than to transform that challenge. They will sharpen the aim and deepen the penetration of telecommunications culture-power into new areas now served mostly (and often less efficiently or more expensively) by print. The over-the-air mass ritual now called television has become essential to commerce, acculturation, and governance. It is most likely to remain basically intact alongside the resurgence of print by electronic means, and to become the object of an increasingly sharp contest for control.

3. The work of Chaffee, Graber, Mannheim, Patterson, Robinson, and others (see, for example, Graber 1980) has established the relevance of television to political orientations and provides a useful starting point for this study.

4. Earlier reports focused on dramatic demonstrations of social power and personal risk (the "Violence Profiles"). In recent years we have used our cumulative data bank of detailed observations based on the analysis of over sixteen hundred programs and fourteen thousand characters, our own surveys, and the extensive archives of survey data available for secondary analysis to investigate television portrayals and related viewer conceptions of women and minorities, aging, scientists and members of other professions, health and medicine, sexual depictions, family images and impact, educational achievement and aspirations, and other issues. Our data collection has been broadly conceived from the beginning so as to permit the analysis of many different trends and features of the world of television and their relationships to the conceptions and attitudes of various groups of viewers.

5. Mainstreaming has been found to explain differential within-group patterns in terms of the cultivation of images of violence, mistrust, and alienation; conceptions of science and scientists; health-related beliefs and practices; sex-role stereotypes; and other issues (Gerbner, Gross, Morgan and Signorielli 1980, 1981b, 1981a; Signorielli 1979).

6. The work of Barnouw (1975), Cantor (1980), and Tuchman (1974) describes in detail the institutional policy process.

7. Heavy viewers are more likely to say they are Democrats within each of the twelve subgroups shown in Table 1, and in all cases but one (respondents under the age of thirty) the relationship is significant. [Note, however, on Table 3, that only 37 percent of light-viewing Democrats and 31 percent of heavy-viewing Democrats call themselves liberals, and that by far the highest ratio of liberals to moderates and conservatives among both heavy and light viewers is found among the college-educated. *Editor's note.*]

8. This result holds even when controlling for residential variation in actual SES within each of the actual SES groups.

9. Political tendency was measured by the question, "We hear a lot of talk these days about liberals and conservatives. I'm going to show you a seven-point scale on which the *political* views that people might hold are arranged from extremely liberal—point 1— to extremely conservative—point 7. Where would you place yourself on this scale?" Self-placements on this scale were recoded into three categories: respondents selecting "extremely liberal," "liberal," and "slightly liberal" (points 1, 2, and 3) were treated as "liberals"; points 5, 6, and 7 were classified as "conservative"; and point 4 represents "moderate, middle-of-the-road." The resulting groupings provide, over the four years combined, 1,611 "liberals" (28.2 percent), 2,254 "moderates" (39.4 percent), and 1,849 "conservatives" (32.4 percent); 306 cases (5.1 percent) have missing data.

10. The tendency for heavy viewers to designate themselves as "moderate" holds up within each of the four years analyzed here, although there are variations in the size of the association (it is weakest in 1977 and strongest in 1978). In addition, this moderating effect seems to be a specific correlate of television viewing, and not a general media-exposure phenomenon: neither radio listening nor newspaper reading is associated with

similar results. The percentage of moderates among light, medium, and heavy radio listeners (defined as for the viewing groups) is 38, 39, and 38, respectively; similarly, 39 percent of both daily and occasional newspaper readers call themselves moderates. Thus, it is television viewing, rather than general media use, that is associated with a self-ascribed "moderate" political disposition. Finally, this finding is replicated in a national survey conducted by Research and Forecasts, Inc., for the Connecticut Mutual Life Insurance Company. The percentage of moderates among light, medium, and heavy viewers in this survey is 41, 48, and 49, respectively. Controlling for party affiliation, the data are virtually identical to those in the GSS.

11. Besides these eight questions, the 1977 GSS contained twenty (mostly nonrepeated) items about attitudes toward blacks, and these were combined into six indices, each having acceptable internal homogeneity. Four of these indices measure support for racial segregation, in terms of interracial marriage, open housing, integrated schools, and avoidance of blacks. A fifth scale deals with respondents' tendencies to keep blacks "in their place," and a sixth measures respondents' agreement with stereotypical explanations for blacks' social disadvantages. As with the eight repeated items, these indices show that, for liberals, greater viewing means greater support for segregation and related manifestations of racism toward blacks. Five out of six relationships are significant among liberals. Yet *none* of the within-group comparisons are significant for moderates or conservatives; five out of six interaction terms are negative, two of them significantly. Once again, heavy viewing cultivates anti-integration and related opinions only among liberals—those who are "otherwise" least opposed to racial equality. Here again, there is not much difference between moderates and conservatives.

12. For homosexuality, respondents indicated whether they felt "sexual relations between two adults of the same sex" are "always wrong," "almost always wrong," "wrong only sometimes," or "not wrong at all"; we focus on those who respond "always wrong." The question was asked in 1977 and 1980. Items measuring approval of legally obtaining an abortion under six specific conditions were included in each of the four GSS years that contained a television viewing question. Respondents were treated as being "against abortion" if they agreed to legal abortions in fewer than three situations *or* only for the three "easiest" situations. Finally, a question on whether or not marijuana should be legalized was included in 1975, 1978, and 1980.

13. The same patterns hold for attitudes toward both premarital and extramarital sex. Light-viewing liberals are much more unlikely to say that these behaviors are "always wrong," while the responses of heavy-viewing liberals approach those of moderates and conservatives. As with busing, moderates and conservatives show significant *negative* associations between amount of viewing and disapproval of premarital sex—another instance of convergence from both directions.

14. A single question (asked in 1977 and 1980) deals with respondents' feelings about communism, on a four-point continuum from "it's the worst kind [of government] of all" to "it's a good form of government." Fifteen questions (all asked in 1977 and 1980) deal with whether each of five types of people should be allowed to (a) make a speech in the respondent's community, (b) have a book in the community's library, and (c) teach in a local college or university. We subdivided the five types into "leftists" (atheists, communists, homosexuals) and "rightists" (racists, militarists), and constructed two indices of respondents' willingness to curtail the freedom of speech of these groups.

15. The same basic patterns also hold in terms of attitudes toward the Equal Rights Amendment (asked only in 1977), but nonsignificantly. Among liberals, 17 percent of light but 20 percent of heavy viewers oppose its passage. For moderates and conservatives—who are more likely to be against the amendment—heavy viewing means

greater support. Among moderates, 28 percent of light and 24 percent of heavy viewers are opposed; among conservatives, 40 percent of light and 32 percent of heavy viewers would not see it passed. A 23 percentage point spread between light-viewing liberals and light-viewing conservatives is cut in half (to 12 points) among heavy viewers.

16. In the 1980 GSS, respondents were asked their position on a seven-point scale, with point 1 equal to "government should provide many fewer services; reduce spending a lot" and point 7 labeled "government should continue to provide services; no reduction in spending." We combined respondents who fell on the upper three points with those who said the amount of taxes they pay is too high, in order to construct a typology of attitudes on spending and taxes. We focus on the one-third (32.1 percent) who take the contradictory position of opposing reductions in spending while claiming their taxes are too high. Forty percent want less spending and lower taxes, 13.9 percent want reduced spending but do *not* feel their taxes are too high, and 13.9 percent want continued spending and do not feel their taxes are too high.

References

Barnouw, Erik. 1975. *Tube of Plenty: The Evolution of American Television*. New York: Oxford University Press.

Barwise, T. P., A. S. C. Ehrenberg, and G. J. Goodhardt. 1982. Report on U.S. television viewing behavior. London Business School.

Cantor, Muriel G. 1980. *Prime-Time Television: Content and Control*, Beverly Hills, Calif.: Sage.

DeFleur, Melvin L., and Lois B. DeFleur. 1967. "The Relative Contribution of Television as a Learning Source for Children's Occupational Knowledge." *American Sociological Review* 32: 777–789.

Entman, Robert M., and David L. Paletz. 1980. "Media and the Conservative Myth." *Journal of Communication* 30(4): 154–65.

Gerbner, George, Larry Gross, Michael Morgan, and Nancy Signorielli. 1980. "The 'Mainstreaming' of America: Violence Profile No. 11." *Journal of Communication* 30(3): 10–29.

———. 1981a. "Health and Medicine on Television." *New England Journal of Medicine* 305(15): 901–904.

———. 1981b. "Scientists on the TV Screen." *Society* 18(4): 41–44.

Gerbner, George, Larry Gross, Nancy Signorielli, and Michael Morgan. 1980. "Aging with Television: Images on Television Drama and Conceptions of Social Reality." *Journal of Communication* 30(1): 37–47.

Gerbner, George, and Nancy Signorielli. 1979. "Women and Minorities in Television Drama 1969–1978." The Annenberg School of Communications, University of Pennsylvania. Mimeo.

Graber, Doris A. 1980. *Mass Media and American Politics*. Washington, D.C.: Congressional Quarterly Press.

Morgan, Michael. 1980. "Longitudinal Patterns of Television Viewing and Adolescent Role Socialization." Unpublished Ph.D dissertation, University of Pennsylvania, 1980.

———. 1982. "Symbolic Victimization and Real-World Fear." Paper presented at the Symposium on Cultural Indicators for the Comparative Study of Culture, Vienna, Austria.

Signorielli, Nancy. 1979. "Television's Contribution to Sex Role Socialization." Paper presented at the Seventh Annual Telecommunications Policy Research Conference, Skytop, Pennsylvania.

Tuchman, Gaye, ed. 1974. *The TV Establishment: Programming for Power and Profit.* Englewood Cliffs, N.J.: Prentice-Hall.

Volgy, Thomas J., and John E. Schwarz. 1980. "TV Entertainment Programming and Sociopolitical Attitudes." *Journalism Quarterly* 57(1): 150–155.

Weigel, Russel H., James W. Loomis, and Matthew J. Soja. 1980. "Race Relations on Prime Time Television." *Journal of Personality and Social Psychology* 39(5): 884–893.

MASS CULTURE AND THE ECLIPSE OF REASON: THE IMPLICATIONS FOR PEDAGOGY

STANLEY ARONOWITZ

In his book *The Eclipse of Reason*, Max Horkheimer, founder of the Frankfurt Institute for Social Research, provided one of the most succinct formulations of the problem engendered by mass culture. According to Horkheimer, the significance of the challenge posed by the massified culture industry to civilization as such consisted in its assault on the capacity to engage in critical thought as a meaningful form of social discourse. Horkheimer cared deeply about the content of critical thought, but with the rise of fascism he became more concerned with the specter of the end of reason itself. In his view, the capacity of humans to distance themselves from the object in order to gain critical perspective upon their social world can no longer be taken for granted. The restricted language and thought codes produced by the reduction of all thought to its technical dimensions reach far into the culture, encompassing schools as well as communications, the public as well as the private spheres of discourse. It is no longer a question of whether ordinary discourse is able to deal effectively with issues of specific ideological and social content. As Jürgen Habermas expressed it, the new situation raises the issue of the competence of people to effectively communicate ideational content. The issue is the capacity for theoretical or conceptual thought itself. When people lack such competence, social action that transcends the struggle for justice within the empirically given rules of social organization and discourse is impossible.

Marcuse asserted the fundamental transformation of the individual in late capitalist society. Using the metaphor of the relation between the gene and the soma, he argued not only that cultural commodities have produced a closed universe from which oppositional ideas are strictly excluded, but also that fundamental changes in the "genetic" structures of humans had occurred such that individuation is foreclosed within the terms set by the system. Within this grim paradigm, the truncated imagination now appears natural. We need not detain ourselves in debate about the "scientific" content of Marcuse's argument, though empirical evidence for his assertions can be adduced from recent psychological research, showing a tendency toward narrowing of perception, imitative patterns of child's play, disruptions of concept formation among schoolchildren, the visual character of thought, and the increasing difficulties experienced by children in performing abstract and logical functions. The research suggests a correlation of television watching (and consumption of mass culture in general) to a tendency

From *College English* 38, no. 8 (1977).

toward literalness in thought. Here, the merging of thought with object seems to have become the new universal of human consciousness.

The litany of complaint that surrounds teaching in the 1970s, particularly English composition, may be ascribed to a perception of many teachers that mass audience culture has disrupted the normal routes to learning. Of course there are problems with the way the perception has been presented in popular and academic journals and other forms. Richard Ohmann and Wayne O'Neil have argued against the claim of growing illiteracy among college students.[1] In their view, there exists little hard evidence that those entering institutions of higher education are increasingly deficient in the skills of writing and reading. Instead, they have adduced evidence to show that the level of reading and writing among minorities as well as those who are "expected" to be literate has advanced slightly in the past decade. Their analysis points to a tendency to legitimate the closing of doors to minorities. They view the current avalanche of demands of parents and educators alike that schools return to the "basics" as a panic born of institutionalized racism expressing both the economic crisis in American society and the specific upsurge of racism in American education.

Of course, neither Ohmann nor O'Neil denies that a more profound illiteracy has afflicted large segments of the American population. Far from having its roots in the alleged runaway permissiveness that may be identified with the revival of progressive education in the 1960s, the new illiteracy is connected neither with mindless liberalism nor with the specific attack on racial minorities and women. In my view, the deeper problem is a gradual but relentless growth of anti-intellectualism in American life, born in part of the traditional antipathy of American ideology to ideas themselves (but this aspect is not new) and in part from the rise of what I will call a *visual culture*, which has increasingly replaced other types of communication, particularly the written and verbal forms.

No one can "prove" with statistics that cognition is in crisis. I will merely ask you to accept this as a hypothesis whose validity resides in the experience of many teachers in two- and four-year colleges, including those characterized as elite schools. I believe the collective perception of composition teachers confirms that what I will describe has reached nearly universal proportions. The explanation I will offer and my prescriptive remarks may be subject to debate, since these are of a more speculative nature (and will be developed more systematically elsewhere).

Put succinctly, students of all social classes exhibit a tendency toward literalness, that is, they seem unable to penetrate beyond the surfaces of things to reach down to those aspects of the object that may not be visible to the senses. "Object" here means that which appears to perception as "natural" or belonging to the social world. Students have a skeptical view, or even seem to boggle at the idea that the imagination, or reason, may be employed to yield knowledge. Moreover, the problem of abstraction becomes a major barrier to analysis because students seem enslaved to the concrete. Finally, teachers notice that many have trouble making connections between two objects or sets of concepts that are not related to each other in an obvious manner.

In short, reality is dissolved into objecthood, whose particular existence defines its boundaries. For those acquainted with the history of American and British philosophy, students exemplify an extreme form of the empiricist epistemology. What the empiricists have claimed for the relation of knowing to the known is internalized as a rigid methodology of knowledge acquisition by many students. The critical project of learning, according to which things are not what they seem to be and abstract concepts such as "society," "capitalism," "history," and other categories not available to the senses are endowed with the status of the real, seems in eclipse.

For those familiar with the environment of the college or university, this condensed description may strike a fairly loud chord. For those who have never encountered the problem of concept formation among their students, I must admit envy. In my several years of teaching both social science and literature, I have never met a class that did not complain with either bitterness or bewilderment that the "reading was too hard," that the ideas associated with critical thinking were beyond their preparation. Students are overwhelmed by the factuality of the observed world and have enormous difficulty making the jump to concepts which may controvert appearances. I refer not only to concepts that have obvious ideological content such as socialism and capitalism, imperialism and national independence, but also to ones like metaphor and metonymy, or even the logical principle of syllogism, that demand some leap beyond experience.

If this metadescription is at all correct, then what is at stake is even the *liberal* tradition of critical thought, much less the more radical effort to encourage social action. Since critical thinking is the fundamental precondition for an autonomous and self-motivated public or citizenry, its decline would threaten the future of democratic social, cultural, and political forms. And such democratic concern does not require a commitment to social change. What is required is a deep caring about the structure of power in society and its wide distribution to all social classes.

Although I assume that the majority of those who disseminate through teaching and scholarship the enlightenment tradition of reason and critical theory accept as their essential goal the development of autonomous activity among large numbers of persons in society, the present situation seems to have generated a deep sense of gloom among my colleagues, rather than a spirited effort to find ways to counter the tendency toward massive indifference to critical thinking. Part of the explanation for the despair lies in the enormity of the task. For it must be admitted at the outset that, compared to the powerful institutions of mass audience culture, the efforts of college teachers can be viewed with some skepticism. However, it is also the case that recent concern with the problem of literacy offers an opportunity—to those who are prepared not to blame the students but rather to identify the issue in different terms—to have some impact. Before proceeding to some proposals, I wish to offer some explanation.

Long before the advent of mass audience culture on the present scale, American ideology offered a model of both pedagogy and society that militantly denied the elementary axioms of European critical thought. The widely influential slogan "Learning by Doing" admittedly has its virtues in comparison to a European high culture that insisted on the bifurcation of mental and manual labor, theory and practice, and the self and society. John Dewey and others who proposed a broad program of American education that stressed its democratic character certainly did not intend more than to find new ways to broaden the constituency for learning. However, the process of concept formation, the reality of abstractions that may have no useful consequences, and the whole Western philosophic tradition were questioned as somehow not relevant to the contemporary problems of democratic education. Dewey's instrumentalism, especially as interpreted by educators, resulted in the development of a curriculum that, far from widening the base of the citizenry in the classical sense of the term, resulted in an educational complement to the specialization and degradation of the labor force in factories and offices.

American educational theory in the twentieth century has been dominated by the idea that learning should be problem-centered rather than concept-centered, and that students should both have fun and understand the practical application of what is learned. Thus even the relatively theoretical disciplines of science and mathematics are taught in public schools in terms of a set of operations that will yield results; the theory of the operation, although sometimes mentioned, is seldom stressed. As for history, social sciences, and language acquisition, elementary and secondary education have adopted methodologies that are at once fragmented, antitheoretical, and skills-oriented. The technicalization of education cannot be blamed entirely for the phenomenon of conceptual illiteracy; it was merely the phenomenal working out of a broad vision of the world that may be characterized as the "mechanization of the world picture" or the triumph of nominalism in social perception.

But technological domination goes beyond the schools. It permeates every sphere of social existence, especially the work situation and what we may designate as leisure activities. The degradation of labor, its routinization by technology, is too well known to be repeated here at length. Nor would it be accurate to claim that the phenomenon of bread and circuses is a late capitalist product. But in the last half of the twentieth century, the degree to which mass audience culture has colonized the social space available to the ordinary person for reading, discussion, and critical thought must be counted as the major event of social history in our time. Television, film, and photography, far from making culture democratic, have fostered the wide dissemination of industrialized entertainment, thereby restricting the capacity of persons to produce their own culture, in the widest meaning of the term. I mean the production of speech that modifies language socially, that expresses, together with popular art, the frustrations and the aspirations of a people. I am referring to patterns of interaction in ordinary situations that allow for a relatively autonomous system of interpersonal communications. I mean the capacity of persons to make inferences, to offer arguments, to develop explanations of social events that may counter those that are considered authoritative.

The culture industry is indeed ubiquitous. It has manufactured a vision of the world, even more than a series of entertainments. The vision is consistent both with the breaking up of reality into interchangeable parts and with the presentation of a world that seems impenetrable. The "news" presented on television is not only ideologically inscribed by the biases of the network, it is denied conceptual depth, both by the mode of discourse itself and by the time frames used for individual stories. Space and time, over and above "messages" with specific content, become the vehicles of inscription.

Of course neither school nor mass culture totally determines the learning process. Consciousness, colonized by the culture industry, has its own moments of resistance. In the absence of a popular democratic movement, however, such as those once fostered by trade unions, populists, and socialists, and offering alternatives to the dominant culture, the weight of mass audience culture on the structure of consciousness becomes ever more powerful.

I wish to suggest that schools, especially the colleges and universities, are now battlegrounds that may help determine the shape of the future. The proliferation of composition programs at all levels of higher education may signal a new effort to extend the technicalization process even further into the humanities. For in the identification of the problem as one of "skills," there has developed a tendency to degrade writing to its functional boundaries instead of seeing it as an expressive and intellectual process. A widespread tendency of those who find themselves working in composition programs has been to interpret their presence as a sign of failure or, alternatively, as a stopgap job before moving on to the teaching and research for which they have been trained: literary criticism or scholarship. The splitting of composition as a course from the study of literature is of course a sign of its technicalization and should be resisted, both because it is an attack against critical thought and because it results in demoralization and alienation from work on the part of teachers.

A programmatic alternative to the splitting of writing into technical functions might begin by recognizing that if the task is to penetrate the apparently opaque "mind set" of students, then the spectacle in which they are caught must be deconstructed. Most students go through their classes as if in a dream. They are bemused by daily interaction as if *it* were the unreality. Many of them live for the spectacle of the television show, the rock concert, the record party, and other mass-cultural activities. The spectacle appears as the real world in which they wake up and participate in the process of living; their nonmedia life is the fiction. If writing is to become part of the critical process, deconstruction of mass audience culture is the first priority. I mean that writing could consist in the first place in analysis of TV shows of the most popular variety, critical interrogation of popular music, and close scrutiny of film genres that approximate mass culture, such as disaster films, horror shows, and adventures. In other words, the job of the teacher is to legitimate mass audience culture in order to criticize and transcend it—or to discover whether genuine expressive forms are repressed within it. For those teachers who claim their personal indifference to these forms and refuse to validate this type of investigation, one can only reply that such a stance may be tantamount to abandoning their students and the critical project as well. But if committed teachers wish to engage students, they could do worse than beginning their own education by learning how to examine the media as an intellectual activity of the highest importance.

It is likely that those who choose this approach will encounter initial resistance by some students. After all, students have already spent more than a dozen years learning what "real" school is. There, mass culture does not appear to be a legitimate subject for investigation. We find that students still have a traditional version of the three R's as interpreted by their teachers, who also share the students' conception of the proper fields of education or research. Thus, in most colleges and universities the outlaw character of media studies is expressed in the refusal of administrations to endow these efforts with departmental standing. Instead they are relegated to the twilight zone of "programs" or sometimes included in the regular departments in the person of an academic specialist who views the media as just one more object of investigation, like literature or sociology.

If what I have described is at all accurate, then the teacher must persuade students of the significance of the study before the study will be meaningful to them. The objects of mass-cultural perception, particularly rock music and television, are so close that achieving critical distance from them requires even more intellectual and emotional effort than literature or math, which are sufficiently distanced by their historical character and academic legitimacy to make them easier to study. Mass-cultural forms have colonized the leisure time activities of youth so completely that giving up, through analysis, the pleasure one gets from them may be painful. Music is employed by many persons as respite from anxieties produced by everyday life, particularly those generated by a relatively uncertain love life, job market, schools, and family. To give up the "pleasure" of the mass-cultural product is tantamount to giving up almost everything that provides a respite from alienated activity. Of course, people jump from one form of alienation to another when they consume rather than produce their culture, but there is a perceived difference between those types of activity called "work" and those called "free time." The ideological content of the linguistic difference can only be discerned by analyzing the function of mass culture in everyday life. Without prejudicing the result, my experience demonstrates that, after some balking, students can become quite involved in really looking at mass culture.

But the problem is not solved merely by showing the ways in which television and other cultural industry products contain serious political and ideological content. Having successfully demystified media content and seen how certain forms such as popular music provide only spurious satisfaction, students are still left to face daily life.

When the safety valves of mass culture have been removed, ordinary existence may be truly intolerable. At this point the investigation may shift to the family, schools, and the world of work. This aspect of the program entails both a sociological and historical examination of these institutions and a personal examination of the ways individuals are influenced by and try to struggle within them. For instance, students may write autobiographical essays focusing on conflicts between peer interaction and interaction with authorities such as parents and teachers. I discovered that almost all students grow up in two worlds: one of school and family, where they feel they are not in control of their lives, and one with friends or by themselves, which they see as more autonomous. The influence of mass culture in narrowing the space between compulsion and freedom begins to appear as children grow older. They become more willing to give up everyday life, which seems to represent experiences of almost unrelieved frustration. Internalizing the ideological and vocational expectations of the adult world becomes more difficult, but as long as radio, TV, records, and spectator sports are available to divert them from the "real world," institutional life is tolerable.

The reconstruction of critical thought may now proceed, since the examination of mass culture and social institutions within a context of personal experience has laid a groundwork for this step. At this juncture, students are writing about their lives and the mediations of experience that have stood between their conscious activity and the outside world. They must now learn what is going on (and how to find out about it) beyond the personal sphere. The next projects concern political, social, and cultural issues, which can be looked at from the perspective of concepts, abstractions, argument, evidence, and the other categories of critical thought. The objects of critical thought become the economy, the international relations of our country, health issues, labor conflicts, race and sex discrimination, and so forth. Students may also take a more comprehensive view of the culture, breaking out of the narrow perspective offered both by mass culture and by the literary studies that are legitimated in traditional colleges. The concept of culture becomes more anthropological; that is, it includes all forms of human activity: human sexuality and human interaction, ideologies, attitudes, and belief systems, and of course language itself as a model for culture. The spiral character of critical thought is demonstrated by a return to everyday relations, but on a new level of abstraction to complement the specificity.

What I have sketched out here may be an entire curriculum for critical thought. And it may go beyond the bureaucratic consignment of "freshman composition" or the humanities core course offered by most universities and colleges. Yet I believe it is a realistic approach to these areas, and corresponds to the contemporary situation of most students at all levels of higher education. It is grounded in the ubiquitous character of mass audience culture and tries to take it out of the realm of just another academic specialty. Unless teachers are willing to help students make everyday life and the social world more urgent than the spectacles of the culture industry, they cannot effectively oppose the transformation of persons into anomic consumers.

Note

1. Richard Ohmann, "The Decline in Literacy Is a Fiction, If Not a Hoax," *Chronicle of Higher Education*, 25 October 1976; and Wayne O'Neil, "Why *Newsweek* Can't Explain Things," *Radical Teacher*, no. 2 (June 1976): 11–15. For a response to Ohmann and O'Neil, see Donald Lazere, "Literacy and Political Consciousness: A Critique of Left Critiques," *Radical Teacher*, no. 8 (May 1978): 15–18, and in the same issue, Wayne O'Neil, "Lazere and Me," p. 19.

Part VII

From the Halls of Montezuma to the Shores of Tripoli: Cultural Imperialism

INTRODUCTION

American cultural imperialism has been one of the most prominent themes in recent left writing, as represented in the readings in this section. The main motifs here are the muting in American culture of our colonialist motives, the ethnocentric image of foreigners in our domestic media, the financial and technological expansion of the American culture industry throughout the world, the propagation of American and capitalist ideology through that expansion, and the militarization of sports and other mass culture.

In a 1979 talk "American Media and Foreign Policy," Noam Chomsky said:

> Any society which is sufficiently powerful to be an active agent in international affairs will develop a system of beliefs and doctrines of quasi-theological character. . . . The society will develop a state religion which has a number of functions. One of them will be to try to disguise as much as possible the actual reality of the exercise of power and the factors that enter into it. And, secondly, it will try to disguise and conceal the motivation that lies behind actions in the international arena—what they are intended to achieve—and what their consequences in fact are. And again, this natural expectation is quite well substantiated by the historical record.
>
> The British empire had its white man's burden. The French empire had its civilizing mission; and the United States' imperial system has had its own system of doctrines which all have to do with the unique benevolence of the United States, its unique role as the only society in world history that doesn't act on the material interests of ruling groups but rather out of commitments to abstract ideals such as freedom, Wilsonian ideals, and so on.[1]

In refutation of conservative claims that the liberal members of the "new class" are hypercritical of America, Chomsky added, "It's true that the intelligentsia are very hypercritical and fiercely independent and the media are critical, but within a very narrow framework of assumptions. Namely within the framework of assumptions that define the state religion."[2]

Among the traits of the American state religion is the exclusion of the words *imperialism* and *colonialism*, like *propaganda* and *capitalism*, from the vocabulary of American news and entertainment media. Even the liberals most critical of recent American interventions in Indochina, Central America, and the Middle East have rarely acknowledged any element of colonialism or defense of corporate interests in this country's motivations; nor is any element of revolt *against* colonialism acknowledged as a motivating force in national liberation movements, which are habitually reduced to mere communist fronts. (The typical left response is then to deny *any* influence of international communism in such movements; the truth is a more problematic mixture than either side usually admits.) Going back at least to the Mexican-American and Spanish-American wars, both contemporary cultural accounts and later historical analyses of foreign adventures have provided some of the most grotesquely sentimental versions of American mythology, albeit no more sentimental than the wartime propaganda of other countries.[3] Recent American debacles in Vietnam, Latin America, and the Middle East have obliged us to turn a more skeptical ear to the glorification of past military conquests in "The Marine Hymn."

Tom Engelhardt ("Ambush at Kamikaze Pass") and Ariel Dorfman and Armand Mattelart ("The Great Parachutist") examine American media stereotypes of foreigners, particularly those of the Third World and nonwhite races that mesh with stereotypes of American blacks, Indians, and Latinos. The kind of gross racism that Engelhardt traces in earlier periods of American culture has by now considerably diminished, although vestiges of it have persisted—during the Vietnam War, for instance, in some media images of the Viet Cong, and, most recently, in the portrayal of Arabs and Islam, as Edward Said has documented in *Orientalism* and *Covering Islam*. The foremost factor in the decline of racism in the United States and elsewhere is undoubtedly the increased self-assertion of nonwhite peoples, but the expansion of worldwide communications media in the last few decades has also been a factor, probably doing more to overcome nationalistic and ethnocentric prejudices, as Tunstall argues ("Media Imperialism?"), than to perpetuate them. Nevertheless, the attitudes of several generations of twentieth-century Americans have been shaped by the earlier patterns of bias.

The works of Dorfman and Mattelart, which view the more chauvinistic period of American culture through Third World eyes, provide an unsettling but purgative antidote to U.S. sociocentrism. What they reveal is not simply the crude racism reviewed by Engelhardt but the more insidious projection on the rest of the world of Anglo and bourgeois norms. In this bleached-out world view, underdeveloped countries exist only as a backdrop for the heroic adventures or exotic vacations of white Americans; Third World peoples—like the North American nonwhites in the episodes of "The Lone Ranger" and other mass culture studied by Dorfman in *The Empire's Old Clothes*—exist only as extras providing local color. The "natives'" own history has been expunged, as has that of colonial exploitation. Before Castro in Cuba, Allende in Chile, the Nicaraguan Sandinistas, and the rebels in El Salvador came to the foreground of news media, most Americans thought of Latin America as a place where carefree natives danced to the latest tropical beat while a comical series of dictators overthrew one another. Even the most liberal Americans traveling to the Caribbean or South America are shocked by the true extent of poverty and by the overwhelmingly nonwhite population. For we were raised on movies like *Blue Skies* (1947) and *Royal Wedding* (1950), featuring Fred Astaire's big production numbers set in Martinique and Haiti, where the natives were miraculously all white, or *There's No Business Like Show Business* (1954), set in another Caribbean paradise, in which white dancers in vaguely hispanic makeup, identified as "Chico" and "Pancho," drooled over Marilyn Monroe singing "Heat Wave."

South Pacific (1949), a more liberal Broadway and Hollywood musical, criticized white American prejudice against Polynesians and miscegenation. But the Polynesians display only adulatory subservience toward the all-white American armed forces. Both intermarriages shown are between white men and nonwhite women. Nellie Forbush nobly comes to accept Emile DeBecque's former marriage to a Polynesian and to adopt their mulatto children, but it is unlikely that the liberalism of the time would have extended to *her* marrying a Polynesian, let alone an American black. (Even in the eighties, several TV sitcoms have shown black children being adopted by white parents or white men marrying black women, but none to date has dared reverse the racial roles.) Indeed, intolerance by American servicepeople toward Polynesians was a far less dangerous subject to broach than racial discrimination within our own troops in World War II. *Casablanca* (1943) was equally liberal in Rick's benevolent paternalism toward Sam. But Sam, referred to by Ingrid Bergman's Ilse as "the boy playing the piano," is portrayed as having no existence other than waiting around to whip out his piano bench and play "As Time Goes By" for the white folks. Least of all is there any hint of identity between him and the Moroccan blacks or Arabs, who have even lower visibility in the film. The backgrounding and servility of non-whites persisted into the eighties in pastiches of earlier films, such as *Raiders of the Lost Ark* and the *Star Wars* series, the latter of which accommodated to the decline of racism by transforming Sam, Tonto, and Punjab into robot and "wookie" sidekicks of the WASP heroes.

The concluding essay in this section by Tunstall surveys and judiciously evaluates a growing body of studies by left critics, led by Herbert Schiller, of the spread to other countries of American industry—through film, popular music, television, other communications technologies, sports and sporting equipment—and the effect on foreign economies and national cultures. As Tunstall indicates, there is general agreement among current critics that American corporate hegemony exists but disagreement about the extent to which American ideology actually dominates. Tunstall notes that the values projected by American culture produce some domestically liberating influences in countries less advanced in economic, racial and sexual equality. Likewise, Michele and Armand Mattelart have analyzed how national corporate elites mediate American culture in Chile and elsewhere, a process that results in "creolization," a hybrid of American and local bourgeois culture.[4]

The relation of sports to imperialism is another disputed topic on the left. Mark Naison's "Sports and the American Empire" reiterates the main lines of argument of many recent critics: that the modern obsession with sports in the United States and elsewhere throughout the West has been engineered by ruling elites as support for both militaristic nationalism and capitalistic aggression (Michael Real interprets football, in the struggle to monopolize the field's property, as a replica of capitalism);[5] that organized sports has served in colonized countries to impose the colonizer's norms; that it has reinforced class, racial, and sexual lines and diverted class conflict into infantile, macho opposition between "our" team and "theirs," between localities, and between nations. Naison, however, presents a more complex view of these patterns than some other left critics have, reflecting the general position of *Radical America*, the journal in which his article first appeared. He argues that each of these negative traits in American sports has also generated positive modes of opposition and assertions of identity by colonial peoples, blacks, women, and the working class. Unfortunately, since 1972, when the article was published, few of the positive tendencies he noted have progressed much; if anything, there has been a regression toward jingoism in both sports and the whole national temper. Although racial integration in sports has certainly increased dramatically, advancing the general acceptance of integration, minorities are still relegated to subordinate roles in many aspects of sports. Christopher Lasch, in *The Culture of Narcissism*, presented another line of disagreement with most left critics, arguing that jingoism in both nationalism and sports has been superseded by the age of multinational corporations and technocratic management of conflict. His case, like Naison's, seemed more plausible in the seventies than it does in the retrograde eighties, when we are confronted with ex-sportscaster Ronald Reagan exhorting Americans to win the cold war "for the Gipper."

Notes

1. Noam Chomsky, "American Media and Foreign Policy," speech at the Cambridge Forum (transcript), p. 2.

2. Ibid., p. 6.

3. On the euphemizing of American imperialism and racism in high school history textbooks, see Frances FitzGerald, *America Revised* (Boston: Atlantic–Little, Brown, 1979).

4. Michele Mattelart, "Notes on Modernity: A Way of Reading Women's Magazines," in *Communication and Class Struggle*, Vol. 1: *Capitalism, Imperialism*, ed. Armand Mattelart and Seth Siegelaub (New York: International General, 1979), pp. 158–170; Armand Mattelart, "Cultural Imperialism," in Mattelart and Siegelaub, *Capitalism, Imperialism*, pp. 57–64; and Armand Mattelart, "Cultural Imperialism, Mass Media, and Class Struggle," *The Insurgent Sociologist* 9, no. 4 (1980): 67–79.

5. Michael Real, "The Super Bowl: Mythic Spectacle," in *Mass-Mediated Culture* (Englewood Cliffs, N.J.: Prentice-Hall, 1977), p. 104.

Further Readings

Boyd-Barrett, J. O. "Cultural Dependency and the Mass Media." In *Culture, Society, and the Media*, ed. Michael Gurevitch, Tony Bennett, James Curran, and Janet Woollacott. New York: Methuen, 1982.

Dorfman, Ariel. "Salvation and Wisdom of the Common Man: The Theology of *The Reader's Digest*." *Praxis*, 1, no. 3 (1976): 41–56.

Erens, Patricia. "Images of Minority and Foreign Groups in American Films: 1958–73." *Jump Cut*, no. 7 (May–July 1975): 19–22.

Franco, Jean. "What's in a Name? Popular Culture Theories and Their Limitations." *Journal of Latin American Popular Culture* 1, no. 1 (1981): 5–14.

Friar, Ralph E., and Natasha A. Friar. *The Only Good Indian . . . : The Hollywood Gospel*. New York: Drama Book Specialists, 1972.

Golding, Peter. "Media Professionalism in the Third World: The Transfer of Ideology." In *Mass Communication and Society*, ed. James Curran, Michael Gurevitch, and Janet Woollacott. London: Open University Press, 1979.

James, C. L. R. *Beyond the Boundary*. New York: Pantheon Books, 1984.

Kunzle, David. "The *Reader's Digest*—A Self Image." *Praxis* 1, no. 3 (1976): 38–40.

Lee, Chin-chuan. *Media Imperialism Reconsidered: The Homogenizing of Television Culture*. Beverly Hills, Calif.: Sage, 1980.

Mattelart, Armand. "Cultural Imperialism, Mass Media and Class Struggle: An Interview with Armand Mattelart." *Insurgent Sociologist* 9, no. 4 (1980): 69–79.

———. *Mass Media, Ideologies, and the Revolutionary Movement*. Atlantic Highlands, N.J.: Humanities Press, 1980.

————. *Multinational Corporations and the Control of Culture: The Ideological Apparatuses of Imperialism.* Atlantic Highlands, N.J.: Humanities Press, 1982.

Mattelart, Armand, and Seth Siegelaub, eds. *Communication and Class Struggle.* Vol. 1: *Capitalism, Imperialism.* New York: International General, 1979.

Pettit, Arthur G. *Images of the Mexican American in Fiction and Film.* College Station: Texas A & M University Press, 1980.

Said, Edward. *Covering Islam.* New York: Pantheon Books, 1981.

————. *Orientalism.* New York: Pantheon Books, 1978.

Schiller, Herbert. *Communication and Cultural Domination.* White Plains, N.Y.: International Arts and Sciences Press, 1976.

————. *Mass Communications and American Empire.* Boston: Beacon Press, 1971.

Smith, Anthony. *The Geopolitics of Information: How Western Culture Dominates the World.* New York: Oxford University Press, 1980.

Smythe, Dallas W. *Dependency Road: Communications, Capitalism, Consciousness, and Canada.* Norwood, N.J.: Ablex, 1981.

Tunstall, Jeremy, and David Walker. *Media Made in California: Hollywood, Politics, and the News.* New York: Oxford University Press, 1981.

AMBUSH AT KAMIKAZE PASS

TOM ENGELHARDT

> *I was visiting an Indian school and a movie was being shown in*
> *the auditorium about the cavalry and the Indians. The cavalry*
> *was, of course, outnumbered and holding an impossible posi-*
> *tion where the Indians had chased them into the rocks. The In-*
> *dians, attempting to sneak up on the cavalry, were being killed,*
> *one every shot. When it finally appeared that the Indians were*
> *going to overrun the army position the ubiquitous cavalry*
> *appeared on the far horizon with their bugle blowing, and*
> *charged to save the beleaguered few. The whole auditorium full*
> *of Indian students cheered.*
>
> OUR BROTHER'S KEEPER: THE INDIAN IN WHITE AMERICA

> *It was a thrilling drama of love and death they saw silently*
> *reeled off; the scenes, laid at the court of an oriental despot,*
> *galloped past, full of gorgeousness and naked bodies, thirst of*
> *power and raving religious self-abnegation, full of cruelty, ap-*
> *petite and deathly lust, and slowing down to give a full view of*
> *the muscular development of the executioner's arms. Con-*
> *structed, in short, to cater to the innermost desires of an*
> *onlooking, international civilization.*
>
> THOMAS MANN, MAGIC MOUNTAIN

"Westerns" may have been America's most versatile art form. For several generations of Americans, westerns provided history lessons, entertainment, and a general guide to the world. They created or recreated a flood of American heroes,
filled popcorned weekends, and overwhelmed untold imaginations. It's as difficult today to imagine movies without them as to think of a luncheonette without
Coca-Cola. In their folksy way, they intruded on our minds. Unobtrusively they
lent us a hand in grinding a lens through which we could view the whole of the
nonwhite world. Their images were powerful; their structure was satisfying; and
at their heart lay one archetypal scene, which went something like this:

White canvas-covered wagons roll forward in a column. White men, on their horses,
ride easily up and down the lines of wagons. Their arms hang loosely near their guns. The
walls of the buttes rise high on either side. Cakey streaks of yellow, rusty red, dried brown
enclose the sun's heat boiling up on all sides. The dust settles on their nostrils, they gag
and look apprehensively toward the heights, hostile and distant. Who's there? Sullenly,
they ride on.

Beyond the buttes, the wagon train moves centrally into the flatlands, like a spear
pointed at the sunset. The wagons circle. Fires are built, guards set. From within this
warm and secure circle, at the center of the plains, the white men (white cameras) stare
out. There, in the enveloping darkness, on the peripheries of human existence, at dawn or
dusk, hooting and screeching, from nowhere, like maggots, swarming, naked, painted,
burning and killing, for no reason, like animals, they would come. The men touch their
gun handles and circle the wagons. From this strategically central position, with good
cover and better machines, today or tomorrow, or the morning after, they will simply mow

From *Bulletin of Concerned Asian Scholars* 3, no. 1 (1971).

them down. Wipe them out. Nothing human is involved. It's a matter of self-defense, no more. Extermination can be the only answer.

There are countless variations on this scene. Often the encircled wagon train is replaced by the surrounded fort; yet only the shape of the object has changed. The fort, like the wagon train, is the focus of the film. Its residents are made known to us. Familiarly, we take in the hate/respect struggle between the civilian scout and the garrison commander; the love relations between the commander's daughter and the young yet-to-prove-himself first lieutenant; the comic routines of the general soldiery. From this central point in our consciousness they sally forth to victory against unknown besiegers with inexplicable customs, irrational desires, and an incomprehensible language (a mixture of pig latin and Pidgin Hollywood).

What does this sort of paradigm do to us? Mostly, it forces us to flip history on its head. It makes the intruder exchange places in our eyes with the one intruded upon. (Who ever heard of a movie in which the Indians wake up one morning to find that, at the periphery of their existences, in their own country, there are new and aggressive beings ready to make war on them, incomprehensible, unwilling to share, out to murder and kill, and so on?) It is the Indians, in these films, who must invade, intrude, break in upon the circle—a circle that contains all those whom the film has already certified as "human." No wonder the viewer identifies with those in the circle, not with the Indians left to patrol enigmatically the bluffs overlooking humanity. In essence, the viewer is forced behind the barrel of a repeating rifle, and it is from that position, through its gun sights, that he receives a picture history of Western colonialism and imperialism. Little wonder that he feels no sympathy for the enemy as they fall before his withering fire—within this cinematic structure, the opportunity for such sympathy simply ceases to exist.

Such an approach not only transforms invasion into an act of self-defense, but it also prepares its audiences for the acceptance of genocide. The theory is simple enough: We may not always be right (there are stupid commanders, for instance), but we are human. By any standards (offered in the film), "they" are not. What, then, are they? They are animate; thus they are, if not human, in some sense animals. And for animals facing a human onslaught, the options are limited. Certain of the least menacing among them can be retained as pets. As a hunter trains his dog, these can be trained to be scouts, tracking down those of their kind who try to escape or resist, or to be porters or servants. Those not needed as pets (who are nonetheless domesticable) can be maintained on preserves. The rest, fit neither for house training nor for cages, must be wiped out.[1]

From the acceptance of such a framework flows the ability to accept as pleasurable, a relief, satisfying, the mass slaughter of the "nonhuman"—the killing, the mowing down of the nonwhite, hundreds to a film, and normally in the scene that barely precedes the positive resolution of the relationships among the whites. Anyone who thinks the body count is a creation of the recent Indochinese war should look at the movies he saw as a kid. It was the implicit rule of those films that no less than ten Indian (or Japanese or Chinese) warriors should fall for each white expendable secondary character.[2]

Just as the style and substance of the Indian wars was a prototype for many later American intrusions into the Third World (particularly the campaigns in the Philippines and Indochina), so movies about those wars provided the prototype from which nearly every American movie about the Third World derived. That these Third World movies are pale reflections of the framework, outlook, and even conventions of the cowboy movie is easy enough to demonstrate. Just a few examples, chosen almost at random from the thirty or forty films I've caught on TV in the last few months, will suffice. Pick your country: the Mexico of toothy Pancho Villan bandits, the North Africa of encircled Foreign Legionnaires, the India of embattled British Lancers, or even South Africa. One would think treatment of South Africa might be rather special, have its own unique features. But lo! We look up, and already the Boers are trekking away in (strange to say) wagons, and yep, there's . . . no, it can't be . . . it is—Susan Hayward. Suddenly, from nowhere, the Zulus appear, hooting and howling, to surround the third-rate wagons of this third-rate movie. And here's that unique touch we've all been waiting for. It seems to be the singular quality of the Zulus that they have no horses and so must circle the wagon train on foot, yelling at the tops of their voices and brandishing their spears. But wait . . . from the distance . . . it's the Transvaal cavalry to the rescue! As they swoop down, one of the Boers leaps on a wagon seat, waving his hat with joy, and calls to his friend in the cavalry, "You've got 'em running, Paul. Keep 'em running, Paul! Run 'em off the end of the earth!" (*Untamed*, 1955).

Or switch to the Pacific. In any one of a hundred World War II flicks, we see a subtle variation on the same encirclement imagery. From the deck of our flagship amid the fleet corralled off the Okinawa coast, we look through our binoculars. The horizon is empty, yet already the radar has picked them up: somewhere beyond human sight, unidentified flying objects. The sirens are howling, the men pouring out of their bunks and helter-skelter into battle gear. At their guns, they look grimly toward the empty sky: the young ensign too eager for his first command, the swabby who got a date with that pretty Wave, the medic whose wife just sent him a "Dear John" letter (he's slated to die heroically). A speck on the horizon. Faces tense up, jokes fall away. It's the Kamikaze! Half-man, half-machine, an incomprehensible human torpedo bearing down from the peripheries of fanatical animate existence to pierce the armored defenses of the forces of Western democracy. The result? Serious damage to several ships, close calls on more, several secondary characters dead, and an incredible number of Japanese planes obliterated from the sky.[3]

That there is no feeling of loss at the obliteration of human torpedoes is hardly surprising. Even in those brief moments when you "meet" the enemy, movies like this make it immaculately clear that he is not only strange, barbarous, hostile, and dangerous, but he has little regard for his own life. Throwing himself on the gatling guns of the British with only spear in hand, or on the ack-ack guns of the Americans with only bomb in portal, he is not acting out of any human emotion. It is not a desire to defend his home, his friends, or his freedom. It has no rational (that is, "human") explanation. It is not even "bravery" as we in the West know it (though similar acts by whites are portrayed heroically). Rather, it is something innate, fanatical, perverse—an inexplicable desire for death, disorder, and destruction.

When the enemy speaks a little English, he often explains this himself. Take, for instance, the captured Japanese officer in *Halls of Montezuma* (1950). The plot is already far advanced. On an island in the Pacific, hours before the big attack, Marines are pinned down by Japanese mortars whose position they cannot locate. Yet if they do not locate them, the attack will fail. The Japanese officer obstinately refuses to help them. Richard Widmark pleads with him, appealing to his life force. "You have a future—to rebuild Japan—to live for." But the officer replies: "Captain, you seem to have forgotten, my people for centuries have thought not of living well but dying well. Have you not studied our Judo, our science? We always take the obvious and reverse it. Death is the basis of our strength." Suddenly a mortar shell explodes above the bunker. Everybody ducks. Rafters fall, dust billows; slowly the air clears; a shocked voice yells out: "My God, the Jap's committed Hari Kari!" Fortunately, the idiot gave it all away. He reminded the Americans of the quirks in the nonwhite mind. As any schoolboy should have known, Orientals think backward. The Japs put their rockets on the front slope of the mountain, not the protected rear slopes as an American would have done. The attack, to the tune of the Marine Hymn, moves forward, preparing to wipe the Japs off the face of the island.

If, in print, such simple idiocy makes you laugh, it probably didn't when you saw the film; nor is it in any way atypical of four decades of action films about Asia. The overwhelmingly present theme of the non-human-ness of the nonwhite prepares us to accept, without flinching, the extermination of our "enemies." (As John Wayne commented in *The Searchers* [1956], there's "humans," and then there's "Comanches.") And just as surely, it helped prepare the ideological way for the leveling and near obliteration of three Asian areas in the course of three decades.

It is useful, in this light, to compare the cinematic treatment of the European front in World Wars I and II with that of the Pacific front. From the silent *Big Parade* on, a common and often moving convention of movies about the wars against Germany went something like this: The allied soldier finds himself caught in a foxhole (trench, farmhouse) with a wounded German soldier. He is about to shoot, when the young, begrimed soldier holds up two fingers in a V, meaning, "Do you have a cigarette?" Though speaking different languages, they exchange family pictures and common memories.[4]

The scene is meant to attest to man's sense of humanity and brotherhood over and above war and national hatred. Until very recently, such a scene simply did not appear in movies about the Japanese front. Between the American and his nonwhite enemy, a bond transcending enmity was hardly even considered. Instead, an analogous scene went something like this: A group of Japanese, shot down in a withering crossfire, lie on the ground either dead or severely wounded. The American soldiers approach, less from humanitarian motives than because they hope to get prisoners and information.[5] One of the Japanese, however, is just playing possum. As the American reaches down to give him water (first aid, a helping hand), he suddenly pulls out a hand grenade (pistol, knife) and, with the

look of a fanatic, tries to blow them *all* to smithereens. He is quickly dispatched (see, for instance, *In Love and War*, 1956).

The theme of alien intruders descending on embattled humans and being obliterated from an earth they clearly are not entitled to is most straightforwardly put in science fiction movies; for monsters turn out to be little more than the metaphysical wing of the Third World. These movies represent as history events that have taken place only in the Western imagination. Thus, the themes of the cowboy (and cowboy–Third World) movie come through in a more primeval way. An overlay of fear replaces the suspense. Metaphorically, the world is the wagon train; the universe, the horizon. (Or, alternatively, the spaceship from earth is the wagon train; an alien planet, the horizon). From that horizon, somewhere at the peripheries of human existence, from the Arctic icecap (*The Thing*, 1951), the desert (*Them*, 1954), the distant past (*The Beast from 20,000 Fathoms*, 1954), the sky (*War of the Worlds*, 1953), at dawn or dusk, hooting and beeping, come the invaders. Enveloping whole armies, they smash through human defenses, forcing the white representatives of the human race to fall back on their inner defense line (perhaps New York or Los Angeles). Imperiling the very heartland of civilized life, they provide only one option—destroy THEM before THEY can destroy us.

In this sort of a movie, the technical problems involved in presenting the extinction of a race for the enjoyment of an audience are simplified.[6] Who would even think about saving the Pod People (*Invasion of the Body Snatchers*, 1956)? Ordinarily the question of alternatives to elimination barely comes to mind. If it does, as in that prototype "modern" sci fi film *The Thing* (James Arness of Matt Dillon fame played the monster), usually the man who wants to save Them ("just talk to Them") is the bad mad scientist as opposed to the good, absent-minded scientist (who probably has the pretty daughter being wooed by the cub reporter).[7]

Unfortunately for American moviemakers, Asians and others could not simply be photographed with three heads, tentacles, and gelatinous bodies. Consequently, other conventions had to be developed (or appropriated) that would clearly differentiate them from "humanity" at large. The first of these was invisibility. In most movies about the Third World, the nonwhites provide nothing more than a backdrop for all-white drama—an element of exotic and unifying dread against which to play out the tensions and problems of the white world. Sometimes, even the locales seem none too distinguishable, not to speak of their black, brown, or yellow inhabitants. It is not surprising, for instance, that the Gable-Harlow movie *Red Dust* (1932), set on an Indochinese rubber plantation (Gable is the foreman), could be transported to Africa without loss two decades later as the Gable-Kelly *Mogambo*. It could as well have been set in Brazil on a coffee plantation, or in Nevada on a cattle ranch.

As George Orwell commented of North Africa in 1939,

All people who work with their hands are partly invisible, and the more important the work they do, the less visible they are. Still, a white skin is always fairly conspicuous. In northern Europe, when you see a labourer ploughing a field, you probably give him a second glance. In a hot country, anywhere south of Gibraltar or east of Suez, the chances are that you don't even see him. I have noticed this again and again. In a tropical landscape one's eye takes in everything except the human beings. It takes in the dried-up soil, the prickly pear, the palm tree and the distant mountain, but it always misses the peasant hoeing at his patch. He is the same colour as the earth, and a great deal less interesting to look at. It is only because of this that the starved countries of Asia and Africa are accepted as tourist resorts.[8]

Theoretically, it should have been somewhat more difficult following the Chinese and Vietnamese revolutions and other uprisings of the oppressed and nonwhite around the world to ignore the people for the scenery. Yet we can't fault Hollywood for its valiant attempt. Generally, American films have hewed with unsurpassed tenacity to this framework, reproducing the white world whole in the Orient, for example, with Asians skittering at the edges of sets as servants or as "scenic" figures of menace. This is even more true in films on Africa, where for generations whites have fought off natives and lions, not necessarily in that order.

A second convention in these films concerns the pecking order of white and nonwhite societies when they come into conflict. It is always a "united front" among whites. Although they are often portrayed as the highly romanticized third-rate flotsam and jetsam of a mythologized American society—adventurers, prostitutes, opportunists, thieves (just as the films themselves, particularly those about Asia, tend to represent the brackish backwater of the American film industry), yet no matter how low, no matter what their internal squabbles, no matter what their hostilities toward one other, in relation to the Third World the whites stand as one: Missionary's daughter and drunken ferryboat captain ("I hate the Reds," he says to her, "because they closed a lot of Chinese ports where they have dames. Chinese, Eurasian, and White Russian. . . . Somebody pinned the bleeding heart of China on your sleeve but they never got around to me" [*Blood Alley*, 1955]); soldier of fortune and adventurer-journalist, natural enemies over the Woman They Both Love (they escape Canton together, avoiding the clutches of the Reds in a stolen boat [*Soldier of Fortune*, 1955]); sheriff, deputies, and captured outlaws (they are surrounded by Mexican bandits [*Bandalero*, 196?]); or on a national level, the British, Americans, and Russians (they must deal with "the chief enemy of the Western World," Mao Tse-tung [*The Chairman*, 1970]). This theme is, of course, simply a variation on a more homegrown variety—the Confederates and Yankees who bury their sectional hatreds to unite against the Indians; the convicts on their way to prison who help the wagon train fight off the Sioux, bringing the women and children to safety, and so forth. (See, for example, *Ambush at Cimarron Pass* [1959], which combines everything in one laughable mess when a Yankee patrol and its prisoner team up with a Confederate rancher to fight off an Apache attack.)

The audience is expected to carry two racial lessons away from this sort of thing. The first is that the presence of the incomprehensible and nonhuman brings out what is "human" in every man. Individual dignity, equality, fraternity—all that on which the West theoretically places premium value is brought sharply into focus at the expense of "alien" beings. The second is the implicit statement that, in a pinch, any white is a step up from the rest of the world. They may be murderers, rapists, and mother-snatchers, but they're ours.

When the inhabitants of these countries emerge from the ferns or their wattled huts and try to climb to the edges of the spotlight, they find the possibilities limited indeed. In this cinematic pick-up-sides, the whites already have two hands on the bat handle before the contest begins. The set hierarchy of roles is structured something like this: All roles of positive authority are reserved for white characters. Among the whites, the men stand triumphantly at the top; their women cringe, sigh, and faint below; and the Asians are left to scramble for what's left, like beggars at a refuse heap.

There is only one category in which a nonwhite is likely to come out top dog—villain. With their stock of fanatical speeches and their propensity for odd tortures, Third World villains provided the American filmmaker with a handy receptacle for his audience's inchoate fears of the unknown and inhuman. Only as the repository for Evil could the nonwhite "triumph" in films. However, this is no small thing; for wherever there is a Third World country, American scriptwriters have created villain slots to be filled by otherwise unemployable actors (though often even these roles are monopolized by whites in yellowface). From area to area, like spirits, their forms change: the Mexican bandit chief with his toothy smile, hearty false laugh, sombrero, and bushy eyebrows (see, for instance, the excellent *Treasure of the Sierra Madre*, 1948; or the awful *Bandalero*); the Oriental warlord with his droopy mustache and shaved head (see *The Left Hand of God*, 1955; *The General Died at Dawn*, 1936; *Shanghai Express*, 1932; *Seven Women*, 1965; and so on ad nauseam); the Indian "khan" or prince with his little goatee and urbane manner (*Khyber Pass*, 1954; *Charge of the Light Brigade*, 1936)—yet their essence remains the same.

Set against their shiny pates or silken voices, their hard eyes and twitching mouths, no white could look anything but good. In *The Left Hand of God*, Humphrey Bogart, the pilot turned opportunistic-warlord advisor turned fraudulent-priest, becomes a literal saint under the leer of Lee J. Cobb's General Yang. In *The Chairman*, Gregory Peck, an "uninvolved" scientist–CIA spy, becomes a boy wonder and living representative of humanity when faced with a ping-pong-playing Mao Tse-tung. How can you lose when the guy you want to double-deal represents a nation that has discovered an enzyme allowing pineapples to grow in Tibet and winter wheat in Mongolia, yet (as one of the Russian agents puts it) is holding it so that the rest of the "underdeveloped" world, "90 percent poor, 90 percent peasant . . . will crawl on their hands and knees to Peking to get it." All in all, these nonwhite representatives of evil provide a backboard off which white Western values can bounce in, registering one more cinematic score for Civilization.

The other group of roles open to nonwhites are roles of helplessness and dependence. At the dingy bottom of the scale of dependence crouch children. Nonwhite children have traditionally been a favorite for screenwriters and directors. Ingrid Bergman helped them across the mountains to safety (*The Inn of the Sixth Happiness*, 1958); Deborah Kerr taught them geography (*The King and I*, 1956); Humphrey Bogart helped them to memorize "My Old Kentucky Home" (*The Left Hand of God*); Carrol Baker went with them on a great trek back to their homelands (*Cheyenne Autumn*, 1964); Richard Widmark took one (a little half-breed orphan girl—sort of the black, one-eyed Jew of the tiny tot's universe) back to the States with him (*55 Days at Peking*); and so on.

Essentially, nonwhite children fulfill the same function and have the same effect as nonwhite villains. They reflect to the white audience just another facet of their own humanity. Of course, if you ignore W. C. Fields, children have had a traditionally cloying place in American films; but in the Third World movie they provide a particularly strong dose of knee-jerk sentiment, allowing the white leads to show the other side of Western civilization. It is their duty not just to exterminate the world's evil forces, but also to give to those less capable (and more needy) than themselves. And who more closely fits such a description than the native child who may someday grow up to emulate us?

While it is children who enable the white authorities to demonstrate their natural impulses toward those who do not resist them but are helpless before them or dependent upon them, it is women who prove the point. Even within the cinematic reflection of the white world, women have seldom held exalted positions. Normally they are daughters of missionaries, sweethearts of adventurers, daughters, nurses, daughters of missionaries, wives on safari, schoolmarms, daughters of missionaries, or prostitutes. (The exceptions usually occur when women come under a "united front" ruling—that is, they confront Asian men, not white men. Then, as with Anna in *The King and I*, while their occupations may not change, they face society on a somewhat different footing.) Several rungs down the social ladder, nonwhite women are left mainly with roles as bargirls, geishas, belly dancers, nurse's aides, missionary converts, harem girls, or prostitutes. In such positions, their significance and status depend totally on the generosity (or lack of generosity) of those white men around whom the movies revolve.

However "well intentioned" the moviemaker, the basic effect of this debased dependency is not changeable. Take that classic schmaltz of the 1950s, *The World of Suzie Wong*. William Holden, a dissatisfied architect-businessman, has taken a year's sabbatical in Hong Kong to find out if he can "make it" as an artist. (It could have been Los Angeles, but then the movie would have been a total zilch.) He meets ***Suzie Wong***, a bargirl who is cute as a Walt Disney button and speaks English with an endearing "Chinese" accent ("Fo' goo'niss sakes," she says over and over at inappropriate moments). He wants her to be his model. She wants to be his "permanent girlfriend." Many traumas later, the moviemakers trundle out their good intentions toward the world's ill-treated masses. They allow Holden to choose Suzie over Kay, the proper, American, upper-class woman who is chasing him as well. This attempt to put down the upper classes for their prejudices toward Chinese and bargirls, however, barely covers over the basic lesson of the movie: a helpless, charming Chinese bargirl *can* be saved by the right white man, purified by association with him, and elevated to dependency on him. (Her bastard child, conveniently brought out for his pity quotient, is also conveniently bumped off by a flash flood, avoiding further knotty problems for the already overtaxed sensibilities of the scriptwriters.) It all comes across as part act of God, part act of white America.

Moving upward toward a peak of Third World success and white condescen-

sion, we discover the role of "sidekick." Indispensable to the sidekick is his un-canny ability to sacrifice his life for his white companion at just the right mo-ment. In this, he must leave the audience feeling that he has repaid the white man something intangible that was owed to him. And in this, too, we find the last major characteristic of Third World roles—expendability. Several classic scenes come to mind. For example, the otherwise pitiful Gunga Din excelled in this skill (*Gunga Din*, 1939): up on a craggy ledge, already dying, yet blowing that bugle like crazy to save the British troops from ambush by the fanatic Kali-worshippers. Or, to bring up still another Third World group, there is the death of the black trainer in *Body and Soul* (1947), which prevents his protégé, the white Heavy-weight Champion of the World (John Garfield), from throwing the big fight; or even, if I remember rightly, Sidney Poitier, Mau Mau initiate, falling on the punji sticks to save the white child of his boyhood friend Rock Hudson (*Something of Value*, 1957). The parts blend into each other: the Filipino guide to the American guerrillas, the Indian pal of the white scout, the Mexican guy with the big gut and sly sense of humor. In the end, Third World characters are considered ex-pendable by both moviemakers and their audiences because they are no more a source of "light" than the moon at night. All are there but to reflect, in differing mirrors, aspects of white humanity.

Although these movies have offered a steady diet of extermination, depen-dency, and expendability over the decades, American moviemakers have not re-mained totally stagnant in their treatment of the Third World and its inhabitants.

They have, over the last forty years, emerged ponderously from a colonial world into a neocolonial one. In the 1930s, the only decade when anything other than second-rate films were made about Asia, moviemakers had no hesitation about expressing an outright contempt for subjugated or powerless Asians; nor did they feel self-conscious about proudly portraying the colonial style in which most Westerners in Asia lived. The train in *Shanghai Express* (1932) is shown in all its "colonial" glory: the Chinese passengers are crammed into crude compartments, while the Westerners eat dinner in their spacious and elegant dining room. Here was the striking contrast between the rulers and the ruled, and nobody saw any reason to hide it.

During this period the European imperial structure in Asia was still unbroken, and colonial paternalism abounded. No one blinked an eye when, in *Wee Willie Winkie* (1937), Shirley Temple asked her grandfather, the British colonel, why he was mad at "Khoda Khan," leader of the warlike tribes on India's northeast border, and he replied, "We're not mad at Khoda Khan. England wants to be friends with all her peoples. But if we don't shoot him, he'll shoot us . . . they've been plundering for so many years, they don't realize they'd be better off planting crops" [a few poppy seeds perhaps?]. Nor were audiences taken aback when Cary Grant called his Indian sidekick a "beastie" (or, alternately, the "regimental beastie") in *Gunga Din*; or when Clark Gable kicked his Indochinese workers out of a ditch (to save them from a storm, of course), calling them similar names (*Red Dust*).

A decade later such scenes and lines would have been gaffes.[9] In the wake of World War II and its flock of anti-Japanese propaganda.flicks (whose progeny were still alive in the early 1960s), the destruction of the British, French, and Dutch empires, the success of the communist revolution in China, the birth and death of dreaded "neutralism," and the rise of the United States to a position of preeminence in the world, new cinematic surfaces were developed to fit over old frames. In their new suits, during the decade of the 1950s, cowboy–Third World movies flourished as never before. A vast quantity of these low-budget (and not-so-low-budget) films burst from Hollywood to flood the country's theaters. In the more "progressive" of them, an India in chains was replaced by a struggling, almost "independent" country; the "regimental beastie," by a Nehru- or Gandhi-type "rebel" leader; the Kali-worshipping, loinclothed fanatic, by Darvee, the Maoist revolutionary ("You cannot make omelettes without breaking eggs"). Yet this sort of exercise was no more than sleight of hand. The Nehru character looked just as ridiculously pompous and imitative as did Gunga Din when he practiced his bugle; nor did the whites monopolize center stage any less (holding, naturally, the key military and police positions); nor could the half-breed woman (Ava Gardner) choose light (the British officer) over darkness (Darvee and his minions) any less (*Bhowani Junction*, 1956). Soon, all this comes to seem about as basic a change in older forms as was the "independence" granted to many former colonies in the real world.

If any new elements were to enter these movies in the 1950s (and early 1960s), it was in the form of changes in relations within the white world, not between the white and nonwhite worlds. These changes, heralded by the "adult western" of the late fifties, have yet to be fully realized in films on Asia; yet there was a certain early (and somewhat aborted) move in this direction in some of the films that appeared about the Korean War (not a particularly popular subject, as might be imagined)—a certain tiredness ("Three world wars in one lifetime" [*Battle Circus*, 1953]) and some doubts. The World War II flick's faith in the war against the "Japs," in a "civilian" army, and in "democracy" comes across tarnished and tired. The "professional" soldier (or flier) takes center stage ("We've gotta do a clean, professional job on those [North Korean] bridges" [*The Bridges at Toko-ri*, 1954]). There is, for instance, no analogue in World War II movies to the following conversation in *The Bridges at Toko-ri*. Mickey Rooney (a helicopter rescue pilot) and William Holden (a flier) have been shot down behind North Korean lines. Surrounded, they wait in a ditch for help to arrive. During a lull in the shooting, they begin to talk:

Holden: I'm a lawyer from Denver, Colorado, Mike. I probably couldn't hit a thing [with this gun] . . .
Rooney: Judas, how'd you ever get out here in a smelly ditch in Korea?
Holden: That's just what I've been asking myself . . . The wrong war in the wrong place and that's the one you're stuck with . . . You fight simply because you are here.

Within minutes, they are both killed by the advancing Korean soldiers.

Yet although the white world might seem tarnished, and its heroes bitter, tired, and ridden with doubts, its relationship to the nonwhite world had scarcely changed. If anything, the introduction of massive air power to Asian warfare had only further reduced the tangential humanity of Asian peoples. For in a movie like *Toko-ri* (as at Danang during the Vietnam War), you never even needed to see the enemy, only charred bodies.

This early attempt, particularly in westerns, to introduce new attitudes in the white world muddied the divisions between stock characters, brought to the fore the hero-as-cynic, and called into question the "humanity" of the whites vis-à-vis one other. Such adjustments in a relatively constant cinematic structure represented an attempt to update a form that the world's reality was rendering increasingly unbelievable. By the early 1960s, the "adult western" had reached a new stage—that of elegy (for instance, *The Man Who Shot Liberty Valence*, 1962). Superficially, such movies seem to represent a state of sentimental mourning for the closing of the frontier and the end of a mythical white frontier life. But indeed, the western as a form was created originally in part to mourn just such a loss to industrial America. The elegiac western of the 1960s was, in fact, mourning its own passing. Today, this form has come to what may be its terminal fruition in America, the "hip" western—*Butch Cassidy and the Sundance Kid* (1969), a parody not of the western but of the elegiac western, since not even that can be taken totally straight any more.[10]

Even in this extension of the western, however, one thing has not changed—the attitude toward the Third World. When, for instance, Butch and Sundance cannot make a go of it in a hemmed-in West, they naturally move on, "invading" Bolivia. In Bolivia, of course, it's the same old local color scene again, with one variation: instead of the two of them killing off hundreds of Bolivians in that old wagon train scene, hundreds of unidentified Bolivians band together to kill *them*. It all boils down to the same thing.

Whatever *Butch Cassidy* may be the end of, I think we stand at the edge of a not totally new but nonetheless yawning abyss—the "sympathetic" film. The first of what I expect will be an onslaught of these movies are appearing now, showing at least pretensions toward changing how we see relationships not only within the white world itself but also between the white and Indian worlds. And what is appearing in westerns today may be the transmuted meat of Asian or African films within the next decade.

A Man Called Horse (1970) is a good example. It seems to have been a sincere and painstaking attempt to make a large-scale, commercially successful movie about the Sioux (before they were overrun by the whites), to show from an Indian point of view their way of life, their rituals (recreated from George Catlin's paintings) and beliefs, their feelings and fears. Yet at every turn the film betrays the edges of older and more familiar frameworks.

It concerns an English lord who is hunting in the American West early in the nineteenth century. Captured by a Sioux raiding party, he is brought back to their village (where the rest of the film takes place). There he becomes a slave (horse) for an Indian woman (Dame Judith Anderson). Already a white "hero" has been slipped into this movie about Indians, betraying an assumption that American audiences could not sustain interest in a film without whites. Given the way we look at these films, he immediately becomes the center of our attention; in the end, you are forced to relate to the Sioux village through his eyes and to relate to the Sioux as they relate to him (aiding him or mistreating him). Furthermore, by following the travails of this lord turned beast-of-burden as he assimilates to the tribe, the movie seems to prove that old adage, "Put a white man among even the best of savages and you have a natural chief." (He kills enemy Indians, goes through the sun initiation ritual, marries the chief's daughter, teaches the tribe British infantry tactics, and, in the end, his wife and adopted mother being dead, he splits for the white world.)

His girlfriend has that Ali McGraw look, which is probably supposed to allow the audience to "identify" better with the Indians but looks about as fitting as it did among the Jews of New Jersey (*Goodbye, Columbus*). Even a stab at righting the wrongs westerns have done to language has a similarly dismal result. The movie's makers, reacting to the common use of Pidgin Hollywood by Indian characters in normal westerns, allow the Sioux in this movie to speak their own language. Because all but two of the characters are Sioux, much of the movie is conducted in the Sioux language. If this were a French movie, there would naturally be subtitles; but as these are Sioux *au naturel*, and as there is already a conveniently English-speaking character, an alternate means is called upon. Another "prisoner" is created, an Indian who spent some time with the French and speaks broken English. At the behest of the English lord, he translates what is necessary to his and our understanding. In this way, the Indians, while retaining the dignity of their own language, are perhaps slightly less able to express themselves comprehensibly in this picture than in a normal western. More important, just as in the normal wagon train scenario, we are forced to see everything through white eyes.[11]

And, as long as the eyes through which we see the world do not change, as long as the old frameworks for movies about the Third World are not thrown away, "intentions" go for little indeed. It is hard even to think of examples of films in which sympathetic intentions are matched by deeds. Certainly one would have to venture beyond the bounds of the United States to find them—perhaps *The Battle of Algiers* (which, in reverse, does for the French colonizers what we were never willing to do for the Indians). Its view begins at least to accord with the brutal history of the Third World, to tell a little what it means, from the point of view of the colonized, to resist, to fight back, to rebel against your occupiers.

American moviemakers, however, are at heart still in love with an era when people could accept the six-year-old Shirley Temple telling Khoda Khan not to make war on the British because "the Queen wants to protect her people and make them rich." In later movies they simply replaced the Queen with (American) technology—machine guns to mow 'em down, band-aids to patch 'em up. This mood is best captured when Humphrey Bogart says, "China's becoming a nightmare, Anne . . . What are we really doing here? . . . We belong back in the States, marrying, raising a family." She replies, "There's too much work to do here . . . The things we're doing here are what they need, whether medicine or grace. And we can give it to them." Of course, the historical joke of this being uttered in China's Sinkiang province in 1947, a time when the unmentioned communist revolution was sweeping through the central provinces, passed the scriptwriters by. Yet, on the whole, just this distance between the film's "message" and Chinese reality about sums up the American approach to the Third World. In the end, no matter where the moviemakers may think their sympathies lie, their films are usually no more than embroideries on a hagiography of "pacification."

Within such a context, there is no possibility for presenting resistance, rebellion, or revolution on the part of the intruded upon in a way that could be even comprehensible, much less sympathetic. Quite the opposite, the moviemakers are usually hell-bent on glorifying those Asians (or other Third Worlders) who allied with the Western invaders, not those who at some point resisted either the invasion or its consequences. However, there is an insoluble contradiction here. The method for judging nonwhites in these films is based on how dependent or independent they are of the white leads and the white world. To the degree that they are dependent, they are seen as closer to humanity. To the degree that they are independent (that is, resist), they are seen as less liable to humanization, or even outright inhuman, and thus open to extermination ("Mitchell, we must stamp this out immediately" [*Gunga Din*]). In other words, there is an inherent bias in these movies toward the glorification of those "natives" who have allied with us. Yet what makes the white hero so appealing is the audience's feeling that no matter how low he sinks, he retains some sense of human dignity. There is always that feeling (as Bogart and countless cowboy stars brought out so well) that, despite appearances, *he is his own man*. No movie Asians linked to the West can ever really be that; they can bask in the light of humanity, but they can never really be much more than imitation humans. In only one nonwhite role is this possibility open: that of the villain (he who refuses white help and actively opposes him). Only the villain, already placed outside the pale of humanity (no pun intended), can be his own man.

The result is a knotty problem. If, on the one hand, those close to the whites are invariably dependent, they cannot be viewed, at least in some way, but with contempt, no matter how the moviemakers go about trying to glorify them. On the other hand, if those most contemptible of nonhumans, the villains, are the only Asians capable of "independence" in these films, they are also the only Asians who are the cinematic equivalents of the white leads. Thus, we cannot help but have a sneaking respect for those who oppose us and a sneaking contempt for those who side with us. (How similar this must have been to the attitudes of many American soldiers in Vietnam toward the National Liberation Front forces on the one hand and the Army of the Republic of [South] Vietnam on the other.) No doubt this contradiction is at least partly responsible for the extremes American moviemakers have gone to in glorifying one and despoiling the other.

What Lewis and Clark's Indian guide Sacajawea was to high school American history texts, Gunga Din was to Third World movies. He makes the classic sacrifice for the white world and in death theoretically proves he is a "better man" than his British mentors. Yet how hollow this "triumph" is for the viewing audience. No one is fooled by the words. Doing his mimic marching shuffle around the corner from the practicing British troops, what a pitiful imitation "human" he appears to be. And even his greatest hopes—to get one toe on the lowest rung of the white regimental ladder as company bugler—leave him second best to any white who comes along. In contrast, the leader of the Kali worshippers (read: native resistance forces) is portrayed in a paroxysm of caricature ("Rise brothers and kill . . . kill for the love of Kali, kill for the love of killing, kill, *kill*, KILL!"). He is a mad murderer, a torturer, a loinclothed savage, a megalomaniac with bulging eyes. Yet he is the only Indian in the film who has the real ability to "love his country" like a white man. "I can die as readily for my country and my fate as you for yours," he says, and voluntarily jumps into the snakepit, yelling "India farewell!"

This inability, despite pulling all the stops, to deny the enemy a certain dignity is not extraordinary. Even Mao Tse-tung, in the otherwise rabid *The Chairman*, proves in some grim sense irrepressible. On the other hand, no matter how charmingly portrayed, our allies' dependency cannot be totally overcome. They are always, in a way, trained spies in the camp of their own people.

American movies about the Third World should not be given more credit than is their due. Despite the impression one might get in the theater, American moviemakers did not invent the world, or even the version of world history they present in their films. They must be given full credit, however, for developing a highly successful and satisfying cinematic form to encapsulate an existing ideological message. With this form they have been able to relegate the great horrors of Western expansion into the rest of the world, and of present-day American hegemony over great hunks of it, to another universe of pleasure and enjoyment. They have successfully tied extermination of nonwhite peoples to laughable relief, and white racial superiority to the natural order of things. They have destroyed any possibility for explaining the various ways in which nonwhite (not to speak of white) people could resist invasion, colonization, exploitation, and even mass slaughter.

Cowboy (–Third World) films make up, in the end, a vast visual "pacification" program that ostensibly describes the rest of the world but in fact is aimed at the millions of people who for several generations have made up the American viewing audience. It's hardly a wonder that Vietnam did not sear the American consciousness. Why should it have? For years, Americans had been watching the whole scene on their movie screens: endless precursors to My Lai, body counts, killing of wounded enemy soldiers, aerial obliteration, and on and on. We had grown used to seeing it, and thrilled with pleasure while reaching for another handful of popcorn.

Such a pacification program is based on the inundation principle. It is a matter not of quality (probably there have been no good films on Asia since the 1930s) but of quantity. So many cowboy–third world movies have rolled factory-style off the production line that the most minute change of plot is hailed as a great innovation. In the end, all the visual "choices" available to a viewer emphasize only the way in which America is strikingly a one-channel country. In fact, it might not be too far wrong to say that although pacification may have failed in Vietnam, its pilot project here in America has generally succeeded—that we are a pacified population, living unknowingly in an occupied country.

Notes

1. The men who historically advocated or pursued such a policy in the American West openly and unashamedly referred to it at the time as an "extermination" policy.

2. One must at least credit director John Ford for keeping the carnage down in several of his films (for example, *She Wore a Yellow Ribbon*, 1949) and for allowing the Indians to emerge victorious, if no more comprehensible, from at least one movie in the history of the western film (*Fort Apache*, 1948).

3. The land equivalent of the kamikaze onslaught is the "banzai!" charge (as in Fuller's *Merrill's Marauders*, 1962).

4. This sense of fraternity with the enemy is somewhat harder to find in Nazi war flicks, but see *The Enemy Below* (1957) for the World War II (and naval) version of the same scene. The last shot is of the opposing American and Nazi commanders, who have

disabled each other's ships and saved each other's lives, standing at the stern, sharing a cigarette and looking out together over the endless sea.

5. This is not to say that Americans are portrayed as lacking generosity. Quite the opposite, humanitarian gestures are second nature to them; however, those gestures tend to be directed toward humans (that is, whites). As in the scene in which Merrill's Marauders, having smashed through a mass of Japanese, are confronted with a wounded comrade: "You wouldn't leave me?" he asks; "We never leave anybody" is the reply.

6. Extermination has, however, been spoken of quite bluntly in certain Third World movies. This was particularly true of those movies made during the war against Japan. Take, for example, *The Purple Heart* (1944), about Japanese attempts to try the Doolittle fliers for "war crimes." At the trial, the leader of the American fliers tells the Japanese judge: "We'll come by night and we'll come by day. We'll blacken your skies and burn your cities to the ground until you get down on your knees and beg for mercy . . . This was your war. You asked for it. You started it . . . and now we won't stop until your crummy little empire is wiped off the face of the earth." The Japanese chief prosecutor immediately commits hara-kari because of loss of face in failing to break the American prisoners. Or again, *Objective Burma* (1945): the American journalist sees tortured and dead American prisoners. In anger, he says, "This was done in cold blood by a people who claim to be civilized . . . Stinking little savages. Wipe 'em out. Wipe 'em off the face of the earth, I say. Wipe 'em off the face of the earth!"

7. Of all the forms discussed, only science fiction films exhibit certain themes that run against this grain. It seems to me there are two sources for this opening toward "deviation." First, in the particularly chilly years of the fifties, antinuclear, antimilitary freaks flocked to this form because its very fantastical nature provided an allegorical legitimacy for their questionable messages. Thus, even the monster-eradication movies often hide a plea for "peace"—that is, deliverance from incompetent military defenders and their nuclear disasters, whose by-products are sci fi's ubiquitous radioactive creatures. Second, a traditional tie-in with the sky, heaven, and God led to a semireligious countertheme of "divine intervention" and human (implicitly, white) inferiority. This conception of wisdom descending from above to straighten out the stupid problems of blundering, incapable humanity is basic to *The Day the Earth Stood Still* (1951), in which "Klaatu" appears from space to tour Washington and plead for nuclear peace (and a fascist robot-police force to patrol the world); or *The Next Voice You Hear* (1950), in which God intervenes in person—via radio.

8. George Orwell, "Marrakech," in *Essays* (New York: Doubleday, 1954), pp. 189–190.

9. There were, of course, some holdovers from the thirties—particularly junk like *Khyber Pass* (1954), in which British lancer Richard Egan, getting ready to capture rebel leaders in a village, tells a fellow officer: "I don't want any of those devils to escape us."

10. Even John Wayne, the last of the cowboy superstars still in the saddle, was forced to mourn his own passing in *True Grit* (1968).

11. For another recent example, see *Tell Them Willie Boy Is Here* (1970); and I feel certain (though I have yet to see it) that *Soldier Blue* (1970) will fall into the same general category.

As for the newness of "sympathetic" films—at least a couple of historical antecedents come to mind: first, *The General Died at Dawn* (1936) with Gary Cooper, and Akim Tamiroff as the warlord Yang (quite the popular name for Hollywood warlords). This Clifford Odets script is heavy with the hand of the thirties Left. ("You ask me why I'm for oppressed people—because I have a background of oppression myself.") But despite its professed sympathy for the oppressed people of China, its protestations of Asian dignity and love for life, and its unbelievably murky politics, it is loaded with all the normal stuff: white-centeredness ("Mr. O'Hara, from the time you leave this room until you deliver the money, the fate of China is in your hands"); a Chinese superevil villain; and a mass suicide scene that could only have taken place among those for whom human life meant nothing at all (in the movie's climactic scene, General Yang, who is to die at dawn, has his troops line up in two facing lines several feet apart and shoot each other)—to name just a few of the more salient points.

For an example from the earlier sixties, see John Ford's "bow" to the tribulations of the Indians, *Cheyenne Autumn* (1964). Exactly the same sort of process occurs, and a good book by Marie Sandoz, written from the viewpoint of the Cheyenne, is destroyed in the bargain. Even its historical ending is twisted to imply that Secretary of the Interior Schultz (Edward G. Robinson) allowed the remnants of the Cheyenne to return to their home-land—which he most definitely did not.

SPORTS AND THE AMERICAN EMPIRE

MARK NAISON

Since the Second World War, sports have become a more visible and important part of American mass culture than ever before in our history. Through television coverage and heavy journalistic promotion, mass spectator sports have been made one of the major psychological reference points for American men, perhaps the single most important focus of emotion and energy in their leisure time. The corporations that finance this activity are capitalized at billions of dollars and are granted political privileges—gifts of land, stadiums constructed at public expense, immunity from antitrust legislation—that are normally extended only to "public utilities." This special status is reinforced by the American educational system, which sponsors an intensive program of spectator sports from grade school up and explicitly seeks to "train" athletes for professional ranks in its higher levels.

The support that organized sports has been given by government, business, and education is not coincidental. The sports industry has been self-consciously used as a safety valve for social discontent and a vehicle for the political and cultural unification of the American population. After the Second World War, sports became one of the major areas for the assimilation of new racial groups (blacks and Latinos) into the mainstream of American life and the incorporation of backward and developing regions (the South and Southwest) into the orbit of modern capitalist relations. Black players began to enter major-league sports in large numbers at the same time (1947–1950) that a series of executive orders "integrated" the U.S. armed forces, and the expansion of professional football and basketball and major-league baseball into the South directly followed the passage of federal civil rights legislation.

In addition, athletic events have increasingly reflected the dynamics of an emergent American imperialism. As the American political economy "internationalized" in the postwar period, many of its most distinctive cultural values and patterns, from consumerism to military preparedness, became integral parts of organized sports. Professional sports events have become "spectacles," the political and cultural impact of which lies as much in the marching bands, cheerleaders, commercial endorsements, and showcasing of politicians and visiting servicemen as in the competition on the field. The spectator is dazzled by an image of American civilization so overwhelming that it seems incomprehensible and futile to try to change it or exist outside its framework.

Nevertheless, the use of organized sports as an instrument of political control and repression has not been entirely successful. The enormous American sports industry has not only failed to defuse social discontent off the field, but it has also found itself increasingly torn by rebellion within its own ranks. The black

From *Radical America*, July–August 1972.

revolt, the antiwar movement, and women's liberation have all had an impact on contemporary sports, an impact that seems to grow progressively stronger the more sports are "capitalized" and exposed in the media. In the last twenty-five years, with more television coverage than ever, sports events have been interrupted by strikes, boycotts, and racial conflict to an unprecedented degree.

In addition, sports, particularly on a local level, continue to serve as vehicles for creativity, self-expression, and cultural growth for oppressed people. In black and white working-class and poor neighborhoods throughout America, participation in sports (as distinct from viewing) serves as a highly affirmative experience that can define communities, express personalities, and help people endure the pains of daily life. In Harlem, for example, basketball is more than just physical exercise and competition, it is a sphere of life in which young men affirmatively experience their blackness, feel the full flowering of their abilities, and experience pride in their origins and community. There is a kind of pathos (which is described in Peter Axheim's excellent book *The City Game*)—that in communities where creative outlets are few, opportunities for mobility limited, and forms of living death legion, a sport should become the focal point of such emotion and energy. But it also represents a triumph of human ingenuity and creativity, an example of people's ability to use an "irrelevant" or even repressive institution as a tool of self-development and solidarity.[1]

In the following pages, I will try to shed some light on the "double-edged" character of organized sports in the contemporary American scene—its emergence as a vehicle for the maintenance of corporate hegemony in America and the Empire, and its transformation into an instrument of political rebellion and the creation of new social relations. This essay is divided into three sections: the first deals with sports as a mirror of America's relationship with the Third World and the American black community, the second with the relationship of the sports industry to the changing position of women in American society, and the third with the effects of expanded media coverage and the corporate rationalization of sports on both athlete and spectator. In each section, we will observe a tension between the expanding use of athletic events to legitimize imperial goals and values, and the growing self-consciousness of groups directly or indirectly oppressed by the American sports industry.

Much of what follows will be highly speculative. It is not so much the product of original research as an effort to synthesize my own experiences as an athlete and sports fan with my readings on the dynamics of American capitalism and the position of black people and women in American society. Its interpretive stance has been greatly influenced by the writings of C. L. R. James, Selma James, and George Rawick and by long and often painful discussions with Paul Buhle. These individuals have enabled me to develop a view of history in which my interest in sports can be accepted as something other than a "political embarrassment" and by which revolution can be seen as a process that continually turns the most repressive aspects of society and culture into instruments of their own destruction. Much of the "inspiration" behind what follows is theirs; the faults are all mine.

SPORTS, DECOLONIZATION, AND THE DYNAMICS OF AMERICAN CAPITALISM: THE BLACK ATHLETE IN AMERICAN SPORTS

The rise of the black athlete has been one of the more dramatic occurrences in postwar professional sports. Since 1947, black football, basketball, and baseball players, once limited to segregated teams, have moved quickly into the major leagues in their respective sports. By the late 1960s, they had become a dominant force, comprising over half the professional basketball players, over one-quarter of baseball and football players, and the majority of "all-stars" in all three sports.[2]

The meaning of this phenomenon has been the subject of much journalistic speculation and barroom debate. The "superiority" of the black athlete has been attributed to everything from extra muscles in the legs to a unique bone structure to a "constitutional ability to remain calm under pressure."[3] However, such biological theories and images represent a fundamental misreading of the character of contemporary professional sports. Team sports are governed by the dynamics of modern industrial life, and they require highly specialized behavior. Professional athletes need far more than natural ability to succeed—as in almost any industrial work situation, athletes must practice their skills steadily, use strategic thinking, and cooperate with teammates and comrades (fellow workers). The rise of the black athlete thus tells us a lot more about the rapid movement of black people into urban society and their creative assimilation of industrial values than it does about inherited racial differences. Blacks now compose almost 40 percent of the work force in the American automobile industry and over half the transit work force in Chicago, New York, and Detroit; yet no one talks about the "natural propensity" of black people for assembly-line work or their "constitutional attraction" to fast-moving vehicles.

The significance of sports in the political modernization of agrarian (and colonial) people has been brilliantly analyzed by C. L. R. James in his history of cricket in the West Indies, *Beyond a Boundary*. As James shows, cricket was one of the primary vehicles by which English culture was transmitted to the West Indies, and West Indian identity was thus forged in a distinctive way. West Indians learned English values and the norms of industrial and commercial life as much on the cricket field as in the school and the workplace, and their success in developing great players and great teams marked their coming of age as a people. When West Indian teams demonstrated their ability to beat the best of the English teams using styles and techniques all their own, it symbolized their mastery of modern social organization, their ability to produce dominant personalities, and the viability of their traditional cultures. Cricket, a sport that had been imported to legitimize English culture and English rule, was thus transformed into a proving ground for West Indian self-government.

With some modifications, the same analysis can help us understand the role that soccer has played in defining "national identity" in South American countries. That game has been taken to unparalleled heights of skill by South American teams who have incorporated the rhythms of dance into their play. The South American soccer leagues bring together, in a creative context, seemingly conflicting elements in their national culture, fusing modern mass society and commercialism (embodied in the huge stadiums, the crowds, and the publicity surrounding the games) with traditional folkways and rivalries. The mixture is an explosive one—full of riots, violent assaults, and stampeding crowds—but it is an accurate mirror of the tensions of contemporary life that these societies experience. In countries such as Brazil, soccer has become an affirmative embodiment of the national experience, in which the personality forms, values, and tensions of modern civilization are played off against the distinctive local cultures—which people must remain in touch with if they are to keep their sense of balance in times of rapid social change.

A more dramatic example of this process can be found in the growing popularity of "American" sports (baseball and basketball) in postwar Japan and the Spanish-speaking Caribbean (Puerto Rico, the Dominican Republic, Cuba, Venezuela, Colombia, Mexico). Baseball came into Japan with the American military occupation and soon became that country's most popular spectator sport. A similar experience took place somewhat earlier in the Caribbean, where baseball was popularized by the increasing number of American corporate and military personnel who entered those countries after the Spanish-American War.[4] The sport became a vehicle of adjustment to American imperialism, its popularity an index of America's success in engendering adulation of its culture and values. Nevertheless, the process that began as imitation soon assumed other proportions. As athletes were produced capable of competing with or beating the Americans (as happened with Caribbean baseball players in the fifties and sixties), and because these "stars" embodied qualities distinctive to the country, the sport became an instrument of national pride and independence. It is no accident that one of Fidel Castro's favorite ways of demonstrating his closeness to the people was to travel around the country playing baseball with workers and peasants, or that Cuba's victory over American volleyball and basketball teams in the Pan-American games was viewed as a symbolic triumph for the revolution.

The experience of black Americans in professional sports has followed a similar dynamic of assimilation and resistance. The integration of black athletes into the major leagues had been fought for years by the black press and the organized left (the *Daily Worker* and the Harlem *People's Voice* had been particularly active in the fight), but its implementation took the form of a calculated edict from the top designed to reinforce the legitimacy of American institutions.[5] Branch Rickey's "pioneering act," carefully cleared with Truman administration leaders, New York City politicians, and local community leaders,[6] was one of a variety of coincident decisions (the executive order desegregating the armed forces and the Truman civil rights act were others) designed to adjust American society to the requirements of the postwar world and to help bring a strategically located black population (increasingly urban and industrial) into the mainstream of American society. With the U.S. economy increasingly dependent on the penetration and control of emerging nations, racial segregation had become a political embarrassment that could be exploited by the Soviet bloc or anticolonial revolutionaries to mobilize resistance to U.S. aims. The more far-sighted American leaders saw the need to create at least a facade of racial equality and harmony in key American institutions, and they were willing to use sports to get that message across to the American public as well as the large international audience.

From the perspective of the black community, integration in sports (as in other areas of life) represented both an opportunity to get a larger share of the rewards of industrial society and an end to irksome racial prohibitions. The black community had had its own professional sports leagues ever since the great migration to the cities after World War I, but these leagues were poorly financed, poorly organized, and unable to provide their players with anywhere near the income of their counterparts in "the majors."[7] Jackie Robinson's signing with the Brooklyn Dodgers in 1947 thus symbolized to black Americans the opening of a whole new era, filled with both opportunities and dangers.[8] They were excited by the chance their best athletes would be getting to "prove themselves" in the ballpark and get into the big money, but they were also concerned about the insults, humiliations, and internal tensions the athletes would have to endure as they confronted white society.

The "case" of Jackie Robinson put all these competing pressures and emotions on the line. When Robinson was chosen to integrate professional baseball—then far and away the most popular American spectator sport—he was faced with incredible mental pressures that almost thrust the question of his physical ability into the background. To succeed, Robinson had to maintain his concentration, his self-discipline, and his enthusiasm for the game in the face of threats, insults, ostracism, and condescension, and he had to live with the knowledge that millions of black people were investing their hopes in his performance while millions of whites were hoping he would fail. Robinson was selected for this task not because he was clearly the best black ball player (Sam Jethroe and Larry Doby had equivalent reputations, and Satchel Paige was a household word),[9] but because he was deemed best equipped to stand the pressure—in short, to function as a symbol of the black community.[10] College-educated, articulate by white standards, possessed of great personal dignity, Robinson survived his ordeal well enough to win "Rookie of the Year" honors and make the All-Star game. To many black people, he became the definitive symbol of their arrival into the mainstream of American life.

But if Robinson's experience represented a vindication of black hopes for a new era in race relations, it also reflected the rather restricted boundaries within which the system intended "racial integration" to occur. To liberal whites, Robinson was the archetypical "acceptable" Negro, a person who fit all the standards of white society and would not rock the boat. In the press, the radio, and the bulletins of the U.S. Information Agency and the Voice of America, he was presented as an example of America's racial progress and of black people's loyalty to the American political system. When Paul Robeson made his famous speech saying that black people would not fight on the U.S. side in a war with the Soviet Union, Robinson was called before the House Un-American Activities Committee to assert that black people identified completely with America and would repudiate Robeson.[11] Under such conditions, whites could easily see racial integration in sports as an opportunity for self-congratulation.

However, the ability of whites to control the context of racial integration in sports was to prove considerably more limited in succeeding years. In the late 1950s two black athletes, Bill Russell in basketball and Jim Brown in football, emerged as dominant figures in their sports in a manner that gave whites little grounds for self-congratulation. Both of these men were intelligent, independent, and fiercely proud; they refused the gratuitous displays of gratitude that sports journalists demanded and made no secret of their distaste for racial discrimination in any form.[12] Their superiority in their respective sports was so great, their reputations so awesome, that they could define the terms on which they interacted with whites to a far greater degree than most Americans, black or white, were used to. Both men were living contradictions to prevailing racial stereotypes and images. Although both were great athletes, the distinctive elements in their superiority were concentration, self-discipline, and an unwavering drive to succeed (classic elements for success in American sports and American capitalist society). Aloof from their teammates, in tune with hidden and internalized sources of energy, they went to incredible lengths to psyche themselves up before games—Russell to the point of having to throw up from nervous tension before every contest. The unwavering dignity and professionalism of these two black men enforced respect even from people who opposed their political positions and their avoidance of journalistic rituals. They helped create a new image of black self-consciousness in America, fully within the framework of American capitalist values and male supremacy but transcendent of the historic racial dynamic that required whites to take the initiative in defining race relations.

An even further step in defining black self-consciousness was taken by Muhammad Ali (born Cassius Clay), a black prizefighter from Louisville, Kentucky. Clay began his career as an exuberant, highly talented youth who alternately delighted and annoyed the American fighting public with his mocking predictions of his opponents' downfall, his poetry, and his complete absence of false modesty ("I'm the greatest"). Although he flouted the unwritten norms of the sports world by his refusal to act humble, he hardly seemed a very threatening figure—indeed, his bragging was regarded benignly by some whites as a reaffirmation of racial stereotypes ("What do you expect from a nigger?") and as a comforting sign of lack of discipline.

It was an incredible shock when Cassius Clay, that laughing, jiving kid, beat the most fearsome heavyweight of his time, Sonny Liston, and then announced that his victory was due to the influence of the Nation of Islam. Changing his name to Muhammad Ali, Clay swore off drinking, smoking, and sexual excess and proclaimed his belief in black independence and racial separation. After a year of fighting under his new banner, Ali was drafted, but he refused to enter the armed forces. The reaction of the sports establishment in America, which had spent millions of dollars promoting Ali as a "fresh new face on the boxing scene," was swift and brutal. Ali lost his license to fight in most of the United

States, was charged with draft evasion, and was almost universally condemned in the press as "ungrateful and unpatriotic."

Throughout, Ali was the decisive psychological victor. He served notice on white America that it could not unopposedly use racial integration on a symbolic level to legitimize its domination of nonwhite peoples. In his public statements, Ali argued that black people had a tie of solidarity with nonwhite people around the world, including the Vietnamese, which transcended any loyalty to the U.S. government. In his speeches, his political actions, and his approach to sports, he embodied the spirit of decolonization—the commitment of oppressed peoples to transform the mechanisms of Western capitalist rule into instruments of popular liberation. He was viewed by young blacks as a symbol of black manhood—a man who combined the survival skills of the ghetto (rapping, psychological warfare, physical strength, the "hustle") with an uncommon self-discipline and willingness to sacrifice wealth for principle. He represented, much like Malcolm X, a new image of *being*, a portent of higher human possibilities.

Ali, like most heroes fortunate enough to avoid assassination, has been cut down to more human proportions in succeeding years. After the initial shock wore off, the American sports establishment, like the American ruling class in general,[13] moved to co-opt black nationalism into the mainstream of American culture and to remove its "revolutionary" implications. As soon as Ali was cleared of his draft charge, athletic commissions throughout the country renewed his license, and sports reporters literally fell over one another trying to interview him and mark his return as "one of the boys." Ali, weary of his ordeal and perhaps somewhat disillusioned by factional struggles in the Nation of Islam, returned to his earlier position as the "darling" of the American press, appearing on talk shows, giving play-by-plays of sports events, even helping to "roast" Sammy Davis, Jr., at the Friars' Club (a humorous ritual honoring entertainers). He never lost his primary sense of commitment to black people, maintaining an intensive schedule of speaking engagements and boxing exhibitions in the black community. But the cutting edge of his rebellion was gone, limited by the inability of the movement to which he was tied to forge a stable political or economic base for black independence in America. He had helped pave the way for the "coming of black men"[14] as a force in American society and had helped legitimize black nationalism as a political and cultural stance (when Lew Alcindor changed his name to Kareem Abdul-Jabbar, sports announcers accepted the change without discussion or protest), but he could not stop the absorption of black people into the sports industry or their acceptance of many of its values.

The political pacification of Muhammad Ali dramatizes some of the most painful dilemmas facing the black movement in America. Although black people have experienced a form of oppression similar to that of their brethren in the Third World, they find it impossible to liberate themselves through a movement of national independence. The dispersion of the black population through the country and its employment in the center of the American industrial infrastructure (heavy industry, government employment, the armed forces) means that the black movement can escape the domination of capital and its attendant social relationships only if capital itself is destroyed. The black revolt in sports, like the black movement as a whole, inevitably becomes a "reform" movement when it does not connect its nationalist aims to a large struggle to transform American society.

There is perhaps no better example of the political limitations of the black revolt in sports (and much of the black movement generally) than the image of male supremacy that it projects. Although the new forms of "social personality" forged by black athletes represent a transcendence of historic patterns of racial control in America, they present no challenge to the domination of men over women on which the very fabric of American capitalism is woven. The Nation of Islam, the organization from which Ali drew strength, inspiration, and political support for his rebellion, has explicitly defined the subordination of black women as a precondition for the liberation of black men. The image of "black manhood" embodied by Jim Brown in his football career, his acting, and his personal life seems to be an Afro-American amalgam of Errol Flynn and James Bond—an image in which women are alternately seen as status symbols, sexual partners, and targets for aggression.

The racial transformation of commercial sports in America, while often disquieting to both the sports establishment and the American public, has thus far been contained within the framework of capitalist and male-supremacist relations. Although black people have been able to use athletics as an arena for self-development, self-expression, and the creative affirmation of black "nationality," they have been unable to transcend the attendant value system which makes domination, competition, and personal profit the highest social ideals.

It remains to be seen whether a similar neutralization can be accomplished with movements for women's liberation. The growing power of women in postwar American life has not been reflected in commercial sports. The massive participation of women in the labor market, and the accompanying, though grudging, democratization of family life that this has produced,[15] have no analogies in the sports world, where the hiring of a few female jockeys and the more vigorous promotion of women's tennis are the only noticeable "reforms." Indeed, the expansion of commercial athletics has been so dramatically impervious to women's influence that questions have been raised as to whether sports, like the "new sexuality," is being used to culturally sustain male-supremacist behavior at a time when an objective social basis for that behavior is diminishing. In any case, the relationship between sports and the women's struggle is an important subject to examine, and I will try to suggest a framework that may make some of the contradictions comprehensible.

SPORTS, WOMEN, AND THE
IDEOLOGY OF DOMINATION

In exposing the relationship between the "sports industries" and the emerging women's struggle, I would like to draw attention to three coincident trends in the postwar political economy. First we must recognize the growing importance of women in the labor market and the effect this has had on male-female relations in the family, the workplace, the educational system, and the bedroom. As Selma

James points out, the entry of women into the labor market during the Second World War "created in women a new awareness of themselves . . . expanded their conception of their capacities, and cracked . . . open the economic basis of the subordination of women." [16] When the pattern persisted after the war (by 1966, one-third of married women were working), it created a crisis of "roles" in both working-class and middle-class families. With the economic basis for male "authoritarianism" in the family (the single paycheck) weakening, male-female relations entered a period of struggle, sometimes hostile and politicized (among the middle class), sometimes veiled behind a mutual concern for survival (among the working class and poor). As James described it: "Men, particularly young men who have been trained to exercise domination, but have had little opportunity to do so, find themselves lost in their relations with these new women." [17] Their diminishing power over their wives and children evokes feelings of frustration that must be exorcised through social activity or rendered insignificant by more satisfying experiences in other spheres of life.

Second, and equally significant for our purposes, has been the increasing bureaucratization and "Taylorization" of factory and office work and the bargaining away by the labor movement of worker control over the quality and pace of production. Between 1940 and 1956, the once-militant CIO unions, with the lure of "high wages," assumed the role of disciplining workers to managerial imperatives of "efficiency" and became what amounted to a middle layer of the managerial bureaucracy. Workers who once had unions or shop committees responsive to their needs found themselves faced with simply another hierarchy of relentless impersonality which did nothing to stop the speedups and changes in production methods that took away what little pride workers had in their job and product. In addition, the growing service sector of the economy brought with it an increasing "proletarianization" of white-collar work, which was reflected in the rise of civil service unions but not in a more satisfying work experience. For the majority of working Americans, craftsmanship, creativity, and feelings of community became experiences sought in leisure activities, not through work. [18]

A third significant phenomenon was the emergence of the United States as a full-blown imperial power, with a political and military "line of defense" on every continent. The entire society was mobilized, behind the banner of anticommunism, to higher levels of effort—as workers, as soldiers, as managers, as consumers. Never in American history had there been so coordinated an effort to discipline the American people to a common cause, in this instance the cause of world domination. Education, music, sports, in fact all aspects of culture became infused with the dynamics of the need to protect the empire.

The psychology of domination thus became an increasingly important theme in American life, but at a time when the historic domination of men over women was diminishing and the control by workers of the productive process was shrinking. As a result, the day-to-day experience of the American male did not confirm what he was constantly told: that he was a hero and a "world runner." Whatever frustrations resulted from this contradiction had to be expressed outside the workplace, where a struggle for greater control of production might reduce "efficiency" or challenge some corporate priorities. One legitimate outlet became

consumerism—which made the accumulation of property, appliances, and hob-
bies a focal point of energy and emotion, but through which more violent,
aggressive feelings could not be fully released. The most socially destructive
feelings, when they were not actually being lived (with wives, children, work
companions, friends, racial and political opponents) found their outlet in two
areas—commercialized sex and commercialized sports, both of which reached
new levels of development in the postwar period.

The use of sports and sexuality as outlets for violent and guilt-provoking feelings is nothing new; they have served that function throughout the history of industrial society and probably much before. Violent games and rituals such as
rugby, hurling, boxing, wrestling, and cock-fighting have been part of the daily
life of European and American working men for centuries, as have prostitution
and pornography in their various forms.

What is new in postwar America is the scale on which they are organized,
their expression in nationwide media (some of which, like television, are new
inventions), and their penetration by corporate values and relations. In the last
twenty years, for example, the imagery of sexual domination and exploitation
has become a major theme in the culture, dominating the consumer market, the
film industry, popular music, and the agencies that define values for courtship,
marriage, and the family (such as popular magazines and medical books).
Women, once seen as the repositories of morality and civilized culture, have
been projected as sexual beings whose new freedom offers men unimagined possibilities for sexual consumption. The advertising industry and magazines like
Playboy offer a new, more hedonistic image of male domination to replace the
declining authority of the family man. With the help of filmmakers, psychia-
trists, and progressive clergymen, these media suggest that every woman should
now provide what men once sought in prostitutes—a seductive, but fundamentally passive, sexuality that would affirm men's feelings of competence. Female
sexuality is projected as a legitimate "catch-all" for male anxieties, a narcotic
that eases the pain of daily existence. In both reality and projective fantasy, men
are encouraged to find in sex and the experience of control (over women, over
themselves) what is lacking in their economic and social life.

The success of this "sexualization" of daily experience is questionable. Despite the incredible propaganda campaign, women have resisted sexual objectification, and most men find it difficult to get their wives and lovers to play the
roles defined in *Playboy*. Nevertheless, what is unattainable in relationships is
made available in fantasy. The growing culture of pornography in America—top-
less dancers, X-rated movies, sex novels and magazines—represent efforts to
provide a vicarious experience that meets male needs for sexual dominance. In
daily life, then, women have won a kind of quiet victory; by their own self-
activity, they have forced the most repressive aspects of the "new sexuality" out
of the household, out of sexual encounters, and into compensatory fantasies, art,
and masturbation.

The growth of commercial athletics in the postwar period mirrors many of the
same developments and the same struggles. The increasing coverage of sports in
the national media, like the increasing use of sexual images and incentives, aims

at the reinforcement of ideals of male dominance that are being undercut in daily life. The major commercial sports—baseball, football, basketball, ice hockey, and auto racing—allow women to participate only as cheerleaders, spectators, and advertising images, a situation that hardly mirrors the increasing participation of women in the job market or the growing influence of women in the family. Moreover, these games are not so much played as they are observed. Unlike tennis, golf, volleyball, table tennis, and softball, games a whole family can participate in and enjoy democratically, these five all-male sports have expanded nationwide, catalyzed the construction of new stadiums, and acquired enormous television, radio, and newspaper coverage—all without a significant increase in the degree to which they are *played*. The American male spends a far greater portion of his time with sports than he did forty years ago, but the greatest proportion of that time is spent in front of a television set observing games that he will hardly ever play.

THE CORPORATE RATIONALIZATION
OF SPORTS: REPRESSION
AND RESISTANCE

The political and psychological implications of the massive promotion of spectator sports are worth investigating in some detail. The major commercial sports, as we have suggested before, are all-male games with a fairly high incidence of violence; they provide emotionally involved spectators with an opportunity to purge themselves of aggressive feelings. Most important, the presentation of these sports is now characterized by corporate forms of organization and military and technological imagery. The man watching a football game on television sees not only huge men smashing each other (just as he would like to do, possibly to his boss, his wife, or his kids) but also the reduplication of military and corporate thinking. Elaborate offensive and defensive "maneuvers," discussions of "field generalship," and analyses of "what it takes to win" reinforce images of strong men running things and legitimize the strategies by which America seeks to maintain its empire. From their former role of simply enshrining willpower, competition, and physical strength, spectator sports in America have come to glorify strategic thinking and technological rationality as contemporary masculine values. The violence, the brutality, and the vicarious identification are still central elements, but they have been appropriated for more sophisticated ends.

This "modernization" of the sports world has had a decisive effect on the life of the professional athlete. As professional (and college) sports have become bigger and bigger business (with television rights, advertising contracts, and huge arenas) athletes have been increasingly subjected to industrial norms and disciplines. From grade school through high school up to college and professional ranks, the "production" of star athletes has been systematized along superficially rational lines. Sports programs in most American schools are tracking systems designed not to maintain physical fitness among their students but to select potential stars for training. On each level, players are disciplined, skills are refined, and the stars are guided to the next level. Those who succeed in sports are often discouraged from serious academic concerns. Arrangements are made to provide tutors, term papers, and "gentlemen's Cs" so that intellectual labors will not interfere with athletic proficiency. In the great sports factories (Syracuse, Michigan, UCLA, and the like), many of the athletes in major sports do not actually attain their degrees.

By the time a player "makes it" to the pro ranks, the pressure on him escalates astronomically. Pro athletes are given training regimens that refine their special skills but can handicap them for life. As Dave Meggysey points out in his excellent book *Out of Their League*, professional football players are forced to strain their bodies beyond physically tolerable limits in both training and games and are given amphetamines to increase their energy level and steroids to help them put on weight. The most famous football coach of modern times, Vince Lombardi, was renowned for insisting that his players perform with sprains, viruses, and broken bones: one of his favorite players, Jerry Kramer, was nicknamed "the Zipper" because he continued to play after many serious operations. Even in sports such as baseball and basketball, which have a lower level of violence than football, players continue to play with injuries that leave them nearly crippled (Mickey Mantle, Tony Oliva, Gus Johnson, and Willis Reed for example), and many become inured to existing with constant pain. The average professional "athlete" is probably less physically healthy than a normal person his age, and considers himself lucky to finish his career without permanent physical and mental damage.

The irony of this situation (not to mention its brutality) is lost on the American sports fan, though. Every weekend tens of millions of men sit before their television sets and in stadiums and arenas, rising with their victories, falling with their defeats, and emerging temporarily purged of their anger, their frustration, their feelings of impotence. Some of them, if they have the energy, go out to the playground and, with each jump shot, base hit, or cross body block, put flesh onto their fantasies. This strange, this sad, this painfully self-deceiving network of rituals is part of the basic fabric of American life—a safety valve for aggression and a crucible for social values organic to modern capitalism. It is a central stabilizing element in American culture: organized and financed by the corporate elite but supported by millions of men because it provides an outlet for overwhelming inner needs.

However, there is growing resistance within the sports world to many of its most repressive cultural and political patterns. Both inside and outside professional sports, the credibility of the sports establishment's values, images, and business practices is being questioned and challenged. This counterstruggle cannot as yet be called a "movement," for it has been diffuse and self-contradictory and has thus far failed to project an alternative vision of athletic activity and organization. But it has forced political conflict and economic struggle into commercial athletics in a way that has undercut the ability of sports to reinforce corporate values and serve as an "escape" from the anxieties of daily life.

Within professional sports proper, the most important sign of resistance has been the growing strength and militancy of the players' associations, culminating in recent baseball strikes. This movement can be seen as a direct response to the proletarianization of athletes in major sports. Although salaries have been increasing rapidly in the postwar period, players have been experiencing the introduction into their lives of "speedup" and scientific management. In all major sports, the athlete's work life has become more difficult and dangerous because of the lengthening of the season and the imposition of new performance norms. Baseball, basketball, and football players all have a longer "regular season" than they did fifteen years ago, and a longer exhibition schedule. In addition, training procedures have been scientifically refined to produce the maximum response from their bodies. Professional athletes are now given IQ and personality tests (the Dallas Cowboys won't let anybody with an IQ of less than 120 play quarterback), trained with machines, given special diets, and bolstered with drugs.

This introduction of corporate discipline into what are fondly called "games" has increased the number of injuries, but it has also brought collective organization into a historically individualistic milieu. Players' organizations, uniting "stars" and journeyman players, have assumed an ever greater bargaining role in major sports, threatening—and recently using—the strike as a weapon to force the owners' hands. Their most basic demand has been for pension plans that provide security for the injured and retired athlete—a demand with great force in a field where the average playing span is four to six years, and where the player is often left physically and mentally unequipped for the job market.

The proletarianization of athletics has also generated more individual forms of resistance. A number of star athletes in major sports have begun to challenge the "reserve clause"—the rule that enables a team to purchase exclusive rights to a player and prevent him from playing for another club unless he is sold or traded. This regulation, with its analogues to slavery, was challenged in the courts by Curt Flood, formerly a star outfielder with the St. Louis Cardinals, and was upheld in 1972 by the Supreme Court. It has been challenged more effectively in practice, however, by professional basketball players who have "jumped" from one basketball league to another in violation of their contracts in order to gain high salaries or more satisfactory living or playing conditions.

In these highly publicized cases, black athletes have taken the lead. Owners, fans, and journalists have attacked free agents for lack of loyalty to their teams and contempt for the traditions of the game, but such criticism has not stopped Flood, Vida Blue, Earl Monroe (who refused to play in Baltimore), Charley Scott, Spencer Haywood, and others from forcing owners to bid against one another for their services. The growing commercialism of sports, as well as its dangers, has removed from the minds of the players such "romanticism" as the leagues try to project and has reduced motivations on all levels to the mere calculation of maximum financial advantage. Star players use their bargaining power increasingly to force teams to give them a share of the profits and to help set them up in business with loans and investments. The black athletes have been most aggressive in this respect, having learned from experience that they are least likely to be "taken care of" by their sports or by private industry when their playing careers are over. Their actions, even when "selfishly" motivated, have helped to strip the aura of sanctity from the sports world and have shown an often unwilling public its true character. It is an excellent example of how capitalism can help dig its own grave through the extension of its own most cherished values.

The increasing "economic chaos" in commercial sports has been paralleled by the beginnings of a political and cultural critique of the sports establishment's values and goals. In recent years, several leading sports figures have taken "unpopular" political stances, and a few have begun to question the function sports are made to serve in American society. Beginning with Muhammad Ali, black athletes have been increasingly outspoken about racism in sports and society and have refused to accept the traditional dictum that "politics" be kept out of the playing field or the sports interview. Black athletes in pro and college ranks give clenched-fist salutes when introduced; use the black handshake in center jumps and other rituals; have pressed steadily for black representation in coaching, announcing, cheerleading, and sports administration; and have generally challenged the illusion that loyalty to the team and sport comes before race, politics, or personal interest. An increasing number of white athletes have also taken political or cultural stances, announcing their opposition to the Vietnam War, their commitment to new life-styles, and their doubts about the brutality or the political uses of athletics.

These actions, however, have not qualitatively changed the character of commercial sports. The sports industry, like the American empire as a whole, manages to stumble through its opposition with its violence, its brutality, and its grim will to prevail yet unchecked. As long as the social relations of contemporary capitalism generate in American men a need for violent outlets and a vicarious experience of mastery, the corporations will be glad to finance the sports industry and mold it in their own image. The rebellion in the sports world must be accompanied by a struggle to transform the most significant institutional centers of American life if it is to humanize this aspect of our culture. Only as creative, cooperative activity begins to govern human relations in production, child-rearing, and sexuality, only as the imperatives of maintaining the empire diminish, can we begin to divest sports of the responsibility for legitimizing violent and dominating behavior and make democratic participation, rather than "rooting," the focal point of athletic involvement.

Slowly, often undramatically, the basis for a new approach to sports is developing. The growing power of women in American society, although it has evoked a counterreaction in many areas, has paved the way for more democratic relations in the family, the educational system, the job market, and politics. The women's movement may often have increased the level of social tension, but it has also certainly begun to help erode the psychological "stake" in authoritarian behavior. In those sectors of society where a conscious women's movement has been strongest and the brutality of daily life least overwhelming (among déclassé or white middle-class youth, for example), women have taken the lead in developing new approaches to sports, exercise, and physical health. In youth communities, on college campuses, and in urban parks where young people congregate, men and women can be seen playing previously male sports (soccer, softball, touch football, basketball) in a newly noncompetitive way, inventing new sports

6

(frisbee), and practicing calisthenics and self-defense (judo, karate, and the like). In addition, people in these groups have begun to challenge patterns of diet, musculature, and physical well-being projected by the consumer culture and have sought a more comfortable relation with both nature and self that looks toward a reduction in the basic sources of violence and aggression.

These new patterns are not capable, in themselves, of providing a model for "athletic revolution." Among the industrial working class and the poor there is justifiable suspicion that the vision of athletics projected by the "counterculture" neglects the opportunities for achievement, self-expression, and communal solidarity that competitive sports can provide. In working-class communities throughout America, sports leagues that place a premium on good fellowship and skill continue to thrive, and it is hard to envision them "withering away" into a hippie paradise where everyone plays at the same level in the interest of cooperation. Nor is this situation necessarily reactionary. As sports critic Jack Scott points out, the disciplined pursuit of athletic excellence is intrinsically no more harmful than the development of scientific, literary, or artistic skill.[19] Rather, the problem has been the context in which such skills have been cultivated and the uses to which they have been put.

If this point is understood, we can help set the stage for a broad attack on the more alienating aspects of American sports and particularly its legitimation of the dominance of men over women. The ability of men to run faster, jump higher, or hit a ball farther offers no more "natural" claim to power in advanced industrial society than does the ability of women to have children, and the one-sided glorification of maleness that pervades American athletics is ripe to be subverted. Women have begun to press for equal opportunity to develop their athletic talents, and have won a few significant victories. In schools throughout the country, women have won the right to play on tennis, golf, and even basketball teams, have organized their own teams in football, basketball, and volleyball, and have begun to raise questions about male domination of athletic departments. In addition, women professionals in tennis and golf have achieved some concessions in their demand for parity with men in the distribution of prize money and have attracted far greater recognition for their performance in the press. These changes are hardly revolutionary, but they do give some indication of the opportunities for concerted action.

The greatest single obstacle to such democratization lies in the structure of the sports industry and the media with which it is allied. At no time has the potential for broad and nondominating athletic participation been so obvious, yet at no time has the sports industry made such a concerted effort to get people to watch rather than play. (There is an average of six hours of sports on television every Saturday and Sunday during most of the year.) The athletic "spectacle" has become the definitive mode of social manipulation for American capitalism, absorbing the viewer's energies in a hypnotic panoply of crowds, contests, and commercials. It can be transcended, but only by activity that strikes at the *need* for this kind of entertainment. A radical transformation of sports must be linked to a larger effort to bring about people's control of production and communication and to develop satisfying proximate relations in the family, the community, and the workplace. The vicarious, abstract stimulation provided by the sports industry will lose much of its appeal when people are involved in struggle and creative activity.

Notes

1. The notion of an instrument of repression (or of socialization to an oppressive system) becoming a tool of liberation has been influenced by George Rawick's discussion of the role of the black church during slavery in *The Makings of the Black Community, from Sundown to Sunup* (Westport, Conn.: Greenwood Press, 1972).

2. Harry Edwards, "The Sources of the Black Athlete's Superiority," *The Black Scholar*, November 1971, p. 34.

3. Ibid., pp. 35–38.

4. Professional baseball leagues had been organized in Cuba as early as 1910, only ten years after the conclusion of the Spanish-American War. From that time on, interest in the game increased steadily, and white and black stars of American teams frequently traveled to Cuba to play there when their seasons were over. Black players in particular cherished this opportunity, for the salaries they received were often higher than those the black teams were paying, and they were received in hotels and restaurants without the humiliation of Jim Crow. Even today the Caribbean leagues (now concentrated in the Dominican Republic, Colombia, and Puerto Rico) offer black players substantially greater opportunity to exercise leadership than do the "majors"—for example, several black players are managers in the winter leagues, a situation that no major-league team has emulated as yet. See Robert W. Petersen, *Only the Ball Was White* (Englewood Cliffs, N.J., 1970) for a good description of the role of black Americans in Caribbean baseball.

5. Both Petersen (ibid., p. 184) and Joseph Starobin, (*American Communism in Crisis, 1943–1956* [Cambridge, 1972], pp. 30–31) mention the role of the *Daily Worker* in pressing the major leagues to enroll black ball players. However Starobin greatly overstates his case when he claims that "this was the almost singlehanded work of the *Daily Worker* sports editor." Black newspapers such as the *Pittsburgh Courier* and the *Chicago Defender* had been pressing this issue for years, as had a radical Harlem daily called the *People's Voice*, which was tied to both Adam Clayton Powell and the Communist party.

6. Petersen, *Only the Ball Was White*, pp. 183–205.

7. As Petersen (ibid.) points out, the black leagues suffered a rapid decline in attendance and interest as soon as significant numbers of black players entered the majors. Only during the Second World War had the leagues attained anywhere near the stability and organization of the majors, and their salaries remained, with one or two exceptions, far below the "big-league" level. There was surprisingly little sentiment on behalf of the retention of the black teams, even in nationalistic communities such as Harlem and the South Side of Chicago. By 1958 there were no black professional baseball teams left on any scale except a Globetrotter-like group called the Indianapolis Clowns.

8. At a dinner honoring Jackie Robinson, Bill Russell made a speech saying that at the time Robinson came into the majors he "was carrying black people on his shoulders."

9. Petersen (*Only the Ball Was White*, p. 193) quotes a black player named Buck Leonard as saying: "We didn't think he was going to get there. We thought we had other ballplayers who were better players than he. We thought maybe they were going to get there, but we didn't think he would."

10. Ibid., p. 189.

11. From "Communist Influence Among Negroes—Fact or Illusion," National Urban

League Pamphlet, 1949. Robinson's statement of July 19, 1949, before the House Un-American Activities Committee was reprinted here in full. The statement was prepared for "Hearings Regarding Communist Infiltration of Minority Groups," during which Robinson said: "I can't speak for fifteen million people any more than any other one person, but I know myself that I've got too much invested for my wife and child and myself in the future of this country, and I and other Americans of many races and faiths have too much invested in this country's welfare to throw it away because of a siren song sung in bass. . . . But that doesn't mean we're going to stop fighting race discrimination in this country until we've got it licked. It means that we're going to fight all the harder because our stake in the future is so big. We can win our fight without the communists, and we don't want their help."

12. Russell asserted: "I had made up my mind that I would not become the bigot's stereotype of the Negro. I would not be the laughing boy, seeking their favors. . . . There were some who expected me to curry favor with them. I had news for them, baby. I didn't and I won't. I wrote some controversial articles, but I believed them at the time. I was talking human rights before it was popular" (Bill Russell with William McSweeney, *Go Up for Glory* [New York, 1966], p. 55).

13. See Robert Allen, *Black Awakening in Capitalist America* (New York, 1969), for the best available analysis of the corporate response to black nationalism.

14. See Vincent Harding's essay "Beyond Chaos: Black History and the Search for the New Land," in *Amistad I* (New York, 1970), for an excellent example of how an extremely sophisticated spokesman for black nationalism sees the black liberation movement of the 1960s as "the coming of black men."

15. See Selma James, "The American Family, Decay and Rebirth," *Radical America*, February 1971.

16. Ibid., p. 13.

17. Ibid., p. 15.

18. Paul Baran and Paul Sweezy, *Monopoly Capital* (New York, 1966), pp. 232, 244.

19. Jack Scott, "Sports Radical Ethic," *Intellectual Digest*, July 1972, pp. 49–50.

INTRODUCTION TO *HOW TO READ DONALD DUCK*

DAVID KUNZLE

The Walt Disney World logo is a terrestrial globe wearing Mickey Mouse ears, enclosed in the letter D.

The presidents change; Disney remains. Forty-six years after the birth of Mickey Mouse, eight years after the death of his master, Disney's may be the most widely known North American name in the world. He is, arguably, the century's most important figure in bourgeois popular culture. He has done more than any single person to disseminate throughout the world certain myths upon which that culture has thrived, notably that of a supposedly universal "innocence," beyond place, beyond time—and beyond criticism.

The myth of U.S. political "innocence" is at last being dismantled, and the reality it masks now lies in significant areas exposed to public view. But the great American dream of cultural innocence still holds a global imagination in thrall. The first major breach into the Disney part of this dream was made by Richard Schickel's *The Disney Version: The Life, Times, Art and Commerce of Walt Disney* (1968). But even this analysis, penetrating and caustic as it is, in many respects remains prey to the illusion that Disney productions, even at their worst, are somehow redeemed by the fact that, made in "innocent fun," they are socially harmless.

Disney is no mean conjuror, and it has taken the Dorfman and Mattelart eye to expose the magician's sleight of hand, to reveal the scowl of capitalist ideology behind the laughing mask, the iron fist beneath the Mouse's glove. The value of their book *How to Read Donald Duck* lies not so much in their analysis of a particular group of comics or even a particular cultural entrepreneur but in the way capitalist and imperialist values are shown to be supported by the culture itself. And the very simplicity of the comics has enabled the authors to make simply visible a very complicated process.

Many cultural critics in the United States bridle at the magician's unctuous patter and shrink from his bland fakery, and in so doing they fail to recognize just what he is faking and the extent to which it is not just things or animatronic robots he manipulates, but people, human beings. Unfortunately, the army of media critics have focused over the past decades principally on "sex and violence" films, "horror comics," and the peculiar inanities of the television sitcom as the great bludgeons of the popular sensibility. If important sectors of the intelligentsia in the United States have been lulled into silent complicity with Disney, it can only be because they share his basic values and see the broad public as enjoying the same cultural privileges. But this complicity becomes positively criminal when their common ideology is imposed on noncapitalist, under-

Excerpted from Ariel Dorfman and Armand Mattelart, *How to Read Donald Duck*, translated and with an Introduction by David Kunzle (New York: International General, 1975).

developed countries with no regard to the grotesque disparity between the Disney dream of wealth and leisure and the *real* needs in the Third World.

It is no accident that the first thoroughgoing analysis of the Disney ideology should come from one of the most economically and culturally dependent colonies of the U.S. empire. *How to Read Donald Duck* was born in the heat of the struggle to free Chile from that dependency, and it has since become, with its eleven Latin American editions, a most potent instrument for the interpretation of bourgeois media in the Third World.

Until 1970, Chile was completely in pawn to U.S. corporate interests, with a foreign debt that ranked second highest per capita in the world. And even under the Popular Unity government (1970–1973), which initiated the peaceful road to socialism, it proved easier to nationalize copper than to free the mass media from U.S. influence. The most popular television channel in Chile imported about half its material from the United States (including "FBI," "Mission: Impossible," and "The Mickey Mouse Club"), and until June 1972, 80 percent of the films shown in the cinemas (Chile had virtually no native film industry) came from the United States. The major chain of newspapers and magazines, including *El mercurio*, was owned by Agustin Edwards, a vice-president of Pepsi Cola who also controlled many of the largest industrial corporations in Chile as a Miami, Florida, resident. With so much of the mass media serving conservative interests, the Popular Unity government tried to reach the people through certain alternative media, such as the poster, the mural, and a new kind of comic book.[1]

The ubiquitous magazine and newspaper kiosks of Chile were emblazoned with the garish covers of U.S. and U.S.-style comics (including some no longer known in the source country): *Superman*, *The Lone Ranger*, *Red Ryder*, *Flash Gordon*, and, of course, the various Disney magazines. In few countries of the world did Disney so completely dominate the so-called children's comic market, a term that in Chile (as in much of the Third World) includes magazines read by adults as well.

Under the aegis of the Popular Unity publishing house Quimantú, however, a forceful resistance to the Disney hegemony soon developed. *How to Read Donald Duck* was part of this cultural offensive, and it became a best-seller immediately on publication in late 1971, and subsequently in other Latin American editions. As a practical alternative a delightful children's comic, *Cabro chico* (Little Kid, on which Dorfman and Mattelart also collaborated), was created, designed to drive a wedge of new values into the U.S.-disneyfied cultural climate of old. Both ventures had to compete in a market in which the bourgeois media were long entrenched and had established their own strictly commercial criteria for the struggle—and both were too successful not to arouse the hostility of the bourgeois press. *El mercurio*, the leading reactionary mass daily in Chile, under the headline "Warning to Parents," denounced them as part of a government "plot" to seize control of education and the media, "brainwash" the young, inject them with "subtle ideological contraband," and "poison" their minds against Disney characters.[2] The article referred repeatedly to "mentors both Chilean and foreign" (that is, the authors of the present work, whose names are of German-Jewish and Belgian origin), appealing to the crudest kind of xenophobia.

Chile Monitor, London, 1974

"Hey, Hegel!
Look what a fat
little worm I've
caught"

"Congratulations,
Marx! I've got a
nice morsel too"

"How dreadful! The
kittens aren't
prepared for this!"

"Go away! Don't
you realize we
aren't scarecrows."

"Gulp! Occasionally
I run up against
guys who are
immune to the
voice of
conscience".

"Get him,comrade!"

"The farmer is
coming with a
shot-gun!"

"Ha! Firearms are
the only thing
these bloody
birds are afraid
of".

The Chilean bourgeois press resorted to the grossest lies, distortions, and scare campaigns in order to undermine confidence in the Popular Unity government, accusing the government of doing what they aspired to do themselves: censor and silence the voice of their opponents. And seeing that, despite their machinations, popular support for the government grew louder every day, they called upon the military to intervene by force of arms.

On September 11, 1973, the Chilean armed forces executed, with U.S. aid, the bloodiest counterrevolution in the history of the continent. Tens of thousands of workers and government supporters were killed. All art and literature favorable to the Popular Unity movement was immediately suppressed. Murals were destroyed. There were public bonfires of books, posters, and comics.[3] Intellectuals of the left were hunted down, jailed, tortured, and killed. Among those persecuted were the authors of this book.

The "state of war" declared by the junta to exist in Chile has been openly declared by the Disney comic too. In a recent issue, the Allende government, symbolized as murderous vultures called Marx and Hegel (meaning, perhaps, Engels), is being driven off by naked force: "Ha! Firearms are the only things these lousy birds are afraid of."

How to Read Donald Duck is now, of course, banned in Chile. To be found in possession of a copy is to risk one's life. By "cleansing" Chile of every trace of Marxist or popular art and literature, the junta are protecting the cultural envoys of their imperial masters. They know what kind of culture best serves their interests, that Mickey and Donald will help keep them in power, hold socialism at bay, and restore "virtue and innocence" to a "corrupted" Chile.

How to Read Donald Duck is an enraged, satirical, and politically impassioned book. The authors' passion derives in part from a sense of personal victimization, for they themselves, brought up on Disney comics and films, were injected with the Disney ideology which they now reject. But this book is much more than that: it is not just Latin American water off a duck's back; the system of domination the U.S. culture imposes so disastrously abroad also has deleterious effects at home, not least among those who work for Disney, that is, those who *produce* his ideology. The circumstances in which Disney products are made ensure that his employees reproduce in their lives and work relations the same system of exploitation to which they, as well as the consumer, are subject.[4]

To locate Disney correctly in the capitalist system would require a detailed analysis of the working conditions at Disney Productions and Walt Disney World. Such a study (which would, necessarily, break through the wall of secrecy behind which Disney operates) does not yet exist, but we may begin to piece together such information as may be gleaned about the circumstances in which the comics are created and about the people who create them—their relationship to their work and to Disney.

Disney does not take the comics seriously; indeed, he hardly even admits publicly of their existence.[5] He is far too concerned with the promotion of films and the amusement parks, his two most profitable enterprises. The comics tag along as an "ancillary activity" of interest only insofar as a new comic title can be used to help keep the name of a new film in the limelight. Royalties from comics constitute a small declining fraction of the revenue from Disney Publications, which constitute a small fraction of the revenue from Ancillary Activities, which constitute a small fraction of the total corporate revenue. Although Disney's share of the market in "educational" and children's books in other formats has increased dramatically, his cut of the total U.S. comics cake has surely shrunk.

In foreign lands, however, the Disney comics trade is still a mouse that roars. Many parts of the world, without access to Disney's films or television shows, know the Disney characters from the comics alone. Those too poor to buy a ticket to the cinema can always get hold of a comic, if not by purchase then by borrowing it from a friend. In the United States, moreover, comic book circulation figures are an inadequate index of the cultural influence of comic book characters. Since no new comedy cartoon shorts have been made of Mickey Mouse since 1948, or of Donald Duck since 1955 (the TV shows carry only reruns), the only place one finds original stories with the classic characters is in the comics. It is thus the comic books and strips that sustain old favorites in the public consciousness (in the United States and abroad) and keep it receptive to the massive merchandising operations that exploit the popularity of those characters.

Disney, like the missionary Peace Corps volunteer or "goodwill ambassador" depicted by his Public Relations agents, has learned the native lingoes—he is fluent in eighteen of them at the moment. In Latin America he speaks Spanish and Portuguese, from magazines that are slightly different from those produced elsewhere and at home. Indeed, there are at least four different Spanish-language editions of the Disney comic. The differences between them do not affect the basic content, and to determine the precise significance of such differences would require an excessive amount of research; but the fact of their existence points up some structural peculiarities in this little corner of Disney's empire. Most notable is the fact that the Disney comic, more than any of his other media, systematically relies on foreign labor in all stages of the production process. Thus the native contributes directly to his own colonization.[6]

Like other multinational corporations, Disney has found it profitable to decentralize operations, allowing considerable organizational and production leeway to his foreign subsidiaries, or "franchises," which are usually locked into the giant popular press conglomerates of their respective countries, like Mondadori in Italy or International Press Corporation in Britain. The Chilean edition is similar to other foreign editions in that it draws its material from several outside sources apart from the United States. Clearly, it is in the interests of the mother country that the various foreign subsidiaries should render mutual assistance to one another, exchanging stories they have imported or produced themselves. Even when foreign editors do not find it convenient to commission stories locally, they can select the type of story or the combination of stories ("story mix") they consider suited to a particular public taste and particular marketing conditions in the country or countries they are serving. They also edit (for instance, delete scenes considered offensive or inappropriate to the national sensibility),[7] have dialogues more or less accurately translated or more or less freely adapted, and add local color (in the literal sense: the pages arrive at the foreign press in the form of black-and-white transparencies, or "mats," which require the addition of color as well as dialogue in the local idiom). Some characters, such as Rockerduck, a free-spending millionaire, Fethry Duck, a "beatnik" type, and O. O. Duck, a silly spy, never caught on at home and are known chiefly, or only, from the foreign editions. The Italians in particular have proven adept in the creation of indigenous characters.

Expressed preferences of foreign editors reveal certain broad differences in taste. Brazil and Italy tend toward more physical violence, more blood and guts; Chile evidently tends (like Scandinavia, Germany, and Holland) to more quiet adventures, aimed (apparently) at a younger age group. Since the military are now in control of education and the mass media in Chile, and are known to be importing Brazilian techniques of repression, one may expect them also to introduce the more violent, Brazilian style of Disney comic.

The tremendous and increasing popularity of Disney abroad is not proportionately matched in the home market, where sales have been dropping, to a degree probably exceeding that of other comic classics, ever since the peak years of the early 1950s. Competition from television is usually cited as a major cause of the slump in the comics market; logistical difficulties of distribution are another; and a third factor, affecting Disney in particular, may be found in the whole cultural shift of the last two decades, which has transformed the tastes of so many American young children and teenagers and which Disney media appear in many respects to have ignored. If the Disney formula has been successfully preserved in the films and amusement parks even within this changing climate, it is by virtue of an increasingly heavy cloak of technical gimmickry that has been thrown over the old content. Thus the comics, bound today to the same production technology (coloring, printing, and so on) as when they started thirty-five years ago, have been unable to keep up with the new entertainment tricks.

The factors that sent the comics trade into its commercial decline in the United States have not weighed to nearly the same extent in the less developed nations of the world. The "cultural lag" (an expression of dominance of the metropolitan center over its colonized areas) is a familiar phenomenon; even in the United States, Disney comics sell proportionately better in the Midwest and South.

By fueling the foreign market from within, the United States has in recent years run into some difficulties. The less profitable domestic market, which Disney does not directly control and which now relies heavily on reprints, might conceivably be allowed to wind down altogether. As the domestic market shrinks, Disney pushes harder abroad, in the familiar mechanism of imperialist capitalism. As the foreign market expands, he is under increasing pressure to keep it dependent on supply from the United States (despite—or because of—the fact that the colonies show, as we have seen, signs of independent productive capacity). But Disney is being faced with a recruitment problem as old workhorses of the profession retire (such as Carl Barks, the creator of the best Donald Duck stories) and others become disillusioned with the low pay and restrictive conditions.

Disney has responded to the need to revitalize domestic production on behalf of the foreign market in a characteristic way: by tightening the rein on worker and product, to ensure that they adhere rigidly to established criteria. Where Disney can exercise direct control, the control must be total.

Prospective freelancers for Disney receive from the Publications Division a sheaf of Comic Book Art Specifications, designed in the first instance for the Comic Book Overseas Program. (Western Publishing, which is not primarily beholden to the foreign market, and which is also trying to attract new talent, although perhaps less strenuously, operates by unwritten and less inflexible rules.) Instead of inviting the invention of new characters and new locales, the Comic Book Art Specifications do exactly the opposite: they insist that only the established characters be used and, moreover, that there be "no upward mobility. The subsidiary figures should never become stars in our stories, they are just extras." This severe injunction seems calculated to repress exactly what in the past gave a certain growth potential and flexibility to the Duckburg cast, whereby a minor character could be upgraded into a major one and might even aspire to a comic book of his own. Nor do these established characters have any room to maneuver even within the hierarchical structure in which they are immutably fixed, for they are restricted to "a set pattern of behavior which must be complied with." The authoritarian tone of this instruction to the story writer seems expressly designed to crush any kind of creative manipulation on his part. He is also discouraged from localizing the action in any way, for Duckburg is explicitly stated to be *not* in the United States, but "everywhere and nowhere." All taint of specific geographical location must be expunged, as must all taint of dialect in the language.

Not only sex, but even love is prohibited (the relationship between Mickey and Minnie, or Donald and Daisy, is "platonic"—but not a platonic form of love). The gun laws outlaw all firearms, but "antique cannons and blunderbusses"; (other) firearms may, under certain circumstances, be waved as a threat, but never used. There are to be no "dirty, realistic business tricks," no "social differences" [8] or "political ideas." Above all, race and racial stereotyping is abolished: "Natives should never be depicted as negroes, Malayans, or singled out as belonging to any particular human race, and under no circumstances should they be characterized as dumb, ugly, inferior or criminal."

As is evident from the analysis in this book, and as is obvious to anyone at all familiar with the comics, none of these rules (with the exception of the sexual prohibition) have been observed in the past, in either Duck or Mouse stories. Indeed, they have been flouted, time and again. Duckburg is identifiable as a typical small Californian or Midwestern town, within easy reach of forest and desert (as is Hemet, California, where Carl Barks lived), and the comics are full of Americanisms, in custom and in language. Detective Mickey carries a revolver when on assignment, and frequently gets shot at. Uncle Scrooge is often guilty of blatantly dirty business tricks, and although defined by the Specifications as "*not* a bad man," he constantly behaves in the most reprehensible manner (for which he is properly reprehended by the younger ducks). The stories are replete with the "social differences" between rich and penniless (Scrooge and Donald), between virtuous Ducks and unshaven thieves; political ideas frequently come to the fore; and, of course, natives are often characterized as dumb, ugly, inferior, and criminal.

The Specifications seem to represent a fantasy on the studio's part, a fantasy of control, of a purity that was never really present. This is how the public is supposed to think of the comics, as of Disney in general; yet the past success of the comics with the public, and their unique character vis-à-vis other comics, has indubitably depended on the prominence given to certain capitalist sociopolitical realities, including financial greed, dirty business tricks, and the denigration of foreign peoples.

. . . .

Dorfman and Mattelart's book studies the Disney productions and their effects on the world. It cannot be a coincidence that much of what they observe in the relationships between the Disney characters can also be found, and maybe even explained, in the organization of work within the Disney industry itself.

Film is a collective process, dependent essentially on teamwork. A good animated cartoon requires the conjunction of many talents. Disney's long-standing public relations image of his studio as one great, happy, democratic family is no more than a smoke screen to conceal the rigidly hierarchical structure, with very poorly paid inkers and colorers (mostly women) at the bottom of the scale and animators (male, of course) at the top, earning five times as much as their assistants. In one instance of a top animator's objecting, on behalf of his assistant, to this gross wage differential, he was fired forthwith.

People were a commodity over which Disney needed absolute control. If a good artist left the studio for another job, he was considered by Disney, if not actually as a thief who had robbed him, then as an accomplice to theft—and he was never forgiven. Disney was the authoritarian father figure, quick to punish youthful rebellion. In postwar years, however, as he grew in fame, wealth, power, and distance, he was no longer regarded by even the most innocent employee as a father figure, but as an uncle—a rich uncle. Always "Walt" to everyone, he had everyone "walt" in.[9] "There's only one S.O.B. in the studio," he said, "and that's me."

For his workers to express solidarity against him was a subversion of his legitimate authority. When members of the Disney studio acted to join an AFL-CIO–affiliated union, he fired them and accused them of being communists or communist sympathizers. Later, in the McCarthy period, he cooperated with the FBI and the House Un-American Activities Committee in the prosecution of an ex-employee for "communism."

Ever since 1935, when the League of Nations recognized Mickey Mouse as an "International Symbol of Good Will," Disney has been an outspoken political figure, and one who has always been able to count on government help. When the Second World War cut off the extremely lucrative European market, which contributed a good half of the corporate income, the U.S. government helped him turn to Latin America. Washington hastened the solution of a strike that was crippling his studio and, at a time when Disney was literally on the verge of bankruptcy, began to commission propaganda films, which became his mainstay for the duration of the war. Nelson Rockefeller, then coordinator of Latin American Affairs, arranged for Disney, as a "goodwill ambassador," to make a film in order to win over hearts and minds vulnerable to Nazi propaganda. The film, called *Saludos amigos*, quite apart from its function as a commercial for Disney, was a diplomatic lesson served on Latin America, and one that is still considered valid today. The live-action travelogue footage of "ambassador" Disney and his artists touring the continent is interspersed with animated sections on "life" in Brazil, Argentina, Peru, and Chile, which define Latin America as the United States wished to see it and as the local peoples were supposed to see it themselves. They are symbolized by comic parrots, merry sambas, luxury beaches, goofy gauchos, and (to show that even the primitives can be modern) a little Chilean plane that braves the terrors of the Andes in order to deliver a single tourist's greeting card. The reduction of Latin America to a series of picture postcards was taken further in a later film, *The Three Caballeros*, and also permeates the comic book stories set in that part of the world.

During the Depression, critics gratefully received such Disney favorites as

Mickey Mouse and the Three Little Pigs as fitting symbols of courageous optimism in the face of great difficulties. Disney always pooh-poohed the idea that his work contained any particular kind of political message, proudly pointing (as proof of his innocence) to the diversity of political ideologies sympathetic to him. Mickey, noted the proud parent, was "one matter upon which the Chinese and Japanese agree." "Mr. Mussolini, Mr. King George and Mr. President Roosevelt" all loved the Mouse; and if Hitler disapproved (Nazi propaganda considered all kinds of mice, even Disney's, to be dirty creatures)—"Well," scolded Walt, "Mickey is going to save Mr. A. Hitler from drowning or something one day. Just wait and see if he doesn't. Then won't Mr. A. Hitler be ashamed!" [10] Come the war, however, Disney was using the Mouse not to save Hitler but to damn him. Mickey became a favorite armed forces mascot; fittingly, the climactic event of the European war, the Normandy landing, was code-named Mickey Mouse.

Among Disney's numerous wartime propaganda films, the most controversial, and in many ways the most important, was *Victory Through Air Power*. Undertaken on Disney's own initiative, this film was designed to support Major Alexander Seversky's theory of the "effectiveness" (that is, in terms of damage-to-cost ratio) of strategic bombing, including the bombing of population centers. It would be unfair to project back onto Disney our own guilt over Dresden and Hiroshima, but it is noteworthy that even at the time a film critic was shocked by Disney's "gay dreams of holocaust." [11] And it is consistent that the maker of such a film should later give active and financial support to some noted proponents of massive strategic and terror bombing of Vietnam, such as Goldwater and Reagan. Disney's support for Goldwater in 1964 was more than the public gesture of a wealthy conservative; he went so far as to wear a Goldwater button while being invested by Johnson with the President's Medal of Freedom. In the 1960 presidential campaign, he was arrogant enough to bully his employees to give money to the Nixon campaign fund, whether they were Republicans or not.

.   .   .   .

The public Disney myth has been fabricated not only from the man's works but also from autobiographical data and personal pronouncements. Disney never separated himself from his work; and there are certain formative circumstances of his life upon which he himself liked to enlarge and which through biographies and interviews have contributed to the public image of both Disney and Disney Productions. This public image was also the man's self-image, and both fed into and upon a dominant North American self-image. Many members of his vast audience interpret their lives as he interpreted his. His innocence is their innocence, and vice versa; his rejection of reality, his yearning for purity, are theirs, too. Their aspirations are the same as his; they, like he, started out in life poor and worked hard in order to become rich—and if he became rich and they didn't, well, maybe luck just wasn't on their side.

Walter Elias Disney was born in Chicago in 1901. When he was four, his father, who had been unable to make a decent living in that city as a carpenter and small building contractor, moved to a farm near Marceline, Missouri. Later, Walt was to idealize life there, remembering it as a kind of Eden (although he had to help in the work), a necessary refuge from the evil world, for he agreed with his father that "after boys reached a certain age they are best removed from the corruptive influences of the big city and subjected to the wholesome atmosphere of the country." [12]

After four years of unsuccessful farming, however, Elias Disney sold his property, and the family returned to the city—this time, Kansas City. There, in addition to going to school, the eight-year-old Walt was forced by his father into brutally hard work as a newspaper delivery boy, for which he had to get up at 3:30 every morning and walk for hours in dark, snowbound streets. [13] The memory haunted him all his life. His father was also in the habit of giving him, for no good reason, beatings with a leather strap, to which Walt submitted "to humor him and keep him happy." This phrase in itself suggests a conscious attempt, on the part of the adult, to avoid confronting the oppressive reality of his childhood.

Walt's mother, meanwhile, is conspicuously absent from his memories, as is his younger sister. All his three elder brothers ran away from home, and it is a remarkable fact that after he became famous, Walt Disney had nothing to do with either of his parents, or indeed with any of his family except his brother Roy, who was eight years older. Indeed, throughout Walt's career, Roy worked as his financial manager, and he was from the very beginning a kind of parent substitute or uncle–father figure. The elimination of true parents, especially the mother, from the comics, and the incidence in the films of mothers dead at the start, dying in the course of events, or cast as wicked stepmothers (*Bambi*, *Snow White*, and especially *Dumbo*), [14] must have held great personal meaning for Disney. The theme has of course long been a constant of world folk literature, but the manner in which it is handled by Disney may tell us a great deal about twentieth-century bourgeois culture. Peculiar to Disney comics, surely, is the fact that the mother is not even technically missing; she is simply nonexistent as a concept. It is possible that Disney truly hated his childhood and feared and resented his parents but could never admit it, seeking through his works to escape from the bitter social realities associated with his upbringing. If he hated being a child, one can also understand why he always insisted that his films and amusement parks were designed in the first place for adults, not children, why he was pleased at the statistics, which showed that for every one child visitor to Disneyland there were four adults, and why he always complained at getting the awards for Best *Children's* Film.

As Dorfman and Mattelart show, the child in the Disney comic is really a mask for adult anxieties; he is an adult self-image. Most critics are agreed that Disney shows little or no understanding of the "real child" or of real childhood psychology and problems.

Disney has also, necessarily, eliminated the biological link between the parent and child—sexuality. The raunchy touch, the barnyard humor of his early films, has long since been sanitized. Disney was the only man in Hollywood to whom you could not tell a dirty joke. His sense of humor, if it existed at all (and many writers on the man have expressed doubts on this score), was always of a markedly "bathroom" or anal kind. Coy anality is the Disney substitute for sexuality; this is notorious in the films, and observable in the comics also. The world of

Disney, inside and outside the comics, is a male one. The Disney organization excludes women from positions of importance. Disney freely admitted, "Girls bored me. They still do." [15] He had very few intimate relationships with women; his daughter's biography contains no hint that there was any real intimacy even within the family circle. Walt's account of his courtship of his wife establishes it as a purely commercial transaction. [16] Walt had hired Lillian Bounds as an inker because she would work for less money than anyone else; he married her when his brother Roy married and moved out because he needed a new roommate and a cook.

But just as Disney avoided the reality of sex and children, so he avoided that of nature. The man who made the world's most publicized nature films, whose work expresses a yearning to return to the purity of natural, rustic living, avoided the countryside. He hardly ever left Los Angeles. His own garden at home was filled with railroad tracks and stock (this was his big hobby). He was interested in nature only in order to tame it, control it, cleanse it. Disneyland and Walt Disney World are monuments to his desire for total control of his environment, and at the end of his life he was planning to turn vast areas of California's loveliest "un-spoiled" mountains, at Mineral King, into a $35 million playground. He had no sense of the special nonhuman character of animals, or of the wilderness; his concern with nature was to anthropomorphize it.

Disney liked to claim that his genius, his creativity, "sprouted from mother earth." [17] Nature was the source of his genius, his genius was the source of his wealth, and his wealth grew like a product of nature, like corn. What made his golden cornfield grow? Dollars. "Dollars," said Disney, in a remark worthy of Uncle Scrooge McDuck, "are like fertilizer—they make things grow." [18]

As Dorfman and Mattelart observe, it is Disney's ambition to render the past like the present, the present like the past, and project both onto the future. Disney has patented—"sewn up all the rights on"—tomorrow as well as today. For, in the jargon of the media, "he has made tomorrow come true today" and "enables one to actually experience the future." His future has taken shape in Walt Disney World in Orlando, Florida, an amusement park that covers an area of once-virgin land twice the size of Manhattan, which in its first year attracted 10.7 million visitors (about the number who visit Washington, D.C., annually). With its own laws, it is a state within a state. It boasts the fifth largest submarine fleet in the world. Distinguished bourgeois architects, town planners, critics, and land specu-lators have hailed Walt Disney World as the solution to the problems of our cities, a prototype for living in the future. EPCOT (Experimental Prototype Community of Tomorrow) is, in the words of a well-known critic, "a *working* community, a vast, living, ever-changing laboratory of urban design . . . [which] understand-ably . . . evades a good many problems—housing, schools, employment, poli-tics and so on. . . . They are in the fun business [emphasis added]." [19] Of course.

The Disney parks have brought the fantasies of the "future" and the "fun" of the comics one step nearer to capitalist "reality." "In Disneyland (the happiest place on earth)," says Public Relations, "you can encounter 'wild' animals and native 'savages' who often display their hostility to your invasion of their jungle privacy. . . . From stockades in Adventureland, you can actually shoot at Indians."

Meanwhile, out there in the *real* real world, the "savages" *are* fighting back.

Notes

1. Cf. Herbert Schiller and Dallas Smythe, "Chile: An End to Cultural Colonialism," *Society*, March 1972, pp. 35–39, 61; and David Kunzle, "Art of the New Chile: Mural, Poster and Comic Book in a 'Revolutionary Process,'" in *Art and Architecture in the Service of Politics*, ed. Henry Millon and Linda Nochlin (Cambridge, Mass.: MIT Press, 1978).

2. *El mercurio* (Santiago, Chile), 13 August 1971. The passage below is slightly abridged from that published on pages 80–81 in the Chilean edition of *How to Read Donald Duck*:

"Among the objectives pursued by the Popular Unity government appears to be the creation of a new mentality in the younger generation. In order to achieve this purpose, typical of all Marxist societies, the authorities are intervening in education and the advertising media and resorting to various expedients.

"Persons responsible to the Government maintain that education shall be one of the means calculated to achieve this purpose. A severe critique is thus being instituted at this level against teaching methods, textbooks, and the attitude of broad sectors of the nation's teachers who refuse to become an instrument of propaganda.

"We register no surprise at the emphasis placed on changing the mentality of schoolchildren, who in their immaturity cannot detect the subtle ideological contraband to which they are being subjected.

"There are however other lines of access being forged to the juvenile mind, notably the magazines and publications which the State publishing house has just launched, under literary mentors both Chilean and foreign, but in either case of proven Marxist militancy.

"It should be stressed that not even the vehicles of juvenile recreation and amusement are exempt from this process, which aims to diminish the popularity of consecrated characters of world literature, and at the same time replace them with new models cooked up by the Popular Unity propaganda experts.

"For some time now the pseudosociologists have been clamoring, in their tortuous jargon, against certain comic books with an international circulation, judged to be disastrous in that they represent vehicles of intellectual colonization for those who are exposed to them. . . . Since clumsy forms of propaganda would not be acceptable to parents and guardians, children are systematically given carefully distilled doses of propaganda from an early age, in order to channel them in later years in Marxist directions.

"Juvenile literature has also been exploited so that the parents themselves should be exposed to ideological indoctrination, for which purpose special adult supplements are included. It is illustrative of Marxist procedures that a State enterprise should sponsor initiatives of this kind, with the collaboration of foreign personnel.

"The program of the Popular Unity demands that the communications media should be educational in spirit. Now we are discovering that this 'education' is no more than the instrument for doctrinaire proselytization imposed from the tenderest years in so insidious and deceitful a form that many people have no idea of the real purposes being pursued by these publications."

It is now widely known, even in the United States, that *El mercurio* was CIA-funded: "Approximately half the CIA funds (one million dollars) were funnelled to the opposition press, notably the nation's leading daily, *El mercurio*" (*Time*, 30 September 1974, p. 29).

3. In autumn 1973, UNESCO voted thirty-two to two to condemn the book burning in Chile. The United States and Taiwan alone voted with the junta.

4. If we continue to refer to Disney Productions after the death of Walt as "Disney" and "he," we do so in response to the fact that his spirit, that of U.S. corporate capitalism, continues to dominate the organization.

5. Neither comic book nor syndicated newspaper strip is mentioned in the company's annual report for 1973. These presumably fall within the category "Publications," which constitutes 17 percent of the group "Ancillary Activities." This group, of which Character Merchandising and Music and Records (27 percent each) are the major constituents, showed an extraordinary increase in activity (up 28 percent over the previous year, up 228 percent over the past four years, the contribution of Publications being proportionate), so as to bring its share of the total corporate revenue of $385 million up to 10 percent.

Written solicitation with Disney Productions regarding income from comic books proved unavailing. The following data have been culled from the press:

The total monthly circulation of Disney comics throughout the world was given in 1962 at fifty million, covering fifty countries and fifteen different languages (*Newsweek*, 31 December 1962, pp. 48–51). These languages now number eighteen: Arabic, Chinese, Danish, Dutch, English, Finnish, Flemish, French, German, Hebrew, Italian, Japanese, Norwegian, Portuguese, Serbo-Croatian, Spanish, Swedish, and Thai. The number of countries served must have risen sharply in the late fifties, to judge by the figures published in 1954 (*Time*, 27 December 1954, p. 42), when thirty million copies of a "single title" (*Walt Disney's Comics and Stories*) were being bought in twenty-six countries every month.

In the United States, discounting special "one-shot" periodicals keyed to current films, the following fourteen comic book titles are now being published under Disney's name: *Aristokittens, Beagle Boys, Chip and Dale, Daisy and Donald, Donald Duck, Huey Dewey and Louie Junior Woodchucks, Mickey Mouse, Moby Duck, Scamp, Supergoof, Uncle Scrooge, Walt Disney Showcase, Walt Disney's Comics and Stories*, and *Walt Disney's Comics Digest*. It should be stressed that although the number of Disney titles has recently increased, their individual size has diminished considerably, as has, presumably, their circulation.

6. Some statistics will reveal the character and extent of foreign participation in the Disney comic, as well as the depth of Disney's penetration into the Latin American continent. In a recent year the Chilean edition, which also serves neighboring Peru, Paraguay, and Argentina, used for its four comics titles (one weekly, three bi-weeklies) totaling 800,000 copies sold per month: 4,400 pages of Disney material, of which well over a third came directly from Disney studios; just over a third from Disney's U.S. franchise, Western Publishing Company; less than a quarter from Italy; and a small fraction from Brazil and Denmark. The Mexican edition (which uses only half as many pages as the Chilean group) takes almost exclusively from the U.S. sources. In contrast, Brazil, with five titles totaling over 2,000,000 copies sold per month, is fairly dependent on Italy (1,000 out of 5,000 pages) and generates 1,100 pages of its own material. Another Latin American edition is that of Colombia. Italy is perhaps the most self-sufficient country of all, producing itself over half of its 5,600 annual pages. France's *Journal de Mickey*, which sells around 340,000 copies weekly, consists of about half Disney and half non-Disney material.

There is a direct reverse-flow back to the mother country in *Disneyland*, a comic for younger readers with more stylish drawing started about 1971, produced entirely in England, and distributed by Fawcett in the United States. This and *Donald and Mickey*, the other major Disney comic serving the non-U.S. English-speaking world, sell around 200,000 copies per week each in the United Kingdom.

7. A collection of such editorial changes might reveal some of the finer and perhaps more surprising nuances of cultural preferences. The social sensibility of the Swedes, for instance, was offended by the inclusion of some realistic scenes of poverty in which the ducklings try to buy gifts for the poor ("Christmas for Shacktown," 1952). By cutting such scenes, the editors rendered the story almost incomprehensible.

A country with a totally different cultural tradition, such as Taiwan, cannot use Disney comics in their original form at all, and the very essence of favorite characters must be changed. Thus Donald becomes a responsible, model parent, admired and obeyed by his little nephews.

8. The contradiction here is nakedly exposed in the version of the Specifications distributed by the Scandinavian Disney publishers: "no social differences (poor kids, arrogant manager, humble servant). . . . Donald Duck, in relation to Uncle Scrooge, is . . . underpaid . . . grossly exploited in unpleasant jobs."

9. That is, "walled in." The pun is that of a studio hand; cited in "Father Goose," *Time*, 27 December 1954, p. 42.

10. Cited by Richard Schickel, *The Disney Version* (New York: Simon & Schuster, 1968), p. 132.

11. Ibid., p. 233.

12. Ibid., p. 35.

13. His father added the money Walt earned to the household budget, so he was essentially unpaid. Newspaper delivery is one of the few legally sanctioned forms of child labor still surviving today. Most parents nowadays (presumably) let their children keep the money they earn and regard the job as a useful form of early ideological training in which the child learns the value and necessity of making a minute personal "profit" out of the labor that enriches the millionaire newspaper publisher.

14. According to Richard Schickel, *Dumbo* is "the most overt statement of a theme that is implicit in almost all the Disney features—the absence of a mother" (*The Disney Version*, p. 225).

15. Ibid., p. 48. Cf. "Top management's roster lists very few Jews, very few Catholics. No blacks. No women"; cited by D. Keith Mono, "A Real Mickey Mouse Operation," *Playboy*, December 1973, p. 328.

16. His daughter's words bear repeating: "Father [was] a low-pressure swain with a relaxed selling technique. That's the way he described it to me. . . . [He was] an unabashed sentimentalist . . . [but] to hear him talk about marrying Mother, you'd think he was after a lifetime's supply of her sister's fried chicken." His proposal came in this form: " 'Which do you think we ought to pay for first, the car or the ring?' " They bought the ring, and on the cheap because it was probably "hot" (Diane Daisy Miller, *The Story of Walt Disney* [New York, 1956], p. 98). According to *Look* magazine (15 July 1955, p. 29), "Lillian Bounds was paid so little, she sometimes didn't bother to cash her paycheck. This endeared her greatly to Roy . . . [who] urged Walt to use his charm to persuade the lady to cash even fewer checks."

17. *Time*, 27 December 1954, p. 42.

18. *Newsweek*, 31 December 1962, pp. 48–51.

19. Peter Blake, in an article for *Architectural Forum*, June 1972.

THE GREAT PARACHUTIST

ARIEL DORFMAN AND ARMAND MATTELART

*"If I were able to produce money with my black magic, I
wouldn't be in the middle of the desert looking for gold,
would I?"*

MAGICA DE SPELL

What are these adventurers escaping from their claustrophobic cities really after?
What is the true motive of their flight from the urban center? Bluntly stated, in
more than 75 percent of our sampling they are looking for gold, in the remaining
25 percent they are competing for fortune—in the form of money or fame—in
the city.

Why should gold, criticized ever since the beginning of a monetary economy
as a contamination of human relations and the corruption of human nature,
mingle here with the innocence of the noble savage (child and people)? Why
should gold, the fruit of urban commerce and industry, flow so freely from these
rustic and natural environments?

The answer to these questions lies in the manner in which our earthly paradise
generates all this raw wealth.

It comes, above all, in the form of hidden treasure. It is to be found in the
Third World, and is magically pointed out by some ancient map, a parchment, an
inheritance, an arrow, or a clue in a picture. After great adventures and obstacles,
and after defeating some thief trying to get there first (disqualified from the prize
because it wasn't his idea but filched from someone else's map), the good Duckburgers appropriate the idols, figurines, jewels, crowns, pearls, necklaces, rubies,
emeralds, precious daggers, and golden helmets.

First of all, we are struck by the *antiquity* of the coveted object. It has lain
buried for thousands of years: within caverns, ruins, pyramids, coffers, sunken
ships, Viking tombs—that is, any place with vestiges of civilized life in the past.
Time separates the treasure from its original owners, who have bequeathed this
unique heritage to the future. Furthermore, this wealth is left without heirs; despite their total poverty, the noble savages take no interest in the gold abounding
so near them (in the sea, in the mountains, under the tree). These ancient civilizations are envisioned, by Disney, to have come to a somewhat catastrophic
end. Whole families exterminated, armies in constant defeat, people forever hiding their treasure, for . . . for whom? Disney conveniently exploits the supposed
total destruction of past civilizations to carve an abyss between the innocent
present-day inhabitants and the previous, but nonancestral, inhabitants. The innocents are not heirs to the past, because that past is not father to the present. It
is, at best, the uncle. There is an empty gap. Whoever arrives first with the brilliant idea and the shovel has the right to take the booty back home. The noble
savages have no history, and they have forgotten their past, which was never

From Ariel Dorfman and Armand Mattelart, *How to Read Donald Duck*, (New York: International
General, 1975). Translated by David Kunzle.

theirs to begin with. By depriving them of their past, Disney destroys their historical memory, in the same way he deprives a child of his parenthood and genealogy—and with the same result: the destruction of their ability to see themselves as a product of history.

It would appear, moreover, that these forgotten peoples never actually produced this treasure. They are consistently described as warriors, conquerors, and explorers, as if they had seized it from someone else. In any event, there is no reference at any time—how could there be, with something that happened so long ago?—to the making of these objects, although they must have been handcrafted. The actual origin of the treasure is a mystery that is never even mentioned. The only legitimate owner of the treasure is the person who had the brilliant idea of tracking it down; he creates it the moment he thinks of setting off in search of it. It never really existed before, anywhere. *The ancient civilization is the uncle of the object, and the father is the man who gets to keep it.* Having discovered it, he rescued it from the oblivion of time.

But even then the object remains in some slight contact with the ancient civilization; it is the last vestige of vanishing faces. So the finder of the treasure has one more step to take. In the vast coffers of Scrooge there is never the slightest trace of the handcrafted object, despite the fact that he brings treasure home from so many expeditions. Only banknotes and coins remain. As soon as the treasure leaves its country of origin for Duckburg, it loses shape and is swallowed up by Scrooge's dollars. It is stripped of the last vestige of that crafted form that might link it to persons, places, and time. It turns into gold without the odor of fatherland or history. Uncle Scrooge can bathe and cavort in his coins and banknotes (in Disney these are no mere metaphors) more comfortably than in spiky idols and jeweled crowns. Everything is transmuted mechanically (but without machines) into a single monetary mold in which the last breath of human life is extinguished. And finally the adventure that led to the relic fades away, together with the relic itself. As treasure buried in the earth it pointed to a past, however remote, and even as treasure in Duckburg (were it to survive in its original form) it would point to the adventure experienced, however remote that might be. Just as the historical memory of the original civilization is blotted out, so is Scrooge's personal memory of his experience. Either way, history is melted down in the crucible of the dollar. The falsity of all the Disney publicity regarding the educational and aesthetic value of these comics, which are touted as journeys through time and space and as aids to the learning of history and geography, stands revealed. For Disney, history exists in order to be demolished, in order to be turned into the dollar that gave birth to it and lays it to rest. Disney even kills archeology, the science of artifacts.

Disneyfication is Dollarfication: all objects (and, as we shall see, actions as well) are transformed into gold. Once this conversion is completed *the adventure is over*: one cannot go further, for gold—ingot or dollar bill—cannot be reduced to a more symbolic level. The only prospect is to go hunting for more of the same, since once it is invested it becomes active, and soon it will start taking sides and enter contemporary history. Better cross it out and start afresh. Add more adventures, which accumulate in aimless and sterile fashion.

So it is not surprising that the hoarder desires to skip these productive phases and go off in search of pure gold.

But even in the treasure hunt the productive process is lacking. On your marks, get set, collect—like fruit picked from a tree. The problem lies not in the actual extraction of the treasure but in discovering its geographical location. Once one has gotten there, the gold—always in nice fat nuggets—is already in the bag, without having raised a single callus on the hand that carries it off. Mining is like abundant agriculture, once one has had the genius to spot the mine. And agriculture is conceived as picking flowers in an infinite garden. There is no effort in the extraction; it is foreign to the material of which the object is made: bland, soft, and unresistant. The mineral is simply playing hide and seek—one needs only cunning to lift it from its sanctuary, not physical labor to shape its content and give it form, changing it from its natural physical-mineral state into something useful to human society. In the absence of this process of transformation, wealth is made to appear as if society creates it by means of the spirit, the idea, the little light bulbs flashing over the characters' heads. Nature apparently delivers the material ready-to-use, as in primitive life, without the intervention of workman and tool. The Duckburgers have airplanes, submarines, radar, helicopters, rockets, but not so much as a stick to open up the earth. Mother Earth is prodigal, and taking in the gold is as innocent as breathing in fresh air. Nature feeds gold to these creatures: it is the only sustenance these aurivores desire.

Now we understand why it is that the gold is found yonder in the world of the noble savage. It cannot appear in the city, because the normal order of life is that of production (although we shall see later how Disney eliminates even this factor in the cities). The origin of this wealth has to appear natural and innocent. Let us place the Duckburgers in the great uterus of history: all comes from nature; nothing is produced by man. The child must be taught (and along the way, the adult convinces himself) that the objects have no history; they arise by enchantment, and are untouched by human hand. The stork brought the gold. It is the immaculate conception of wealth.

The production process in Disney's world is natural, not social. And it is magical. All objects arrive on parachutes, are conjured out of hats, are presented as gifts in a nonstop birthday party, are spread out like mushrooms. Mother Earth gives all: pick her fruits and be rid of guilt. No one is getting hurt.

Gold is produced by some inexplicable, miraculous natural phenomenon. Like rain, wind, snow, waves, an avalanche, a volcano, or like another planet.

"What is that falling from the sky?"

"Hardened raindrops . . . Ouch! Or molten metal."

"It can't be. It's gold coins. Gold!"

"Hurray! A rain of gold! Just look at that rainbow."

"We must be having visions, Uncle Scrooge. It can't be true."

But it is.

Like bananas, like copper, like tin, like cattle. One sucks the milk of gold from the earth. Gold is claimed from the breast of nature without the mediation of work. The claimants have clearly acquired the rights of ownership thanks to their native genius, or else thanks to their accumulated suffering (an abstracted form of work, as we explain below).

It is not superhuman magic, like that of the witch Magica de Spell, for example, that creates the gold. This kind of magic, distilled from the demon of technology, is merely a parasite upon nature. Man cannot counterfeit the wealth. He has to get it through some other charmed source, the natural one, in which he does not have to intervene but only deserve.

An example: Donald and nephews, followed by Magica, search for the rainbow's end, behind which, according to the legend, is hidden a pot of gold, the direct fruit of nature. Although our heroes do not exactly find the mythical treasure, they return with another kind of "pot of gold": fat commercial profits. How did this happen? Uncle Scrooge's airplane, loaded with lemon seeds, accidently inseminated the Sahara Desert, and when Magica de Spell provoked a rainstorm, within minutes the whole area became an orchard of lemon trees. The seeds (i.e., ideas) come from abroad, magic or accident sows them, and the useless, underdeveloped desert soil makes them grow. "Come on, boys!" cries Donald, "let's start picking lemons. And take them to the town to sell." Work is minimal and a pleasure; the profit is tremendous.

This does not happen only in distant places, but also in Duckburg, at its beaches, woods, and mountains. Donald and Gladstone, for example, go on a beachcombing expedition to see who can come up with the most valuable find to give to Daisy and win her company for lunch. The sea successively washes up huge seashells, a giant snail, a "very valuable" ancient Indian seashell necklace, rubber boats (one each for Gladstone and Donald), a rubber elephant loaded with tropical fruits, papayas and mangoes, an Alaskan kayak, a mirror, and an ornamental comb. The sea is a cornucopia; generous nature showers abundance upon man—and in the Third World, in a particularly exotic form. In and beyond Duckburg, it is always nature that mediates between man and wealth.

It is surely undeniable nowadays that all real and concrete human achievements derive from effort and work. Although nature provides the raw materials, people must struggle to make a living from them. If this were not so, we would still be in Eden.

In the world of Disney, however, no one has to work in order to produce. There is a constant round of buying, selling, and consuming, but to all appearances, none of the products involved has required any effort whatsoever to make. Nature is the great labor force, producing objects of human and social utility as if they were natural.

The human origin of the product—be it table, house, car, clothing, gold, coffee, wheat, or maize (which, according to one comic strip, comes from *granaries*, direct from warehouses, rather than from the fields)—has been suppressed. The process of production has been eliminated, as has all reference to its genesis; the actors, the objects, the circumstances of the process never existed. What in fact has been erased is the paternity of the object, and the possibility to link it to the process of production.

This brings us back to the curious Disney family structure, with its absence of natural paternity. The simultaneous lack of direct biological production and direct economic production is not coincidental. They both coincide and reinforce a dominant ideological structure, which also seeks to eliminate the working class, the true producer of objects, and with it, the class struggle.

Disney exorcises history, magically expelling the socially (and biologically) reproductive element, leaving amorphous, rootless, and inoffensive products— without sweat, without blood, without effort, and without the misery they inevitably sow in the life of the working class. The object produced is truly fantastic; it is purged of unpleasant associations, which are relegated to an invisible background of dreary, sordid slumland living. Disney uses the imagination of the child to eradicate all reference to the real world. The products of history that "people" and pervade the world of Disney are incessantly bought and sold. But Disney has appropriated these products and the work that brought them into being, just as the bourgeoisie has appropriated the products and labor of the working class. The situation is ideal for the bourgeoisie: they get the product without the workers. Even on the rare occasion when a factory does appear (for example, a brewery in one strip), there is never more than one workman, and he always seems to be acting as caretaker. His role appears to be little more than that of a policeman protecting the autonomous and automated factory of his boss. This is the world the bourgeoisie have always dreamed of, one in which a man can amass great wealth without ever facing its producer and product: the worker. Objects are cleansed of guilt. It is a world of pure surplus without the slightest suspicion of a worker demanding the slightest reward. The proletariat, born of the contradictions of the bourgeois regime, sells its labor "freely" to the highest bidder, who transforms the labor into wealth for his own social class. In the Disney world, the proletariat is expelled from the society it created, thus ending all antagonisms, conflicts, class struggle, and indeed, the very concept of social class. Disney's is a world of bourgeois interests with the cracks in the structure repeatedly papered over. In the imaginary realm of Disney, the rosy publicity fantasy of the bourgeoisie is realized to perfection: wealth without wages, deodorant without sweat. Gold becomes a toy, and the characters who play with it are amusing children; after all, the way the world goes, they aren't doing any harm to anyone . . . within *that* world. But in *this* world there is harm in dreaming and realizing the dream of a particular class as if it were the dream of the whole of humanity.

There is a term that would be like dynamite to Disney, like a scapulary to a vampire, like electricity convulsing a frog: social class. That is why Disney must publicize his creations as universal, beyond frontiers; they reach all homes, they reach all countries. O immortal Disney, international patrimony, reaching all children everywhere, everywhere, everywhere.

Marx had a word—"fetishism"—for the process that separates the product (accumulated work) from its origin and expresses it as gold, abstracting it from the actual circumstances of production. It was Marx who discovered that behind his gold and silver the capitalist conceals the whole process of accumulation which he achieves at the worker's expense (surplus value). The words "precious metals," "gold," and "silver" are used to hide from the worker the fact that he is being robbed, and that the capitalist is no mere accumulator of wealth but the appropriator of the product of social production. The transformation of the worker's labor into gold fools him into believing that it is gold that is the true generator of wealth and source of production.

Gold, in sum, is a *fetish*, the supreme fetish, and in order for the true origin of wealth to remain concealed, all social relations, all people, are *fetishized*.

Since gold is the actor, director, and producer of this film, humanity is reduced to the level of a thing. Objects possess a life of their own, and humanity controls neither its products nor its own destiny. The Disney universe is proof of the internal coherence of the world ruled by gold and an exact reflection of the political design it reproduces.

Nature, by taking over human production, makes it evaporate. But the products remain. What for? To be consumed. Of the capitalist process that goes from production to consumption, Disney knows only the second stage. This is consumption rid of the original sin of production, just as the son is rid of the original sin of sex, represented by his father, and just as history is rid of the original sin of class and conflict.

Let us look at the social structure in the Disney comic. For example, the professions. In Duckburg, everyone seems to belong to the tertiary sector, that is, those who sell their services: hairdressers, real estate and tourist agencies, salespeople of all kinds (especially shop assistants selling sumptuous objects, and vendors going from door-to-door), nightwatchmen, waiters, delivery boys, and people attached to the entertainment business. These fill the world with objects and more objects, which are never produced but always purchased. There is a constant repetition of the act of buying. But this mercantile relationship is not limited to the level of objects. Contractual language permeates the most commonplace forms of human intercourse. People see themselves as buying each other's services or selling themselves. It is as if the only security were to be found in the language of money. All human interchange is a form of commerce; people are like a purse, an object in a shop window, or coins constantly changing hands.

"It's a deal." " 'What the eye doesn't see . . . you can take for free'—I should patent that saying." "You must have spent a fortune on this party, Donald." These are explicit examples, although it is generally implicit that all activity revolves around money, status or the status-giving object, and the competition for them.

The world of Walt, in which every word advertises something or somebody, is under an intense compulsion to consume. The Disney vision can hardly transcend consumerism when it is fixated on selling itself along with other merchandise. Sales of the comic are fostered by the so-called Disneyland Clubs, which are heavily advertised in the comics and are financed by commercial firms who offer cut rates to members. The absurd ascent from corporal to general, right up to chief-of-staff, is achieved exclusively by purchasing Disneyland comics and sending in the coupons. It offers no benefits, except the incentive to continue buying the magazine. The solidarity which it appears to promote among readers simply traps them in the buying habit.

Surely it is not good for children to be surreptitiously injected with a permanent compulsion to buy objects they don't need. This is Disney's sole ethical code: consumption for consumption's sake. But to keep the system going, throw the things away (rarely are objects shown being enjoyed, even in the comic), and buy the same thing, only slightly different, the next day. Let money change hands, and if it ends up fattening the pockets of Disney and his class, so be it.

Disney creatures are engaged in a frantic chase for money. As we are in an amusement world, allow us to describe the land of Disney as a carousel of consumerism. Money is the goal everyone strives for, because it manages to embody all the qualities of their world. To start with the obvious, its powers of acquisition are unlimited, encompassing the affection of others, security, influence, authority, prestige, travel, vacation, leisure, and to temper the boredom of living, entertainment. The only access to these things is through money, which comes to symbolize the good things of life, all of which can be bought.

But who decides the distribution of wealth in the world of Disney? By what criteria is one placed at the top or the bottom of the pile?

Let us examine some of the mechanisms involved. Geographical distance separates the potential owner, who takes the initiative, from the ready-to-use gold that passively awaits him. But this distance in itself is insufficient to create obstacles and suspense along the way. So a *thief* after the same treasure appears on the scene. Chief of the criminal gangs are the Beagle Boys, but there are innumerable other professional crooks, luckless buccaneers, and decrepit eagles, along with the inevitable Black Pete. To these we may add Magica de Spell, Big Bad Wolf, and some lesser thieves of the forest, like Brer Bear and Brer Fox.

They are all oversize, dark, ugly, ill-educated, unshaven, stupid (they never have a good idea), clumsy, dissolute, greedy, conceited (always toadying each other), and unscrupulous. They are lumped together in groups and are individually indistinguishable. The professional crooks, like the Beagle Boys, are conspicuous for their prison identification number and burglar's mask. Their criminality is innate: "Shut up," says a cop seizing a Beagle Boy, "you weren't born to be a guard. Your vocation is jailbird."

Crime is the only work they know; otherwise, they are slothful unto eternity. Big Bad Wolf reads a book all about disguises (printed by Confusion Publishers): "At last I have found the perfect disguise: no one will believe that Big Bad Wolf is capable of working." So he disguises himself as a worker. With his moustache, hat, overalls, barrow, and pick and shovel, he sees himself as quite the Southern convict on a road gang.

As if their criminal record were not sufficient to impress upon us the illegitimacy of their ambitions, they are constantly pursuing the treasure already amassed or preempted by others. The Beagle Boys versus Scrooge McDuck are the best example, the others being mere variations on this central theme. In a world so rich in maps and badly kept secrets, it is a statistical improbability and seems unfair that the villains should not occasionally, at least, get hold of a parchment first. Their inability to deserve this good fortune is another indication that there is no question of them changing their status. Their fate is fruitless robbery or intent to rob, constant arrest or constant escape from jail (perhaps there are so many of them that jail can never hold them all?). They are a constant threat to those who had the idea of hunting for gold.

The only obstacle to the adventurer's getting his treasure is not a very realistic one. The sole purpose of the presence of the villain is to legitimate the right of the other to appropriate the treasure. Occasionally the adventurer is faced with a moral dilemma: his gold or someone else's life. He always chooses in favor of the life, although he somehow never has to sacrifice the gold (the choice was not very real—the dice were loaded). But he can at least confront evil temptations, whereas the villains, with a few exceptions, never have a chance to search their conscience and rise above their condition.

Disney can conceive of no other threat to wealth than theft. His obsessive need to criminalize any person who infringes the laws of private property invites us to look at these villains more closely. The darkness of their skin, their ugliness, the disorder of their dress, their stature, their reduction to numerical categories, their moblike character, and the fact that they are "condemned" in perpetuity all add up to a stereotypical stigmatization of the bosses' real enemy, the one who truly threatens his property.

But the real-life enemy of the wealthy is not the thief. Were there only thieves about him, the man of property could convert history into a struggle between legitimate owners and criminals, who are to be judged according to the property laws he, the owner, has established. But reality is different. The element that truly challenges the legitimacy and necessity of the monopoly of wealth, and is capable of destroying it, is the working class, whose only means of liberation is to liquidate the economic base of the bourgeoisie and abolish private production. Since the moment the bourgeoisie began exploiting the proletariat, the former has tried to reduce the resistance of the latter, and indeed, the class struggle itself, to a battle between good and evil, as Marx showed in his analysis of Eugene Sue's serial novels.[1] The moral label is designed to conceal the root of the conflict, which is economic, and at the same time to censure the actions of the class enemy.

In Disney, then, the working class has been split into two groups: criminals in the city, and noble savages in the countryside. Since the Disney worldview emasculates violence and social conflicts, even the urban rogues are conceived as naughty children ("boys"). As the anti-model, they are always losing, being spanked, and celebrating their stupid ideas by dancing in circles, hand in hand. They are expressions of the bourgeois desire to portray workers' organizations as a motley mob of crazies.

Thus, when Scrooge is confronted by the possibility that Donald has taken to thieving, he says "My nephew, a robber? Before my own eyes? I must call the police and the lunatic asylum. He must have gone mad." This statement reflects the reduction of criminal activity to a psychopathic disease rather than the result of social conditioning. The bourgeoisie converts the defects of the working class, which are the outcome of the exploitation of this class, into moral blemishes and objects of derision and censure so as to weaken the working class and conceal its exploitation. The bourgeoisie even imposes its own values on the ambitions of the enemy, who, incapable of originality, steal in order to become millionaires themselves and join the exploiting class. Never are workers depicted as trying to improve society. This caricature, which twists every characteristic capable of lending the worker dignity and respect—and thereby, identity within a social class—turns that worker into a spectacle of mockery and contempt. (And parenthetically, in the modern technological era, the daily mass culture diet of the bourgeoisie still consists of the same mythic caricatures that arose during the late-nineteenth-century machine age.)

The criterion for dividing good from bad is honesty, that is, the respect for private property. Thus, in "Honesty Rewarded," the nephews find a ten-dollar bill and fight for it, calling each other "thief," "crook," and "villain." But Donald intervenes: such a sum, found in the city, must have a legal owner, who must be traced. This is a titanic task, for all the big, ugly, violent, dark-skinned people try to steal the money for themselves. The worst is one who wants to steal the note in order to "buy a pistol to rob the orphanage." Peace finally returns (significantly, Donald was reading *War and Peace* in the first scene) when the true owner of the money appears. She is a poor little girl, famished and ragged, the only case of social misery in our entire sample. "This was all that mommy had left, and we haven't eaten all day long."

Just as the "good" foreigners defended the simple natives of the Third World, now they protect another little native, the underprivileged mite of the big city. The nephews have behaved like saints (they actually wear halos in the last picture) because they have recognized the right of each and all to possess the money they already own. There is no question of an unjust distribution of wealth: if everyone were like the honest ducklings rather than the ugly cheats, the system would function perfectly. The little girl's problem is not her poverty, it is having *lost* the only money her family had (which presumably will last forever, or else they will starve and the whole house of Disney will come tumbling down). To avoid war and preserve social peace, everyone should deliver unto others what is already theirs. The ducklings decline the monetary reward offered by Donald: "We already have our reward. Knowing that we have helped make someone happy." But the act of charity underlines the moral superiority of the givers and justifies the mansion to which they return after their "good works" in the slums. If they hadn't returned the banknote, they would have descended to the level of the Beagle Boys and would not be worthy enough to win the treasure hunt. The path to wealth lies through charity, which is a good moral investment. The number of lost children, injured lambs, old ladies needing help to cross the street, is an index of the requirements for entry into the "good guys club"—after one has already been nominated by another "good guy." In the absence of active virtue, Good Works are the proof of moral superiority.

Prophetically, Alexis de Tocqueville wrote in his *Democracy in America*, "By this means, a kind of virtuous materialism may ultimately be established in the world, which would not corrupt, but enervate the soul, and noiselessly unbend its springs of action." It is a pity that the Frenchman who wrote this in the mid–nineteenth century did not live to visit the land of Disney, where his words have been burlesqued in a great idealistic cock-a-doodle-doo.

Thus the winners are announced in advance. In this race for money, where all the contestants are apparently in the same position, what is the factor that decides that this one wins and the other one loses? If goodness and truth are on the side of the "legitimate" owner, how does someone else take ownership of the property?

Nothing could be simpler and more revealing: they can't. The bad guys (who, remember, behave like children) are bigger, stronger, faster, and armed; the good guys have the advantage of superior intelligence, and use it mercilessly. The bad guys rack their brains desperately for ideas (in one strip, "I have a terrific plan in my head," says one, scratching it like a halfwit, "Are you sure you have a head, 176–716?"). Their brainlessness is *invariably* what leads to their downfall. They are caught in a double bind: if they use only their legs, they won't get there; if they use their heads as well, they won't get there either. Nonintellectuals by definition, their ideas can never prosper. Thinking won't do you bad guys any good, better rely on those arms and legs, eh? The little adventurers will always have a better and more brilliant idea, so there's no point in competing with them. They hold a monopoly on thought, brains, words, and, for that matter, on the meaning of the world at large. It's their world, they must know it better than you bad guys, right?

There can be only one conclusion: behind good and evil are hidden not only the social antagonists but also a definition of them in terms of soul versus body, spirit versus matter, brain versus muscle, and intellectual versus manual work. It is a division of labor that cannot be questioned. The good guys have "cornered the knowledge market" in their competition against the muscle-bound brutes.

But there is more. Since the laboring classes are reduced to mere legs running for a goal they will never reach, the bearers of ideas are left as the legitimate owners of the treasure. They won in a fair fight. And not only that, it was the power of their ideas that created the wealth to begin with, and inspired the search and proved, once again, the superiority of mind over matter. Exploitation has been justified, the profits of the past have been legitimated, and ownership is found to confer exclusive rights on the retention and increase of wealth. If the bourgeoisie now controls the capital and the means of production, it is not because it exploited anyone or accumulated wealth unfairly.

Disney, throughout his comics, implies that capitalist wealth originates under the same circumstances he portrays in his comics. It was always the ideas of the bourgeoisie that gave it the advantage in the race for success, and nothing else.

And those ideas shall, in the end, rise up in its defense.

Note

1. Karl Marx, *The Holy Family* (1845); cf. Marcelin Pleynet, "A propos d'une analyse des *Mystères de Paris*, par Marx dans *La sainte famille*," *La nouvelle critique* (Paris), 1968.

MEDIA IMPERIALISM?

JEREMY TUNSTALL

THE TELEVISION
IMPERIALISM THESIS

Many people over the past hundred years have pointed out the importance of American (and British) media in the world.[1] The most carefully researched work on this topic is still Thomas Guback's *The International Film Industry* (1969), which analyzes Hollywood dominance in the Western European film industries since 1945. Herbert Schiller's *Mass Communications and American Empire*, also by an American and also published in 1969, is a rare exception to the general lack of Marxist empirical accounts.[2] Schiller's thesis—that American television exports are part of an attempt by the American military industrial complex to subjugate the world—has been followed by other related work. Alan Wells's *Picture Tube Imperialism?* (1972) pursues the television imperialism thesis in Latin America.

Schiller's first contention is that despite the apparently commercial character of U.S. telecommunications, the American radio spectrum has increasingly come under the control of the federal government in general and the secretary of defense in particular. The major concern of domestic American radio and television is to sell receiving sets and advertise goods. The educational stations of early American radio were lost as a consequence of this commercialism and greed, and Schiller would like to see a return to a more educational and less commercial emphasis. Since 1950 and increasingly since the Cuban Bay of Pigs fiasco of 1961, Schiller sees American television as having come under the control of Washington; for example, RCA (which controls the NBC television and radio networks) is a major defense contractor—and consequently beholden to, and uncritical of, the federal government.

The great expansion of American television into the world around 1960—equipment, programming, and advertising—is seen by Schiller as part of a general effort of the American military industrial complex to subject the world to military control, electronic surveillance, and homogenized American commercial culture. American television program exports, through their close connection with the manufacture of television receiving sets and American advertising agencies, are also seen as the spearhead for an American consumer goods invasion of the world. This export boom has, and is intended to have, the effect of muting political protest in much of the world; local and authentic culture in many countries is driven to the defensive by homogenized American culture. Traditional national drama and folk music retreat before "Peyton Place" and "Bonanza." So powerful is the thrust of American commercial television that few nations can resist. Even nations that deliberately choose not to have commercial broadcasting find their policies being reversed by American advertising agencies

From Jeremy Tunstall, *The Media Are American* (New York: Columbia University Press, 1977).

within their borders and by pirate radio stations from without. Commercial radio and television received from neighboring countries tend to a "domino effect," by which commercial radio spreads remorselessly into India, and commercial television spreads from one West European country to the next. With the exception of the communist countries, and perhaps Japan, few nations can resist.

During the 1960s, Schiller argued, American policy came to focus even more strongly on subjugating and pacifying the poor nations; and in this strategy space satellites were to play a key part. The U.S. government placed its telecommunications satellite policy in the hands of the giant electronics companies (AT & T, IT & T, RCA) and then negotiated with the Western nations INTELSAT arrangements that gave the United States dominance of world communications; ultimately the policy was to beam American network television complete with commercials straight into domestic television sets around the world. The homogenization of world culture would then be complete. False consciousness would be plugged via satellite into every human home.

Alan Wells elaborates how American television imperialism works in Latin America. Latin American television has, since its birth, been dominated by U.S. finance, companies, technology, and programming and, above all, by New York advertising agencies and practices. There is a very substantial direct ownership interest on the part of the United States in Latin American television stations. "Worldvision," an ominously titled subsidiary of the ABC network, plays a dominant role in Latin America; American advertising agencies not only produce most of the very numerous commercial breaks but also sponsor, shape, and determine the whole pattern of programming and importing from the United States. Indeed, "approximately 80 per cent of the hemisphere's current programs—including "The Flintstones," "I Love Lucy," "Bonanza," and "Route 66"—were produced in the United States."[3] This near-monopoly of North American television programming within South America distorts entire economies away from "producerism" and toward "consumerism." Madison Avenue picture tube imperialism has triumphed in every Latin American country except Cuba.

THE TELEVISION IMPERIALISM
THESIS: TOO STRONG
AND TOO WEAK

The Schiller-Wells account exaggerates the strength of American television, partly because some of their quoted figures are unreliable; they concentrate on the high point of American television exports in the mid-1960s. They also tend to accept too easily the promotional optimism of a company like ABC, whose Worldvision remained a paper "network" only. Sometimes, too, their logic is faulty; they complain that in the poor countries only the very rich can buy television anyhow, but then they see television as subverting the whole nation. Nevertheless, the American influence on world television—even if not so great as these authors argue—has been very considerable.

At the same time, these authors' argument is also too weak. They scarcely notice the tendency of television merely to repeat a previous pattern of radio and feature films. This television imperialism thesis ignores the much earlier pattern of the press and news agencies, which quite unambiguously did have an imperial character—although these empires were European ones, mainly British, but also French, Dutch, Belgian, Portuguese.

Tapio Varis has produced the first reasonably comprehensive mapping of worldwide television import patterns. Varis found for 1971 (the year before Wells's book was published) that the television channels in the larger Latin American countries (such as Argentina, Colombia, and Mexico) imported between 10 and 39 percent of programming. The only one of seven Latin American countries in the Varis study to import 80 percent of programming was Guatemala.[4] Varis also found that a substantial proportion of television imports came from countries other than the United States, including such Latin American countries as Mexico.

Nevertheless, the Varis study did document American television exports around the world on an enormous scale:

Many of the developing countries use much imported material, but—with the exception of a number of Latin American countries and a few Middle East countries—television is still of minor importance in most parts of the developing world; when it is available, it is for the most part merely a privilege of the urban rich.

The United States and the People's Republic of China are examples of countries which currently use little foreign material—at least compared with the total amount of their own programming. Japan and the Soviet Union also produce most of their own programs. Most other nations, however, are heavy purchasers of foreign material. Even in an area as rich as Western Europe, imported programs account for about one-third of total transmission time.

Most nonsocialist countries purchase programs mainly from the United States and the United Kingdom. In Western Europe for example, American produced programs account for about half of all imported programs, and from 15 to 20 per cent of total transmission time. The socialist countries also use American and British material, but only TV Belgrade uses as large a share of American programs as the Western European countries.

The real social and political impact of imported programs may be greater than might be inferred from the volume of imported material, because of audience viewing patterns and the placing of foreign programming. Available studies about prime-time programming in various countries tend to show that the proportion of foreign material during these hours is considerably greater than at other times.

For each country surveyed, we looked at the categories into which imported programs fell. Program imports are heavily concentrated on serials and series, long feature films, and entertainment programs.[5]

A more recent study by Elihu Katz, George Wedell, and their colleagues traces the history of both radio and television in ten Latin American, Asian, and African countries, as well as Cyprus.[6] This study attributes a considerably larger place to British influence. The Katz-Wedell study suggests that the television imperialism thesis takes too little account of radio and of differences both within and between nations. It also strongly confirms that there was a high point of American influence on world television at some point in the 1960s. Central to the Katz-Wedell study is the notion of "phases of institutionalization." First there was a direct transfer or adoption of a metropolitan—usually American, British, or French—model of broadcasting, with radio setting the pattern for television. Next there was a phase of adapting this system to the local society. And ultimately a new "sense of direction" was introduced by the government—this typically involved removing any remaining vestiges of direct foreign ownership and increasing the direct control of government. This third phase typically occurred around 1970, which was about when the Schiller and Wells works were being published; thus some of their arguments are invalid because incomplete.

Katz and Wedell focus heavily on the receiving countries and are excellent at detailing the endless muddles, confusion, indecisions, self-deception, conflicting goals, conflicting ministries—in short, the general chaos that seems to characterize the appearance of television. Katz and Wedell reject any strong television imperialism thesis, and they tend to see the American and British exporters of television models and styles as no less muddled and self-deceiving than the importers.

Nevertheless, despite their implicit rejection of much of the television imperialism thesis, Katz and Wedell do provide much descriptive material which fits the thesis quite well. The importance of production (transmission and studio) technology is confirmed. Like the other students of television exports, they look with horror on the weight of commercial advertising, the predominance of American entertainment series, and the relative absence in most countries of high-quality educational or cultural television programming.

. . . .

SOME APPEALS OF HOLLYWOOD
ENTERTAINMENT

Many countries failed around 1920 to grasp the near impossibility of shutting out Hollywood films. Later, especially in the 1930s, some countries began to develop coherent policies for such resistance. But having made noncommercial arrangements for broadcasting, most of these same countries then failed to recognize that a state controlled broadcasting system also would face an importing dilemma. Thus the same state broadcasting systems that in the late 1940s were taken unawares by music imports were later taken unawares by television imports.

The most successful resistance to Hollywood imports in the 1930s occurred in the Soviet Union, Japan, and Germany. These governments all saw Hollywood imports in political as well as cultural terms; all these countries had substantial economic resources—and their governments were willing to pay the price of maintaining major domestic film industries.

Television was invariably established as an offshoot of radio, a decision that confused and weakened initial resistance to American television imports. Most countries outside Latin America had a public service (or BBC) style of radio. European and other state broadcasting organizations overestimated their ability to resist importing Hollywood materials and styles; and in countries where a domestic mini-Hollywood has been painfully established, broadcasting organizations typically failed to grasp the relevance of this hard-won domestic experience.

The importing of entertainment materials has primarily been of pop music records, feature films, recorded television drama series, and recorded entertainment shows. Much of this material adopts the form of a fictional story—children's programming, comic strips, women's magazine fiction, and paperback books. In these fictional stories the American media present their characteristic themes of status, success, personal qualities, sex roles, youth, and ethnicity. The response of foreign consumers will depend partly on their own ethnicity, age, and sex. In Europe, imported material reaches the entire population, but outside Europe those most heavily exposed to imported media are mainly urban, employed in the modern economy, and relatively youthful, with higher-than-average incomes. In Latin America, Asia, and Africa the typical consumer of imported media will be a young white-collar worker or a factory worker—not an elderly peasant in a remote rural area. Many of these urban consumers will themselves have a personal history of social and geographical mobility, and may respond to these themes in American media. Many will be women, often escaping from traditional views of appropriate women's roles, and the portrayal of women in American media output may be appealing.

People in authority may not like emphasis on upward social mobility, relative freedom for women, and support of the young against the old. Hollywood's favorable portrayal of people with white skins and its much less favorable portrayal until recently of people with black skins must have led to very mixed responses. Within many countries in Latin America, the Arab world, and Asia, there are people of both lighter and darker skin color—so the possibilities for racial identification and antagonism even within a single country are quite complex.

The appeal of stylized violence to the frustrated urban youth of many lands cannot be better illustrated than by the many imitations of the American western. Some of the most obvious are the Italian and Spanish—"spaghetti" and "paella"—westerns. There have also been many Asian imitations of the western, including Chinese films made in Shanghai in the interwar period, Japanese historical films, and more recently the kung-fu (or "chop suey") westerns of Hong Kong.

The various mini-Hollywoods of the world have copied the phenomenon of the star, and in many countries the most popular single star performer is a local national. But Hollywood established the first star system around 1920 and has managed to convince the world that it still has a uniquely large supply of uniquely dazzling stars. Part of the glamor of the Hollywood star lies in his or her stardom itself—fame and fortune not only in the United States, but all around the world. This factor of stardom in many countries as an integral part of star appeal was already evident in 1920, when Douglas Fairbanks and Mary Pickford visited Europe ostensibly on their honeymoon:

The crowds were so thick outside their suite at the Ritz-Carlton in New York before they sailed that they couldn't leave the hotel. Word was called ahead to England, France, Holland, Switzerland, and Italy that Doug and Mary were coming. . . .

They first stopped at the Ritz in London and crowds thousands deep waited all night to catch sight of their idols. Doug delighted in carrying Mary through the pressing throngs in London and later in Paris. . . . Doug and Mary escaped to the cottage of Lord Northcliffe on the Isle of Wight only to be discovered surrounded by hundreds of fans at dawn one morning.

These scenes were repeated on the Continent and not really discouraged by Mary and Doug. . . . In Lugano, Switzerland, and Venice, Florence and Rome the fans hailed "Maria e Lampo" (for "lightning," which is what Douglas was called in Italian). In Paris one afternoon they were afraid to leave their suite at the Hotel Crillon, the crowds were so thick, but they announced their intention of visiting Les Halles one morning and took satisfaction in stopping all traffic. . . .

Only in Germany, the so recent enemy, were they ignored, and neither Doug nor Mary could stand it. . . .

Word of the triumphal tour came back to New York through the newspapers, and America wasn't to be outdone in honoring the pair of cinema artists.[7]

Charlie Chaplin was greeted by equally enormous European crowds. Mary Pickford and Douglas Fairbanks also visited the Soviet Union, where in 1925 their films still dominated local screens, and they were again greeted by huge crowds.

All of this was powerfully encouraged by the Hollywood publicity mills, the result of operating publicity across a continent of daily newspapers; Hollywood also drew on the techniques of "advancing" presidential campaigns and theatrical tours. The arrival of famous faces from six thousand miles away must have seemed more dramatic than any arrival of a star in one European country coming from another. These Hollywood stars also had an excuse for perpetual movement—a continuous succession of photogenic arrivals and departures— just like their film selves.

The Hollywood star arriving on a publicity trip in Europe was the inheritor of an established tradition of exotic American publicity trips to Europe. Increasingly during the latter half of the nineteenth century, American minstrels, celebrities, circus freaks, founders of new religions, and Wild West entertainers had arrived to entertain the staid Europeans with the latest American exotica. Douglas Fairbanks established a pattern by which the indication of success in such a trip was the number of kings and queens met in Europe and subsequently invited back for visits to Los Angeles.

The same thing continues still as waves of American singers, dancers, actors, actresses, and celebrities come remorselessly fluttering out of the western sky— here today in Europe and gone tomorrow around the world. The same preceding and succeeding waves of publicity operate; only now the old traditions of shipboard interviews and arrivals and departures for the benefit of the local press have been substituted by the rituals of the airport and the television chat show.

The status themes, the stars' personalities, the intimate career details are put on display. The star modestly admits to the two hundredth interviewer how she was just so lucky to get her latest and best-yet part. The media audience is invited to identify with the star, who is so dazzlingly successful and yet not so very different from you or me—who is indeed sincerely worried about her next show, film, or record.

Success in the media has long been one of the staple topics of the American media. And as the American media have moved out onto the world scene, media-success-on-the-world-scene has become a staple media topic: "Yes, darling, already doing good business in Japan and Sweden, not released here until tomorrow."

.   .   .   .

CULTURAL IMPERIALISM VERSUS
AUTHENTIC LOCAL CULTURE

The cultural imperialism thesis claims that authentic, traditional, and local culture in many parts of the world is being battered out of existence by the indiscriminate dumping of large quantities of slick commercial and media products, mainly from the United States. Those who make this argument most forcibly tend to favor restrictions on media imports, as well as the deliberate preservation of authentic and traditional culture.

This problem of cultural identity is part of a larger problem of national identity. The United States, Britain, and France belong to a minority of the world's nations in having a fairly strong national identity. Almost all their citizens speak roughly the same language; but even in these countries there are major internal frictions—regional, ethnic, language, and social class differences. And even this degree of national identity has only been achieved after several centuries of national existence, including civil war often followed by the brutal subjugation of regional and ethnic minorities. Countries that have an unusually strong national identity also happen to have the longest traditions of the press and other media, conducted primarily in a single national language.

The strength of national identity is less marked in Latin America, either despite, or possibly because of, the use of Spanish as the language of all but one of the largest countries. In much of eastern, central, and parts of northern Europe there are two, three, or more separate languages, religions, and cultural traditions within a single state. The Soviet Union has this pattern on an even larger scale, as does India and some other Asian countries. There are similarly sharp cleavages within many Arab countries; and in Africa, national identity is least strong of all.

The variety of languages within many nation states is at once a major factor in "cultural imperialism" and in lack of national identity. There are also very big differences between urban and rural areas, a very uneven pattern of development between some backward areas and other areas with exportable resources. Peasants' rebellions, guerrilla uprisings, palace revolutions, and even large-scale civil wars are a recent experience or an immediate realistic prospect in many lands. In the many countries where the prime object of policy is to reduce the threat of armed conflict, the need to strengthen "authentic culture" may not be seen as critical.

The most authentic and traditional culture often seems—and not only to the ruling elite—to be also the most inappropriate. This is not merely because traditional culture sanctions what would now be called civil war. Traditional culture is also typically archaic, does not fit with contemporary notions of justice or equality, and depends on religious beliefs that have long been in decline. Many traditional cultures were primarily carried by a small elite of scholars and priests, who often used languages which few other people understood. Not only Arab and Hindu cultures but many others as well ascribed a fixed subservient position to women, the young, and the occupationally less favored. It is precisely these unpopular characteristics of much authentic culture that make the imported media culture so popular by contrast.

The variety in traditional cultures is clearly enormous, but two relatively common types of music can be used as illustration. One is the type of traditional opera found in a number of Asian countries; such traditional opera is musically complex, often having its own specialized acting traditions as well as its own musical instruments. Both its total repertoire and its total audience are often quite small. Such music belongs to a traditional hierarchical society that has long been in decline. Clearly it is unlikely to become a hit parade or television staple; it has to compete, moreover, with Beethoven and Mozart as well as with the Beatles and the movies.

A second common type of traditional music is found in many parts of Africa and some parts of Asia. This music is less complex and depends on simpler instruments; the music both appeals to and is produced by the ordinary people. The music is indeed an integral part of the major individual (birth, marriage, death) and collective (especially harvest) events and symbolism of ordinary life. It is often played for a few days or a few weeks on end. It has influenced jazz and all subsequent Western popular music; but in its authentic and traditional form it is difficult to adapt to media usage—although many African radio services do broadcast such music, and it is often popular especially in the immediate area from which it originates.

Another difficulty of "authentic culture" is that one might expect there to be some level of regional culture, beyond the tribal or national but smaller than the international. There is indeed quite a lot of radio listening across national boundaries, although many governments and broadcasting organizations wish to discourage it. Many nations in the world, both "old" and "new," have uneasy relations with their neighbors. Subjecting the neighbor's citizens to your media while protecting your own citizens from his media is a common purpose of radio policy.

The debate about cultural imperialism and authentic culture is reminiscent of, and related to, another debate about "mass society," mass culture, and indeed the "mass media." The term "mass" has a long intellectual genealogy of its own— and has long been used by both left and right with various shades of meaning and implication.[8] When this debate dealt with Europe and the United States it was confused enough. But the same debate, transposed to Asia and Africa, gets even more confused. It is precisely the highly educated elite in Asian and African countries who are the most active consumers of imported—and presumably "low, brutal and commercial"—media, whereas the rural dwellers—short of land, food, literacy, income, life expectation, birth control devices, and so on— are the main consumers of traditional and "authentic" culture.

T. W. Adorno at one time claimed that even a symphony concert when broadcast on radio was drained of significance; many mass culture critics also had very harsh things to say about the large audiences that went to western and crime films in the 1930s—films which yet other cultural experts have subsequently decided were masterpieces after all. Even more bizarre, however, is the Western intellectual who switches off the baseball game, turns down the hi-fi, or pushes aside the Sunday magazine and pens a terse instruction to the developing world to get back to its tribal harvest ceremonials or funeral music.

Such a caricature illustrates that the real choice probably lies with hybrid forms. In many countries older cultural forms often continue in vigorous existence, although modified by Western influences. Pop music often takes this form; "Eastern westerns" or the Latin American *telenovelas* are other examples. The debate then, should be about whether such hybrid forms are primarily traditional and "authentic" or merely translations or imitations of Anglo-American forms.

POLITICS AND INEQUALITY

How do the Anglo-American media affect politics or inequality within an importing country? Do they, as the media imperialism thesis implies, buttress reactionary politicians and solidify inequalities? Or do they have democratic and egalitarian implications?

Among nineteenth-century elites in Europe, one of the main anxieties about the American press was its lack of respect for established practices and people. Charles Dickens, returning from the United States in 1842, expressed these anxieties with vigor and clarity:

Among the herd of journals which are published in the States there are some, the reader scarcely need be told, of character and credit. From personal intercourse with accomplished gentlemen connected with publications of this class, I have derived both pleasure and profit. But the name of these is Few, and of the other Legion; and the influence of the good, is powerless to counteract the mortal poison of the bad.

Among the gentry of America; among the well-informed and moderate; in the learned professions; at the bar and on the bench: there is, and there can be, but one opinion, in reference to the vicious character of these infamous journals. It is sometimes contended—I will not say strangely, for it is natural to seek excuses for such a disgrace—that their influence is not so great as a visitor would suppose. I must be pardoned for saying that there is no warrant for this plea, and that every fact and circumstance tends directly to the opposite conclusion.

When any man, of any grade of desert in intellect or character, can climb to any public distinction, no matter what, in America, without first grovelling down upon the earth, and bending the knee before this monster of depravity; when any private excellence is safe from its attacks; when any social confidence is left unbroken by it, or any tie of social decency and honour is held in the least regard . . . then, I will believe that its influence is lessening, and men are returning to their manly senses. But while that Press has its evil eye in every house, and its black hand in every appointment in the state, from a president to a postman; while, with ribald slander for its only stock in trade, it is the standard literature of an enormous class, who must find their reading in a newspaper, or they will not read at all; so long must its odium be upon the country's head, and so long must the evil it works, be plainly visible in the Republic.

To those who are accustomed to the leading English journals, or to the respectable journals of the Continent of Europe, to those who are accustomed to anything else in print and paper; it would be impossible, without an amount of extract for which I have neither space nor inclination, to convey an adequate idea of this frightful engine in America.

Responses to imported American media continue to be related to attitudes toward currently prevalent inequalities. But it would be quite misleading to think in terms of media imports always favoring the poor at the expense of the rich. Even within the United States the media are primarily aimed at the middle of the population, not at its very poorest members. In terms of England in 1842, or Western Europe today, imports of American media may quite realistically be seen as potentially hostile to established elites. But the emphasis of these media on success and status favors the new rich more than the old poor. These media also present a heavily *urban* view of life.

In multi-party nations of western Europe, and perhaps to some extent in Eastern Europe as well, imports of American media materials may tend toward democratizing and egalitarian effects. Such commercial infusions will tend to influence, if not the basic substance of political power within importing countries, then at least the *styles* politicians use in presenting themselves to local and national publics. Increased amounts of market-oriented media fare—more entertaining entertainment, and more "neutral" news—will tend to make the more obviously political party fare seem less entertaining and more obviously dull and unattractive. Thus politicians try to dress up their political messages in more entertaining and neutral-looking packages. This in turn implies the use of PR and market research skills—in presenting the chief executive and his supporters, but also in presenting and shaping policies in even the most complex and delicate areas.

In multi-party countries, the rise of commercial or mainly advertising-financed media and the decline of party or government-financed media may become cumulative. Politically or government-controlled media tend to become less attractive to audiences, hence less important to politicians, and so on. More and more politicians use the techniques and the advice of advertising, market research, and public relations, and the argument is heard (and heeded) that media that are obviously controlled by government or party constitute bad political strategy. There is a gradual change by which politicians and governments in multi-party countries seek accommodations within an increasingly commercial pattern of media.

But in poorer African and Asian nations, infusions of Western media may indeed buttress and extend existing inequalities. Since these imported media are consumed mainly by the urban and relatively affluent, and since importing becomes a substitute for providing cheap domestic media to most areas, inequality may be increased. In many poor countries, also, the media are controlled by the government; the national media may become a key instrument through which a small affluent elite maintains itself in power. This view of the media as prime defenders of the status quo is often shared by politicians in power and illustrated by the heavy military guard found outside many capital city radio stations.

Thus foreign media may in some affluent countries favor more equality, but in other less affluent countries favor more inequality. In yet other countries, such as those of Latin America, both sorts of effects may occur at the same time. For example, it may be true that, in general, the imported media tip the scales away from the country and in favor of the city; but within the heavily populated Latin American cities those same media might have an egalitarian effect.

ONE MEDIA IMPERIALIST,
OR A DOZEN?

The media imperialism thesis does not confront the presence of strong regional exporters in various parts of the world. Mexico and Argentina have a tradition of exporting media to their neighbors, Egypt exports to the Arab world, and Indian films and records go to many countries in Africa and Asia. Not only the United States, Britain, and France, but also West Germany, Italy, Spain, and Japan all export some media. Even Sweden has its own little media empire in Scandinavia. And the Soviet Union has strong media markets in Eastern Europe.

This phenomenon can be seen as running counter to the media imperialist thesis—showing that American and British media exports have many substantial rivals. But there are also grounds for seeing Mexican or Egyptian or even Indian exports as an indirect extension of Anglo-American influence. *The countries that are strongly regional exporters of media tend themselves to be unusually heavy importers of American media.*

Italy in 1972 was, after the United States, the largest exporter of feature films, with considerable strength in every world region. Yet the United States was the source for over half of Italy's imports, and for an unusually high proportion of Britain's, Mexico's, and India's imports as well. Other strong film exporters— Japan, Egypt, and West Germany—were strong importers of U.S. films. Only the Soviet Union, among major film exporters, imports virtually nothing from Hollywood.

By 1972 the majority of films made in Britain were Hollywood-financed and -distributed, as was a substantial proportion of Italian and French films (including Italian-French coproductions subsidized by both governments). And all of the major film exporters in the world (except the Soviet Union) take around three-quarters of their film imports from the United States, Great Britain, Italy, and France combined. Thus almost all significant film exporters in the world are themselves open to heavy current Hollywood influence. The strength of Soviet film exports in Eastern Europe is noticeably weaker than Hollywood's unassisted export strength in all world regions apart from Eastern Europe.

These data, incidentally, illustrate that television is not necessarily the best example for the media imperialist thesis. The continuing extent of Hollywood feature film exports around the world is all the more remarkable because Hollywood has here retained its export leadership for sixty years.

The television imperialism thesis, then, cannot be considered merely for television alone. A more historical approach, covering all media, is required. We must also note, for example, the intentions of both exporters and importers, and we must recognize as well that many social consequences are unintended. Nevertheless, the Schiller thesis has a number of strengths, especially in taking the whole world for its unit of analysis—and Schiller's domino theory of American media influence is one illustration of the benefits of so doing.

In my view, the Anglo-American media are connected with imperialism, British imperialism. But these media exports both predate and still run ahead of the general American economic presence overseas or the multinational company phenomenon. Schiller attributes too many of this world's ills to television. He also has an unrealistic view of returning to traditional cultures, many of which, although authentic, are dead. In my view, a non-American way out of the media box is difficult to discover because that box was built in the first place by Americans, or Anglo-Americans. The only way out is to construct a new box, and this, with the possible exception of the Chinese, no nation seems willing to do.

Notes

1. The present author first came across this phenomenon in the case of British advertising agencies. See Jeremy Tunstall, *The Advertising Man in London Advertising Agencies* (London: Chapman & Hall, 1964), pp. 33–35, 140–141, 156–157, 224–226.

2. The shortage of Marxist empirically based accounts of this topic is illustrated in *Marxism and the Mass Media: Towards a Basic Bibliography*, vol. 3 (Paris: International General, 1974), which contains 453 references.

3. Alan Wells, *Picture-Tube Imperialism? The Impact of U.S. Television on Latin America* (Maryknoll, N.Y.: Orbis Books, 1972), p. 121.

4. Kaarle Nordenstreng and Tapio Varis, *Television Traffic—A One-Way Street?* (Paris: UNESCO, 1974), p. 14.

5. Tapio Varis, "Global Traffic in Television," *Journal of Communication* 24 (1974): 107.

6. E. Katz, E. G. Wedell, M. J. Pilsworth, and D. Shinar, *Broadcasting and National Development* (manuscript).

7. Robert Windeler, *Mary Pickford, Sweetheart of the World* (London: Allen, 1975), pp. 119–121.

8. Leon Bramson, *The Political Context of Sociology* (Princeton, N.J.: Princeton University Press, 1961).

Part VIII

Alternatives and
Cultural Activism

INTRODUCTION

What would American socialists replace capitalist mass culture with, other than bureaucratic state monopoly and Soviet-style commissars? The goal of a communications system in a democratic socialist society would be to maximize freedom of political and cultural expression, public participation, and dialogue and debate among a full range of ideological viewpoints. The model for such a system would have a pluralistic structure, something like that envisioned by Robert Cirino ("An Alternative American Communications System") and Christopher Jencks ("Should News Be Sold for Profit?") here: a multi-channeled, multi-ideological national public communications network, supplemented by a diversity of nonprofit media financed by local communities (like WNYC in New York), public corporations such as PBS, direct support from listeners and viewers (Pacifica Radio, cable TV), universities and school systems, worker and consumer cooperatives, trade unions, and other interest groups. Private businesses and capitalist ideologists would retain a voice, but only in proportion to their reduced role in the society as a whole—in contrast to their present virtual monopoly on mass communication—and limitations on extreme wealth would curb the influence of the rich in politics, media, and culture. For example, either political campaign advertising on television and radio could be illegalized, as it has been in many democracies, or else stations could be required to provide equal time for response to all political ads, as well as to ideological ads such as Mobil Oil's or any other disputable commercials. Better yet, political or commercial advertisers could be obliged to debate their critics face to face. A healthier climate of national dialogue could further be fostered by instituting the regular practice of direct, televised questioning of officeholders (starting with the president), news reporters, and commentators by opponents from both the other major party and minority parties ranging from far left to far right.

The recent experience of other democracies suggests that the best system is one that encourages competition between public and commercial media, with democratic safeguards to ensure that neither overpowers the other. Sober-minded socialists recognize that any such system would have its own flaws; there is no certainty that it would be an improvement in any given respect over the present system; however, like the socialist ideal in general, in allowing goals to be set that meet social needs—rather than focusing only on profits—such a system could provide *possibilities* for improvement that are precluded by the structure of capitalism.

Within the limits of the possible under present-day American capitalism, the immediate project of left cultural activism must be modest: to explore means of expanding alternative media and to gain more of a hearing for socialist views in diverse fields, including those covered in each of the articles in this section. In all of these fields, the deck is stacked economically and politically against innovation; yet the actual projects described by Spark, Davis, and Kellner in this section, and Zipes in Part 5, along with many others described in the further readings—such as John Downing's *Radical Media: The Political Experience of*

Alternative Communication and David Armstrong's *A Trumpet to Arms: Alternative Media in America*—indicate a heartening range of possibilities if only we can exercise sufficient hope, imagination, and willpower to achieve them.

In terms of pedagogical practice, what kind of rhetorical framework can be set up for college courses in various disciplines to foster debate between other approaches to mass media or popular culture and the one presented in this collection? Kampf's course on sports suggests one model; others follow below. To supplement these suggestions, several useful books addressed to teachers, some with classroom exercises, are listed in the further readings.

To begin with advertising, the kind of favorable attitudes expressed in McQuade and Atwan's *Popular Writing in America* and Marsden's "Popular Culture and the Teaching of English" (with equal time limited to one article in each volume criticizing subliminal techniques of persuasion) can be balanced against the critical classroom activities suggested in the full-length version of Richard Ohmann's "Doublespeak and Ideology in Ads" in *Teaching About Doublespeak*.[1] Criticism of the economic functions of advertising within the capitalist system needs to be aired—functions such as the artificial stimulation of demand to absorb surplus production; the encouragement of waste, planned obsolescence, and resource depletion; the creation of the illusion of differences within an inefficient multiplicity of essentially similar products; and the facilitation of excessively high pricing and monopolization of the market by brand-name products. Defenders of advertising will argue that all of its negative traits are justifiable within the imperatives of capitalist economy because advertising stimulates production, which results (theoretically) in lower prices and higher employment.

At this point, either capitalism must be accepted as a given in our society or else the discussion must lead into the larger issue of socialist alternatives to capitalist production and marketing. To facilitate this debate, students might evaluate defenses of capitalism by Democratic and Republican political leaders, establishment media such as *Time*, or authors like Milton and Rose Friedman, William F. Buckley, Jr., or George Gilder, in comparison to the case for socialism as stated in such books as Michael Lerner's *The New Socialist Revolution*, Martin Carnoy and Derek Shearer's *Economic Democracy*, Steve Rosskamm Shalom's *Socialist Visions*, Alec Nove's *Feasible Socialism*, or the many works of Michael Harrington, Irving Howe, Christopher Lasch, and Stanley Aronowitz.[2]

Turning to the study of political propaganda and news reporting, as part of a unit in a composition class on diction or semantics, students can look for examples in political speeches or writings and in television or print news of inaccurate, ambiguous, or slanted uses of such terms as *liberal, conservative,* and *radical, free enterprise, capitalism, communism, socialism, fascism, democracy,* and *the free world.* On politically biased or censored news, virtually all recent debate has been in terms of liberal versus conservative bias. To put the debate into the context of capitalist versus socialist bias, exercises along the lines of Cirino's "An Alternative American Communications System" can be devised. In order for teachers to expose themselves and students to socialist perspectives on political issues, the books we customarily read can be supplemented by ones from publishers open to left viewpoints, including South End Press, Routledge and Kegan Paul, Monthly Review Press, Ramparts Press, International Publishers, Pathfinder Press, Methuen, Ablex, Basil Blackwell, Beacon Press, Bergin and Garvey, Lawrence Hill, and Seabury Press. To the mainstream weekly, monthly, and quarterly journals, both popular and scholarly, can be added those listed in the further readings. After regular exposure to these publications, readers will likely find them no more slanted toward socialism than most liberal-to-conservative periodicals are toward capitalism and one or the other of the establishment parties.

The selections and recommended further readings in this volume on television and film entertainment, popular music, sports, and mass-mediated religion can be studied for their distinctive rhetorical viewpoint on the relation of these media to capitalist economics and ideology and on the role of class, sexual, and racial divisions in both capitalism and media. (More recent models for such study can be found in current issues of left periodicals that are devoted exclusively to one of these topics—for example, *Jump Cut* and *Cineaste* on film—or that carry regular back-of-the-book features on culture, such as *In These Times*, the *Village Voice*, and *Mother Jones*.)

For example, consider Marsden's discussion of television production: "Our Popular Culture is created by the combined creative efforts of many people and it involves their working together for the benefit of all. The finished product is the most entertaining and culturally significant product the cast and crew are able to produce within the tight schedules and other limitations placed upon them." [3] Classroom analysis of Marsden might call attention to his omission, among the limitations placed on production, of censorship by sponsors, producers, networks, local stations, and pressure groups. Contrasting left sources such as Todd Gitlin's "Television's Screens: Hegemony in Transition" (Part 4) and Michael Real's *Mass-Mediated Culture* describe the pressures applied, for instance, by the American Medical Association and law enforcement agencies to turn TV medical and police serials into propaganda for the professional establishment. [4] The psychological effects of television and film violence have been widely treated in textbooks, but liberal and conservative accounts rarely place such analyses within the context provided by George Gerbner on authoritarianism or Herbert Marcuse, in works such as *An Essay on Liberation* and *Repressive Tolerance,* on the institutionalized aggression and destructiveness fostered by capitalism.

For more creative activities, students might write scenarios for familiar TV shows and films from differing political viewpoints, as Cirino does. Or they might take part in some of the many current movements for media activism, such as those described by the authors in this section, including theater, film, radio, and television collectives, cable and open-studio TV production groups, networks for increased citizen access to commercial media through free speech messages and other public service broadcasting (along with the same kind of pressure applied by right-wing groups such as Accuracy in Media), groups concerned with investigating local media for sex and race bias in hiring and programming, and organizations to facilitate expanded uses of computer networks and citizens band radio.

The movement for cultural activism is closely allied to a grouping of American educators, including Ira Shor, Stanley Aronowitz, Henry Giroux, Michael Apple, Jonathan Kozol, and the editors of *Radical Teacher*, who, following the Brazilian Paulo Freire, seek alternate modes of literacy and learning that are active rather than passive, that serve to empower students personally and politically rather than fit them into the established order. They do not advocate the touchy-feely permissiveness of some of the educational experiments of the sixties; rather, they insist upon a rigorous curriculum close to the model of classic liberal education, but freed from its traditional class bias and enabling all citizens to develop the critical thinking necessary to resist the reproduction of capitalist hierarchies in the work force, mass-mediated politics and culture, and the educational system itself.

Beyond these immediate possibilities within the present realities of capitalist society, the larger vision of an alternative system of communication and culture, utopian as it may seem, must be sustained as an essential part of the platform for any future left renaissance in America. Democratic socialist alternatives are sneeringly dismissed by the neoconservative Dr. Panglosses who proclaim that Ronald Reagan's vision of American capitalism and its international empire is the best of all possible worlds, as well as by those leftists who pose international communism as its inevitable replacement—while both sides push the world toward total massification, militarization, and nuclear confrontation. But all the derision by these "realists" cannot stifle the persistent human instinct that a better world and a more humane culture must be possible, and that they are worth struggling for.

Notes

1. Donald McQuade and Robert Atwan, eds., *Popular Writing in America*, 2d ed. (New York: Oxford University Press, 1980); Michael T. Marsden, Introduction to "Popular Culture and the Teaching of English" (special issue), *Arizona English Bulletin* 17, no. 3 (1975).

2. Michael Lerner, *The New Socialist Revolution* (New York: Delta, 1973); Martin Carnoy and Derek Shearer, *Economic Democracy* (White Plains, N.Y.: Sharpe, 1980); Steve Rosskamm Shalom, *Socialist Visions* (Boston: South End Press, 1983); Alec Nove, *Feasible Socialism* (London: George Allen and Unwin, 1983).

3. Marsden, "Popular Culture," p. 4.

4. Michael Real, "Marcus Welby and the Medical Genre," *Mass-Mediated Culture* (Englewood Cliffs, N.J.: Prentice-Hall, 1977), pp. 118–139.

Further Readings

Books and Articles on Cultural Activism

Armstrong, David. *A Trumpet to Arms: Alternate Media in America*. Boston: South End Press, 1984.

Boyte, Harry C., and Sara M. Evans. "Strategies in Search of America: Cultural Radicalism, Populism, and Democratic Culture." *Socialist Review*, nos. 75–76 (May–August 1984): 73–102.

Butler, Matilda, and William Paisley. *Women and the Mass Media–Sourcebook for Research and Action*. New York: Human Sciences Press, 1980.

Cantarow, Ellen. "Dubious Battles: How a Small Tenants' Newspaper in Massachusetts Tried to Create a Socialist Journalism." *Radical Teacher* 1, no. 1 (1975): 2–9.

Davis, R. G. *The San Francisco Mime Troupe: The First Ten Years*. Palo Alto, Calif.: Ramparts Press, 1975.

Downing, John. *Radical Media: The Political Experience of Alternative Communication*. Boston: South End Press, 1984.

Hedemann, Ed, ed. *War Resisters League Organizer's Manual*. New York: War Resisters League, 1981. [War Resisters League, 339 Lafayette St., New York, NY 10012; includes a chapter on media activism.]

Hirsch, Glenn, and Alan Lewis. *Strategies for Access to Public Service Advertising*. San Francisco: Public Media Center.

Johnson, Nicholas. *How to Talk Back to Your Television Set*. New York: Bantam Books, 1970.

———. *Test Pattern for Living*. New York: Bantam Books, 1972.

Kessler, Lauren. *The Dissident Press: Alternative Journalism in American Society*. Beverly Hills, Calif.: Sage, 1984.

Klein, Maxine. *Theater for the 98%*. Boston: South End Press, 1984.

Lesnick, Henry, ed. *Guerrilla Street Theater*. New York: Avon Books, 1973.

Mattelart, Armand, and Seth Siegelaub, eds. *Communication and Class Struggle*. Vol. 2: *Liberation, Socialism*. New York: International General, 1980.

Peck, Abe. *Uncovering the Sixties: The Life and Times of the Underground Press*. New York: Pantheon Books, 1984.

Picard, Robert G. *The Press and the Decline of Democracy: The Democratic Socialist Response*. Westport, Conn.: Greenwood Press, 1985.

Polansky, Jonathan, and Michael Singsen. *Talking Back: Public Media Center's Guide to Broadcasting and the Fairness Doctrine for People Who Are Mad as Hell and Aren't Going to Take It Anymore*. San Francisco: Public Media Center, 1983.

Shapiro, Andrew O. *Media Access: Your Rights to Express Your Views on Radio and Television*. Boston: Little, Brown, 1976.

Van Blum, Paul. *The Critical Vision: A History of Social and Political Art in the U.S.* Boston: South End Press, 1981.

Wilkinson, Edymion. *The People's Comic Book*. Garden City, N.Y.: Doubleday, 1973.

Willett, John, ed. *Brecht on Theatre*. New York: Hill & Lang, 1964.

Books and Articles on Critical Education in Media and Mass Culture

Aronowitz, Stanley, and Henry Giroux. *Education Under Siege: The Conservative, Liberal, and Radical Debate Over Schooling*. South Hadley, Mass.: Bergin & Garvey, 1985.

Apple, Michael. *Education and Power*. Boston: Routledge & Kegan Paul, 1982.

———. *Ideology and Curriculum*. Boston: Routledge & Kegan Paul, 1979.

———, ed. *Cultural and Economic Reproduction in Education*. Boston: Routledge & Kegan Paul, 1982.

Chorbajian, Leon. "Teaching the Sociology of Sports." *Radical Teacher*, no. 15 (December 1979): 35–37.

Dieterich, Daniel. *Teaching About Doublespeak*. Urbana, Ill.: National Council of Teachers of English, 1976.

Freire, Paulo. *Education for Critical Consciousness*. New York: Seabury Press, 1974.

———. *The Politics of Education: Culture, Power, and Liberation*. South Hadley, Mass.: Bergin & Garvey, 1985.

Freire, Paulo and Donald Macedo. *Literacy: Reading the Word & the World*. South Hadley, Mass.: Bergin & Garvey, 1986.

Giroux, Henry. *Ideology, Culture, and the Process of Schooling*. Philadelphia: Temple University Press, 1981.

Harty, Sheila. *Hucksters in the Classroom: A Review of Industry Propaganda in Schools*. Washington, D.C.: Center for the Study of Responsive Law, 1979.

Kozol, Jonathan. *Illiterate America*. Garden City, N.Y.: Anchor Press/Doubleday, 1985.

———. *The Night Is Dark and I Am Far from Home*. Boston: Houghton Mifflin, 1975.

Livingston, David, and Contributors. *Critical Pedagogy and Cultural Power*. South Hadley, Mass.: Bergin & Garvey, 1986.

Norton, Theodore Mills, and Bertell Ollman. *Studies in Socialist Pedagogy*. New York: Monthly Review Press, 1978.

Ohmann, Richard. *Politics of Letters*. Middletown, Conn.: Wesleyan University Press, 1987.

Schrank, Jeffrey. *Deception Detection*. Boston: Beacon Press, 1979.

Shor, Ira. *Critical Teaching and Everyday Life*. Boston: South End Press, 1980.

Shor, Ira, and Paulo Freire. *A Pedagogy for Liberation: Dialogues on Transforming Education*. South Hadley, Mass.: Bergin & Garvey, 1986.

Left Journals on Politics and Culture

The Black Scholar
Box 7106
San Francisco, CA 94120

Cineaste
200 Park Ave. South
New York, NY 10003

Covert Action Information Bulletin
P. O. Box 50272
Washington, DC 20004

The Daily World
Longview Publishing Co., Inc.
239 West 23rd St.
New York, NY 10011

Democratic Left
853 Broadway, Suite 801
New York, NY 10033

Discourse
P. O. Box 4667
Berkeley, CA 94704

Dollars & Sense
38 Union Square
Somerville, MA 02143

Feminist Studies
Women's Study Program

University of Maryland
College Park, MD 20742

Grand Street
50 Riverside Drive
New York, NY 10024

The Guardian
33 West 17th St.
New York, NY 10011

In These Times
Institute for Public Affairs
1300 W. Belmont
Chicago, IL 60657

Insurgent Sociologist
Department of Sociology
University of Oregon
Eugene, OR 97403

Jump Cut
P. O. Box 865
Berkeley, CA 94701

Left Curve
P. O. Box 472
Oakland, CA 94604

Media Culture and Society
School of Communications

Polytechnic of Central London
18–22 Riding House Street
London W1P 7PD
England

Mediations
Marxist Literary Group
Department of Literature (D-007)
University of California at San Diego
La Jolla, CA 92093

The Militant
Militant Publishing Association
14 Charles Lane
New York, NY 10014

The Minnesota Review
Department of English
SUNY Stony Brook
Stony Brook, NY 11794

Monthly Review
62 West 14th St.
New York, NY 10011

Mother Jones
1663 Mission St.
San Francisco, CA 94103

The Nation
72 Fifth Ave.
New York, NY 10011

New German Critique
Telos Press
431 East 12 St.
New York, NY 10009

New Left Review
7 Carlyle St.
London W1V 6NL
England

New Politics
P. O. Box 98
Brooklyn, NY 11231

The People
Socialist Labor Party
914 Industrial Ave.
Palo Alto, CA 94303

The People's World
Pacific Publishing Foundation, Inc.
1819 Tenth St.
Berkeley, CA 94710

Politics and Society
Geron-X, Inc.
Box 1108
Los Altos, CA 94022

Praxis
P. O. Box 1280
Santa Monica, CA 90406

The Progressive
409 E. Main St.
Madison, WI 53703

Public Citizen
P. O. Box 19404
Washington, DC 20036

Radical America
Alternative Education Project, Inc.
38 Union Square
Somerville, MA 02143

Radical History Review
445 West 59th St.
New York, NY 10019

Radical Teacher
P. O. Box 102
Kendall Square Post Office
Cambridge, MA 02142

Resist Newsletter
38 Union Square
Somerville, MA 02143

Review of Radical Political Economics
41 Union Square West, Room 901
New York, NY 10013

Rock and Roll Confidential
P. O. Box 1073
Maywood, NJ 07607

Science Fiction Studies
English Department
Indiana State University
Terre Haute, IN 47809
and
McGill University
Montreal, Quebec
Canada H3A 2T6

Science and Society
Room 4331, John Jay College
CUNY, 445 West 59th St.
New York, NY 10019

Screen (incorporating *Screen Education*)
29 Old Compton St.
London W1V 5PL
England

Signs
University of Chicago
5801 Ellis Ave.
Chicago, IL 60637

Socialist Affairs
Socialist International
301 Metcalfe St.
Ottawa, Ontario
Canada K2P 1R9

Socialist Review
3202 Adeline St.
Berkeley, CA 94703

Social Text
P. O. Box 450
70 Greenwich Ave.
New York, NY 10011

Tabloid
P. O. Box 3243
Stanford, CA 94305

Telos
431 East 12th St.
New York, NY 10009

Theory and Society
The Elsevier Scientific Publishing Co.
Box 211
Amsterdam, Netherlands

Theory, Culture, and Society
Department of Administrative
and Social Studies
Teeside Polytechnic
Middlesborough
Cleveland TS1 3BA
England

Tikkun
5100 Leona Street
Oakland, CA 94619

The Village Voice
842 Broadway
New York, NY 10003

Working Papers in Cultural Studies
Center for Contemporary
Cultural Studies
University of Birmingham
P. O. Box 363
Birmingham B15 2TT
England

Media Activist Organizations and Journals

Access
Telecommunications Research
and Actions Center (TRAC)
Box 12038
Washington, DC 20005

Alternative Media
Alternative Press Syndicate
P. O. Box 1347, Ansonia Station
New York, NY 10011

Alternative Media Information Center
121 Fulton St., Seventh Floor
New York, NY 10038

Alternative Press Center
P. O. Box 33109, Dept. L
Baltimore, MD 21218

Bread and Roses (A Cultural Project
of the National Union of Hospital
and Health Care Employees)

% Publishing Center for
Cultural Resources
625 Broadway
New York, NY 10012

Building Economic Alternatives
Co-op America
2100 M St., N.W., Suite 310
Washington, DC 20063

CableScan
Foundation for Community Service
Cable TV
5616 Geary Blvd., Suite 212
San Francisco, CA 94121

California Newsreel
630 Natoma St.
San Francisco, CA 94103

Center for Social Research and
Education
3202 Adeline St.
Berkeley, CA 94703

Community Television Review
National Federation of Local
Cable Programmers
3700 Far Hills Ave.
Kettering, OH 45429

Direct Cinema Limited
P. O. Box 69589
Los Angeles, CA 90069

Educators for Social Responsibility
23 Garden St.
Cambridge, MA 02138

Equal Time
P. O. Box 1462
Madison, WI 53701

Fairness and Accuracy in Reporting
666 Broadway
New York, NY 10012

Fine Line Productions
1101 Masonic Ave.
San Francisco, CA 94114

International Association of Machinists
and Aerospace Workers
IAM Media Project
Machinists Building
1300 Connecticut Avenue
Washington, DC 20036

Media Access Project
1609 Connecticut Ave., N.W.
Washington, DC 20009

Media Alliance
Fort Mason Center
Building D
San Francisco, CA 94123

Media Network
Center for Study of Filmed History, Inc.
208 West 13th St.
New York, NY 10011

National Writers Union
13 Astor Place, Seventh Floor
New York, NY 10003

New Day Films
853 Broadway, Suite 1210
New York, NY 10003

New Options Newsletter
P. O. Box 19324
Washington, DC 20036

Paper Tiger TV
165 West 91st St.
New York, NY 10024

Public Citizen, Inc.
P. O. Box 7229
Baltimore, MD 21218

Public Media Center
466 Green St.
San Francisco, CA 94133

Quarterly Review of Doublespeak
Committee on Public Doublespeak
National Council of Teachers of English
1111 Kenyon Road
Urbana, IL 61801

Teachers and Writers Collaborative
84 Fifth Ave.
New York, NY 10011

Telecommunications Research
and Action Center
P. O. Box 12038
Washington, DC 20005

Union for Democratic Communications
5338 College Avenue
#C
Oakland, CA 94513

Video Networks
Bay Area Video Coalition
1111 17th St.
San Francisco, CA 94107

We Will Not Be Disappeared
A Directory of Arts Activism
c/o *Cineaste*
P. O. Box 2242
New York, NY 10009

SHOULD NEWS BE SOLD FOR PROFIT?

CHRISTOPHER JENCKS

Walter Powell's article on media conglomerates [in Part 1 above] raises serious questions about the way in which America gathers and distributes news. Few American journalists are satisfied with existing arrangements, and many have chronic fantasies about starting their own newspaper or magazine (though few, it seems, imagine starting an organization to produce television news). But despite perpetual grousing, American journalists seldom discuss how news ought to be collected and distributed in a democratic society. Unlike their European counterparts, they have made no political effort to improve existing institutional arrangements.

Having begun my career in journalism, I find this reluctance to think about alternatives both puzzling and discouraging. Why, for example, are so few journalists disturbed by the fact that news is collected and distributed for private profit? Other professions, though frequently avaricious, at least recognize that the organizations through which they deliver services—universities, hospitals, courts—run better on a nonprofit basis. Why shouldn't newspapers, news magazines, or television news be run the same way?

Eliminating the profit motive does not imply public ownership or control of the news media. It is quite compatible with the present method of financing the collection and distribution of news, which depends in large part on intermingling news with commercial advertising. Nor does eliminating the profit motive imply dismantling existing news organizations; it would simply mean lending these organizations enough money to buy out their stockholders and then running them on a break-even basis.

Let me begin by conceding what many readers might not concede, namely that the profit motive is the best-known method of making an organization give its customers what they want when they want it. News is no exception to this rule. Profit-oriented news media are concerned with maximizing advertising revenue. To accomplish this they tinker endlessly with both the format and the substance of the news in order to attract the largest and most affluent audience they can. Such efforts appear quite successful; if public enlightenment depended simply on getting as many people as possible to read newspapers and watch television news, there would not be much basis for complaint against the existing system.

But what the public wants is not always what it needs. And when a profit-oriented organization has to choose between giving people what they want or giving them what they need, it almost always chooses to gratify wants. The argument that people don't know what is good for them is, of course, hard to reconcile with conventional democratic ideas. Democracy assumes that in the last analysis

From *Working Papers*, July–August 1979.

people are the best—perhaps the only—judge of their own needs. Those who believe in democracy are rightly suspicious of experts who claim to know the public's needs better than the public itself does. But while skepticism is certainly warranted, a closed mind is not. We all know of instances in which people want things that are bad for them. The task of social reform is to deal with such situations without doing more harm than good.

In the case of news, the conflict between what we want and what we need derives from well-known human weaknesses: exhaustion and laziness. Most of us read newspapers and watch television in the morning when we are half-awake or after a tiring day's work. Our appetite for difficult ideas or moral ambiguity is even lower than usual at these times. A news organization seeking to maximize its audience therefore finds that it pays to make the news simple and exciting, not complex or challenging.

Those who manage the news media justify this approach by arguing that the public is divided into two distinct groups: a small number of "intellectuals" who want detailed information, careful analysis, and moral challenge, and a much larger group of "ordinary people" who want quick summaries, simple concepts, and moral reassurance. Defenders of the present system then describe their critics as elitists who don't understand ordinary folks. But this argument is too simple. Eggheads and yahoos certainly exist. For the most part, though, this is a schism *within* the mind of each reader or viewer. "Intellectuals" are hardly immune to the appeal of easy entertainment, as the fascination with Watergate attested; and although "ordinary people" often prefer entertainment, most also have a certain appetite for education—for experiences that literally "lead them out" of the narrow confines of their everyday lives. Furthermore—and this is the crucial point—most people regard their impulse to be educated as more creditable than their impulse to be entertained. We are proud of the moments when we rise to an intellectual or moral challenge. The moments when we ignore or avoid such challenges, while far more numerous, leave us with no comparable sense of satisfaction. Thus, although it is true that most people want the news to be entertaining most of the time, it is also true that most people "want to want" the news to be enlightening.

An organization that collects and distributes the news therefore faces an uncomfortable choice. One alternative is to ask as little as possible of its audience, thus maximizing its size but losing its respect. Television networks have gone this route and have learned to live with the fact that even the most assiduous viewers have a low opinion of the medium. Newspaper chains, which seldom care about the respect of local readers and usually see each local paper as a "profit center" rather than a community service, tend to go the same route.

The other alternative is for a news organization to seek the respect of its audience and worry about audience size only insofar as that is essential to solvency. Public television sometimes adopts this stance. But public television has kept itself financially precarious by refusing to accept most forms of advertising. A number of family-controlled papers, such as the *New York Times*, the *Washington Post*, and the *Los Angeles Times*, also seem to value their reputation more than they value maximum profits—though all strive to ensure "adequate" profits. If all newspapers were produced on a nonprofit basis, I think they would place far more emphasis on winning the public's long-term respect and far less on maximizing audience size. The same is probably true of television news. The lure of profit is one of the few motives strong enough to make an organization pursue policies that risk public contempt. Eliminate this motive and you shift the balance toward respectability.

Eliminating the profit motive would create a crisis of legitimacy in existing news organizations. Instead of letting their shareholders choose their directors, these organizations would have to select trustees in some other way. Furthermore, once they defined their official purpose as "public service" rather than private profit, tremendous controversy would arise about what the public really needed and who should define these needs. The experience of other nonprofit organizations, such as universities and hospitals, suggests that in the long run the professional staff would probably acquire a major role in running the organizations and deciding what was really "news," regardless of how trustees were selected. This would be a drastic change. Today's news organizations treat journalists as hired help, not professionals, and give them very little voice in running the organizations they work for.

What distinguishes a profession is its ability to convince other people that only members of the profession know enough to evaluate practitioners' work. This claim allows the profession to exercise significant control over its members' careers. Doctors or lawyers, for example, can expect those who hire them when they finish school to be doctors or lawyers themselves. This same pattern will persist throughout their careers. If they make a serious mistake, those who evaluate its seriousness will again be doctors or lawyers, unless they end up in a malpractice suit. Scholars, too, can expect those who hire and promote them to be mainly fellow scholars. Journalists, by contrast, must entrust their careers to the judgment of corporate managers. These managers are often called "editors," which makes them sound vaguely like fellow professionals. Indeed, often they are former journalists as well, but that is no more relevant than the fact that the managers of universities are called "deans" and are often former scholars. A manager inevitably comes to identify with the organization, not with a former craft. If journalists wanted professional autonomy comparable to scholars, they would have to ensure that their careers depended largely on judgments made by other working journalists, not by editors or other corporate managers.

A journalist's claim to autonomy differs from that of most professions, however, in that it does not rest on strictly technical expertise. A journalist is more like a teacher than a scholar. Like teachers, journalists seek to instruct their audience and must often try to get people to absorb ideas they don't find intrinsically interesting. Unlike teachers, journalists cannot force people to pay attention by giving exams on their material. They are therefore under constant pressure to bring everything down to the level of the least attentive reader or viewer—much as teachers are under pressure to bring everything down to the level of the least attentive student. Some measure of professional autonomy would give journalists the short-run protection they need in order to persuade the public to accept their judgments about what is worth knowing over the long run. If the news media operated on a nonprofit basis, journalists would almost certainly be better protected in this respect.

If one is convinced that the news media should be nonprofit, the next question is how we might get from here to there. In the case of television, the change could be relatively simple. Congress could instruct the Federal Communications Commission to reserve certain hours of the day for national and local news and to restrict broadcasting during these hours to nonprofit organizations, which would lease broadcasting facilities from existing commercial stations. CBS, NBC, and ABC News would presumably separate from their profit-making parents, establish themselves as independent nonprofits, and apply for the right to broadcast national news. Under the FCC's present, rather arbitrary, licensing procedures, these new nonprofits would probably get their licenses and continue to enjoy oligopolistic privileges. Local television news organizations would presumably go the same route. The main change would be in the internal operation of these groups.

The transition to nonprofit status would be somewhat more complicated in the case of newspapers and newsmagazines. In the print media the division between news and entertainment is not so clear-cut, and separating the two functions is probably impractical. An entire publication would therefore have to be converted to nonprofit status. The most politically promising way to do this would be to allow shareholders to convert their stock to government-guaranteed bonds on favorable terms. Such conversion might be made mandatory when the shareholder died or wanted to transfer the shares.

Such changes are hardly imminent. The question, however, is not whether they are imminent but whether they would be desirable. If a consensus were to emerge among journalists that news *ought* not to be sold for profit like shoes or deodorant, I suspect journalists could alter other people's views rather quickly. At the moment, journalists are not even thinking about such questions.

AN ALTERNATIVE AMERICAN COMMUNICATIONS SYSTEM

ROBERT CIRINO

Entertainment and news reporting are both treated the same as any other commodity in the United States: the product that sells is produced, that which doesn't sell isn't. To make money in the mass media, entertainment and news have to attract the kind and size of audience that advertisers are willing to pay big money for. Five million readers or viewers might like a magazine or program, but if it doesn't generate enough advertising money it is dead. The management of news and entertainment is viewed as a business decision similar to a style or color change in next year's automobiles, made for the purpose of maximizing profit.

Entertainment and news are truly part of the marketplace of commodities. The people are given choices among products that can produce a profit. But entertainment and news are also important channels, if not the most important, for transmitting political ideas. Therefore, they are a vital part of the marketplace of ideas as well as of commodities. This creates a seemingly insoluble problem, because a free marketplace of ideas does not and cannot exclude viewpoints representing alternatives to the status quo simply because they don't appeal to the majority or bring in advertising revenue. Nor can a free marketplace censor any views opposing their ideological interests, as is the case under our present system of private corporate ownership and sponsorship.

What democratic alternatives to our present commercial communications system are conceivable? Any alternative is apt to entail a paternalistic, elite model of management operation, where objective professionals try to make decisions fair to all viewpoints, or else a spectrum-sharing model of management, where each representative viewpoint programs and produces its own mass media entertainment, news, and public affairs. At this point it is relevant to survey what kinds of systems and management theories have been adopted by the various democratic nations. In all democracies, the publishing of daily newspapers is left mainly to the commodity marketplace, and these papers tend to support the prevailing political and economic system. However, in most democracies other than the United States, unions and political parties representing the entire spectrum also publish daily newspapers, with or without advertising support. Thus a real choice of political perspectives is provided in daily newspapers, rather than a limited choice encompassing a moderately liberal or conservative viewpoint clothed in a style of objectivity. Understandably, in these countries there is little demand for the government to support public newspapers to guarantee a variety of voices. However, Italy, Norway, Finland, and the Netherlands do give some government subsidies to political parties in order to guarantee that the public will have exposure to newspapers that represent political outlooks other than those represented in the commercial enterprises.

From *College English* 38, no. 8 (1977).

Broadcasting is a different matter. Many democracies do not permit private ownership of broadcasting at all, and nearly all have some sort of public broadcasting system. The public systems in the United States, England, Japan, and Australia follow the paternalistic, elitist model. In contrast, the public system in the Netherlands follows a spectrum-sharing model, with broadcasting access, technology, and production capacity divided among four different broadcasting societies, each representing a different basic viewpoint. Groups representing views other than the four main ones are given a smaller amount of access to produce and present their programs. Recently, the public systems in Italy, France, and Belgium have accepted the principle of spectrum sharing and have made some moves to share communication power among contrasting viewpoints.

In terms of funding, the United States is far behind in its support of public broadcasting. Whereas Japan provides $2.90, England $3.29, and Canada $6.00 per person per year, the United States provides less than $2.00. It is clear that in contrast to the systems in every other democracy, the Public Broadcasting Service (PBS) in the United States is not funded to compete with commercial programming or designed to provide the public with exposure to viewpoints that are excluded or neglected by the commercial marketplace of ideas. Furthermore, PBS has become increasingly dependent on corporate funding, and its management and policies have been steadily moving toward an approximation of the commercial networks. As a result, most Americans are exposed only to those communications products that prove themselves profitable as commodities and favorable to the ideology of corporate ownership and advertisers.

I now want to propose an alternative to the present broadcasting system in the United States, called the United States Broadcasting Corporation (USBC), intended to supplement, not replace, the present system. Although I am only discussing broadcasting, the same system can equally well be extended to newspapers, magazines, books, and films.

I have tried to design a system that would offer the public real competition among representative viewpoints in entertainment, news, and public affairs. I do not have high expectations that such a system will ever be established in our country; there are just too many powerful interests that do not want to subject their ideas or policies to the risky competition and unpredictable outcome that are part of any real debate. They stand to lose enormous wealth and power if they do not win public approval. Such wealthy individuals and groups have the political power to kill any proposal for such a system and, much more important, the communication power to create public attitudes hostile to such a system. So, I offer the alternative system not in the expectation that it will ever be accepted, but in the spirit of providing a concrete alternative for the purpose of illustrating what real competition would be like, what kinds of choices it would offer, and how far our present system is from offering any real or fair debate in news or entertainment.

Contrary to the philosophy of the present public broadcasting system, the new USBC operates on the assumption that the different representative viewpoints can compete equally for public approval only if each is allowed to produce and control its own news and entertainment. It rejects the operating assumption of the present system, which holds that so-called objective or neutral professionals can present fairly those viewpoints they either despise or do not espouse themselves. The new system assumes that bias is natural and inevitable, that the problem is not to eliminate, conceal, or deny bias but to reveal it—to make sure that all biases are made equally available to the public.

Therefore, the new USBC will consist of four separate and independent networks representing different positions—socialist, liberal, conservative, libertarian. Each network will have the same amount of money to hire its own staff and artists and to produce its own news, public affairs, and entertainment programs for television and radio. Nationwide, two channels will be used; the socialists and conservatives will alternate every other day on one channel and the libertarians and liberals will alternate on the second channel. Broadcast frequencies are more plentiful on radio, therefore each network will produce daily programs for its own nationwide radio network. The above requires that the technical capacity and audience reach of the new USBC be equal to that of commercial broadcasting, just as the British Broadcasting Corporation (BBC) in England is technically fully competitive on radio and TV with commercial broadcasting.

The board of directors for each network will be made up of seven representatives chosen by each of seven national magazines that clearly represent the viewpoint of the particular network. In addition, each political party that legally qualified candidates for national offices on more than fifteen state ballots in the most recent election will select a representative to serve on the network that it feels best represents its political viewpoint. Each network must have at least one minority member and a minimum of two women on its board.

The new USBC will accept no advertising. And in sharp contrast to the present system, it will accept no sponsorship of particular programs by corporations, foundations, or other organizations. In this way it will eliminate the present circumstance allowing special interest groups to influence programming decisions. Foundations, corporations, and labor unions that want to contribute to public broadcasting may do so, but their money will be equally divided among all four networks to be used as each sees fit.

Regular financing for the USBC will come from small taxes on the profits of commercial broadcasts, on gross receipts of advertising, on gross receipts of radio and TV sales, and on a national lottery (when and if established). Additional funds, if needed, will come from the federal budget, to be granted on a five-year basis. Such financing will further guarantee the editorial independence of the networks from possible pressures by the Senate or the executive branch. The present system is subjected to and influenced by subtle and heavy-handed pressure from Congress, the president, and private donors. The new USBC will be totally independent of such stifling financial pressures.

The present system operates under a statutory requirement to produce "fair" programs. This is ridiculous, since it is impossible for any single production or network to be fair to all viewpoints. The new USBC, with its four competing networks *taken as a whole*, will automatically produce a fair debate without any need for a statutory requirement or regulation by the Federal Communications Commission (FCC). In fact, no government regulation of any kind will be necessary to ensure fairness.

Like nearly every other public broadcasting system in democracies throughout the world, the USBC will not allow politicians, political parties, or any outside interests to buy time. Outside interests may produce a program in hopes of giving or selling it to the networks, but it is up to each network to decide whether to present the program. No equal time requirement is necessary because every legally qualified candidate would have no problem finding one of the networks willing to invite him or her to take part in a debate, discussion, or question-and-answer session.

How would the new system change things? Just what can Americans expect from television and radio that they do not now see or hear from either the commercial or public broadcasting system? And how might this different programming affect people and society?

With the four new networks devoting a substantial portion of television time to public affairs, the commercial networks can finally feel free to drop out of public affairs programming altogether. They might feel greatly relieved, because documentaries, special news coverage, and public affairs programs cause them to lose money and expose them to hostile charges of bias. Network news, instead of feeling a certain obligation to cover important events, can emphasize the sensational, entertaining tidbits of news—the human interest, trivia, tragedy, or accident story. In this way they can perhaps reach new highs in popularity ratings and advertising income, and the public, being aware of the fact that they are not really getting the important news from the networks, can turn elsewhere for this if they so desire.

Every night the public will have at least two hours of prime-time documentaries to choose from. At present few hours of prime-time programming on either commercial or public broadcasting offer documentaries, and most of these are rather tame or dishonestly "balanced" to avoid offending anyone who might bring charges of "bias" against a network.

No longer will there be a fuss about whether the president's televised speeches should require a response by opposing spokespersons. Each network will make that decision, putting on as many spokespersons as it wishes. No longer will a president be able to get public support for his policies and behavior through the use of lies and distortions of language and facts. Responded to by opposition spokespersons from the entire spectrum, he will have to win public support in an arena of real debate.

Children's television will change markedly. The commercial networks, which recently have been losing money on children's television because of the many reforms forced on them by angry parents, can drop out of the business, leaving it to the four new networks. Their programs, uninterrupted by ads selling sugared goodies and expensive toys, will be produced for the benefit of children, not for the purpose of attracting a large audience of children in order to deliver their impressionable minds to advertisers.

Finally, and most importantly, entertainment programs for everyone will reflect *the power and dignity of belief and commitment* rather than the present artificiality and compromise of artistic integrity that is usually practiced in order to attract a large audience. There will be no need to censor or regulate violence and sex or to set up voluntary industry "codes" with which to placate complainers.

Since the four new networks cannot make any profit from exploiting violence and sex, these two essential elements of life will be dealt with honestly. They will be included in programs not just to gain high ratings but to communicate important beliefs about the relationship between sex, violence, and society. Although much violence and sex may remain in entertainment, it is unlikely that it will be so highly glamorized. The commercial networks will of course still use spurious and glamorized violence and sex to get high ratings, but at least the public will be able to tune in to entertainment produced to communicate human ideas and feelings rather than to corral majorities.

Let us imagine what kind of live television coverage the four USBC networks would have offered during a noteworthy week and compare it to what the commercial networks actually offered. This analysis, incidentally, can serve as a model for similar exercises by students in composition classes, who might likewise enjoy and benefit from writing scenarios with political viewpoints that differ from those of current newspapers or magazines, television entertainment shows, or films.

During the week of November 11–17, 1973, Secretary of State Henry Kissinger was visiting China. At its Rome headquarters, the United Nations Food and Agricultural Organization was having its biannual conference meeting. In London, socialist heads of state from eighteen nations were having a meeting of the Socialist International. And also in England, the royal wedding of Princess Anne was taking place. All three networks (ABC, CBS, and NBC) decided to give live coverage to the royal wedding.

In the United States, congressional committees were investigating corporate participation in the Watergate affair, wasteful defense spending, and corruption in the Small Business Administration. And Skylab 3, representing the nation's sixteenth manned space effort, was scheduled to blast off at 9:01 Friday morning. All three networks decided to give live coverage to the spaceship launch.

On Saturday all three networks covered, live, President Nixon's press conference before the Associated Press Managing Editors Association. One network (CBS) followed the press conference with live coverage of analysis by network journalists. The other two (ABC and NBC) ended live coverage immediately after the newscast.

The networks' reports of the royal wedding and the space launch were presented ostensibly as nonpolitical, objective programming. However, viewers of the space launch may have been influenced to believe that the right technological mastery rather than the right social or economic policy can best solve our country's problems—in other words, the technological response is more important than the political response. As a result of the added importance that live coverage bestows on manned space flights, many Americans may feel a sense of patriotic pride or believe that success or failure in space is a symbolic indication of America's success or failure as a nation. In other words, this selection and treatment of events served as covert propaganda for American nationalism and the aerospace industry. The choice to cover the wedding, uncritically emphasizing its glamor, was a tacit approval of royal splendor.

The live coverage of the wedding and the space launch was itself an incredible display of television technology providing the public the chance to witness events as they were actually happening. Who could possibly complain about being able to view such events? But if one imagines the potential of live coverage to expand the public's perspectives and knowledge at the same time it is providing live entertainment, there are plenty of reasons for finding fault with the decisions to televise live the royal wedding and space launch. This same money and technology could have been used to offer the public live coverage of other events of equal or greater significance. Perhaps those events (the Kissinger trip, the Watergate hearings, the Food and Agricultural Organization meeting) were not as spectacular, but they could still have been covered in an entertaining and informative manner. In fact, earlier live coverage of the Watergate hearings proved that even Senate hearings can attract a large audience.

An equally valid proposal is that no live coverage at all should have been offered during the week, that instead, the money and technology should have been allocated to the production of several special documentaries on cultural events or contemporary issues. Since Americans have been offered hundreds of hours of live space coverage, and the wedding was of little significance to the United States, special coverage—delayed rather than live—would have given adequate coverage and saved millions of dollars.

Accepting for a moment the questionable decisions that were made, it can still be argued that the public was being force-fed, since all three networks covered the same events. It seems like a restriction of entertainment options as well as an incredible waste of television resources just to offer duplicate coverage.

By televising press conferences arranged and controlled by the president, television is allowing presidents to manipulate images and restrict ideas, follow-up, and response. Viewers may come to think that the objective-style analysis of network journalists offers sufficient balance to offset the president's appearance. Those watching the networks that offer no commentary at all may feel that neither analysis nor a response from opposition spokespersons is needed to achieve fairness. If television refused to grant live coverage to such controlled events, the president would have to accept a format more conducive to vigorous questioning and response. By not giving live coverage to opposing responses, television is in effect saying that the president is a very special person, one who is above partisan politics, one who is above the democratic process of debate. The networks are thus taking a very decided stand in favor of exalting the office of the president. This is a controversial matter in itself, for opposition spokespersons would say that the president already has too much power and that affording him special television treatment helps him to use this power in dangerous, unchecked ways.

Aware of all the events that lend themselves to coverage, and aware of what the others have decided to cover, how would the live coverage of the different USBC networks differ from each other—and from the actual live coverage offered by the commercial networks? Although some of these meetings of congressional committees and international organizations were held behind closed doors, the organizations involved would probably be more than happy to open up many sessions if they were promised live coverage. It also seems safe to assume that they would arrange these open hearings at times that would attract the largest possible audience.

THE SOCIALIST NETWORK

After the commercial networks have announced the live coverage for the week, the socialist network schedules live coverage of the Socialist International meeting in London, the Senate Watergate hearings, and the response of a leading socialist to the president's news conference.

Besides covering the open meeting discussions between socialist leaders, live coverage from London includes many interviews of socialist heads of state. Commentary and taped background features compare the different socialist programs and policies of quasi-socialist and socialist countries represented at the meeting. Other short features show how these socialist-oriented countries have distributed health, housing, television, and other vital services according to human need, on a nonprofit basis. This is compared to how the capitalist countries distribute such services for profit, according to who can pay, with the accompanying neglect of people, young and old, who cannot afford to pay. The underlying theme of these short fill-in features is that capitalism offers the privileged a chance to accumulate wealth, luxuries, and power for themselves, whereas socialism offers everyone in society meaningful work—not for the purpose of accumulating private gain, but for improving life for everyone.

During breaks in the Watergate hearings, commentators fill in the gaps by explaining that Watergate is an inevitable by-product of an election system that allows those with money to purchase communication power and political favor. They justify their coverage by claiming that these Watergate hearings, focusing on how corporations gave huge sums of money to Nixon's reelection committee, are the most important of all because they show the ultimate source of corruption in America. They note the funny coincidence that the commercial networks stopped live coverage of the hearings just before some of their large corporate advertisers were going to be questioned about their illegal contributions.

THE LIBERTARIAN NETWORK

Following the announcements of the commercial networks and the socialist network, the libertarian network schedules live coverage of the meetings of the Food and Agricultural Organization in Rome, the congressional hearings on corruption in the Small Business Administration, and the response of a leading libertarian to the president's press conference.

Although not supporters of the United Nations, the libertarians use the meeting of the U.N. Food and Agricultural Organization as a dramatic vehicle for focusing the public's attention on agricultural production, world starvation, and population growth. Background features compare agricultural production of capitalist farms with that of collective farms and focus on the role of individual incentive and private capital in increasing productivity. Interviews with agricultural experts help fill in gaps between coverage of official discussions.

The live coverage of the Small Business Administration hearings prove every bit as fascinating as the earlier Watergate hearings. Witnesses reveal how some SBA offices were infiltrated by organized crime, others tell of kickbacks to officials handling loans to certain businesses, and some reveal how banks were able to defraud the government by having the SBA absorb losses banks incurred by being unable to collect on loans they made to businesses that failed. One case revealed how one company got over $3 million in loans and rent money from the SBA and is now unable to repay. Libertarian commentators fill in the gaps during breaks in the hearing, pointing out that the whole sordid mess is what one can expect when the government gets involved in helping businesses and banks.

THE LIBERAL NETWORK

Following the other networks, the liberal network announces live coverage of Kissinger's arrival in China, the congressional investigations of Defense Department spending, and the response of a leading liberal senator to the president's news conference.

Liberal China experts provide background and commentary to supplement coverage of Kissinger's activities and meetings with Chinese leaders. On-the-spot tours of streets, factories, schools, and communes make this live coverage something of an educational experience for the viewer. The overall bias of the coverage and commentary is one that favors the Kissinger trip and expanding relations with China.

Although not quite as entertaining as the Watergate hearings, coverage of Senator Proxmire's Joint Economic Committee investigations into Defense Department contracting is fascinating and revealing. Government auditors reveal that in some cases the Pentagon paid five times more for weapons and electrical equipment when it bought them from a single noncompetitive bidder than when it asked for competitive bids. Further testimony indicates that on the average the Pentagon paid more than double the price for noncompetitive single-supplier contracts. Liberal commentators fill in the gaps by revealing other examples of wasteful spending, and they stress the need for drastic reform in the awarding of weapons contracts to single noncompetitive suppliers.

THE CONSERVATIVE NETWORK

The conservative network decides to cover Kissinger's last day in China. Contrary to the earlier liberal network coverage in China, this coverage, with its conservative experts on communism, does not approve of either the secretary of state's trip or expanding relations with China. Coverage shows Chinese schools, factories, and communes but emphasizes the totalitarian and propagandistic elements more than the liberal network did.

Breaks in the Watergate hearings are filled by commentators who point out that the lesson of Watergate is not that the American system is basically corrupt, but that certain individuals violate ethical standards. They claim that many Democrats have done similar things in the past but have been ignored by the liberal press. The overall attitude is that these investigations show that the American system can work to clean its own house, not that fundamental changes in the system are needed.

Like the other networks, this one is giving live coverage to the response of one of its leading spokespersons (a senator) to the presidential news conference.

The foregoing sketch of the USBC's structure and programming is meant only to be suggestive, not definitive, and could well be combined with other alternative plans. One such plan, proposed by Donald Lazere, would replace the present structure of news reporting and political debate with daily newscasts and newspaper reports by a panel of reporters and commentators representing diverse political viewpoints, and would replace the unchallenged speeches and news conferences of office-holding politicians with regular broadcast debates and cross-examination by political opponents of both major and minor parties. Any such alternatives, of course, are utopian to the extent that it is virtually impossible to bring them into being against the opposition of the vested economic and political interests that monopolize communication under the capitalist system. Nevertheless, being able to conceptualize preferable alternatives is an essential first step toward our attaining the understanding and asserting the will to make whatever political changes are necessary to effect these alternatives.

PACIFICA RADIO AND THE POLITICS OF CULTURE

CLARE SPARK

The Pacifica Foundation, with FM radio stations in Berkeley (KPFA), Los Angeles (KPFK), New York (WBAI), Houston (KPFT), and Washington, D.C. (WPFW), has the potential to be the most influential alternative institution in American mass media. Its first station, KPFA, was founded in 1949 by a radical pacifist, poet, and former commercial broadcaster, Lew Hill. Hill envisioned a radio station to counter cold war ideology, with listener sponsorship and worker management keeping it honest and independent. The original Pacifica charter expressed Hill's concerns: to study the causes of philosophical, religious, racial, and national antagonisms in the interests of world peace; to disseminate news and analysis that was being suppressed in commercial media; and to foster new art forms.

Since 1949, Pacifica radio has led the media in its coverage of the antinuclear, civil rights, black power, feminist, gay rights, ecology and labor movements. Pacifica's commitment against imperialism and its outstanding coverage of opposition to the war in Vietnam in the sixties and seventies brought it national renown. Over the years, however, a lack of clearly defined programming policies caused internal dissension and a drift away from Lew Hill's original vision. Was Pacifica to be a community-access open forum, an instrument for social change, or both? Did the charter mandate any particular principles and standards? What was the relation of the stations, staffed largely by the white middle class, to the culturally diverse audience they were trying to build?

In April 1981, all the Pacifica program directors met to discuss these issues. It was agreed that Pacifica's "mission" was all but lost and that the charter required affirmation and reinterpretation to establish a basis for unity within the organization. Pacifica should, we concluded, promote critical, independent thought. Its "pluralism" should be realized within a general opposition to racism, sexism, and imperialism. We would try to unify the audience by recreating the historical experience of peoples who had been denied access to mass media and whose cultures had been submerged and twisted. Since elitist, racist, and sexist beliefs and behavior were still present at all the stations, it was necessary to plan programs of continuing education and consciousness-raising. This direction did not preclude the airing of music, drama, and other performing arts that expressed the full spectrum of dominant, submerged, and oppositional culture; culture, however, would be subject to the same critical analysis as politics: the study of ideology and consciousness would be a high priority. We would attempt to activate the listeners, stimulating them to set agendas for programming and develop sharper critical tools to evaluate existing programs and thereby to participate more fully in the creation of an alternative, progressive culture. Listener call-ins would not be limited to "talk shows" but would be encouraged on many news and cultural programs as well, and the studio itself would become a center for political and cultural activism.

I had been volunteering and working at KPFK since 1969; in 1981 I was hired as program director with a mandate to implement these goals. Over the next eighteen months, KPFK dramatically increased its listener support, garnered favorable press coverage, diversified its audiences, and, naturally, stirred up controversy. Collaborations with many progressive scholars, journalists, and activists led to innovative cultural and political coverage. Every peace organization in Southern California participated in our Peace Festivals. There were popular live teach-ins on El Salvador, the arms race, reproductive rights, Northern Ireland, South Africa, and Reaganomics and the future of the corporate state. The June 12, 1982, New York peace demonstration was supported by week-long programming about the nuclear age. Some of the highlights of KPFK's cultural criticism included studies of the politics of literacy, the militarization of consciousness, the culture of narcissism, romantic necrophilia in the sentimental culture of nineteenth-century America (the foundation of much current pop culture), and profiles of John Lennon, Jimi Hendrix, Phil Ochs, and Randy Newman.

The problems we faced at the station during this period became a microcosm of the dilemmas implicit not only in Pacifica's charter but in left cultural politics in general. A major question we had to deal with was whether one medium can serve as both an instrument for social change—in our case representing a leftist viewpoint (albeit a broad, nonsectarian one)—and a community-access open forum. A system of communications more rational than the commercial American one, which leaves room for neither alternative, would allow for both in separate media, thus resolving the problems Pacifica faced in trying to combine the two. A case for Pacifica as a platform for committed left views can be made by analogy with print media's journals of opinion or with the widespread networks of right-wing and Christian broadcasting in America; it can also be made in terms of the need for counterbalance to the self-proclaimed nonpartisanship of commercial media, which in practice are partisan organs of the political mainstream that shut out explicit critical questioning of capitalism and of Americans' nationalistic biases. Our conception of Pacifica in this light was not as a monolithic organ of leftist propaganda but as a center that would permit the formulation of a cogent ideological perspective on political and cultural issues—a perspective allowing full room for debate from both within and outside the left. To this end, we regularly carried libertarian commentaries and were open to criticism of our views from the political mainstream—far more open than the mainstream media are to criticism from the left.

Of course, commitment to a left viewpoint does not necessarily preclude open community access; indeed, a crucial project of left cultural politics is to empower audiences. But what about the right-wing zealots, racists, and sexists in the audience? Is a leftist medium responsible for empowering them also? Although the parochially separated branches of American media have tended to keep right-wing populists from listening to or participating in Pacifica stations, my answer in principle is yes, we should reach out to them, attempt to show them their common ground with disfranchised working people, minorities, and women, and try to persuade them that the forces oppressing them are caused not by the left but by the workings of the capitalist system. If the views such people expressed on the air were bigoted, we would not censor them, but we would also not let them go unchallenged.

Another possible conflict in the conception of Pacifica as a vanguard medium as opposed to a community-access forum lay in the class and cultural differences between programmers and audience. If we aired progressive "authorities" as political or cultural analysts, weren't they bound to be more literate than many in the audience we were trying to reach? And given the association of higher education with higher social classes, weren't such analysts likely to further alienate working-class audience members? Aren't the very issues that these analysts address of interest and accessible mainly to the middle class and "highbrows"? In practice, these questions caused surprisingly little conflict. The overwhelming response from listeners was gratitude for the airing of the kind of serious political and cultural dialogue the commercial media patronizingly believe is over the head of their audience. Diverse sectors of our audience contributed viewpoints in call-ins and letters that were no less valuable than those of our broadcasters, and the heated exchange of views created an on-the-air energy level far beyond anything in commercial broadcasting.

A far greater source of conflict in practice involved the various modes of left sectarianism that worked against Pacifica's commitment to healing the divisions among disfranchised peoples. I was particularly concerned with the divisiveness of the cultural nationalists and separatists, who tended to dominate programming about women and blacks and who resisted debate with or airing of integrationists—for example, the producer of a reggae special who refused to include any discussion of sexism or commercialism in reggae culture. My view was that since such problems could not be easily resolved or glossed over, they should at least be addressed openly.

The airing of such problems produced enormously exciting broadcasting, but factionalism within the station's personnel took its toll. Conflicts also arose with the Pacifica board of directors and their appointed station managers, who unfortunately had become self-perpetuating bureaucracies unto themselves, not accountable either to workers or to listener-sponsors, and who were moving, during these financially pressing times, to seek corporate funding and a "safer" kind of broadcasting similar to National Public Radio. Beginning in fall 1982, a series of purges and resignations tore KPFK apart; I was among those fired. At this writing, in 1984, KPFK and Pacifica are still functioning, though at a reduced level of *esprit de corps* and sense of mission. Such are the hazards, to paraphrase Trotsky, of trying to create socialism in one radio station!

Perhaps the obstacles to bucking the whole system of American capitalism and its media institutions are simply insurmountable at this time. Right-wingers and left-wingers alike tend to blame the left's failures on its own flaws, such as its fatal proneness to factional splintering. But this weakness is undoubtedly due in large measure to the objective situation of left movements, which by necessity consist of coalitions of large numbers of relatively powerless, divided individuals. Political rightists are united by power and wealth; they can hire field troops.

The left's troops, however, are volunteers; they have to earn at least a subsistence living within the system while they struggle to change it. As Michael Lerner has observed, powerlessness is as corruptive as power, though in different ways.[1] With oppositional media like KPFK so rare, and so many disfranchised groups in the world, power struggles are bound to erupt. Nevertheless, the temporary successes achieved at KPFK, and the valuable lessons learned in the process of trial and error, provide overwhelming confirmation that the struggle for alternative media and political visions is a valid one.

The following are excerpts from the monthly column I wrote in the KPFK program guide in 1981 and 1982, addressing these and related issues more fully.

"Listening to Clio: Radical History, Not Rhetoric" (KPFK Folio, *June 1981*)

I. The Vanguard. The Pacifica agenda—our legal mandate—is the most humane, most highly evolved project of its kind that I know. It is unambiguous in its language and intent: the study of the causes of conflict, with the goal of a lasting understanding among all peoples. Pacifica programs and programmers, therefore, are mandated to create programs and social processes that show what people must do to *heal* conflicts. People whose agenda it is to *exacerbate* conflict in order to perpetuate structures of domination are, it seems to us, not to be in control of our air (i.e., present themselves as representing Pacifica or as exempt from critical dialogue). Rather, such people are to be the subjects and objects of our collective inquiry.

II. Legitimacy. Pacifica legitimizes its authority through a historical and dialectical approach to politics and culture alike. As part of the professional development of all Pacifica personnel (and, by extension, the audience), it is expected that all attempts will be made to remedy the classist, racist, sexist educations that shaped most of us—this by reading labor history, women's history, ethnic group history, and so on, by attending workshops, and by participating in in-service training. Without personal transformations and increased sensitivity to the particular historical experience of our audiences, we cannot fulfill our charter, let alone perform outreach and self-criticism.

III. Tokenism. It follows from the above that by isolating class, race, gender, and labor questions to ghettoized programming—that is, by not integrating these questions into the way we analyze and create *all* our programming—we only perpetuate preexisting divisions and the pitting of groups against each other as they fight for turf. This has been the strategy of co-optation since the sixties, and it has fragmented the staff and audience and, we believe, turned off large portions of our constituency. The integration of class, gender, and race into a coherent analysis of society and conflict requires a sophistication barely and rarely achieved by radical scholars. It must, however, be a Pacifica project to strive for such analyses and syntheses.

"Pacifica Arts Programming and the Pacifica Charter" (KPFK Folio, *July 1981*)

Pacifica programs in the arts will attend to what is new, important, and enduring in American and international culture while:

1. Providing artists with direct access to publics so that they may explain their work and intentions; such views will then be contrasted with official interpretations and the responses of varied publics.

2. Examining how received ideas, cultural institutions, and routines affect artistic decisions, or, as Raymond Williams would say, what the pressures and limits are that determine cultural practices. How autonomous can artists be? What interests oppose and limit artistic "freedom"? How do mainstream, alternative, and oppositional art forms differ or blend?

3. Locating recent cultural events within American social history and within the interplay among "high," "commercial," and "indigenous" or "folk" cultures.

4. Reviewing relations between vanguard artists and their audiences (Renato Poggioli's Romantic adventurism, agonism, antagonism, and nihilism) and discovering which artists are challenging those relations by finding new audiences and new social roles.

5. Analyzing the "frames" in which institutions—media, museums, schools —present cultural events and artifacts. How do such factors as museum installations, the syntax of exhibition labels, the paradigms that determine significance and that explain how history happens and how society works shape the experience of the public? How do audiences accept, reject, and transform cultural messages?

6. Investigating how cultural institutions have been responding to the aspirations and demands of sixties-style liberation movements. What are the limits of reform? What assumptions about the artist in society are contained within the demands of independent producers and community groups? What is the range of art-historical and political opinion that supports or opposes public pressures on artists and arts institutions? Is there a contradiction between "democracy" and "excellence"?

7. Demonstrating how the arts can mystify or clarify consciousness. The imagination contains possibilities for both deception and transcendence; similarly, a radio program can mystify the social processes that create culture, simultaneously reinforcing dependency on "experts" who explain the world to their own liking. Can Pacifica programs embody social processes that enhance the audience's capacity to formulate independent critical judgments?

Pacifica and Cultural Politics. The diffuseness of our grass roots funding enables us to pose these critical questions and to support challenging art and criticism. Similarly, we are free to analyze the discourses of more constrained artists, groups, and institutions as they debate questions of the arts and social policy. These are the questions we should be asking about the politics of arts funding, including our own. My remarks draw on my experiences as a consultant to the National Endowment for the Arts (NEA), an arts reporter, and producer of radio documentaries on the politics of culture.

The survival of culture in America appears increasingly to depend on the (now jeopardized) willingness of government bodies to vote dollars for the arts. I have attended innumerable conferences, legislative hearings, and NEA policy discussions and conducted many interviews with government officials, arts administrators, and other institutional policy makers. I have also interviewed a cross-section of artists and community groups seeking to reform existing arts institutions. Pacifica should be asking: In what terms are the arts discussed? How is the arts public imagined? To what extent do the funding sources set limits on what arts will be preserved or generated and how they will be presented? What are reformers asking for, and which of their demands are likely to be met? What do various publics think the arts are about? Why are some people polarized around issues of censorship and cultural imperialism? In short, what has "democratization" of the arts come to signify? What could "democratization" be like at Pacifica?

Unlike more compromised organizations, Pacifica has the capacity to clarify what is now a very murky set of debates by examining the historical roots of current conflicts and consensuses in the politics of culture. We may look at art-making as an ongoing social process. We may take the imagination—which either embraces or rejects "art"—to have a *social history*. To elaborate, art (and I mean all the arts) is still talked about as if it were more or less *good*, as if it were created by more or less *great* individuals (situated in cultural history but not in social history), as if it had universal, timeless value and significance. There is the certified art object, always "good"; and there is the audience, "good" only insofar as it has been "developed" to apprehend the art object's "aesthetic qualities."

There is another way to think and talk about art and the audience. Art objects can be conceived as social artifacts, art-making as a social process with social roots and social consequences, and the imaginations of artists and audiences as having social histories, which determine whether relations will be friendly, ambivalent, or antagonistic. This critical, historical methodology does *not* dissolve the achievements of individual artists; on the contrary, it deepens and extends textual meanings. But in the "critical" approach, the moral component shifts away from the "goodness" of taste toward the dilemmas of people accepting or resisting established authority, perpetuating or challenging class, racial, and gender stereotypes, and engaging, evading, or transforming those social conflicts in which the artist is embroiled—and in which he or she has a stake.

Here are some examples of how arts policies are discussed and how the social function of the arts has been construed by groups with differing social commitments. In recent studies, the sociologists Paul Di Maggio and Michael Useem observe that the audience for the "high" arts is overwhelmingly elite.[2] They suggest that more "education" and "outreach," as well as additional funding for participatory and community arts, will be needed if the arts are to be "democratized." Di Maggio and Useem do discuss the ways elites block access to the arts (and their reasons for doing so), but they do not explore the ideological content of artworks, that is, the class monopoly of creativity in general, or the ways artworks may affirm values and ideas antagonistic to democracy. Their omission is striking in view of the criticisms leveled at arts institutions by activists and scholars since the sixties. For instance, the January 1980 policy review panel of NEA's Media Arts urged that agency to stop "cultural imperialism," in other words, to counter the tendency of dominant institutions to present the high arts of Western Europe (and their offspring) as the yardstick by which all other cultural artifacts are to be measured for "quality." The racially diverse review panel declined to rubber-stamp current government funding patterns but rather made the undoubtedly utopian demand that the U.S. government respond vigorously to the needs and experiences of women, labor, and people of color. Had the panel continued this discussion, it might have revealed divergent and incompatible views concerning the social value of artworks.

Consider now some left-wing opinions on the role of the "vanguard." Stalinists see the vanguard arts as the dying wail of bourgeois society and as the carrier of values inimical to the interests of workers—hence, for example, their call for "proletarian literature." Trotsky refrained from prescribing "themes" for "poets," but asked all artists to be sensitive to the social conditions of creation and not to undermine the revolution. "We ought," he concluded, "to have a watchful revolutionary censorship, and a broad and flexible policy in the field of art, free from petty partisan maliciousness." The critical theorists of the Frankfurt School tend to see the high arts as the repositories of the truths capitalism represses in everyday life.

Unlike the followers of Herbert Marcuse, cultural nationalists and separatists reject the high arts as instruments of white male domination and embrace only those "traditions" they perceive as reflecting purely "black," "hispanic," or "female" experience—dismissing the rest of culture as meretricious at worst, irrelevant at best. The cultural nationalist position, as I have described it, seems intolerant and philistine. But consider what it is reacting to. I recently heard a long retrospective of the work and career of George Gershwin, produced and written by Miles Kreuger and presented by National Public Radio. Kreuger framed his program to carry this message: Gershwin's early death halted his inexorable upward progress toward the writing of truly good music—symphonies and more operas. Now, one could argue that Gershwin's early work was musically as brilliant as the late. And where did Gershwin's music come from? There was only one passing (and belated) reference to the importance of Afro-American culture to Gershwin's work, and no discussion at all of the interactions between black and Jewish entertainers in the early twentieth century. Kreuger was equally oblivious to Gershwin's problematic relations with women and the sexism of his collaborators' lyrics. The program comprised, in short, nothing but voyeuristic anecdotes, adulation, and laments for unwritten American symphonic masterpieces. And Kreuger's work exemplifies the rule, not the exception—not that this should surprise us: it is to be expected that government- and corporation-funded "public" media would encourage fans to look for heroes.

The positions I have sketched here are (mostly) comforting in their simplicity, soothingly unambiguous, and well tailored to the rapid-fire headline style of modern mass media. Pacifica must not shrink from its obligation to provide a more subtle, thoughtful discourse on the meanings, uses, and abuses of the arts in society.

[In September of 1981, KPFK's special teach-in on Southern Africa was immediately followed by "The Big Broadcast," a weekly program that celebrated "the golden age of radio." The selection that evening was "Amos 'n' Andy." The debates engendered by this excruciating juxtaposition continue. Should the program have been played only within a critical context, or is it an infringement of free speech to place any restrictions whatever on the mode of its presentation? This is an extreme example of a persistent and unresolved dispute in "alternative" media. To the politically conscious, the culture that shaped us—and to which many of us are still partially attached—is frequently repressive to women, people of color, and labor. The question for alternative media practitioners is, can racism, sexism, and class elitism be removed by fiat from above? Are there less authoritarian, perhaps less moralistic approaches that support a changing, more progressive consciousness? The following articles proposed alternative relations and attitudes toward the "audience" and a non-punitive environment in which staff and listeners might consciously participate in their "self-transformations."]

"Two-Way Communication, Free Speech, and the Marketplace of Ideas"
(KPFK Folio, August 1982)

Recent Pacifica programming has dealt with the clash between strict civil libertarians on the one hand and women and members of ethnic minorities on the other as they argue about the persistence of stereotypes in all forms of media. Some reformers strive to replace "negative" images with "positive" images and "role models" and ask the state to enforce the removal of media perceived as damaging to them and their children. Civil libertarians, however, worry about enlarging the power of the state to control media, pointing out that "censorship" further empowers the right to stifle dissident perspectives. Some libertarians argue that there should be a "marketplace of ideas" in which contending points of view clash, the best ones prevailing. It is this argument I wish to examine.

First and most obviously, precious few people have access to this "marketplace." Would that women, people of color, and workers in general had the resources and technology to challenge official reality with *their* experiences of the world. The second point is more subtle. As one of the lawyers on the Pacifica/ ACLU Bill of Rights Education Project observed, there is an assumption in the "marketplace of ideas" argument that everyone who debates there is "rational," that is, capable of reasoning and separating fantasy from reality.

"Consciousness" exists as a tension between reason and objectivity on the one hand and the distortions created by media and our irrational processes on the other (irrational processes created in a society that subjugates women, people of color, and nature, that defines upper-class white males as rational and the oppressed as irrational). Intellectual and emotional development consists of bringing these irrational and unconscious processes to light. Alternative media must similarly bring those representatives of the "irrational"—women, people of color, labor—out of the shadows of public life and onto center stage, into formats that do not predefine them as cranks and deviants. Under such conditions, gender and racial stereotypes may start to dissolve because the power relations that created and perpetuated them are at least momentarily modified.

What about "objectivity"? Some Pacifica listeners have complained that left-wing news and analysis is "biased," as opposed to the "balanced" news they believe the networks provide. One answer has been that everyone is "subjective," that is, to a degree biased and irrational; Pacifica is simply more up front. A better approach might be to examine "objectivity" as practiced by the dominant media, *as if* there were no world of facts and experience out there, ready to be marshaled, evaluated, and argued over as to its meaning and significance. "Reason," "objectivity," and "balance," then, are not the exclusive possessions of powerful white males; rather, they are the always-imperfect outcomes of social processes that should involve all people in free-wheeling debates and in which no thoughts or feelings are deemed off-limits. In such a context, divisive political labels start to look less important than the persuasive power of arguments and the respect for human frailty and human solidarity that the contending parties represent. Such strategies should build, not diminish, audiences, for they embody fairness and empathy.

The media reformers are making unrealistic demands, because established media are structurally unable and unwilling to abolish sexism and racism from their airwaves. Even at Pacifica we have insufficiently considered the extent to which we replicate the authoritarian styles of commercial media and "public" television and radio. Film, TV, and radio, as currently designed, are *one-way* communication—implicitly authoritarian, no matter how progressive the veneer of particular programs. For instance, if we experience media alone, we are isolated in our perceptions and thus more susceptible to being pushed around—both by the program and by our own unconscious resistances to challenging material. Furthermore, although listeners are fully capable of articulating their criticisms, needs, interests, and dilemmas, they are excluded from decision making affecting program selection, direction, and emphasis. Listener phone-ins help, but they are not enough.

Pacifica radio has the potential to become more and more "two-way" and thus might help end that isolation and facilitate the development of critical consciousness (a precondition for autonomy and self-determination). Media reformers should be supporting *us* while demanding that we continually question the power relations implicit in our technology and forms of communication. Only media controlled by people whose goal it is to empower each other, to help each other to see beyond the narrow stereotypes of race, class, and gender, can meet the demands of those who would abolish defamatory material. And as long as the state and the corporations control mass media, the challenging and controversial works that challenge all forms of domination will be marginalized or starved to death. Effective media reform is thus inseparable from radical politics.

"I Am Not Your Mother and This Is Not a Test" (KPFK Folio, *September 1981*)
This month I want to reflect on bureaucracy and the psychology of the marketplace, on how the sixties slogan of "trust the process" may or may not contradict the structures of domination we've come to identify as insufferable. This is not an abstract lesson in social theory—I want to apply this analysis to two questions in particular that are of concern now at KPFK: (1) why many people lack the wish or the confidence to telephone our talk shows; and (2) how we are to accomplish our goal to integrate "minorities" in a new way, one that will not perpetuate existing structures of domination.

Consider self-confidence; consider what the psychologists call basic trust.

Courageously, let us contemplate our bureaucratized market society, where everything and everyone is measured and tested, pigeonholed and tracked; where everyone seems to be on the make; where you can't tell your friends from your enemies; where the world (which is a *phase* in history *made by people*) appears intractable, permanent, hostile, and alien. This world, so accurately described by Hobbes as "the war of all against all," is said by the official culture to be naturally harmonious and free—thanks either to the laws of the unimpeded free market or to the presence of institutions that arbitrate and resolve conflict. (Normal people find true love in this context.)

Somebody please tell me how, in a society where power and privilege are monopolized by one class, one gender, and one race, we should believe that these class institutions will resolve conflicts in favor of anyone but the owning class? Enter Pacifica and its grand plan to develop autonomy and critical consciousness in the audience, to integrate women, minorities, and white working-class males in new ways. Why should people trust us, given the rich history of bamboozlement these groups have experienced? The institutions created for "their own good"—schools, family welfare programs—turned out to be agencies of social control; in the name of individual success, people, in unions or as tokens, were co-opted and thereby had to relinquish the community networks that helped them to survive in America—then they were paraded as proof that "the system works." Or, from the left, women, minorities, and white male workers frequently experience elitism in the form of insensitive terminology ("false consciousness"), paternalism, tactical rigidity, dilettantism, Third World–ism (concern with the faraway unmatched by the support of causes in the bedroom or backyard), or "going native"—escaping the iron cages to wallow in *their* music, *their* food, *their* sex, *their* tragedy.

Back to our original question. Are we asking our women/minority/working-class listeners to call KPFK and risk getting trashed again? Pacifica claims to embody social processes that people can trust; yet I fear we will replicate these old sadomasochistic strategies unless there is a lot of introspection and self-criticism —I know I have participated in every one of these "class" actions. At some point one must say, "Enough. I'm going to change, however long and painful that process is." Former masochists, like myself, will try to find supportive structures that help us all find more authentic, egalitarian ways of being together. This is what I want for our radio station: not the bogus perfect happy family thrust on us by mass media, but a creative community. To attain that, we must change the way we imagine our capacities and measure our talents—all of us. The reluctance to take such a drastic step comes from the psychology of the marketplace. To transcend the market mentality, we have to understand how bureaucracy has penetrated every aspect of existence. The bureaucrats define reality, and they gain our acquiescence in this reality, through tests that they devise and we trust as accurate gauges of our "potential." We are isolated in these tests, "on our own." Having internalized our success or failure in the tests, we can be relied upon to limit our expectations, not to be surprised when our "reach exceeds our grasp." And so we wait for heaven.

What if, as the alternative to bureaucracy, we were to shift our focus from the performance of the tested, isolated individual to the group? What if we evaluated the group as successful only insofar as it accurately describes social reality; as it demonstrates its capacity to care for each and every member; as it honors the uniqueness of each person—including unique perspectives and vision; as it resonates with loveliness and pain? I believe that such a community would embody processes that foster independence and authenticity (defined as the right to tell the truth without being abandoned), that in such circumstances people, finding that they are not required to cut off vital parts of themselves in order to function, who are *not being tested as a prelude to rejection*, find that they have inner resources and capacities hitherto invisible to them, or perhaps that have been hidden from a hostile world.

What I am saying is this: unless Pacifica can represent alternative social relations, all the integration plans, bibliographies, resource networks, affirmative action hires, and so on will be for naught. We'll wake up every day and it will still be business as usual. So I want each of us who loves the radio station, who cherishes it as the only authentic culture in America, to ask just how much we are willing to support each other in the process of growth and change. How much pain can we endure as we examine all that class baggage? For myself, I can say, hesitantly and timidly, I am starting to trust the process.

[Among my duties as program director was the formulation of theme programming for the four-week-long fund drives that took place twice a year. I was so impressed by Peter Lyman's essay "The Politics of Anger: On Silence, Ressentiment, and Political Speech," in the *Socialist Review*, no. 57 (1981), that I thought we should program the fall fund drive around the issues he had raised. The programmers were asked to look for the sources of apathy, nihilism, and despair in American culture and politics, and then to survey contemporary social movements to discover to what extent they were considering these mass political emotions as they attempted to mobilize their constituencies. The article that follows was my contribution to the debate over whether the expression of anger is a political tool or a political nemesis. It begins with an excerpt of Lyman's article.]

"Speaking Our Anger" (KPFK Folio, November 1981)
Nietzsche defines anger as the pathos of subordination, and argues that rage may lead beyond angry speech and aggressive action to a self-destructive adaptation to subordination through the internalization of rage. He calls this silent rage "ressentiment," and argues that it is the dominant political emotion of modernity. "Ressentiment" is literally a political neurosis; like a neurosis, the past becomes a trauma that dominates the present and future, for every event recapitulates the unresolved injury. Speech and action to change the future are impossible, because memory is incomplete for the wounded ego that refuses to remember the trauma and surrender; thus the victim cannot learn from the past, only suffer it. "Ressentiment" is an unconscious rage which creates a dramaturgy of revenge out of the everyday world, but this revenge is acted out unconsciously as a latent motivation hiding beneath seemingly ordinary speech and action. It is a rage that cannot live up to the courage of its convictions, cannot speak its anger in public, but it is manifested in a free-floating anxiety ready to be mobilized around any cause that brings injury on its object. The world of "ressentiment" is not moral, but moralistic, containing a quality of latent aggression, of inflexible righteousness, a need to impose order upon the world, and a need to find catharsis.

Nietzsche's thought on the political power of repressed anger has important consequences, for silence may be as important a text of anger as is vehement speech. Anger
may manifest itself indirectly, as a latent motive that silently introduces powerful and dangerous emotional currents into politics. While we learn from Freud that political anger
may have its source in a personal neurosis, we learn from Nietzsche that political anger
may manifest itself silently, indirectly, or even in self-destructive psychological symptoms.

As we continue to ponder the question of our continued survival and growth
(especially in the face of growing competition from National Public Radio), we
find it ever more necessary to articulate what it is that makes us genuinely alternative and responsive to the subscribers who have supported Pacifica since 1949.
It seems to me that what is most novel about Pacifica is our view of the audience
and its role in creating and sustaining us and in guiding the direction of our programs. We think about the *activity* of our Pacifica "family" and the *passivity*—
perhaps the immobility—of those who listen but contribute neither money nor
labor to our ongoing existence. We wonder why people do not avail themselves of
such political processes as exist in our country. In his essay on self-destructive
political anger, Peter Lyman has disconcertingly forced us to wonder about the
motives we bring to our work at Pacifica and about why some social movements
"burn out." If we conceal from the audience and from ourselves the sources of
our own indignation, can we expect them to open their hearts and purses to us?
Can we expect them to think more independently about ideology and consciousness, about how early family experiences affect future political participation?

The rage and impotence described by Peter Lyman need not be terminal, but
it must be identified, and its origins traced back into the family. Cultural criticism on Pacifica radio is in a unique position to do just that, for unlike other
media, it is our project to liberate one another from oppressive institutions, not to
perpetuate their illegitimate control.

Whether their "worlds" were "moral" or "moralistic," people have "spoken
their anger" at Pacifica. They have been heard. Perhaps some have been changed
in the process of changing the society. If we want to build a larger, more robust
and expressive liberated community, we should be looking at all the ways we, as
"alternative" media people, have been trapped in social relations and institutional practices of the dominant culture. I will end with the concluding remarks
from a 1976 essay of mine about how artists might function in alternative media,
called "Masochism Builds Character." Lyman's concerns resonate in this call for
a theory and practice for alternative media that directly challenge the false gentility, secrecy, and evasiveness of bourgeois culture.

> It is the people who tolerate the government, which in turn tol-
> erates opposition within the framework determined by the con-
> stituted authorities.
>
> —HERBERT MARCUSE

There are styles of discourse—conventional ways of relating to people, subject
matter, technology. The forms, the amenities, the rules of decorum mask the
power relations between the artists and the audience. In 1973 at the Aspen De-

sign Conference, drama and movie critic John Simon received a standing ovation for a speech entitled "The Death of the Audience," in which he denounced the cultural movements of the sixties and condemned the mob. Warning against the fatal extremes of "apathy" and "participation mania," Simon described the proprieties of art-communication: something "analogous to the sexual act," in which the "audience, a female figure," must have a certain "attitude," without which there can be no "erection," no "insemination," and no "conception."

The "artist," he said, "is a male figure" that "impregnates the audience with his vision." The recommended demeanor for the audience—oh, cautious Muse—is passive, receptive attentiveness. She must neither lie there "like a piece of wood" nor behave like a "mad nymphomaniac . . . jumping up and down like a whirling dervish," lest the artist be unable "to stick it into her." Simon also "thank[ed] God and women's liberation . . . that no one will now be insulted to be compared to a female figure"—and I'm sure that none of us will misinterpret his colorful use of metaphor. I'll never forget the end of his speech, his eyes shut as he blissfully recited from Rilke, in German. He didn't notice that the sound system had gone awry. His lips just kept on moving.

I have been describing some of the obstacles to communication that impede the development of a praxis for alternative media. They derive from a history most of us share: authoritarian child-rearing. Beneath the sexist imagery of that *Übermensch* Simon lurk the rigidity and insensibility of authoritarian character structure. Simon can't perform unless the audience agrees not to talk back. Authoritarians are terrified of dissent because they have been punished for childhood strivings for independence, for sexuality, aggression, and self-assertion. So they tune out by selectively listening, by selectively feeling the impact of only those ideas and emotions that won't offend the man with the whip: the angry god, the boss, the state—the stand-ins for the introjected punitive father. Finally they, too, become the angry god, to propitiate the insatiable tyrant by reproducing themselves in his image.

Legitimate authority derives from the *conscious* consent of the governed and needs no sticks or whips to enforce cooperation. Developing open and reciprocal relations with our "audience" is necessary if we are to uproot, expose, and eventually destroy the illegitimate control that pervades everyday life. Authoritarians, with their protective armor, cannot be active listeners. Active listening requires openness to new or unsettling ideas; it requires the training and opportunity to evaluate these ideas, then to feed that evaluation (which may take the form of "art") back to the "teacher," who in turn is open to modifying her or his thought and behavior to growth, to becoming more conscious. How else can we build a creative community? How else can we invent a flexible new politics?

Understanding and applying the principle of community feedback strikes at elitism, the bulwark of any society that confuses leadership with rule by force. The "star system" undermines reciprocity and subverts the collective processes that spur invention and excellence. Stars are to be eternally, uncritically admired, from a great distance. Star-gazing distracts us from this world and blurs its contradictions, anesthetizes us to our own pain and the hurts we inflict on others.

By creating fixed stars and phony reconciliations, monopoly capitalism tries to block socialism; it formulates the perfect denouement: a curtsy of aggression turned against the self. Open communication thrusts the creative imagination into politics, potentiates community, brings history back to life, and annihilates the ending.

Notes

1. Michael Lerner, *Surplus Powerlessness* (Oakland, Calif.: Institute for Labor and Mental Health, 1986).

2. Paul di Maggio and Michael Useem, "The Arts in Class Reproduction," in Michael W. Apple, ed., *Cultural and Economic Reproduction in Education* (London: Routledge & Kegan Paul, 1982), pp. 181–201; "Elitists and Populists: Politics for Art's Sake," *Working Papers for a New Society*, no. 6 (September 1978): 23–31; "Social Class and Arts Consumption: The Origins and Consequences of Class Differences in Exposure to the Arts in America," *Theory and Society*, no. 5 (1978): 141–161.

A COURSE ON SPECTATOR SPORTS

LOUIS KAMPF

Although I make my living as a teacher of literature, I have taught a course on mass spectator sports for the last four years. I intend to teach the course again. My reasons for doing so are serious, and derive from my political concerns as a socialist. I want to educate myself, to begin with, about an important area of culture: polls show, after all, that most people read little more than the sports section in their newspapers; I, for one, eagerly scan the latest sports results before I turn to the front of the paper. I also want the opportunity to talk to students I ordinarily don't get to talk to: those who may not have the slightest interest in literature or high culture but are passionate about sports.

Mass sports—both spectator and participatory—play an important role in our culture and in the political economy. Playing in a softball league may be one of the few ways of getting away from the miseries of the office, the factory, school, or one's family. How many boys from low-income families clutch to the reality of the American dream in the form of the multimillion-dollar contracts signed by the likes of Catfish Hunter, Joe Namath, and Julius Erving? And why the millions of fans? Rooting for a favorite team is one of the few ways left to show group loyalty. But that yearning for group loyalty also allows entrepreneurs to exploit the culture of masses of people. In the current stage of capitalist development, sports is one area of the service sector still capable of expansion. Several years ago, *Fortune* reported that Japanese capitalists are now stressing "quality of life investments." The qualities referred to are illustrated by the more than ten thousand bowling alleys built in Japan in 1970. In the United States there is now a booming business in tennis equipment. To create the boom, working-class prejudices against tennis had to be broken down; furthermore, spectator etiquette had to be transformed from a norm of restrained clapping for a well-executed shot to one of raucous applause for one's favorite player or team. How were such transformations engineered? Teaching this course, I hoped, would lead me to some answers for such questions.

I also meant to learn something about myself. I'm a professional: an intellectual with a proper degree of skepticism. Yet sports has a nagging hold on me. It played a significant role in shaping my consciousness as I grew up. I can't shake its effects, and I still find myself rooting for some team or other, even though I know the whole spectator sports business is a rip-off.

Then, I was intrigued by the role sports had played in the development of class consciousness during the rise of industrial capitalism. We have difficulty explaining how class consciousness develops, or fails to develop, or is displaced by false consciousness. Modern mass spectator sports and large-scale organized recreational activities came into existence in the West—especially in England and the

From *College English* 38, no. 8 (1977).

United States—as the industrial revolution hit its full stride in the nineteenth century. By 1850 it had become a diversion for the urban masses. Industrialization brought huge numbers of people from rural communities to the cities, tearing them away from the entertainments of the village green, the inn, or the tavern. Those concerned with the maintenance of public order were afraid that this displaced mass of humanity would tend to dissolve into an unruly mob. The YMCA movement was one type of response. Sports and recreation were consciously used to keep working people off the streets, out of trouble, and wrapped up in anything but their most vital political concerns. The organization of professional baseball teams in the United States and football (soccer) clubs in England and Scotland probably had some significant impact on the development of working-class consciousness. Class consciousness is advanced and solidified through the institutions workers develop: unions, fraternal organizations, social clubs, even sports associations. The teams in the baseball and football leagues, however, elicited loyalties that cut across class lines; you rooted for Brooklyn, or Liverpool, or New York. In Glasgow, one football club was Catholic, the other Protestant: a match between them had working-class Protestants and Catholics at each others' throats. Prizefighters in New York and Chicago punched, butted, and gouged for the greater glory of the ethnic groups the newspapers said they represented. Loyalty to the team or the individual performer, not social class, helped mass sports to become *subjectively* the most important life activity for millions in the working class as the elements of autonomy, creativity, and play became increasingly separated from work—in other words, as work became tedious labor. If a person's subjective life is absorbed by a diversion from the very element that defines his or her social class—that is, work—then class consciousness has lost its foundation in objective fact. That is not the whole story, of course. For one thing, sports also became an important instrument of sex role differentiation and male supremacy. I wanted to learn more about such interrelationships.

Finally, I wondered how my practice as radical activist and organizer, both on and off campus, might relate to sports. If I were involved in a community project, how would I relate to the sports activities in that community? How might I write about sports in a community newspaper? Should I try to organize a campaign supporting girls' attempts to get into the Little League?

THE COURSE

I made it very clear that anyone who did not take the course seriously would be asked to leave. Many students have told me that I should have been more strict about enforcing this rule. The procedure is unpleasant; but the students have to know that the course is not a gag—though it may be fun.

The course's chief requirement was that each student participate in a group research project to be presented to the rest of the class. I gave the class a list of suggested topics, to which the students added. The class then divided itself into groups according to preference for a particular research topic. The groups met regularly. Each group was also in charge of teaching one or more readings. The research topics chosen over the first two terms were sex roles and sports; sports heroes; why hockey is more popular than basketball in Boston; betting in various cultures; a class analysis of bettors at a nearby racetrack; sports as big business; self-competitive sports; regional and national differences in the popularity of certain sports.

Finding appropriate readings for the course was difficult. Little of value has been written about sports. Naturally, sports magazines, newspapers, popular sports biographies and autobiographies, and children's books are worth studying because millions read them. We do not really know what they do to people's heads, so there are serious questions to be asked. However, many students resented being asked to read more than a small amount of trash. The students and I read the sports section in the papers as well as some magazines and wrote comments about them in journals we kept for that purpose. I read the students' journals once a week and handed out copies of my own journal to everyone in class.

As a guide for class discussion, I gave the students a list of questions to ask themselves, including: What is a sports fan? Why am I one? What are the motives for sports—pleasure? challenge? escape? fame? Why win? Does competition need to be antagonistic? What do I experience when playing or watching—joy? love? hate? curiosity? detachment? anger? anything else? Does my social background have anything to do with the sports I enjoy?

THE READINGS AND CLASS DISCUSSION

1. Arthur Miller: *Death of a Salesman*

The play broadly draws the apparent parallel between success in football and success in business. The parallel turns out to be an illusion that allows the salesman to continue believing in the American Dream. In discussing the play, the students quite naturally, and without my prompting, raised most of the social, political, and psychological issues I wanted the course to focus on. Most of the students saw themselves in the play and wondered how their own interest in sports was related to their notions of success and their relationships to their parents. Discussion of the play was not nearly so lively the second time the course was given, however. Most of the students, it turned out, had read and discussed the play in high school, which apparently dampened their interest.

2. The History of American Sports

I had to give a long lecture on the history of sports in the United States, since there was no reading I could assign on the subject that was both reasonably short and accurate. Some of the topics I tried to cover were: the development of mass recreation and entertainment in general; how development of these, as well as of mass sports, was a function of urbanization, which process broke up traditional village and town entertainments; the relation of ideologies about work and recreation to the changing labor needs of industrial capitalism; the rise of professional recreationists as a response to urban unrest; the class structure of sports activities (which social class played or watched what sports); investment patterns in sports (the role, for example, of early trolley companies in building sports facilities at the edge of town, a trolley ride away). I concluded the survey with the formation of the National Baseball League in 1876. It became the model for all leagues in Europe and the Americas. Gamblers put the league together. It was an act of capitalist rationalization: if the gamblers were going to take bets on baseball games, they had to be sure the games were actually going to be played. Having a league with more or less permanently stationed teams also made fan loyalty possible. With rationalization of enterprise and fan loyalty to the team we have the beginning of the modern sports era. The combination made large-scale investments possible; consequently, it also opened the possibility for the extensive manipulation of people's consciousness.

3. David Mandell: *The Nazi Olympics*

This is a pedestrian and thin history of the modern Olympics. I had hoped that the book would begin a discussion of nationalism and sports. Alas, it bombed. The students could not take it seriously and therefore found it difficult to relate the historical events to themselves. The fiction of *Death of a Salesman* had seemed more real to them.

Given this failure, I eliminated Mandell's book the second time I taught the course. Instead, the students read two short essays: Gerald Ford's "In Defense of the Competitive Urge"—a compendium of most of the common inanities about sports building national character, preparing us to fight the enemy, teaching us how to do well in business, and being vital in maintaining law and order. And Marie Hart's "Sport: Women Sit in the Back of the Bus"—an intelligent analysis of sexism in sports and of how the urge to win relates to the machismo that is so prevalent in public and private life. The two essays made a useful contrast and led to a rich discussion of the relationship of sexism and sports to political and social life.

4. Louis Kampf: "What's
   Happened to Baseball?"

I could not find an appropriate reading about baseball, so I wrote this brief essay for the occasion. In it I discussed baseball's changes in organization and audience since the early 1940s, when I first began to follow and play the game. I especially emphasized the disappearance of minor, semipro, and local leagues, of the Negro leagues, and of large-scale participation by adults in sandlot ball. The discussion was reasonable, but not fervent. The students took baseball for granted—an old uncle—and therefore could not expend much energy on it. Most interesting was the discussion of the relationship of various ethnic and racial groups to this almost exclusively American game, nearly incomprehensible to most Europeans.

The second time I taught the course I decided to take a chance with Roger Kahn's *The Boys of Summer*. It didn't work. Most of the students could not identify with Kahn's nostalgia for the Brooklyn Dodgers of the 1950s; they found his autobiographical digressions irrelevant, even impertinent; and, worst of all, Kahn's attempt at literary sophistication kept them from focusing on the social issues that are the heart of the book.

5. Jerry Kramer, ed.: *Lombardi:*
    Winning Is the Only Thing

This is a collection of evaluations of Vince Lombardi by some of the players he coached, several of which are surprisingly honest and perceptive. Since Lombardi was a sentimental fascist who loved children, pregnant women, and General MacArthur, the book led students to dwell on the authoritarian aspects of organized sports.

The next year I substituted Kramer's *Instant Replay*, his diary of a season played under Lombardi in Green Bay. The book touches on most of the issues one needs to discuss about football: violence, spectator fanaticism, sexism, racism, football as a business venture and a means of social mobility, and so on. Kramer is an intelligent propagandist for football and the social system, and therefore a very useful witness. I did have occasional difficulties in keeping the discussion from bogging down in the details of football strategy.

6. Gary Shaw: *Meat on the Hoof*

This is one player's very moving account of growing up with football in Texas. Shaw describes how the game infantilized him, destroyed his capacity for non-authoritarian human relationships and love, and corrupted his perceptions of the social and political world around him. A nervous breakdown led to an attempt to restructure his life. He then discusses alternatives to the way players and spectators now experience football. The book gripped most of the students. Some couldn't quite believe Shaw's gruesome account of football training. Primarily, it led students to think about what sports is doing to their own world of feeling and sexuality, and how such matters of the emotions relate to the politics of their country.

7. Old Boxing Movies

One student's father, a former prizefighter, ran a bar in New Bedford, Massachusetts, which showed boxing movies from the 1920s and 1930s. The student screened some of them for class. New Bedford has a large Portuguese immigrant population, which takes to boxing as Irish, Jewish, and Italian neighborhoods did in the past. The class, therefore, had a context within which it was able to discuss how boxing had changed, since New Bedford's boxing scene is a relic of a lost world. Most of the discussion focused on ethnic and class loyalties. The dominant feeling in class was that boxing heroes gave ethnic and racial minorities a false sense of power.

The next time I taught the course I tried to get some students to do a research project on the New Bedford boxing scene. Unfortunately, there were no volunteers.

8. Jackie Stewart: *Faster*

The second time I taught the course, I wanted the class to discuss auto racing. The book is one year's diary of the Grand Prix circuit by the greatest Formula I driver of the last decade. Stewart is brashly honest about his expensive tastes, his love of money, and his desire to do business and rub shoulders with the powerful and wealthy. During the season he describes, several of his friends were killed in racing accidents. Now the several varieties of auto racing constitute the most popular spectator sport in the United States. Success is based on skill, mechanical ingenuity, and the availability of money rather than on physical power. Death is a real possibility, and serious injury is always on everyone's mind. Spectator loyalty is fierce, occasionally even nasty. Yet little happened in class discussion. I wound up trying to convince the students that auto racing was worthy of their attention. I'm not sure what went wrong, though I suspect it had something to do with the social origins of the students—a matter to which I'll return further on.

9. "The Only Game in Town"

This *Sports Illustrated* article tells of the cultural hold ice hockey has on a small Canadian town. Hockey has become the town's model for most aspects of everyday life. It gives people their sense of identity, and is used to gloss over social and political conflict. Class discussion tended to become fixated on hockey violence, which was then very much in the news. However, the service a sport can render to a town's power structure and for received morality did not go without attention. One group of students looked into the financing of hockey rinks in Massachusetts and discovered that several corporations were using state funds to make sizable profits.

10. David Wolf: *Foul*

The book is about Connie Hawkins, once the most spectacular basketball player around. Hawkins, who grew up in Brooklyn's black Bedford-Stuyvesant ghetto, had been falsely accused of taking a bribe to shave points in high school. Vindication came slowly, and most of Hawkins's prime years were wasted clowning around with the Harlem Globetrotters. Along with his description of these events, Wolf gets into the nature of college recruiting, racism in major sports, the culture of schoolyard basketball, and the social function of style. The students were gripped by the book. The discussion occasionally tended to get away from basketball and to concentrate on racism in the United States. Once again, the issue of how athletic prowess can give a minority a false sense of power came up.

11. The Reports

They were a mixed bag: some very useful, others less so. The students agreed that they got a great deal out of working in groups. Generally they felt good about having done a piece of work they were interested in and reporting on it to their fellow students. I learned a good deal from a number of them. Most of the reports made clear that the students had learned to look at sports as a social, political, and economic phenomenon.

12. Course Summary

We spent several hours summarizing the content of the course, and considering how it might be improved. I introduced some themes which I thought had emerged time and again during the course and which expressed tensions within the culture of industrial capitalism:

Sports is part of the country's economic base; it is also part of its cultural superstructure. Awareness of this dual function creates emotional difficulties for many people.

In an industrial capitalist society sport is supposed to be a form of personal escape from the prison of work. Yet people—and especially performing athletes—are constantly reminded that winning at sports is a patriotic duty and a training school for one's life, which will be competitive.

Play apparently allows the individual freedom and autonomy. Yet it is used to teach children that they must obey rules.

Team sports stress the primacy of the group. Yet one is rewarded for individual accomplishment; a giant ego is a prerequisite for stardom in sports.

13. Additional Readings

The only additional books I put on reserve were

Foster Rhea Dulles: *America Learns to Play*
Dulles, a conservative diplomatic historian, wrote this long history of recreation in the United States as a lark. Being a conservative, he really believes that sports ought to be an important instrument of social control. As a result, he is quite clear and accurate about the social function of modern mass sports.
Paul Hoch: *Rip-Off the Big Game*
Hoch's Marxist analysis of contemporary spectator sports is essentially accurate, though occasionally vulgar and glib. I could not use it as a primary text in the course because Hoch assumes that the reader is on his side politically. Most of my students were not.

As I mentioned earlier, little worth reading has been written about sports. Some useful theoretical work, heavily influenced by Marcuse, has been published in French, German, and Italian journals. However, they assume a solid knowledge of Marxism—something I could hardly expect of my students. As for the literature in professional sociological and psychological journals, it is dominated by quantitative studies that avoid most of the central issues I tried to raise in the course.

What have I learned? A great deal, though not as much as I would have liked. In preparing for the course it was fascinating to read some of the materials in the New York Public Library's section on play and recreation. The recreation movement was (and is) even more nationalistic, authoritarian, sexist, and anti-working class than I had anticipated. I learned how very aware the ruling class was in the nineteenth century of having to try and control the culture of the working class. Toward this end, business groups pulled no punches in enlisting the church, the schools, the police, and the new profession of recreationists to do their share in bringing about the sports explosion in the United States. I did not learn much about the role of sports in political organizing. One needs the example of practice, and few community groups have had the time or energy to experiment with sports programs. As for the radical community newspapers in my area, cultural matters hardly ever seem to get into their pages. I asked the class to try to develop alternate models for community sports, but they were not interested in utopian fantasies. Finally, I learned how deeply sexism and gay-baiting is built into our culture of sports: machismo reigns supreme.

As for the students, they began to perceive that cultural life does not take place in a realm separate from practical life. Ordinarily, we place our activities in two separate and sealed spheres: there is going to work, cooking dinner, fixing the door, shoveling snow, filling out tax forms (practical life), and there is listening to music, reading, playing cards, watching a basketball game, going to the movies (culture or recreation). The former are activities necessary for survival; the latter are what we survive for. At the end of a wearying day, we turn on the tube to watch the Knicks play the Celts. The practical world is forgotten, and we are in the realm of the aesthetic—of culture. The two spheres seem to be absolutely separate. I think most of my students learned that this is a mystification, that the realm of culture is not an escape from practical life, that, indeed, the two are intimately related. For one thing, many of the lessons taught by spectator and participatory sports (competitiveness, winning at any cost) apply to practical life. Every president since Franklin D. Roosevelt has used the language of competitive sports to describe the practice of politics. And isn't the football game a rehearsal for the rounds of daily life? (A current country-western hit begins, "Drop-kick me Jesus through the goal posts of life.") For another, my students agreed that their leisure activities contribute to the well-being of the capitalist economy. More subtly, they began to see that their energies and loyalties were being channeled into activities (rooting for the home team, grinding hours of practice for a swimming meet) acceptable to those who wield political and economic power. If one's capacity for devotion is dedicated to the cause of the Red Sox, it is less likely to be engaged by the cause of social justice. The leisure activity that had seemed autonomous—what one freely chose to do on one's own time—turned out to be a component of the practical life from which it was to be an escape. "If I'm to understand the workings of capitalism," one of my students wrote in her journal, "I have to grasp what's involved in my buying the equipment to play badminton in the backyard, and why I do it."

I intend to keep teaching and changing this course. I hope others who share my perspective will have the inclination and time to teach similar or related courses. I would like to hear from them.

RETHINKING GUERRILLA THEATER, 1971, 1985

R. G. DAVIS

1971

Guerrilla theater was intended to be an alternative to bourgeois theatre; instead, it has become a parallel, slipping in and out of existence, used by the egocentric, manhandled by the outraged children of the rich, even expounded upon by the meatballs of fashionable theater. Its original intention was to describe a radical political perspective for a type of theater that would live outside the oppressive culture of capitalism. To continue that direction, it will have to become far more dialectical and less didactic, understand its claims to Marxism, and expel from its ranks the fatheads of freakdom who incorrectly assume that images will destroy international corporate empires. In the hope of creating a more effective radical theater, the following essay analyzes some of the vagaries of guerrilla theater.

Muddle

Ideas are fluid, but too often they are squeezed out of context to suit contradictory needs. My 1965 guerrilla theater essay (in the *Tulane Drama Review*) was a description of what the San Francisco Mime Troupe had done. The essay was neither a symbolic definition nor a manifesto: we declared that we had been involved for five years in a new mode of theatrical endeavor and we sounded the alarm for others to take up the struggle. The gestalt of our activity was guerrilla-like. The content, form, acting techniques, life-style, and aims of the Mime Troupe constituted the guerrilla life of a theater in an alien society. Since the publication of that essay, guerrilla theater aberrations have been plentiful: Diggers and Yippies [1] who think politics is a theatrical splash; liberal thespians who make guerrilla theater into a "symbolic action"; and instant revolutionary-agitproppers who perform but ignore the representational nature and requisites of theater.

In 1966 and 1967 the Mime Troupe continued developing its style in the parks and across the country. In 1968 we ran out of energy and stopped to examine our progress. Sensing tne general misconception of guerrilla theater, and concerned about the Mime Troupe's developing pseudorevolutionary rhetoric, I wrote another essay, "Cultural Revolution USA . . . One Step—1968," which addressed the problem: "Can the term 'guerrilla theatre,' which describes activity on the cultural front in the USA, actually come close to the activity of an armed revolutionary foco [movement or party]?"

This essay originally appeared in *Performance* 1, no. 1 (1971). It also appears in R. G. Davis, *The San Francisco Mime Troupe: The First Ten Years* (Palo Alto: Ramparts Press, 1975). The 1985 postscript was written for this collection.

Agitprop

Agitprop is agitational propaganda. Agitprop theater is made up of skits performed by people who, like their audience, are directly engaged in the content of the skit. For example, Teatro Campesino, when performing in Delano, California, in 1965–1967, presented agitational propaganda for the members of the Farm Workers Association (NFWA). Their songs and *actos* (Luis Valdez's descriptive word for social skits with signs: Brecht/Cantinflas vignettes with immediately recognizable characters, placards on chests, who get into political confrontations with other characters) were designed to inform the workers of union negotiations, grievances, and programs. The performers were engaged in organizing work, and their *actos* were extensions of that work.

Agitprop done on the street for unrecognizable yet amorphously familiar audiences is not the same. The conditions have changed when players of the middle class play for unknown people vaguely described as Americans against the Vietnam War. Still further removed from agitprop are those so-called guerrilla theater groups who surprise people in the midst of their daily routines by creating a theatrical situation where performers and audience are mixed. Often the skit happens so rapidly that the audience doesn't know it has been hit until the piece is over. The people, mildly duped, are supposed to become conscious of their responsibility and guilt. Acting more like bandits than guerrillas and, like newspaper headlines, shouting images rather than telling news, these groups try to "sell" their product through moral suasion and personal confrontation—both ideals of the bourgeois culture (like attacking a balloon with another balloon).

.   .   .   .

Even at its best, agitational propaganda is not revolutionary art. It supports rather than examines, explains rather than analyzes. It can be only a temporary form for the group it performs to (farm workers' theater for farm workers). Didactic rather than dialectical, agitprop often skips over fundamental problems to facilitate immediate gains. Its very particularity limits its usefulness and longevity. The organization's immediate pressures are as constricting as the urgency of immediate explanations. Cesar Chavez often asked the members of the Teatro to return to face-to-face organizing and picket line work, thereby interrupting rehearsals and sometimes complicating tour dates. When the Teatro began to consider its role as important as the union's, a conflict of interest set in and the Teatro severed its ties with the union in order to grow politically and theatrically.

The Teatro Campesino left Delano not because it emphatically disagreed with Chavez and the Farm Workers Movement–Luis Valdez, Augustín Lira, and others in the Teatro did not oppose improvements in the farm workers' existence; they all come from the same blood, they understand the oppression. They left because they could not develop their theater; they could not speak out on Vietnam (the Kennedys supported Chavez and the war); they could not discuss or parody the Catholic Church (the Virgen de Guadalupe led the Peregrination to Sacramento). When the Teatro moved out of Delano, they moved from agitational propaganda to cultural propaganda. They now perform plays or *actos* related to the cultural problems of the larger, more amorphous community of the Chicanos of Aztlan.

Shortsighted political organizing, precisely the kind of political conceptualization that arises in this Protestant, anticultural, antisensual country, fails to recognize that political changes are directly related to the prevailing cultural hegemony. One of the few communists (since Marx) who understood this, the Italian Antonio Gramsci, wrote: "The populace . . . changes concepts with great difficulty, and never by accepting concepts in their 'pure' form, so to speak, but always in some eclectic combination."

Theater of the Yippies

The Yippies have taken the life-style acting of the Diggers (ca. 1966) and the theatrics of the 1940s and used both for politics. They assume that media actions will make changes: "If it appears in the newspapers, it happened, Ronny," Jerry Rubin told me in jest and belief. They read the *New York Daily News*, watch commercial TV, and attend Hollywood movies to understand the nature of Amerika. Their intention is to use the information they collect from these sources to create an Amerikan revolution. Their motives are left and unimpeachable—they do use themselves in the fight for change. But we must look at their tactics, not their motives. Do they accomplish what they plan?

McLuhan has defined television as a causal element rather than a transfer machine. TV, under the umbrella of McLuhan's pop thoughts, made Nixon lose the presidency in 1960 and win it in 1968. Surely TV must be more principled than that! McLuhan does not consider who owns television. He fails to concern himself with the corporate entities that control programming and the price of images, and thus their content. The mass media are not owned by the people, as we should know from the FCC regulations and the content of any TV channel, radio station, or newspaper. Advertisers own it. They rent the space. If you can't rent space, you must do somersaults to obtain coverage. Somersaults create news, and created news adds spice to the commercials. The object of privately manipulated mass media is not to distribute news but to create demand for consumer products.

Yippies run into camera range as often as possible because they believe (or believed) the media are a tool at their disposal. Agnew and Nixon believe the same thing, the difference being that Agnew and Nixon have accountable and legal power to follow up their attacks, while the Yippies can only hope the kids are getting the message (or the inside dope). Yippie actions are not guerrilla theater but mind-benders, one-liners, image-breakers. When only Abbie Hoffman's voice came over the TV talk show because his American flag shirt had been blacked out, the majority of viewers planned to watch the same "exciting" talk show the next night. Lenny Bruce, the trampoline of the Yippie mind, was not a revolutionary but a brilliant nightclub comic. Lenny Bruce's awesome contradiction was that he was a stand-up comic, a one-man individualistic speedfreak testimonial in a nightclub! He fell out a window! Dick Gregory, in contrast, gave up nightclubs. He realized that the content of his political rap was *not* possible in a nightclub. The Yippies fail to recognize the medium of their message. When Yippies assume that Woodstock is their own Nation, it is a conceit made foolish by *Life* and Warner Brothers.

Liberal "Guerrillas"

A liberal like Richard Schechner of the Performance Group feels a twinge of contradiction when teaching a useless course at a large university. An event interrupts his class, so he and others stomp out and purge themselves. He labels this action guerrilla theater:

One of the basics of guerrilla theatre is that you use what is at hand. The murders were at hand, and they were used. I found out about Kent State during my seminar on Performance Theory at NYU at 6:00 P.M., May 4. Someone came into the class and handed out a leaflet. . . . A general meeting was called for 7:30. . . We decided to start a guerrilla theatre. I got to the microphone and announced that decision.[2]

Marc Estrin, director of the American Playground (a theater in Washington, D.C., and at Goddard College), another liberal, takes the concept of theater as politics even further than Schechner. Estrin talks of "infiltration scenarios"; his "actors" infiltrate a public place and bring the "audience" at that location to the point of confrontation and awareness.

SCENE: Any public park across from a public building. . . . A man arrives in the park carrying a largish canvas and all the accoutrements of a Sunday painter. He sets up his easel and begins to sketch the building. He is quite friendly to all onlookers and especially friendly to the park police. . . . He works slowly and with great accuracy, laying out his lines as if to produce a work for the public library. . . . What is important is that he establish beyond doubt his legitimacy in the park, his friendliness with the police and passersby, his solid technique—his existence as a genuine painter who has a right to be doing what he is doing. To as many people as possible: "I'll see you tomorrow," "Come back later and see how I'm doing," etc. Over the course of the next few days . . . the painting begins to transform into a scene appropriate to the subject matter—on the White House balcony babies are napalmed, from the roof ICBMs emerge, as a grotesque Nixon and Laird oversee the operations. The painting becomes a mirror reflecting the inner truth behind the marble facade.

The painter attempts to be as friendly to onlookers, especially the police, as he was before, but he will find that the nature of their response to him has changed. He may even find that he is no longer allowed to paint in the park without a permit or somesuch. . . . He should follow up his expulsion from the park with TV and radio interviews. Money from the sale of the now-famous painting is donated to the Movement.[3]

Estrin is not a revolutionary, but neither is he a rightist provocateur. He would like to make people more aware: "The war is on while you're having fun." When the time comes, he hopes to put theater and people into the right scenario, the right location, and create a political event. He considered People's Park a good piece of theater. Estrin—like Schechner, a director who first approached theater through fantasy and literature—reads newspaper accounts of political activities as *tales*; politics is not connected to reality, politics is theatrical. Liberal thinkers are good souls. Their motives are idealistic and, actually, they are correct in their analyses of U.S. electoral politics. Certainly the "politics" of Reagan, Murphy, McCall of Oregon (all former television performers) is *tale*, show biz, image-making. Yet Estrin's analysis is within the framework of American politics, just as is Agnew's or Reagan's; he would make the system work better, not overturn it.

Other avant-gardists in theater and dance point to their efforts to increase communication between viewer and doer as some kind of "revolutionary" new-wave concept. This technical innovation, like improvisational theater, in bourgeois circumstances only sustains and increases the empathetic responses of all concerned; it doesn't change consciousness on a conceptual level, nor does it motivate social action.

Radical and Hit-and-Run Agitproppers

If the political Yippies and Diggers are not theatrical but are merely media mindbenders, and the liberal guerrillas serve only to support the system, what about those radical theater workers who call themselves guerrillas? Because a theater group is antiestablishment doesn't mean that it is a revolutionary guerrilla group per se. The theater we see practiced by radicals is most often agitprop; the current San Francisco Mime Troupe, Third World Revolutionists, and Pageant Players all give performances that are like briefings before an audience destined for a particular mission. This type of agitprop traditionally supports the existing ideas of its audience; the presentation is like psychodrama. The Chicano followers of the Teatro Campesino, in twelve or fifteen *teatros* over the West Coast, suffer from the same affliction. Rather than a demonstration of insight we see an expression of outrage, as the groups pseudopsychologically describe the oppression of the Chicano.

The hit-and-run agitproppers (or instant street-theater skit groups) that spring up at demonstrations often try to smash complacency and, like the liberals, "spoil people's fun." People engaged in street theater often rely on slogans that neither clarify their own political position nor present a theatrically interesting event. The act of doing illegal hit-and-run theatrical skits exaggerates this activity's importance. The content is less significant than the "moment." Although this is a step in the right direction, it's only a misdemeanor, not a felony.

Some publicity stunts, of course, can have political repercussions: for example, the military recruiter who received a pie in the face. Mark Rudd describes the event:

At a meeting of SDS Draft Committee . . . the question came up of what to do when the head of the Selective Service System for N.Y.C. came to speak at Columbia. Someone suggested that SDS greet the Colonel by attacking him physically. . . . The idea was defeated by a vote of thirty to one. . . . It was decided that the Draft Committee would be present at the speech to "ask probing questions." Several SDS members and nonmembers then organized clandestinely the attack on the Colonel. In the middle of the speech, a mini-demonstration appeared in the back of the room with a fife and drum, flags, machine guns, and noisemakers. As attention went to the back, a person in the front row stood up and placed a lemon-meringue pie in the Colonel's face. Everyone split.[4]

The pie incident was gloriously media-oriented. The recruiter was in total focus when his image was blown with lemon pie. But he changed his shirt and returned. He wasn't implacably stopped; his job wasn't taken over, nor was his own relationship to his role seriously threatened. In other words, his power was not touched. The pie thrown to embarrass (a liberal radical pie protest) did, however, puncture the Colonel's anal holiness and express the outrage of all the students.

All the whoop and whipped cream about "do your own thing" or "do something" has, at its base, a positive response to dull speech making and dull organizing, but the incident must be understood. Not all pies work, and the overexerted exhortations to act like a madman in politics (the Artaudian disease) don't lead to concrete power. The yippies get coverage. Liberal theater-guerrillas make people "aware"; radical theater-guerrillas protest and agitprop in the wind.

Guerrilla Theater—What Was It?

In 1965 we declared it possible to create theater and some life without elaborate buildings and loads of money. But what was the goal of doing this? In 1965 I stated that our purpose was to teach, direct toward change, be an example of change. In 1968 I added the thought: We must take power. In 1970 I stopped and asked: Could we do all the above?

Worried that the call to action might lead to activism for its own sake, soaked with the moral justifications of a "guerrilla way of life," in 1968 I suggested we consider the problem of power in relation to teaching, directing toward change, and being an example of change. I had grown worried because, in the late sixties, we were moving in zippy political and consumer currents; instant revolutionaries, psychedelic visionaries, and rock millionaires impressed all of us, and there was little time for reflection. The media became so ubiquitous that the difference between stage and street dissolved. Life-style acting, a slogan of the poetically crude communists, smogged all thoughts.

The Berliner Ensemble is the only example we have so far of an aggressive, dynamic teaching machine.[5] During Brecht's lifetime, the Ensemble came dangerously close to Antonio Gramsci's idea of truth, rather than Ulbricht's,[6] but who got the lesson here? Bentley? Esslin?[7] While the Ensemble carved a place in history, we were swinging large slogans at square hegemony and calling for revolution of *consciousness*. . . . Actors, writers, or directors who confuse theatrical representations with life will struggle desperately to approach reality and become speedfreak schizophrenics.

Onward

The path of relevant political theater is away from naturalism toward epic theater. Guerrilla theater, a reaction to bourgeois theater, produced a step in the right direction, but the slogans were not meaningful enough to take root, and consciousness did not change anything but hairstyles. We have treated our audiences to an ad agency–like bombardment—by telling the "truth," protesting the "outrages," and showing examples of purity—as if our "product" could be sold like cigarettes, cars, or consumptive goods. The first step is to avoid sloganeering, easy access to information, or one-liners. An audience is more than a group of consumers, and we, as performers, are in need of a technique far greater than that of commodity manipulators.

We have not understood or believed the lessons of the past: We must come to the inevitable conclusion that the guerrilla fighter is a social reformer, that he takes up arms responding to the angry protest of the people against their oppressors.—*Che*

There can be no revolutionary movement without revolutionary theory.—*Lenin*

The truth is revolutionary.—*Gramsci*

What we do next should neither sustain prevailing conditions nor attempt to blow people's minds. Bourgeois consciousness is deep and complex. Radical theater must bring people to the point of demanding change, through giving them knowledge of the processes of their condition. Imperialism is a far larger tiger than the "bosses," the "Establishment," or the face of Truman/Eisenhower/Kennedy/Johnson/Nixon. Therefore, our weapons must deal with computerized exploitation, as well as rotten personal habits. To become an effective instrument of social criticism or revolutionary culture, a theater has to develop a tangible theory manifested in practice. It must be conceived with intelligent care and great love. For those of us who consider revolutionary culture neither a gimmick nor an extension of bourgeois careerism but rather a process of thought leading to the dissolution of imperialism's hegemony, dialectical materialism (yeah, Marx) has to become the source of our inspiration.

1985: WHERE ARE WE NOW?

In the second term of Reagan's presidency, where the "me" generation of the 1970s has turned into the "mean" generation of the 1980s, a reexamination of the 1960s is taking place. The fashion of the 1950s has been exhausted; now forward to films, books, re-visits, re-visions, and college courses on the 1960s. Recent political activism on the campuses against apartheid warms the hearts of the "street-demonstrating peoples," but demonstrations *for* Nicaragua and *against* the bombing in El Salvador appear sparse. And although students are known to be the first to erupt—in Greece, Nicaragua, Cuba, Paris, Berkeley, Columbia— student radicalism is erratic, tuned to quarter or semester systems. Long-term insiders such as Nader's Raiders have proved that legal, administrative, and lobbying pressure produces corporate hiccups. These two paths are, in their own ways, effective; yet no matter what path is taken, the substantive problem remains. Do we have a deep and comprehensive enough critique of both the right and the liberals, and sufficient channels for communicating it to a wide audience, to make any significant changes? David Wellman (a 1960s activist who is now a professor at the University of California, Santa Cruz) has noted that "the sixties left critique of the liberals has been taken over by the right."

While preparing material for a film series on the 1960s at U.C. Berkeley's Pacific Film Archive, I did some rereading and studying. One article, by Stephen Bronner in *Social Text*, discussed the profoundly non-Marxist 1960s, steeped in activism that often ran itself in circles; yet, says Bronner, "it was the New Left which decisively helped to build a legitimate concern for the oppressed people of the Third World in its struggles against the Vietnam War and American incursions into Latin America to undermine progressive governments. . . . This anti-imperialist sensibility has so far helped impede the worst excesses of the American government in Central America."[8] Another assessment by Fredric Jameson, in *The 60s Without Apology*,[9] places the decade in a periodized view of history: "We have described the 60's as a moment in which the enlargement of capitalism on a global scale simultaneously produced an immense freeing or unbinding of social energies, a prodigious release of untheorized new forces: the ethnic forces of black and 'minority' third world movements everywhere, regionalisms, the development of new and militant bearers of 'surplus consciousness' in the student and women's movements, as well as in a host of struggles of other kinds." However, "the great explosions of the 60's have led, in the worldwide economic crisis, to powerful restorations of the social order and a renewal of the repressive power of the various state apparatuses." What, then, happened to all the liberating actions? William C. Dowling, in a review of Jameson's thoughts, says that collective transformation of social reality was turned into a mere ideology of personal and individual ecstasy. And with the current parade of fashions, ice cream stands, and gourmet restaurants, is that not partially true? Jameson ends his article with the observation that the 1960s was a superstructural movement, whereas global capitalism in the 1980s may "unify the unequal, fragmented, or local resistances" into a traditional division of upper, middle, and working classes.

Jameson projects future economic developments that in turn may affect cultural shifts; Bronner's more activist stance is closer to my own work and what I find many others now doing. Bronner's essay concludes on the thought, "If a new consciousness is to emerge, it becomes necessary to reappropriate a revolutionary history—which even includes that of the bourgeoisie on the rise—whose values have been surrendered or ignored in the name of the exigencies of the present."[10]

And speaking of reviewing the past, the San Francisco Mime Troupe, which I left in 1970, remains a fixture of the Bay Area scene. An American now living in Ireland who is writing a book about theater in the United States recently came through this area. We talked, and I asked him what he thought of the Mime Troupe. He said, "They target their audience and play to them—nothing radical about it at all." I thought he was perceptive. I would add one more observation: their stories are liberal, while their image is radical. In a decade of image and not substance, they get away with it. The offshoots of the Mime Troupe are few. "Modern Times" in New York and "Del Arte" in Northern California were both formed by ex-Troupers: the first is a two-person operation whose dramatic subjects have been apartheid and atomic destruction; the second is like a bunch of cracked brains run amok, doing Commedia dell'Arte characters with animals, Indians, and tricks of any kind. They follow the tradition developed in the Bay Area of skilled animators with little to tell.

My latest information about Peter Schumann of Bread and Puppet Theatre, who in the 1960s was the creator of emblematic pacifist images for demonstrations, concerns his recent trip to Nicaragua. His big puppets, religious homilies, and encouraging rural religiosity unite sympathetically with liberation theology in Central America. A recent picture book of Bread and Puppet in Nicaragua attests to his successes in a religious and radical environment.

Guerrilla theater was dead here until Reagan came along. The other day a

friend told me of her daughter who was in a group "guerrillarizing bus passengers with Contra and Nicaragua battles," much as Mark Estrin was doing in
the 1960s.

The Chicano theater movement has to deal with the commercial success (*Zoot
Suit* on Broadway and in film) of Luis Valdez, whose conservatism is self-serving.
His cultural nationalism doesn't represent the campesinos any more than does
Linda Chavez, who does civil rights PR for the Reagan administration.

The East Coast theater groups once associated with radical theater are no
longer. Richard Schechner of the Performance Group was superseded by Spauld-
ing Gray and a group of Performance Artists. Joe Chaiken long since disbanded
Open Theatre, respectably closing down the operation when it no longer functioned. Provisional, in Los Angeles, did the same. The Living Theatre came
back to the United States from its peregrinations in Europe and did not do so
well; Julian Beck died of cancer. The new younger resident theaters (funded by
NEA, state, local, and private foundations) are made up of liberals with the ambitions of young corporate executives. The best are producing socialist imports
from England in a soft-centered manner.

Liberal and left theater people always talk of Brecht, Weill, and Eisler, and
everyone including Peter Brook and Yale drama critic Richard Gilman call Brecht
"a Genius" and then go ahead and create or support theatre that is entirely opposite to everything epic theater stood for. *Evita* and *Sweeney Todd* have taken
every theatrical innovation that Piscator or Brecht ever created and souped it up
with slimy sentimentality and reactionary fantasy. Young left theater people,
then, are not entirely to blame for having trouble understanding anything called
"political theater."

Not only is there much less insight in theater today, but there is a lack of relevant criticism as well. A volume by Hal Foster, *The Anti-Aesthetic—Essays on
Postmodern Culture*, states in the preface: "The essays that follow are diverse.
Many subjects are discussed (architecture, sculpture, painting, photography, music, film . . .), but as practices transformed, not as ahistorical categories." [11] No
mention of theater, that minor art in the U.S.A. And perhaps herein is the reason
such piddling efforts by a few tiny protest theater groups are acceptable as left
culture—when they are so illiterate, unintelligent, hysterical, and, at best,
naively agitprop. Would that my criticism were moderated by being a voice
among many.

Documentary films are filling the gap where theater and demonstrations once
held sway. These nostalgic and empathetic products move audiences to tears and
memories without providing critical insight. These films turn elements of the left
into commodities, rendering the experience similar to a wake for the dead. One
rare gem in the midst of this nostalgia is a film by J. P. Gorin, a documentary in
which he investigates his *own* motives as well as those of the subject: *Poto and
Copango* is politically relevant simply because the filmmaker enters the discourse of subject/object in a way CBS and PBS never do.

Protest music functions in the same chord and harmonic structure as commercial sound; the texts are rhymed couplets that unite hope and utopia. Pete Seeger
tops the charts for those over fifty, and Bruce Springsteen for many other hun-

dreds of thousands. Nueva Canción, the Spanish version of 1960s folk music, with lyrics about Central and South American revolutionary struggles, is emotive, based on the same limited structure employed in left music ever since the Almanac Singers. Crashing contradictions arise: a Nicaraguan band touring the United States wanted to play advanced trash—their current sound-fusion music—but the North Americans didn't want that commercial junk, they wanted the sentimental protest music.

What is artistically interesting? Some of the performance artists and two or three of the imagistic theaters are playing with different materials and a few new thoughts. The movement as a whole is a challenge to the melodramatic plays of the legitimate theater. Most American playwrights are still investigating the disappeared family in the first act and nothing in the second. Imagistic theater can take on society and the world. However, limited by its background in the visual arts, its vision is narrowly aestheticized.

Left art (not culture) in the 1985 U.S.A. is at this juncture, in my opinion, inadequate to engage political issues in any intelligent, dialectical materialist manner; therefore, one has to look elsewhere. The joining of East German playwright Heiner Müller, an unorthodox bolshevik who is produced on both sides of the wall, and imagistic theater's international star Robert Wilson for the production *Civil Wars* (executed in seven countries but barred from the international arts festival staged in conjunction with the 1984 Olympics in Los Angeles) comes at a time when Reagan is forcing a lot of people to figure out what "working class" means while at the same time scaring them away from Marxism with a reheated cold war. Perhaps Müller's impacted poetry will inform Wilson's dancing aesthetic and thereby expand our revolutionary spirits.

Where else is the progressive theater? In Colombia, for one, where Santiago García, director of Teatro Candalaria in Bogotá, Enrique Buenaventura, playwright and director of Teatro Experimental de Cali, and the Teatro Popular movement (160 groups!) are all active. They have developed a popular-new-collective theatrical approach derived from Marx, Brecht, and the poor of Colombia, and replete with theoretical and practical examples, they influence all the cultural work in Colombia. In addition, they have been supportive of the Nuevo Teatro Movement in Cuba and aided the nascent cultural work in Nicaragua. The images of Buenaventura's plays are far more flamboyant and less impacted than those of Müller, although both are post-Brechtians.

To what extent the Colombian model, or perhaps Dario Fo, a Marxist Italian farceur, or some other outspoken socialist theatrical creator is an appropriate model for the United States is a question too elaborate for discussion here. Let me briefly suggest that our unique artistic job is to find distinctive forms through which to challenge the multinational corporations we are all so intimately in touch with and controlled by. Before we can take on the question of how to deliver the "new political insight," or what audience or constituency should be addressed, we have to face up to corporate culture and corporate imperialism; this the arts specifically are barely capable of doing, given their limited forms and need to stir up the emotions. Melodrama, nostalgic documentaries, and folk songs are fun for the folk, yet they are hardly capable of combating corporate exploitation.

Notes

1. The Diggers, a free-food distributing group, and the Yippies (Youth International Party) were 1960s countercultural activists originating in the San Francisco area.—Ed.

2. Richard Schechner, *The Drama Review* (Spring 1970): 163.

3. Mark Estrin, "Four Guerrilla Pieces," *The Drama Review* (Spring 1969): 72.

4. Marc Rudd, "Columbia: Notes on the Spring Rebellion," in *The New Left Reader*, ed. Carl Oglesby (New York: Grove Press, 1969), pp. 92–93.

5. The Berliner Ensemble was the theater Brecht established in East Germany after World War II. It was based on Brecht's principle of "epic theatre," a politically committed and instructive form of drama, subverting naturalistic conventions and distancing, or "estranging," audiences from facile empathy with illusionary plots and characters, even if these appeared in plays with leftist themes. See Dana Polan's "Bertolt Brecht and Daffy Duck: Toward a Politics of Self-Reflexive Cinema?" in Part 5.—Ed.

6. Walter Ulbricht, Communist Party leader in the German Democratic Republic.—Ed.

7. Eric Bentley and Martin Esslin, the two critics of Brecht whose interpretations have been most influential in the United States.—Ed.

8. Stephen Eric Bronner, "Reconstructing the Experiment: Politics, Ideology, and the American New Left," *Social Text*, no. 8 (Winter 1983–1984): 139.

9. Fredric Jameson, "Periodizing the 60s," in *The 60s Without Apology*, ed. Sohnya Sayres, Anders Stephanson, Stanley Aronowitz, and Fredric Jameson (Minneapolis: University of Minnesota Press, 1984), p. 208.

10. Bronner, "Reconstructing the Experiment," p. 141.

11. Hal Foster, *The Anti-Aesthetic: Essays on Postmodern Culture* (Port Townsend, Wash.: Bay Press, 1983): p. xii.

PUBLIC ACCESS TELEVISION: ALTERNATIVE VIEWS

DOUGLAS KELLNER

A community will evolve only when a people control their own communications.

FRANTZ FANON

The rapid expansion of public access television in recent years provides new possibilities for progressives to produce video programming cutting against the conservative programming that dominates mainstream television in the United States. Progressive access programming is now being cablecast regularly in such places as New York, Atlanta, Madison, Urbana, and Austin. In this article, I shall discuss public access television in the context of the new possibilities for left intervention in broadcast media made possible by access television, and shall provide examples of progressive programming based on a media project that I am involved with in Austin.[1]

CABLE, PUBLIC ACCESS, AND THE POSSIBILITY OF LEFT INTERVENTION

When cable television began to be widely introduced in the early 1970s, the Federal Communications Commission (FCC) mandated that "beginning in 1972, new cable systems (and after 1977, all cable systems) in the 100 largest television markets be required to provide channels for government, for educational purposes, and most importantly, for public access." This suggested, in fact, that cable systems should make available three public access channels to be used for state and local government, education, and community public access use. "Public access" was construed to mean that the cable company should make available equipment and airtime so that literally anybody could make use of the access channel and say and do anything they wished on a first-come, first-served basis, subject only to obscenity and libel laws. Managing the access channel required, in most cases, setting up a local organization to manage the access system.

In the beginning few, if any, cable systems made as many as three channels available, but some systems began offering one or two access channels in the early to mid 1970s. The availability of access channels depended, for the most part, on the political clout of local government and committed, often unpaid, local groups to convince a cable company (almost all of which are privately owned) to make available an access channel.[2] Here in Austin, for example, a small group of video activists formed Austin Community Television in 1970 and began broadcasting with their own equipment through the cable system that year. Eventually they raised grants to support their activities, buy equipment, and pay regular employees salaries. A new cable contract signed in the early 1980s called for the cable company to provide $500,000 a year for access, and after a difficult political struggle, which I shall mention later, they were able to get at least $300,000 a year to support their activities.

A 1979 Supreme Court decision, however, struck down the 1972 FCC ruling on the grounds that the FCC didn't have the authority to mandate access, an authority that supposedly belongs to the U.S. Congress.[3] Nonetheless, cable was expanding so rapidly and becoming such a high-growth, competitive industry that city governments considering cable systems were besieged by companies making lucrative offers (twenty- to eighty-channel cable systems) and were able to negotiate access channels and financial support for a public access system. Consequently, public access grew significantly during the early 1980s.

Where public access systems are operative, leftists have promising, though insufficiently explored, possibilities to produce and broadcast their own television programs. In Austin, for example, there have been weekly antinuclear programs, black and Chicano series, gay programs, countercultural and anarchist programs, an atheist program, occasional feminist programs, and a weekly left news magazine, "Alternative Views," which has produced over 250 hour-long videocassettes from 1978 to the present on a wide variety of topics. Two surveys, one undertaken by the University of Texas and another commissioned by the cable company, indicate that from ten to thirty thousand Austin viewers watch the show each week, and that public access programming in general receives about 7 percent of the audience. National surveys of viewer preferences for cable programs also indicate that public access is a high priority for many viewers.[4] Thus there is definitely a receptive and growing audience for public access television, and the possibility of left production of alternative television programs should be a much higher priority for radical media politics.

"ALTERNATIVE VIEWS"

The program I've been involved with, "Alternative Views," has gained a national reputation and a large and loyal audience. Although we began, in 1978, with no television experience and no resources, we immediately began producing a weekly program, using video equipment and tapes at the University of Texas and the broadcast and editing facilities of Austin Community Television. In fact, a group wishing to make access programming need have no technical experience or even financial resources to begin producing public access television where there is an access system in place that will make equipment, technical personnel, and videotapes available. Some systems charge money for use of facilities or charge a fee for use of airtime, but in the 1980s competitive bidding among cable systems for the most lucrative franchises caused many cable systems to offer free use of equipment, personnel, and airtime. In these situations, then, radicals can make use of public access facilities without technical expertise, television experience, or financial resources.

Many access systems also offer training programs in how to use the media for groups or individuals wanting to be in control of their own programs from conception through final editing. And with the rapid decline in equipment costs, it has even become possible for some groups to purchase their own video equipment. During its first two years, the "Alternative Views" group made the program literally on a zero budget, using University of Texas and Austin Community Television tapes and equipment. From the third year to the present we have raised around $2,000 a year, which allows us to own our own tapes and make copies available to sympathetic groups. We have also obtained tax-deductible nonprofit status and have applied to various foundations for grants to expand our operation.

Eventually we wish to own our own equipment, but for now we are able to make a weekly program using equipment available to the community. Such conditions make it possible for progressive groups to produce video programs for public access television and other projects on a very low budget. Moreover, tape acquisition often requires far less money than does production of many print media projects. Consequently, the cost of producing videotapes for public access is not necessarily prohibitive, and groups who want to explore the possibilities of producing public access television should look into the availability of equipment in their area or the costs of buying their own tapes and equipment.

From the beginning we were convinced that, despite our lack of previous television experience, we were making programs of interest to the community and that we were gaining an appreciative audience. On our first program, in October 1978, we had as guest an Iranian student who discussed opposition to the shah and the possibility of his overthrow as well as a detailed discussion of the Sandinistas' struggle to overthrow Somoza—weeks before the national broadcast media discovered these movements. We then had two programs on nuclear energy and energy alternatives—topics that later became central for the U.S. left—with, among other guests, Austinite Ray Reece, whose book *The Sun Betrayed* (Boston: South End Press, 1980) later became a definitive text on corporate control and suppression of solar energy. On early shows we also had long interviews with former senator Ralph Yarborough, a Texas progressive responsible for such legislation as the National Defense–Education Act—who we learned had never before been interviewed in depth for television. We also had an electrifying two-hour, two-part interview with former CIA official John Stockwell, who described how he was drafted into the CIA at the University of Texas and then discussed CIA recruitment, indoctrination, activities, and his own experiences in Africa, Vietnam, and Angola. His experiences in Angola led him finally to quit the CIA and write his book *In Search of Enemies*, which exposed the Angola operation he had been in charge of. Stockwell concluded with a long history of CIA abuses and his arguments for why the CIA should be shut down and a new intelligence service developed.

Responses to our shows were tremendously positive, and so we began taping interviews regularly with people who visited Austin as well as with local activists involved in various struggles. We also decided to vary our format, using documentary films, slide shows, raw video footage, and other visual material to enhance the visual aspect of our program. In addition, one of our members, Frank Morrow, became skilled at editing and developed some impressive montages of documentary and interview material to illustrate the topics being discussed.

Once the project got under way, we had little difficulty finding topics, people, or resources. We discovered that anyone we wished to interview was happy to come on our program, and after we began gaining recognition, local groups and individuals called us regularly to provide topics, speakers, films, or other video-material. We encouraged some local groups to make their own weekly shows, and a variety of peace, countercultural, gay, antinuke, chicano, anti-Klan, and other groups have indeed done so. And we have continued to serve as an umbrella organization, producing programs for over one hundred local groups using their speakers and film or video materials.

Over the years we have also had hour-long interviews with antiwar and anti-nuclear activists including Helen Caldecott, George Wald, Daniel Ellsberg, Michael Klare, David Dellinger, and many representatives of the European peace movement; we have talked with such American New Left activists as David McReynolds, Stokley Carmichael, Greg Calvert, and Dr. Spock; many feminist, gay, and union activists and representatives of local progressive groups have ap-peared on our show; and officials from the Soviet Union, Nicaragua, Allende's government in Chile, the democratic front in El Salvador, and many other Third World countries and revolutionary movements have been featured as well. In ad-dition, we have shown many documentaries and films provided by various film-makers and groups, and have made some video documentaries ourselves on a variety of topics. We have also worked with raw video footage of the bombing of Lebanon and the aftermath of the massacres at Sabra and Shatilla, of the killing of five communist labor organizers by the Ku Klux Klan in Greensboro, North Carolina, and of counterrevolutionary activity in Nicaragua.

Most of this material would not be shown on network television, or would be severely cut and censored; thus, the only real possibility today of having alter-native television is through public access/cable television. Obviously, progressive groups who want to carry out access projects need to develop a sustained com-mitment to radical media politics and explore local possibilities for intervention. We began at "Alternative Views" with a group of eight, but since most were graduate students, only two of us have been active throughout the entire project. Many people have worked with us over the years, and we now have a support group, Friends of Alternative Views, that regularly contributes money and helps with fundraising, publicity, and other projects. The first few years some internal conflicts arose concerning topics, format, and organization, but we worked through these problems and over the last few years have functioned rather smoothly in our internal politics. External problems, however, have emerged, both here in Austin and elsewhere in the United States; I shall call attention to these in the conclusion.

PUBLIC ACCESS TELEVISION:
PROBLEMS AND CHALLENGES

Once progressive public access television became more widespread and popular in Austin, it was, of course, subject to political counterattacks. The conservative daily newspaper in town, for instance, the *Austin American-Statesman*, pub-lished frequent denunciations of public access television to the effect that it was controlled by the "lunatic" fringe of "socialists, atheists, and radicals" and was not representative of the community as a whole—a lie, since many conservative church groups, business groups, and political groups also make use of access. The allegedly poor technical quality was attacked along with the "irresponsibility" of many of the programs (in fact, technical quality has been constantly improving).

In 1983 these criticisms were repeated with regard to Austin Community Television in editorials and articles in the more liberal monthly magazines *Texas Monthly* and *Third Coast*. At this point the criticisms carried some threat, because Austin Community Television was in the process of applying for a five-year renewal of their contract as access manager; certain interests in the community, however, desired to eliminate ACTV and find another access manager and system controlled by city government and local media interests. After an intense political struggle, the city cable commission and city council approved the renewal of the Austin Community Television access management. For the time being, then, our access system remains in the control of the community and open to whoever wants to use it, on either a regular or an occasional basis.

Struggles like these indicate that the left can successfully mobilize coalitions and alliances and be an effective force in local politics. Here in Austin, a "progressive coalition" has successfully beaten business-oriented candidates in city council elections and has won referendums on community issues in over half the electoral struggles in the last five years or so—in a city where business interests previously dominated local politics completely.

Other U.S. cities have not been so fortunate. The cable company in San Diego reportedly took over their access center after gaining a long-term renewal of their contract; a company recently bought out the San Antonio cable company and threatened to refuse to honor the terms of the previous contract, which mandated several access channels; Warner's Communications is threatening to renege on earlier contract obligations, which might threaten public access in their systems; many cable companies have never provided access channels and some rigidly control the access channels and would probably not permit a program like "Alternative Views" to be broadcast. Many cities do have relatively open access channels, however, and wherever possible, the left should start to use this vehicle of political communication and attempt to develop a national public access network through which tapes can be exchanged and circulated.

Beginnings in this direction are being discussed by various groups, including our own, which is working on developing a national network. In spring 1984 we sent packages of five tapes to contacts in Dallas and San Antonio, and in fall 1984 we began regularly sending tapes to Fayetteville, Atlanta, Minneapolis, Pittsburgh, and Urbana. In 1985–86 we added access systems in Boston, Cincinnati, Atlanta, San Diego, Portland, New York, and several other cities to our network, and we are now negotiating with groups in other cities who are interested in sponsoring our program on a regular weekly basis. In fact, groups or individuals who would be interested in sponsoring our program in their areas are invited to write to us, and we would also like to hear from individuals or groups who have programs they would like to include in our series or who have ideas about a possible progressive access network.

In discussions with Dee Dee Halleck of Paper Tiger Television in New York and with participants of the Union for Democratic Communications conference in Washington in October 1984, we have begun to explore with other groups the possibility of renting a couple of hours of weekly satellite time on one of the PBS transponders so that progressive access programming could be beamed to homes with satellite receivers all over the country. In 1986, Paper Tiger Television received a grant that made possible a ten-week pilot satellite television series to which access groups nationwide contributed material. They enlisted the support of various access systems in broadcasting, or taping for replay later, the programming we would send up by satellite on a weekly basis. Preliminary inquiries suggest that renting satellite time for access programming is not prohibitively expensive; thus, a grant of some $10,000 or $15,000 a year might make it possible for hundreds of thousands of people around the country to receive progressive television in their homes.

HOW TO PRODUCE LOCAL ACCESS PROGRAMMING

I would like to conclude with some comments on how the left might make use of public access television in situations in which cable television and at least the technical potential for public access already exist. First, groups must explore the availability of an access channel and approach the people in charge of it. Proposals should be made concerning the type of programming the group wants to produce, and the group must see if equipment, training, and tapes are available to use. Many video activists and public access systems are open to leftist projects— more so, for the most part, than are the establishment media. (At least this is the U.S. experience, as radicals have regularly produced programs in such places as Austin, Atlanta, New York, Madison, Pittsburgh, Appalachia, and Montana.)

For example, Paper Tiger Television in New York does regular critiques of mainstream mass media, and other New York groups feature regular left-wing shows on Nicaragua, American labor, Northern Ireland, and New York politics. A Pittsburgh group offers labor-oriented programming, and Appleshop TV in Kentucky does local documentary programming from a left perspective.[5]

If an access system exists, alliances must be made with access and video people before project development proceeds. Next, a group must decide if they wish to produce only occasional programs or to develop a regular weekly, bi-weekly, or monthly series. We began producing weekly one-hour programs as soon as we got the access channel to agree to broadcast our program, and our programming organization, philosophy, and projects were developed as we went on. Some might, however, find it more practical to have a more fully developed project outlined before beginning. In any case, we believe that it is best to attempt to undertake a weekly program, played at the same day and time every week, in order to build up an audience. The talk show format is, of course, the easiest to adopt and might make a good beginning, though more imaginative uses of video should be developed as experience and expertise expand. Many groups and individuals are happy to provide copies of their films and videocassettes for broadcast on public access. Then, as the project progresses, the group may want to develop its own documentaries, to mix documentary, film, and discussion formats, and to edit in titles, slides, and other images to make use of the video format. It should be noted that for such a project to succeed, one or more individuals must be strongly committed to investing time and labor to the planning, shooting, and editing of the programs. ("Alternative Views" has only been able to succeed thanks to the commitment of Frank Morrow, who has dedicated countless hours to every aspect of the programs.)

Once the project is under way, the group should apply for nonprofit, tax-deductible status from the IRS, which helps in fundraising activities and makes possible purchase of bulk-mailing permits. As a nonprofit organization we have regular fundraising benefits, organize publicity, solicit contributions, have a support group that contributes money to us yearly, and apply for various local and national foundation grants. A steering committee of the Alternative Information Network (our umbrella organization, founded by Mike Jankowski) meets annually to discuss finances, programming, and the political effects of "Alternative Views." Those most active in producing the program on a weekly basis meet regularly to plan programming and to attempt to improve the show. Two of us regularly produce the show and do the interviewing; a revolving group of people provides news reports from left media and regular in-depth analysis of issues such as U.S. policy in Central America, the arms race, the CIA and FBI, civil liberties, and other issues of importance. Such sustained commitment is necessary to ensure the success of any access series, as are contacts and cooperation with local political groups and individuals; such groups contact us regularly and send representatives to discuss their local organizing and political efforts.

Indeed, we do not see our program as a substitute for political organization and struggle, but rather as a vehicle for local political groups to use the media to provide information about their struggles and to involve people in their efforts. Almost every group that has appeared on our program has reported that appearing on public access television is a useful organizing and recruiting tool, judging by the many phone calls and letters they receive indicating interest in their activities. We also regularly show our tapes in high schools and at the university and make them available to local groups. Our tapes on Central America, for instance, have been frequently shown in churches and elsewhere as part of educational and organizing efforts. We also make ourselves and guests on our program available to groups to discuss the issues we deal with, specific programs, or public access television itself. Thus public access programming goes beyond broadcasting and reaches into community politics and organizing, serving as a useful tool for political education and organizing.

To conclude, public access television is still in a relatively primitive state here in the United States, and it is just beginning in Europe. Although public access is absent or restricted in some parts of the country, where it does exist it provides the one potential opening for left participation in the commercial and state broadcasting system. Thus progressive groups and individuals who wish to communicate their ideas and visions to a mass audience should consider how they might use public access television in politically progressive ways. It is self-defeating simply to dismiss broadcast media as tools of manipulation and to embrace print media as the only tools of communication open to the left; most people get their news and information from television, which plays a decisive role in defining political realities, shaping public opinion, and determining what is real and legitimate. If the left wants to play a role in American political life, we must come to terms with the realities of electronic communication and develop strategies to make use of new technologies and possibilities for intervention. Surveys have shown that people take more seriously individuals, groups, and politics that appear on television. The right has been making effective use of new communication technologies and media; for this very reason, the left can no longer afford the luxury of remaining distant from broadcast media or contemptuously dismissing television. The 1980s confront the left with both new challenges and new dangers, and if we want to survive and expand, we must increase our mass base and make our struggles known to more segments of the population. Risk exists, of course, that time and energies spent in other projects may be lost in frustrating media politics; but the risk must be taken if the left wants to grow during the 1980s and begin to intervene more effectively in the changing technological and political environment of the future.

Notes

1. The Alternative Information Network has been amassing material concerning radical media politics and progressive use of public access television and other new media of communication for production of a future book. Readers who have material on these topics, or who would like to correspond with us, can write: Alternative Information Network, P.O. Box 7279, Austin, Texas 78713.

For an earlier discussion of the need for a radical media politics and intervention in broadcasting, see my articles "TV, Ideology, and Emancipatory Popular Culture," *Socialist Review* 45 (November–December 1979), and "Network Television and American Society," *Theory and Society* 10 (January–February 1981). See also Armand Mattelart and Seth Siegelaub, eds., *Communication and Class Struggle.* Vol. 2: *Liberation, Socialism* (New York: International General, 1980); this valuable anthology contains a vast amount of material on left media politics and projects but, unfortunately, nothing on the potential progressive uses of public access television.

2. A directory of access systems put out by the National Federation of Local Cable Programmers, *The Video Register, 1983–84,* claims that there are over seven hundred access facilities operative in the United States. Some of these systems, however, are limited to a channel for time, weather, and announcements of local activities. In any case, although it is quite difficult to ascertain exactly how many full-blown access centers are operative, the number is clearly growing.

3. On the 1979 Supreme Court decision, see Josh Koenig, "Court Strikes Down FCC Access Rules," *Community Television Review* (Spring 1979).

4. A survey by the ELRA Group of East Lansing, Michigan, indicates that access is rated the fifth most popular category of television programming (ahead of sports, women's and children's programs, religious programs, and so on) and that 63 percent of those surveyed had an interest in access programming. Local surveys in Austin have confirmed that access programs have a potentially large audience.

5. It is difficult to get up-to-date information on the state of local access projects.

Journals such as *Access*, *The Independent*, *Alternative Media*, and *Community Television Review* and newsletters like those published by the National Federation of Local Cable Programmers and other local access groups have some material, but it is hard to get an overview. Material on ten access projects in the mid-1970s is surveyed in Chuck Anderson, *Video Power* (New York: Praeger, 1975), which also has suggestions on how to develop grassroots video projects. Material on early access projects can be found in issues of *Radical Software* (1970–1975), in Michael Shamberg, *Guerrilla Television* (New York: Holt, Rinehart & Winston, 1971); and in H. Allan Frederiksen, *Community Access Video* (Menlo Park, Calif.: Nowells Publications, 1972). A good review and critique of these projects is found in Bob Jacobson, "Video at the Crossroads," *Jump Cut*, no. 1 (May–June 1974). Suggestions on how to set up an access system and provide quality community programming is found in Monroe Price and John Wicklein, *Cable Television: A Guide for Citizen Action* (Philadelphia: Pilgrim Press, 1972); information on setting up a community media center is found in A. C. Lynn Zelmer, *Community Media Handbook* (Metuchen, N.J.: Scarecrow Press, 1979); and a booklet by Evonne Ianacone, *Changing More Than the Channel*, provides a "Citizen's Guide to Forming a Media Access Group," though it does not really focus on how to develop a public access program. The National Federation of Local Cable Programmers also provides guides concerning the production of access television, as do some other sources. We would appreciate receiving copies of such guides, as people frequently write and ask us for material on how to set up an access center or how to produce an access program, and we are forced to refer them to material that might not be up-to-date or directly relevant to their interests.

Designer: Betty Gee
Compositor: G&S Typesetters, Inc.
Printer: Murray Printing Company
Binder: Murray Printing Company
Text: 10/12 Times Roman
Display: Garamond Condensed